The Life of Abraham Lincoln;

WARD H. LAMON

THE LIFE

OF

ABRAHAM LINCOLN;

FROM

HIS BIRTH TO HIS INAUGURATION AS PRESIDENT.

BY

WARD H. LAMON.

WITH ILLUSTRATIONS.

BOSTON:

JAMES R. OSGOOD AND COMPANY,

(LATE TICKNOR & FIELDS, AND FIELDS, OSGOOD, & CO.)

1872.

Boston:
Stereotyped and Printed by Rand, Avery, & Co.

PREFACE.

IN the following pages I have endeavored to give the life of Abraham Lincoln, from his birth to his inauguration as President of the United States. The reader will judge the character of the performance by the work itself: for that reason I shall spare him the perusal of much prefatory explanation.

At the time of Mr. Lincoln's death, I determined to write his history, as I had in my possession much valuable material for such a purpose. I did not then imagine that any person could have better or more extensive materials than I possessed. I soon learned, however, that Mr. William H. Herndon of Springfield, Ill., was similarly engaged. There could be no rivalry between us; for the supreme object of both was to make the real history and character of Mr. Lincoln as well known to the public as they were to us. He deplored, as I did, the many publications pretending to be biographies which came teeming from the press, so long as the public interest about Mr. Lincoln excited the hope of gain. Out of the mass of works which appeared, of one only — Dr. Holland's — is it possible to speak with any degree of respect.

Early in 1869, Mr. Herndon placed at my disposal his remarkable collection of materials, — the richest, rarest, and fullest collection it was possible to conceive. Along with them came an offer of hearty co-operation, of which I have availed myself so extensively, that no art of mine would serve to conceal it. Added to my own collections, these acquisitions have enabled me to do what could not have been done before, — prepare an authentic biography of Mr. Lincoln.

Mr. Herndon had been the partner in business and the intimate personal associate of Mr. Lincoln for something like a quarter of a century; and Mr.

iii

Lincoln had lived familiarly with several members of his family long before their individual acquaintance began. New Salem, Springfield, the old judicial circuit, the habits and friends of Mr. Lincoln, were as well known to Mr. Herndon as to himself. With these advantages, and from the numberless facts and hints which had dropped from Mr. Lincoln during the confidential intercourse of an ordinary lifetime, Mr. Herndon was able to institute a thorough system of inquiry for every noteworthy circumstance and every incident of value in Mr. Lincoln's career.

The fruits of Mr. Herndon's labors are garnered in three enormous volumes of original manuscripts and a mass of unarranged letters and papers. They comprise the recollections of Mr. Lincoln's nearest friends; of the surviving members of his family and his family-connections; of the men still living who knew him and his parents in Kentucky; of his schoolfellows, neighbors, and acquaintances in Indiana; of the better part of the whole population of New Salem; of his associates and relatives at Springfield; and of lawyers, judges, politicians, and statesmen everywhere, who had any thing of interest or moment to relate. They were collected at vast expense of time, labor, and money, involving the employment of many agents, long journeys, tedious examinations, and voluminous correspondence. Upon the value of these materials it would be impossible to place an estimate. That I have used them conscientiously and justly is the only merit to which I lay claim.

As a general thing, my text will be found to support itself; but whether the particular authority be mentioned or not, it is proper to remark, that each statement of fact is fully sustained by indisputable evidence remaining in my possession. My original plan was to verify every important statement by one or more appropriate citations; but it was early abandoned, not because it involved unwelcome labor, but because it encumbered my pages with a great array of obscure names, which the reader would probably pass unnoticed.

I dismiss this volume into the world, with no claim for it of literary excellence, but with the hope that it will prove what it purports to be, — a faithful record of the life of Abraham Lincoln down to the 4th of March, 1861.

                                                    WARD H. LAMON.
WASHINGTON CITY, May, 1872.

LIST OF ILLUSTRATIONS.

TABLE OF CONTENTS.

CHAPTER I.

CHAPTER II.

CHAPTER III.

CHAPTER IV.

CHAPTER V.

CHAPTER VI.

CHAPTER VII.

CHAPTER VIII.

CHAPTER IX.

CHAPTER X.

CHAPTER XI.

CHAPTER XII.

CHAPTER XIII.

CHAPTER XIV.

CHAPTER XV.

CHAPTER XVI.

CHAPTER XVII.

CHAPTER XVIII.

CHAPTER XIX.

CHAPTER XX.

LIFE OF ABRAHAM LINCOLN.

CHAPTER I.

ABRAHAM LINCOLN was born on the twelfth day of February, 1809. His father's name was Thomas Lincoln, and his mother's maiden name was Nancy Hanks. At the time of his birth, they are supposed to have been married about three years. Although there appears to have been but little sympathy or affection between Thomas and Abraham Lincoln, they were nevertheless connected by ties and associations which make the previous history of Thomas Lincoln and his family a necessary part of any reasonably full biography of the great man who immortalized the name by wearing it.

Thomas Lincoln's ancestors were among the early settlers of Rockingham County in Virginia; but exactly whence they came, or the precise time of their settlement there, it is impossible to tell. They were manifestly of English descent; but whether emigrants directly from England to Virginia, or an offshoot of the historic Lincoln family in Massachusetts, or of the highly-respectable Lincoln family in Pennsylvania, are questions left entirely to conjecture. We have absolutely no evidence by which to determine them. Thomas Lincoln himself stoutly denied that his progenitors were either

1

Quakers or Puritans; but he furnished nothing except his own word to sustain his denial: on the contrary, some of the family (distant relatives of Thomas Lincoln) who remain in Virginia believe themselves to have sprung from the New-England stock. They found their opinion solely on the fact that the Christian names given to the sons of the two families were the same, though only in a few cases, and at different times. But this might have arisen merely from that common religious sentiment which induces parents of a devotional turn to confer scriptural names on their children, or it might have been purely accidental. Abrahams, Isaacs, and Jacobs abound in many other families who claim no kindred on that account. In England, during the ascendency of the Puritans, in times of fanatical religious excitement, the children were almost universally baptized by the names of the patriarchs and Old-Testament heroes, or by names of their own pious invention, signifying what the infant was expected to do and to suffer in the cause of the Lord. The progenitors of all the American Lincolns were Englishmen, and they may have been Puritans. There is, therefore, nothing unreasonable in the supposition that they began the practice of conferring such names before the emigration of any of them; and the names, becoming matters of family pride and family tradition, have continued to be given ever since. But, if the fact that Christian names of a particular class prevailed among the Lincolns of Massachusetts and the Lincolns of Virginia at the same time is no proof of consanguinity, the identity of the surname is entitled to even less consideration. It is barely possible that they may have had a common ancestor; but, if they had, he must have lived and died so obscurely, and so long ago, that no trace of him can be discovered. It would be as difficult to prove a blood relationship between all the American Lincolns, as it would be to prove a general cousinship among all the Smiths or all the Joneses.[1] A patronymic so common as Lincoln, derived from a large geographical

---

[1] At the end of this volume will be found a very interesting account of the family, given by Mr. Lincoln himself. The original is in his own handwriting, and is here reproduced in fac-simile.

division of the old country, would almost certainly be taken by many who had no claim to it by reason of descent from its original possessors.

Dr. Holland, who, of all Mr. Lincoln's biographers, has entered most extensively into the genealogy of the family, says that the father of Thomas was named Abraham; but he gives no authority for his statement, and it is as likely to be wrong as to be right. The Hankses — John and Dennis — who passed a great part of their lives in the company of Thomas Lincoln, tell us that the name of his father was Mordecai; and so also does Col. Chapman, who married Thomas Lincoln's step-daughter. The rest of those who ought to know are unable to assign him any name at all. Dr. Holland says further, that this Abraham (or Mordecai) had four brothers, — Jacob, John, Isaac, and Thomas; that Isaac went to Tennessee, where his descendants are now; that Thomas went to Kentucky after his brother Abraham; but that Jacob and John " are supposed to have " remained in Virginia.[1] This is doubtless true, at least so far as it relates to Jacob and John; for there are at this day numerous Lincolns residing in Rockingham County, — the place from which the Kentucky Lincolns emigrated. One of their ancestors, Jacob, — who seems to be the brother referred to, — was a lieutenant in the army of the Revolution, and present at the siege of Yorktown. His military services were made the ground of a claim against the government, and Abraham Lincoln, whilst a representative in Congress from Illinois, was applied to by the family to assist them in prosecuting it. A correspondence of some length ensued, by which the presumed relationship of the parties was fully acknowledged on both sides. But, unfortunately, no copy of it is now in existence. The one preserved by the Virginians was lost or destroyed during the late war. The family, with perfect unanimity, espoused the cause of the Confederate States, and suffered many losses in consequence . of which these interesting papers may have been one.

[1] The Life of Abraham Lincoln, by J. G. Holland, p. 20.

Abraham (or Mordecai) the father of Thomas Lincoln, was the owner of a large and fertile tract of land on the waters of Linnville's Creek, about eight miles north of Harrisonburg, the court-house town of Rockingham County. It is difficult to ascertain the precise extent of this plantation, or the history of the title to it, inasmuch as all the records of the county were burnt by Gen. Hunter in 1864. It is clear, however, that it had been inherited by Lincoln, the emigrant to Kentucky, and that four, if not all, of his children were born upon it. At the time Gen. Sheridan received the order " to make the Valley of the Shenandoah a barren waste," this land was well improved and in a state of high cultivation; but under the operation of that order it was ravaged and desolated like the region around it.

Lincoln, the emigrant, had three sons and two daughters. Thomas was the third son and the fourth child. He was born in 1778; and in 1780, or a little later, his father removed with his entire family to Kentucky.

Kentucky was then the paradise of the borderer's dreams. Fabulous tales of its sylvan charms and pastoral beauties had for years been floating about, not only along the frontiers of Pennsylvania, Virginia, and North Carolina, but farther back in the older settlements. For a while it had been known as the " Cane Country," and then as the " Country of Kentucky." Many expeditions were undertaken to explore it; two or three adventurers, and occasionally only one at a time, passing down the Ohio in canoes. But they all stopped short of the Kentucky River. The Indians were terrible; and it was known that they would surrender any other spot of earth in preference to Kentucky. The canes that were supposed to indicate the promised land — those canes of wondrous dimensions, that shot up, as thick as they could stand, from a soil of inestimable fertility — were forever receding before those who sought them. One party after another returned to report, that, after incredible dangers and hardships, they had met with no better fortune than that which had attended the efforts of their predecessors, and that they had utterly failed to find the " canes." At last they were actually found by Simon Kenton, who stealthily planted a little patch of corn, to see how the stalk that bore the yellow grain would grow beside its " brother " of the wilderness. He was one day leaning against the stem of a great tree, watching his little assemblage of sprouts, and wondering at the strange fruitfulness of the earth which fed them, when he heard a footstep behind him. It was the great Daniel Boone's. They united their fortunes for the present, but subsequently each of them became the chief of a considerable settlement. Kenton's trail had been down the Ohio, Boone's from North Carolina; and from both those directions soon came hunters, warriors, and settlers to join them. But the Indians had no thought of relinquishing their fairest hunting-grounds without a long and desperate struggle. The rich carpet of natural grasses which fed innumerable herds of buffalo, elk, and deer, all the year round; the grandeur of its primeval forests, its pure fountains, and abundant streams, — made it even more desirable to them than to the whites. They had long contended for the possession of it; and no tribe, or confederacy of tribes, had ever been able to hold it to the exclusion of the rest. Here, from time immemorial, the northern and southern, the eastern and western Indians had met each other in mortal strife, mutually shedding the blood which ought to have been husbanded for the more deadly conflict with a common foe. The character of this savage warfare had earned for Kentucky the appellation of " the dark and bloody ground; " and, now that the whites had fairly begun their encroachments upon it, the Indians were resolved that the phrase should lose none of its old significance. White settlers might therefore count upon fighting for their lives as well as their lands.

Boone did not make his final settlement till 1775. The Lincolns came about 1780. This was but a year or two after Clark's expedition into Illinois; and it was long, long before St. Clair's defeat and Wayne's victory. Nearly the whole of the north-west territory was then occupied by hostile Indians. Kentucky volunteers had yet before them many a day of hot and bloody work on the Ohio, the Muskingum, and the Miami, to say nothing of the continual surprises to which they were subjected at home. Every man's life was in his hand. From cabin to cabin, from settlement to settlement, his trail was dogged by the eager savage. If he went to plough, he was liable to be shot down between the handles ; if he attempted to procure subsistence by hunting, he was hunted himself. Unless he abandoned his " clearing " and his stock to almost certain devastation, and shut up himself and his family in a narrow " fort," for months at a time, he might expect every hour that their roof would be given " to the flames, and their flesh to the eagles."

To make matters worse, " the western country," and particularly Kentucky, had become the rendezvous of Tories, runaway conscripts, deserters, debtors, and criminals. Gen. Butler, who went there as a Commissioner from Congress, to treat with certain Indian tribes, kept a private journal, in which he entered a very graphic, but a very appalling description of the state of affairs in Kentucky. At the principal " points," as they were called, were collected hungry speculators, gamblers, and mere desperadoes, — these distinctions being the only divisions and degrees in society. Among other things, the journal contains a statement about land-jobbing and the traffic in town lots, at Louisville, beside which the account of the same business in " Martin Chuzzlewit " is absolutely tame. That city, now one of the most superb in the Union, was then a small collection of cabins and hovels, inhabited by a class of people of whom specimens might have been found a few months ago at Cheyenne or Promontory Point. Notwithstanding the high commissions borne by Gen. Butler and Gen. Parsons, the motley inhabitants of Louisville flatly refused even to notice them. They would probably have sold them a " corner lot " in a swamp, or a " splendid business site " in a mud-hole ; but for mere civilities there was no time. The whole population were so deeply engaged in drinking, card-playing, and selling town lots to each other, that they persistently refused to pay any attention to three men who were drowning in the river near by, although their dismal cries for help were distinctly heard throughout the "city."

On the journey out, the Lincolns are said to have endured many hardships and encountered all the usual dangers, including several skirmishes with the Indians. They settled in Mercer County, but at what particular spot is uncertain. Their house was a rough log-cabin, their farm a little clearing in the midst of a vast forest. One morning, not long after their settlement, the father took Thomas, his youngest son, and went to build a fence, a short distance from the house; while the other brothers, Mordecai and Josiah, were sent to another field, not far away. They were all intent about their work, when a shot from a party of Indians in ambush broke the "listening stillness" of the woods. The father fell dead; Josiah ran to a stockade two or three miles off; Mordecai, the eldest boy, made his way to the house, and, looking out from the loophole in the loft, saw an Indian in the act of raising his little brother from the ground. He took deliberate aim at a silver ornament on the breast of the Indian, and brought him down. Thomas sprang toward the cabin, and was admitted by his mother, while Mordecai renewed his fire at several other Indians that rose from the covert of the fence or thicket. It was not long until Josiah returned from the stockade with a party of settlers; but the Indians had fled, and none were found but the dead one, and another who was wounded and had crept into the top of a fallen tree.

When this tragedy was enacted, Mordecai, the hero of it, was a well-grown boy. He seems to have hated Indians ever after with a hatred which was singular for its intensity, even in those times. Many years afterwards, his neighbors believed that he was in the habit of following peaceable Indians, as they passed through the settlements, in order to get surreptitious shots at them; and it was no secret that he had killed more than one in that way.[2]

Immediately after the death of her husband, the widow

abandoned the scene of her misfortunes, and removed to Washington County, near the town of Springfield, where she lived until the youngest of her children had grown up. Mordecai and Josiah remained there until late in life, and were always numbered among the best people in the neighborhood. Mordecai was the eldest son of his father; and under the law of primogeniture, which was still a part of the Virginia code, he inherited some estate in lands. One of the daughters wedded a Mr. Krume, and the other a Mr. Brumfield.

Thomas seems to have been the only member of the family whose character was not entirely respectable. He was idle, thriftless, poor, a hunter, and a rover. One year he wandered away off to his uncle, on the Holston, near the confines of Tennessee. Another year he wandered into Breckinridge County, where his easy good-nature was overcome by a huge bully, and he performed the only remarkable achievement of his life, by whipping him. In 1806, we find him in Hardin County, trying to learn the carpenter's trade. Until then, he could neither read nor write; and it was only after his marriage that his ambition led him to seek accomplishments of this sort.

Thomas Lincoln was not tall and thin, like Abraham, but comparatively short and stout, standing about five feet ten inches in his shoes. His hair was dark and coarse, his complexion brown, his face round and full, his eyes gray, and his nose large and prominent. He weighed, at different times, from one hundred and seventy to one hundred and ninety-six. He was built so "tight and compact," that Dennis Hanks declares he never could find the points of separation between his ribs, though he felt for them often. He was a little stoop-shouldered, and walked with a slow, halting step. But he was sinewy and brave, and, his habitually peaceable disposition once fairly overborne, was a tremendous man in a rough-and-tumble fight. He thrashed the monstrous bully of Breckinridge County in three minutes, and came off without a scratch.

His vagrant career had supplied him with an inexhaustible fund of anecdotes, which he told cleverly and well. He loved to sit about at " stores," or under shade-trees, and " spin yarns," — a propensity which atoned for many sins, and made him extremely popular. In politics, he was a Democrat, — a Jackson Democrat. In religion he was nothing at times, and a member of various denominations by turns, — a Free-Will Baptist in Kentucky, a Presbyterian in Indiana, and a Disciple — vulgarly called Campbellite — in Illinois. In this latter communion he seems to have died.

It ought, perhaps, to be mentioned, that both in Virginia and Kentucky his name was commonly pronounced " Linckhorn," and in Indiana, " Linckhern." The usage was so general, that Tom Lincoln came very near losing his real name altogether. As he never wrote it at all until after his marriage, and wrote it then only mechanically, it was never spelled one way or the other, unless by a storekeeper here and there, who had a small account against him. Whether it was properly " Lincoln," " Linckhorn," or " Linckhern," was not definitely settled until after Abraham began to write, when, as one of the neighbors has it, " he remodelled the spelling and corrected the pronunciation."

By the middle of 1806, Lincoln had acquired a very limited knowledge of the carpenter's trade, and set up on his own account; but his achievements in this line were no better than those of his previous life. He was employed occasionally to do rough work, that requires neither science nor skill; but nobody alleges that he ever built a house, or pretended to do more than a few little odd jobs connected with such an undertaking. He soon got tired of the business, as he did of every thing else that required application and labor. He was no boss, not even an average journeyman, nor a steady hand. When he worked at the trade at all, he liked to make common benches, cupboards, and bureaus; and some specimens of his work of this kind are still extant in Kentucky and Indiana, and bear their own testimony to the quality of their workmanship.

Some time in the year 1806 he married Nancy Hanks. It was in the shop of her uncle, Joseph Hanks, at Elizabethtown, in Hardin County, that he had essayed to learn the trade. We have no record of the courtship, but any one can readily imagine the numberless occasions that would bring together the niece and the apprentice. It is true that Nancy did not live with her uncle; but the Hankses were all very clannish, and she was doubtless a welcome and frequent guest at his house. It is admitted by all the old residents of the place that they were honestly married, but precisely when or how no one can tell. Diligent and thorough searches by the most competent persons have failed to discover any trace of the fact in the public records of Hardin and the adjoining counties. The license and the minister's return in the case of Lincoln and Sarah Johnston, his second wife, were easily found in the place where the law required them to be; but of Nancy Hanks's marriage there exists no evidence but that of mutual acknowledgment and cohabitation. At the time of their union, Thomas was twenty-eight years of age, and Nancy about twenty-three.

Lincoln had previously courted a girl named Sally Bush, who lived in the neighborhood of Elizabethtown; but his suit was unsuccessful, and she became the wife of Johnston, the jailer. Her reason for rejecting Lincoln comes down to us in no words of her own; but it is clear enough that it was his want of character, and the "bad luck," as the Hankses have it, which always attended him. Sally Bush was a modest and pious girl, in all things pure and decent. She was very neat in her personal appearance, and, because she was particular in the selection of her gowns and company, had long been accounted a "proud body," who held her head above common folks. Even her own relatives seem to have participated in this mean accusation; and the decency of her dress and behavior appear to have made her an object of common envy and backbiting. But she had a will as well as principles of her own, and she lived to make them both serviceable to the neglected and destitute son of Nancy Hanks. Thomas Lincoln took another wife, but he always loved Sally Bush as much as he was capable of loving anybody; and years afterwards, when her husband and his wife were both dead, he returned suddenly from the wilds of Indiana, and, representing himself as a thriving and prosperous farmer, induced her to marry him. It will be seen hereafter what value was to be attached to his representations of his own prosperity.

Nancy Hanks, who accepted the honor which Sally Bush refused, was a slender, symmetrical woman, of medium stature, a brunette, with dark hair, regular features, and soft, sparkling hazel eyes. Tenderly bred she might have been beautiful; but hard labor and hard usage bent her handsome form, and imparted an unnatural coarseness to her features long before the period of her death. Toward the close, her life and her face were equally sad; and the latter habitually wore the woful expression which afterwards distinguished the countenance of her son in repose.

By her family, her understanding was considered something wonderful. John Hanks spoke reverently of her " high and intellectual forehead," which he considered but the proper seat of faculties like hers. Compared with the mental poverty of her husband and relatives, her accomplishments were certainly very great; for it is related by them with pride and delight that she could actually read and write. The possession of these arts placed her far above her associates, and after a little while even Tom began to meditate upon the importance of acquiring them. He set to work accordingly, in real earnest, having a competent mistress so near at hand; and with much effort she taught him what letters composed his name, and how to put them together in a stiff and clumsy fashion. Henceforth he signed no more by making his mark; but it is nowhere stated that he ever learned to write any thing else, or to read either written or printed letters.

Nancy Hanks was the daughter of Lucy Hanks. Her mother was one of four sisters, — Lucy, Betsy, Polly, and

Nancy. Betsy married Thomas Sparrow; Polly married Jesse Friend, and Nancy, Levi Hall. Lucy became the wife of Henry Sparrow, and the mother of eight children. Nancy the younger was early sent to live with her uncle and aunt, Thomas and Betsy Sparrow. Nancy, another of the four sisters, was the mother of that Dennis F. Hanks whose name will be frequently met with in the course of this history. He also was brought up, or was permitted to come up, in the family of Thomas Sparrow, where Nancy found a shelter.

Little Nancy became so completely identified with Thomas and Betsy Sparrow that many supposed her to have been their child. They reared her to womanhood, followed her to Indiana, dwelt under the same roof, died of the same disease, at nearly the same time, and were buried close beside her. They were the only parents she ever knew; and she must have called them by names appropriate to that relationship, for several persons who saw them die, and carried them to their graves, believe to this day that they were, in fact, her father and mother. Dennis Hanks persists even now in the assertion that her name was Sparrow; but Dennis was pitiably weak on the cross-examination: and we shall have to accept the testimony of Mr. Lincoln himself, and some dozens of other persons, to the contrary.

All that can be learned of that generation of Hankses to which Nancy's mother belonged has now been recorded as fully as is compatible with circumstances. They claim that their ancestors came from England to Virginia, whence they migrated to Kentucky with the Lincolns, and settled near them in Mercer County. The same, precisely, is affirmed of the Sparrows. Branches of both families maintained a more or less intimate connection with the fortunes of Thomas Lincoln, and the early life of Abraham was closely interwoven with theirs.

Lincoln took Nancy to live in a shed on one of the alleys of Elizabethtown. It was a very sorry building, and nearly bare of furniture. It stands yet, or did stand in 1866, to witness for itself the wretched poverty of its early inmates. It is about fourteen feet square, has been three times removed, twice used as a slaughter-house, and once as a stable. Here a daughter was born on the tenth day of February, 1807, who was called Nancy during the life of her mother, and after her death Sarah.

But Lincoln soon wearied of Elizabethtown and carpenterwork. He thought he could do better as a farmer; and, shortly after the birth of Nancy (or Sarah), removed to a piece of land on the south fork of Nolin Creek, three miles from Hodgensville, within the present county of La Rue, and about thirteen miles from Elizabethtown. What estate he had, or attempted to get, in this land, is not clear from the papers at hand. It is said he bought it, but was unable to pay for it. It was very poor, and the landscape of which it formed a part was extremely desolate. It was then nearly destitute of timber, though it is now partially covered in spots by a young and stunted growth of post-oak and hickory. On every side the eye rested only upon weeds and low bushes, and a kind of grass which the present owner of the farm describes as "barren grass." It was, on the whole, as bad a piece of ground as there was in the neighborhood, and would hardly have sold for a dollar an acre. The general appearance of the surrounding country was not much better. A few small but pleasant streams — Nolin Creek and its tributaries — wandered through the valleys. The land was generally what is called "rolling;" that is, dead levels interspersed by little hillocks. Nearly all of it was arable; but, except the margins of the watercourses, not much of it was sufficiently fertile to repay the labor of tillage. It had no grand, unviolated forests to allure the hunter, and no great bodies of deep and rich soils to tempt the husbandman. Here it was only by incessant labor and thrifty habits that an ordinary living could be wrung from the earth.

The family took up their residence in a miserable cabin, which stood on a little knoll in the midst of a barren glade.

A few stones tumbled down, and lying about loose, still indicate the site of the mean and narrow tenement which sheltered the infancy of one of the greatest political chieftains of modern times. Near by, a "romantic spring" gushed from beneath a rock, and sent forth a slender but silvery stream, meandering through those dull and unsightly plains. As it furnished almost the only pleasing feature in the melancholy desert through which it flowed, the place was called after it, "Rock Spring Farm." In addition to this single natural beauty, Lincoln began to think, in a little while, that a couple of trees would look well, and might even be useful, if judiciously planted in the vicinity of his bare house-yard. This enterprise he actually put into execution; and three decayed pear-trees, situated on the "edge" of what was lately a rye-field, constitute the only memorials of him or his family to be seen about the premises. They were his sole permanent improvement.

In that solitary cabin, on this desolate spot, the illustrious Abraham Lincoln was born on the twelfth day of February, 1809.

The Lincolns remained on Nolin Creek until Abraham was four years old. They then removed to a place much more picturesque, and of far greater fertility. It was situated about six miles from Hodgensville, on Knob Creek, a very clear stream, which took its rise in the gorges of Muldrews Hill, and fell into the Rolling Fork two miles above the present town of New Haven. The Rolling Fork emptied into Salt River, and Salt River into the Ohio, twenty-four miles below Louisville. This farm was well timbered, and more hilly than the one on Nolin Creek. It contained some rich valleys, which promised such excellent yields, that Lincoln bestirred himself most vigorously, and actually got into cultivation the whole of six acres, lying advantageously up and down the branch. This, however, was not all the work he did, for he still continued to pother occasionally at his trade; but, no matter what he turned his hand to, his gains were equally insignificant. He was satisfied with indifferent shelter, and a diet of " corn-bread and milk " was all he asked. John Hanks naively observes, that " happiness was the end of life with him." The land he now lived upon (two hundred and thirty-eight acres) he had pretended to buy from a Mr. Slater. The deed mentions a consideration of one hundred and eighteen pounds. The purchase must have been a mere speculation, with all the payments deferred, for the title remained in Lincoln but a single year. The deed was made to him Sept. 2, 1813; and Oct. 27, 1814, he conveyed two hundred acres to Charles Milton for one hundred pounds, leaving thirty-eight acres of the tract unsold. No public record discloses what he did with the remainder. If he retained any interest in it for the time, it was probably permitted to be sold for taxes. The last of his voluntary transactions, in regard to this land, took place two years before his removal to Indiana; after which, he seems to have continued in possession as the tenant of Milton.

In the mean time, Dennis Hanks endeavored to initiate young Abraham, now approaching his eighth year, in the mysteries of fishing, and led him on numerous tramps up and down the picturesque branch, — the branch whose waters were so pure that a white pebble could be seen in a depth of ten feet. On Nolin he had hunted ground-hogs with an older boy, who has since become the Rev. John Duncan, and betrayed a precocious zest in the sport. On Knob Creek, he dabbled in the water, or roved the hills and climbed the trees, with a little companion named Gallaher. On one occasion, when attempting to " coon " across the stream, by swinging over on a sycamore-tree, Abraham lost his hold, and, tumbling into deep water, was saved only by the utmost exertions of the other boy. But, with all this play, the child was often serious and sad. With the earliest dawn of reason, he began to suffer and endure; and it was that peculiar moral training which developed both his heart and his intellect with such singular and astonishing rapidity. It is not likely that Tom

Lincoln cared a straw about his education. He had none himself, and is said to have admired " muscle " more than mind. Nevertheless, as Abraham's sister was going to school for a few days at a time, he was sent along, as Dennis Hanks remarks, more to bear her company than with any expectation or desire that he would learn much himself. One of the masters, Zachariah Riney, taught near the Lincoln cabin. The other, Caleb Hazel, kept his school nearly four miles away, on the " Friend " farm ; and the hapless children were compelled to trudge that long and weary distance with spelling-book and " dinner," — the latter a lunch of corn-bread, Tom Lincoln's favorite dish. Hazel could teach reading and writing, after a fashion, and a little arithmetic. But his great qualification for his office lay in the strength of his arm, and his power and readiness to " whip the big boys."

But, as time wore on, the infelicities of Lincoln's life in this neighborhood became insupportable. He was gaining neither riches nor credit ; and, being a wanderer by natural inclination, began to long for a change. His decision, however, was hastened by certain troubles which culminated in a desperate combat between him and one Abraham Enlow. They fought like savages ; but Lincoln obtained a signal and permanent advantage by biting off the nose of his antagonist, so that he went bereft all the days of his life, and published his audacity and its punishment wherever he showed his face. But the affray, and the fame of it, made Lincoln more anxious than ever to escape from Kentucky. He resolved, therefore, to leave these scenes forever, and seek a roof-tree beyond the Ohio.

It has pleased some of Mr. Lincoln's biographers to represent this removal of his father as a flight from the taint of slavery. Nothing could be further from the truth. There were not at the time more than fifty slaves in all Hardin County, which then composed a vast area of territory. It was practically a free community. Lincoln's more fortunate relatives in other parts of the State were slaveholders ; and there is not the slightest evidence that he ever disclosed any conscientious scruples concerning the "institution."

The lives of his father and mother, and the history and character of the family before their settlement in Indiana, were topics upon which Mr. Lincoln never spoke but with great reluctance and significant reserve.

In his family Bible he kept a register of births, marriages, and deaths, every entry being carefully made in his own handwriting. It contains the date of his sister's birth and his own; of the marriage and death of his sister; of the death of his mother; and of the birth and death of Thomas Lincoln. The rest of the record is almost wholly devoted to the Johnstons and their numerous descendants and connections. It has not a word about the Hankses or the Sparrows. It shows the marriage of Sally Bush, first with Daniel Johnston, and then with Thomas Lincoln; but it is entirely silent as to the marriage of his own mother. It does not even give the date of her birth, but barely recognizes her existence and demise, to make the vacancy which was speedily filled by Sarah Johnston.[1]

An artist was painting his portrait, and asked him for a sketch of his early life. He gave him this brief memorandum: "I was born Feb. 12, 1809, in the then Hardin County, Kentucky, at a point within the now county of La Rue, a mile or a mile and a half from where Hodgens Mill now is. My parents being dead, and my own memory not serving, I know of no means of identifying the precise locality. It was on Nolin Creek."

To the compiler of the "Dictionary of Congress" he gave the following: "Born Feb. 12, 1809, in Hardin County, Kentucky. Education defective. Profession, a lawyer. Have been a captain of volunteers in the Black-Hawk War. Postmaster at a very small office. Four times a member of the Illinois Legislature, and was a member of the Lower House of Congress."

---

[1] The leaf of the Bible which contains these entries is in the possession of Col. Chapman.

To a campaign biographer who applied for particulars of his early history, he replied that they could be of no interest; that they were but

" The short and simple annals of the poor."

" The chief difficulty I had to encounter," writes this latter gentleman, " was to induce him to communicate the homely facts and incidents of his early life. He seemed to be painfully impressed with the extreme poverty of his early surroundings, the utter absence of all romantic and heroic elements; and I know he thought poorly of the idea of attempting a biographical sketch for campaign purposes. . . . Mr. Lincoln communicated some facts to me about his ancestry, which he did not wish published, and which I have never spoken of or alluded to before. I do not think, however, that Dennis Hanks, if he knows any thing about these matters, would be very likely to say any thing about them."

CHAPTER II.

THOMAS LINCOLN was something of a waterman. In the frequent changes of occupation, which had hitherto made his life so barren of good results, he could not resist the temptation to the career of a flat-boatman. He had accordingly made one, or perhaps two trips to New Orleans, in the company and employment of Isaac Bush, who was probably a near relative of Sally Bush. It was therefore very natural, that when, in the fall of 1816, he finally determined to emigrate, he should attempt to transport his goods by water. He built himself a boat, which seems to have been none of the best, and launched it on the Rolling Fork, at the mouth of Knob Creek, a half-mile from his cabin. Some of his personal property, including carpenter's tools, he put on board, and the rest he traded for four hundred gallons of whiskey. With this crazy boat and this singular cargo, he put out into the stream alone, and floating with the current down the Rolling Fork, and then down Salt River, reached the Ohio without any mishap. Here his craft proved somewhat rickety when contending with the difficulties of the larger stream, or perhaps there was a lack of force in the management of her, or perhaps the single navigator had consoled himself during the lonely voyage by too frequent applications to a portion of his cargo: at all events, the boat capsized, and the lading went to the bottom. He fished up a few of the tools " and most of the whiskey," and, righting the little boat, again floated down to a landing at Thompson's Ferry, two and a half miles west of Troy, in

Perry County, Indiana. Here he sold his treacherous boat, and, leaving his remaining property in the care of a settler named Posey, trudged off on foot to select "a location" in the wilderness. He did not go far, but found a place that he thought would suit him only sixteen miles distant from the river. He then turned about, and walked all the way back to Knob Creek, in Kentucky, where he took a fresh start with his wife and her children. Of the latter there were only two, — Nancy (or Sarah), nine years of age, and Abraham, seven. Mrs. Lincoln had given birth to another son some years before, but he had died when only three days old. After leaving Kentucky, she had no more children.

This time Lincoln loaded what little he had left upon two horses, and "packed through to Posey's." Besides clothing and bedding, they carried such cooking utensils as would be needed by the way, and would be indispensable when they reached their destination. The stock was not large. It consisted of "one oven and lid, one skillet and lid, and some tin-ware." They camped out during the nights, and of course cooked their own food. Lincoln's skill as a hunter must now have stood him in good stead.

Where he got the horses used upon this occasion, it is impossible to say ; but they were likely borrowed from his brother-in-law, Krume, of Breckinridge County, who owned such stock, and subsequently moved Sarah Johnston's goods to Indiana, after her marriage with Lincoln.

When they got to Posey's, Lincoln hired a wagon, and, loading on it the whiskey and other things he had stored there, went on toward the place which has since become famous as the "Lincoln Farm." He was now making his way through an almost untrodden wilderness. There was no road, and for a part of the distance not even a foot-trail. He was slightly assisted by a path of a few miles in length, which had been "blazed out" by an earlier settler named Hoskins. But he was obliged to suffer long delays, and cut out a passage for the wagon with his axe. At length, after many detentions and difficulties he reached the point where he intended to make his future home. It was situated between the forks of Big Pigeon and Little Pigeon Creeks, a mile and a half east of Gentryville, a village which grew up afterwards, and now numbers about three hundred inhabitants. The whole country was covered with a dense forest of oaks, beeches, walnuts, sugar-maples, and nearly all the varieties of trees that flourish in North America. The woods were usually open, and devoid of underbrush; the trees were of the largest growth, and beneath the deep shades they afforded was spread out a rich greensward. The natural grazing was very good, and hogs found abundant sustenance in the prodigious quantity of mast. There was occasionally a little glade or prairie set down in the midst of this vast expanse of forest. One of these, not far from the Lincoln place, was a famous resort for the deer, and the hunters knew it well for its numerous " licks." Upon this prairie the militia " musters " were had at a later day, and from it the south fork of the Pigeon came finally to be known as the " Prairie Fork."

Lincoln laid off his curtilage on a gentle hillock having a slope on every side. The spot was very beautiful, and the soil was excellent. The selection was wise in every respect but one. There was no water near, except what was collected in holes in the ground after a rain; but it was very foul, and had to be strained before using. At a later period we find Abraham and his step-sister carrying water from a spring situated a mile away. Dennis Hanks asserts that Tom Lincoln " riddled his land like a honeycomb," in search of good water, and was at last sorely tempted to employ a Yankee, who came around with a divining-rod, and declared that for the small consideration of five dollars in cash, he would make his rod point to a cool, flowing spring beneath the surface.

Here Lincoln built " a half-faced camp," — a cabin enclosed on three sides and open on the fourth. It was built, not of logs, but of poles, and was therefore denominated a " camp," to distinguish it from a " cabin." It was about fourteen feet square, and had no floor. It was no larger than the first house he lived in at Elizabethtown, and on the whole not as good a shelter. But Lincoln was now under the influence of a transient access of ambition, and the camp was merely preliminary to something better. He lived in it, however, for a whole year, before he attained to the dignity of a residence in a cabin. " In the mean time he cleaned some land, and raised a small crop of corn and vegetables."

In the fall of 1817, Thomas and Betsy Sparrow came out from Kentucky, and took up their abode in the old camp which the Lincolns had just deserted for the cabin. Betsy was the aunt who had raised Nancy Hanks. She had done the same in part for our friend Dennis Hanks, who was the offspring of another sister, and she now brought him with her. Dennis thus became the constant companion of young Abraham ; and all the other members of that family, as originally settled in Indiana, being dead, Dennis remains a most important witness as to this period of Mr. Lincoln's life.

Lincoln's second house was a " rough, rough log " one : the timbers were not hewed; and until after the arrival of Sally Bush, in 1819, it had neither floor, door, nor window. It stood about forty yards from what Dennis Hanks calls that " darned little half-faced camp," which was now the dwelling of the Sparrows. It was " right in the bush," — in the heart of a virgin wilderness. There were only seven or eight older settlers in the neighborhood of the two Pigeon Creeks. Lincoln had had some previous acquaintance with one of them, — a Mr. Thomas Carter; and it is highly probable that nothing but this trivial circumstance induced him to settle here.[1]

The nearest town was Troy, situated on the Ohio, about half a mile from the mouth of Anderson Creek. Gentryville had as yet no existence. Travelling was on horseback or on foot, and the only resort of commerce was to the packhorse or the canoe. But a prodigious immigration was now

[1] The principal authorities for this part of our narrative are necessarily Dennis and John Hanks; but their statements have been carefully collated with those of other persons, both in Kentucky and Indiana.

sweeping into this inviting country. Harrison's victories over the Indians had opened it up to the peaceful settler; and Indiana was admitted into the Union in 1816, with a population of sixty-five thousand. The county in which Thomas Lincoln settled was Perry, with the county-seat at Troy; but he soon found himself in the new county of Spencer, with the court-house at Rockport, twenty miles south of him, and the thriving village of Gentryville within a mile and a half of his door.

A post-office was established at Gentryville in 1824 or 1825. Dennis Hanks helped to hew the logs used to build the first storeroom. The following letter from Mr. David Turnham, now of Dale, Spencer County, presents some interesting and perfectly authentic information regarding the village and the settlements around it in those early times: —

"Yours of the 5th inst. is at hand. As you wish me to answer several questions, I will give you a few items of the early settlement of Indiana.

"When my father came here in the spring of 1819, he settled in Spencer County, within one mile of Thomas Lincoln, then a widower. The chance for schooling was poor; but, such as it was, Abraham and myself attended the same schools.

"We first had to go seven miles to mill; and then it was a hand-mill that would grind from ten to fifteen bushels of corn in a day. There was but little wheat grown at that time; and, when we did have wheat, we had to grind it on the mill described, and use it without bolting, as there were no bolts in the country. In the course of two or three years, a man by the name of Huffman built a mill on Anderson River, about twelve miles distant. Abe and I had to do the milling on horseback, frequently going twice to get one grist. Then they began building horse-mills of a little better quality than the hand-mills.

"The country was very rough, especially in the low lands, so thick with bush that a man could scarcely get through on foot. These places were called Roughs. The country abounded in game, such as bears, deer, turkeys, and the smaller game.

"About the time Huffman built his mill, there was a road laid out from Corydon to Evansville, running by Mr. Lincoln's farm, and through what is now Gentryville. Corydon was then the State capital.

"About the year 1823, there was another road laid out from Rockport to Bloomington, crossing the aforesaid at right angles, where Gentryville now stands. James Gentry entered the land; and in about a year Gideon Romine brought goods there, and shortly after succeeded in getting a post-office, by the name of Gentryville Post-office. Then followed the laying out of lots, and the selling of them, and a few were improved. But for some cause the lots all fell back to the original owner. The lots were sold in 1824 or 1825. Romine kept goods there a short time, and sold out to Gentry, but the place kept on increasing slowly. William Jones came in with a store, that made it improve a little faster, but Gentry bought him out. Jones bought a tract of land one-half mile from Gentryville, moved to it, went into business there, and drew nearly all the custom. Gentry saw that it was ruining his town: he compromised with Jones, and got him back to Gentryville; and about the year 1847 or 1848 there was another survey of lots, which remains.

"This is as good a history of the rise of Gentryville as I can give, after consulting several of the old settlers.

"At that time there were a great many deer-licks; and Abe and myself would go to those licks sometimes, and watch of nights to kill deer, though Abe was not so fond of a gun as I was. There were ten or twelve of these licks in a small prairie on the creek, lying between Mr. Lincoln's and Mr. Wood's (the man you call Moore). This gave it the name of Prairie Fork of Pigeon Creek.

"The people in the first settling of this country were very sociable, kind, and accommodating; but there was more drunkenness and stealing on a small scale, more immorality, less religion, less well-placed confidence."

The steps taken by Lincoln to complete his title to the land upon which he settled are thus recited by the Commissioner of the General Land Office : —

" In reply to the letter of Mr. W. H. Herndon, who is writing the biography of the late President, dated June 19, 1865, herewith returned, I have the honor to state, pursuant to the Secretary's reference, that on the 15th of October, 1817, Mr. Thomas Lincoln, then of Perry County, Indiana, entered under the old credit system, —

" 1. The South-West Quarter of Section 32, in Township 4, South of Range 5 West, lying in Spencer County, Indiana.

" 2. Afterwards the said Thomas Lincoln relinquished to the United States the *East* half of said South-West Quarter ; and the amount paid thereon was passed to his credit to complete payment of the *West* half of said South-West Quarter of Section 32, in Township 4, South of Range 5 West ; and accordingly a patent was issued to said Thomas Lincoln for the latter tract. The patent was dated June 6, 1827, and was signed by John Quincy Adams, then President of the United States, and countersigned by George Graham, then Commissioner of the General Land Office." [1]

It will be observed, that, although Lincoln squatted upon the land in the fall of 1816, he did not enter it until October of the next year ; and that the patent was not issued to him until June, 1827, but a little more than a year before he left it altogether. Beginning by entering a full quarter section, he was afterwards content with eighty acres, and took eleven years to make the necessary payments upon that. It is very probable that the money which finally secured the patent was furnished by Gentry or Aaron Grigsby, and the title passed out of Lincoln in the course of the transaction. Dennis Hanks says, " He settled on a piece of government land, — eighty acres. This land he afterwards bought under the Two-Dollar Act ; was to pay for it in instalments ; one-half he paid,

---

[1] The patent was issued to Thomas Lincoln *alias* Linckhern.

the other half he never paid, and finally lost the whole of the land."

For two years Lincoln continued to live along in the old way. He did not like to farm, and he never got much of his land under cultivation. His principal crop was corn; and this, with the game which a rifleman so expert would easily take from the woods around him, supplied his table. It does not appear that he employed any of his mechanical skill in completing and furnishing his own cabin. It has already been stated that the latter had no window, door, or floor. But the furniture — if it may be called furniture — was even worse than the house. Three-legged stools served for chairs. A bedstead was made of poles stuck in the cracks of the logs in one corner of the cabin, while the other end rested in the crotch of a forked stick sunk in the earthen floor. On these were laid some boards, and on the boards a "shake-down" of leaves covered with skins and old petticoats. The table was a hewed puncheon, supported by four legs. They had a few pewter and tin dishes to eat from, but the most minute inventory of their effects makes no mention of knives or forks. Their cooking utensils were a Dutch oven and a skillet. Abraham slept in the loft, to which he ascended by means of pins driven into holes in the wall.

In the summer of 1818, the Pigeon-Creek settlements were visited by a fearful disease, called, in common parlance, "the milk-sickness." It swept off the cattle which gave the milk, as well as the human beings who drank it. It seems to have prevailed in the neighborhood from 1818 to 1829; for it is given as one of the reasons for Thomas Lincoln's removal to Illinois at the latter date. But in the year first mentioned its ravages were especially awful. Its most immediate effects were severe retchings and vomitings; and, while the deaths from it were not necessarily sudden, the proportion of those who finally died was uncommonly large.[1] Among the num-

[1] The peculiar disease which carried off so many of Abraham's family, and induced the removal of the remainder to Illinois, deserves more than a passing allusion. The

ber who were attacked by it, and lingered on for some time in the midst of great sufferings, were Thomas and Betsy

following, regarding its nature and treatment, is from the pen of an eminent physician of Danville. Illinois : —

WARD H. LAMON, ESQ.

DEAR SIR, — Your favor of the 17th inst. has been received. You request me to present you with my theory in relation to the origin of the disease called " milk-sickness," and also a " general statement of the best treatment of the disease," and the proportion of fatal cases.

I have quite a number of cases of the so-called disease in Danville, Ill., and its vicinity ; but perhaps you are not aware, that, between the great majority of the medical faculty in this region of country and myself, there is quite a discrepancy of opinion. They believe in the existence of the disease in Vermilion County ; while, on the contrary, I am firmly of opinion, that, instead of genuine milk-sickness, it is only a modified form of *malarial* fever with which we here have to contend. Though sceptical of its existence in this part of the country, we have too much evidence from different intelligent sources to doubt, for a moment, that, in many parts of the West and South-west, there is a distinct malady, witnessed more than fifty years ago, and different from every other heretofore recognized in any system of Nosology.

In the opinion of medical men, as well as in that of the people in general, where milk-sickness prevails, cattle, sheep, and horses contract the disease by feeding on wild pasture-lands ; and, when those pastures have been enclosed and cultivated, the cause entirely disappears. This has also been the observation of the farmers and physicians of Vermilion County. Illinois. From this it might be inferred that the disease had a vegetable origin. But it appears that it prevails as early in the season as March and April in some localities ; and I am informed that, in an early day, say thirty-five or forty years ago, it showed itself in the winter-time in this county. This seems to argue that it may be produced by water holding some mineral substance in solution. Even in this case, however, some vegetable producing the disease may have been gathered and preserved with the hay on which the cattle were fed at the time ; for in that early day the farmers were in the habit of cutting wild grass for their stock. On the whole. I am inclined to attribute the cause to a vegetable origin.

The symptoms of what is called milk-sickness in this county — and they are similar to those described by authors who have written on the disease in other sections of the Western country — are a whitish coat on the tongue. burning sensation of the stomach severe vomiting, obstinate constipation of the bowels. coolness of the extremities. great restlessness and jactitation, pulse rather small, somewhat more frequent than natural, and slightly corded. In the course of the disease, the coat on the tongue becomes brownish and dark, the countenance dejected, and the prostration of the patient is great. A fatal termination may take place in sixty hours, or life may be prolonged for a period of fourteen days. These are the symptoms of the acute form of the disease. Sometimes it runs into the chronic form, or it may assume that form from the commencement ; and. after months or years, the patient may finally die. or recover only a partial degree of health.

The treatment which I have found most successful is pills composed of calomel and opium. given at intervals of two, three, or four hours, so as to bring the patient pretty strongly under the influence of opium by the time the second or third dose had been administered ; some effervescing mixture, *pro re nata ;* injections ; castor oil, when the stomach will retain it ; blisters to the stomach ; brandy or good whiskey freely administered throughout the disease ; and quinine after the bowels have been moved.

Under the above treatment, modified according to the circumstances, I would not expect to lose more than one case in eight or ten, as the disease manifests itself in this county. . . .

As ever, THEO. LEMON.

Sparrow and Mrs. Nancy Lincoln. It was now found expedient to remove the Sparrows from the wretched " half-faced camp," through which the cold autumn winds could sweep almost unobstructed, to the cabin of the Lincolns, which in truth was then very little better. Many in the neighborhood had already died, and Thomas Lincoln had made all their coffins out of "green lumber cut with a whip-saw." In the mean time the Sparrows and Nancy were growing alarmingly worse. There was no physician in the county, — not even a pretender to the science of medicine; and the nearest regular practitioner was located at Yellow Banks, Ky., over thirty miles distant. It is not probable that they ever secured his services. They would have been too costly, and none of the persons who witnessed and describe these scenes speak of his having been there. At length, in the first days of October, the Sparrows died; and Thomas Lincoln sawed up his green lumber, and made rough boxes to enclose the mortal remains of his wife's two best and oldest friends. A day or two after, on the 5th of October, 1818, Nancy Hanks Lincoln rested from her troubles. Thomas Lincoln took to his green wood again, and made a box for Nancy. There were about twenty persons at her funeral. They took her to the summit of a deeply-wooded knoll, about half a mile south-east of the cabin, and laid her beside the Sparrows. If there were any burial ceremonies, they were of the briefest. But it happened that a few months later an itinerant preacher, named David Elkin, whom the Lincolns had known in Kentucky, wandered into the settlement; and he either volunteered or was employed to preach a sermon, which should commemorate the many virtues and pass in silence the few frailties of the poor woman who slept in the forest. Many years later the bodies of Levi Hall and his wife, Nancy Hanks, were deposited in the same earth with that of Mrs. Lincoln. The graves of two or three children belonging to a neighbor's family are also near theirs. They are all crumbled in, sunken, and covered with wild vines in deep and tangled mats. The great trees were originally cut away to make a small cleared space for this primitive graveyard; but the young dog-woods have sprung up unopposed in great luxuriance, and in many instances the names of pilgrims to the burial-place of the great Abraham Lincoln's mother are carved in their bark. With this exception, the spot is wholly unmarked. Her grave never had a stone, nor even a board, at its head or its foot; and the neighbors still dispute as to which one of those unsightly hollows contains the ashes of Nancy Lincoln.

Thirteen months after the burial of Nancy Hanks, and nine or ten months after the solemnities conducted by Elkin, Thomas Lincoln appeared at Elizabethtown, Ky., in search of another wife. Sally Bush had married Johnston, the jailer, in the spring of the same year in which Lincoln had married Nancy Hanks. She had then rejected him for a better match, but was now a widow. In 1814 many persons in and about Elizabethtown had died of a disease which the people called the "cold plague," and among them the jailer. Both parties being free again, Lincoln came back, very unexpectedly to Mrs. Johnston, and opened his suit in an exceedingly abrupt manner. "Well, *Miss* Johnston," said he, "I have no wife, and you have no husband. I came a purpose to marry you: I knowed you from a gal, and you knowed me from a boy. I have no time to lose; and, if you are willin', let it be done straight off." To this she replied, "Tommy, I know you well, and have no objection to marrying you; but I cannot do it straight off, as I owe some debts that must first be paid." "The next morning," says Hon. Samuel Haycraft, the clerk of the courts and the gentleman who reports this quaint courtship, "I issued his license, and they were married *straight* off on that day, and left, and I never saw her or Tom Lincoln since." From the death of her husband to that day, she had been living, "an honest, poor widow," "in a round log-cabin," which stood in an "alley" just below Mr. Haycraft's house. Dennis Hanks says that it was only "on the earnest solicitation of her friends" that Mrs. Johnston consented to marry Lincoln. They all liked Lincoln, and it was with a member of her family that he had made several voyages to New Orleans. Mr. Helm, who at that time was doing business in his uncle's store at Elizabethtown, remarks that "life among the Hankses, the Lincolns, and the Enlows was a long ways below life among the Bushes." Sally was the best and the proudest of the Bushes; but, nevertheless, she appears to have maintained some intercourse with the Lincolns as long as they remained in Kentucky. She had a particular kindness for little Abe, and had him with her on several occasions at Helm's store, where, strange to say, he sat on a nail-keg, and ate a lump of sugar, "just like any other boy."

Mrs. Johnston has been denominated a "poor widow;" but she possessed goods, which, in the eyes of Tom Lincoln, were of almost unparelleled magnificence. Among other things, she had a bureau that cost forty dollars; and he informed her, on their arrival in Indiana, that, in his deliberate opinion, it was little less than sinful to be the owner of such a thing. He demanded that she should turn it into cash, which she positively refused to do. She had quite a lot of other articles, however, which he thought well enough in their way, and some of which were sadly needed in his miserable cabin in the wilds of Indiana. Dennis Hanks speaks with great rapture of the "large supply of household goods" which she brought out with her. There was "one fine bureau, one table, one set of chairs, one large clothes-chest, cooking utensils, knives, forks, bedding, and other articles." It was a glorious day for little Abe and Sarah and Dennis when this wondrous collection of rich furniture arrived in the Pigeon Creek settlement. But all this wealth required extraordinary means of transportation; and Lincoln had recourse to his brother-in-law, Ralph Krume, who lived just over the line, in Breckinridge County. Krume came with a four-horse team, and moved Mrs. Johnston, now Mrs. Lincoln, with her family and effects, to the home of her new husband in Indiana. When she got there, Mrs. Lincoln was much "surprised" at the contrast between the glowing representations which her husband had made to her before leaving Kentucky and the real poverty and meanness of the place. She had evidently been given to understand that the bridegroom had reformed his old Kentucky ways, and was now an industrious and prosperous farmer. She was scarcely able to restrain the expression of her astonishment and discontent; but, though sadly overreached in a bad bargain, her lofty pride and her high sense of Christian duty saved her from hopeless and useless repinings. On the contrary, she set about mending what was amiss with all her strength and energy. Her own goods furnished the cabin with tolerable decency. She made Lincoln put down a floor, and hang windows and doors. It was in the depth of winter; and the children, as they nestled in the warm beds she provided them, enjoying the strange luxury of security from the cold winds of December, must have thanked her from the bottoms of their newly-comforted hearts. She had brought a son and two daughters of her own, — John, Sarah, and Matilda; but Abe and his sister Nancy (whose name was speedily changed to Sarah), the ragged and hapless little strangers to her blood, were given an equal place in her affections. They were half naked, and she clad them from the stores of clothing she had laid up for her own. They were dirty, and she washed them; they had been ill-used, and she treated them with motherly tenderness. In her own modest language, she "made them look a little more human." "In fact," says Dennis Hanks, "in a few weeks all had changed; and where every thing was wanting, now all was snug and comfortable. She was a woman of great energy, of remarkable good sense, very industrious and saving, and also very neat and tidy in her person and manners, and knew exactly how to manage children. She took an especial liking to young Abe. Her love for him was warmly returned, and continued to the day of his death. But few children loved their parents as he loved his step-mother. She soon dressed him up in entire new clothes, *and from that time on he appeared to lead a new life*. He was encouraged by her to study, and any wish on his part was gratified when it could be done. The two sets of children got along finely together, as if they had all been the children of the same parents. Mrs. Lincoln soon discovered that young Abe was a boy of uncommon natural talents, and that, if rightly trained, a bright future was before him, and she did all in her power to develop those talents." When, in after years, Mr. Lincoln spoke of his " saintly mother," and of his " angel of a mother," he referred to this noble woman,[1] who first made him feel " like a human being," — whose goodness first touched his childish heart, and taught him that blows and taunts and degradation were not to be his only portion in the world.[2]

" When I landed in Indiana," says Mrs. Lincoln, " Abe was about nine years old, and the country was wild and desolate." It is certain enough that her presence took away much that was desolate in his lot. She clothed him decently, and had him sent to school as soon as there was a school to send him to. But, notwithstanding her determination to do the best for him, his advantages in this respect were very limited. He had already had a few days', or perhaps a few weeks' experience, under the discipline of Riney and Hazel, in Kentucky; and, as he was naturally quick in the acquisition of any sort of knowledge, it is likely that by this time he could read and write a little. He was now to have the benefit of a few months more of public instruction; but the poverty of the family, and the necessity for his being made to work at home in the shop and on the farm, or abroad as a hired boy, made his attendance at school, for any great length of time, a thing impossible. Accordingly, all his school-days added together would not make a single year in the aggregate.

---

[1] The author has many times heard him make the application. While he seldom, if ever, spoke of his own mother, he loved to dwell on the beautiful character of Sally Bush.

[2] The following description of her personal appearance is from the pen of her granddaughter, the daughter of Dennis Hanks: —

" His wife, my grandmother, is a very tall woman; straight as an Indian, fair complexion, and was, when I first remember her, very handsome, sprightly, talkative, and proud; wore her hair curled till gray; is kind-hearted and very charitable, and also very industrious." — MRS. H. A. CHAPMAN.

Abraham began his irregular attendance at the nearest school very soon after he fell under the care of the second Mrs. Lincoln. It was probably in the winter of 1819, she having come out in the December of that year. It has been seen that she was as much impressed by his mental precocity as by the good qualities of his heart.

Hazel Dorsey was his first master.[1] He presided in a small house near the Little Pigeon Creek meeting-house, a mile and a half from the Lincoln cabin. It was built of unhewn logs, and had " holes for windows," in which " greased paper " served for glass. The roof was just high enough for a man to stand erect. Here he was taught reading, writing, and ciphering. They spelled in classes, and " trapped " up and down. These juvenile contests were very exciting to the participants ; and it is said by the survivors, that Abe was even then the equal, if not the superior, of any scholar in his class.

The next teacher was Andrew Crawford. Mrs. Gentry says he began pedagogue in the neighborhood in the winter of 1822–3, whilst most of his other scholars are unable to fix an exact date. He " kept " in the same little schoolhouse which had been the scene of Dorsey's labors, and the windows were still adorned with the greased leaves of old copybooks that had come down from Dorsey's time. Abe was now in his fifteenth year, and began to exhibit symptoms of gallantry toward the weaker sex, as we shall presently discover. He was growing at a tremendous rate, and two years later attained his full height of six feet four inches. He was long, wiry, and strong ; while his big feet and hands, and the length of his legs and arms, were out of all proportion to his small trunk and head. His complexion was very swarthy, and Mrs. Gentry says that his skin was shrivelled and yellow even then. He wore low shoes, buckskin breeches, linsey-woolsey shirt, and a cap made of the skin of an opossum or a coon. The breeches clung close to his thighs and legs, but

[1] The account of the schools is taken from the Grigsbys, Turnham, and others, who attended them along with Abe, as well as from the members of his own family.

3

failed by a large space to meet the tops of his shoes. Twelve inches remained uncovered, and exposed that much of "shinbone, sharp, blue, and narrow."[1] "He would always come to school thus, good-humoredly and laughing," says his old friend, Nat Grigsby. "He was always in good health, never was sick, had an excellent constitution, and took care of it."

Crawford taught "manners." This was a feature of backwoods education to which Dorsey had not aspired, and Crawford had doubtless introduced it as a refinement which would put to shame the humbler efforts of his predecessor. One of the scholars was required to retire, and re-enter as a polite gentleman is supposed to enter a drawing-room. He was received at the door by another scholar, and conducted from bench to bench, until he had been introduced to all the "young ladies and gentlemen" in the room. Abe went through the ordeal countless times. If he took a serious view of the business, it must have put him to exquisite torture; for he was conscious that he was not a perfect type of manly beauty, with his long legs and blue shins, his small head, his great ears, and shrivelled skin. If, however, it struck him as at all funny, it must have filled him with unspeakable mirth, and given rise to many antic tricks and sly jokes, as he was gravely led about, shamefaced and gawky, under the very eye of the precise Crawford, to be introduced to the boys and girls of his most ancient acquaintance.

But, though Crawford inculcated manners, he by no means neglected spelling. Abe was a good speller, and liked to use his knowledge, not only to secure honors for himself, but to help his less fortunate schoolmates out of their troubles, and he was exceedingly ingenious in the selection of expedients for conveying prohibited hints. One day Crawford gave out the difficult word *defied*. A large class was on the floor, but they all provokingly failed to spell it. D-e-f-i-d-e, said one; d-e-f-y-d-e, said another; d-e-f-y-d, — d-e-f-y-e-d, cried another and another. But it was all wrong: it was

[1] " They had no woollen clothing in the family until about the year 1824." — DENNIS HANKS.

shameful, that, among all these big boys and girls, nobody
could spell "defied;" ● Crawford's wrath gathered in
clouds over his terrible brow. He made the helpless culprits
shake with fear. He declared he would keep the whole class
in all day and all night, if "defied" was not spelled. There
was among them a Miss Roby, a girl fifteen years of age,
whom we must suppose to have been pretty, for Abe was
evidently half in love with her. "I saw Lincoln at the window," says she: "he had his finger in his eye, and a smile on
his face; I instantly took the hint, that I must change the
letter y into an i. Hence I spelled the word, — the class let
out. I felt grateful to Lincoln for this simple thing."

Nat Grigsby tells us, with unnecessary particularity, that
"essays and poetry were not taught in this school." "Abe
took it (them) up on his own account." He first wrote short
sentences against "cruelty to animals," and at last came forward with a regular "composition" on the subject. He was
very much annoyed and pained by the conduct of the boys,
who were in the habit of catching terrapins, and putting
coals of fire on their backs. "He would chide us," says Nat,
"tell us it was wrong, and would write against it."

The third and last school to which Abe went was taught
by a Mr. Swaney, in 1826. To get there, he had to travel
four and a half miles; and this going back and forth so great
a distance occupied entirely too much of his time. His attendance was therefore only at odd times, and was speedily
broken off altogether. The schoolhouse was much like the
other one near the Pigeon Creek meeting-house, except
that it had two chimneys instead of one. The course of
instruction was precisely the same as under Dorsey and Crawford, save that Swaney, like Dorsey, omitted the great department of "manners." "Here," says John Hoskins, the son of
the settler who had "blazed out" the trail for Tom Lincoln,
"we would choose up, and spell as in old times every Friday
night." Hoskins himself tore down "the old schoolhouse"
long since, and built a stable with the logs. He is now half
sorry for his haste, and reverently presented Mr. Herndon a

piece of the wood as a precious memento of his old friend Abe. An oak-tree, blackened and killed by the smoke that issued from the two chimneys, spreads its naked arms over the spot where the schoolhouse stood. Among its roots is a fine, large spring, over whose limpid waters Abe often bent to drink, and laughed at the reflection of his own homely face.

Abe never went to school again in Indiana or elsewhere. Mr. Turnham tells us, that he had excelled all his masters, and it was "no use" for him to attempt to learn any thing from them. But he continued his studies at home, or wherever he was hired out to work, with a perseverance which showed that he could scarcely live without some species of mental excitement. He was by no means fond of the hard manual labor to which his own necessities and those of his family compelled him. Many of his acquaintances state this fact with strong emphasis, — among them Dennis Hanks and Mrs. Lincoln. His neighbor, John Romine, declares that Abe was "awful lazy. He worked for me; was always reading and thinking; used to get mad at him. He worked for me in 1829, pulling fodder. I say Abe was awful lazy: he would laugh and talk and crack jokes and tell stories all the time; didn't love work, but did dearly love his pay. He worked for me frequently, a few days only at a time. . . . Lincoln said to me one day, that his father taught him to work, but never learned him to love it."

Abe loved to lie under a shade-tree, or up in the loft of the cabin, and read, cipher, and scribble. At night he sat by the chimney "jamb," and ciphered, by the light of the fire, on the wooden fire-shovel. When the shovel was fairly covered, he would shave it off with Tom Lincoln's drawing-knife, and begin again. In the daytime he used boards for the same purpose, out of doors, and went through the shaving process everlastingly. His step-mother[1] repeats often, that " he read

[1] Whenever Mrs. Sarah Lincoln speaks, we follow her implicitly. Regarding Abe's habits and conduct at home, her statement is a very full one. It is, however, confirmed and supplemented by all the other members of the family who were alive in 1866.

every book he could lay his hand on." She says, " Abe read diligently. . . . He read every book he could lay his hands on ; and, when he came across a passage that struck him, he would write it down on boards if he had no paper, and keep it there until he did get paper. Then he would re-write it, look at it, repeat it. He had a copy-book, a kind of scrap-book, in which he put down all things, and thus preserved them."

John Hanks came out from Kentucky when Abe was four-teen years of age, and lived four years with the Lincolns. We cannot describe some of Abe's habits better than John has described them for us : " When Lincoln — Abe and I — returned to the house from work, he would go to the cupboard, snatch a piece of corn-bread, take down a book, sit down on a chair, cock his legs up high as his head, and read. He and I worked barefooted, grubbed it, ploughed, mowed, and cra-dled together ; ploughed corn, gathered it, and shucked corn. Abraham read constantly when he had an opportunity."

Among the books upon which Abe " laid his hands " were " Æsop's Fables," " Robinson Crusoe," Bunyan's " Pilgrim's Progress," a " History of the United States," and Weems's " Life of Washington." All these he read many times, and transferred extracts from them to the boards and the scrap-book. He had procured the scrap-book because most of his literature was borrowed, and he thought it profitable to take copious notes from the books before he returned them. David Turnham had bought a volume of " The Revised Statutes of Indiana ; " but, as he was " acting constable " at the time, he could not lend it to Abe. But Abe was not to be baffled in his purpose of going through and through every book in the neighborhood ; and so, says Mr. Turnham, " he used to come to my house and sit and read it." [1] Dennis Hanks would fain have us believe that he himself was the purchaser of this book, and that he had stood as a sort of first preceptor to Abe in the science of law. " I had like to forgot," writes

[1] He also read at Turnham's house Scott's Lessons and Sindbad the Sailor.

Dennis, with his usual modesty, " How did Abe get his knowledge of law ?   This is the fact about it.   I bought the 'Statute of Indiana,' and from that he learned the principles of
law, and also myself.   Every man should become acquainted
of the principles of law."   The Bible, according to Mrs. Lincoln, was not one of his studies : " he sought more congenial
books."   At that time he neither talked nor read upon religious subjects.   If he had any opinions about them, he kept
them to himself.

Abraham borrowed Weems's " Life of Washington " from his
neighbor, old Josiah Crawford, — not Andrew Crawford, the
school-teacher, as some of his biographers have it.   The
" Life " was read with great avidity in the intervals of work,
and, when not in use, was carefully deposited on a shelf, made
of a clapboard laid on two pins.   But just behind the shelf
there was a great crack between the logs of the wall ; and one
night, while Abe was dreaming in the loft, a storm came up,
and the rain, blown through the opening, soaked his precious
book from cover to cover.   Crawford was a sour and churlish
fellow at best, and flatly refused to take the damaged book
back again.   He said, that, if Abe had no money to pay for
it, he could work it out.   Of course, there was no alternative ;
and Abe was obliged to discharge the debt by " pulling fodder " three days, at twenty-five cents a day.   Crawford afterwards paid dearly for his churlishness.

At home, with his step-mother and the children, he was the
most agreeable fellow in the world.   " He was always ready to
do every thing for everybody."   When he was not doing some
special act of kindness, he told stories or " cracked jokes."
" He was as full of his yarns in Indiana as ever he was in
Illinois."   Dennis Hanks was a clever hand at the same business, and so was old Tom Lincoln.   Among them they must
have made things very lively, during the long winter evenings,
for John Johnston and the good old lady and the girls.

Mrs. Lincoln was never able to speak of Abe's conduct to
her without tears.   In her interview with Mr. Herndon, when

MRS. SARAH LINCOLN, MOTHER OF THE PRESIDENT.

the sands of her life had nearly run out, she spoke with deep emotion of her own son, but said she thought that Abe was kinder, better, truer, than the other. Even the mother's instinct was lost as she looked back over those long years of poverty and privation in the Indiana cabin, when Abe's grateful love softened the rigors of her lot, and his great heart and giant frame were always at her command. " Abe was a poor boy," said she; "and I can say what scarcely one woman — a mother — can say in a thousand. Abe never gave me a cross word or look, and never refused, in fact or appearance, to do any thing I requested him. I never gave him a cross word in all my life. . . . His mind and mine — what little I had — seemed to run together. . . . He was here after he was elected President." (At this point the aged speaker turned away to weep, and then, wiping her eyes with her apron, went on with the story). " He was dutiful to me always. I think he loved me truly. I had a son, John, who was raised with Abe. Both were good boys; but I must say, both now being dead, that Abe was the best boy I ever saw, or expect to see. I wish I had died when my husband died. I did not want Abe to run for President; did not want him elected; was afraid somehow, — felt in my heart; and when he came down to see me, after he was elected President, I still felt that something told me that something would befall Abe, and that I should see him no more."

Is there any thing in the language we speak more touching than that simple plaint of the woman whom we must regard as Abraham Lincoln's mother? The apprehension in her " heart" was well grounded. She " saw him no more." When Mr. Herndon rose to depart, her eyes again filled with tears; and, wringing his hands as if loath to part with one who talked so much of her beloved Abe, she said, " Good-by, my good son's friend. Farewell."

Abe had a very retentive memory. He frequently amused his young companions by repeating to them long passages from the books he had been reading. On Monday mornings he would mount a stump, and deliver, with a wonderful approach to exactness, the sermon he had heard the day before. His taste for public speaking appeared to be natural and irresistible. His step-sister, Matilda Johnston, says he was an indefatigable " preacher." " When father and mother would go to church, Abe would take down the Bible, read a verse, give out a hymn, and we would sing. Abe was about fifteen years of age. He preached, and we would do the crying. Sometimes he would join in the chorus of tears. One day my brother, John Johnston, caught a land terrapin, brought it to the place where Abe was preaching, threw it against the tree, and crushed the shell. It suffered much, — quivered all over. Abe then preached against cruelty to animals, contending that an ant's life was as sweet to it as ours to us."

But this practice of " preaching " and political speaking, into which Abe had fallen, at length became a great nuisance to old Tom. It distracted everybody, and sadly interfered with the work. If Abe had confined his discourses to Sunday preaching, while the old folks were away, it would not have been so objectionable. But he knew his power, liked to please everybody, and would be sure to set up as an orator wherever he found the greatest number of people together. When it was announced that Abe had taken the " stump " in the harvest-field, there was an end of work. The hands flocked around him, and listened to his curious speeches with infinite delight. " The sight of such a thing amused all," says Mrs. Lincoln ; though she admits that her husband was compelled to break it up with the strong hand ; and poor Abe was many times dragged from the platform, and hustled off to his work in no gentle manner. [1]

Abe worked occasionally with Tom Lincoln in the shop ; but he did it reluctantly, and never intended to learn even so much of the trade as Lincoln was able to teach him. The rough work turned out at that shop was far beneath his am-

[1] We are told by Col. Chapman that Abe's father habitually treated h'm with great barbarity. Dennis Hanks insists that he loved him sincerely. but admits that he now and then knocked him from the fence for merely answering traveller's questions about the roads.

bition, and he had made up his mind to lead a life as wholly unlike his father's as he could possibly make it. He therefore refused to be a carpenter. But he could not afford to be idle ; and, as soon as he was able to earn wages, he was hired out among the neighbors. He worked for many of them a few months at a time, and seemed perfectly willing to transfer his services wherever they were wanted, so that his father had no excuse for persecuting him with entreaties about learning to make tables and cupboards.

Abe was now becoming a man, and was, in fact, already taller than any man in the neighborhood. He was a universal favorite, and his wit and humor made him heartily welcome at every cabin between the two Pigeon Creeks. Any family was glad when "Abe Linkern" was hired to work with them ; for he did his work well, and made them all merry while he was about it. The women were especially pleased, for Abe was not above doing any kind of "chores" for them. He was always ready to make a fire, carry water, or nurse a baby. But what manner of people were these amongst whom he passed the most critical part of his life ? We must know them if we desire to know him.

There lived in the neighborhood of Gentryville a Mrs. Elizabeth Crawford, wife to the now celebrated Josiah with the sour temper and the blue nose. Abe was very fond of her, and inclined to "let himself out" in her company. She fortunately possessed a rare memory, and Mr. Herndon's rich collection of manuscripts was made richer still by her contributions. We have from her a great mass of valuable, and sometimes extremely amusing, information. Among it is the following graphic, although rude, account of the Pigeon Creek people in general : —

"You wish me to tell you how the people used to go to meeting, — how far they went. At that time we thought it nothing to go eight or ten miles. The old ladies did not stop for the want of a shawl, or cloak, or riding-dress, or two horses, in the winter-time ; but they would put on their hus-

bands' old overcoats, and wrap up their little ones, and take
one or two of them up on their beasts, and their husbands
would walk, and they would go to church, and stay in the
neighborhood until the next day, and then go home. The old
men would start out of their fields from their work, or out of
the woods from hunting, with their guns on their shoulders,
and go to church. Some of them dressed in deer-skin pants
and moccasins, hunting-shirts with a rope or leather strap
around them. They would come in laughing, shake hands all
around, sit down and talk about their game they had killed,
or some other work they had done, and smoke their pipes together with the old ladies. If in warm weather, they would
kindle up a little fire out in the meeting-house yard, to light
their pipes. If in winter-time, they would hold church in some
of the neighbors' houses. At such times they were always
treated with the utmost of kindness: a bottle of whiskey, a
pitcher of water, sugar and glass, were set out, or a basket of
apples, or turnips, or some pies and cakes. Apples were scarce
them times. Sometimes potatoes were used as a treat. (I
must tell you that the first treat I ever received in old Mr.
Linkern's house, that was our President's father's house, was
a plate of potatoes, washed and pared very nicely, and handed
round. It was something new to me, for I never had seen a
raw potato eaten before. I looked to see how they made use
of them. They took off a potato, and ate them like apples.)
Thus they spent the time till time for preaching to commence,
then they would all take their seats : the preacher would take
his stand, draw his coat, open his shirt-collar, commence service by singing and prayer; take his text and preach till the
sweat would roll off in great drops. Shaking hands and
singing then ended the service. The people seemed to enjoy
religion more in them days than they do now. They were
glad to see each other, and enjoyed themselves better than
they do now."

Society about Gentryville was little different from that of
any other backwoods settlement of the same day. The houses

were scattered far apart; but the inhabitants would travel long distances to a log-rolling, a house-raising, a wedding, or any thing else that might be turned into a fast and furious frolic. On such occasions the young women carried their shoes in their hands, and only put them on when about to join the company. The ladies drank whiskey-toddy, while the men took it straight; and both sexes danced the live-long night, barefooted, on puncheon floors.

The fair sex wore "cornfield bonnets, scoop-shaped, flaring in front, and long though narrow behind." Shoes were the mode when entering the ball-room; but it was not at all fashionable to scuff them out by walking or dancing in them. "Four yards of linsey-woolsey, a yard in width, made a dress for any woman." The waist was short, and terminated just under the arms, whilst the skirt was long and narrow. "Crimps and puckering frills" it had none. The coats of the men were home-made; the materials, jeans or linsey-woolsey. The waists were short, like the frocks of the women, and the long "claw-hammer" tail was split up to the waist. This, however, was company dress, and the hunting-shirt did duty for every day. The breeches were of buck-skin or jeans; the cap was of coon-skin; and the shoes of leather tanned at home. If no member of the family could make shoes, the leather was taken to some one who could, and the customer paid the maker a fair price in some other sort of labor.

The state of agriculture was what it always is where there is no market, either to sell or buy; where the implements are few and primitive, and where there are no regular mechanics. The Pigeon Creek farmer "tickled" two acres of ground in a day with his old shovel-plough, and got but half a crop. He cut one acre with his sickle, while the modern machine lays down in neat rows ten. With his flail and horse tramping, he threshed out fifteen bushels of wheat; while the machine of to-day, with a few more hands, would turn out three hundred and fifty. He "fanned" and "cleaned with a sheet." When he wanted flour, he took his team and went to a "horse-mill," where he spent a whole day in converting fifteen bushels of grain.[1]

The minds of these people were filled with superstitions, which most persons imagine to be, at least, as antiquated as witch-burning. They firmly believed in witches and all kind of witch-doings. They sent for wizards to cure sick cattle. They shot the image of the witch with a silver ball, to break the spell she was supposed to have laid on a human being. If a dog ran directly across a man's path whilst he was hunting, it was terrible "luck," unless he instantly hooked his two little fingers together, and pulled with all his might, until the dog was out of sight. There were wizards who took charmed twigs in their hands, and made them point to springs of water and all kinds of treasure beneath the earth's surface. There were "faith doctors," who cured diseases by performing mysterious ceremonies and muttering cabalistic words. If a bird alighted in a window, one of the family would speedily die. If a horse breathed on a child, the child would have the whooping-cough. Every thing must be done at certain "times and seasons," else it would be attended with "bad luck." They must cut trees for rails in the early part of the day, and in "the light of the moon." They must make fence in "the light of the moon;" otherwise, the fence would sink. Potatoes and other roots were to be planted in the "dark of the moon," but trees, and plants which bore their fruits above ground, must be "put out in the light of the moon." The moon exerted a fearful influence, either kindly or malignant, as the good old rules were observed or not. It was even required to make soap "in the light of the moon," and, moreover, it must be stirred only one way, and by one person. Nothing of importance was to be begun on Friday. All enterprises inaugurated on that day went fatally amiss. A horse-colt could be begotten only "in the dark of the moon,"

---

[1] " Size of the fields from ten, twelve. sixteen, twenty. Raised corn mostly; some wheat, — enough for a cake on Sunday morning. Hogs and venison hams were legal tender, and coon-skins also. We raised sheep and cattle, but they did not fetch much. Cows and calves were only worth six dollars; corn, ten cents; wheat, twenty-five cents at that time." — DENNIS HANKS.

and animals treated otherwise than " according to the signs in the almanac " were nearly sure to die.

Such were the people among whom Abe grew to manhood. With their sons and daughters he went to school. Upon their farms he earned his daily bread by daily toil. From their conversation he formed his earliest opinions of men and things, the world over. Many of their peculiarities became his ; and many of their thoughts and feelings concerning a multitude of subjects were assimilated with his own, and helped to create that unique character, which, in the eyes of a great host of the American people, was only less curious and amusing than it was noble and august.

His most intimate companions were of course, for a long time, the members of his own family. The reader already knows something of Thomas Lincoln, and that pre-eminently good woman, Sally Bush. The latter, we know, washed, clothed, loved, and encouraged Abe in well-doing, from the moment he fell in her way. How much he owed to her goodness and affection, he was himself never able to estimate. That it was a great debt, fondly acknowledged and cheerfully repaid as far as in him lay, there can be no doubt. His own sister, the child of Nancy Hanks, was warmly attached to him. Her face somewhat resembled his. In repose it had the gravity which they both, perhaps, inherited from their mother ; but it was capable of being lighted almost into beauty by one of Abe's ridiculous stories or rapturous sallies of humor. She was a modest, plain, industrious girl, and is kindly remembered by all who knew her. She was married to Aaron Grigsby at eighteen, and a year after died in child-bed. Like Abe, she occasionally worked out at the houses of the neighbors, and at one time was employed in Mrs. Crawford's kitchen, while her brother was a laborer on the same farm. She lies buried, not with her mother, but in the yard of the old Pigeon Creek meeting-house. It is especially pleasing to read the encomiums lavished upon her memory by the Grigsbys; for between the Grigsbys on one side, and Abe and his step-brother on the other, there once subsisted a fierce feud.

As we have already learned from Dennis Hanks, the two families — the Johnstons and the Lincolns — "got along finely together." The affectionate relations between Abe and his two step-sisters were the subject of common remark throughout the neighborhood. One of them married Dennis Hanks, and the other Levi Hall, or, as he is better known, Squire Hall, — a cousin of Abe. Both these women (the latter now Mrs. Moore) furnished Mr. Herndon very valuable memoirs of Abe's life whilst he dwelt under the same roof with them; and they have given an account of him which shows that the ties between them were of the strongest and tenderest kind. But what is most remarkable in their statements is, that they never opened their lips without telling how worthy of everybody's love their mother was, and how Abe revered her as much as they did. They were interesting girls, and became exemplary women.

John D. Johnston, the only son of Mrs. Lincoln, was not the best boy, and did not grow to be the best man, in all the Pigeon Creek region. He had no positive vice, except idleness, and no special virtue but good temper. He was not a fortunate man; never made money; was always needy, and always clamoring for the aid of his friends. Mr. Lincoln, all through John's life, had much trouble to keep him on his legs, and succeeded indifferently in all his attempts. In a subsequent chapter a letter will be given from him, which indirectly portrays his step-brother's character much better than it can be done here. But, as youths, the intimacy between them was very close; and in another place it will appear that Abe undertook his second voyage to New Orleans only on condition that John would go along.

But the most constant of his companions was his jolly cousin, Dennis Hanks. Of all the contributors to Mr. Herndon's store of information, good, bad, and indifferent, concerning this period of Mr. Lincoln's life, Dennis is the most amusing, insinuating, and prolific. He would have it distinctly understood that the well of his memory is the only proper

DENNIS F. HANKS.

source whence any thing like truth may be drawn.[1] He has covered countless sheets of paper devoted to indiscriminate laudations of Abe and all his kindred. But in all this he does not neglect to say a word for himself.

At one place, "his cousin, Dennis Hanks," is said to have taught Abe to read and write. At another, he is represented as the benevolent purchaser of the volumes from which Abe (and Dennis too) derived a wonderfully clear and accurate conception of the science of law. In all studies their minds advanced *pari passu*. Whenever any differences are noted (and they are few and slight), Dennis is a step ahead, benignantly extending a helping hand to the lagging pupil behind. But Dennis's heart is big and kind: he defames no one; he is merely a harmless romancer. In the gallery of family portraits painted by Dennis, every face looks down upon us with the serenity of innocence and virtue. There is no spot on the fame of any one of them. No family could have a more vigorous or chivalrous defender than he, or one who repelled with greater scorn any rumor to their discredit. That Enlow story! Dennis almost scorned to confute it; but, when he did get at it, he settled it by a magnificent exercise of inven-

[1] The following random selections from his writings leave us no room to doubt Dennis's opinion of his own value: —

"William, let in, don't keep any thing back, for I am in for the whole hog sure; for I know nobody can do any for you much, for all they know is from me at last. Every thing you see is from my notes, — this you can tell yourself.

"I have in my possession a little book, the private life of A. Lincoln, comprising a full life of his early years, and a succinct record of his career as statesman and President, by O. J. Victor, author of Lives of Garibaldi, Winfield Scott, John Paul Jones, &c., New York, Beadle and Company, publishers, No. 118 Williams Street. Now, sir, I find a great many things pertaining to Abe Lincoln's life that is not true. If you would like to have the book, I will mail it to you. I will say this much to you: if you don't have my name very frequently in your book, it won't go at all; for I have been East for two months, have seen a great many persons in that time, stating to them that there would be a book, 'The Life of A. Lincoln,' published, giving a full account of the family, from England to this country. Now, William, if there be any thing you want to know, let me know: I will give you all the information I can.

"I have seen a letter that you wrote to my daughter, Harriet Chapman, of inquiry about some things. I thought you were informed all about them. I don't know what she has stated to you about your questions; but you had better consult me about them.

"Billy, it seems to me, from the letters that you write to me asking questions, that you ask the same questions over several times. How is this? Do you forget, or are you like the lawyer, trying to make me cross my path, or not? Now, I *will*. Look below for the answer."

tive genius. He knew "this Abe Enlow" well, he said, and
he had been dead precisely fifty-five years. But, whenever
the truth can be told without damage to the character of a
Lincoln or a Hanks, Dennis will tell it candidly enough, provided there is no temptation to magnify himself. His testimony, however, has been sparingly used throughout these
pages ; and no statement has been taken from him unless it
was more or less directly corroborated by some one else.
The better part of his evidence Mr. Herndon took the precaution of reading carefully to John Hanks, who pronounced
it substantially true ; and that circumstance gives it undeni-
able value.

When Thomas and Betsy Sparrow died in the fall of 1818,
Dennis was taken from the "little half-faced camp," and
became one of the Lincoln family. Until Thomas Lincoln's
second marriage, Dennis, Abe, and Sarah were all three poor,
ragged, and miserable together. After that, Dennis got along
better, as well as the rest. He was a lively, volatile, sympathetic fellow, and Abe liked him well from the beginning.
They fished, hunted, and worked in company ; loafed at the
grocery, where Dennis got drunk, and Abe told stories ; talked
politics with Col. Jones ; " swapped jokes " with Baldwin the
blacksmith ; and faithfully attended the sittings of the nearest
justice of the peace, where both had opportunities to correct
and annotate the law they thought they had learned from the
" Statute of Indiana." Dennis was kind, genial, lazy, brim-
ming over with humor, and full of amusing anecdotes. He
revelled in song, from the vulgarest ballad to the loftiest hymn
of devotion ; " from " The turbaned Turk, that scorns the
world," to the holiest lines of Doctor Watts. These qualities
marked him wherever he went ; and in excessive good-nature,
and in the ease with which he passed from the extreme of
rigor to the extreme of laxity, he was distinguished above the
others of his name.

There was one Hanks, however, who was not like Dennis,
or any other Hanks we know any thing about : this was
" old John," as he is familiarly called in Illinois, — a sober,

honest, truthful man, with none of the wit and none of the
questionable accomplishments of Dennis. He was the son of
Joseph, the carpenter with whom Tom Lincoln learned the
trade. He went to Indiana to live with the Lincolns when
Abe was fourteen years of age, and remained there four years.
He then returned to Kentucky, and subsequently went to
Illinois, where he was speedily joined by the old friends he
had left in Indiana. When Abe separated from the family,
and went in search of individual fortune, it was in company
with " old John." Together they split the rails that did so
much to make Abe President; and " old John " set the ball
in motion by carrying a part of them into the Decatur Convention on his own broad shoulders. John had no education
whatever, except that of the muscles and the heart. He
could neither read nor write; but his character was pure and
respectable, and Lincoln esteemed him as a man, and loved
him as a friend and relative.

About six years after the death of the first Mrs. Lincoln,
Levi Hall and his wife and family came to Indiana, and settled
near the Lincolns. Mrs. Hall was Nancy Hanks, the mother
of our friend Dennis, and the aunt of Nancy Hanks, the
mother of Abraham Lincoln. She had numerous children by
her husband. One of them, Levi, as already mentioned, married one of Abe's step-sisters, while Dennis, his half-brother,
married the other one. The father and mother of the Halls
speedily died of the milk-sickness, but Levi was for many
years a constant companion of Abe and Dennis.

In 1825 Abraham was employed by James Taylor, who
lived at the mouth of Anderson's Creek. He was paid six
dollars a month, and remained for nine months. His principal business was the management of a ferry-boat which Mr.
Taylor had plying across the Ohio, as well as Anderson's
Creek. But, in addition to this, he was required to do all
sorts of farm-work, and even to perform some menial services
about the house. He was hostler, ploughman, ferryman, out
of doors, and man-of-all-work within doors. He ground
corn with a hand-mill, or " grated " it when too young to be

4

ground; rose early, built fires, put on the water in the kitchen, "fixed around generally," and had things prepared for cooking before the mistress of the house was stirring. He slept up stairs with young Green Taylor, who says that he usually read "till near midnight," notwithstanding the necessity for being out of his bed before day. Green was somewhat disposed to ill-use the poor hired boy, and once struck him with an ear of hard corn, and cut a deep gash over his eye. He makes no comment upon this generous act, except that "Abe got mad," but did not thrash him.

Abe was a hand much in demand in "hog-killing time." He butchered not only for Mr. Taylor, but for John Woods, John Duthan, Stephen McDaniels, and others. At this he earned thirty-one cents a day, as it was considered "rough work."

For a long time there was only one person in the neighborhood for whom Abe felt a decided dislike; and that was Josiah Crawford, who had made him "pull fodder," to pay for the Weems's "Washington." On that score he was "hurt" and "mad," and often declared "he would have revenge." But being a poor boy, — a circumstance of which Crawford had already taken shameful advantage to extort three days' labor, — he was glad to get work any place, and frequently "hired to his old adversary." Abe's first business in his employ was daubing his cabin, which was built of logs, unhewed, and with the bark on. In the loft of this house, thus finished by his own hands, he slept for many weeks at a time. He spent his evenings as he did at home, — writing on wooden shovels or boards with "a coal, or keel, from the branch." This family was rich in the possession of several books, which Abe read through time and again, according to his usual custom. One of them was the "Kentucky Preceptor," from which Mrs. Crawford insists that he "learned his school orations, speeches, and pieces to write." She tells us also that "Abe was a sensitive lad, never coming where he was not wanted;" that he always lifted his hat, and bowed, when he made his appearance; and that " he was tender and kind," like his sister, who was at the same time her maid-of-all-work. His pay was twenty-five cents a day; "and, when he missed time, he would not charge for it." This latter remark of good Mrs. Crawford reveals the fact that her husband was in the habit of docking Abe on his miserable wages whenever he happened to lose a few minutes from steady work.

The time came, however, when Abe got his " revenge " for all this petty brutality. Crawford was as ugly as he was surly. His nose was a monstrosity, — long and crooked, with a huge, misshapen " stub " at the end, surmounted by a host of pimples, and the whole as " blue " as the usual state of Mr. Crawford's spirits. Upon this member Abe levelled his attack in rhyme, song, and " chronicle ; " and, though he could not reduce the nose, he gave it a fame as wide as to the Wabash and the Ohio. It is not improbable that he learned the art of making the doggerel rhymes in which he celebrated Crawford's nose from the study of Crawford's own " Kentucky Preceptor." At all events, his sallies upon this single topic achieved him great reputation as a " poet " and a wit, and caused Crawford intolerable anguish.

It is likely that Abe was reconciled to his situation in this family by the presence of his sister, and the opportunity it gave him of being in the company of Mrs. Crawford, for whom he had a genuine attachment; for she was nothing that her husband was, and every thing that he was not. According to her account, he split rails, ploughed, threshed, and did whatever else he was ordered to do; but she distinctly affirms that " Abe was no hand to pitch into his work like killing snakes." He went about it ": calmly," and generally took the opportunity to throw " Crawford " down two or three times " before they went to the field." It is fair to presume, that, when Abe managed to inveigle his disagreeable employer into a tussle, he hoisted him high and threw him hard, for he felt that he had no reason to be careful of his bones. After meals Abe " hung about," lingered long to gossip and joke with the women; and these pleasant, stolen conferences were generally broken up with the exclamation, "Well, this won't buy the child a coat!" and the long-legged hired boy would stride away to join his master.

In the mean time Abe had become, not only the longest, but the strongest, man in the settlement. Some of his feats almost surpass belief, and those who beheld them with their own eyes stood literally amazed. Richardson, a neighbor, declares that he could carry a load to which the strength of " three ordinary men " would scarcely be equal. He saw him quietly pick up and walk away with " a chicken-house, made of poles pinned together, and covered, that weighed at least six hundred, if not much more." At another time the Richardsons were building a corn-crib: Abe was there; and, seeing three or four men preparing " sticks " upon which to carry some huge posts, he relieved them of all further trouble by shouldering the posts, single-handed, and walking away with them to the place where they were wanted. " He could strike with a mall," says old Mr. Wood, " a heavier blow than any man. . . . He could sink an axe deeper into wood than any man I ever saw."

For hunting purposes, the Pigeon Creek region was one of the most inviting on earth. The uplands were all covered with an original growth of majestic forest trees,[1] whilst on the hillsides, and wherever an opening in the woods permitted the access of sunlight, there were beds of fragrant and beautiful wild-flowers, presenting, in contrast with the dense green around them, the most brilliant and agreeable effects. Here the game had vast and secluded ranges, which, until very recently, had heard the report of no white man's gun. In Abe's time, the squirrels, rabbits, partridges, and other varieties of smaller game, were so abundant as to be a nuisance. They devastated grain-fields and gardens; and

---

[1] " Now about the timber: it was black walnut and black oak, hickory and jack oak, elm and white oak. undergrowth, logwood in abundance. grape-vines and shoe-make bushes, and milk-sick plenty. All my relations died of that disease on Little Pigeon Creek, Spencer County."—DENNIS HANKS.

while they were seldom shot for the table, the settlers frequently devised the most cunning means of destroying them in great quantities, in order to save the growing crops. Wild turkeys and deer were the principal reliance for food; but besides these were the bears, the wild-cats, and the panthers.[1] The scream of the latter, the most ferocious and bloodthirsty of the cat kind, hastened Abe's homeward steps on many a dark night, as he came late from Dave Turnham's, "Uncle" Wood's, or the Gentryville grocery. That terrific cry appeals not only to the natural fear of the monster's teeth and claws, but, heard in the solitude of night and the forest, it awakens a feeling of superstitious horror, that chills the heart of the bravest.

Everybody about Abe made hunting a part of his business.[2] Tom Lincoln and Dennis Hanks doubtless regaled him continually with wonderful stories of their luck and prowess; but he was no hunter himself, and did not care to learn. It is true, that, when a mere child, he made a fortunate shot at a flock of wild turkeys, through a crack in the wall of the "half-faced cabin;"[3] and that, when grown up, he went for coons occasionally with Richardson, or watched deer-licks with Turnham; but a true and hearty sportsman he never was. As practised on this wild border, it was a solitary, unsociable way of spending time, which did not suit his nature; and, besides, it required more exertion than he was willing to make without due compensation. It could not be said that Abe was indolent; for he was alert, brisk, active, about every thing that he made up his mind to do. His step was very quick; and, when he had a sufficient object in view, he strode out on

[1] "No Indians there when I first went to Indiana: I say, no, none. I say this: bear, deer, turkey, and coon, wild-cats, and other things, and frogs." — DENNIS HANKS.

[2] "You say, What were some of the customs? I suppose you mean take us all together. One thing I can tell you about: we had to work very hard cleaning ground for to keep body and soul together; and every spare time we had we picked up our rifle, and brought in a fine deer or turkey; and in the winter-time we went a coon-hunting, for coon-skins were at that time considered legal tender, and deer-skins and hams. I tell you, Billy, I enjoyed myself better then than I ever have since." — DENNIS HANKS.

[3] "No doubt about the A. Lincoln's killing the turkey. He done it with his father's rifle, made by William Lutes, of Bullitt County, Kentucky. I have killed a hundred deer with her myself; turkeys too numerous to mention." — DENNIS HANKS.

his long, muscular legs, swinging his bony arms as he moved along, with an energy that put miles behind him before a lazy fellow like Dennis Hanks or John Johnston could make up his mind to start. But, when he felt that he had time to spare, he preferred to give it to reading or to " talk ; " and, of the two, he would take the latter, provided he could find a person who had something new or racy to say. He liked excessively to hear his own voice, when it was promoting fun and good fellowship ; but he was also a most rare and attentive listener. Hunting was entirely too " still " an occupation for him.

All manner of rustic sports were in vogue among the Pigeon Creek boys. Abe was especially formidable as a wrestler; and, from about 1828 onward, there was no man, far or near, that would give him a match. " Cat," " throwing the mall," " hopping and half-hammon " (whatsoever that may mean), and " four-corner bull-pen " were likewise athletic games in high honor.[1]

All sorts of frolics and all kinds of popular gatherings, whether for work or amusement, possessed irresistible attractions for Abe. He loved to see and be seen, to make sport and to enjoy it. It was a most important part of his education that he got at the corn-shuckings, the log-rollings, the shooting-matches, and the gay and jolly weddings of those early border times. He was the only man or boy within a wide compass who had learning enough to furnish the literature for such occasions ; and those who failed to employ his talents to grace or commemorate the festivities they set on foot were sure to be stung by some coarse but humorous lampoon from his pen. In the social way, he would not suffer himself to be slighted with impunity ; and, if there were any who did not enjoy his wit, they might content themselves with being the subjects of it. Unless he received some very pointed intimation that his presence was not wanted, he was

[1] " You ask, What sort of plays ? What we called them at that time were ' bull-pen,' ' corner and cat,' ' hopping and half-hammon ; ' playing at night ' old Sister Feby.' This I know, for I took a hand myself ; and, wrestling, we could throw down anybody." — DENNIS HANKS.

among the first and earliest at all the neighborhood routs; and when his tall, singular figure was seen towering amongst the hunting-shirts, it was considered due notice that the fun was about to commence. "Abe Linkhern," as he was generally called, made things lively wherever he went: and, if Crawford's blue nose happened to have been carried to the assembly, it quickly subsided, on his arrival, into some obscure corner; for the implacable "Linkhern" was apt to make it the subject of a jest that would set the company in a roar. But when a party was made up, and Abe left out, as sometimes happened through the influence of Crawford, he sulked, fumed, "got mad," nursed his anger into rage, and then broke out in songs or "chronicles," which were frequently very bitter, sometimes passably humorous, and invariably vulgar.

At an early age he began to attend the "preachings" round-about, but principally at the Pigeon Creek church, with a view to catching whatever might be ludicrous in the preacher's air or matter, and making it the subject of mimicry as soon as he could collect an audience of idle boys and men to hear him. A pious stranger, passing that way on a Sunday morning, was invited to preach for the Pigeon Creek congregation; but he banged the boards of the old pulpit, and bellowed and groaned so wonderfully, that Abe could hardly contain his mirth. This memorable sermon was a great favorite with him; and he frequently reproduced it with nasal tones, rolling eyes, and all manner of droll aggravations, to the great delight of Nat Grigsby and the wild fellows whom Nat was able to assemble. None that heard him, not even Nat himself (who was any thing but dull), was ever able to show wherein Abe's absurd version really departed from the original.

The importance of Gentryville, as a "centre of business," soon began to possess the imaginations of the dwellers between the two Pigeon Creeks. Why might it not be a great place of trade? Mr. Gentry was a most generous patron; it was advantageously situated where two roads crossed; it already had a blacksmith's shop, a grocery, and a store. Jones, it is

true, had once moved away in a sulk, but Mr. Gentry's fine
diplomacy had quickly brought him back, with all his goods
and talents unreservedly devoted to the " improvement of the
town ; " and now, since there was literally nothing left to
cloud the prospects of the " point," brisk times were expected
in the near future.

Dennis Hanks, John Johnston, Abe, and the other boys
in the neighborhood, loitered much about the store, the grocery, and the blacksmith's shop, at Gentryville. Dennis in-
genuously remarks, " Sometimes we spent a little time at
grog, pushing weights, wrestling, telling stories." The time
that Abe " spent at grog " was, in truth, a " little time." He
never liked ardent spirits at any period of his life ; but " he
did take his dram as others did."[1] He was a natural politician, intensely ambitious, and anxious to be popular. For
this reason, and this alone, he drank with his friends, although
very temperately. If he could have avoided it without giving offence, he would gladly have done so. But he coveted
the applause of his pot companions, and, because he could not
get it otherwise, made a faint pretence of enjoying his liquor
as they did. The " people " drank, and Abe was always for
doing whatever the " people " did. All his life he held that
whatsoever was popular — the habit or the sentiment of the
masses — could not be essentially wrong. But, although a
whiskey-jug was kept in every ordinarily respectable household, Abe never tasted it at home. His step-mother thought
he carried his temperance to extremes.

Jones, the great Jones, without whom it was generally
agreed that Gentryville must have gone into eclipse, but with
whom, and through whom, it was somehow to become a sort of
metropolitan cross-roads, — Jones was Abe's friend and men-
tor from the moment of their acquaintance. Abe is even said
to have " clerked for him ; " that is, he packed and unpacked
boxes, ranged goods on the shelves, drew the liquids in the
cellar, or exhibited the stone and earthen ware to purchasers ;

[1] The fact is proved by his most intimate acquaintances, both at Gentryville and New
Salem.

but in his service he was never promoted to keeping accounts, or even to selling the finer goods across the counter.[1] But Mr. Jones was very fond of his "clerk,"—enjoyed his company, appreciated his humor, and predicted something great for him. As he did not doubt that Abe would one day be a man of considerable influence, he took pains to give him correct views of the nature of American institutions. An ardent Jackson man himself, he imparted to Abe the true faith, as delivered by that great democratic apostle; and the traces of this teaching were never wholly effaced from Mr. Lincoln's mind. Whilst he remained at Gentryville, his politics accorded with Mr. Jones's; and, even after he had turned Whig in Illinois, John Hanks tells us that he wanted to whip a man for traducing Jackson. He was an eager reader of newspapers whenever he could get them, and Mr. Jones carefully put into his hands the kind he thought a raw youth should have. But Abe's appetite was not to be satisfied by what Mr. Jones supplied; and he frequently borrowed others from "Uncle Wood," who lived about a mile from the Lincoln cabin, and for whom he sometimes worked.

What manner of man kept the Gentryville grocery, we are not informed. Abe was often at his place, however, and would stay so long at nights, "telling stories" and "cracking jokes," that Dennis Hanks, who was ambitious in the same line, and probably jealous of Abe's overshadowing success, "got mad at him," and "cussed him." When Dennis found himself thrown in the shade, he immediately became virtuous, and wished to retire early.

John Baldwin, the blacksmith, was one of Abe's special friends from his boyhood onward. Baldwin was a story-teller and a joker of rare accomplishments; and Abe, when a very little fellow, would slip off to his shop and sit and listen to

---

[1] "Lincoln drove a team, cut up pork, and sold goods for Jones. Jones told me that Lincoln read all his books, and I remember History of United States as one. Jones often said to me, that Lincoln would make a great man one of these days,—had said so long before, and to other people,—said so as far back as 1828-9."—DOUGHERTY.

him by the hour. As he grew up, the practice continued as of old, except that Abe soon began to exchange anecdotes with his clever friend at the anvil. Dennis Hanks says Baldwin was his "*particular* friend," and that " Abe spent a great deal of his leisure time with him." Statesmen, plenipotentiaries, famous commanders, have many times made the White House at Washington ring with their laughter over the quaint tales of John Baldwin, the blacksmith, delivered second-hand by his inimitable friend Lincoln.

Abe and Dave Turnham had one day been threshing wheat,— probably for Turnham's father, — and concluded to spend the evening at Gentryville. They lingered there until late in the night, when, wending their way along the road toward Lincoln's cabin, they espied something resembling a man lying dead or insensible by the side of a mud-puddle. They rolled the sleeper over, and found in him an old and quite respectable acquaintance, hopelessly drunk. All efforts failed to rouse him to any exertion on his own behalf. Abe's companions were disposed to let him lie in the bed he had made for himself; but, as the night was cold and dreary, he must have frozen to death had this inhuman proposition been equally agreeable to everybody present. To Abe it seemed utterly monstrous; and, seeing he was to have no help, he bent his mighty frame, and, taking the big man in his long arms, carried him a great distance to Dennis Hanks's cabin. There he built a fire, warmed, rubbed, and nursed him through the entire night, — his companions of the road having left him alone in his merciful task. The man often told John Hanks, that it was mighty " clever in Abe to tote him to a warm fire that cold night," and was very sure that Abe's strength and benevolence had saved his life.

Abe was fond of music, but was himself wholly unable to produce three harmonious notes together. He made various vain attempts to sing a few lines of " Poor old Ned," but they were all equally ludicrous and ineffectual. " Religious songs did not appear to suit him at all," says Dennis Hanks; but of profane ballads and amorous ditties he knew the words of a vast number. When Dennis got happy at the grocery, or passed the bounds of propriety at a frolic, he was in the habit of raising a charming carol in praise of the joys which enter into the Mussulman's estate on earth, — of which he has vouchsafed us only three lines, —

> " The turbaned Turk that scorns the world,
> And struts about with his whiskers curled,
> For no other man but himself to see."

It was a prime favorite of Abe's; and Dennis sang it with such appropriate zest and feeling, that Abe never forgot a single word of it while he lived.

Another was, —

> " Hail Columbia, happy land!
> If you ain't drunk, I'll be damned," —

a song which Dennis thinks should be warbled only in the "fields;" and tells us that they knew and enjoyed "all such [songs] as this." Dave Turnham was also a musical genius, and had a "piece" beginning, —

> " There was a Romish lady
> Brought up in popery,"

which Abe thought one of the best he ever heard, and insisted upon Dave's singing it for the delectation of old Tom Lincoln, who relished it quite as much as Abe did.[1]

Mrs. Crawford says, that Abe did not attempt to sing much

---

[1] "I recollect some more: —

> ' Come, thou Fount of every blessing,
> Tune my heart to sing thy praise.'

> ' When I can read my title clear
> To mansions in the skies! '

> ' How tedious and tasteless the hours.'

> ' Oh! to grace how great a debtor! '

Other little songs I won't say any thing about: they would not look well in print; but I could give them." — DENNIS HANKS.

about the house : he was probably afraid to indulge in such offensive gayeties in the very habitation of the morose Crawford.   According to Dennis Hanks, his melody was not of the sort that hath power to charm the savage ; and he was naturally timid about trying it upon Crawford.   But, when he was freed from those chilling restraints, he put forth his best endeavors to render " one [song] that was called ' William Riley,' and one that was called ' John Anderson's Lamentations,' and one that was made about Gen. Jackson and John Adams, at the time they were nominated for the presidency."

The Jackson song indicated clearly enough Abe's steadiness in the political views inculcated by Jones.   Mrs. Crawford could recollect but a single stanza of it : —

> " Let auld acquaintance be forgot,
> And never brought to mind,
> And Jackson be our President,
> And Adams left behind."

In the text of " John Anderson's Lamentations," — a most distressful lyric to begin with, — Abe was popularly supposed to have interpolated some lines of his own, which conclusively attested his genius for poetic composition.   At all events, he sang it as follows : —

> " O sinners ! poor sinners, take warning by me :
> The fruits of transgression behold now, and see ;
> My soul is tormented, my body confined,
> My friends and dear children left weeping behind.

> " Much intoxication my ruin has been,
> And my dear companion hath barbarously slain :
> In yonder cold graveyard the body doth lie ;
> Whilst I am condemned, and shortly must die.

> " Remember John Anderson's death, and reform
> Before death overtakes you, and vengeance comes on.
> My grief's overwhelming ; in God I must trust :
> I am justly condemned ; my sentence is just.

" I am waiting the summons in eternity to be hurled ;
Whilst my poor little orphans are cast on the world.
I hope my kind neighbors their guardeens will be,
And Heaven, kind Heaven, protect them and me."

In 1826 Abe's sister Nancy (or Sarah) was married to
Aaron Grigsby; and the festivities of the occasion were made
memorable by a song entitled, "Adam and Eve's Wedding
Song," which many believed Abe had himself composed.
The conceits embodied in the doggerel were old before Abe
was born; but there is some intrinsic as well as extraneous
evidence to show that the doggerel itself was his. It was
sung by the whole Lincoln family, before Nancy's marriage
and since, but by nobody else in the neighborhood.

ADAM AND EVE'S WEDDING SONG.

When Adam was created, he dwelt in Eden's shade,
As Moses has recorded, and soon an Eve was made.
    Ten thousand times ten thousand
    Of creatures swarmed around
    Before a bride was formed,
    And yet no mate was found.

    The Lord then was not willing
    The man should be alone,
    But caused a sleep upon him,
    And took from him a bone,

    And closed the flesh in that place of;
    And then he took the same,
    And of it made a woman,
    And brought her to the man.

    Then Adam he rejoiced
    To see his loving bride,
    A part of his own body,
    The product of his side.

    This woman was not taken
    From Adam's feet, we see;
    So he must not abuse her,
    The meaning seems to be.

> This woman was not taken
> From Adam's head, we know;
> To show she must not rule him,
> 'Tis evidently so.
>
> This woman she was taken
> From under Adam's arm;
> So she must be protected
> From injuries and harm.

"It was considered at that time," says Mr. Richardson, "that Abe was the best penman in the neighborhood. One day, while he was on a visit at my mother's, I asked him to write some copies for me. He very willingly consented. He wrote several of them, but one of them I have never forgotten, although a boy at the time. It was this: —

> ' Good boys who to their books apply
> Will all be great men by and by.' "

Here are two original lines from Abe's own copy-book, probably the first he ever had, and which must not be confounded with the famous scrap-book in which his step-mother, lost in admiration of its contents, declares he " entered all things : " —

> " Abraham Lincoln, his hand and pen:
> He will be good, but God knows when."

Again, —

> " Abraham Lincoln is my name,
> And with my pen I write the same :
> I will be a good boy, but God knows when."

The same book contains the following, written at a later day, and with nothing to indicate that any part of it was borrowed : —

> " Time! what an empty vapor 'tis !
> And days how swift they are !
> Swift as an Indian arrow,
> Fly on like a shooting-star.
> The present moment just is here,
> Then slides away in haste,
> That we can never say they're ours,
> But only say they are past."

Abe wrote many "satires" and "chronicles," which are only remembered in fragments by a few old persons in the neighborhood. Even if we had them in full, they were most of them too indecent for publication. Such, at least, was the character of "a piece" which is said to have been "exceedingly humorous and witty," touching a church trial, wherein Brother Harper and Sister Gordon were the parties seeking judgment. It was very coarse, but it served admirably to raise a laugh in the grocery at the expense of the church.

His chronicles were many, and on a great variety of subjects. They were written, as his early admirers love to tell us, "in the scriptural style;" but those we have betray a very limited acquaintance with the model. In these "chapters" was celebrated every event of importance that took place in the neighborhood: weddings, fights, Crawford's nose, Sister Gordon's innocence, Brother Harper's wit, were all served up, fresh and gross, for the amusement of the groundlings.

Charles and Reuben Grigsby were married about the same time, and, being brothers, returned to their father's house with their brides upon the same day. The infare, the feast, the dance, the ostentatious retirement of the brides and grooms, were conducted in the old-fashioned way of all new countries in the United States, but a way which was bad enough to shock Squire Western himself. On this occasion Abe was not invited, and was very "mad" in consequence. This indignation found vent in a highly-spiced piece of descriptive writing, entitled "The Chronicles of Reuben," which are still in existence.

But even "The Chronicles," venomous and highly successful as they were, were totally insufficient to sate Abe's desire for vengeance on the Grigsbys. They were important people about Gentryville, and the social slight they had given him stung him bitterly. He therefore began on "Billy" in rhyme, after disposing of Charles and Reuben "in scriptural style." Mrs. Crawford attempted to repeat these verses to Mr. Herndon; but the good old lady had not proceeded far, when she blushed very red, and, saying that they were hardly decent,

proposed to tell them to her daughter, who would tell them to
her husband, who would write them down and send them to
Mr. Herndon. They are probably much curtailed by Mrs.
Crawford's modesty, but still it is impossible to transcribe
them. We give what we can to show how the first steps of
Abe's fame as a great writer were won. It must be admitted
that the literary taste of the community in which these rhymes
were popular could not have been very high.

"I will tell you about Joel and Mary: it is neither a joke
or a story, for Reuben and Charles has married two girls,
but Billy has married a boy."

> " The girls he had tried on every side,
>   But none could he get to agree :
>   All was in vain ; he went home again,
>   And, since that, he is married to Natty.

> " So Billy and Natty agreed very well,
>   And mamma's well pleased at the match :
>   The egg it is laid, but Natty's afraid
>   The shell is so soft it never will hatch ;
>   But Betsey she said, ' You cursed bald head,
>   My suitor you never can be ;
>   Besides ' " —

Abe dropped " The Chronicles " at a point on the road
where he was sure one of the Grigsbys would find them.
The stratagem succeeded, and that delicate " satire " produced
the desired effect. The Grigsbys were infuriated, — wild
with a rage which would be satisfied only when Abe's face
should be pounded into a jelly, and a couple of his ribs cracked
by some member of the injured family. Honor, according to
the Pigeon Creek code, demanded that somebody should be
" licked " in expiation of an outrage so grievous, — if not Abe,
then some friend of Abe's, whom he would depute to stand
the brunt in his stead. " Billy," the eldest of the brothers,
was selected to challenge him. Abe accepted generally ;
that is, agreed that there should be a fight about the matter
in question. It was accordingly so ordered : the ground was
selected a mile and a half from Gentryville, a ring was

marked out, and the bullies for twenty miles around attended. The friends of both parties were present in force, and excitement ran high. When the time arrived for the champions to step into the ring, Abe displayed his chivalry in a manner that must have struck the bystanders with admiration. He announced, that whereas Billy was confessedly his inferior in size, shape, and talents, unable to hit with pen or fist with any thing like his power, therefore he would forego the advantage which the challenge gave him, and "turn over" his step-brother, John Johnston, to do battle in his behalf. If this near relative should be sacrificed, he would abide the issue: he was merely anxious to see a fair and honorable fight. This proposition was considered highly meritorious, and the battle commenced on those general terms. John started out with fine pluck and spirit; but in a little while Billy got in some clever hits, and Abe began to exhibit symptoms of great uneasiness. Another pass or two, and John flagged quite decidedly, and it became evident that Abe was anxiously casting about for some pretext to break the ring. At length, when John was fairly down, and Billy on top, and all the spectators cheering, swearing, and pressing up to the very edge of the ring, Abe cried out that " Bill Boland showed foul play," and, bursting out of the crowd, seized Grigsby by the heels, and flung him off. Having righted John, and cleared the battle-ground of all opponents, "he swung a whiskey-bottle over his head, and swore that he was the big buck of the lick." It seems that nobody of the Grigsby faction, not one in that large assembly of bullies, cared to encounter the sweep of Abe's tremendously long and muscular arms; and so he remained master of the " lick." He was not content, however, with a naked triumph, but vaunted himself in the most offensive manner. He singled out the victorious but cheated Billy, and, making sundry hostile demonstrations, declared that he could whip him then and there. Billy meekly said " he did not doubt that," but that, if Abe would make things even between them by fighting with pistols, he would not be slow to grant him a meeting. But Abe replied that he was not going " to fool away his life on a single shot ; " and so Billy was fain to put up with the poor satisfaction he had already received.

At Gentryville " they had exhibitions or speaking meetings." " Some of the questions they spoke on were. The Bee and the Ant, Water and Fire : another was, Which had the most right to complain, the Negro or the Indian? Another, " Which was the strongest, Wind or Water ? " [1] The views which Abe then entertained on the Indian and the negro question would be intensely interesting now.   But just fancy him discoursing on wind and water ! What treasures of natural science, what sallies of humor, he must have wasted upon that audience of bumpkins ! A little farther on, we shall see that Abe made pretensions to an acquaintance with the laws of nature which was considered marvellous in that day and generation.

Dennis Hanks insists that Abe and he became learned men and expert disputants, not by a course of judicious reading, but by attending " speech-makings, gatherings," &c.

" How did Lincoln and yourself learn so much in Indiana under such disadvantages ? " said Mr. Herndon to Dennis, on one of his two oral examinations. The question was artfully put ; for it touched the jaunty Dennis on the side of his vanity, and elicited a characteristic reply.   " We learned," said he, " by sight, scent, and hearing. We heard all that was said, and talked over and over the questions heard ; wore them slick, greasy, and threadbare.   Went to political and other speeches and gatherings, as you do now : we would hear all sides and opinions, talk them over, discuss them, agreeing or disagreeing. Abe, as I said before, was originally a Democrat after the order of Jackson, so was his father, so we all were. . . . He preached, made speeches, read for us, ex-

---

[1] " Lincoln did write what is called 'The Book of Chronicles,'—a satire on the Grigsbys and Josiah Crawford,— not the schoolmaster, but the man who loaned Lincoln 'The Life of Washington.' The satire was good, sharp, cutting: it hurt us then, but it is all over now. There is no family in the land who, after this, loved Lincoln so well, and who now look upon him as so great a man. We all voted for him, —all that could, —children and grandchildren, first, last, and always." —NAT GRIGSBY.

plained to us, &c. . . . Abe was a cheerful boy, a witty boy, was humorous always; sometimes would get sad, not very often. . . . Lincoln would frequently make political and other speeches to the boys: he was calm, logical, and clear always. He attended trials, went to court always, read the Revised Statute of Indiana, dated 1824, heard law speeches, and listened to law trials, &c. Lincoln was lazy, a very lazy man. He was always reading, scribbling, writing, ciphering, writing poetry, and the like. . . . In Gentryville, about one mile west of Thomas Lincoln's farm, Lincoln would go and tell his jokes and stories, &c., and was so odd, original, and humorous and witty, that all the people in town would gather around him. He would keep them there till midnight. I would get tired, want to go home, cuss Abe most heartily. Abe was a good talker, a good reader, and was a kind of newsboy."

Boonville was the court-house town of Warrick County, and was situated about fifteen miles from Gentryville. Thither Abe walked whenever he had time to be present at the sittings of the court, where he could learn something of public business, amuse himself profitably, and withal pick up items of news and gossip, which made him an interesting personage when he returned home. During one of these visits he watched, with profound attention, the progress of a murder trial, in which a Mr. John Breckenridge was counsel for the defence. At the conclusion of the latter's speech, Abe, who had listened, literally entranced, accosted the man of eloquence, and ventured to compliment him on the success of his effort. " Breckenridge looked at the shabby boy " in amazement, and passed on his way. But many years afterwards, in 1862, when Abe was President, and Breckenridge a resident of Texas, probably needing executive clemency, they met a second time; when Abe said, " It was the best speech that I up to that time had ever heard. If I could, as I then thought, make as good a speech as that, my soul would be satisfied."

It is a curious fact, that through all Abe's childhood and boyhood, when he seemed to have as little prospect of the Presidency as any boy that ever was born, he was in the habit of saying, and perhaps sincerely believing, that that great prize would one day be his.   When Mrs. Crawford reproved him for "fooling," and bedevilling the girls in her kitchen, and asked him "what he supposed would ever become of him," he answered that "he was going to be President of the United States." [1]

Abe usually did the milling for the family, and had the neighbor boy, Dave Turnham, for his companion.   At first they had to go a long distance, at least twelve or thirteen miles, to Hoffman's, on Anderson's Creek ; but after a while a Mr. Gordon (the husband of Sister Gordon, about whom the "witty piece" was written) built a horse-mill within a few miles of the Lincolns.   Here Abe had come one day with a grist, and Dave probably with him.   He had duly hitched his "old mare," and started her with great impatience ; when, just as he was sounding another "cluck," to stir up her imperturbable and lazy spirit, she let out with her heels, and laid Abe sprawling and insensible on the ground.   He was taken up in that condition, and did not recover for many minutes ; but the first use made of returning sense was to finish the interrupted "cluck."   He and Mr. Herndon had many learned discussions in their quiet little office, at Springfield, respecting this remarkable phenomenon, involving so nice a question in "psychology."

Mr. William Wood, already referred to as "Uncle Wood," was a genuine friend and even a patron of Abe's.   He lived only about a mile and a half from the Lincolns, and frequently had both old Tom and Abe to work for him, — the one as a rough carpenter, and the other as a common laborer.   He says that Abe was in the habit of carrying "his pieces" to him for criticism and encouragement.   Mr. Wood took at least two newspapers, — one of them devoted to politics, and

---

[1] He frequently made use of similar expressions to several others.

one of them to temperance. Abe borrowed them both, and, reading them faithfully over and over again, was inspired with an ardent desire to write something on the subjects of which they treated. He accordingly composed an article on temperance, which Mr. Wood thought " excelled, for sound sense, any thing that the paper contained." It was forwarded, through the agency of a Baptist preacher, to an editor in Ohio, by whom it was published, to the infinite gratification of Mr. Wood and his *protégé*. Abe then tried his hand on " national politics," saying that " the American Government was the best form of government for an intelligent people ; that it ought to be kept sound, and preserved forever ; that general education should be fostered and carried all over the country ; that the Constitution should be saved, the Union perpetuated, and the laws revered, respected, and enforced." This article was consigned, like the other, to Mr. Wood, to be ushered by him before the public. A lawyer named Pritchard chanced to pass that way, and, being favored with a perusal of Abe's " piece," pithily and enthusiastically declared, " The world can't beat it." " He begged for it," and it was published in some obscure paper ; this new success causing the author a most extraordinary access of pride and happiness.

But in 1828 Abe had become very tired of his home. He was now nineteen years of age, and becoming daily more restive under the restraints of servitude which bound him. He was anxious to try the world for himself, and make his way according to his own notions. " Abe came to my house one day," says Mr. Wood, " and stood round about, timid and shy. I knew he wanted *something*, and said to him, 'Abe, what's your case ? ' He replied, ' Uncle, I want you to go to the river, and give me some recommendation to some boat.' I remarked, ' Abe, your age is against you : you are not twenty yet.' ' I know that, but I want a start,' said Abe. I concluded not to go for the boy's good." Poor Abe ! old Tom still had a claim upon him, which even Uncle Wood would not help him to evade. He must wait a few weary

months more before he would be of age, and could say he was
his own man, and go his own way. Old Tom was a hard task-
master to him, and, no doubt, consumed the greater part, if
not all, of his wages.

In the beginning of March, 1828, Abe went to work for old
Mr. Gentry, the proprietor of Gentryville. Early in the next
month, the old gentleman furnished his son Allen with a boat,
and a cargo of bacon and other produce, with which he was
to go on a trading expedition to New Orleans, unless the
stock was sooner exhausted. Abe, having been found faithful
and efficient, was employed to accompany the young man as
a " bow-hand," to work the " front oars." He was paid eight
dollars per month, and ate and slept on board. Returning,
Gentry paid his passage on the deck of a steamboat.

While this boat was loading at Gentry's Landing, near
Rockport, on the Ohio, Abe saw a great deal of the pretty
Miss Roby, whom he had saved from the wrath of Crawford
the schoolmaster, when she failed to spell " defied." She
says, " Abe was then a long, thin, leggy, gawky boy, dried up
and shrivelled." This young lady subsequently became the
wife of Allen Gentry, Abe's companion in the projected voyage. She probably felt a deep interest in the enterprise in
hand, for the very boat itself seems to have had attractions
for her. " One evening," says she, " Abe and I were sitting
on the banks of the Ohio, or rather on the boat spoken of : I
said to Abe that the sun was going down. He said to me,
' That's not so : it don't really go down ; it seems so. The
earth turns from west to east, and the revolution of the
earth carries us under as it were : we do the sinking as you
call it. The sun, as to us, is comparatively still ; the sun's
sinking is only an appearance.' I replied, ' Abe, what a fool
you are !' I know now that I was the fool, not Lincoln. I am
now thoroughly satisfied that Abe knew the general laws of
astronomy and the movements of the heavenly bodies. He
was better read then than the world knows, or is likely to
know exactly. No man could talk to me that night as he did,

unless he had known something of geography as well as astronomy. He often and often commented or talked to me about what he had read, — seemed to read it out of the book as he went along, — did so to others. He was the learned boy among us unlearned folks. He took great pains to explain; could do it so simply. He was diffident then too." [1]

The trip of Gentry and Lincoln was a very profitable one, and Mr. Gentry, senior, was highly gratified by the result. Abe displayed his genius for mercantile affairs by handsomely putting off on the innocent folks along the river some counterfeit money which a shrewd fellow had imposed upon Allen. Allen thought his father would be angry with him for suffering himself to be cheated; but Abe consoled him with the reflection that the "old man" wouldn't care how much bad money they took in the course of business if they only brought the proper amount of good money home.[2]

At Madame Bushane's plantation, six miles below Baton Rouge, they had an adventure, which reads strangely enough in the life of the great emancipator. The boat was tied up to the shore, in the dead hours of the night, and Abe and Allen were fast asleep in the "cabin," in the stern, when they were startled by footsteps on board. They knew instantly that it was a gang of negroes come to rob, and perhaps to murder them. Allen, thinking to frighten the intruders, cried out, "Bring the guns, Lincoln; shoot them!" Abe came without a gun, but he fell among the negroes with a huge bludgeon, and belabored them most cruelly. Not content with beating them off the boat, he and Gentry followed them far back into the country, and then, running back to

---

[1] "When he appeared in company, the boys would gather and cluster around him to hear him talk. . . . Mr. Lincoln was figurative in his speeches, talks, and conversations. He argued much from analogy, and explained things hard for us to understand by stories, maxims, tales, and figures. He would almost always point his lesson or idea by some story that was plain and near us, that we might instantly see the force and bearing of what he said." — NAT GRIGSBY.

[2] "Gentry (Allen) was a great personal friend of Mr. Lincoln. He was a Democrat, but voted for Lincoln, sacrificing his party politics to his friendship. He says that on that trip they sold some of their produce at a certain landing, and by accident or fraud the bill was paid in counterfeit money. Gentry was grieving about it; but Lincoln said, ·Never mind, Allen: it will accidentally slip out of our fingers before we get to New Orleans, and then old Jim can't quarrel at us.' Sure enough, it all went off like hot cakes. I was told this in Indiana by many people about Rockport." — HERNDON. It must be remembered that counterfeit money was the principal currency along the river at this period.

their craft, hastily cut loose and made rapid time down the river, fearing lest they should return in greater numbers to take revenge. The victory was complete; but, in winning it, Abe received a scar which he carried with him to his grave.

"When he was eighteen years old, he conceived the project of building a little boat, and taking the produce of the Lincoln farm down the river to market. He had learned the use of tools, and possessed considerable mechanical talent, as will appear in some other acts of his life. Of the voyage and its results, we have no knowledge; but an incident occurred before starting which he related in later life to his Secretary of State, Mr. Seward, that made a very marked and pleasant impression upon his memory. As he stood at the landing, a steamer approached, coming down the river. At the same time two passengers came to the river's bank who wished to be taken out to the packet with their luggage. Looking among the boats at the landing, they singled out Abraham's, and asked him to scull them to the steamer. This he did; and, after seeing them and their trunks on board, he had the pleasure of receiving upon the bottom of his boat, before he shoved off, a silver half-dollar from each of his passengers. 'I could scarcely believe my eyes,' said Mr. Lincoln, in telling the story. 'You may think it was a very little thing,' continued he, 'but it was a most important incident in my life. I could scarcely believe that I, a poor boy, had earned a dollar in less than a day. The world seemed wider and fairer to me. I was a more hopeful and confident being from that time.'"[1]

If Mr. Lincoln ever made the statement for which Mr. Seward is given as authority, he drew upon his imagination for the facts. He may have sculled passengers to a steamer when he was ferryman for Taylor, but he never made a trip like the one described; never built a boat until he went to Illinois; nor did he ever sell produce on his father's account, for the good reason that his father had none to sell.

[1] Holland's Life of Lincoln, p. 33.

CHAPTER III.

ABE and Gentry returned from New Orleans some time in June, 1828, having been gone not quite three months. How much longer he remained in the service of Gentry, or whether he remained at all, we are unable to say; but he soon took up his old habits, and began to work around among his neighbors, or for his father, precisely as he had done before he got his partial glimpse of the great world down the river.

In the fall of 1829, Mr. Wood saw him cutting down a large tree in the woods, and whip-sawing it into planks. Abe said the lumber was for a new house his father was about to build; but Tom Lincoln changed his mind before the house was half done, and Abe sold his plank to Josiah Crawford, " the book man," who worked them into the south-east room of his house, where relic-seekers have since cut pieces from them to make canes.

In truth, the continued prevalence of that dreadful disease, the milk-sickness, with which Nancy Hanks and the Sparrows and the Halls had all died, was more than a sufficient reason for a new removal, now in contemplation by Thomas Lincoln. Every member of his family, from the first settlement in Indiana, except perhaps Abe and himself, had suffered with it. The cattle, which, it is true, were of little pecuniary value, and raised with great ease and little cost, were swept away by it in great numbers throughout the whole neighborhood. It was an awful scourge, and common prudence suggested flight. It is wonderful that it took a constitu-

73

tional mover thirteen years to make up his mind to escape from it.[1]

In the spring of 1830, before the winter had fairly broken up, he and Abe, and Dennis Hanks and Levi Hall, with their respective families, thirteen in all, took the road for Illinois. Dennis and Levi, as already stated, were married to the daughters of Mrs. Lincoln. Hall had one son, and Dennis a considerable family of sons and daughters. Sarah (or Nancy) Lincoln, who had married Aaron Grigsby, was now dead.

John Hanks had gone to the new country from Kentucky in the fall of 1828, and settled near Decatur, whence he wrote Thomas Lincoln all about it, and advised him to come there. Dennis, whether because of the persuasions of John, or some observations made in a flying trip on his own account, was very full of the move, and would hear to no delay. Lincoln sold his farm to Gentry, senior, if, indeed, he had not done so before, and his corn and hogs to Dave Turnham. The corn brought only ten cents a bushel, and, according to the price-list furnished by Dennis Hanks, the stock must have gone at figures equally mean.

Lincoln took with him to Illinois " some stock-cattle, one horse, one bureau, one table, one clothes-chest, one set of chairs, cooking utensils, clothing," &c. The goods of the three families — Hanks, Hall, and Lincoln — were loaded on a wagon belonging to Lincoln. This wagon was " ironed," a noticeable fact in those primitive days, and " was positively the first one that he (Lincoln) ever owned." It was drawn by four yoke of oxen, — two of them Lincoln's, and two of them Hanks's.

---

[1] " What made Thomas Lincoln leave? The reason is this: we were perplexed by a disease called milk-sick. I myself being the oldest, I was determined to leave, and hunt a country where the milk-sick was not. I married his eldest daughter. I sold out, and they concluded to go with me. Billy, I was tolerably popular at that time, for I had some money. My wife's mother could not think of parting with her, and we ripped up stakes, and started to Illinois, and landed at Decatur. This is the reason for leaving Indiana. I am to blame for it, if any. As for getting more land, this was not the case, for we could have entered ten thousand acres of the best land. When we left, it was on account of the milk. Billy, I had four good milch cows, too, with it in one week, and eleven young calves. This was enough to run me. Besides, liked to have lossed my own life with it. This reason was enough (ain't it?) for leaving." — DENNIS HANKS.

We have no particulars of the journey, except that Abe held the "gad," and drove the team; that the mud was very deep, that the spring freshets were abroad, and that in crossing the swollen and tumultuous Kaskaskia, the wagon and oxen were nearly swept away. On the first day of March, 1830, after fifteen days' tedious and heavy travel, they arrived at John Hanks's house, four miles north-west of Decatur. Lincoln settled (if any thing he did may be called settling) at a point ten miles west of Decatur. Here John Hanks had cut some logs in 1829, which he now gave to Lincoln to build a house with. With the aid of John, Dennis, Abe, and Hall, a house was erected on a small bluff, on the north bank of the north fork of the Sangamon. Abe and John took the four yoke of oxen and " broke up " fifteen acres of land, and then split rails enough to fence it in.

Abe was now over twenty-one. There was no " Uncle Wood to tell him that his age was against him : " he had done something more than his duty by his father ; and, as that worthy was now again placed in a situation where he might do well if he chose, Abe came to the conclusion that it was time for him to begin life on his own account. It must have cost him some pain to leave his good step-mother ; but, beyond that, all the old ties were probably broken without a single regret. From the moment he was a free man, foot-loose, able to go where, and to do what, he pleased, his success in those things which lay nearest his heart — that is, public and social preferment — was astonishing to himself, as well as to others.

It is with great pleasure that we dismiss Tom Lincoln, with his family and fortunes, from further consideration in these pages. After Abraham left him, he moved at least three times in search of a " healthy " location, and finally got himself fixed near Goose Nest Prairie, in Coles County, where he died of a disease of the kidneys, in 1851, at the ripe old age of seventy-three. The little farm (forty acres) upon which his days were ended, he had, with his usual improvidence, mortgaged to the School Commissioners for two hundred dollars, —

its full value. Induced by love for his step-mother, Abraham had paid the debt, and taken a deed for the land, " with a reservation of a life-estate therein, to them, or the survivor of them." At the same time (1841), he gave a helping hand to John Johnston, binding himself to convey the land to him, or his heirs, after the death of " Thomas Lincoln and his wife," upon payment of the two hundred dollars, which was really advanced to save John's mother from utter penury. No matter how much the land might appreciate in value, John was to have it upon these terms, and no interest was to be paid by him, " except after the death of the survivor, as aforesaid." This, to be sure, was a great bargain for John, but he made haste to assign his bond to another person for " fifty dollars paid in hand."

As soon as Abraham got a little up in the world, he began to send his step-mother money, and continued to do so until his own death ; but it is said to have " done her no good," for it only served to tempt certain persons about her, and with whom she shared it, to continue in a life of idleness. At the close of the Black Hawk War, Mr. Lincoln went to see them for a few days, and afterwards, when a lawyer, making the circuits with the courts, he visited them whenever the necessities of his practice brought him to their neighborhood. He did his best to serve Mrs. Lincoln and her son John, but took little notice of his father, although he wrote him an exhortation to believe in God when he thought he was on his death-bed.

But in regard to the relations between the family and Abe, after the latter began to achieve fame and power, nobody can tell the truth more clearly, or tell it in a more interesting and suggestive style, than our friend Dennis, with whom we are now about to part forever. It will be seen, that, when information reached the " Goose Nest Prairie " that Abe was actually chosen President of the United States, a general itching for public employment broke out among the Hankses, and that an equally general disappointment was the result. Doubtless all of them had expectations somewhat like Sancho Panza's, when he went to take the government of his island, and John Hanks, at least, would not have been disappointed but for the little disability which Dennis mentions in the following extract : —

"Did Abraham Lincoln treat John D. Johnston well?" "I will say this much about it. I think Abe done more for John than he deserved. John thought that Abe did not do enough for the old people. They became enemies a while on this ground. I don't want to tell all the things that I know : it would not look well in history. I say this : Abe treated John well."

"What kind of a man was Johnston?"—"I say this much : A kinder-hearted man never was in Coles County, Illinois, nor an honester man. I don't say this because he was my brother-in-law : I say it, knowing it. John did not love to work any the best. I flogged him for not working."

"Did Thomas Lincoln treat Abe cruelly?"—"He loved him. I never could tell whether Abe loved his father very well or not. I don't think he did, for Abe was one of those forward boys. I have seen his father knock him down off the fence when a stranger would ask the way to a neighbor's house. Abe always would have the first word. The old man loved his children."

"Did any of the Johnston family ask for office?"—"No! Thomas Johnston went to Abe : he got this permit to take daguerrotypes in the army; this is all, for they are all dead except John's boys. They did not ask for any."

"Did you or John Hanks ask Lincoln for any office?"--"I say this : that John Hanks, of Decatur, did solicit him for an Indian Agency ; and John told me that Abe as good as told him he should have one. But John could not read or write. I think this was the reason that Abe did not give John the place.

" As for myself, I did not ask Abe right out for an office, only this : I would like to have the post-office in Charleston; this was my wife that asked him. He told her that much was understood, — as much as to say that I would get it.   I did not care much about it."

" Do you think Lincoln cared much for his relations ? " — " I will say this much : when he was with us, he seemed to think a great deal of us ; but I thought sometimes it was hypocritical, but I am not sure."

Abe left the Lincoln family late in March, or early in April. He did not go far away, but took jobs wherever he could get them, showing that he had separated himself from the family, not merely to rove, but to labor, and be an independent man. He made no engagement of a permanent character during this summer : his work was all done " by the job."   If he ever split rails for Kirkpatrick, over whom he was subsequently elected captain of a volunteer company about to enter the Black Hawk War, it must have been at this time ; but the story of his work for Kirkpatrick, like that of his making " a crap of corn" for Mr. Brown, is probably apocryphal.[1]   All this while he clung close to John Hanks, and either worked where he did, or not far away.   In the winter following, he was employed by a Major Warrick to make rails, and walked daily three miles to his work, and three miles back again.

" After Abe got to Decatur," says John Hanks, " or rather to Macon (my country), a man by the name of Posey came into our neighborhood, and made a speech : it was a bad one, and I said Abe could beat it.   I turned down a box, or keg, and Abe made his speech.   The other man was a candidate. Abe wasn't.   Abe beat him to death, his subject being the navigation of the Sangamon River.   The man, after the speech was through, took Abe aside, and asked him where he had learned so much, and how he did so well.   Abe replied, stating his manner and method of reading, and what he had read.   The man encouraged Lincoln to persevere."

In February, 1831, a Mr. Denton Offutt wanted to engage John Hanks to take a flatboat to New Orleans.   John was not well disposed to the business ; but Offutt came to the

[1] See Holland's Life of Lincoln, p. 40.

house, and would take no denial; made much of John's fame as a river-man, and at length persuaded him to present the matter to Abe and John Johnston. He did so. The three friends discussed the question with great earnestness: it was no slight affair to them, for they were all young and poor. At length they agreed to Offutt's proposition, and that agreement was the turning-point in Abe's career. They were each to receive fifty cents a day, and the round sum of sixty dollars divided amongst them for making the trip. These were wages such as Abe had never received before, and might have tempted him to a much more difficult enterprise. When he went with Gentry, the pay was only eight dollars a month, and no such company and assistance as he was to have now. But Offutt was lavish with his money, and generous bargains like this ruined him a little while after.

In March, Hanks, Johnston, and Lincoln went down the Sangamon in a canoe to Jamestown (then Judy's Ferry), five miles east of Springfield. Thence they walked to Springfield, and found Mr. Offutt comforting himself at "Elliott's tavern in Old Town." He had contracted to have a boat ready at the mouth of Spring Creek, but, not looking after it himself, was, of course, "disappointed." There was only one way out of the trouble : the three hands must build a boat. They went to the mouth of Spring Creek, five miles north of Springfield, and there consumed two weeks cutting the timber from "Congress land." In the mean time, Abe walked back to Judy's Ferry, by way of Springfield, and brought down the canoe which they had left at the former place. The timber was hewed and scored, and then "rafted down to Sangamontown." At the mouth of Spring Creek they had been compelled to walk a full mile for their meals ; but at Sangamontown they built a shanty, and boarded themselves. "Abe was elected cook," and performed the duties of the office much to the satisfaction of the party. The lumber was sawed at Kirkpatrick's mill, a mile and a half from the shanty. Laboring under many disadvantages like this, they managed

6

to complete and launch the boat in about four weeks from the time of beginning.

Offutt was with the party at this point. He " was a Whig, and so was Abe; but he (Abe) could not hear Jackson wrongfully abused, especially where a lie and malice did the abuse." Out of this difference arose some disputes, which served to enliven the camp, as well as to arouse Abe's ire, and keep him in practice in the way of debate.

In those days Abe, as usual, is described as being "funny, jokey, full of yarns, stories, and rigs ;" as being " long, tall, and green," " frequently quoting poetry," and " reciting prose-like orations." They had their own amusements. Abe extracted a good deal of fun out of the cooking; took his " dram " when asked to, and played " seven up " at night, at which he made " a good game."

A juggler gave an exhibition at Sangamontown, in the upper room of Jacob Carman's house. Abe went to it, dressed in a suit of rough blue jeans. He had on shoes, but the trousers did not reach them by about twelve inches ; and the naked shin, which had excited John Romine's laughter years ago in Indiana, was still exposed. Between the roundabout and the waist of the trousers, there was another wide space uncovered ; and, considering these defects, Mr. Lincoln's attire was thought to be somewhat inelegant, even in those times. His hat, however, was a great improvement on coonskins and opossum. It was woollen, broad-brimmed, and low-crowned. In this hat the " showman cooked eggs." Whilst Abe was handing it up to him, after the man had long solicited a similar favor from the rest of the audience, he remarked, " Mister, the reason I didn't give you my hat before was out of respect to your eggs, not care for my hat."

Loaded with barrel-pork, hogs, and corn, the boat set out from Sangamontown as soon as finished. Mr. Offutt was on board to act as his own merchant, intending to pick up additions to his cargo along the banks of the two Illinois rivers down which he was about to pass. On the 19th of April they arrived at New Salem, a little village destined to be the scene of the seven eventful years of Mr. Lincoln's life, which immediately followed the conclusion of the present trip. Just below New Salem the boat "stuck," for one night and the better part of a day on Rutledge's mill-dam, — one end of it hanging over the dam, and the other sunk deep in the water behind. Here was a case for Abe's ingenuity, and he exercised it with effect. Quantities of water were being taken in at the stern, the lading was sliding backwards, and every thing indicated that the rude craft was in momentary danger of breaking in two, or sinking outright. But Abe suggested some unheard-of expedient for keeping it in place while the cargo was shifted to a borrowed boat, and then, boring a hole in that part of the bottom extending over the dam, he "rigged up" an equally strange piece of machinery for tilting and holding it while the water ran out. All New Salem was assembled on shore, watching the progress of this singular experiment, — and with one voice affirm that Abe saved the boat; although nobody is able to tell us precisely how.[1] The adventure turned Abe's thoughts to the class of difficulties, one of which he had just surmounted; and the result of his reflections was "an improved method for lifting vessels over shoals."[2] Offutt declared that when he got back from New

---

[1] Many persons at New Salem describe in full Abe's conduct on this occasion.

[2] "Occupying an ordinary and commonplace position in one of the show-cases in the targe hall of the Patent Office, is one little model which, in ages to come, will be prized as at once one of the most curious and one of the most sacred relics in that vast museum of unique and priceless things. This is a plain and simple model of a steamboat, roughly fashioned in wood, by the hand of Abraham Lincoln. It bears date in 1849, when the inventor was known simply as a successful lawyer and rising politician of Central Illinois. Neither his practice nor his politics took up so much of his time as to prevent him from giving much attention to contrivances which he hoped might be of benefit to the world, and of profit to himself.

"The design of this invention is suggestive of one phase of Abraham Lincoln's early life, when he went up and down the Mississippi as a flat-boatman, and became familiar with some of the dangers and inconveniences attending the navigation of the Western rivers. It is an attempt to make it an easy matter to transport vessels over shoals and snags, and sawyers. The main idea is that of an apparatus resembling a noiseless bellows, placed on each side of the hull of the craft, just below the water-line, and worked by an odd but not complicated system of ropes, valves, and pulleys. When the keel of the vessel grates against the sand or obstruction, these bellows are to be filled with air; and, thus buoyed

6

Orleans, he would build a steamboat for the navigation of the Sangamon, and make Abe the captain; he would build it with runners for ice, and rollers for shoals and dams, for with "Abe in command, by thunder, she'd have to go."

Over the dam, and in the deep pool beyond, they reloaded, and floated down to Blue Bank, a mile above the mouth of Salt Creek, where Offutt bought some more hogs. But the hogs were wild, and refused to be driven. Abe again came to the rescue; and, by his advice, their eyes were sewed up with a needle and thread, so that, if the animals fought any more, they should do it in the dark. Abe held their heads, and John Hanks their tails, while Offutt did the surgery. They were then thrown into a cart, whence Abe took them, one by one, in his great arms, and deposited them on board.

From this point they sped very rapidly down the Sangamon and the Illinois. Having constructed curious-looking sails of plank, "and sometimes cloth," they were a "sight to see," as they "rushed through Beardstown," where "the people came out and laughed at them." They swept by Alton and Cairo, and other considerable places, without tying up, but stopped at Memphis, Vicksburg, and Natchez.

In due time they arrived at New Orleans. "There it was," says John Hanks, "we saw negroes chained, mal-

up, the ship is expected to float lightly and gayly over the shoal, which would otherwise have proved a serious interruption to her voyage.

"The model, which is about eighteen or twenty inches long, and has the air of having been whittled with a knife out of a shingle and a cigar-box, is built without any elaboration or ornament, or any extra apparatus beyond that necessary to show the operation of buoying the steamer over the obstructions. Herein it differs from very many of the models which share with it the shelter of the immense halls of the Patent Office, and which are fashioned with wonderful nicety and exquisite finish, as if much of the labor and thought and affection of a lifetime had been devoted to their construction. This is a model of a different kind; carved as one might imagine a retired rail-splitter would whittle, strongly, but not smoothly, and evidently made with a view solely to convey, by the simplest possible means, to the minds of the patent authorities, an idea of the purpose and plan of the simple invention. The label on the steamer's deck informs us that the patent was obtained; but we do not learn that the navigation of the Western rivers was revolutionized by this quaint conception. The modest little model has reposed here sixteen years; and, since it found its resting-place here on the shelf, the shrewd inventor has found it his task to guide the Ship of State over shoals more perilous, and obstructions more obstinate, than any prophet dreamed of when Abraham Lincoln wrote his bold autograph on the prow of this miniature steamer." — *Correspondent Boston Advertiser.*

MR. LINCOLN AS A FLATBOAT-MAN.

treated, whipped, and scourged. Lincoln saw it; his heart bled, said nothing much, was silent from feeling, was sad. looked bad, felt bad, was thoughtful and abstracted. I can say, knowing it, that it was on this trip that he formed his opinions of slavery. It run its iron in him then and there, — May, 1831. I have heard him say so often and often."

Some time in June the party took passage on a steamboat going up the river, and remained together until they reached St. Louis, where Offutt left them, and Abe, Hanks, and Johnston started on foot for the interior of Illinois. At Edwardsville, twenty-five miles out, Hanks took the road to Springfield, and Abe and Johnston took that to Coles County, where Tom Lincoln had moved since Abraham's departure from home.

Abe never worked again in company with his friend and relative, good old John Hanks. Here their paths separated: Abe's began to ascend the heights, while John's continued along the common level. They were in the Black Hawk War during the same campaign, but not in the same division. But they corresponded, and, from 1833, met at least once a year, until Abe was elected President. Then Abe, delighting to honor those of his relatives who were worthy of it, invited John to go with him to see his step-mother. John also went to the inauguration at Washington, and tells, with pardonable pride, how he " was in his [Abe's] rooms several times." He then retired to his old home in Macon County, until the assassination and the great funeral, when he came to Springfield to look in the blackened face of his old friend, and witness the last ceremonies of his splendid burial.

Scarcely had Abe reached Coles County, and begun to think what next to turn his hand to, when he received a visit from a famous wrestler, one Daniel Needham, who regarded him as a growing rival, and had a fancy to try him a fall or two. He considered himself " the best man " in the country, and the report of Abe's achievements filled his big breast with envious pains. His greeting was friendly and hearty, but his challenge was rough and peremptory. Abe valued his popularity among " the boys " too highly to decline it, and met him by public appointment in the "greenwood," at Wabash Point, where he threw him twice with so much ease that Needham's pride was more hurt than his body. "Lincoln," said he, "you have thrown me twice, but you can't whip me."—"Needham," replied Abe, "are you satisfied that I can throw you? If you are not, and must be convinced through a threshing, I will do that, too, for your sake." Needham had hoped that the youngster would shrink from the extremity of a fight with the acknowledged "bully of the patch;" but finding him willing, and at the same time magnanimously inclined to whip him solely for his *own good*, he concluded that a bloody nose and a black eye would be the reverse of soothing to his feelings, and therefore surrendered the field with such grace as he could command.

CHAPTER IV.

ON the west bank of the Sangamon River, twenty miles north-west of Springfield, a traveller on his way to Havana will ascend a bluff one hundred feet higher than the low-water mark of the stream. On the summit he will find a solitary log-hut. The back-bone of the ridge is about two hundred and fifty feet broad where it overlooks the river; but it widens gradually as it extends westerly toward the remains of an old forest, until it terminates in a broad expanse of meadow. On either side of this hill, and skirting its feet north and south, run streams of water in very deep channels, and tumble into the Sangamon almost within hearing. The hill, or more properly the bluff, rises from the river in an almost perpendicular ascent. "There is an old mill at the foot of the bluff, driven by water-power. The river washes the base of the bluff for about four hundred yards, the hill breaking off almost abruptly at the north. The river along this line runs about due north: it strikes the bluff coming around a sudden bend from the south-east, the river being checked and turned by the rocky hill. The mill-dam running across the Sangamon River just at the mill checks the rapidity of the water. It was here, and on this dam, that Mr. Lincoln's flatboat 'stuck on the 19th of April, 1831.' The dam is about eight feet high, and two hundred and twenty feet long, and, as the old Sangamon rolls her turbid waters over the dam, plunging them into the whirl and eddy beneath, the roar and hiss of waters, like the low, continuous, distant thunder, can be distinctly heard through the whole village, day and night, week-day and Sunday, spring and fall, or other high-water time. The river, at the base of the bluff, is about two hundred and fifty feet wide, the mill using up thirty feet, leaving the dam only about two hundred and twenty feet long."

In every direction but the West, the country is broken into hills or bluffs, like the one we are attempting to describe, which are washed by the river, and the several streams that empty into it in the immediate vicinity. Looking across the river from bluff to bluff, the distance is about a thousand yards; while here and there, on both banks, are patches of rich alluvial bottom-lands, eight or nine hundred yards in width, enclosed on one side by the hills, and on the other by the river. The uplands of the eastern bank are covered with original forests of immemorial age; and, viewed from "Salem Hill," the eye ranges over a vast expanse of green foliage, the monotony of which is relieved by the alternating swells and depressions of the landscape.

On the ridge of that hill, where the solitary cabin now stands, there was a few years ago a pleasant village. How it vanished like a mist of the morning, to what distant places its inhabitants dispersed, and what became of the dwellings they left behind, shall be questions for the local antiquarian. We have no concern with any part of the history, except that part which began in the summer of 1831 and ended in 1837, — the period during which it had the honor of sheltering a man whose enduring fame contrasts strangely with the evanescence of the village itself.

In 1829 James Rutledge and John Cameron built the mill on the Sangamon, and laid off the town on the hill. The place was then called Cameron's Mill; but in process of time, as cabins, stores, and groceries were added, it was dignified by the name of New Salem. "I claim," says one of the gentlemen who established the first store, "to be the explorer and discoverer of New Salem as a business point. Mr. Hill (now dead) and myself purchased some goods at Cincinnati, and shipped them to St. Louis, whence I set out on a voyage of

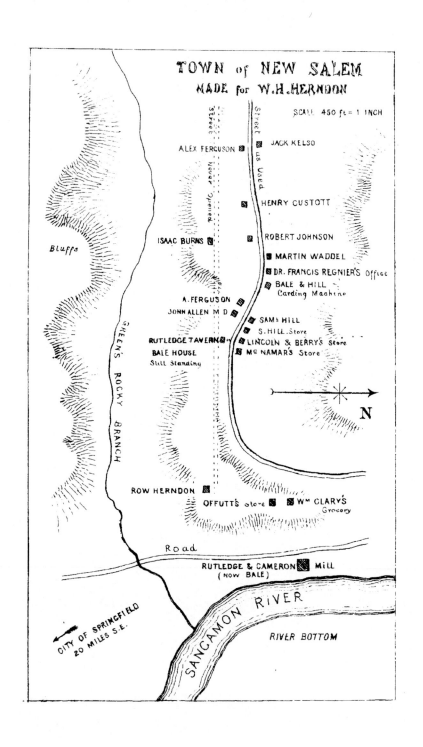

TOWN of NEW SALEM
MADE for W. H. HERNDON

SCALE 450 ft = 1 INCH

JACK KELSO

ALEX FERGUSON

HENRY CUSTOTT

ROBERT JOHNSON

ISAAC BURNS

MARTIN WADDEL

DR. FRANCIS REGNIER'S Office

BALE & HILL
Carding Machine

A. FERGUSON

JOHN ALLEN M D

SAM: HILL

S. HILL Store

RUTLEDGE TAVERNS

LINCOLN & BERRY'S Store

BALE HOUSE
Still Standing

Mc NAMAR'S Store

Bluffs

GREEN'S ROCKY BRANCH

Street

Street as Used

N

ROW HERNDON

OFFUTT'S store

Wm CLARY'S
Grocery

Road

RUTLEDGE & CAMERON MILL
(NOW BALE)

SANGAMON RIVER

CITY OF SPRINGFIELD
20 MILES S.E.

RIVER BOTTOM

discovery on the prairies of Illinois. . . . I, however, soon
came across a noted character who lives in this vicinity, by
the name of Thomas Wadkins, who set forth the beauties
and other advantages of Cameron's Mill, as it was then called.
I accordingly came home with him, visited the locality, contracted for the erection of a magnificent storehouse for the
sum of fifteen dollars; and, after passing a night in the prairie,
reached St. Louis in safety. Others soon followed."

In 1836 New Salem contained about twenty houses, inhabited by nearly a hundred people; but in 1831 there could not
have been more than two-thirds or three-fourths that number.
Many of the houses cost not more than ten dollars, and none
of them more than one hundred dollars.

When the news flew through the country that the mill-dam
was broken, the people assembled from far and near, and made
a grand frolic of mending it. In like manner, when a new
settler arrived, and the word passed around that he wanted
to put up a house, everybody came in to the "raising;" and,
after behaving like the best of good Samaritans to the new
neighbor, they drank whiskey, ran foot-races, wrestled, fought,
and went home.

"I first knew this hill, or bluff," says Mr. Herndon, in his
remarkable lecture on Ann Rutledge, "as early as 1829. I
have seen it in spring-time and winter, in summer-time and
fall. I have seen it in daylight and night-time; have seen it
when the sward was green, living, and vital; and I have seen
it wrapped in snow, frost, and sleet. I have closely studied
it for more than five long years. . . .

"As I sat on the verge of the town, in presence of its ruins,
I called to mind the street running east and west through the
village, the river eastward; Green's Rocky Branch, with its
hills, southward; Clary's Grove, westerly about three miles;
Petersburg northward, and Springfield south-east; and now
I cannot exclude from my memory or imagination the forms,
faces, voices, and features of those I once knew so well. In
my imagination the village perched on the hill is astir with
the hum of busy men, and the sharp, quick buzz of women;

and from the country come men and women on foot or on horseback, to see and be seen, to hear and to be heard, to barter and exchange what they have with the merchant and the laborer. There are Jack Armstrong and William Green, Kelso and Jason Duncan, Alley and Carman, Hill and McNamar, Herndon and Rutledge, Warburton and Sincho, Bale and Ellis, Abraham and Ann. Oh, what a history!"

In those days, which in the progressive West would be called ancient days, New Salem was in Sangamon County, with Springfield as the county-seat. Springfield itself was still a mere village, having a population of one thousand, or perhaps eleven hundred. The capital of the State was yet at Vandalia, and waited for the parliamentary tact of Abraham Lincoln and the "long nine" to bring it to Springfield. The same influence, which, after long struggles, succeeded in removing the capital, caused the new County of Menard to be erected out of Sangamon in 1839, of which Petersburg was made the county-seat, and within which is included the barren site of New Salem.

In July or August, 1831, Mr. Lincoln made his second appearance at New Salem. He was again in company with Denton Offutt, who had collected some goods at Beardstown, and now proposed to bring them to this place. Mr. Lincoln undoubtedly came there in the service of Offutt, but whilst the goods were being transported from Beardstown he seemed to be idling about without any special object in view. Many persons who saw him then for the first time speak of him as "doing nothing." He has given some encouragement to this idea himself by the manner in which he habitually spoke of his advent there, — describing himself as coming down the river after the winter of the deep snow, like a piece of "floating driftwood" borne along by the freshet, and accidentally lodged at New Salem.

On the day of the election, in the month of August, as Minter Graham, the school-teacher, tells us, Abe was seen loitering about the polling-place. It must have been but a few days after his arrival in the town, for nobody knew that

he could write. They were " short of a clerk " at the polls;
and, after casting about in vain for some one competent to fill
the office, it occurred to one of the judges that perhaps the
tall stranger possessed the needful qualifications. He thereupon accosted him, and asked if he could write. He replied,
" Yes, a little." — " Will you act as clerk of the election to-
day?" said the judge. " I will try," returned Abe, "and do the
best I can, if you so request." He did try accordingly, and,
in the language of the schoolmaster, " performed the duties
with great facility, much fairness and honesty and impartiality. This was the first public official act of his life. I
clerked with him," says Mr. Graham, swelling with his theme,
" on the same day and at the same polls. The election-books
are now in the city of Springfield, Ill., where they can be
seen and inspected any day."

Whilst Abe was " doing nothing," or, in other words, waiting for Offutt's goods, one Dr. Nelson, a resident of New Salem, built a flatboat, and, placing his family and effects upon
it, started for Texas. But as the Sangamon was a turbulent
and treacherous stream at best, and its banks were now full
to overflowing, Nelson needed a pilot, at least as far as Beardstown. His choice fell upon Abe, who took him to the mouth of
the doubtful river in safety, although Abe often declared that
he occasionally ran out into the prairie at least three miles
from the channel. Arriving at Beardstown, Nelson pushed
on down the Illinois, and Abe walked back to New Salem.

The second storekeeper at New Salem was a Mr. George
Warburton; but, " the country not having improved his morals
in the estimation of his friends," George thought it advisable
to transfer his storeroom and the remnant of his stock to
Offutt. In the mean time, Offutt's long-expected goods were
received from Beardstown. Abe unpacked them, ranged
them on the shelves, rolled the barrels and kegs into their
places, and, being provided with a brand-new book, pen, and
ink, found himself duly installed as " first clerk " of the principal mercantile house in New Salem. A country store is an

indescribable collection of miscellanies, — groceries, dry goods, hardware, earthenware, and stoneware, cups and saucers, plates and dishes, coffee and tea, sugar and molasses, boots and shoes, whiskey and lead, butter and eggs, tobacco and gunpowder, with an endless list of things unimaginable except by a housewife or a "merchant." Such was the store to the charge of which Abe was now promoted, — promoted from the rank of a common laborer to be a sort of brevet clerk.

But Offutt's ideas of commerce were very comprehensive; and, as "his business was already considerably scattered about the country," he thought he would scatter a little more. He therefore rented the mill at the foot of the hill, from Cameron and Rutledge, and set Abe to overlooking that as well as the store. This increase of business, however, required another clerk, and in a few days Abe was given a companion in the person of W. G. Green. They slept together on the same cot in the store; and as Mr. Green observes, by way of indicating the great intimacy that subsisted between them, "when one turned over, the other had to do so likewise." To complete his domestic arrangements, Abe followed the example of Mr. Offutt, and took boarding at John Cameron's, one of the owners of the mill.

Mr. Offutt is variously, though not differently, described as a "wild, harum-scarum, reckless fellow;" a "gusty, windy, brain-rattling man;" a "noisy, unsteady, fussy, rattle-brained man, wild and improvident." If anybody can imagine the character indicated by these terms, he can imagine Mr. Offutt, — Abe's employer, friend, and patron. Since the trip on the flatboat, his admiration for Abe had grown to be boundless. He now declared that "Abe knew more than any man in the United States;" that "he would some day be President of the United States," and that he could, at that present moment, outrun, whip, or throw down any man in Sangamon County. These loud boasts were not wasted on the desert air: they were bad seed sown in a rank soil, and speedily raised up a crop of sharp thorns for both Abe and Offutt. At New Salem, honors such as Offutt accorded to Abe were to be won before they were worn.

Bill Clary made light of Offutt's opinion respecting Abe's prowess; and one day, when the dispute between them had been running high in the store, it ended by a bet of ten dollars on the part of Clary that Jack Armstrong was "a better man." Now, "Jack was a powerful twister," "square built, and strong as an ox." He had, besides, a great backing; for he was the chief of the "Clary's Grove boys," and the Clary's Grove boys were the terror of the countryside. Although there never was under the sun a more generous parcel of ruffians than those over whom Jack held sway, a stranger's introduction was likely to be the most unpleasant part of his acquaintance with them. In fact, one of the objects of their association was to "initiate or naturalize new-comers," as they termed the amiable proceedings which they took by way of welcoming any one ambitious of admittance to the society of New Salem. They first bantered the gentleman to run a foot-race, jump, pitch the mall, or wrestle; and, if none of these propositions seemed agreeable to him, they would request to know what he would do in case another gentleman should pull his nose, or squirt tobacco-juice in his face. If he did not seem entirely decided in his views as to what should properly be done in such a contingency, perhaps he would be nailed in a hogshead, and rolled down New-Salem hill; perhaps his ideas would be brightened by a brief ducking in the Sangamon; or perhaps he would be scoffed, kicked, and cuffed by a great number of persons in concert, until he reached the confines of the village, and then turned adrift as being unfit company for the people of that settlement. If, however, the stranger consented to engage in a tussle with one of his persecutors, it was usually arranged that there should be "foul play," with nameless impositions and insults, which would inevitably change the affair into a fight; and then, if the subject of all these practices proved indeed to be a man of mettle, he would be promptly received into "good society," and in all probability would never have better friends on earth than the roystering fellows who had contrived his torments.

Thus far Abe had managed to escape "initiation" at the hands of Jack and his associates. They were disposed to like him, and to take him on faith, or at least to require no further evidence of his manhood than that which rumor had already brought them. Offutt, with his busy tongue, had spread wide the report of his wondrous doings on the river; and, better still, all New Salem, including many of the "Clary's Grove boys," had witnessed his extraordinary feats of strength and ingenuity at Rutledge's mill-dam. It was clear that no particular person was "spoiling" for a collision with him; and an exception to the rule might have been made in his favor, but for the offensive zeal and confidence of his employer.

The example of Offutt and Clary was followed by all the "boys;" and money, knives, whiskey, and all manner of things, were staked on the result of the wrestle. The little community was excited throughout, and Jack's partisans were present in great numbers; while Offutt and Bill Green were about the only persons upon whom Abe could rely if the contest should take the usual turn, and end in a fight. For these, and many other reasons, he longed to be safely and honorably out of the scrape; but Offutt's folly had made it impossible for him to evade the conflict without incurring the imputation, and suffering the penalties, of cowardice. He said, "I never tussle and scuffle, and I will not: I don't like this wooling and pulling." But these scruples only served to aggravate his case; and he was at last forced to take hold of Jack, which he did with a will and power that amazed the fellows who had at last baited him to the point of indignation. They took "side holds," and stood struggling, each with tremendous but equal strength, for several minutes, without any perceptible advantage to either. New trips or unexpected twists were of no avail between two such experienced wrestlers as these. Presently Abe profited by his height and the length of his arms to lift Jack clear off the ground, and, swinging him about, thought to land him on his back; but this feat was as futile as the rest, and left Jack standing as square and as firm as ever. "Now, Jack," said Abe, "let's quit: you can't throw me, and I can't throw you." But Jack's partisans, regarding this overture as a signal of the enemy's distress, and being covetous of jack-knives, whiskey, and "smooth quarters," cheered him on to greater exertions. Rendered desperate by these expectations of his friends, and now enraged at meeting more than his match, Jack resolved on "a foul," and, breaking holds, he essayed the unfair and disreputable expedient of "legging." But at this Abe's prudence deserted him, and righteous wrath rose to the ascendent. The astonished spectators saw him take their great bully by the throat, and, holding him out at arm's-length, shake him like a child. Then a score or two of the boys cried "Fight!" Bill Clary claimed the stakes, and Offutt, in the fright and confusion, was about to yield them; but "Lincoln said they had not won the money, and they should not have it; and, although he was opposed to fighting, if nothing else would do them, he would fight Armstrong, Clary, or any of the set." Just at this juncture James Rutledge, the original proprietor of New Salem, and a man of some authority, "rushed into the crowd," and exerted himself to maintain the peace. He succeeded; but for a few moments a general fight was impending, and Abe was seen with his back against Offutt's store "undismayed" and "resolute," although surrounded by enemies.[1]

Jack Armstrong was no bad fellow, after all. A sort of Western John Browdie, stout and rough, but great-hearted, honest, and true: his big hand, his cabin, his table, and his purse were all at the disposal of a friend in need. He possessed a rude sense of justice, and felt an incredible respect for a man who would stand single-handed, stanch, and defiant, in the midst of persecutors and foes. He had never disliked Abe, and had, in fact, looked for very clever things from him, even before his title to respectability had been made so

---

[1] Of the fight and what followed, we have the particulars from many persons who were witnesses.

incontestably clear; but his exhibition of pluck and muscle on this occasion excited Jack to a degree of admiration far beyond his power to conceal it. Abe's hand was hardly removed from his throat, when he was ready to grasp it in friendship, and swear brotherhood and peace between them. He declared him, on the spot, "the best fellow that ever broke into their settlement;" and henceforth the empire was divided, and Jack and Abe reigned like two friendly Cæsars over the roughs and bullies of New Salem. If there were ever any dissensions between them, it was because Jack, in the abundance of his animal spirits, was sometimes inclined to be an oppressor, whilst Abe was ever merciful and kind; because Jack would occasionally incite the "boys" to handle a stranger, a witless braggart, or a poor drunkard with a harshness that shocked the just and humane temper of his friend, who was always found on the side of the weak and the unfortunate. On the whole, however, the harmony that subsisted between them was wonderful. Wherever Lincoln worked, Jack "did his loafing;" and, when Lincoln was out of work, he spent days and weeks together at Jack's cabin, where Jack's jolly wife, "old Hannah," stuffed him with bread and honey, laughed at his ugliness, and loved him for his goodness.

Abe rapidly grew in favor with the people in and around New Salem, until nearly everybody thought quite as much of him as Mr. Offutt did. He was decidedly the most popular man that ever lived there. He could do more to quell a riot, compromise a feud, and keep peace among the neighbors generally, than any one else; and these were of the class of duties which it appears to have been the most agreeable for him to perform. One day a strange man came into the settlement, and was straightway beset by the same fellows who had meditated a drubbing for Abe himself. Jack Armstrong, of course, "had a difficulty with him;" "called him a liar, coward," and various other names not proper for print; but the man, finding himself taken at a disadvantage, "backed up to a woodpile," got a stick, and "struck Jack a blow that brought him to the ground." Being "as strong as two men, Jack wanted to whip the man badly," but Abe interfered, and, managing to have himself made "arbitrator," compromised the difficulty by a practical application of the golden rule. " Well, Jack," said he, " what did you say to the man ? " Whereupon Jack repeated his words. " Well, Jack," replied Abe, " if you were a stranger in a strange place, as this man is, and you were called a d—d liar, &c., what would you do ? " — " Whip him, by God ! " — " Then this man has done no more to you than you would have done to him." — " Well, Abe," said the honest bruiser, " it's all right," and, taking his opponent by the hand, forgave him heartily, and " treated." Jack always treated his victim when he thought he had been too hard upon him.

Abe's duties in Offutt's store were not of a character to monopolize the whole of his time,[1] and he soon began to think that here was a fine opportunity to remedy some of the defects in his education. He could read, write, and cipher as well as most men ; but as his popularity was growing daily, and his ambition keeping pace, he feared that he might shortly be called to act in some public capacity which would require him to speak his own language with some regard to the rules of the grammar, — of which, according to his own confession, he knew nothing at all. He carried his troubles to the school-master, saying, " I have a notion to study English grammar." — " If you expect to go before the public in any capacity," replied Mr. Graham, " I think it the best thing you can do." — " If I had a grammar," replied Abe, " I would commence now." There was no grammar to be had about New Salem ; but the schoolmaster, having kept the run of that species of property, gladdened Abe's heart by telling him that he knew where there was one. Abe rose from the breakfast at which he was sitting, and learning that the book was at Vaner's, only

---

[1] " During the time he was working for Offutt, and hands being scarce, Lincoln turned in and cut down trees, and split enough rails for Offutt to make a pen sufficiently large to contain a thousand hogs. The pen was built under New-Salem hill, close to the mill. . . . I know where those rails are now; are sound to-day."—MINTER GRAHAM.

six miles distant, set off after it as hard as he could tramp. It seemed to Mr. Graham a very little while until he returned and announced, with great pleasure, that he had it. "He then turned his immediate and most undivided attention" to the study of it. Sometimes, when business was not particularly brisk, he would lie under a shade-tree in front of the store, and pore over the book; at other times a customer would find him stretched on the counter intently engaged in the same way. But the store was a bad place for study; and he was often seen quietly slipping out of the village, as if he wished to avoid observation, when, if successful in getting off alone, he would spend hours in the woods, "mastering a book," or in a state of profound abstraction. He kept up his old habit of sitting up late at night; but, as lights were as necessary to his purpose as they were expensive, the village cooper permitted him to sit in his shop, where he burnt the shavings, and kept a blazing fire to read by, when every one else was in bed. The Greens lent him books; the schoolmaster gave him instructions in the store, on the road, or in the meadows: every visitor to New Salem who made the least pretension to scholarship was waylaid by Abe, and required to explain something which he could not understand. The result of it all was, that the village and the surrounding country wondered at his growth in knowledge, and he soon became as famous for the goodness of his understanding as for the muscular power of his body, and the unfailing humor of his talk.

Early in the spring of 1832, some enterprising gentlemen at Springfield determined to try whether the Sangamon was a navigable stream or not. It was a momentous question to the dwellers along the banks; and, when the steamboat "Talisman" was chartered to make the experiment, the popular excitement was intense, and her passage up and down was witnessed by great concourses of people on either bank. It was thought that Abe's experience on this particular river would render his assistance very valuable; and, in company with some others, he was sent down to Beardstown, to meet the " Talisman," and pilot her up. With Abe at the helm, she ran with comparative ease and safety as far as the New-Salem dam, a part of which they were compelled to tear away in order to let the steamer through. Thence she went on as high as Bogue's mill; but, having reached that point, the rapidly-falling water admonished her captain and pilots, that, unless they wished her to be left there for the season, they must promptly turn her prow down stream. For some time, on the return trip, she made not more than three or four miles a day, " on account of the high wind from the prairie." " I was sent for, being an old boatman," says J. R. Herndon, " and I met her some twelve or thirteen miles above New Salem. . . . We got to Salem the second day after I went on board. When we struck the dam, she hung. We then backed off, and threw the anchor over the dam, and tore away a part of the dam, and, raising steam, ran her over the first trial. As soon as she was over, the company that chartered her was done with her. I think the captain gave Mr. Lincoln forty dollars to run her down to Beardstown. I am sure I got forty dollars to continue on her until we landed at Beardstown. We that went down with her walked back to New Salem."

7

CHAPTER V.

IN the spring of 1832, Mr. Offutt's business had gone to ruin : the store was sold out, the mill was handed over to its owners, Mr. Offutt himself departed for parts unknown, and his " head clerk " was again out of work. Just about that time a governor's proclamation arrived, calling for volunteers to meet the famous chief Black Hawk and his warriors, who were preparing for a grand, and, in all likelihood, a bloody foray, into their old hunting-grounds in the Rock-river country.

Black Hawk was a large Indian, of powerful frame and commanding presence. He was a soldier and a statesman. The history of his diplomacy with the tribes he sought to confederate shows that he expected to realize on a smaller scale the splendid plans of Pontiac and Tecumseh. In his own tongue he was eloquent, and dreamed dreams which, amongst the Indians, passed for prophecy. The prophet is an indispensable personage in any comprehensive scheme of Indian politics, and no chief has ever effected a combination of formidable strength without his aid. In the person of Black Hawk, the chief and the prophet were one. His power in both capacities was bent toward a single end, — the great purpose of his life, — the recovery of his birthplace and the ancient home of his people from the possession of the stranger.

Black Hawk was born on the Rock River in Wisconsin, in the year 1767. His grandfather lived near Montreal, whence his father Pyesa had emigrated, but not until he had become thoroughly British in his views and feelings. All his life

98

BLACK HAWK, THE INDIAN CHIEF.

long he made annual journeys to the councils of the tribes at Malden, where the gifts and persuasions of British agents confirmed him in his inclination to the British interests. When Pyesa was gathered to his fathers, his son took his place as the chief of the Sacs, hated the Americans, loved the friendly English, and went yearly to Malden, precisely as he thought Pyesa would have had him do. But Black Hawk's mind was infinitely superior to Pyesa's: his sentiments were loftier, his heart more susceptible; he had the gift of the seer, the power of the orator, with the high courage and the profound policy of a born warrior and a natural ruler. He " had brooded over the early history of his tribe; and to his views, as he looked down the vista of years, the former times seemed so much better than the present, that the vision wrought upon his susceptible imagination, which pictured it to be the Indian golden age. He had some remembrance of a treaty made by Gen. Harrison in 1804, to which his people had given their assent; and his feelings were with difficulty controlled, when he was required to leave the Rock-river Valley, in compliance with a treaty made with Gen. Scott. That valley, however, he peacefully abandoned with his tribe, on being notified, and went to the west of the Mississippi; but he had spent his youth in that locality, and the more he thought of it, the more determined he was to return thither. He readily enlisted the sympathies of the Indians, who are ever prone to ponder on their real or imaginary wrongs; and it may be readily conjectured that what Indian counsel could not accomplish, Indian prophecy would." [1] He had moved when summoned to move, because he was then unprepared to fight; but he utterly denied that the chiefs who seemed to have ceded the lands long years before had any right to cede them, or that the tribe had ever willingly given up the country to the stranger and the aggressor. It was a fraud upon the simple Indians: the old treaty was a great lie, and the signatures it purported to have, made with marks and primitive devices, were not attached in good

[1] Schoolcraft's History of the Indian Tribes.

faith, and were not the names of honest Sacs.   No : he would
go over the river, he would have his own; the voice of the
Great Spirit was in the air wherever he went; it was in his
lodge through all the night-time, and it said " Go ;" and Black
Hawk must needs rise up and tell the people what the voice
said.

It was by such arguments as these that Black Hawk easily
persuaded the Sacs.   But hostilities by the Sacs alone would
be a hopeless adventure.   He must find allies.   He looked
first to their kindred, the Foxes, who had precisely the same
cause of war with the Sacs, and after them to the Winnebagoes, Sioux, Kickapoos, and many others.   That Black
Hawk was a wise and valiant leader, all the Indians conceded; and his proposals were heard by some of the tribes
with eagerness, and by all of them with respect.   At one
time his confederacy embraced nine tribes, — the most formidable in the North-west, if we exclude the Sioux and the
Chippewas, who were themselves inclined to accede.   Early
in 1831, the first chief of the Chippewas exhibited a miniature tomahawk, red with vermilion, which, having been
accepted from Black Hawk, signified an alliance between
them; and away up at Leech Lake, an obscure but numerous
band showed some whites a few British medals painted in
imitation of blood, which meant that they were to follow the
war-paths of Black Hawk.

In 1831 Black Hawk had crossed the river in small force,
but had retired before the advance of Gen. Gaines, commanding
the United States post at Rock Island.   He then promised to
remain on the other side, and to keep quiet for the future.   But
early in the spring of 1832 he re-appeared with greater numbers, pushed straight into the Rock-river Valley, and said he
had " come to plant corn."   He was now sixty-seven years of
age: he thought his great plots were all ripe, and his allies fast
and true.   They would fight a few bloody battles, and then
he would sit down in his old age and see the corn grow where
he had seen it in his youth.   But the old chief reckoned too
much upon Indian fidelity: he committed the fatal error

of trusting to their patriotism instead of their interests. Gen. Atkinson, now in command at Rock Island, set the troops in motion: the governor issued his call for volunteers; and, as the Indians by this time had committed some frightful barbarities, the blood of the settlers was boiling, and the regiments were almost instantly filled with the best possible material. So soon as these facts became known, the allies of Black Hawk, both the secret and the open, fell away from him, and left him, with the Sacs and the Foxes, to meet his fate.

In the mean time Lincoln had enlisted in a company from Sangamon. He had not been out in the campaign of the previous year, but told his friend Row Herndon, that, if he had not been down the river with Offutt, he would certainly have been with the boys in the field. But, notwithstanding his want of military experience, his popularity was so great, that he had been elected captain of a militia company on the occasion of a muster at Clary's Grove the fall before. He was absent at the time, but thankfully accepted and served. Very much to his surprise, his friends put him up for the captaincy of this company about to enter active service. They did not organize at home, however, but marched first to Beardstown, and then to Rushville in Schuyler County, where the election took place. Bill Kirkpatrick was a candidate against Lincoln, but made a very sorry showing. It has been said that Lincoln once worked for Kirkpatrick as a common laborer, and suffered some indignities at his hands; but the story as a whole is supported by no credible testimony. It is certain, however, that the planks for the boat built by Abe and his friends at the mouth of Spring Creek were sawed at the mill of a Mr. Kirkpatrick. It was then, likely enough, that Abe fell in the way of this man, and learned to dislike him. At all events, when he had distanced Kirkpatrick, and was chosen his captain by the suffrages of men who had been intimate with Kirkpatrick long before they had ever heard of Abe, he spoke of him spitefully, and referred in no gentle terms to some old dispute. " Damn him," said he to Green, " I've beat him: he used me badly in our settlement for my toil."

Capt. Lincoln now made a very modest speech to his comrades, reciting the exceeding gratification their partiality afforded him, how undeserved he thought it, and how wholly unexpected it was. In conclusion, " he promised very plainly that he would do the best he could to prove himself worthy of that confidence."

The troops rendezvoused at Beardstown and Rushville were formed into four regiments and a spy battalion. Capt. Lincoln's company was attached to the regiment of Col. Samuel Thompson. The whole force was placed under the command of Gen. Whiteside, who was accompanied throughout the campaign by the governor in person.

On the 27th of April, the army marched toward the mouth of Rock River, by way of Oquaka on the Mississippi. The route was one of difficulty and danger, a great part of it lying through a country largely occupied by the enemy. The men were raw, and restive under discipline. In the beginning they had no more respect for the "rules and regulations" than for Solomon's Proverbs, or the Westminster Confession. Capt. Lincoln's company is said to have been a particularly "hard set of men," who recognized no power but his. They were fighting men, and but for his personal authority would have kept the camp in a perpetual uproar.

At the crossing of Henderson River, — a stream about fifty yards wide, and eight or ten feet deep, with very precipitous banks, — they were compelled to make a bridge or causeway with timbers cut by the troops, and a filling-in of bushes, earth, or any other available material. This was the work of a day and night. Upon its completion, the horses and oxen were taken from the wagons, and the latter taken over by hand. But, when the horses came to cross, many of them were killed in sliding down the steep banks. "While in camp here," says a private in Capt. Lincoln's company, "a general order was issued prohibiting the discharge of fire-arms within fifty steps of the camp. Capt. Lincoln disobeyed the order by

firing his pistol within ten steps of the camp, and for this violation of orders was put under arrest for that day, and his
sword taken from him; but the next day his sword was
restored, and nothing more was done in the matter."

From Henderson River the troops marched to Yellow
Banks, on the Mississippi. "While at this place," Mr. Ben
F. Irwin says, "a considerable body of Indians of the Chero-
kee tribe came across the river from the Iowa side, with the
white flag hoisted. These were the first Indians we saw.
They were very friendly, and gave us a general war-dance.
We, in return, gave them a Sucker ho-down. All enjoyed
the sport, and it is safe to say no man enjoyed it more than
Capt. Lincoln."

From Yellow Banks, a rapid and exhaustive march of a few
days brought the volunteers to the mouth of Rock River,
where "it was agreed between Gen. Whiteside and Gen.
Atkinson of the regulars, that the volunteers should march
up Rock River, about fifty miles, to the Prophet's Town, and
there encamp, to feed and rest their horses, and await the
arrival of the regular troops, in keel-boats, with provisions.
Judge William Thomas, who again acted as quartermaster to
the volunteers, made an estimate of the amount of provisions
required until the boats could arrive, which was supplied; and
then Gen. Whiteside took up his line of march." [1]   But Capt.
Lincoln's company did not march on the present occasion with
the alacrity which distinguished their comrades of other corps.
The orderly sergeant attempted to "form company," but the
company declined to be formed; the men, oblivious of wars
and rumors of wars, mocked at the word of command, and
remained between their blankets in a state of serene repose.
For an explanation of these signs of passive mutiny, we must
resort again to the manuscript of the private who gave the
story of Capt. Lincoln's first arrest. "About the — of April,
we reached the mouth of Rock River. About three or four
nights afterwards, a man named Rial P. Green, commonly
called 'Pot Green,' belonging to a Green-county company,

---

[1] Ford's History of Illinois, chap. iv.

came to our company, and waked up the men, and proposed
to them, that, if they would furnish him with a tomahawk
and four buckets, he would get into the officers' liquors, and
supply the men with wines and brandies. The desired articles
were furnished him; and, with the assistance of one of our
company, he procured the liquors. All this was entirely
unknown to Capt. Lincoln. In the morning, Capt. Lincoln
ordered his orderly to form company for parade; but when
the orderly called the men to 'parade,' they called 'parade,'
too, but couldn't fall into line. The most of the men were un-
mistakably drunk. The rest of the forces marched off, and left
Capt. Lincoln's company behind. The company didn't make
a start until about ten o'clock, and then, after marching about
two miles, the drunken ones lay down and slept their drunk
off. They overtook the forces that night. Capt. Lincoln was
again put under arrest, and was obliged to carry a wooden
sword for two days, and this although Capt. Lincoln was
entirely blameless in the matter."

When Gen. Whiteside reached Prophetstown, where he
was to rest until the arrival of the regulars and the supplies,
he disregarded the plan of operations concerted between him
and Atkinson, and, burning the village to the ground, pushed
on towards Dixon's Ferry, forty miles farther up the river.
Nearing that place, he left his baggage-wagons behind: the
men threw away their allotments of provisions, or left them
with the wagons; and in that condition a forced march was
made to Dixon. There Whiteside found two battalions
of mounted men under Majors Stillman and Bailey, who
clamored to be thrown forward, where they might get up an
independent but glorious " brush " with the enemy on comparatively private account. The general had it not in his
heart to deny these adventurous spirits, and they were
promptly advanced to feel and disclose the Indian force supposed to be near at hand. Stillman accordingly moved up
the bank of " Old Man's Creek " (since called " Stillman's
Run "), to a point about twenty miles from Dixon, where, just
before nightfall, he went into camp, or was about to do so,

when several Indians were seen hovering along some raised ground nearly a mile distant. Straightway Stillman's gallant fellows remounted, one by one, or two and two, and, without officers or orders, galloped away in pursuit. The Indians first shook a red flag, and then dashed off at the top of their speed. Three of them were overtaken and killed: but the rest performed with perfect skill the errand upon which they were sent; they led Stillman's command into an ambuscade, where lay Black Hawk himself with seven hundred of his warriors. The pursuers recoiled, and rode for their lives: Black Hawk bore down upon Stillman's camp; the fugitives, streaming back with fearful cries respecting the numbers and ferocity of the enemy, spread consternation through the entire force. Stillman gave a hasty order to fall back; and the men fell back much faster and farther than he intended, for they never faced about, or so much as stopped, until they reached Whiteside's camp at Dixon. The first of them reached Dixon about twelve o'clock; and others came straggling in all night long and part of the next day, each party announcing themselves as the sole survivors of that stricken field, escaped solely by the exercise of miraculous valor.[1] The affair is

[1] "It is said that a big, tall Kentuckian, with a very loud voice, who was a colonel of the militia, but a private with Stillman, upon his arrival in camp, gave to Gen. Whiteside and the wondering multitude the following glowing and bombastic account of the battle. 'Sirs,' said he, 'our detachment was encamped amongst some scattering timber on the north side of Old Man's Creek, with the prairie from the north gently sloping down to our encampment. It was just after twilight, in the gloaming of the evening, when we discovered Black Hawk's army coming down upon us in solid column: they displayed in the form of a crescent upon the brow of the prairie, and such accuracy and precision of military movements were never witnessed by man; they were equal to the best troops of Wellington in Spain. I have said that the Indians came down in solid column, and displayed in the form of a crescent; and, what was most wonderful, there were large squares of cavalry resting upon the points of the curve, which squares were supported again by other columns fifteen deep, extending back through the woods, and over a swamp three-quarters of a mile, which again rested upon the main body of Black Hawk's army bivouacked upon the banks of the Kishwakee. It was a terrible and a glorious sight to see the tawny warriors as they rode along our flanks attempting to outflank us with the glittering moonbeams glistening from their polished blades and burnished spears. It was a sight well calculated to strike consternation into the stoutest and boldest heart; and accordingly our men soon began to break in small squads for tall timber. In a very little time the rout became general. The Indians were on our flanks, and threatened the destruction of the entire detachment. About this time Major Stillman, Col. Stephenson, Major Perkins, Capt. Adams, Mr. Hackelton, and myself, with some others, threw ourselves into the rear to rally the fugitives and protect the retreat. But in a short time all my companions fell, bravely fighting hand to hand with the savage

known to history as Stillman's Defeat." " Old John Hanks"
was in it, and speaks of it with shame and indignation,
attributing the disaster to "drunken men, cowardice, and
folly," though in this case we should be slow to adopt his
opinion. Of folly, there was, no doubt, enough, both on the
part of Whiteside and Stillman; but of drunkenness no
public account makes any mention, and individual cowardice
is never to be imputed to American troops. These men were
as brave as any that ever wore a uniform, and some of them
performed good service afterwards; but when they went into
this action, they were "raw militia,"—a mere mob; and no
mob can stand against discipline, even though it be but the
discipline of the savage.

The next day Whiteside moved with all possible celerity
to the field of Stillman's disaster, and, finding no enemy, was
forced to content himself with the melancholy duty of bury-
ing the mutilated and unsightly remains of the dead. All of
them were scalped; some had their heads cut off, others had
their throats cut, and others still were mangled and dishon-
ored in ways too shocking to be told.

The army was now suffering for want of provisions. The
folly of the commander in casting off his baggage-train for
the forced march on Dixon, the extravagance and improvidence of the men with their scanty rations, had exhausted the
resources of the quartermasters, and, " except in the messes

enemy, and I alone was left upon the field of battle. About this time I discovered not far
to the left, a corps of horsemen which seemed to be in tolerable order. I immediately
deployed to the left, when, leaning down and placing my body in a recumbent posture
upon the mane of my horse, so as to bring the heads of the horsemen between my eye and
the horizon, I discovered by the light of the moon that they were gentlemen who did
not wear hats, by which token I knew they were no friends of mine. I therefore made a
retrograde movement, and recovered my former position, where I remained some time,
meditating what further I could do in the service of my country, when a random ball came
whistling by my ear, and plainly whispered to me, " Stranger, you have no further business
here." Upon hearing this, I followed the example of my companions in arms, and broke
for tall timber, and the way I run was not a little, and quit.'
" This colonel was a lawyer just returning from the circuit, with a slight wardrobe and
' Chitty's Pleadings ' packed in his saddle-bags, all of which were captured by the Indians.
He afterwards related, with much vexation, that Black Hawk had decked himself out in
his finery, appearing in the woods amongst his savage companions dressed in one of the
colonel's ruffled shirts drawn over his deer-skin leggings, with a volume of ' Chitty's
Pleadings ' under each arm."— *Ford's History of Illinois.*

of the most careful and experienced," the camp was nearly destitute of food. " The majority had been living on parched corn and coffee for two or three days;" but, on the morning of the last march from Dixon, Quartermaster Thomas had succeeded in getting a little fresh beef from the only white inhabitant of that country, and this the men were glad to eat without bread. " I can truly say I was often hungry," said Capt. Lincoln, reviewing the events of this campaign. He was, doubtless, as destitute and wretched as the rest, but he was patient, quiet, and resolute. Hunger brought with it a discontented and mutinous spirit. The men complained bitterly of all they had been made to endure, and clamored loudly for a general discharge. But Capt. Lincoln kept the " even tenor of his way;" and, when his regiment was disbanded, immediately enlisted as a private soldier in another company.

From the battle-field Whiteside returned to his old camp at Dixon, but determined, before doing so, to make one more attempt to retrieve his ill-fortune. Black Hawk's pirogues were supposed to be lying a few miles distant, in a bend of the Rock River; and the capture of these would serve as some relief to the dreary series of errors and miscarriages which had hitherto marked the campaign. But Black Hawk had just been teaching him strategy in the most effective mode, and the present movement was undertaken with an excess of caution almost as ludicrous as Stillman's bravado. " To provide as well as might be against danger, one man was started at a time in the direction of the point. When he would get a certain distance, keeping in sight, a second would start, and so on, until a string of men extending five miles from the main army was made, each to look out for Indians, and give the sign to right, left, or front, by hanging a hat on a bayonet, — erect for the front, and right or left, as the case might be. To raise men to go ahead was with difficulty done, and some tried hard to drop back; but we got through safe, and found the place deserted, leaving plenty of Indian signs, — a dead dog and several scalps taken in Stillman's defeat, as we supposed them to have been taken." After this, the last of Gen. Whiteside's futile attempts, he returned to the battle-field, and thence to Dixon, where he was joined by Atkinson with the regulars and the long-coveted and much-needed supplies.

One day, during these many marches and countermarches, an old Indian found his way into the camp, weary, hungry, and helpless. He professed to be a friend of the whites; and, although it was an exceedingly perilous experiment for one of his color, he ventured to throw himself upon the mercy of the soldiers. But the men first murmured, and then broke out into fierce cries for his blood. "We have come out to fight the Indians," said they, "and by God we intend to do it!" The poor Indian, now, in the extremity of his distress and peril, did what he ought to have done before: he threw down before his assailants a soiled and crumpled paper, which he implored them to read before his life was taken. It was a letter of character and safe-conduct from Gen. Cass, pronouncing him a faithful man, who had done good service in the cause for which this army was enlisted. But it was too late: the men refused to read it, or thought it a forgery, and were rushing with fury upon the defenceless old savage, when Capt. Lincoln bounded between them and their appointed victim. "Men," said he, and his voice for a moment stilled the agitation around him, "*this must not be done: he must not be shot and killed by us.*" — "But," said some of them, "the Indian is a damned spy." Lincoln knew that his own life was now in only less danger than that of the poor creature that crouched behind him. During the whole of this scene Capt. Lincoln seemed to "rise to an unusual height" of stature. The towering form, the passion and resolution in his face, the physical power and terrible will exhibited in every motion of his body, every gesture of his arm, produced an effect upon the furious mob as unexpected perhaps to him as to any one else. They paused, listened, fell back, and then sullenly obeyed what seemed to be the voice of reason, as well as authority. But there were still some murmurs of disappointed rage, and half-suppressed exclamations, which looked towards vengeance of some kind. At length one of the men, a little bolder than the rest, but evidently feeling that he spoke for the whole, cried out, "This is cowardly on your part, Lincoln!" Whereupon the tall captain's figure stretched a few inches higher again. He looked down upon these varlets who would have murdered a defenceless old Indian, and now quailed before his single hand, with lofty contempt. The oldest of his acquaintances, even Bill Green, who saw him grapple Jack Armstrong and defy the bullies at his back, never saw him so much "aroused" before. "If any man thinks I am a coward, let him test it," said he. "Lincoln," responded a new voice, "you are larger and heavier than we are." — "This you can guard against: choose your weapons," returned the rigid captain. Whatever may be said of Mr. Lincoln's choice of means for the preservation of military discipline, it was certainly very effectual in this case. There was no more disaffection in his camp, and the word "coward" was never coupled with his name again. Mr. Lincoln understood his men better than those who would be disposed to criticise his conduct. He has often declared himself, that his life and character were both at stake, and would probably have been lost, had he not at that supremely critical moment forgotten the officer and asserted the man. To have ordered the offenders under arrest would have created a formidable mutiny; to have tried and punished them would have been impossible. They could scarcely be called soldiers: they were merely armed citizens, with a nominal military organization. They were but recently enlisted, and their term of service was just about to expire. Had he preferred charges against them, and offered to submit their differences to a court of any sort, it would have been regarded as an act of personal pusillanimity, and his efficiency would have been gone forever.

Lincoln was believed to be the strongest man in his regiment, and no doubt was. He was certainly the best wrestler in it, and after they left Beardstown nobody ever disputed the fact. He is said to have "done the wrestling for the company;" and one man insists that he *always* had a handkerchief tied around his person, in readiness for the sport. For a while

it was firmly believed that no man in the *army* could throw
him down. His company confidently pitted him " against the
field," and were willing to bet all they had on the result. At
length, one Mr. Thompson came forward and accepted the
challenge. He was, in fact, the most famous wrestler in the
Western country. It is not certain that the report of his
achievements had ever reached the ears of Mr. Lincoln or his
friends ; but at any rate they eagerly made a match with him
as a champion not unworthy of their own. Thompson's
power and skill, however, were as well known to certain persons in the army as Mr. Lincoln's were to others. Each side
was absolutely certain of the victory, and bet according to their
faith. Lincoln's company and their sympathizers put up all
their portable property, and some perhaps not their own,
including " knives, blankets, tomahawks," and all the most
necessary articles of a soldier's outfit.

When the men first met, Lincoln was convinced that he
could throw Thompson ; but, after tussling with him a brief
space in presence of the anxious assemblage, he turned to his
friends and said, " This is the most powerful man I ever had
hold of. He will throw me, and you will lose your all, unless
I act on the defensive." He managed, nevertheless, " to hold
him off for some time ; " but at last Thompson got the " crotch
hoist " on him, and, although Lincoln attempted with all his
wonderful strength to break the hold by " sliding " away, a
few moments decided his fate : he was fairly thrown. As it
required two out of three falls to decide the bets, Thompson and he immediately came together again, and with very
nearly the same result. Lincoln fell under, but the other
man fell too. There was just enough of uncertainty about it
to furnish a pretext for a hot dispute and a general fight.
Accordingly, Lincoln's men instantly began the proper preliminaries to a fracas. " We were taken by surprise," says
Mr. Green, " and, being unwilling to give up our property
and lose our bets, got up an excuse as to the result. We
declared the fall a kind of dog-fall ; did so apparently angrily."
The fight was coming on apace, and bade fair to be a big and

bloody one, when Lincoln rose up and said, "Boys, the man actually threw me once fair, broadly so; and the second time, this very fall, he threw me fairly, though not so apparently so." He would countenance no disturbance, and his unexpected and somewhat astonishing magnanimity ended all attempts to raise one.

Mr. Lincoln's good friend, Mr. Green, the principal, though not the sole authority for the present account of his adventure in behalf of the Indian and his wrestle with Thompson, mentions one important incident which is found in no other manuscript, and which gives us a glimpse of Mr. Lincoln in a scene of another sort. "One other word in reference to Mr. Lincoln's care for the health, welfare, and justice to his men. Some officers of the United States had claimed that the regular army had a preference in the rations and pay. Mr. Lincoln was ordered to do some act which he deemed unauthorized. He, however, obeyed, but went to the officer and said to him, 'Sir, you forget that we are not under the rules and regulations of the War Department at Washington; are only volunteers under the orders and regulations of Illinois. Keep in your own sphere, and there will be no difficulty; but resistance will hereafter be made to your unjust orders: and, further, my men must be equal in all particulars, in rations, arms, camps, &c., to the regular army. The man saw that Mr. Lincoln was right, and determined to have justice done. Always after this we were treated equally well, and just as the regular army was, in every particular. This brave, just, and humane act in behalf of the volunteers at once attached officers and rank to him, as with hooks of steel."

When the army reached Dixon, the almost universal discontent of the men had grown so manifest and so ominous, that it could no longer be safely disregarded. They longed "for the flesh-pots of Egypt," and fiercely demanded their discharge. Although their time had not expired, it was determined to march them by way of Paw-Paw Grove to Ottawa, and there concede what the governor feared he had no power to withhold.

" While on our march from Dixon to Fox River," says Mr. Irwin, " one night while in camp, which was formed in a square enclosing about forty acres, our horses, outside grazing, got scared about nine o'clock; and a grand stampede took place. They ran right through our lines in spite of us, and ran over many of us. No man knows what noise a thousand horses make running, unless he had been there: it beats a young earthquake, especially among scared men, and certain they were scared then. We expected the Indians to be on us that night. Fire was thrown, drums beat, fifes played, which added additional fright to the horses. We saw no real enemy that night, but a line of battle was formed. There were no eyes for sleep that night: we stood to our posts in line; and what frightened the horses is yet unknown."

" During this short Indian campaign," continues the same gentleman, " we had some hard times, — often hungry; but we had a great deal of sport, especially of nights, — foot-racing, some horse-racing, jumping, telling anecdotes, in which Lincoln beat all, keeping up a constant laughter and good-humor all the time; among the soldiers some card-playing, and wrestling, in which Lincoln took a prominent part. I think it safe to say he was never thrown in a wrestle. [Mr. Irwin, it seems, still regards the Thompson affair as " a dog-fall."] While in the army, he kept a handkerchief tied around him near all the time for wrestling purposes, and loved the sport as well as any one could. He was seldom ever beat jumping. During the campaign, Lincoln himself was always ready for an emergency. He endured hardships like a good soldier: he never complained, nor did he fear danger. When fighting was expected, or danger apprehended, Lincoln was the first to say, ' Let's go.' He had the confidence of every man of his company, and they strictly obeyed his orders at a word. His company was all young men, and full of sport.

· · · · · · ·

" One night in Warren County, a white hog — a young sow — came into our lines, which showed more good sense, to my mind, than any hog I ever saw. This hog swam creeks and rivers, and went with us clear through to, I think, the mouth of Fox River; and there the boys killed it, or it would doubtless have come home with us. If it got behind in daylight as we were marching, which it did sometimes, it would follow on the track, and come to us at night. It was naturally the cleverest, friendly-disposed hog any man ever saw, and its untimely death was by many of us greatly deplored, for we all liked the hog for its friendly disposition and good manners; for it never molested any thing, and kept in its proper place."

On the 28th of May the volunteers were discharged. The governor had already called for two thousand more men to take their places; but, in the mean time, he made the most strenuous efforts to organize a small force out of the recently discharged, to protect the frontiers until the new levies were ready for service. He succeeded in raising one regiment and a spy company. Many officers of distinction, among them Gen. Whiteside himself, enlisted as private soldiers, and served in that capacity to the end of the war. Capt. Lincoln became Private Lincoln of the "Independent Spy Company," Capt. Early commanding; and, although he was never in an engagement, he saw some hard service in scouting and trailing, as well as in carrying messages and reports.

About the middle of June the new troops were ready for the field, and soon after moved up to Rock River. Meanwhile the Indians had overrun the country. "They had scattered their war-parties all over the North from Chicago to Galena, and from the Illinois River into the Territory of Wisconsin; they occupied every grove, waylaid every road, hung around every settlement, and attacked every party of white men that attempted to penetrate the country." There had been some desultory fighting at various points. Capt. Snyder, in whose company Gen. Whiteside was a private, had met the Indians at Burr Oak Grove, and had a sharp engagement; Mr. St. Vrain, an Indian agent, with a small party of assistants, had been treacherously murdered near Fort Armstrong; several men had been killed at the lead mines, and the Wisconsin volunteers under Dodge had signally punished

8

the Indians that killed them; Galena had been threatened and Fort Apple, twelve miles from Galena, had sustained a bloody siege of fifteen hours; Capt. Stephenson of Galena had performed an act which "equalled any thing in modern warfare in daring and desperate courage," by driving a party of Indians larger than his own detachment into a dense thicket, and there charging them repeatedly until he was compelled to retire, wounded himself, and leaving three of his men dead on the ground.

Thenceforward the tide was fairly turned against Black Hawk. Twenty-four hundred men, under experienced officers, were now in the field against him; and, although he succeeded in eluding his pursuers for a brief time, every retreat was equivalent to a reverse in battle, and all his manœuvres were retreats. In the latter part of July he was finally overtaken by the volunteers under Henry, along the bluffs of the Wisconsin River, and defeated in a decisive battle. His ruin was complete: he abandoned all hope of conquest, and pressed in disorderly and disastrous retreat toward the Mississippi, in vain expectation of placing that barrier between him and his enemy.

On the fourth day, after crossing the Wisconsin, Gen. Atkinson's advance reached the high grounds near the Mississippi. Henry and his brigade, having won the previous victory, were placed at the rear in the order of march, with the ungenerous purpose of preventing them from winning another. But Black Hawk here resorted to a stratagem which very nearly saved the remnant of his people, and in the end completely foiled the intentions of Atkinson regarding Henry and his men. The old chief, with the high heart which even such a succession of reverses could not subdue, took twenty warriors and deliberately posted himself, determined to hold the army in check or lead it away on a false trail, while his main body was being transferred to the other bank of the river. He accordingly made his attack in a place where he was favored by trees, logs, and tall grass, which prevented the discovery of his numbers. Finding his advance engaged,

Atkinson formed a line of battle, and ordered a charge ; but Black Hawk conducted his retreat with such consummate skill that Atkinson believed he was just at the heels of the whole Indian army, and under this impression continued the pursuit far up the river.

When Henry came up to the spot where the fight had taken place, he readily detected the trick by various evidences about the ground. Finding the main trail in the immediate vicinity, he boldly fell upon it without orders, and followed it until he came up with the Indians in a swamp on the margin of the river, where he easily surprised and scattered them. ・ Atkinson, hearing the firing in the swamp, turned back, and arrived just in time to assist in the completion of the massacre. A few of the Indians had already crossed the river : a few had taken refuge on a little willow island in the middle of the stream. The island was charged, — the men wading to it in water up to their arm-pits, — the Indians were dislodged and killed on the spot, or shot in the water while attempting to swim to the western shore. Fifty prisoners only were taken, and the greater part of these were squaws and children. This was the battle of the Bad Axe, — a terrific slaughter, considering the numbers engaged, and the final ruin of Black Hawk's fortunes.

Black Hawk and his twenty warriors, among whom was his own son, made the best of their way to the Dalles on the Wisconsin, where they seem to have awaited passively whatever fate their enemies should contrive for them. There were some Sioux and Winnebagoes in Atkinson's camp, — men who secretly pretended to sympathize with Black Hawk, and, while acting as guides to the army, had really led it astray on many painful and perilous marches. It is certain that Black Hawk had counted on the assistance of those tribes ; but after the fight on the Wisconsin, even those who had consented to act as his emissaries about the person of the hostile commander not only deserted him, but volunteered to hunt him down. They now offered to find him, take him, and bring him in, provided that base and cowardly service should

be suitably acknowledged.   They were duly employed. Black
Hawk became their prisoner, and was presented by them to
the Indian agent with two or three shameless and disgusting
speeches from his captors.   He and his son were carried to
Washington City, and then through the principal cities of the
country, after which President Jackson released him from cap-
tivity, and sent him back to his own people.   He lived to be
eighty years old, honored and beloved by his tribe, and after
his death was buried on an eminence overlooking the Mississippi, with such rites as are accorded only to the most distinguished of native captains, — sitting upright in war dress and
paint, covered by a conspicuous mound of earth.

We have given a rapid and perhaps an unsatisfactory sketch
of the comparatively great events which brought the Black
Hawk War to a close.   So much at least was necessary, that
the reader might understand the several situations in which
Mr. Lincoln found himself during the short term of his second
enlistment.   We fortunately possess a narrative of his individual experience, covering the whole of that period, from
the pen of George W. Harrison, his friend, companion, and
messmate.   It is given in full; for there is no part of it that
would not be injured by the touch of another hand.   It is an
extremely interesting story, founded upon accurate personal
knowledge, and told in a perspicuous and graphic style, admirably suited to the subject.

" The new company thus formed was called the ' Independent Spy Company;' not being under the control of any
regiment or brigade, but receiving orders directly from the
commander-in-chief, and always, when with the army, camping
within the lines, and having many other privileges, such as
never having camp-duties to perform, drawing rations as much
and as often as we pleased, &c.   Dr. Early (deceased) of
Springfield was elected captain.   Five members constituted
a tent, or ' messed ' together.   Our mess consisted of Mr.
Lincoln, Johnston (a half-brother of his), Fanchier, Wyatt, and
myself.   The ' Independent Spy Company ' was used chiefly
to carry messages, to send an express, to spy the enemy, and

to ascertain facts. I suppose the nearest we were to doing battle was at Gratiot's Grove, near Galena. The spy company of Posey's brigade was many miles in advance of the brigade, when it stopped in the grove at noon for refreshments. Some of the men had turned loose their horses, and others still had theirs in hand, when five or six Sac and Fox Indians came near them. Many of the white men broke after them, some on horseback, some on foot, in great disorder and confusion, thinking to have much sport with their prisoners immediately. The Indians thus decoyed them about two miles from the little cabins in the grove, keeping just out of danger, when suddenly up sprang from the tall prairie grass two hundred and fifty painted warriors, with long spears in hand, and tomahawks and butcher-knives in their belts of deer-skin and buffalo, and raised such a yell that our friends supposed them to be more numerous than Black Hawk's whole clan, and, instantly filled with consternation, commenced to retreat. But the savages soon began to spear them, making it necessary to halt in the flight, and give them a fire, at which time they killed two Indians, one of them being a young chief gayly apparelled. Again, in the utmost horror, such as savage yells alone can produce, they fled for the little fort in the grove. Having arrived, they found the balance of their company, terrified by the screams of the whites and the yells of the savages, closely shut up in the double cabin, into which *they* quickly plunged, and found the much-needed respite. The Indians then prowled around the grove, shooting nearly all the company's horses, and stealing the balance of them. There, from cracks between the logs of the cabin, three Indians were shot and killed in the act of reaching for the reins of bridles on horses. They endeavored to conceal their bodies by trees in an old field which surrounded the fort; but, reaching with sticks for bridles, they exposed their heads and necks, and all of them were shot with two balls each through the neck. These three, and the two killed where our men wheeled and fired, make five Indians known to be killed; and on their retreat from the prairie to the grove, five

white men were cut into small pieces.   The field of this action
is the greatest battle-ground we saw.   The dead still lay
unburied until after we arrived at sunrise the next day.   The
forted men, fifty strong, had not ventured to go out until they
saw us, when they rejoiced greatly that friends and not dreaded
enemies had come.   They looked like men just out of cholera,
— having passed through the cramping stage.   The only part
we could then act was to seek the lost men, and with hatchets
and hands to bury them.   We buried the white men, and
trailed the dead young chief where he had been drawn on the
grass a half-mile, and concealed in the thicket.   Those who
trailed this once noble warrior, and found him, were Lincoln,
I think, Wyatt, and myself.   By order of Gen. Atkinson, our
company started on this expedition one evening, travelled all
night, and reached Gratiot's at sunrise.   A few hours after,
Gen. Posey came up to the fort with his brigade of nearly
a thousand men, when he positively refused to pursue the Indians, — being strongly solicited by Capt. Early, Lincoln, and
others, — squads of Indians still showing themselves in a
menacing manner one and a half miles distant.

" Our company was disbanded at Whitewater, Wis., a short
time before the massacre at Bad Axe by Gen. Henry ; and
most of our men started for home on the following morning ;
but it so happened that the night previous to starting on this
long trip, Lincoln's horse and mine were stolen, probably by
soldiers of our own army, and we were thus compelled to
start outside the cavalcade ; but I laughed at our fate, and he
joked at it, and we all started off merrily.   But the generous
men of our company walked and rode by turns with us ; and
we fared about equal with the rest.   But for this generosity,
our legs would have had to do the better work ; for in that
day, this then dreary route furnished no horses to buy or to
steal ; and, whether on horse or afoot, we always had company,
for many of the horses' backs were too sore for riding.

"Thus we came to Peoria: here we bought a canoe, in
which we two paddled our way to Pekin.   The other members of our company, separating in various directions, stimu-

lated by the proximity of home, could never have consented to travel at our usual tardy mode. At Pekin, Lincoln made an oar with which to row our little boat, while I went through the town in order to buy provisions for the trip. One of us pulled away at the one oar, while the other sat astern to steer, or prevent circling. The river being very low was without current, so that we had to pull hard to make half the speed of legs on land, — in fact, we let her float all night, and on the next morning always found the objects still visible that were beside us the previous evening. The water was remarkably clear, for this river of plants, and the fish appeared to be sporting with us as we moved over or near them.

" On the next day after we left Pekin, we overhauled a raft of saw-logs, with two men afloat on it to urge it on with poles and to guide it in the channel. We immediately pulled up to them and went on the raft, where we were made welcome by various demonstrations, especially by that of an invitation to a feast on fish, corn-bread, eggs, butter, and coffee, just prepared for our benefit. Of these good things we ate almost immoderately, for it was the only warm meal we had made for several days. While preparing it, and after dinner, Lincoln entertained them, and they entertained us for a couple of hours very amusingly.

" This slow mode of travel was, at the time, a new mode, and the novelty made it for a short time agreeable. We descended the Illinois to Havana, where we sold our boat, and again set out the old way, over the sand-ridges for Petersburg. As we drew near home, the impulse became stronger, and urged us on amazingly. The long strides of Lincoln, often slipping back in the loose sand six inches every step, were just right for me; and he was greatly diverted when he noticed me behind him stepping along in his tracks to keep from slipping.

" About three days after leaving the army at Whitewater, we saw a battle in full operation about two miles in advance of us. Lincoln was riding a young horse, the property of

L. D. Matheny. I was riding a sprightly animal belonging to John T. Stuart. At the time we came in sight of the scene, our two voluntary footmen were about three-fourths of a mile in advance of us, and we about half a mile behind most of our company, and three or four on foot still behind us, leading some sore-backed horses. But the owners of our horses came running back, and, meeting us all in full speed, rightfully ordered us to dismount. We obeyed : they mounted, and all pressed on toward the conflict, — they on horseback, we on foot. In a few moments of hard walking and terribly close observation, Lincoln said to me, 'George, this can't be a very dangerous battle.' Reply : 'Much shooting, nothing falls.' It was at once decided to be a sham for the purpose of training cavalry, instead of Indians having attacked a few white soldiers, and a few of our own men, on their way home, for the purpose of killing them."

CHAPTER VI.

THE volunteers from Sangamon returned to their homes shortly before the State election, at which, among other officers, assembly-men were to be chosen. Lincoln's popularity had been greatly enhanced by his service in the war, and some of his friends urged him with warm solicitations to become a candidate at the coming election. He prudently resisted, and declined to consent, alleging in excuse his limited acquaintance in the county at large, until Mr. James Rutledge, the founder of New Salem, added the weight of his advice to the nearly unanimous desire of the neighborhood. It is quite likely that his recent military career was thought to furnish high promise of usefulness in civil affairs; but Mr. Rutledge was sure that he saw another proof of his great abilities in a speech which Abe was induced to make, just about this time, before the New-Salem Literary Society. The following is an account of this speech by R. B. Rutledge, the son of James:—

"About the year 1832 or 1833, Mr. Lincoln made his first effort at public speaking. A debating club, of which James Rutledge was president, was organized, and held regular meetings. As he arose to speak, his tall form towered above the little assembly. Both hands were thrust down deep in the pockets of his pantaloons. A perceptible smile at once lit up the faces of the audience, for all anticipated the relation of some humorous story. But he opened up the discussion in splendid style, to the infinite astonishment of his friends. As he warmed with his subject, his hands would forsake his pockets and would enforce his ideas by awkward gestures, but would very soon seek their easy resting-places. He pursued the question with reason and argument so pithy and forcible that all were amazed.   The president at his fire-side, after the meeting, remarked to his wife, that there was more in Abe's head than wit and fun; that he was already a fine speaker; that all he lacked was culture to enable him to reach the high destiny which he knew was in store for him. From that time Mr. Rutledge took a deeper interest in him.

"Soon after Mr. Rutledge urged him to announce himself as a candidate for the Legislature.   This he at first declined to do, averring that it was impossible to be elected.   It was suggested that a canvass of the county would bring him prominently before the people, and in time would do him good.   He reluctantly yielded to the solicitations of his friends, and made a partial canvass."

In those days political animosities were fierce enough; but, owing to the absence of nominating conventions, party lines were not, as yet, very distinctly drawn in Illinois.   Candidates announced themselves; but, usually, it was done after full consultation with influential friends, or persons of considerable power in the neighborhood of the candidate's residence.   We have already seen the process by which Mr. Lincoln was induced to come forward.   There were often secret combinations among a number of candidates, securing a mutual support; but in the present case there is no trace of such an understanding.

This (1832) was the year of Gen. Jackson's election.   The Democrats stigmatized their opponents as "Federalists," while the latter were steadily struggling to shuffle off the odious name.   For the present they called themselves Democratic Republicans; and it was not until 1833 or 1834, that they formally took to themselves the designation of Whig.   The Democrats were known better as Jackson men than as Democrats, and were inexpressibly proud of either name.   Four or five years afterward their enemies invented for their benefit the meaningless and hideous word "Locofoco."

Since 1826 every general election in the State had resulted in a Democratic victory. The young men were mostly Democrats; and the most promising talents in the State were devoted to the cause, which seemed destined to achieve success wherever there was a contest. In a new country largely peopled by adventurers from older States, there were necessarily found great numbers who would attach themselves to the winning side merely because it was the winning side.

It is unnecessary to restate here the prevailing questions in national politics, — Jackson's stupendous struggle with the bank, " hard money," " no monopoly," internal improvements, the tariff, and nullification, or the personal and political relations of the chieftains, — Jackson, Clay, and Calhoun. Mr. Lincoln will shortly disclose in one of his speeches from the stump which of those questions were of special interest to the people of Illinois, and consequently which of them principally occupied his own attention.

The Democrats were divided into " whole-hog men " and " nominal Jackson men; " the former being thoroughly devoted to the fortunes and principles of their leader, while the latter were willing to trim a little for the sake of popular support. It is probable that Mr. Lincoln might be fairly classed as a " nominal Jackson man," although the precise character of some of the views he then held, or is supposed to have held, on national questions, is involved in considerable doubt. He had not wholly forgotten Jones, or Jones's teachings. He still remembered his high disputes with Offutt in the shanty at Spring Creek, when he effectually defended Jackson against the " abuse " of his employer. He was not Whig, but " Whiggish," as Dennis Hanks expresses it. It is not likely that a man who deferred so habitually to the popular sentiment around him would have selected the occasion of his settlement in a new place to go over bodily to a hopeless political minority. At all events, we have at least three undisputed facts, which make it plain that he then occupied an intermediate position between the extremes of all parties. First, he received the votes of all parties at New Salem; second, he was the next year appointed postmaster by Gen. Jackson; and, third, the Democrats ran him for the legislature two years afterwards; and he was elected by a larger majority than any other candidate.

"Our old way of conducting elections," says Gov. Ford, "required each aspirant to announce himself as a candidate. The most prudent, however, always consulted a little caucus of select, influential friends. The candidates then travelled around the county, or State, in proper person, making speeches, conversing with the people, soliciting votes, whispering slanders against their opponents, and defending themselves against the attacks of their adversaries; but it was not always best to defend against such attacks. A candidate in a fair way to be elected should never deny any charge made against him; for, if he does, his adversaries will prove all that they have said, and much more. As a candidate did not offer himself as the champion of any party, he usually agreed with all opinions, and promised every thing demanded by the people, and most usually promised, either directly or indirectly, his support to all the other candidates at the same election. One of the arts was to raise a quarrel with unpopular men who were odious to the people, and then try to be elected upon the unpopularity of others, as well as upon his own popularity. These modes of electioneering were not true of all the candidates, nor perhaps of half of them, very many of them being gentlemen of first-class integrity."

That portion of the people whose influence lay in their fighting qualities, and who were prone to carry a huge knife in the belt of the hunting-shirt, were sometimes called the "butcher-knife boys," and sometimes "the half-horse and half-alligator men." This class, according to Gov. Ford, "made a kind of balance-of-power party." Their favorite was sure of success; and nearly all political contests were decided by "butcher-knife influence." "In all elections and in all enactments of the Legislature, great pains were taken by all candidates, and all men in office, to make their course and measures acceptable " to these knights of steel and muscle.

At a later date they enjoyed a succession of titles, such as
" barefoot boys," " the flat-footed boys," and " the big-pawed
boys."

In those times, Gov. Ford avers that he has seen all the
rum-shops and groceries of the principal places of a county
chartered by candidates, and kept open for the gratuitous
accommodation of the free and independent electors for several weeks before the vote. Every Saturday afternoon the
people flocked to the county-seat, to see the candidates, to
hear speeches, to discuss prospects, to get drunk and fight.
" Toward evening they would mount their ponies, go reeling
from side to side, galloping through town, and throwing up
their caps and hats, screeching like so many infernal spirits
broke loose from their nether prison ; and thus they separated for their homes." These observations occur in Ford's
account of the campaign of 1830, which resulted in the
choice of Gov. Reynolds, — two years before Mr. Lincoln
first became a candidate, — and lead us to suppose that the
body of electors before whom that gentleman presented
himself were none too cultivated or refined.

Mr. Lincoln's first appearance on the stump, in the course
of the canvass, was at Pappsville, about eleven miles west
of Springfield, upon the occasion of a public sale by the
firm of Poog & Knap. The sale over, speech-making was
about to begin, when Mr. Lincoln observed strong symptoms
of inattention in his audience, who had taken that particular
moment to engage in what Mr. James A. Herndon pronounces
" a general fight." Lincoln saw that one of his friends was
suffering more than he liked in the *mêlée ;* and, stepping into
the crowd, he shouldered them sternly away from his man,
until he met a fellow who refused to fall back : him he seized
by the nape of the neck and the seat of his breeches, and
tossed him " ten or twelve feet easily." After this episode,
— as characteristic of him as of the times, — he mounted the
platform, and delivered, with awkward modesty, the following speech : —

" Gentlemen and Fellow-Citizens, I presume you all know

who I am. I am humble Abraham Lincoln. I have been solicited by many friends to become a candidate for the Legislature. My politics are short and sweet, like the old woman's dance. I am in favor of a national bank. I am in favor of the internal-improvement system and a high protective tariff. These are my sentiments and political principles. If elected, I shall be thankful; if not, it will be all the same."

In these few sentences Mr. Lincoln adopted the leading principles of the Whig party,— Clay's "American System" in full. In his view, as we shall see by another paper from him when again a candidate in 1834, the internal-improvement system required the distribution of the proceeds of the sales of the public lands amongst the States. He says nothing of South Carolina, of nullification, of disunion; and on these subjects it is quite probable his views were like Mr. Webster's, and his sympathies with Jackson. The opinions announced in this speech, on all the subjects touched by the speaker, were as emphatically Whig as they could be made in words; yet as far as they related to internal improvements, and indirectly favored the increase of bank issues, they were such as most of the "nominal Jackson men" in Illinois professed to hold, and such as they united with the Whigs to enforce, then and afterwards, in the State Legislature. The "whole-hog men" would have none of them, and therein lay the distinction. Although the Democratic party continued to have a numerical majority for many years in the Legislature, the nominal men and the Whigs coalesced to control legislation in accordance with Whig doctrines. Even with such a record made and making by them, the "nominal men" persisted in calling themselves Democrats, while Jackson was vetoing the Maysville Road Bill, grappling with the National Bank, and exposing the oppressive character of the Tariff Act then in force, which imposed the highest scale of duties since the first enactment for "protection" in 1816. It was their practice to run men like themselves for the State offices where the chances of a plain-spoken Whig were hopeless; and, by means of the "nominal" character of the candidate, secure enough Democratic votes, united with the Whigs, to elect him. In the very next canvass Mr. Lincoln himself was taken up by such a combination and triumphantly elected. Such things were made feasible by the prevalent mode of making nominations without the salutary intervention of regular party conventions and committees. We repeat that Mr. Lincoln's position was midway between the extremes in local politics.

His friend, Mr. A. Y. Ellis, who was with him during a part of this campaign, says, " He wore a mixed jeans coat, claw-hammer style, short in the sleeves, and bobtail, —in fact, it was so short in the tail he could not sit on it, —flax and tow linen pantaloons, and a straw hat. I think he wore a vest, but do not remember how it looked. He then wore pot-metal boots.

" I accompanied him on one of his electioneering trips to Island Grove; and he made a speech which pleased his party friends very well indeed, though some of the Jackson men tried to make sport of it. He told several anecdotes in his speech, and applied them, as I thought, very well. He also told the boys several stories which drew them after him. I remember them; but modesty and my veneration for his memory forbid me to relate them."

Mr. J. R. Herndon, his friend and landlord, heard him make several speeches about this time, and gives us the following extract from one, which seems to have made a special impression upon the minds of his auditors: " Fellow-citizens, I have been told that some of my opponents have said that it was a disgrace to the county of Sangamon to have such a looking man as I am stuck up for the Legislature. Now, I thought this was a free country: that is the reason I address you to-day. Had I have known to the contrary, I should not have consented to run; but I will say one thing, let the shoe pinch where it may: when I have been a candidate before you some five or six times, and have been beaten every time, I will consider it a disgrace, and will be sure never to try it again; but I am bound to beat that man if I am beat myself. Mark that!"

These were not the only speeches he made in furtherance
of his present claims, but they are all of which we have any
intelligible account. There was one subject upon which he
felt himself peculiarly competent to speak, — the practical
application of the "internal-improvement system" to the
river which flowed by the doors of the constituency he
addressed. He firmly believed in the right of the Legislature
of the State or the Congress of the United States to appropriate the public money to local improvements for the sole
advantage of limited districts ; and that he believed it good
policy to exercise the right, his subsequent conduct in the
Legislature, and an elaborate speech in Congress, are sufficient
proof. In this doctrine he had the almost unanimous support
of the people of Illinois. Almost every man in the State was
a speculator in town lots or lands. Even the farmers had
taken up or held the very lands they tilled with a view to a
speculation in the near future. Long after the Democratic
party in the South and East, leaving Mr. Calhoun in a state of
isolation, had begun to inculcate different views of constitutional power and duty, it was a dangerous thing for a politician in Illinois to intimate his agreement with them. Mr.
Lincoln knew well that the policy of local improvement at
the general expense was at that moment decidedly the most
popular platform he could mount; but he felt that this was not
enough for his individual purposes, since it was no invention
of his, and belonged to nearly everybody else as much as to
him. He therefore prudently ingrafted upon it a hobby of
his own: " The Improvement of the Sangamon River," — a
plan to straighten it by means of cuts, to clear out its obstructions, and make it a commercial highway at the cost of the
State. That the idea was nearly, if not quite impracticable,
the trip of " The Talisman " under Mr. Lincoln's piloting,
and the fact that the river remained unimproved during all
the years of the " internal-improvement " mania, would seem
to be pretty clear evidence. But the theme was agreeable to
the popular ear, and had been dear to Lincoln from the
moment he laid his eyes on the Sangamon. It was the great

topic of his speech against Posey and Ewing in Macon County, when, under the auspices of John Hanks, he " beat " those professional politicians so completely that they applauded him themselves. His experience in navigating the river was not calculated to make him forget it, and it had occupied his thoughts more or less from that day forward. Now that it might be turned to good use, where he was personally interested, he set about preparing a written address on it, and on some other questions of local interest, upon which he bestowed infinite pains. The " grammatical errors " in the first draft were corrected by Mr. McNamar, the pioneer of New Salem as a business point, and the gentleman who was destined to be Mr. Lincoln's rival in the most important love-affair of his life. He may have consulted the schoolmaster also; but, if he had done so, it is hardly to be surmised that the schoolmaster would have left so important a fact out of his written reminiscences. It is more probable that Mr. Lincoln confined his applications for assistance on this most important matter to the quarter where he could get light on politics as well as grammar. However that may have been, the following is the finished paper : —

To the People of Sangamon County.

Fellow-Citizens, — Having become a candidate for the honorable office of one of your Representatives in the next General Assembly of this State, in accordance with an established custom and the principles of true republicanism, it becomes my duty to make known to you, the people, whom I propose to represent, my sentiments with regard to local affairs.

Time and experience have verified to a demonstration the public utility of internal improvements. That the poorest and most thinly-populated countries would be greatly benefited by the opening of good roads, and in the clearing of navigable streams within their limits, is what no person will deny. Yet it is folly to undertake works of this or any other kind, without first knowing that we are able to finish them, — as half-finished work generally proves to be labor lost. There cannot justly be any objection to having railroads and canals, any more than to other good things, provided they cost nothing. The only objection is to paying for them; and the objection arises from the want of ability to pay.

With respect to the County of Sangamon, some more easy means of communication than it now possesses, for the purpose of facilitating the task of exporting the surplus products of its fertile soil, and importing necessary articles from abroad, are indispensably necessary. A meeting has been held of the citizens of Jacksonville and the adjacent country, for the purpose of deliberating and inquiring into the expediency of constructing a railroad from some eligible point on the Illinois River, through the town of Jacksonville, in Morgan County, to the town of Springfield, in Sangamon County. This is, indeed, a very desirable object. No other improvement that reason will justify us in hoping for can equal in utility the railroad. It is a never-failing source of communication between places of business remotely situated from each other. Upon the railroad the regular progress of commercial intercourse is not interrupted by either high or low water, or freezing weather, which are the principal difficulties that render our future hopes of water communication precarious and uncertain.

Yet however desirable an object the construction of a railroad through our country may be; however high our imaginations may be heated at thoughts of it, — there is always a heart-appalling shock accompanying the account of its cost, which forces us to shrink from our pleasing anticipations. The probable cost of this contemplated railroad is estimated at $290,000; the bare statement of which, in my opinion, is sufficient to justify the belief that the improvement of the Sangamon River is an object much better suited to our infant resources.

Respecting this view, I think I may say, without the fear of being contradicted, that its navigation may be rendered completely practicable as high as the mouth of the South

Fork, or probably higher, to vessels of from twenty-five to thirty tons' burden, for at least one-half of all common years, and to vessels of much greater burden a part of the time. From my peculiar circumstances, it is probable, that for the last twelve months I have given as particular attention to the stage of the water in this river as any other person in the country. In the month of March, 1831, in company with others, I commenced the building of a flatboat on the Sangamon, and finished and took her out in the course of the spring. Since that time I have been concerned in the mill at New Salem. These circumstances are sufficient evidence that I have not been very inattentive to the stages of the water. The time at which we crossed the mill-dam being in the last days of April, the water was lower than it had been since the breaking of winter in February, or than it was for several weeks after. The principal difficulties we encountered in descending the river were from the drifted timber, which obstructions all know are not difficult to be removed. Knowing almost precisely the height of water at that time, I believe I am safe in saying that it has as often been higher as lower since.

From this view of the subject, it appears that my calculations with regard to the navigation of the Sangamon cannot but be founded in reason; but, whatever may be its natural advantages, certain it is, that it never can be practically useful to any great extent, without being greatly improved by art. The drifted timber, as I have before mentioned, is the most formidable barrier to this object. Of all parts of this river, none will require so much labor in proportion to make it navigable, as the last thirty or thirty-five miles; and going with the meanderings of the channel, when we are this distance above its mouth we are only between twelve and eighteen miles above Beardstown, in something near a straight direction; and this route is upon such low ground as to retain water in many places during the season, and in all parts such as to draw two-thirds or three-fourths of the river-water at all high stages.

This route is on prairie land the whole distance; so that it appears to me, by removing the turf a sufficient width, and damming up the old channel, the whole river in a short time would wash its way through, thereby curtailing the distance, and increasing the velocity of the current, very considerably: while there would be no timber on the banks to obstruct its navigation in future; and, being nearly straight, the timber which might float in at the head would be apt to go clear through. There are also many places above this where the river, in its zigzag course, forms such complete peninsulas, as to be easier to cut at the necks than to remove the obstructions from the bends, which, if done, would also lessen the distance.

What the cost of this work would be, I am unable to say. It is probable, however, that it would not be greater than is common to streams of the same length. Finally, I believe the improvement of the Sangamon River to be vastly important and highly desirable to the people of the county; and, if elected, any measure in the Legislature having this for its object, which may appear judicious, will meet my approbation and shall receive my support.

It appears that the practice of drawing money at exorbitant rates of interest has already been opened as a field for discussion; so I suppose I may enter upon it without claiming the honor, or risking the danger, which may await its first explorer. It seems as though we are never to have an end to this baneful and corroding system, acting almost as prejudicial to the general interests of the community as a direct tax of several thousand dollars annually laid on each county, for the benefit of a few individuals only, unless there be a law made fixing the limits of usury. A law for this purpose, I am of opinion, may be made, without materially injuring any class of people. In cases of extreme necessity, there could always be means found to cheat the law; while in all other cases it would have its intended effect. I would favor the passage of a law on this subject which might not be very easily evaded. Let it be such that the labor and difficulty of evading it could only be justified in cases of greatest necessity.[1]

Upon the subject of education, not presuming to dictate any plan or system respecting it, I can only say that I view it as the most important subject which we as a people can be engaged in. That every man may receive at least a moderate education, and thereby be enabled to read the histories of his own and other countries, by which he may duly appreciate the value of our free institutions, appears to be an object of vital importance, even on this account alone, to say nothing of the advantages and satisfaction to be derived from all being able to read the Scriptures and other works, both of a religious and moral nature, for themselves.

For my part, I desire to see the time when education—and, by its means, morality, sobriety, enterprise, and industry— shall become much more general than at present, and should be gratified to have it in my power to contribute something to the advancement of any measure which might have a tendency to accelerate the happy period.

With regard to existing laws, some alterations are thought to be necessary. Many respectable men have suggested that our estray laws — the law respecting the issuing of executions, the road-law, and some others — are deficient in their present form, and require alterations. But, considering the great probability that the framers of those laws were wiser than myself, I should prefer not meddling with them, unless they were first attacked by others; in which case I should feel it both a privilege and a duty to take that stand, which, in my view, might tend most to the advancement of justice.

But, fellow-citizens, I shall conclude. Considering the great degree of modesty which should always attend youth,

---

[1] Until the year 1833 there had been no legal limit to the rate of interest to be fixed by contract. But usury had been carried to such an unprecedented degree of extortion and oppression as to cause the Legislature to enact severe usury laws, by which all interest above twelve per cent was condemned. It had been no uncommon thing before this to charge one hundred and one hundred and fifty per cent, and sometimes two and three hundred per cent. But the common rate of interest, by contract, had been about fifty per cent. — *Ford's History*, page 236.

it is probable I have already been more presuming than becomes me. However, upon the subjects of which I have treated, I have spoken as I have thought. I may be wrong in regard to any or all of them; but, holding it a sound maxim, that it is better only sometimes to be right than at all times wrong, so soon as I discover my opinions to be erroneous, I shall be ready to renounce them.

Every man is said to have his peculiar ambition. Whether it be true or not, I can say, for one, that I have no other so great as that of being truly esteemed of my fellow-men, by rendering myself worthy of their esteem. How far I shall succeed in gratifying this ambition is yet to be developed. I am young, and unknown to many of you. I was born, and have ever remained, in the most humble walks of life. I have no wealthy or popular relations or friends to recommend. My case is thrown exclusively upon the independent voters of the county; and, if elected, they will have conferred a favor upon me, for which I shall be unremitting in my labors to compensate. But, if the good people in their wisdom shall see fit to keep me in the background, I have been too familiar with disappointments to be very much chagrined.

Your Friend and Fellow-Citizen,

A. LINCOLN.

New Salem, March 9, 1832.

Mr. Lincoln was defeated at the election, having four hundred and seventy votes less than the candidate who had the highest number. But his disappointment was softened by the action of his immediate neighbors, who gave him an almost unanimous support. With three solitary exceptions, he received the whole vote of his precinct, — two hundred and seventy-seven, — being one more than the whole number cast for both the candidates for Congress.

CHAPTER VII.

THE results of the canvass for the Legislature were precisely such as had been predicted, both by Mr. Lincoln and Mr. Rutledge: he had been defeated, as he expected himself; and it had done "him much good," in the politician's sense, as promised by Mr. Rutledge. He was now somewhat acquainted with the people outside of the New Salem district, and generally marked as a young man of good parts and popular manners. The vote given him at home demonstrated his local strength, and made his favor a thing of value to the politicians of all parties.

Soon after his return from the army, he had taken quarters at the house of J. R. Herndon, who loved him then, and always, with as much sincerity as one man can love another. Mr. Herndon's family likewise "became much attached to him." He "nearly always had one" of Herndon's children "around with him." Mr. Herndon says of him further, that he was "at home wherever he went;" making himself wonderfully agreeable to the people he lived with, or whom he happened to be visiting. Among other things, "he was very kind to the widow and orphan, and chopped their wood."

Lincoln, as we have seen already, was not enamored of the life of a common laborer, — mere hewing and drawing. He preferred to clerk, to go to war, to enter politics, — any thing but that dreary round of daily toil and poor pay. But he was now, as he would say, "in a fix:" clerks were not wanted every day in New Salem, and he began to cast about

for some independent business of his own, by which he could
earn enough to pay board and buy books. In every community where he had lived, "the merchant" had been the principal man. He felt that, in view of his apprenticeship under
those great masters, Jones and Offutt, he was fully competent
to "run a store," and was impatient to find an opening in
that line.

Unfortunately for him, the circumstances of the business
men of New Salem were just then peculiarly favorable to his
views. At least three of them were as anxious to sell out as
Lincoln was to buy.

Lincoln, as already stated, was at this time living with
"Row" Herndon. Row and his brother "Jim" had taken
"a store down to New Salem early in that year." But Jim
"didn't like the place," and sold out his interests to an idle,
convivial fellow, named Berry. Six weeks later Row Herndon grew tired of his new partner, and sold his interest to
Lincoln. The store was a mixed one, — dry goods and groceries.

About the same time Mr. Radford, who kept one of the
New Salem groceries, fell into disfavor with the "Clary's
Grove Boys," who generously determined that he should
keep a grocery no longer. They accordingly selected a convenient night for breaking in his windows, and, in their own
elegant phrase, "gutting his establishment." Convinced that
these neighborly fellows were inclined to honor him with further attentions, and that his bones might share the fate of his
windows, Radford determined to sell out with the earliest
dawn of the coming day. The next day he was standing
disconsolate in the midst of his wreck, when Bill Green rode
up. Green thought he saw a speculation in Radford's distress, and offered him four hundred dollars for the whole concern. Radford eagerly closed with him; and in a few minutes
Green owned the grocery, and Radford was ready for the
road to a more congenial settlement. It is said that Green
employed Lincoln to make an inventory of the stock. At all
events, Lincoln was satisfied that Green's bargain was a very

good one, and proposed that he and Berry should take it off his hands at a premium of two hundred and fifty dollars. Radford had Green's note for four hundred dollars; but he now surrendered, it and took Lincoln & Berry's for the same amount, indorsed by Green; while Lincoln & Berry gave Green a note for two hundred and fifty dollars, the latter's profit in the trade.

Mr. Rutledge "also owned a small grocery in the village;" and this was speedily absorbed by the enterprising firm of Lincoln & Berry, who now had the field to themselves, being sole proprietors " of the only store of the kind in New Salem."

Whether Mr. Lincoln sold liquor by the dram over the counter of this shop remains, and will forever remain, an undetermined question. Many of his friends aver that he did, and as many more aver that he did not. When Douglas, with that courtesy for which he distinguished himself in the debates with Lincoln, revived the story, Lincoln replied, that, even if it were true, there was but little difference between them; for, while he figured on one side of the counter, Douglas figured on the other. It is certain liquors were a part of the stock of all the purchases of Lincoln & Berry. Of course they sold them by the quantity, and probably by the drink. Some of it they *gave* away, for no man could keep store without setting out the customary dram to the patrons of the place.[1]

---

[1] Here is the evidence of James Davis, a Democrat, "aged sixty," who is willing to "give the Devil his due:" —

"Came to Clary's Grove in 1829; knew Lincoln well; knew Jim and Row Herndon: they sold out to Berry, — one of them did; afterwards the other sold out to Lincoln. The store was a mixed one, — dry goods, a few groceries, such as sugar, salt, &c., and whiskey solely kept for their customers, or to sell by the gallon, quart, or pint, — not otherwise. The Herndons probably had the Blankenship goods. Radford had a grocery-store, — salt, pepper, and suchlike things, with whiskey. It is said Green bought this out, and instantly sold to Berry & Lincoln. Lincoln & Berry broke. Berry subsequently kept a doggery, a whiskey saloon, as I do now, or did. Am a Democrat; never agreed in politics with Abe. He was an honest man. Give the Devil his due; he never sold whiskey by the dram in New Salem! I was in town every week for years; knew, I think, all about it. I always drank my dram, and drank at Berry's often; ought to know. Lincoln got involved, I think, in the first operation. Salem Hill was a barren."

The difficulty of gathering authentic evidence on this subject is well illustrated in the following extract from Mr. George Spears of Petersburg: —

"I took my horse this morning, and went over to New Salem, among the P——s and

All that winter (1832–3) Lincoln struggled along with a bad partner, and a business which began wrong, and grew worse every day. Berry had no qualities which atoned for his evil habits. He preferred to consume the liquors on hand rather than to sell them, and exerted himself so successfully, that in a few months he had ruined the credit of the firm, squandered its assets, and destroyed his own health. The "store" was a dead failure; and the partners were weighed down with a parcel of debts, against which Lincoln could scarcely have borne up, even with a better man to help him. At last they sold out to two brothers named Trent. The Trents continued the business for a few months, when they broke up and ran away. Then Berry, encouraged by the example of the Trents, "cleared out" also, and, dying soon after, left poor Lincoln the melancholy task of settling up the affairs of their ill-starred partnership.

In all the preceding transactions, the absence of any cash consideration is the one thing very striking. It is a fair illustration of the speculative spirit pervading the whole people. Green bought from Radford on credit; Lincoln & Berry bought from Green on credit; they bought from the Herndons on credit; they bought from Rutledge on credit; and they sold to the Trents on credit. Those that did not die or run away had a sad time enough in managing the debts resulting from their connection with this unlucky grocery. Radford assigned Lincoln & Berry's note to a Mr. Van Bergen, who got judgment on it, and swept away all Lincoln's little personal property, including his surveying instruments, — his very means of livelihood, as we shall see at another place. The Herndons owed E. C. Blankenship for the goods they sold, and assigned Lincoln & Berry's note in payment. Mr. Lincoln struggled to pay, by slow degrees, this harassing debt to Blankenship, through many long and weary years. It

A——s, and made all the inquiries I could, but could learn nothing. The old ladies would begin to count up what had happened in New Salem when such a one of their children was born, and such a one had a bastard; but it all amounted to nothing. I could arrive at no dates, only when those children were born. Old Mrs. Potter affirms that Lincoln did sell liquors in a grocery. I can't tell whether he did or not."

was not until his return from Congress, in 1849, that he got the last dollar of it discharged. He paid Green *his* note of two hundred and fifty dollars, in small instalments, beginning in 1839, and ending in 1840. The history of his debt to Rutledge is not so well known. It was probably insignificant as compared with the others ; and Mr. Rutledge proved a generous creditor, as he had always been a kind and considerate friend.

Certain that he had no abilities for trade, Mr. Lincoln took the best resolution he could have formed under the circumstances. He sat down to his books just where he was, believing that knowledge would be power, and power profit. He had no reason to shun his creditors, for these were the men of all others who most applauded the honesty of his conduct at the period of his greatest pecuniary misfortune. He talked to them constantly of the "old debt," " the national debt," as he sometimes called it, — promised to pay when he could, and they devoutly relied upon every word he said.

Row Herndon moved to the country, and Lincoln was compelled to change his boarding-place. He now began to live at a tavern for the first time in his life. It was kept by various persons during his stay, — first, it seems, by Mr. Rutledge, then by Henry Onstatt, and last by Nelson Alley. It was a small log-house, covered with clapboards, and contained four rooms.

Lincoln began to read law while he lived with Herndon. Some of his acquaintances insist that he began even earlier than this, and assert, by way of proof, that he was known to borrow a well-worn copy of Blackstone from A. V. Bogue, a pork-dealer at Beardstown. At all events, he now went to work in earnest, and studied law as faithfully as if he had never dreamed of any other business in life. As a matter of course, his slender purse was unequal to the purchase of the needful books : but this circumstance gave him little trouble ; for, although he was short of funds, he was long in the legs, and had nothing to do but to walk off to Springfield, where his friend, John T. Stuart, cheerfully supplied his wants. Mr.

Stuart's partner, H. C. Dummer, says, "He was an uncouth-looking lad, did not say much, but what he did say he said straight and sharp."

"He used to read law," says Henry McHenry, "in 1832 or 1833, barefooted, seated in the shade of a tree, and would grind around with the shade, just opposite Berry's grocery-store, a few feet south of the door." He occasionally varied the attitude by lying flat on his back, and "*putting his feet up the tree,*" — a situation which might have been unfavorable to mental application in the case of a man with shorter extremities.

"The first time I ever saw Abe with a law-book in his hand," says Squire Godbey, "he was sitting astride of Jake Bales's woodpile in New Salem. Says I, 'Abe, what are you studying?'—'Law,' says Abe. 'Great God Almighty!' responded I." It was too much for Godbey: he could not suppress the blasphemy at seeing such a figure acquiring science in such an odd situation.

Minter Graham asserts that Abe did a little "of what we call sitting up to the fine gals of Illinois;" but, according to other authorities, he always had his book with him "when in company," and would read and talk alternately. He carried it along in his walks to the woods and the river; read it in daylight under the shade-tree by the grocery, and at night by any friendly light he could find, — most frequently the one he kindled himself in the shop of his old benefactor, the cooper.

Abe's progress in the law was as surprising as the intensity of his application to study. He never lost a moment that might be improved. It is even said that he read and recited to himself on the road and by the wayside as he came down from Springfield with the books he had borrowed from Stuart. The first time he went up he had "mastered" forty pages of Blackstone before he got back. It was not long until, with his restless desire to be doing something practical, he began to turn his acquisitions to account in forwarding the business of his neighbors. He wrote deeds, contracts, notes, and other legal papers, for them, "using a small dictionary and an old form-book;" "petifogged" incessantly before the justice of the peace, and probably assisted that functionary in the administration of justice as much as he benefited his own clients.   This species of country "student's" practice was entered upon very early, and kept up until long after he was quite a distinguished man in the Legislature.   But in all this he was only trying himself: as he was not admitted to the bar until 1837, he did not regard it as legitimate practice, and never charged a penny for his services.   Although this fact is mentioned by a great number of persons, and the generosity of his conduct much enlarged upon, it is seriously to be regretted that no one has furnished us with a circumstantial account of any of his numerous cases before the magistrate.

But Mr. Lincoln did not confine himself entirely to the law. He was not yet quite through with Kirkham nor the schoolmaster.   The "valuable copy" of the grammar "he delighted to peruse" is still in the possession of R. B. Rutledge, with the thumb-marks of the President all over it.   "He also studied natural philosophy, chemistry, astronomy, &c.   He had no regular teacher, but perhaps received more assistance from Minter Graham than from any other person."

He read with avidity all the newspapers that came to New Salem, — chiefly "The Sangamon Journal," "The Missouri Republican," and "The Louisville Journal." [1] The latter was his favorite: its wit and anecdotes were after his own heart; and he was a regular subscriber for it through several years when he could ill afford a luxury so costly.

Mr. Lincoln was never a profound historical student: if he happened to need historical facts for the purposes of a political or legal discussion, he read them on the spur of the occasion. For this reason his opinions of current affairs all through his life were based more upon individual observation and reflection than upon scientific deductions from the experience of the world.   Yet at this time, when he probably felt more

---

[1] According to Mr. McNamar, Lincoln took "The Sangamon Journal" and "The Louisville Journal" from 1832 to 1837; and Hill and Bale took "The Missouri Republican" and "The Cincinnati Gazette." "The Missouri Republican" was first issued as a daily in September, 1836. Its size was then twenty-five by thirty-six inches.

keenly than ever after the want of a little learning to embel-
lish the letters and speeches he was ambitious to compose, he
is said to have read Rollin's "Ancient History," Gibbon's
"Rise and Fall of the Roman Empire," and similar works,
with great diligence and care. The books were borrowed
from William Green, Bowlin Greene, and other parties in
and about New Salem.

But he greatly preferred literature of another sort, such as
Mrs. Lee Hentz's novels; some of which he found among the
effects of Mr. Ellis, at the time his companion and occasional
bedfellow. "He was very fond," Mr. Ellis declares, "of short
stories, one and two columns long, — like ' Cousin Sally Dil-
lard,' ' Becky Wilson's Courtship,' ' The Down-easter and
the Bull,' ' How a bashful man became a married man, with
five little bashful boys, and how he and his red-headed wife
became Millerites, and before they were to ascend agreed to
make a clean breast of it to each other ;' and how, when the
old lady was through, the Down-easter earnestly wished that
Gabriel might blow his horn without delay." One New Salem-
ite insists that Mr. Lincoln told this latter story "with embezzle-
ments" (embellishments), and therefore he is firmly convinced
that Mr. Lincoln "had a hand" in originating it. The cata-
logue of literature in which he particularly delighted at New
Salem is completed by the statement of Mr. Rutledge, that
he took great pleasure in "Jack Downing's Letters."

Mr. Lincoln still relished a popular song with a broad
"point" or a palpable moral in it as much as he had ever
enjoyed the vocal efforts of Dennis Hanks and his rollicking
compeers of the Gentryville grocery. He even continued
his own unhappy attempts, although with as little success as
before, and quite as much to the amusement of his friends.
To the choice collection of miscellaneous ballads acquired in
Indiana, he now added several new favorites, like "Old Sukey
Blue Skin," and some selections from the "Missouri Harmony," with variations by himself. He was also singularly fond
of an Irish song, "which tells how St. Patrick came to be
born on the 17th day of March."

"You ask me," says Mr. Ellis, "if I remember the first time I saw Mr. Lincoln. Yes, I do. . . . I was out collecting back tax for Gen. James D. Henry. I went from the tavern down to Jacob Bales's old mill, and then I first saw Mr. Lincoln. He was sitting on a saw-log talking to Jack and Rial Armstrong and a man by the name of Hohammer. I shook hands with the Armstrongs and Hohammer, and was conversing with them a few minutes, when we were joined by my old friend and former townsman, George Warburton, pretty tight as usual; and he soon asked me to tell him the old story about Ben Johnson and Mrs. Dale's blue dye, &c., which I did. And then Jack Armstrong said, 'Lincoln, tell Ellis the story about Gov. J. Sichner, his city-bred son, and his nigger Bob;' which he did, with several others, by Jack's calling for them. I found out then that Lincoln was a cousin to Charley Hanks of Island Grove. I told him I knew three of the boys, — Joe, Charley, and John, — and his uncle, old Billy Hanks, who lived up on the North Fork of the Sangamon River, afterwards near Decatur."[1]

This interview took place shortly after the Black Hawk War; but it was not until the next year (1833), the period at which we have now arrived, that Lincoln and Ellis became "intimate." At that time Ellis went there to keep a store, and boarded "at the same log-tavern" where Lincoln was. Lincoln, being "engaged in no particular business," merely endeavoring to make a lawyer, a surveyor, and a politician of himself, gave a great deal of his time to Ellis and Ellis's business. "He also used to assist me in the store," says this

[1] "I myself knew old Billy Hanks, his mother's brother, and he was a very sensible old man. He was father to Mrs. Dillon, on Spring Creek; and Charley, Billy, jr., and John were his sons: they were all low-flung. — could neither read nor write. Some of them used to live in Island Grove, Sangamon County. . . . I remember the time that Lincoln and E. D. Baker ran in convention, to decide who should run for Congress in old Sangamon; that some of Baker's friends accused Mr. Lincoln of belonging to a proud and an aristocratic family, — meaning the Edwardses and Todds, I suppose; and, when it came to Mr. Lincoln's ears, he laughed heartily, and remarked, 'Well, that sounds strange to me: I do not remember of but one that ever came to see me, and while he was in town he was accused of stealing a jew's-harp.' Josh Speed remembers his saying this. I think you ought to remember it. Beverly Powell and myself lived with Bell and Speed, and I think he said so in their store. After that a Miss Hanks came to spend the winter with Mrs. Lincoln." — A. Y. ELLIS.

new friend, " on busy days, but he always disliked to wait on the ladies : he preferred trading with the men and boys, as he used to say. I also remember that he used to sleep in the store, on the counter, when they had too much company at the tavern.

" I well remember how he was dressed : he wore flax and tow linen pantaloons, — I thought about five inches too short in the legs, — and frequently he had but one suspender, no vest or coat. He wore a calico shirt, such as he had in the Black Hawk War ; coarse brogans, tan color ; blue yarn socks, and straw hat, old style, and without a band.

" Mr. Lincoln was in those days a very shy man of ladies. On one occasion, while we boarded at this tavern, there came a family, containing an old lady and her son and three stylish daughters, from the State of Virginia, and stopped there for two or three weeks ; and, during their stay, I do not remember of Mr. Lincoln ever eating at the same table when they did. I then thought it was on account of his awkward appearance and his wearing apparel."

There lived at New Salem at this time, and for some years afterward, a festive gentleman named Kelso, a school-teacher, a merchant, or a vagabond, according to the run of his somewhat variable " luck." When other people got drunk at New Salem, it was the usual custom to tussle and fight, and tramp each other's toes, and pull each other's noses ; but, when Kelso got drunk, he astonished the rustic community with copious quotations from Robert Burns and William Shakspeare, — authors little known to fame among the literary men of New Salem. Besides Shakspeare and Burns, Mr. Kelso was likewise very fond of fishing, and could catch his game " when no other man could get a bite." Mr. Lincoln hated fishing with all his heart. But it is the testimony of the country-side, from Petersburg to Island Grove, that Kelso " drew Lincoln after him by his talk ; " that they became exceedingly intimate ; that they loitered away whole days together, along the banks of the quiet streams ; that Lincoln learned to love inordinately our " divine William " and

"Scotia's Bard," whom his friend mouthed in his cups, or expounded more soberly in the intervals of fixing bait and dropping line. Finally he and Kelso boarded at the same place; and with another "merchant," named Sincho, of tastes congenial and wits as keen as Kelso's, they were "always found together, battling and arguing." Bill Green ventures the opinion, that Lincoln's incessant reading of Shakspeare and Burns had much to do in giving to his mind the "sceptical" tendency so fully developed by the labors of his pen in 1834–5, and in social conversations during many years of his residence at Springfield.

Like Offutt, Kelso disappeared suddenly from New Salem, and apparently from the recollection of men. Each with a peculiar talent of his own, kind-hearted, eccentric creatures, no man's enemy and everybody's prey, they strolled out into the great world, and left this little village to perish behind them. Of Kelso a few faint traces have been found in Missouri; but if he ever had a lodging more permanent than the wayside tavern, a haystack, or a hedge, no man was able to tell where it was. Of Offutt not a word was ever heard: the most searching and cunning inquiries have failed to discover any spot where he lingered for a single hour; and but for the humble boy, to whom he was once a gentle master, no human being that knew him then would bestow a thought upon his name. In short, to use the expressive language of Mr. Lincoln himself, he literally "petered out."

Mr. Lincoln was often annoyed by "company." His quarters at the tavern afforded him little privacy, and the shade of the tree in front of the grocery was scarcely a sufficiently secluded situation for the purposes of an ardent student. There were too many people to wonder and laugh at a man studying law with "his feet up a tree;" too many to worry him for the stories and jokes which it was supposed he could furnish on demand. For these reasons it became necessary that he should "retire to the country occasionally to rest and study." Sometimes he went to James Short's on the Sand Ridge; sometimes to Minter Graham's; sometimes to Bowlin

Greene's; sometimes to Jack Armstrong's, and as often,
perhaps, to Able's or Row Herndon's. All of these men
served him faithfully and signally at one time and another,
and to all of them he was sincerely attached. When Bowlin
Greene died, in 1842, Mr. Lincoln, then in the enjoyment of
great local reputation, undertook to deliver a funeral oration
over the remains of his beloved friend; but, when he rose to
speak, his voice was choked with deep emotion: he stood a
few moments, while his lips quivered in the effort to form the
words of fervent praise he sought to utter, and the tears ran
down his yellow and shrivelled cheeks. Some of those who
came to hear him, and saw his tall form thus sway in silence
over the body of Bowlin Greene, say he looked so helpless,
so utterly bereft and pitiable, that every heart in the audience
was hushed at the spectacle. After repeated efforts, he found
it impossible to speak, and strode away, openly and bitterly
sobbing, to the widow's carriage, in which he was driven from
the scene. Mr. Herndon's papers disclose less than we
should like to know concerning this excellent man: they
give us only this burial scene, with the fact that Bowlin
Greene had loaned Mr. Lincoln books from their earliest
acquaintance, and on one occasion had taken him to his home,
and cared for him with the solicitude of a devoted friend
through several weeks of great suffering and peril. The circumstances of the attempted eulogy are mentioned here to
show the relations which subsisted between Mr. Lincoln and
some of the benefactors we have enumerated.

But all this time Mr. Lincoln had a living to make, a running board-bill to pay, and nothing to pay it with. He was, it
is true, in the hands of excellent friends, so far as the greater
part of his indebtedness was concerned; but he was industrious by nature, and wanted to be working, and paying as he
went. He would not have forfeited the good opinion of those
confiding neighbors for a lifetime of ease and luxury. It was
therefore a most happy thing for him, and he felt it to be so,
when he attracted the attention of John Calhoun, the surveyor of Sangamon County.

Calhoun was the type of a perfect gentleman, — brave, courteous, able, and cultivated. He was a Democrat then, and a Democrat when he died. All the world knows how he was president of the Lecompton Convention; how he administered the trust in accordance with his well-known convictions; and how, after a life of devotion to Douglas, he was adroitly betrayed by that facile politician, and left to die in the midst of obloquy and disaster. At the time we speak of, he was one of the most popular men in the State of Illinois, and was one of the foremost chieftains of the political party which invariably carried the county and the district in which Mr. Lincoln lived. He knew Lincoln, and admired him. He was well assured that Lincoln knew nothing of surveying; but he was equally certain that he could soon acquire it. The speculative fever was at its height; he was overrun with business: the country was alive with strangers seeking land; and every citizen was buying and selling with a view to a great fortune in the " flush times " coming. He wanted a deputy with common sense and common honesty: he chose Lincoln, because nobody else possessed these qualities in a more eminent degree. He hunted him up; gave him a book; told him to study it, and said, that, as soon as he was ready, he should have as much work as he could do.

Lincoln took the book, and " retired to the country; " that is, he went out to Minter Graham's for about six weeks, in which time, by the aid of that good master, he became an expert surveyor, and was duly appointed Calhoun's deputy. Of course he made some money, merely his pay for work; but it is a remarkable fact, that, with his vast knowledge of the lands in Sangamon and adjacent counties, he never made a single speculation on his own account. It was not long until he acquired a considerable private business. The accuracy of his surveys were seldom, if ever, questioned. Disputes regarding "corners" and "lines" were frequently submitted to his arbitration; and the decision was invariably accepted as final. It often happened that his business kept him away from New Salem, and his other studies, for weeks at a time; but all this while he was gathering friends against the day of election.

In after years — from 1844 onward — it was his good or bad fortune frequently to meet Calhoun on the stump; but he never forgot his benefaction to him, and always regarded him as the ablest and best man with whom he ever had crossed steel. To the day of Calhoun's death they were warmly attached to each other. In the times when it was most fashionable and profitable to denounce Calhoun and the Lecompton Constitution, when even Douglas turned to revile his old friend and coadjutor, Mr. Lincoln was never known to breathe a word of censure on his personal character.

On the 7th of May, 1833, Mr. Lincoln was appointed postmaster at New Salem. His political opinions were not extreme; and the Jackson administration could find no man who was at the same time more orthodox and equally competent to perform the duties of the office. He was not able to rent a room, for the business is said to have been carried on in his hat; but, from the evidence before us, we imagine that he kept the office in Mr. Hill's store, Mr. Hill's partner, McNamar, having been absent since 1832. He held the place until late in 1836, when New Salem partially disappeared, and the office was removed to Petersburg. For a little while before his own appointment, he is said to have acted as "deputy-postmaster" under Mr. Hill.

The mail arrived duly once a week; and the labors of distributing and delivering it were by no means great. But Mr. Lincoln was determined that the dignity of the place should not suffer while he was the incumbent. He therefore made up for the lack of real business by deciphering the letters of the uneducated portion of the community, and by reading the newspapers aloud to the assembled inhabitants in front of Hill's store.

But his easy good-nature was sometimes imposed upon by inconsiderate acquaintances; and Mr. Hill relates one of the devices by which he sought to stop the abuse. "One Elmore Johnson, an ignorant but ostentatious, proud man, used

to go to Lincoln's post-office every day, — sometimes three or
four times a day, if in town, — and inquire, 'Any thing for
me?' This bored Lincoln, yet it amused him. Lincoln
fixed a plan, — wrote a letter to Johnson as coming from a
negress in Kentucky, saying many good things about opossum, dances, corn-shuckings, &c.; 'John's! come and see
me; and old master won't kick you out of the kitchen any
more!' Elmore took it out; opened it; couldn't read a
word; pretended to read it; went away; got some friends
to read it: they read it correctly; he thought the reader was
fooling him, and went to others with the same result. At
last he said he would get *Lincoln* to read it, and presented it
to Lincoln. It was almost too much for Lincoln, but he read
it. The man never asked afterwards, 'Any thing here for
me?'"

It was in the latter part of 1834 that Mr. Lincoln's personal
property was sold under the hammer, and by due process of
law, to meet the judgment obtained by Van Bergen on the
note assigned to him by Radford. Every thing he had was
taken; but it was the surveyor's instruments which it hurt
him most to part with, for by their use he was making a
tolerable living, and building up a respectable business. This
time, however, rescue came from an unexpected quarter.

When Mr. Lincoln first came to New Salem, he employed
a woman to make him a pair of pantaloons, which, probably
from the scarcity of material, were cut entirely too short, as
his garments usually were. Soon afterwards the woman's
brother came to town, and she pointed Abe out to him as
he walked along the street. The brother's name was James
Short. "Without the necessity of a formal introduction,"
says Short, "we fell in together, and struck up a conversation,
the purport of which I have now forgotten. He made a
favorable impression upon me by his conversation on first
acquaintance through his intelligence and sprightliness, which
impression was deepened from time to time, as I became better
acquainted with him." This was a lucky "impression" for
Abe. Short was a fast friend, and in the day of trouble a

sure and able one.   At the time the judgment was obtained, Short lived on the Sand Ridge, four miles from New Salem; and Lincoln was in the habit of walking out there almost daily.   Short was then unconscious of the main reason of Mr. Lincoln's remarkable devotion to him: there was a lady in the house whom Lincoln secretly but earnestly loved, and of whom there is much to be said at another place.   If the host had known every thing, however, poor Abe would have been equally welcome; for he made himself a strangely agreeable guest here, as he did everywhere else.   In busy times he pulled off his roundabout, and helped Short in the field with more energy than any hired man would have displayed. "He was," said Short, "the best hand at husking corn on the stalk I ever saw.   I used to consider myself very good; but he would gather two loads to my one."

These visits increased Short's disposition to serve him; and it touched him sorely when he heard Lincoln moaning about the catastrophe that hung over him in the form of Van Bergen's judgment.   "An execution was issued," says he, "and levied on Lincoln's horse, saddle, bridle, compass, chain, and other surveyor's instruments.   He was then very much discouraged, and said he would let the whole thing go by the board.   He was at my house very much, — half the time.   I did all I could to put him in better spirits.   I went on the delivery-bond with him; and when the sale came off, which Mr. Lincoln did not attend, I bid in the above property at a hundred and twenty dollars, and immediately gave it up again to him.   Mr. Lincoln afterwards repaid me when he had moved to Springfield.   Greene also turned in on this judgment his horse, saddle, and bridle at a hundred and twenty-five dollars; and Lincoln afterwards repaid him."

But, after all, Mr. Lincoln had no friend more intimate than Jack Armstrong, and none that valued him more highly. Until he finally left New Salem for Springfield, he "rusticated" occasionally at Jack's hospitable cabin, situated "four miles in the country," as the polished metropolitans of New Salem would say. Jack's wife, Hannah, before alluded to, liked Abe, and enjoyed his visits not less than Jack did. "Abe would come out to our house," she says, "drink milk, eat mush, corn-bread, and butter, bring the children candy, and rock the cradle while I got him something to eat. . . . I foxed his pants; made his shirts . . . He has gone with us to father's; he would tell stories, joke people, girls and boys, at parties. He would nurse babies, — do any thing to accommodate anybody. . . . I had no books about my house; loaned him none. We didn't think about books and papers. We worked; had to live. Lincoln has staid at our house two or three weeks at a time."

If Jack had "to work to live," as his wife has it, he was likewise constrained to fight and wrestle and tumble about with his unhappy fellow-citizens, in order to enjoy the life he earned by labor. He frequently came "to town," where his sportive inclinations ran riot, except as they were checked and regulated by the amicable interposition of Abe, — the prince of his affections, and the only man who was competent to restrain him.

"The children at school had made a wide sliding walk," from the top of Salem Hill to the river-bank, down which they rode on sleds and boards, — a distance of two hundred and fifty or three hundred yards. Now, it was one of the suggestions of Jack's passion for innocent diversion to nail up in hogsheads such of the population as incurred his displeasure, and send them adrift along this frightful descent. Sol. Spears and one Scanlon were treated to an adventure of this kind; but the hogshead in which the two were caged "leaped over an embankment, and came near killing Scanlon." After that the sport was considered less amusing, and was very much discouraged by that portion of the community who feared, that, in the absence of more convenient victims, "the boys" might light on them. Under these circumstances, Jack, for once in his life, thought it best to abandon coercion, and negotiate for subjects. He selected an elderly person of bibulous proclivities, and tempted him with a great temptation. ' Old man Jordan *agreed* to be rolled down the hill for a gallon of whiskey ; " but Lincoln, fully impressed with the brutality of the pastime, and the danger to the old sot, " stopped it." Whether he did it by persuasion or force, we know not, but probably by a judicious employment of both.

" I remember once," says Mr. Ellis, " of seeing Mr. Lincoln out of temper, and laughing at the same time. It was at New Salem. The boys were having a jollification after an election. They had a large fire made of shavings and hemp-stalks ; and some of the boys made a bet with a fellow that I shall call ' Ike,' that he couldn't run his little bob-tail pony through the fire. Ike took them up, and trotted his pony back about one hundred yards, to give him a good start, as he said. The boys all formed a line on either side, to make way for Ike and his pony. Presently here he come, full tilt, with his hat off ; and, just as he reached the blazing fire, Ike raised in his saddle for the jump straight ahead ; but pony was not of the same opinion, so he flew the track, and pitched poor Ike into the devouring element. Mr. Lincoln saw it, and ran to his assistance, saying, ' You have carried this thing far enough.' I could see he was mad, though he could not help laughing himself. The poor fellow was considerably scorched about the head and face. Jack Armstrong took him to the doctor, who shaved his head to fix him up, and put salve on the burn. I think Mr. Lincoln was a little mad at Armstrong, and Jack himself was very sorry for it. Jack gave Ike next morning a dram, his breakfast, and a seal-skin cap, and sent him home."

One cold winter day, Lincoln saw a poor fellow named "Ab Trent" hard at work chopping up " a house," which Mr. Hill had employed him to convert into firewood. Ab was barefooted, and shivered pitifully while he worked. Lincoln watched him a few moments, and asked him what he was to get for the job. Ab answered, ' One dollar ; ' and, pointing to his naked and suffering feet, said that he wished to buy a pair of shoes. Lincoln seized the axe, and, ordering the boy to comfort himself at the nearest fire, chopped up ' the house' so fast that Ab and the owner were both amazed when they saw it done." According to Mr. Rutledge, " Ab remembered this act with the liveliest gratitude. Once he, being a cast-iron Democrat, determined to vote against his party and for Mr. Lincoln ; but the friends, as he afterwards said with tears in his eyes, made him drunk, and he had voted against Abe. Thus he did not even have an opportunity to return the noble conduct of Mr. Lincoln by this small measure of thanks."

We have given some instances of Mr. Lincoln's unfailing disposition to succor the weak and the unfortunate. He never seems to have hesitated on account of actual or fancied danger to himself, but boldly espoused the side of the oppressed against the oppressor, whoever and whatever the latter might be. In a fisticuff or a rough-and-tumble fight, he was one of the most formidable men of the region in which he lived. It took a big bully, and a persevering one, to force him into a collision ; but, being in, his enemy found good reason to beware of him. He was cool, calculating, but swift in action, and terribly strong. Nevertheless, he never promoted a quarrel, and would be at infinite trouble any time to compose one. An unnecessary broil gave him pain ; and whenever there was the slightest hope of successful mediation, whether by soft speech or by the strong hand, he was instant and fearless for peace. His good-nature, his humor, his fertility in expedients, and his alliance, offensive and defensive, with Jack Armstrong, made him almost irresistible in his benevolent efforts to keep the ordinary ruffian of New Salem within decent bounds. If he was talking to Squire Godbey or Row Herndon (each of them give incidents of the kind), and he heard the sounds or saw the signs which betoken a row in the street, he would jump up, saying, " Let's go and stop it." He would push through the " ring " which was generally formed around the combatants, and, after separating the latter, would demand a truce and "a talk ; " and so soon as he got them to talking, the victory was his. If it happened to

be rough Jack himself who was at the bottom of the disturbance, he usually became very much ashamed of his conduct,
and offered to " treat," or do any thing else that would atone
for his brutality.

Lincoln has often been seen in the old mill on the river-
bank to lift a box of stones weighing from a thousand to
twelve hundred pounds. Of course it was not done by a
straight lift of the hands : he " was harnessed to the box with
ropes and straps." It was even said he could easily raise a
barrel of whiskey to his mouth when standing upright, and
take a drink out of the bung-hole ; but of course one cannot
believe it. Frequent exhibitions of such strength doubtless
had much to do with his unbounded influence over the
rougher class of men.

He possessed the judicial quality of mind in a degree so
eminent, and it was so universally recognized, that he never
could attend a horse-race without being importuned to act as
a judge, or witness a bet without assuming the responsibility
of a stakeholder. " In the spring or summer of 1832," says
Henry McHenry, " I had a horse-race with George Warburton. I got Lincoln, who was at the race, to be a judge of
the race, much against his will and after hard persuasion.
Lincoln decided correctly ; and the other judge said, ' Lincoln
is the fairest man I ever had to deal with : if Lincoln is in
this county when I die, I want him to be my administrator,
for he is the only man I ever met with that was wholly and
unselfishly honest.' " His ineffable purity in determining the
result of a scrub-race had actually set his colleague to thinking
of his latter end.

But Lincoln endured another annoyance much worse than
this. He was so generally esteemed, and so highly admired,
that, when any of his neighbors had a fight in prospect, one
of the parties was sure to insist upon his acting as his second.
Lincoln was opposed to fights, but there were some fights that
had to be fought ; and these were " set," a day fixed, and the
neighborhood notified. In these cases there was no room for
the offices of a mediator ; and when the affair was pre-ordained,

" and must come off," Mr. Lincoln had no excuse for denying the request of a friend.

" Two neighbors, Harry Clark and Ben Wilcox," says Mr. Rutledge, " had had a lawsuit. The defeated declared, that, although he was beaten in the suit, he could whip his opponent. This was a formal challenge, and was at once carried to the ears of the victor (Wilcox), and as promptly accepted. The time, place, and seconds were chosen with due regularity; Mr. Lincoln being Clark's, and John Brewer, Wilcox's second. The parties met, stripped themselves all but their breeches, went in, and Mr. Lincoln's principal was beautifully whipped. These combats were conducted with as much ceremony and punctiliousness as ever graced the duelling-ground. After the conflict, the seconds conducted their respective principals to the river, washed off the blood, and assisted them to dress. During this performance, the second of the party opposed to Mr. Lincoln remarked, ' Well, Abe, my man has whipped yours, and I can whip you.' Now, this challenge came from a man who was very small in size. Mr. Lincoln agreed to fight, provided he would chalk out his size on Mr. Lincoln's person, and every blow struck outside of that mark should be counted foul. After this sally, there was the best possible humor, and all parties were as orderly as if they had been engaged in the most harmless amusement."

In 1834 Lincoln was again a candidate for the Legislature, and this time was elected by a larger majority than any other man on the ticket. By this time the party with which he acted in the future was " discriminated as Whig; " and he did not hesitate to call himself a Whig, although he sought and received the votes of a great many Democrats. Just before the time had arrived for candidates to announce themselves, he went to John T. Stuart, and told him " the Democrats wanted to run him." He made the same statement to Ninian W. Edwards. Edwards and Stuart were both his personal and political friends, and they both advised him to let the Democrats have their way. Major Stuart's advice was certainly disinterested; for, in pursuance of it, two of the Whig candidates, Lincoln and Dawson, made a bargain with the Democrats which very nearly proved fatal to Stuart himself. He was at that time the favorite candidate of the Whigs for the Legislature; but the conduct of Lincoln and Dawson so demoralized the party, that his vote was seriously diminished. Up to this time Sangamon had been stanchly Democratic; but even in this election of 1834 we perceive slight evidences of that party's decay, and so early as 1836 the county became thoroughly Whig.

We shall give no details of this campaign, since we should only be repeating what is written of the campaign of 1832. But we cannot withhold one extract from the reminiscences of Mr. Row Herndon: —

"He (Lincoln) came to my house, near Island Grove, during harvest. There were some thirty men in the field. He got his dinner, and went out in the field where the men were at work. I gave him an introduction, and the boys said that they could not vote for a man unless he could make a hand. 'Well, boys,' said he, 'if that is all, I am sure of your votes.' He took hold of the cradle, and led the way all the round with perfect ease. The boys were satisfied, and I don't think he lost a vote in the crowd.

"The next day was speaking at Berlin. He went from my house with Dr. Barnett, the man that had asked me who this man Lincoln was. I told him that he was a candidate for the Legislature. He laughed and said, 'Can't the party raise no better material than that?' I said, 'Go to-morrow, and hear all before you pronounce judgment.' When he came back, I said, 'Doctor, what say you now?' 'Why, sir,' said he, ' he is a perfect take-in: he knows more than all of them put together.' "

Lincoln got 1,376 votes, Dawson 1,370, Carpenter 1,170, Stuart 1,164. Lincoln was at last duly elected a Representative by a very flattering majority, and began to look about for the pecuniary means necessary to maintain his new dignity. In this extremity he had recourse to an old friend named Coleman Smoot.

One day in 1832, while he was clerking for Offutt, a stranger came into the store, and soon disclosed the fact that his name was Smoot. Abe was behind the counter at the moment; but, hearing the name, he sprang over and introduced himself. Abe had often heard of Smoot, and Smoot had often heard of Abe. They had been as anxious to meet as ever two celebrities were; but hitherto they had never been able to manage it. "Smoot," said Lincoln, after a steady survey of his person, "I am very much disappointed in you: I expected to see an old Probst of a fellow." (Probst, it appears, was the most hideous specimen of humanity in all that country.) "Yes," replied Smoot; "and I am equally disappointed, for I expected to see a good-looking man when I saw you." A few neat compliments like the foregoing laid the foundation of a lasting intimacy between the two men, and in his present distress Lincoln knew no one who would be more likely than Smoot to respond favorably to an application for money.

"After he was elected to the Legislature," says Mr. Smoot, "he came to my house one day in company with Hugh Armstrong. Says he, 'Smoot, did you vote for me?' I told him I did. 'Well,' says he, 'you must loan me money to buy suitable clothing, for I want to make a decent appearance in the Legislature.' I then loaned him two hundred dollars, which he returned to me according to promise."

The interval between the election and his departure for the seat of government was employed by Mr. Lincoln partly in reading, partly in writing.

The community in which he lived was pre-eminently a community of free-thinkers in matters of religion; and it was then no secret, nor has it been a secret since, that Mr. Lincoln agreed with the majority of his associates in denying to the Bible the authority of divine revelation. It was his honest belief, — a belief which it was no reproach to hold at New Salem, Anno Domini 1834, and one which he never thought of concealing. It was no distinction, either good or bad, no honor, and no shame. But he had made himself thoroughly familiar with the writings of Paine and Volney, — the "Ruins"

by one, and " The Age of Reason" by the other.   His mind
was full of the subject, and he felt an itching to write.   He
did write, and the result was a "little book."   It was probably merely an extended essay; but it is ambitiously spoken of
as " a book " by himself and by the persons who were made
acquainted with its contents.   In this work he intended to
demonstrate, —

" First, that the Bible was not God's revelation ; and,

" Secondly, that Jesus was not the Son of God."

These were his leading propositions, and surely they were
comprehensive enough ; but the reader will be better able to
guess at the arguments by which they were sustained, when he
has examined some of the evidence recorded in Chapter XIX.

No leaf of this little volume has survived.   Mr. Lincoln
carried it in manuscript to the store of Mr. Samuel Hill,
where it was read and discussed.   Hill was himself an unbeliever, but his son considered this book "infamous."   It is
more than probable that Hill, being a warm personal friend of
Lincoln, feared that the publication of the essay would some
day interfere with the political advancement of his favorite.
At all events, he snatched it out of his hand, and thrust it into
the fire, from which not a shred escaped.   The sequel will
show that even Mr. Hill's provident forethought was not altogether equal to the prevention of the injury he dreaded.

CHAPTER VIII.

THE reader is already familiar with the name of James Rutledge, the founder of New Salem, and the owner in part of the famous mill on the Sangamon. He was born in South Carolina, and was of the illustrious Rutledge family of that State. From South Carolina he emigrated to Kentucky, and thence to Illinois. In 1828 he settled at New Salem, built the mill and laid out the village in conjunction with Mr. Cameron, a retired minister of the Cumberland Presbyterians. Mr. Rutledge's character seems to have been pure and high; for wherever his name occurs in the voluminous records before us, — in the long talks and the numerous epistles of his neighbors, — it is almost invariably coupled with some expression of genuine esteem and respect.

At one time, and along with his other business, — which appears to have been quite extensive and various, — Mr. Rutledge kept the tavern, the small house with four rooms on the main street of New Salem, just opposite Lincoln's grocery. There Mr. Lincoln came to board late in 1832, or early in 1833. The family consisted of the father, mother, and nine children, — three of them born in Kentucky and six in Illinois; three grown up, and the rest quite young. Ann, the principal subject of this chapter, was the third child. She was born on the 7th of January, 1813, and was about nineteen years of age when Mr. Lincoln came to live in the house.

When Ann was a little maiden just turned of seventeen, and still attending the school of that redoubtable pedagogue Minter Graham, there came to New Salem a young gentleman

159

of singular enterprise, tact, and capacity for business. He is identical with the man whom we have already quoted as "the pioneer of New Salem as a business point," and who built the first storehouse there at the extravagant cost of fifteen dollars. He took boarding with Mr. Rutledge's friend and partner, James Cameron, and gave out his name as John McNeil. He came to New Salem with no other capital than good sense and an active and plucky spirit; but somehow fortune smiled indiscriminately on all his endeavors, and very soon — as early as the latter part of 1832 — he found himself a well-to-do and prosperous man, owning a snug farm seven miles north of New Salem, and a half-interest in the largest store of the place. This latter property his partner, Samuel Hill, bought from him at a good round sum; for McNeil now announced his intention of being absent for a brief period, and his purpose was such that he might need all his available capital.

In the mean time the partners, Hill and McNeil, had both fallen in love with Ann Rutledge, and both courted her with devoted assiduity. But the contest had long since been decided in favor of McNeil, and Ann loved him with all her susceptible and sensitive heart. When the time drew near for McNeil to depart, he confided to Ann a strange story, — and, in the eyes of a person less fond, a very startling story. His name was not John McNeil at all, but John McNamar. His family was a highly respectable one in the State of New York; but a few years before his father had failed in business, and there was great distress at home. He (John) then conceived the romantic plan of running away, and, at some undefined place in the far West, making a sudden fortune with which to retrieve the family disaster. He fled accordingly, changed his name to avoid the pursuit of his father, found his way to New Salem, and — she knew the rest. He was now able to perform that great act of filial piety which he set out to accomplish, would return at once to the relief of his parents, and, in all human probability, bring them back with him to his new home in Illinois. At all events, she might look for his return as speedily as the journey could be made with ordinary diligence; and thenceforward there should be no more partings between him and his fair Ann. She believed this tale, because she loved the man that told it; and she would have believed it all the same if it had been ten times as incredible. A wise man would have rejected it with scorn, but the girl's instinct was a better guide; and McNamar proved to be all that he said he was, although poor Ann never saw the proof which others got of it.

McNamar rode away "on old Charley," an antiquated steed that had seen hard usage in the Black Hawk War. Charley was slow, stumbled dreadfully, and caused his rider much annoyance and some hard swearing. On this provoking animal McNamar jogged through the long journey from New Salem to New York, and arrived there after many delays, only to find that his broken and dispirited father was fast sinking into the grave. After all his efforts, he was too late: the father could never enjoy the prosperity which the long-absent and long-silent son had brought him. McNamar wrote to Ann that there was sickness in the family, and he could not return at the time appointed. Then there were other and still other postponements; "circumstances over which he had no control" prevented his departure from time to time, until years had rolled away, and Ann's heart had grown sick with hope deferred. She never quite gave him up, but continued to expect him until death terminated her melancholy watch. His inexplicable delay, however, the infrequency of his letters, and their unsatisfactory character, — these and something else had broken her attachment, and toward the last she waited for him only to ask a release from her engagement, and to say that she preferred another and a more urgent suitor. But without his knowledge and formal renunciation of his claim upon her, she did not like to marry; and, in obedience to this refinement of honor, she postponed her union with the more pressing lover until Aug. 25, 1835, when, as many persons believe, she died of a broken heart.

11

Lincoln's friend Short was in some way related to the Rutledges, and for a while Lincoln visited Ann two or three times a week at his house. According to him, " Miss Rutledge was a good-looking, smart, lively girl, a good housekeeper, with a moderate education, and without any of the so-called accomplishments." L. M. Greene, who knew her well, talks about her as " a beautiful and very amiable young woman ; " and " Nult " Greene is even more enthusiastic. " This young lady," in the language of the latter gentleman, " was a woman of exquisite beauty ; but her intellect was quick, sharp, deep, and philosophic, as well as brilliant. She had as gentle and kind a heart as an angel, full of love, kindliness, and sympathy. She was beloved by everybody, and everybody respected and loved her, so sweet and angelic was she. Her character was more than good : it was positively noted throughout the county. She was a woman worthy of Lincoln's love." McNamar, her unfortunate lover, says, " Miss Ann was a gentle, amiable maiden, without any of the airs of your city belles, but winsome and comely withal ; a blonde in complexion, with golden hair, cherry-red lips, and a bonny blue eye." Even the women of the neighborhood united with the men to praise the name of this beautiful but unhappy girl. Mrs. Hardin Bale " knew her well. She had auburn hair, blue eyes, fair complexion ; was a slim, pretty, kind, tender, good-hearted woman ; in height about five feet three inches, and weighed about a hundred and twenty pounds. She was beloved by all who knew her. McNamar, Hill, and Lincoln all courted her near the same time. She died as it were of grief. Miss Rutledge was beautiful." Such was Ann Rutledge, the girl in whose grave Mr. Lincoln said, " My heart lies buried."

When Mr. Lincoln first saw Ann, she was probably the most refined woman with whom he had then ever spoken, — a modest, delicate creature, fascinating by reason of the mere contrast with the rude people by whom they were both surrounded. She had a secret, too, and a sorrow, — the unexplained and painful absence of McNamar, — which no doubt made her all the more interesting to him whose spirit was often even more melancholy than her own. It would be hard to trace the growth of such an attachment at a time and place so distant; but that it actually grew, and became an intense and mutual passion, the evidence before us is painfully abundant.

Mr. Lincoln was always welcome at the little tavern, at Short's on the Sand Ridge, or at the farm, half a mile from Short's, where the Rutledges finally abode. Ann's father was his devoted friend, and the mother he called affectionately "Aunt Polly." It is probable that the family looked upon McNamar's delay with more suspicion than Ann did herself. At all events, all her adult relatives encouraged the suit which Lincoln early began to press; and as time, absence, and apparent neglect, gradually told against McNamar, she listened to him with augmenting interest, until, in 1835, we find them formally and solemnly betrothed. Ann now waited only for the return of McNamar to marry Lincoln. David Rutledge urged her to marry immediately, without regard to any thing but her own happiness; but she said she could not consent to it until McNamar came back and released her from her pledge. At length, however, as McNamar's re-appearance became more and more hopeless, she took a different view of it, and then thought she would become Abe's wife as soon as he found the means of a decent livelihood. "Ann told me once," says James M. in a letter to R. B. Rutledge, in coming from camp-meeting on Rock Creek, "that engagements made too far ahead sometimes failed; that one *had* failed (meaning her engagement with McNamar), and gave me to understand, that, as soon as certain studies were completed, she and Lincoln would be married."

In the summer of 1835 Ann showed unmistakable symptoms of failing health, attributable, as most of the neighborhood believed, to the distressing attitude she felt bound to maintain between her two lovers. On the 25th of August, in that year, she died of what the doctors chose to call "brain-fever." In a letter to Mr. Herndon, her brother says, "You suggest that the probable cause of Ann's sickness was her conflicts, emotions, &c. As to this I cannot say. I, however, have my own private convictions. The character of her sickness was brain-fever." A few days before her death Lincoln was summoned to her bedside. What happened in that solemn conference was known only to him and the dying girl. But when he left her, and stopped at the house of John Jones, on his way home, Jones saw signs of the most terrible distress in his face and his conduct. When Ann actually died, and was buried, his grief became frantic: he lost all self-control, even the consciousness of identity, and every friend he had in New Salem pronounced him insane, mad, crazy. " He was watched with especial vigilance," as William Green tells us, " during storms, fogs, damp, gloomy weather, for fear of an accident." At such times he raved piteously, declaring, among other wild expressions of his woe, ' I can never be reconciled to have the snow, rains, and storms to beat upon her grave ! ' "

About three-quarters of a mile below New Salem, at the foot of the main bluff, and in a hollow between two lateral bluffs, stood the house of Bowlin Greene, built of logs and weather-boarded. Thither the friends of Lincoln, who apprehended a total abdication of reason, determined to transport him, partly for the benefit of a mere change of scene, and partly to keep him within constant reach of his near and noble friend, Bowlin Greene. During this period of his darkened and wavering intellect, when " accidents " were momentarily expected, it was discovered that Bowlin Greene possessed a power to persuade and guide him proportioned to the affection that had subsisted between them in former and better times. Bowlin Greene came for him, but Lincoln was cunning and obstinate : it required the most artful practices of a general conspiracy of all his friends to " disarm his suspicions," and induce him to go and stay with his most anxious and devoted friend. But at last they succeeded ; and Lincoln remained down under the bluff for two or three weeks, the object of undisguised solicitude and of the strictest surveillance. At the end of that time his mind seemed to be restored, and it was thought safe to let him go back to his old haunts, —

to the study of law, to the writing of legal papers for his
neighbors, to pettifogging before the justice of the peace, and
perhaps to a little surveying.   But Mr. Lincoln was never
precisely the same man again.   At the time of his release he
was thin, haggard, and careworn, — like one risen from the
verge of the grave.   He had always been subject to fits of
great mental depression, but after this they were more frequent
and alarming.   It was then that he began to repeat, with a
feeling which seemed to inspire every listener with awe, and
to carry him to the fresh grave of Ann at every one of his
solemn periods, the lines entitled, " Immortality ; or, Oh ! why
should the spirit of mortal be proud ? "   None heard him but
knew that he selected these curiously empty, yet wonderfully
sad, impressive lines, to celebrate a grief which lay with continual heaviness on his heart, but to which he could not with
becoming delicacy directly allude.   He muttered them as he
rambled through the woods, or walked by the roaring Sangamon.   He was heard to murmur them to himself as he
slipped into the village at nightfall, after a long walk of
six miles, and an evening visit to the Concord graveyard ; and
he would suddenly break out with them in little social assem-
blies after noticeable periods of silent gloom.   They came
unbidden to his lips, while the air of affliction in face and gesture, the moving tones and touching modulations of his voice,
made it evident that every syllable of the recitation was
meant to commemorate the mournful fate of Ann.   The poem
is now his : the name of the obscure author is forgotten, and
his work is imperishably associated with the memory of a
great man, and interwoven with the history of his greatest
sorrow.   Mr. Lincoln's adoption of it has saved it from mer-
ited oblivion, and translated it from the " poet's corner " of
the country newspaper to a place in the story of his own life,
— a story that will continue to be written, or written about,
as long as our language exists.

Many years afterwards, when Mr. Lincoln, the best lawyer
of his section, with one exception, travelled the circuit with the
court and a crowd of his jolly brethren, he always rose early, be

fore any one else was stirring, and, raking together a few glowing coals on the hearth, he would sit looking into them, musing
and talking with himself, for hours together. One morning,
in the year of his nomination, his companions found him in
this attitude, when " Mr. Lincoln repeated aloud, and at
length, the poem ' Immortality,' " indicating his preference for
the two last stanzas, but insisting that the entire composition
" sounded to him as much like true poetry as any thing that
he had ever heard."

In Carpenter's " Anecdotes and Reminiscences of President
Lincoln," occurs the following passage : —

" The evening of March 22, 1864, was a most interesting
one to me. I was with the President alone in his office for
several hours. Busy with pen and papers when I went in,
he presently threw them aside, and commenced talking to me
of Shakspeare, of whom he was very fond. Little ' Tad,'
his son, coming in, he sent him to the library for a copy of
the plays, and then read to me several of his favorite passages.
Relapsing into a sadder strain, he laid the book aside, and,
leaning back in his chair, said, —

" ' There is a poem which has been a great favorite with me
for years, which was first shown to me when a young man by
a friend, and which I afterwards saw and cut from a newspaper, and learned by heart. I would,' he continued, ' give a
great deal to know who wrote it; but I have never been able
to ascertain.'

" Then, half closing his eyes, he repeated the verses to me : —

> " ' Oh! why should the spirit of mortal be proud?
> Like a swift-fleeting meteor, a fast-flying cloud,
> A flash of the lightning, a break of the wave,
> He passeth from life to his rest in the grave.
>
> The leaves of the oak and the willow shall fade,
> Be scattered around, and together be laid;
> And the young and the old, and the low and the high,
> Shall moulder to dust, and together shall lie.

The infant a mother attended and loved;
The mother that infant's affection who proved;
The husband that mother and infant who blest, —
Each, all, are away to their dwellings of rest.

[The maid on whose cheek, on whose brow, in whose eye,
Shone beauty and pleasure, her triumphs are by;
And the memory of those who loved her and praised,
Are alike from the minds of the living erased.]

The hand of the king that the sceptre hath borne,
The brow of the priest that the mitre hath worn,
The eye of the sage, and the heart of the brave,
Are hidden and lost in the depths of the grave.

The peasant whose lot was to sow and to reap,
The herdsman who climbed with his goats up the steep,
The beggar who wandered in search of his bread,
Have faded away like the grass that we tread.

[The saint who enjoyed the communion of Heaven,
The sinner who dared to remain unforgiven,
The wise and the foolish, the guilty and just,
Have quietly mingled their bones in the dust.]

So the multitude goes, like the flower or the weed,
That withers away to let others succeed;
So the multitude comes, even those we behold,
To repeat every tale that has often been told.

For we are the same our fathers have been;
We see the same sights our fathers have seen;
We drink the same stream, we view the same sun,
And run the same course our fathers have run.

The thoughts we are thinking our fathers would think;
From the death we are shrinking our fathers would shrink;
To the life we are clinging they also would cling;
But it speeds from us all like a bird on the wing.

They loved, but the story we cannot unfold;
They scorned, but the heart of the haughty is cold;
They grieved, but no wail from their slumber will come;
They joyed, but the tongue of their gladness is dumb.

> They died, ay, they died: we things that are now,
> That walk on the turf that lies over their brow,
> And make in their dwellings a transient abode,
> Meet the things that they met on their pilgrimage road.
>
> Yea, hope and despondency, pleasure and pain,
> Are mingled together in sunshine and rain;
> And the smile and the tear, the song and the dirge,
> Still follow each other like surge upon surge.
>
> 'Tis the wink of an eye, 'tis the draught of a breath,
> From the blossom of health to the paleness of death,
> From the gilded saloon to the bier and the shroud, —
> Oh! why should the spirit of mortal be proud?'"

It was only a year or two after the death of Ann Rutledge that Mr. Lincoln told Robert L. Wilson, a distinguished colleague in the Legislature, parts of whose letter will be printed in another place, that, although "he appeared to enjoy life rapturously," it was a mistake; that, "when alone, he was so overcome by mental depression, that he never dared to carry a pocket-knife." And during all Mr. Wilson's extended acquaintance with him he never did own a knife, notwithstanding he was inordinately fond of whittling.

Mr. Herndon says, "He never addressed another woman, in my opinion, 'Yours affectionately,' and generally and characteristically abstained from the use of the word '*love.*' That word cannot be found more than a half-dozen times, if that often, in all his letters and speeches since that time. I have seen some of his letters to other ladies, but he never says 'love.' He never ended his letters with 'Yours affectionately,' but signed his name, 'Your friend, A. Lincoln.'"

After Mr. Lincoln's election to the Presidency, he one day met an old friend, Isaac Cogdale, who had known him intimately in the better days of the Rutledges at New Salem. "Ike," said he, "call at my office at the State House about an hour by sundown. The company will then all be gone."

Cogdale went according to request; "and sure enough," as he expressed it, "the company dropped off one by one, including Lincoln's clerk."

"'I want to inquire about old times and old acquaintances,' began Mr. Lincoln. 'When we lived in Salem, there were the Greenes, Potters, Armstrongs, and Rutledges. These folks have got scattered all over the world, — some are dead. Where are the Rutledges, Greenes, &c. ?'

"After we had spoken over old times," continues Cogdale, — "persons, circumstances, — in which he showed a wonderful memory, I then dared to ask him this question : —

"'May I now, in turn, ask you one question, Lincoln?'

"'Assuredly. I will answer your question, if a fair one, with all my heart.'

"'Well, Abe, is it true that you fell in love and courted Ann Rutledge?'

"'It is true, — true: indeed I did. I have loved the name of Rutledge to this day. I have kept my mind on their movements ever since, and love them dearly.'

"'Abe, is it true,'" still urged Cogdale, "that you ran a little wild about the matter?'

"'I did really. I ran off the track. It was my first. I loved the woman dearly. She was a handsome girl; would have made a good, loving wife; was natural and quite intellectual, though not highly educated. I did honestly and truly love the girl, and think often, often, of her now.'"

A few weeks after the burial of Ann, McNamar returned to New Salem. He saw Lincoln at the post-office, and was struck with the deplorable change in his appearance. A short time afterwards Lincoln wrote him a deed, which he still has, and prizes highly, in memory of his great friend and rival. His father was at last dead; but he brought back with him his mother and her family. In December of the same year his mother died, and was buried in the same graveyard with Ann. During his absence, Col. Rutledge had occupied his farm, and there Ann died; but "the Rutledge farm" proper adjoined this one to the south. "Some of Mr. Lincoln's corners, as a surveyor, are still visible on lines traced by him on both farms."

On Sunday, the fourteenth day of October, 1866, William

H. Herndon knocked at the door of John McNamar, at his residence, but a few feet distant from the spot where Ann Rutledge breathed her last. After some preliminaries not necessary to be related, Mr. Herndon says, " I asked him the question : —

" ' Did you know Miss Rutledge ? If so, where did she die ? '

" He sat by his open window, looking westerly ; and, pulling me closer to himself, looked through the window and said, ' There, by that,' — choking up with emotion, pointing his long forefinger, nervous and trembling, to the spot, — ' there, by that currant-bush, she died. The old house in which she and her father died is gone.'

.   .   .   .

" After further conversation, leaving the sadness to momentarily pass away, I asked this additional question : —

" ' Where was she buried ? '

" ' In Concord burying-ground, one mile south-east of this place.' "

Mr. Herndon sought the grave. " S. C. Berry," says he, " James Short (the gentleman who purchased in Mr. Lincoln's compass and chain in 1834, under an execution against Lincoln, or Lincoln & Berry, and gratuitously gave them back to Mr. Lincoln), James Miles, and myself were together.

" I asked Mr. Berry if he knew where Miss Rutledge was buried, — the place and exact surroundings. He replied, ' I do. The grave of Miss Rutledge lies just north of her brother's, David Rutledge, a young lawyer of great promise, who died in 1842, in his twenty-seventh year.'

" The cemetery contains but an acre of ground, in a beautiful and secluded situation. A thin skirt of timber lies on the east, commencing at the fence of the cemetery. The ribbon of timber, some fifty yards wide, hides the sun's early rise. At nine o'clock the sun pours all his rays into the cemetery. An extensive prairie lies west, the forest north, a field on the east, and timber and prairie on the south. In this lonely ground lie the Berrys, the Rutledges, the Clarys, the Armstrongs, and the Joneses, old and respected citizens, — pioneers of an early day. I write, or rather did write, the original draught of this description in the immediate presence of the ashes of Miss Ann Rutledge, the beautiful and tender dead. The village of the dead is a sad, solemn place. Its very presence imposes truth on the mind of the living writer. Ann Rutledge lies buried north of her brother, and rests sweetly on his left arm, angels to guard her. The cemetery is fast filling with the hazel and the dead."

A lecture delivered by William H. Herndon at Springfield, in 1866, contained the main outline, without the minuter details, of the story here related. It was spoken, printed, and circulated without contradiction from any quarter. It was sent to the Rutledges, McNeeleys, Greenes, Short, and many other of the old residents of New Salem and Petersburg, with particular requests that they should correct any error they might find in it. It was pronounced by them all truthful and accurate; but their replies, together with a mass of additional evidence, have been carefully collated with the lecture, and the result is the present chapter. The story of Ann Rutledge, Lincoln, and McNamar, as told here, is as well proved as the fact of Mr. Lincoln's election to the Presidency.

CHAPTER IX.

FOLLOWING strictly the chronological order hitherto observed in the course of this narrative, we should be compelled to break off the story of Mr. Lincoln's love-affairs at New Salem, and enter upon his public career in the Legislature and before the people. But, while by that means we should preserve continuity in one respect, we should lose it in another; and the reader would perhaps prefer to take in at one view all of Mr. Lincoln's courtships, save only that one which resulted in marriage.

Three-quarters of a mile, or nearly so, north of Bowlin Greene's, and on the summit of a hill, stood the house of Bennett Able, a small frame building eighteen by twenty feet. Able and his wife were warm friends of Mr. Lincoln; and many of his rambles through the surrounding country, reading and talking to himself, terminated at their door, where he always found the latch-string on the outside, and a hearty welcome within. In October, 1833, Mr. Lincoln met there Miss Mary Owens, a sister of Mrs. Able, and, as we shall presently learn from his own words, admired her, although not extravagantly. She remained but four weeks, and then went back to her home in Kentucky.

Miss Owens's mother being dead, her father married again; and Miss Owens, for good reasons of her own, thought she would rather live with her sister than with her stepmother. Accordingly, in the fall of 1836, she re-appeared at Able's, passing through New Salem on the day of the presidential election, where the men standing about the polls stared and wondered at her "beauty." Twenty eight or nine years of age, "she was," in the language of Mr. L. M. Greene, "tall and portly; weighed about one hundred and twenty pounds, and had large blue eyes, with the finest trimmings I ever saw. She was jovial, social, loved wit and humor, had a liberal English education, and was considered wealthy. Bill," continues our excellent friend, "I am getting old; have seen too much trouble to give a lifelike picture of this woman. I won't try it. None of the poets or romance-writers has ever given to us a picture of a heroine so beautiful as a good description of Miss Owens in 1836 would be."

Mrs. Hardin Bale, a cousin to Miss Owens, says "she was blue-eyed, dark-haired, handsome, — not pretty, — was rather large and tall, handsome, truly handsome, matronly looking, over ordinary size in height and weight. . . . Miss Owens *was* handsome, that is to say, noble-looking, matronly seeming."

Respecting her age and looks, Miss Owens herself makes the following note, Aug. 6, 1866: —

"Born in the year eight; fair skin, deep-blue eyes, with dark curling hair; height five feet five inches, weighing about one hundred and fifty pounds."

Johnson G. Greene is Miss Owens's cousin; and, whilst on a visit to her in 1866, he contrived to get her version of the Lincoln courtship at great length. It does not vary in any material part from the account currently received in the neighborhood, and given by various persons, whose oral or written testimony is preserved in Mr. Herndon's collection of manuscripts. Greene (J. G.) described her in terms about the same as those used by Mrs. Bale, adding that "she was a nervous and muscular woman," very "intellectual," — "the most intellectual woman he ever saw," — "with a forehead massive and angular, square, prominent, and broad."

After Miss Owens's return to New Salem, in the fall of 1813, Mr. Lincoln was unremitting in his attentions; and wherever she went he was at her side. She had many relatives in the neighborhood, — the Bales, the Greenes, the Grahams: and, if she went to spend an afternoon or an evening with any of these, Abe was very likely to be on hand to conduct her home. He asked her to marry him; but she prudently evaded a positive answer until she could make up her mind about questionable points of his character. She did not think him coarse or cruel; but she did think him thoughtless, careless, not altogether as polite as he might be, — in short, "deficient," as she expresses it, "in those little links which make up the great chain of woman's happiness." His heart was good, his principles were high, his honor sensitive; but still, in the eyes of this refined young lady, he did not seem to be quite the gentleman. "He was lacking in the smaller attentions;" and, in fact, the whole affair is explained when she tells us that "*his education was different from*" hers.

One day Miss Owens and Mrs. Bowlin Greene were making their way slowly and tediously up the hill to Able's house, when they were joined by Lincoln. Mrs. Bowlin Greene was carrying "a great big fat child, heavy, and crossly disposed." Although the woman bent pitiably under her burden, Lincoln offered her no assistance, but, dropping behind with Miss Owens, beguiled the way according to his wishes. When they reached the summit, "Miss Owens said to Lincoln laughingly, 'You would not make a good husband. Abe.' They sat on the fence; and one word brought on another, till a split or breach ensued."

Immediately after this misunderstanding, Lincoln went off toward Havana on a surveying expedition, and was absent about three weeks. On the first day of his return, one of Able's boys was sent up "to town" for the mail. Lincoln saw him at the post-office, and "asked if Miss Owens was at Mr. Able's." The boy said "Yes." — "Tell her," said Lincoln, "that I'll be down to see her in a few minutes." Now, Miss Owens had determined to spend that evening at Minter Graham's; and when the boy gave in the report, "she thought a moment, and said to herself, 'If I can draw Lincoln up there to Graham's, it will be all right.'" This scheme was to operate as a test of Abe's love; but it shared the fate

of some of "the best-laid schemes of mice and men," and
went "all agley."

Lincoln, according to promise, went down to Able's, and
asked if Miss Owens was in. Mrs. Able replied that she had
gone to Graham's, about one and a half miles from Able's due
south-west. Lincoln said, "Didn't she know I was coming?" Mrs. Able answered, "No;" but one of the children
said, "Yes, ma, she did, for I heard Sam tell her so." Lincoln sat a while, and then went about his business. "The
fat was now in the fire. Lincoln thought, as he was extremely
poor, and Miss Owens very rich, it was a fling on him on
that account. Abe was mistaken in his guesses, for wealth
cut no figure in Miss Owens's eyes. Miss Owens regretted
her course. Abe would not bend; and Miss Owens wouldn't.
She said, if she had it to do over again she would play the
cards differently. . . . She had two sons in the Southern
army. She said that if either of them had got into difficulty, she would willingly have gone to old Abe for relief."

In Miss Owens's letter of July 22, 1866, it will be observed
that she tacitly admitted to Mr. Gaines Greene "the circumstances in connection with Mrs. Greene and child." Although she here denies the precise words alleged to have been
used by her in the little quarrel at the top of the hill, she
does not deny the impression his conduct left upon her mind,
but presents additional evidence of it by the relation of
another incident of similar character, from which her inferences were the same.

Fortunately we are not compelled to rely upon tradition,
however authentic, for the facts concerning this interesting
episode in Mr. Lincoln's life. Miss Owens is still alive to tell
her own tale, and we have besides his letters to the lady herself. Mr. Lincoln wrote his account of it as early as 1838.
As in duty bound, we shall permit the lady to speak first.
At her particular request, her present name and residence
are suppressed.

———, May 1, 1866.

Mr. W. H. HERNDON.

Dear Sir, — After quite a struggle with my feelings, I have at last decided to send you the letters in my possession written by Mr. Lincoln, believing, as I do, that you are a gentleman of honor, and will faithfully abide by all you have said.

My associations with your lamented friend were in Menard County, whilst visiting a sister, who then resided near Petersburg. I have learned that my maiden name is now in your possession; and you have ere this, no doubt, been informed that I am a native Kentuckian.

As regards Miss Rutledge, I cannot tell you any thing, she having *died* previous to my acquaintance with Mr. Lincoln; and I do not now recollect of ever hearing him mention her name. Please return the letters at your earliest convenience.

Very respectfully yours,
MARY S. ———.

———, May 22, 1866.

Mr. W. H. HERNDON.

My dear Sir, — Really you catechise me in true lawyer style; but I feel you will have the goodness to excuse me if I decline answering all your questions in detail, being well assured that few women would have ceded as much as I have under all the circumstances.

You say you have heard why our acquaintance terminated as it did. I, too, have heard the same bit of gossip; but I never used the remark which Madam Rumor says I did to Mr. Lincoln. I think I did on one occasion say to my sister, who was very anxious for us to be married, that I thought Mr. Lincoln was deficient in those little links which make up the chain of woman's happiness, — at least, it was so in my case. Not that I believed it proceeded from a lack of goodness of heart: but his training had been different from mine; hence there was not that congeniality which would otherwise have existed.

From his own showing, you perceive that his heart and hand were at my disposal; and I suppose that my feelings were not sufficiently enlisted to have the matter consummated. About the beginning of the year 1833 I left Illinois, at which time our acquaintance and correspondence ceased without ever again being renewed.

My father, who resided in Green County, Kentucky, was a gentleman of considerable means; and I am persuaded that few persons placed a higher estimate on education than he did

Respectfully yours,
MARY S. ———.

————, July 22, 1866.

Mr. W. H. Herndon.

Dear Sir, — I do not think that you are pertinacious in asking the question relative to old Mrs. Bowlin Greene, because I wish to set you right on that question. Your information, no doubt, came through my cousin, Mr. Gaines Greene, who visited us last winter. Whilst here, he was laughing at me about Mr. Lincoln, and among other things spoke about the circumstance in connection with Mrs. Greene and child. My impression is now that I tacitly admitted it, for it was a season of *trouble* with me, and I gave but little heed to the matter. We never had any *hard feelings* toward each other that I know of. On no occasion did I say to Mr. Lincoln that I did not believe he would make a kind husband, because he did not tender his services to Mrs. Greene in helping of her carry her babe. As I said to you in a former letter, I thought him lacking in smaller attentions. One circumstance presents itself just now to my mind's eye. There was a company of us going to Uncle Billy Greene's. Mr. Lincoln was riding with me; and we had a very bad branch to cross. The other gentlemen were very officious in seeing that their partners got over safely. We were behind, he riding in, never looking back to see how I got along. When I rode up beside him, I remarked, "You are a nice fellow! I suppose you did not care whether my neck was broken or not." He laughingly replied (I suppose by way of compliment) that he knew I was plenty smart to take care of myself.

In many things he was sensitive, almost to a fault. He told me of an incident: that he was crossing a prairie one day, and saw before him "a hog mired down," to use his own language. He was rather "fixed up;" and he resolved that he would pass on without looking towards the shoat. After he had gone by, he said the feeling was irresistible; and he had to look back, and the poor thing seemed to say wistfully, "There, now, my last hope is gone;" that he deliberately got down, and relieved it from its difficulty.

In many things we were congenial spirits. In politics we saw eye to eye, though since then we differed as widely as the South is from the North. But methinks I hear you say, "Save me from a political woman!" *So say I.*

The last message I ever received from him was about a year after we parted in Illinois. Mrs. Able visited Kentucky; and he said to her in Springfield, "Tell your sister that I think she was a great fool, because she did not stay here, and marry me." Characteristic of the man.

Respectfully yours,

Mary S. ————.

————————

Vandalia, Dec. 13, 1836.

Mary, — I have been sick ever since my arrival, or I should have written sooner. It is but little difference, however, as I have very little even yet to write. And more, the longer I can avoid the mortification of looking in the post-office for your letter, and not finding it, the better. You see I am mad about that *old letter* yet. I don't like very well to risk you again. I'll try you once more, anyhow.

The new State House is not yet finished, and consequently the Legislature is doing little or nothing. The Governor delivered an inflammatory political message, and it is expected there will be some sparring between the parties about it as soon as the two Houses get to business. Taylor delivered up his petitions for the new county to one of our members this morning. I am told he despairs of its success, on account of all the members from Morgan County opposing it. There are names enough on the petition, I think, to justify the members from our county in going for it; but if the members from Morgan oppose it, which they say they will, the chance will be bad.

Our chance to take the seat of government to Springfield is better than I expected. An internal-improvement convention was held here since we met, which recommended a loan of several million of dollars, on the faith of the State, to construct railroads. Some of the Legislature are for it, and some against it: which has the majority I cannot tell. There is great strife and struggling for the office of the United States Senator here at this time. It is probable we shall ease their pains in a few days. The opposition men have no candidate of their own; and consequently they will smile as complacently at the angry snarl of the contending Van-Buren candidates and their respective friends, as the Christian does at Satan's rage. You recollect that I mentioned at the outset of this letter that I had been unwell. That is the fact, though I believe I am about well now; but that, with other things I cannot account for, have conspired, and have gotten my spirits so low that I feel that I would rather be any place in the world than here. I really cannot endure the thought of staying here ten weeks. Write back as soon as you get this, and, if possible, say something that will please me; for really I have not been pleased since I left you. This letter is so dry and stupid that I am ashamed to send it, but with my present feelings I cannot do any better.

Give my best respects to Mr. and Mrs. Able and family.

Your friend,
LINCOLN.

SPRINGFIELD, May 7, 1837.

MISS MARY S. OWENS.

Friend Mary, — I have commenced two letters to send you before this, both of which displeased me before I got half done, and so I tore them up. The first I thought was not serious enough, and the second was on the other extreme. I shall send this, turn out as it may.

This thing of living in Springfield is rather a dull business, after all; at least, it is so to me. I am quite as lonesome here as I ever was anywhere in my life. I have been spoken to by but one woman since I've been here, and should not have been by her, if she could have avoided it. I've never been to church yet, nor probably shall not be soon. I stay away because I am conscious I should not know how to behave myself.

I am often thinking about what we said of your coming to live at Springfield. I am afraid you would not be satisfied. There is a great deal of flourishing about in carriages here, which it would be your doom to see without sharing it. You would have to be poor, without the means of hiding your poverty. Do you believe you could bear that patiently? Whatever woman may cast her lot with mine, should any ever do so, it is my intention to do all in my power to make her happy and contented; and there is nothing I can imagine that would make me more unhappy than to fail in the effort. I know I should be much happier with you than the way I am, provided I saw no signs of discontent in you. What you have said to me may have been in the way of jest, or I may have misunderstood it. If so, then let it be forgotten; if otherwise, I much wish you would think seriously before you decide. For my part, I have already decided. What I have said I will most positively abide by, provided you wish it. My opinion is, that you had better not do it. You have not been accustomed to hardship, and it may be more severe than you now imagine. I know you are capable of thinking correctly on any subject; and, if you deliberate maturely upon this before you decide, then I am willing to abide your decision.

You must write me a good long letter after you get this. You have nothing else to do; and, though it might not seem interesting to you after you have written it, it would be a good deal of company to me in this "busy wilderness." Tell your sister, I don't want to hear any more about selling out and moving. That gives me the hypo whenever I think of it.

Yours, &c.,

LINCOLN.

———

SPRINGFIELD, Aug. 16, 1837.

FRIEND MARY, — You will no doubt think it rather strange that I should write you a letter on the same day on which we parted; and I can only account for it by supposing that seeing you lately makes me think of you more than usual; while at our late meeting we had but few expressions of thoughts. You must know that I cannot see you, or think of you, with entire indifference; and yet it may be that you are mistaken in regard to what my real feelings toward you are. If I knew you were not, I should not trouble you with this letter. Perhaps any other man would know enough without further information; but I consider it *my* peculiar right to plead ignorance, and your bounden duty to allow the plea. I want in all cases to do right; and most particularly so in all cases with women. I want, at this particular time, more than any thing else, to do right with you: and if I *knew* it would be doing right, as I rather suspect it would, to let you alone, I would do it. And, for the purpose of making the matter as plain as possible, I now say that you can now drop the subject, dismiss your thoughts (if you ever had any) from me forever, and leave this letter unanswered, without calling forth one accusing murmur from me. And I will even go further, and say, that, if it will add any thing to your comfort or peace of mind to do so, it is my sincere wish that you should. Do not understand by this that I wish to cut your acquaintance. I mean no such thing. What I do wish is, that our further acquaintance shall depend upon yourself. If such further acquaintance would constitute nothing to your happiness, I am sure it would not to mine. If you feel yourself in any degree bound to me, I am now willing to release you, provided you wish it; while, on the other hand, I am willing, and even anxious, to bind you faster, if I can be convinced that it will, in any considerable degree, add to your happiness. This, indeed, is the whole question with me. Nothing would make me more miserable than to believe you miserable, — nothing more happy than to know you were so.

In what I have now said, I think I cannot be misunderstood; and to make myself understood is the only object of this letter.

If it suits you best to not answer this, farewell. A long life and a merry one attend you. But, if you conclude to write back, speak as plainly as I do. There can be neither harm nor danger in saying to me any thing you think, just in the manner you think it.

My respects to your sister.   Your friend,

LINCOLN.

After his second meeting with Mary, Mr. Lincoln had little time to prosecute his addresses in person; for early in December he was called away to his seat in the Legislature; but, if his tongue was silent in the cause, his pen was busy.

During the session of the Legislature of 1836–7, Mr. Lincoln made the acquaintance of Mrs. O. H. Browning, whose husband was also a member. The acquaintance ripened into friendship, and that winter and the next Mr. Lincoln spent a great deal of time in social intercourse with the Brownings. Mrs. Browning knew nothing as yet of the affair with Miss Owens; but as the latter progressed, and Lincoln became more and more involved, she noticed the ebb of his spirits, and often rallied him as the victim of some secret but consuming passion. With this for his excuse, Lincoln wrote her, after the adjournment of the Legislature, a full and connected account of the manner in which he had latterly been making "a fool of" himself. For many reasons the publication of this letter is an extremely painful duty. If it could be withheld, and the act decently reconciled to the conscience of a biographer professing to be honest and candid, it should never see the light in these pages. Its grotesque humor, its coarse exaggerations in describing the person of a lady whom the writer was willing to marry, its imputation of toothless and weather-beaten old age to a woman really young and handsome, its utter lack of that delicacy of tone and sentiment which one naturally expects a gentleman to adopt when he thinks proper to discuss the merits of his late mistress, — all these, and its defective orthography, it would certainly be more agreeable to suppress than to publish. But, if we begin by omitting or mutilating a document which sheds so broad a light upon one part of his life and one phase of his character, why may we not do the like as fast and as often as the temptations arise? and where shall the process cease? A biography worth writing at all is worth writing fully and honestly; and the writer who suppresses or mangles the truth is no better than he who bears false witness in any other capacity.

In April, 1838, Miss Owens finally departed from Illinois; and in that same month Mr. Lincoln wrote Mrs. Browning: —

SPRINGFIELD, April 1, 1838.

DEAR MADAM, —Without appologising for being egotistical, I shall make the history of so much of my life as has elapsed since I saw you the subject of this letter. And, by the way, I now discover, that, in order to give a full and inteligible account of the things I have done and suffered *since* I saw you, I shall necessarily have to relate some that happened *before*.

It was, then, in the autumn of 1836, that a married lady of my acquaintance, and who was a great friend of mine, being about to pay a visit to her father & other relatives residing in Kentucky, proposed to me that on her return she would bring a sister of hers with her on condition that I would engage to become her brother-in-law with all convenient despatch. I, of course, accepted the proposal, for you know I could not have done otherwise, had I really been averse to it; but privately, between you and me, I was most confoundedly well pleased with the project. I had seen the said sister some three years before, thought her inteligent and agreeable, and saw no good objection to plodding life through hand in hand with her. Time passed on, the lady took her journey, and in due time returned, sister in company, sure enough. This astonished me a little; for it appeared to me that her coming so readily showed that she was a trifle too willing; but, on reflection, it occurred to me that she might have been prevailed on by her married sister to come, without any thing concerning me ever having been mentioned to her; and so I concluded, that, if no other objection presented itself, I would consent to waye this. All this occurred to me on *hearing* of her arrival in the neighborhood; for, be it remembered, I had not yet *seen* her, except about three years previous, as above mentioned. In a few days we had an interview; and, although I had seen her before, she did not look as my imagination had pictured her. I knew she was oversize, but she now appeared a fair match for Falstaff. I knew she was called an "old maid," and I felt no doubt of the truth of at least half of the appelation; but now, when I beheld her, I could not for my life avoid thinking of my mother; and this, not from withered features, for her skin was too full of fat to permit of its contracting into wrinkles, but from her want of teeth, weather-beaten appearance in general, and from a kind of notion that ran in my head that *nothing* could have commenced at the size of infancy and reached her present bulk in less than thirty-five or forty years; and, in short, I was not at all pleased with her. But what could I do? I had told her sister that I would take her for better or for worse; and I made a point of honor and conscience in all things to stick to my word, especially if others had been induced to act on it, which in this case I had no doubt they had; for I was now fairly convinced that no other man on earth would have her, and hence the conclusion that they were bent on holding me to my bargain. "Well," thought I, "I have said it, and, be the consequences what they may, it shall not be my fault if I fail to do it." At once I determined to consider her my wife; and, this done, all my powers of discovery were put to work in search of perfections in her which might be fairly sett off against her defects. I tried to imagine her handsome, which, but for her unfortunate corpulency, was actually true. Exclusive of this, no woman that I have ever seen has a finer face. I also tried to convince myself that the mind was much more to be valued than the person; and in this she was not inferior, as I could discover, to any with whom I had been acquainted.

Shortly after this, without attempting to come to any positive understanding with her, I sat out for Vandalia, when and where you first saw me. During my stay there I had letters from her which did not change my opinion of either her intelect or intention, but, on the contrary, confirmed it in both.

All this while, although I was fixed, "firm as the surge-repelling rock," in my resolution, I found I was continually repenting the rashness which had led me to make it. Through life, I have been in no bondage, either real or imaginary, from the thraldom of which I so much desired to be free. After my return home, I saw nothing to change my opinions of her in any particular. She was the same, and so was I. I now spent my time in planing how I might get along through life after my contemplated change of circumstances should have taken place, and how I might procrastinate the evil day for a time, which I really dreaded as much, perhaps more, than an Irishman does the halter.

After all my suffering upon this deeply-interesting subject, here I am, wholly, unexpectedly, completely, out of the "scrape;" and I now want to know if you can guess how I got out of it, — out, clear, in every sense of the term; no violation of word, honor, or conscience. I don't believe you can guess, and so I might as well tell you at once. As the lawyer says, it was done in the manner following, to wit: After I had delayed the matter as long as I thought I could in honor do (which, by the way, had brought me round into the last fall), I concluded I might as well bring it to a consuma-tion without further delay; and so I mustered my resolution, and made the proposal to her direct: but, shocking to relate, she answered, No. At first I supposed she did it through an affectation of modesty, which I thought but ill became her under the peculiar circumstances of her case; but, on my renewal of the charge, I found she repeled it with greater firmness than before. I tried it again and again, but with the same success, or rather with the same want of success.

I finally was forced to give it up; at which I verry unexpectedly found myself mortified almost beyond endurance. I was mortified, it seemed to me, in a hundred different ways. My vanity was deeply wounded by the reflection that I had so long been too stupid to discover her intentions, and at the same time never doubting that I understood them perfectly; and also that she, whom I had taught myself to believe nobody else would have, had actually rejected me with all my fancied greatness. And, to cap the whole, I then, for the first time, began to suspect that I was really a little in love with her. But let it all go. I'll try and outlive it. Others have been made fools of by the girls; but this can never with truth be said of me. I most emphatically, in this instance, made a fool of myself. I have now come to the conclusion never again to think of marrying, and for this reason: I can never be satisfied with any one who would be blockhead enough to have me.

When you receive this, write me a long yarn about something to amuse me. Give my respects to Mr. Browning.

Your sincere friend,

A. LINCOLN.

MRS. O. H. BROWNING.

CHAPTER X.

THE majority of Mr. Lincoln's biographers — and they are many and credulous — tell us that he *walked* from New Salem to Vandalia, a distance of one hundred miles, to take his seat, for the first time, in the Legislature of the State. But that is an innocent mistake; for he was resolved to appear with as much of the dignity of the senator as his circumstances would permit. It was for this very purpose that he had borrowed the two hundred dollars from Coleman Smoot; and, when the choice between riding and walking presented itself, he sensibly enough got into the stage, with his new clothes on, and rode to the scene of his labors.

When he arrived there, he found a singular state of affairs. Duncan had been chosen Governor at the recent August election by "the whole-hog Jackson men;" but he was absent in Congress during the whole of the campaign; and, now that he came to the duties of his office, it was discovered that he had been all the while an anti-Jackson man, and was quite willing to aid the Whigs in furtherance of some of their worst schemes. These schemes were then just beginning to be hatched in great numbers; but in due time they were enacted into laws, and prepared Illinois with the proper weights of public debt and " rag " currency, to sink her deeper than her neighbors into the miseries of financial ruin in 1837. The speculating fever was just reaching Illinois; the land and town-lot business had barely taken shape at Chicago; and State banks and multitudinous internal improvements were yet to be invented. But this Legislature was a very wise one

184

in its own conceit, and was not slow to launch out with the first of a series of magnificent experiments. It contented itself, however, with chartering a State bank, with a capital of one million five hundred thousand dollars; rechartering, with a capital of three hundred thousand dollars, the Shawneetown Bank, which had broken twelve years before; and providing for a loan of five hundred thousand dollars, on the credit of the State, wherewith to make a beginning on the Illinois and Michigan Canal. The bill for the latter project was drawn and introduced by Senator James M. Strode, the gentleman who described with such moving eloquence the horrors of Stillman's defeat. These measures Gov. Ford considers " the beginning of all the bad legislation which followed in a few years, and which, as is well known, resulted in general ruin." Mr. Lincoln favored them all, and faithfully followed out the policy of which they were the inauguration at subsequent sessions of the same body. For the present, nevertheless, he was a silent member, although he was assigned a prominent place on the Committee on Public Accounts and Expenditures. The bank-charters were drawn by a Democrat who hoped to find his account in the issue; all the bills were passed by a Legislature " nominally " Democratic; but the Board of Canal Commissioners was composed exclusively of Whigs, and the Whigs straightway assumed control of the banks.

It was at a special session of this Legislature that Lincoln first saw Stephen A. Douglas, and, viewing his active little person with immense amusement, pronounced him " the *least* man he ever saw." Douglas had come into the State (from Vermont) only the previous year, but, having studied law for several months, considered himself eminently qualified to be State's attorney for the district in which he lived, and was now come to Vandalia for that purpose. The place was already filled by a man of considerable distinction; but the incumbent remaining at home, possibly in blissful ignorance of his neighbor's design, was easily supplanted by the supple Vermonter.

It is the misfortune of legislatures in general, as it was in those days the peculiar misfortune of the Legislature of Illinois, to be beset by a multitude of gentlemen engaged in the exclusive business of "log-rolling." Chief among the "rollers" were some of the most "distinguished" members, each assisted by an influential delegation from the district, bank, or "institution" to be benefited by the legislation proposed. An expert "log-roller," an especially wily and persuasive person, who could depict the merits of his scheme with roseate but delusive eloquence, was said to carry "a gourd of 'possum fat," and the unhappy victim of his art was said to be "*greased and swallowed.*"

It is not to be supposed that anybody ever succeeded in anointing a single square inch of Mr. Lincoln's person with the "fat" that deluded; but historians aver that "the Long Nine," of whom he was the longest and cleverest, possessed "gourds" of extraordinary dimensions, and distributed "grease" of marvellous virtues. But of that at another place.

In 1836 Mr. Lincoln was again a candidate for the Legislature; his colleagues on the Whig ticket in Sangamon being, for Representatives, John Dawson, William F. Elkin, N. W. Edwards, Andrew McCormick, Dan Stone, and R. L. Wilson; and for Senators, A. G. Herndon and Job Fletcher. They were all elected but one, and he was beaten by John Calhoun.

Mr. Lincoln opened the campaign by the following manifesto : —

NEW SALEM, June 13, 1836.

To THE EDITOR OF "THE JOURNAL."

In your paper of last Saturday, I see a communication over the signature of "Many Voters," in which the candidates who are announced in the "Journal" are called upon to "show their hands." Agreed. Here's mine.

I go for all sharing the privileges of the government who assist in bearing its burdens. Consequently, I go for admitting all *whites* to the right of suffrage who pay taxes or bear arms (*by no means excluding females*).

If elected, I shall consider the whole people of Sangamon my constituents, as well those that oppose as those that support me.

While acting as their Representative, I shall be governed by their will on all subjects upon which I have the means of knowing what their will is;

and upon all others I shall do what my own judgment teaches me will best advance their interests. Whether elected or not, I go for distributing the proceeds of the sales of the public lands to the several States, to enable our State, in common with others, to dig canals and construct railroads without borrowing money and paying the interest on it.

If alive on the first Monday in November, I shall vote for Hugh L. White for President.

Very respectfully,

A. LINCOLN.

The elections were held on the first Monday in August, and the campaign began about six weeks or two months before. Popular meetings were advertised in "The Sangamon Journal" and "The State Register," — organs of the respective parties. Not unfrequently the meetings were joint, — composed of both parties, — when, as Lincoln would say, the candidates "put in their best licks," while the audience "rose to the height of the great argument" with cheers, taunts, cat-calls, fights, and other exercises appropriate to the free and untrammelled enjoyment of the freeman's boon.

The candidates travelled from one grove to another on horseback; and, when the "Long Nine" (all over six feet in height) took the road, it must have been a goodly sight to see.

"I heard Lincoln make a speech," says James Gourly, "in Mechanicsburg, Sangamon County, in 1836. John Neal had a fight at the time: the roughs got on him, and Lincoln jumped in and saw fair play. We staid for dinner at Green's, close to Mechanicsburg, — drank whiskey sweetened with honey. There the questions discussed were internal improvements, Whig principles." (Gourly was a great friend of Lincoln's, for Gourly had had a foot-race "with H. B. Truett, now of California," and Lincoln had been his "judge;" and it was a remarkable circumstance, that nearly everybody for whom Lincoln "judged" came out ahead.)

"I heard Mr. Lincoln during the same canvass," continues Gourly. "It was at the Court House, where the State House now stands. The Whigs and Democrats had a general quarrel then and there. N. W. Edwards drew a pistol on Achilles Morris." But Gourly's account of this last scene is

unsatisfactory, although the witness is willing; and we turn
to Lincoln's colleague, Mr. Wilson, for a better one. "The
Saturday evening preceding the election the candidates were
addressing the people in the Court House at Springfield. Dr.
Early, one of the candidates on the Democratic side, made
some charge that N. W. Edwards, one of the candidates on
the Whig side, deemed untrue. Edwards climbed on a table,
so as to be seen by Early, and by every one in the house, and
at the top of his voice told Early that the charge was false.
The excitement that followed was intense, — so much so, that
fighting men thought that a duel must settle the difficulty.
Mr. Lincoln, by the programme, followed Early. He took
up the subject in dispute, and handled it fairly, and with
such ability that every one was astonished and pleased. So
that difficulty ended there. Then, for the first time, developed by the excitement of the occasion, he spoke in that
tenor intonation of voice that ultimately settled down into
that clear, shrill monotone style of speaking that enabled his
audience, however large, to hear distinctly the lowest sound
of his voice."

It was during this campaign, possibly at the same meeting, that Mr. Speed heard him reply to George Forquer.
Forquer had been a leading Whig, one of their foremost men
in the Legislature of 1834, but had then recently changed
sides, and thereupon was appointed Register of the Land
Office at Springfield. Mr. Forquer was an astonishing man:
he not only astonished the people by "changing his coat in
politics," but by building the best frame-house in Springfield,
and erecting over it the only lightning-rod the entire region
could boast of. At this meeting he listened attentively to
Mr. Lincoln's first speech, and was much annoyed by the
transcendent power with which the awkward young man
defended the principles he had himself so lately abandoned.
"The speech" produced a profound impression, "especially
upon a large number of Lincoln's friends and admirers, who
had come in from the country" expressly to hear and ap-
plaud him.

" At the conclusion of Lincoln's speech " (we quote from Mr. Speed), " the crowd was dispersing, when Forquer rose and asked to be heard. He commenced by saying that the young man would have to be taken down, and was sorry that the task devolved upon him. He then proceeded to answer Lincoln's speech in a style, which, while it was able and fair, yet, in his whole manner, asserted and claimed superiority. Lincoln stood near him, and watched him during the whole of his speech. When Forquer concluded, he took the stand again. I have often heard him since, in court and before the people, but never saw him appear so well as upon that occasion. He replied to Mr. Forquer with great dignity and force; but I shall never forget the conclusion of that speech. Turning to Mr. Forquer, he said, that he had commenced his speech by announcing that ' this young man would have to be taken down.' Turning then to the crowd, he said, ' It is for you, not for me, to say whether I am up or down. The gentleman has alluded to my being a young man : I am older in years than I am in the tricks and trades of politicians. I desire to live, and I desire place and distinction as a politician; but I would rather die now, than, like the gentleman, live to see the day that I would have to erect a lightning-rod to protect a guilty conscience from an offended God.' "

He afterwards told Speed that the sight of that same rod " had led him to the study of the properties of electricity and the utility of the rod as a conductor."

Among the Democratic orators stumping the county at this time was Dick Taylor, a pompous gentleman, who went abroad in superb attire, ruffled shirts, rich vest, and immense watch-chains, with shining and splendid pendants. But Dick was a severe Democrat in theory, made much of " the hard-handed yeomanry," and flung many biting sarcasms upon the aristocratic pretensions of the Whigs, — the " rag barons " and the manufacturing " lords." He was one day in the midst of a particularly aggravating declamation of this sort, " when Abe began to feel devilish, and thought he would take the wind out of Dick's sails by a little sport." He therefore " edged " slyly up to the speaker, and suddenly catching his vest by the lower corner, and giving it a sharp pull upward, it opened wide, and out fell upon the platform, in full view of the astonished audience, a mass of ruffled shirt, gold watch, chains, seals, and glittering jewels. Jim Matheny was there, and nearly broke his heart with mirth. "The crowd couldn't stand it, but shouted uproariously." It must have been then that Abe delivered the following speech, although Ninian W. Edwards places it in 1840 : —

"While he [Col. Taylor] was making these charges against the Whigs over the country, riding in fine carriages, wearing ruffled shirts, kid gloves, massive gold watch-chains, with large gold seals, and flourishing a heavy gold-headed cane, he [Lincoln] was a poor boy, hired on a flatboat at eight dollars a month, and had only one pair of breeches to his back, and they were buckskin, — 'and,' said Lincoln, 'if you know the nature of buckskin, when wet and dried by the sun, they will shrink, — and mine kept shrinking, until they left several inches of my legs bare between the tops of my socks and the lower part of my breeches ; and, whilst I was growing taller, they were becoming shorter, and so much tighter, that they left a blue streak around my legs that can be seen to this day. If you call this aristocracy, I plead guilty to the charge.' "

Hitherto Sangamon County had been uniformly Democratic ; but at this election the Whigs carried it by an average majority of about four hundred, Mr. Lincoln receiving a larger vote than any other candidate. The result was in part due to a transitory and abortive attempt of the anti-Jackson and anti-Van-Buren men to build up a third party, with Judge White of Tennessee as its leader. This party was not supposed to be wedded to the "specie circular," was thought to be open to conviction on the bank question, clamored loudly about the business interests and general distress of the country, and was actually in favor of the distribution of the proceeds of the sales of the public lands. In the nomenclature of Illinois, its members might have been called "nominal Jackson men;" that is to say, men who continued to act with the Democratic party, while disavowing its cardinal principles, — traders, trimmers, cautious schismatics who argued the cause of Democracy from a brief furnished by the enemy. The diversion in favor of White was just to the hand of the Whigs, and they aided it in every practicable way. Always for an expedient when an expedient would answer, a compromise when a compromise would do, the "hand" Mr. Lincoln "showed" at the opening of the campaign contained the "White" card among the highest of its trumps. "If alive on the first Monday in November, I shall vote for Hugh L. White for President." A number of local Democratic politicians assisting him to play it, it won the game in 1836, and Sangamon County went over to the Whigs.

At this election Mr. Douglas was made a Representative from Morgan County, along with Col. Hardin, from whom he had the year before taken the State's attorneyship. The event is notable principally because Mr. Douglas was nominated by a convention, and not by the old system of self-announcement, which, under the influence of Eastern immigrants, like himself, full of party zeal, and attached to the customs of the places whence they came, was gradually but surely falling into disfavor. Mr. Douglas served only one session, and then became Register of the Land Office at Springfield. The next year he was nominated for Congress in the Peoria District, under the convention system, and in the same year Col. Stephenson was nominated for Governor in the same way. The Whigs were soon compelled to adopt the device which they saw marshalling the Democrats in a state of complete discipline; whilst they themselves were disorganized by a host of volunteer candidates and the operations of innumerable cliques and factions. At first "it was considered a Yankee contrivance," intended to abridge the liberties of the people; but the Whig "people" were as fond of victory, offices, and power as their enemies were, and in due time they took very kindly to this effectual means of gaining them. A speech of Ebenezer Peck of Chicago, "before a great meeting of the lobby, during the special session of 1835-6 at Vandalia," being a production of special ingenuity and power, is supposed to have contributed largely to the introduction of the convention system into the middle and southern parts of the State. Mr. Peck was then a fervent Democrat, whom the Whigs delighted to malign as a Canadian monarchist; but in after times he was the fast and able friend of their great leader, Abraham Lincoln.

One of the first and worst effects of the stricter organization of parties in Illinois, as well as in other States, was the strong diversion of public attention from State to Federal affairs. Individual candidates were no longer required to "show their hands:" they accepted "platforms" when they accepted nominations; and without a nomination it was mere quixotism to stand at all. District, State, and national conventions, acting and re-acting upon one another, produced a concert of sentiment and conduct which overlaid local issues, and repressed independent proceedings. This improved party machinery supplied the readiest and most effective means of distributing the rapidly-increasing patronage of the Federal Executive; and those who did not wish to be cut off from its enjoyment could do no less than re-affirm with becoming fervor, in their local assemblages, the latest deliverance of the faith by the central authority. The promoters of heresies and schisms, the blind leaders who misled a county or a State convention, and seduced it into the declaration of principles of its own, had their seats contested in the next general council of the party, were solemnly sat upon, condemned, "delivered over to Satan to be buffeted," and cast out of the household of faith, to wander in the wilderness and to live upon husks. It was like a feeble African bishop imputing heresy to the Christian world, with Rome at its head. A man like Mr. Lincoln, who earnestly "desired place and distinction as a politician," labored without hope while his party affinities remained the subject of a reasonable doubt. He must be "a whole-hog man" or nothing, a Whig or a

Democrat. Mr. Lincoln chose his company with commendable decision, and wasted no tender regrets upon his "nominal" Democratic friends. For White against Harrison, in November, 1836, he led the Whigs into action when the Legislature met in December; and when the hard-cider campaign of 1840 commenced, with its endless meetings and processions, its coon-skins and log-cabins, its intrigue, trickery, and fun, his musical voice rose loudest above the din for "Old Tippecanoe;" and no man did better service, or enjoyed those memorable scenes more, than he who was to be the beneficiary of a similar revival in 1860.

When this legislature met in the winter of 1836–7, the bank and internal-improvement infatuation had taken full possession of a majority of the people, as well as of the politicians. To be sure, "Old Hickory" had given a temporary check to the wild speculations in Western land by the specie circular, about the close of his administration, whereby gold and silver were made "land-office money;" and the Government declined to exchange any more of the public domain for the depreciated paper of rotten and explosive banks. Millions of notes loaned by the banks on insufficient security or no security at all were by this timely measure turned back into the banks, or converted to the uses of a more legitimate and less dangerous business. But, even if the specie circular had not been repealed, it would probably have proved impotent against the evils it was designed to prevent, after the passage of the Act distributing among the States the surplus (or supposed surplus) revenues of the Federal Government.

The last dollar of the old debt was paid in 1833. There were from time to time large unexpended and unappropriated balances in the treasury. What should be done with them? There was no sub-treasury as yet, and questions concerning the mere safe-keeping of these moneys excited the most tremendous political contests. The United States Bank had always had the use of the cash in the treasury in the form of deposits; but the bank abused its trust, — used its enormous power over the currency and exchanges of the country to

achieve political results in its own interest, and, by its mani-
fold sins and iniquities, compelled Gen. Jackson to remove the
deposits.   Ultimately the bank took shelter in Pennsylvania,
where it began a new fraudulent life under a surreptitious
clause tacked to the end of a road law on its passage through
the General Assembly.   In due time the "beast," as Col.
Benton loved to call it, died in its chosen lair a shameful
and ignominious death, cheating the public with a show of
solvency to the end, and leaving a fine array of bill-holders
and depositors to mourn one of the most remarkable delusions
of modern times.

Withdrawn, or rather withheld (for they were never withdrawn), from the Bank of the United States, the revenues
of the Federal Government were deposited as fast as they
accrued in specie-paying State banks.   They were paid in the
notes of the thousand banks, good, bad, and indifferent, whose
promises to pay constituted the paper currency of the day.
It was this money which the Whigs, aided by Democratic
recusants, proposed to give away to the States.   They passed
an Act requiring it to be *deposited* with the States, — osten-
sibly as a safe and convenient method of keeping it; but
nobody believed that it would ever be called for, or paid if it
was.   It was simply an extraordinary largess; and pending
the very embarrassment caused by itself, when the government had not a dollar wherewith to pay even a pension, and
the temporary expedient was an issue of treasury notes against
the better judgment of the party in power, the possibility of
withdrawing these deposits was never taken into the account.
The Act went into effect on the 1st of January, 1837, and
was one of the immediate causes of the suspension and disasters of that year.   "The condition of our deposit banks was
desperate, — wholly inadequate to the slightest pressure on
their vaults in the ordinary course of business, much less that
of meeting the daily government drafts and the approaching
deposit of near forty millions with the States."   Nevertheless,
the deposits began at the rate of ten millions to the quarter.
The deposit banks "blew up;" and all the others, including

that of the United States, closed their doors to customers and bill-holders, which gave them more time to hold public meetings, imputing the distress of the country to the hard-money policy of Jackson and Van Buren, and agitating for the re-charter of Mr. Biddle's profligate concern as the only remedy human ingenuity could devise.

It was in the month previous to the first deposit with the States, — about the time when Gov. Ford says, "lands and town-lots were the only articles of export" from Illinois; when the counters of Western land-offices were piled high with illusory bank-notes in exchange for public lands, and when it was believed that the West was now at last about to bound forward in a career of unexampled prosperity, under the forcing process of public improvements by the States, with the aid and countenance of the Federal Government,—that Mr. Lincoln went up to attend the first session of the new Legislature at Vandalia. He was big with projects: his real public service was just now about to begin. In the previous Legislature he had been silent, observant, studious. He had improved the opportunity so well, that of all men in this new body, of equal age in the service, he was the smartest parliamentarian and the cunningest "log-roller." He was fully determined to identify himself conspicuously with the "liberal" legislation in contemplation, and dreamed of a fame very different from that which he actually obtained as an antislavery leader. It was about this time that he told his friend, Mr. Speed, that he aimed at the great distinction of being called "the De Witt Clinton of Illinois."

Meetings with a view to this sort of legislation had been held in all, or nearly all, the counties in the State during the preceding summer and fall. Hard-money, strict-construction, no-monopoly, anti-progressive Democrats were in a sad minority. In truth, there was little division of parties about these matters which were deemed so essential to the prosperity of a new State. There was Mr. Lincoln, and there was Mr. Douglas, in perfect unison as to the grand object to be accomplished, but mortally jealous as to which should take the lead in accomplishing it. A few days before the Legislature assembled, " a mass convention " of the people of Sangamon County " instructed " their members " to vote for a *general system of internal improvements.*" The House of Representatives organized in the morning; and in the evening its hall was surrendered to a convention of delegates from all parts of the State, which " devised and recommended to the Legislature a system of internal improvements, the chief feature of which was, that it should be commensurate with the wants of the people." This result was arrived at after two days of debate, with " Col. Thomas Mather, of the State Bank, as president."

Mr. Lincoln served on the Committee on Finance, and was a most laborious member, instant in season and out of season, for the great measures of the Whig party. It was to his individual exertion that the Whigs were indebted in no small degree for the complete success of their favorite schemes at this session. A railroad from Galena to the mouth of the Ohio was provided for ; another from Alton to Shawneetown ; another from Alton to Mount Carmel ; another from Alton to the eastern boundary of the State towards Terre Haute ; another from Quincy by way of Springfield to the Wabash ; another from Bloomington to Pekin ; another from Peoria to Warsaw, — in all about thirteen hundred miles. But in this comprehensive " system," " commensurate with the wants of the people," the rivers were not to be overlooked ; and accordingly the Kaskaskia, the Illinois, the Great Wabash, the Little Wabash, and the Rock rivers were to be duly improved. To set these little matters in motion, a loan of eight millions of dollars was authorized ; and, to complete the canal from Chicago to Peru, another loan of four millions of dollars was voted at the same session, — two hundred thousand dollars being given as a gratuity to those counties which seemed to have no special interest in any of the foregoing projects. Work on all these roads was to commence, not only at the same time, but at both ends of each road, and at all the river-crossings. There were as yet no surveys of any route, no estimates, no reports of engineers, or even unprofessional viewers. " Progress " was not to wait on trifles ; capitalists were supposed to be lying in wait to catch these precious bonds ; the money would be raised in a twinkling, and being applied with all the skill of " a hundred De Witt Clintons," — a class of gentlemen at that time extremely numerous and obtrusive, — the loan would build the railroads, the railroads would build cities, cities would create farms, foreign capital would rush to so inviting a field, the lands would be taken up with marvellous celerity, and the " land-tax " going into a sinking fund, *that*, with some tolls and certain sly speculations to be made by the State, would pay principal and interest of the debt without ever a cent of taxation upon the people. In short, everybody was to be enriched, while the munificence of the State in selling its credit and spending the proceeds would make its empty coffers overflow with ready money. It was a dark stroke of statesmanship, a mysterious device in finance, which, whether from being misunderstood, or from being mismanaged, bore from the beginning fruits the very reverse of those it had promised.

A Board of Canal Commissioners was already in existence ; but now were established, as necessary parts of the new "system," a Board of Fund Commissioners and a Board of Commissioners of Public Works.

The capital stock of the Shawneetown Bank was increased to one million seven hundred thousand dollars, and that of the State Bank to three million one hundred thousand dollars. The State took the new stock, and proposed to pay for it " with the surplus revenues of the United States, and the residue by a sale of State bonds." The banks were likewise made fiscal agencies, to place the loans, and generally to manage the railroad and canal funds. The career of these banks is an extremely interesting chapter in the history of Illinois, — little less so than the rise and collapse of the great internal-improvement system. But, as it has already a place in a chronicle of wider scope and greater merit than this, it is enough to say that in due time they went the way of their kind, — the State lost by them, and they lost by the State, in morals as well as in money.

The means used in the Legislature to pass the "system" deserve some notice for the instruction of posterity. " First, a large portion of the people were interested in the success of the canal, which was threatened, if other sections of the State were denied the improvements demanded by them ; and thus the friends of the canal were forced to log-roll for that work by supporting others which were to be ruinous to the country. Roads and improvements were proposed everywhere, to enlist every section of the State. Three or four efforts were made to pass a smaller system; and, when defeated, the bill would be amended by the addition of other roads, until a majority was obtained for it. Those counties which could not be thus accommodated were to share in the fund of two hundred thousand dollars. Three roads were appointed to terminate at Alton, before the Alton interest would agree to the system. The seat of government was to be removed to Spring- field. Sangamon County, in which Springfield is situated, was then represented by two Senators and seven Representatives, called the 'Long Nine,' all Whigs but one. Amongst them were some dexterous jugglers and managers in politics, whose whole object was to obtain the seat of government for Spring- field. This delegation, from the beginning of the session, threw itself as a unit in support of, or in opposition to, every local measure of interest, but never without a bargain for votes in return on the seat-of-government question. Most of the other counties were small, having but one Representative and many of them with but one for a whole representative district; and this gave Sangamon County a decided prepon- derance in the log-rolling system of those days. It is worthy of examination whether any just and equal legislation can ever be sustained where some of the counties are great and powerful, and others feeble. But by such means 'The Long- Nine' rolled along like a snowball, gathering accessions of strength at every turn, until they swelled up a considerable party for Springfield, which party they managed to take almost as a unit in favor of the internal-improvement system, in return for which the active supporters of that system were to vote for Springfield to be the seat of government. Thus it was made to cost the State about six millions of dollars to remove the seat of government from Vandalia to Springfield, half of which sum would have purchased all the real estate in that town at three prices ; and thus by log-rolling on the canal measure; by multiplying railroads; by terminating three railroads at Alton, that Alton might become a great city in opposition to St. Louis; by distributing money to some of the counties to be wasted by the county commissioners ; and by giving the seat of government to Springfield, — was the whole State bought up, and bribed to approve the most senseless and disastrous policy which ever crippled the energies of a growing country." [1]

Enumerating the gentlemen who voted for this combination of evils, — among them Stephen A. Douglas, John A. Mc-Clernand, James Shields, and Abraham Lincoln, — and reciting the high places of honor and trust to which most of them have since attained, Gov. Ford pronounces " all of them spared monuments of popular wrath, evincing how safe it is to a politician, but how disastrous it may be to the country, to keep along with the present fervor of the people."

" It was a maxim with many politicians just to keep along even with the humor of the people, right or wrong ; " and this maxim Mr. Lincoln held then, as ever since, in very high estimation. But the " humor" of his constituents was not only intensely favorable to the new scheme of internal improvements : it was most decidedly their " humor " to have the capital at Springfield, and to make a great man of the legislator who should take it there. Mr. Lincoln was doubtless thoroughly convinced that the popular view of all these matters was the right one ; but, even if he had been unhappily afflicted with individual scruples of his own, he would have deemed it but simple duty to obey the almost unanimous voice of his constituency. He thought he never could serve them better than

[1] Ford's History of Illinois.

by giving them just what they wanted; and that to collect the will of his people, and register it by his own vote, was the first and leading obligation of a representative. It happened that on this occasion the popular feeling fell in very pleasantly with his young dream of rivalling the fame of Clinton; and here, also, was a fine opportunity of repeating, in a higher strain and on a loftier stage, the ingenious arguments, which, in the very outset of his career, had proved so hard for "Posey and Ewing," when he overthrew those worthies in the great debate respecting the improvement of the Sangamon River.

"The Internal-Improvement Bill," says Mr. Wilson (one of the "Long Nine"), "and a bill to permanently locate the seat of government of the State, were the great measures of the session of 1836–7. Vandalia was then the seat of government, and had been for a number of years. A new state house had just been built. Alton, Decatur, Peoria, Jacksonville, Illiapolis, and Springfield were the points seeking the location, if removed from Vandalia. The delegation from Sangamon were a unit, acting in concert in favor of the permanent location at Springfield. The bill was introduced at an early day in the session, to locate, by a joint vote of both Houses of the Legislature. The friends of the other points united to defeat the bill, as each point thought the postponement of the location to some future period would give strength to their location. The contest on this bill was long and severe. Its enemies laid it on the table twice, — once on the table to the fourth day of July, and once indefinitely postponed it. To take a bill from the table is always attended with difficulty; but when laid on the table to a day beyond the session, or when indefinitely postponed, it requires a vote of reconsideration, which always is an intense struggle. In these dark hours, when our bill to all appearances was beyond resuscitation, and all our opponents were jubilant over our defeat, and when friends could see no hope, Mr. Lincoln never for one moment despaired; but, collecting his colleagues to his room for consultation, his practical common sense, his thorough knowledge of human nature, then made him an overmatch for his compeers, and for any man that I have ever known."

" We surmounted all obstacles, passed the bill, and, by a joint vote of both Houses, located the seat of government of the State of Illinois at Springfield, just before the adjournment of the Legislature, which took place on the fourth day of March, 1837. The delegation acting during the whole session upon all questions as a unit, gave them strength and influence, that enabled them to carry through their measures and give efficient aid to their friends. The delegation was not only remarkable for their numbers, but for their length, most of them measuring six feet and over. It was said at the time that that delegation measured fifty-four feet high. Hence they were known as ' *The Long Nine.*' So that during that session, and for a number of years afterwards, all the bad laws passed at that session of the Legislature were chargeable to the management and influence of ' The Long Nine.' . . .

" He (Mr. Lincoln) was on the stump and in the halls of the Legislature a ready debater, manifesting extraordinary ability in his peculiar manner of presenting his subject. He did not follow the beaten track of other speakers and thinkers, but appeared to comprehend the whole situation of the subject, and take hold of its principles. He had a remarkable faculty for concentration, enabling him to present his subject in such a manner, as nothing but conclusions were presented."

It was at this session of the Legislature, March 3, 1837, that Mr. Lincoln began that antislavery record upon which his fame through all time must chiefly rest. It was a very mild beginning; but even that required uncommon courage and candor in the day and generation in which it was done.

The whole country was excited concerning the doctrines and the practices of the Abolitionists. These agitators were as yet but few in numbers: but in New England they comprised some of the best citizens, and the leaders were persons

of high character, of culture and social influence; while, in
the Middle States, they were, for the most part, confined to
the Society of Friends, or Quakers. All were earnest, active,
and uncompromising in the propagation of their opinions; and,
believing slavery to be the " sum of all villanies," with the utmost pertinacity they claimed the unrestricted right to disseminate their convictions in any manner they saw fit, regardless
of all consequences. They paid not the slightest heed to the
wishes or the opinions of their opponents. They denounced
all compromises with an unsparing tongue, and would allow
no law of man to stand, in their eyes, above the law of God.

George Thompson, identified with emancipation in the
British West Indies, had come and gone. For more than a
year he addressed public meetings in New England, the
Central States, and Ohio, and contributed not a little to the
growing excitement by his fierce denunciations of the slaveholding class, in language with which his long agitation in
England had made him familiar. He was denounced, insulted,
and mobbed; and even in Boston he was once posted as an
" infamous foreign scoundrel," and an offer was made of a hundred dollars to " snake him out " of a public meeting. In
fact, Boston was not at all behind other cities and towns in
its condemnation of the Abolitionists. A great meeting in
Faneuil Hall, called by eighteen hundred leading citizens, —
Whigs and Democrats, — condemned their proceedings in language as strong and significant as Richard Fletcher, Peleg
Sprague, and Harrison Gray Otis could write it. But Garrison
still continued to publish " The Liberator," filling it with all
the uncompromising aggressiveness of his sect, and distributing
it throughout the Southern States. It excited great alarm in
the slaveholding communities where its secret circulation, in
the minds of the slaveholders, tended to incite the slaves to
insurrections, assassinations, and running away; but in the
place where it was published it was looked upon with general
contempt and disgust. When the Mayor of Baltimore wrote
to the Mayor of Boston to have it suppressed, the latter (the
eloquent Otis) replied, " that his officers had ferreted out the

paper and its editor, whose office was an obscure hole; his only visible auxiliary a negro boy; his supporters a few insignificant persons of all colors."

At the close of the year 1835, President Jackson had called the attention of Congress to the doings of these people in language corresponding to the natural wrath with which he viewed the character of their proceedings. " I must also," said he, "invite your attention to the painful excitements in the South by attempts to circulate through the mails inflammatory appeals addressed to the passions of slaves, in prints and various sorts of publications calculated to stimulate them to insurrection, and to produce all the horrors of civil war. It is fortunate for the country that the good sense, the generous feeling, and deep-rooted attachment of the people of the non-slaveholding States to the Union and their fellow-citizens of the same blood in the South have given so strong and impressive a tone to the sentiments entertained against the proceedings of the misguided persons who have engaged in these unconstitutional and wicked attempts, and especially against the emissaries from foreign parts, who have dared to interfere in this matter, as to authorize the hope that these attempts will no longer be persisted in. . . . I would therefore call the special attention of Congress to the subject, and respectfully suggest the propriety of passing such a law as will prohibit, under severe penalties, the circulation in the Southern States, through the mail, of incendiary publications, intended to instigate the slaves to insurrection."

Mr. Clay said the sole purpose of the Abolitionists was to array one portion of the Union against the other. " With that in view, in all their leading prints and publications, the alleged horrors of slavery are depicted in the most glowing and exaggerated colors, to excite the imaginations and stimulate the rage of the people of the Free States against the people of the slaveholding States. . . . Why are the Slave States wantonly and cruelly assailed? Why does the abolition press teem with publications tending to excite hatred and animosity on the part of the Free States against the Slave

States? . . . Why is Congress petitioned? Is their purpose to appeal to our understanding, and actuate our humanity? And do they expect to accomplish that purpose by holding us up to the scorn and contempt and detestation of the people of the Free States and the whole civilized world? . . . Union on the one side will beget union on the other. . . . One section will stand in menacing, hostile array against another; the collision of opinion will be quickly followed by the clash of arms."

Mr. Everett, then (1836) Governor of Massachusetts, informed the Legislature, for the admonition of these unsparing agitators against the peace of the South, that "every thing that tends to disturb the relations created by this compact [the Constitution] is at war with its spirit ; and whatever, by direct and necessary operation, is calculated to excite an insurrection among the slaves, has been held by highly respectable legal authority an offence against the peace of this Commonwealth, which may be prosecuted as a misdemeanor at common law." It was proposed in the Legislature to pass an act defining the offence with more certainty, and attaching to it a severer penalty. The Abolitionists asked to be heard before the committee ; and Rev. S. J. May, Ellis Gray Loring, Prof. Charles Follen, Samuel E. Sewell, and others of equal ability and character, spoke in their behalf. They objected to the passage of such an act in the strongest terms, and derided the value of a Union which could not protect its citizens in one of their most cherished rights. During the hearing, several bitter altercations took place between them and the chairman.

In New York, Gov. Marcy called upon the Legislature "to do what may be done consistently with the great principles of civil liberty, to put an end to the evils which the Abolitionists are bringing upon us and the whole country." The "character" and the "interests" of the State were equally at stake, and both would be sacrificed unless these furious and cruel fanatics were effectually suppressed.

In May, 1836, the Federal House of Representatives resolved, by overwhelming votes, that Congress had no right to interfere with slavery in the States, or in the District of Columbia, and that henceforth all abolition petitions should be laid on the table without being printed or referred. And, one day later than the date of Mr. Lincoln's protest, Mr. Van Buren declared in his inaugural, that no bill abolishing slavery in the District of Columbia, or meddling with it in the States where it existed, should ever receive his signature. "There was no other form," says Benton, "at that time, in which slavery agitation could manifest itself, or place it could find a point to operate; the ordinance of 1787 and the compromise of 1820 having closed up the Territories against it. Danger to slave property in the States, either by direct action, or indirectly through the District of Columbia, were the only points of expressed apprehension."

Abolition agitations fared little better in the twenty-fifth Congress than in the twenty-fourth. At the extra session in September of 1837, Mr. Slade of Vermont introduced two petitions for the abolition of slavery in the District of Columbia; but, after a furious debate and a stormy scene, they were disposed of by the adoption of the following: —

"*Resolved*, That all petitions, memorials, and papers, touching the abolition of slavery, or the buying, selling, or transferring of slaves, in any State, District, or Territory, of the United States, be laid on the table, without being debated, printed, read, or referred; and that no further action whatever shall be had thereon."

In Illinois, at the time we speak of (March, 1837), an Abolitionist was rarely seen, and scarcely ever heard of. In many parts of the State such a person would have been treated as a criminal. It is true, there were a few Covenanters, with whom hatred of slavery in any form and wherever found was an essential part of their religion. Up to 1824 they had steadily refused to vote, or in any other way to acknowledge the State government, regarding it as " an heathen and unbaptized institution," because the Constitution failed to recognize " Jesus Christ as the head of the government, and the Holy Scriptures as the only rule of faith and practice." It was

only when it was proposed to introduce slavery into Illinois
by an alteration of that "heathen" Constitution, that the
Covenanters consented to take part in public affairs.   The
movement which drew them out proved to be a long and
unusually bitter campaign, lasting full eighteen months, and
ending in the fall of 1824, with a popular majority of several
thousand against calling a convention for the purpose of
making Illinois a Slave State.   Many of the antislavery leaders
in *this* contest — conspicuous among whom was Gov. Coles —
were gentlemen from Slave States, who had emancipated their
slaves before removal, and were opposed to slavery, not upon
religious or moral grounds, but because they believed it would
be a material injury to the new country.   Practically no other
view of the question was discussed; and a person who should
have undertaken to discuss it from the "man and brother"
stand-point of more modern times would have been set down
as a lunatic.   A clear majority of the people were against
the introduction of slavery into their own State; but that
majority were fully agreed with their brethren of the minority,
that those who went about to interfere with slavery in the
most distant manner in the places where it already existed
were deserving of the severest punishment, as the common
enemies of society.   It was in those days a mortal offence to
call a man an Abolitionist, for Abolitionist was synonymous
with thief.   Between a band of men who stole horses and a
band of men who stole negroes, the popular mind made small
distinctions in the degrees of guilt.   They were regarded as
robbers, disturbers of the peace, the instigators of arson, murder, poisoning, rape; and, in addition to all this, traitors to the
government under which they lived, and enemies to the Union
which gave us as a people liberty and strength.   In testimony
of these sentiments, Illinois enacted a "black code" of most
preposterous and cruel severity, — a code that would have
been a disgrace to a Slave State, and was simply an infamy
in a free one.   It borrowed the provisions of the most revolt-
ing laws known among men, for exiling, selling, beating, bedevilling, and torturing negroes, whether bond or free.   Under

this law Gov. Coles, the leader of the antislavery party, who had emancipated his slaves, and settled them around him in his new home, but had neglected to file a bond with the condition that his freedmen should behave well and never become a charge upon the public, was fined two hundred dollars in each case; and, so late as 1852, the writer of these pages very narrowly escaped the same penalty for the same offence.

In 1835–36 Rev. Elijah P. Lovejoy had been publishing a moderately antislavery paper at St. Louis. But the people of that city did not look with favor upon his enterprise; and, after meeting with considerable opposition, in the summer of 1836 he moved his types and press across the river to Alton, Ill. Here he found an opposition more violent than that from which he had fled. His press was thrown into the river the night after its arrival; and he was informed that no abolition paper would be allowed in the town. The better class of citizens, however, deprecated the outrage, and pledged themselves to reimburse Mr. Lovejoy, in case he would agree not to make his paper an abolition journal. Mr. Lovejoy assured them it was not his purpose to establish such a paper in Alton, but one of a religious character: at the same time he would not give up his right as an American citizen to publish whatever he pleased on any subject, holding himself answerable to the laws of his country in so doing. With this general understanding, he was permitted to go forward. He continued about a year, discussing in his paper the slavery question occasionally; not, however, in a violent manner, but with a tone of moderation. This policy, however, was not satisfactory: it was regarded as a violation of his pledge; and the contents of his office were again destroyed. Mr. Lovejoy issued an appeal for aid to re-establish his paper, which met with a prompt and generous response. He proposed to bring up another press, and announced that armed men would protect it: meantime, a committee presented him with some resolutions adopted at a large meeting of the citizens of Alton, reminding him that he had previously given a pledge that in his paper he would refrain from advocating abolitionism, and also censuring him for not having kept his promise, and desiring to know if he intended to continue the publication of such doctrines in the future. His response consisted of a denial of the right of any portion of the people of Acton to prescribe what questions he should or should not discuss in his paper. Great excitement followed: another press was brought up on the 21st of September, which shortly after followed the fate of its predecessors. Another arrived Nov. 7, 1837, and was conveyed to a stone warehouse by the riverside, where Mr. Lovejoy and a few friends (some of them not Abolitionists) resolved to defend it to the last. That night they were attacked. First there was a brief parley, then a volley of stones, then an attempt to carry the building by assault. At this juncture a shot was fired out of a second-story window, which killed a young man in the crowd. It was said to have been fired by Lovejoy; and, as the corpse was borne away, the wrath of the populace knew no bounds. It was proposed to get powder from the magazine, and blow the warehouse up. Others thought the torch would be a better agent; and, finally, a man ran up a ladder to fire the roof. Lovejoy came out of the door, and, firing one shot, retreated within, where he rallied the garrison for a sortie. In the mean time many shots were fired both by the assailants and the assailed. The house was once actually set on fire by one person from the mob, and saved by another. But the courage of Mr. Lovejoy's friends was gradually sinking, and they responded but faintly to his strong appeals for action. As a last resource, he rushed to the door with a single companion, gun in hand, and was shot dead on the threshold. The other man was wounded in the leg, the warehouse was in flames, the mob grew more ferocious over the blood that had been shed, and riddled the doors and windows with volleys from all sorts of fire-arms. The Abolitionists had fought a good fight; but seeing now nothing but death before them, in that dismal, bloody, and burning house, they escaped down the river-bank, by twos and threes, as best they could, and their press was tumbled after them, into the river. And thus ended the first attempt to establish an abolition paper in Illinois. The result was certainly any thing but encouraging, and indicated pretty clearly what must have been the general state of public feeling throughout the State in regard to slavery agitation.

In fact, no State was more alive to the necessity of repressing the Abolitionists than Illinois; and accordingly it was proposed in the Legislature to take some action similar to that which had been already taken, or was actually pending, in the legislatures of sister Commonwealths, from Massachusetts through the list. A number of resolutions were reported, and passed with no serious opposition. The record does not disclose the precise form in which they passed; but that is of little consequence now. That they were extreme enough may be gathered from the considerate language of the protest, and from the fact that *such a protest* was considered necessary at all. The protest was undoubtedly the product of Mr. Lincoln's pen, for his adroit directness is seen in every word of it. He could get but one man — his colleague, Dan Stone — to sign with him.

MARCH 3, 1837.

The following protest was presented to the House, which was read, and ordered to be spread on the journals, to wit: —

Resolutions upon the subject of domestic slavery having passed both branches of the General Assembly at its present session, the undersigned hereby protest against the passage of the same.

They believe that the institution of slavery is founded on both injustice and bad policy; but that the promulgation of abolition doctrines tends rather to increase than abate its evils.

They believe that the Congress of the United States has no power, under the Constitution, to interfere with the institution of slavery in the different States.

They believe that the Congress of the United States has the power, under the Constitution, to abolish slavery in the District of Columbia, but that the power ought not to be exercised, unless at the request of the people of the District.

The difference between these opinions and those contained in the said resolutions is their reason for entering this protest.

(Signed)				DAN STONE,
					A. LINCOLN,
			Representatives from the County of Sangamon.

Mr. Lincoln says nothing here about slavery in the Territories. The Missouri Compromise being in full force, and regarded as sacred by all parties, it was one of its chief effects that both sections were deprived of any pretext for the agitation of that question, from which every statesman, Federalist or Republican, Whig or Democratic, apprehended certain disaster to the Union. Neither would Mr. Lincoln suffer himself to be classed with the few despised Quakers, Covenanters, and Puritans, who were so frequently disturbing the peace of the country by abolition-memorials to Congress and other public bodies. Slavery, says the protest, is wrong in principle, besides being bad in economy; but "the promulgation of abolition doctrines" is still worse. In the States which choose to have it, it enjoys a constitutional immunity beyond the reach of any " higher law ; " and Congress must not touch it, otherwise than to shield and protect it. Even in the District of Columbia, Mr. Lincoln and Dan Stone would leave it entirely to the will of the people. In fact, the whole paper, plain and simple as it is, seems to have been drawn with no object but to avoid the imputation of extreme views on either side. And from that day to the day of his inauguration, Mr. Lincoln never saw the time when he would have altered a word of it. He never sided with the Lovejoys. In his eyes their work tended "rather to increase than to abate" the evils of slavery, and was therefore unjust, as well as futile. Years afterwards he was the steady though quiet opponent of Owen Lovejoy, and declared that Lovejoy's nomination for Congress over Leonard Swett "almost turned him blind." When, in 1860, the Democrats called Mr. Lincoln an Abolitionist, and cited the protest of 1837 to support the charge, friends pointed to the exact language of the document as his complete and overwhelming refutation.

On the 10th of May, the New York banks suspended specie payments, and two days afterwards the Bank of the United States and the Philadelphia banks did likewise. From these the stoppage and the general ruin, among business men and speculators alike, spread throughout the country. Nevertheless, the Fund Commissioners of Illinois succeeded in placing a loan during the summer, and before the end of the year work had begun on many railroads. " Money was as plenty as dirt. Industry, in place of being stimulated, actually languished. We exported nothing, and every thing was paid for by the borrowed money expended among us." And this money was bank-paper, such as a pensioner upon the Government of the United States scorned to take in payment of his gratuity, after the deposit banks had suspended or broken, with thirty-two millions of Government money· in their possession.

The banks which had received such generous legislation from the Legislature that devised the internal-improvement system were not disposed to see that batch of remarkable enterprises languish for want of their support. One of them took at par and sold nine hundred thousand dollars of bonds ; while the other took one million seven hundred and sixty-five thousand dollars, which it used as capital, and expanded its business accordingly. But the banks were themselves in greater danger than the internal-improvement system. If the State Bank refused specie payments for sixty days, its charter was forfeited under the Act of Assembly. But they were the main-stay of all the current speculations, public and private ; and having besides large sums of public money in their hands, the governor was induced to call a special session of the Legislature in July, 1837, to save them from impending dissolution. This was done by an act authorizing or condoning the suspension of specie payments. The governor had not directly recommended this, but he had most earnestly recommended the repeal or modification of the internal-improvement system ; and *that* the Legislature positively refused. This wise body might be eaten by its own dogs, but it was determined not to eat *them ;* and in this direction there was no prospect of relief for two years more. According to Gov. Ford, the cool, reflecting men of the State anxiously hoped that their rulers might be able to borrow no more money, but in this they were immediately and bitterly disappointed. The United

States Bank took some of their bonds. Some were sold at par in this country, and others at nine per cent discount in Europe.

In 1838, a governor (Carlin) was elected who was thought by many to be secretly hostile to the "system;" and a new Legislature was chosen, from which it was thought something might be hoped. Mr. Lincoln was again elected, with a reputation so much enhanced by his activity and address in the last Legislature, that this time he was the candidate of his party for speaker. The nomination, however, was a barren honor, and known to be such when given. Col. Ewing was chosen by a plurality of one, — two Whigs and two Democrats scattering their votes. Mr. Lincoln kept his old place on the Finance Committee. At the first session the governor held his peace regarding the "system;" and, far from repealing it, the Legislature added a new feature to it, and voted another $800,000.

But the Fund Commissioners were in deep water and muddy water: they had reached the end of their string. The credit of the State was gone, and already were heard murmurs of repudiation. Bond County had in the beginning pronounced the system a swindle upon the people; and Bond County began to have admirers. Some of the bonds had been lent to New York State banks to start upon; and the banks had presently failed. Some had been sold on credit. Some were scattered about in various places on special deposit. Others had been sent to London for sale, where the firm that was selling them broke with the proceeds of a part of them in their hands. No expedients sufficed any longer. There was no more money to be got, and nothing left to do, but to "wind up the system," and begin the work of common sense by providing for the interest on the sums already expended. A special session of the Legislature in 1838–9 did the "winding up," and thenceforth, for some years, there was no other question so important in Illinois State politics as how to pay the interest on the vast debt outstanding for this account. Many gentlemen discovered that De Witt Clintons were rare.

and in certain contingencies very precious. Among these must have been Mr. Lincoln. But being again elected to the Legislature in 1840, again the acknowledged leader and candidate of his party for speaker, he ventured in December of that year to offer an expedient for paying the interest on the debt; but it was only an expedient, and a very poor one, to avoid the obvious but unpopular resort of direct taxation.

"Mr. Lincoln moved to strike out the bill and amendment, and insert the following : —

"An Act providing for the payment of interest on the State debt.

"SECTION 1. — Be it enacted by the people of the State of Illinois represented in the General Assembly, that the governor be authorized and required to issue, from time to time, such an amount of State bonds, to be called the 'Illinois Interest Bonds,' as may be absolutely necessary for the payment of the interest upon the lawful debt of the State, contracted before the passage of this Act.

"SECTION 2. — Said bonds shall bear interest at the rate of   per cent per annum, payable half-yearly at   , and be re-imbursable in   years from their respective issuings.

"SECTION 3. — That the State's portion of the tax hereafter arising from all lands which were not taxable in the year one thousand eight hundred and forty is hereby set apart as an exclusive fund for the payment of interest on the said 'Illinois Interest Bonds;' and the faith of the State is hereby pledged that said fund shall be applied to that object, and no other, except at any time there should be a surplus; in which case such surplus shall became a part of the general funds of the treasury.

"SECTION 4. — That hereafter the sum of thirty cents for each hundred dollars' worth of all taxable property shall be paid into the State treasury; and no more than forty cents for each hundred dollars' worth of such taxable property shall be levied and collected for county purposes."

It was a loose document. The governor was to determine the "amount" of bonds "necessary," and the sums for which they should be issued. Interest was to be paid only upon the "lawful" debt; and the governor was left to determine what part of it *was* lawful, and what unlawful. The last section lays a specific tax; but the proceeds are in no way connected with the "interest bonds."

"Mr. Lincoln said he submitted this proposition with great diffidence. He had felt his share of the responsibility devolving upon us in the present crisis; and, after revolving in his mind every scheme which seemed to afford the least prospect of relief, he submitted this as the result of his own deliberations.

"The details of the bill might be imperfect; but he relied upon the correctness of its general features.

"By the plan proposed in the original bill of hypothecating our bonds, he was satisfied we could not get along more than two or three months before some other step would be necessary: another session would have to be called, and new provisions made.

"It might be objected that these bonds would not be salable, and the money could not be raised in time. He was no financier; but he believed these bonds thus secured would be equal to the best in market. A perfect security was provided for the interest; and it was this characteristic that inspired confidence, and made bonds salable. If there was any distrust, it could not be because our means of fulfilling promises were distrusted. He believed it would have the effect to raise our other bonds in market.

"There was another objection to this plan, which applied to the original bill; and that was as to the impropriety of borrowing money to pay interest on borrowed money, — that we are hereby paying compound interest. To this he would reply, that, if it were a fact that our population and wealth were increasing in a ratio greater than the increased interest hereby incurred, then this was not a good objection. If our increasing means would justify us in deferring to a future time the resort to taxation, then we had better pay compound interest than resort to taxation now. He was satisfied, that, by a direct tax now, money enough could not be collected to pay the accruing interest. The bill proposed to provide in this way for interest not otherwise provided for. It was not intended to apply to those bonds for the interest on which a security had already been provided.

"He hoped the House would seriously consider the proposition. He had no pride in its success as a measure of his own, but submitted it to the wisdom of the House, with the hope, that, if there was any thing objectionable in it, it would be pointed out and amended."

Mr. Lincoln's measure did not pass. There was a large party in favor, not only of passing the interest on the State debt, which fell due in the coming January and July, but of repudiating the whole debt outright. Others thought the State ought to pay, not the full face of its bonds, but only the amount received for them; while others still contended that, whereas, many of the bonds had been irregularly, illegally, and even fraudulently disposed of, there ought to be a particular discrimination made against *these*, and these only. "At last Mr. Cavarly, a member from Green, introduced a bill of two sections, authorizing the Fund Commissioners to hypothecate internal-improvement bonds to the amount of three hundred thousand dollars, and which contained the remarkable provision, that the proceeds were to be applied by that officer to the payment of all interest *legally* due on the public debt; thus shifting from the General Assembly, and devolving on the Fund Commissioner, the duty of deciding on the legality of the debt. Thus, by this happy expedient, conflicting opinions were reconciled without direct action on the matter in controversy, and thus the two Houses were enabled to agree upon a measure to provide temporarily for the interest on the public debt. The Legislature further provided, at this session, for the issue of interest bonds, to be sold in the market at what they would bring; and an additional tax of ten cents on the hundred dollars' worth of property was imposed and pledged, to pay the interest on these bonds. By these contrivances, the interest

for January and July, 1841, was paid.   The Fund Commissioner hypothecated internal-improvement bonds for the
money first due; and his successor in office, finding no sale
for Illinois stocks, so much had the credit of the State
fallen, was compelled to hypothecate eight hundred and four
thousand dollars of interest bonds for the July interest.   On
this hypothecation he was to have received three hundred
and twenty-one thousand six hundred dollars, but was never
paid more than two hundred and sixty-one thousand five
hundred dollars.   These bonds have never been redeemed
from the holders, though eighty of them were afterwards
repurchased, and three hundred and fifteen thousand dollars
of them were received from the Shawneetown Bank for State
stock in that institution." [1]

This session (the session of 1840–1) had been called two
weeks earlier than usual, to provide for the January interest
on the debt.   But the banks had important business of their
own in view, and proceeded to improve the occasion.   In
1837, and every year since then, the banks had succeeded in
getting acts of the Legislature which condoned their suspension of specie payments.   But, by the terms of the last act,
their charters were forfeited unless they resumed before the
adjournment of the next session.   The Democrats, however,
maintained that the present special session was *a session* in
the sense of the law, and that, before its adjournment, the
banks must hand out " the hard," or die.   On the other hand,
the Whigs held this session, and the regular session which
began on the first Monday in December, to be one and the
same, and proposed to give the banks another winter's lease
upon life and rags.   But the banks were a power in the
land, and knew how to make themselves felt.   They were the
depositories of the State revenues.   The auditor's warrants
were drawn upon them, and the members of the Legislature
paid in their money.   The warrants were at a discount of fifty
per cent; and, if the banks refused to cash them, the members
would be compelled to go home more impecunious than they

[1] Ford's History of Illinois.

came. The banks, moreover, knew how to make "opportune loans to Democrats;" and, with all these aids, they organized a brilliant and eventually a successful campaign. In the eyes of the Whigs they were "the institutions of the country," and the Democrats were guilty of incivism in attacking them. But the Democrats retorted with a string of overwhelming slang about rag barons, rags, printed lies, bank vassals, ragocracy, and the "British-bought, bank, blue-light, Federal, Whig party." It was a fierce and bitter contest; and, witnessing it, one might have supposed that the very existence of the State, with the right to life, liberty, and the pursuit of happiness, depended upon the result. The Democrats were bent upon carrying an adjournment *sine die;* which, according to their theory, killed the banks. To defeat this, the Whigs resorted to every expedient of parliamentary tactics, and at length hit upon one entirely unknown to any of the standard manuals: they tried to absent themselves in sufficient numbers to leave no quorum behind. "If the Whigs absented themselves," says Mr. Gillespie, a Whig member, "there would not be a quorum left, even with the two who should be deputed to call the ayes and noes. The Whigs immediately held a meeting, and resolved that they would all stay out, except Lincoln and me, who were to call the ayes and noes. We appeared in the afternoon: motion to adjourn *sine die* was made, and we called the ayes and noes. The Democrats discovered the game, and the sergeant-at-arms was sent out to gather up the absentees. There was great excitement in the House, which was then held in a church at Springfield. We soon discovered that several Whigs had been caught and brought in, and that the plan had been spoiled; and we — Lincoln and I — determined to leave the hall, and, going to the door, found it locked, and then raised a window and jumped out, but not until the Democrats had succeeded in adjourning. Mr. Gridley of McLean accompanied us in our exit. . . . I think Mr. Lincoln always regretted that he entered into that arrangement, as he deprecated every thing that savored of the revolutionary."

In the course of the debate on the Apportionment Bill, Mr. Lincoln had occasion to address the House in defence of "The Long Nine," who were especially obnoxious to the Democrats. The speech concluded with the following characteristic passage : —

"The gentleman had accused old women of being partial to the number nine ; but this, he presumed, was without foundation. A few years since, it would be recollected by the House, that the delegation from this county were dubbed by way of eminence 'The Long Nine,' and, by way of further distinction, he had been called 'The Longest of the Nine.' Now," said Mr. Lincoln, "I desire to say to my friend from Monroe (Mr. Bissell), that if any woman, old or young, ever thought there was any peculiar charm in this distinguished specimen of number nine, I have as yet been so unfortunate as not to have discovered it." (Loud applause.)

But this Legislature was full of excitements. Besides the questions about the public debt and the bank-charters, the Democrats proposed to legislate the Circuit judges out of office, and reconstruct the Supreme Court to suit themselves. They did this because the Supreme judges had already decided one question of some political interest against them, and were now about to decide another in the same way. The latter was a question of great importance ; and, in order to avoid the consequences of such a decision, the Democrats were eager for the extremest measures.

The Constitution provided that all free white male *inhabitants* should vote upon six months' residence. This, the Democrats held, included aliens ; while the Whigs held the reverse. On this grave judicial question, parties were divided precisely upon the line of their respective interests. The aliens numbered about ten thousand, and nine-tenths of them voted steadily with the Democracy. Whilst a great outcry concerning it was being made from both sides, and fierce disputes raged in the newspapers and on the stump, two Whigs at Galena got up an amicable case, to try it in a quiet way before a Whig judge, who held the Circuit Courts in their neighborhood. The judge decided for his friends, like a man that he was. The Democrats found it out, and raised a popular tumult about it that would have put Demetrius the silversmith to shame. They carried the case to the Supreme Court, where it was argued before the Whig majority, in December, 1839, by able and distinguished counsellors, — Judge Douglas being one of them; but the only result was a continuance to the next June. In the mean time Judge Smith, the only Democrat on the bench, was seeking favor with his party friends by betraying to Douglas the secrets of the consultation-room. With his aid, the Democrats found a defect in the record, which sent the case over to December, 1840, and adroitly secured the alien vote for the great elections of that memorable year. The Legislature elected then was overwhelmingly Democratic; and, having good reason to believe that the aliens had small favor to expect from this court, they determined forthwith to make a new one that would be more reasonable. There were now nine Circuit judges in the State, and four Supreme judges, under the Act of 1835. The offices of the Circuit judges the Democrats concluded to abolish, and to create instead nine Supreme judges, who should perform circuit duties. This they called "reforming the judiciary;" and "thirsting for vengeance," as Gov. Ford says, they went about the work with all the zeal, but with very little of the disinterested devotion, which reformers are generally supposed to have. Douglas, counsel for one of the litigants, made a furious speech "in the lobby," demanding the destruction of the court that was to try his cause; and for sundry grave sins which he imputed to the judges he gave Smith — his friend Smith — as authority. It was useless to oppose it: this "reform" was a foregone conclusion. It was called the "Douglas Bill;" and Mr. Douglas was appointed to one of the new offices created by it. But Mr. Lincoln, E. D. Baker, and other Whig members, entered upon the journal the following protest: —

"For the reasons thus presented, and for others no less apparent, the undersigned cannot assent to the passage of the bill, or permit it to become a law without this evidence of their disapprobation; and they now protest against the re-organization of the judiciary: Because

"1st. It violates the great principles of free government by subjecting the judiciary to the Legislature.

"2d. It is a fatal blow at the independence of the judges and the constitutional term of their offices.

"3d. It is a measure not asked for, or wished for, by the people.

"4th. It will greatly increase the expense of our courts, or else greatly diminish their utility.

"5th. It will give our courts a political and partisan character, thereby impairing public confidence in their decisions.

"6th. It will impair our standing with other States and the world.

"7th. It is a party measure for party purposes, from which no practical good to the people can possibly arise, but which may be the source of immeasurable evils.

"The undersigned are well aware that this protest will be altogether unavailing with the majority of this body. The blow has already fallen ; and we are compelled to stand by, the mournful spectators of the ruin it will cause."

Mr. Lincoln was elected in 1840, to serve, of course, until the next election in August, 1842; but for reasons of a private nature, to be explained hereafter, he did not appear during the session of 1841-2.

In concluding this chapter, taking leave of New Salem, Vandalia, and the Legislature, we cannot forbear another quotation from Mr. Wilson, Lincoln's colleague from Sangamon, to whom we are already so largely in debt: —

"In 1838 many of the Long Nines were candidates for re-election to the Legislature. A question of the division of the county was one of the local issues. Mr. Lincoln and myself, among others, residing in the portion of the county sought to be organized into a new county, and opposing the division, it became necessary that I should make a special canvass through the north-west part of the county, then known as

Sand Ridge. I made the canvass; Mr. Lincoln accompanied me ; and, being personally well acquainted with every one, we called at nearly every house. At that time it was the universal custom to keep some whiskey in the house, for private use and to treat friends. The subject was always mentioned as a matter of etiquette, but with the remark to Mr. Lincoln, 'You never drink, but maybe your friend would like to take a little.' I never saw Mr. Lincoln drink. He often told me he never drank ; had no desire for drink, nor the companionship of drinking men. Candidates never treated anybody in those times unless they wanted to do so.

"Mr. Lincoln remained in New Salem until the spring of 1837, when he went to Springfield, and went into the law-office of John T. Stuart as a partner in the practice of law, and boarded with William Butler.

"During his stay in New Salem he had no property other than what was necessary to do his business, until after he stopped in Springfield. He was not avaricious to accumulate property, neither was he a spendthrift. He was almost always during those times hard up. He never owned land.

"The first trip he made around the circuit after he commenced the practice of law, I had a horse, saddle, and bridle, and he had none. I let him have mine. I think he must have been careless, as the saddle skinned the horse's back.

"While he lived in New Salem he visited me often. He would stay a day or two at a time : we generally spent the time at the stores in Athens. He was very fond of company : telling or hearing stories told was a source of great amusement to him. He was not in the habit of reading much, — never read novels. Whittling pine boards and shingles, talking and laughing, constituted the entertainment of the days and evenings.

"In a conversation with him about that time, he told me, that, although he appeared to enjoy life rapturously, still he was the victim of terrible melancholy. He sought company, and indulged in fun and hilarity without restraint, or stint as to time ; but when by himself, he told me that he was so overcome by mental depression that he never dared carry a knife in his pocket; and as long as I was intimately acquainted with him, previous to his commencement of the practice of the law, he never carried a pocket-knife. Still he was not misanthropic: he was kind and tender-hearted in his treatment to others.

" In the summer of 1837 the citizens of Athens and vicinity gave the delegation then called the 'Long Nine' a public dinner, at which Mr. Lincoln and all the others were present. He was called out by the toast, 'Abraham Lincoln, one of Nature's noblemen.' I have often thought, that, if any man was entitled to that compliment, it was he."

CHAPTER XI.

UNDER the Act of Assembly, due in great part to Mr. Lincoln's exertions, the removal of the archives and other public property of the State from Vandalia to Springfield began on the fourth day of July, 1839, and was speedily completed. At the time of the passage of the Act, in the winter of 1836–7, Mr. Lincoln determined to follow the capital, and establish his own residence at Springfield. The resolution was natural and necessary ; for he had been studying law in all his intervals of leisure, and wanted a wider field than the justice's court at New Salem to begin the practice. Henceforth Mr. Lincoln might serve in the Legislature, attend to his private business, and live snugly at home. In addition to the State courts, the Circuit and District Courts of the United States sat here. The eminent John McLean of Ohio was the justice of the Supreme Court who sat in this circuit, with Judge Pope of the District Court, from 1839 to 1849, and after that with Judge Drummond. The first terms of these courts, and the first session of the Legislature at Springfield, were held in December, 1839. The Senate sat in oné church, and the House in another.

Mr. Lincoln got his license as an attorney early in 1837, " and commenced practice regularly as a lawyer in the town of Springfield in March" of that year. His first case was that of Hawthorne *vs.* Wooldridge, dismissed at the cost of the plaintiff, for whom Mr. Lincoln's name was entered. There were then on the list of attorneys at the Springfield bar many names of subsequent renown. Judge Stephen T.

Logan was on the bench of the Circuit Court under the Act of 1835. Stephen A. Douglas had made his appearance as the public prosecutor at the March term of 1836; and at the same term E. D. Baker had been admitted to practice. Among the rest were John T. Stuart, Cyrus Walker, S. H. Treat, Jesse B. Thomas, George Forquer, Dan Stone, Ninian W. Edwards, John J. Hardin, Schuyler Strong, A. T. Bledsoe, and Josiah Lamborn.

By this time Mr. Lincoln enjoyed considerable local fame as a politician, but none, of course, as a lawyer. He therefore needed a partner, and got one in the person of John T. Stuart, an able and distinguished Whig, who had relieved his poverty years before by the timely loan of books with which to study law, and who had from the first promoted his political fortunes with zeal as disinterested as it was effective. The connection promised well for Mr. Lincoln, and no doubt did well during the short period of its existence. The court-room was in Hoffman's Row; and the office of Stuart & Lincoln was in the second story above the court-room. It was a "little room," and generally a "dirty one." It contained "a small dirty bed," — on which Lincoln lounged and slept, — a buffalo-robe, a chair, and a bench. Here the junior partner, when disengaged from the cares of politics and the Legislature, was to be found pretty much all the time, "reading, abstracted and gloomy." Springfield was a small village, containing between one and two thousand inhabitants. There were no pavements: the street-crossings were made of "chunks," stones, and sticks. Lincoln boarded with Hon. William Butler, a gentleman who possessed in an eminent degree that mysterious power which guides the deliberations of party conventions and legislative bodies to a foregone conclusion. Lincoln was very poor, worth nothing, and in debt, — circumstances which are not often alleged in behalf of the modern legislator; but "Bill Butler" was his friend, and took him in with little reference to board-bills and the settlement of accounts. According to Dr. Jayne, he "fed and clothed him for years;" and this signal service, rendered at a very critical time, Mr. Lincoln forgot wholly when he was in Congress, and Butler wanted to be Register of the Land Office, as well as when he was President of the United States, and opportunities of repayment were multitudinous. It is doubtless all true; but the inference of personal ingratitude on the part of Mr. Lincoln will not bear examination. It will be shown at another place that Mr. Lincoln regarded all public offices within his gift as a sacred trust, to be administered solely for the people, and as in no sense a fund upon which he could draw for the payment of private accounts. He *never* preferred his friends to his enemies, but rather the reverse, as if fearful that he might by bare possibility be influenced by some unworthy motive. He was singularly cautious to avoid the imputation of fidelity to his friends at the expense of his opponents.

In Coke's and Blackstone's time the law was supposed to be " a jealous mistress; " but in Lincoln's time, and at Springfield, she was any thing but exacting. Politicians courted her only to make her favor the stepping-stone to success in other employments. Various members of that bar have left great reputations to posterity, but none of them were earned solely by the legitimate practice of the law. Douglas is remembered as a statesman, Baker as a political orator, Hardin as a soldier, and some now living, like Logan and Stuart, although eminent in the law, will be no less known to the history of the times as politicians than as lawyers. Among those who went to the law for a living, and to the people for fame and power, was Mr. Lincoln. He was still a member of the Legislature when he settled at Springfield, and would probably have continued to run for a seat in that body as often as his time expired, but for the unfortunate results of the " internal-improvement system," the hopeless condition of the State finances, and a certain gloominess of mind, which arose from private misfortunes that befell him about the time of his retirement. We do not say positively that these were the reasons why Mr. Lincoln made no effort to be re-elected to the Legislature of 1840; but a careful study of all the circum-

stances will lead any reasonable man to believe that they
were.   He was intensely ambitious, longed ardently for place
and distinction, and never gave up a prospect which seemed
to him good when he was in a condition to pursue it with
honor to himself and fairness to others.   Moreover State politics were then rapidly ceasing to be the high-road to fame and
fortune.   Although the State of Illinois was insolvent, unable
to pay the interest on her public debt, and many were talking about repudiating the principal, the great campaign of
1840 went off upon national issues, and little or nothing was
said about questions of State policy.   Mr. Lincoln felt and
obeyed this tendency of the public mind, and from 1837
onward his speeches — those that were printed and those that
were not — were devoted chiefly, if not exclusively, to Federal
affairs.

In January, 1837, he delivered a lecture before the Springfield Lyceum on the subject of the "*Perpetuation of our Free
Institutions.*"   As a mere declamation, it is unsurpassed in
the annals of the West.   Although delivered in mid-winter,
it is instinct with the peculiar eloquence of the most fervid
Fourth of July.

"In the great journal of things," began the orator, "happening under the sun, we, the American People, find our
account running under date of the nineteenth century of the
Christian era.   We find ourselves in the peaceful possession of
the fairest portion of the earth, as regards extent of territory,
fertility of soil, and salubrity of climate.   We find ourselves
under the government of a system of political institutions
conducing more essentially to the ends of civil and religious
liberty than any of which the history of former times tells us.
We, when mounting the stage of existence, found ourselves
the legal inheritors of these fundamental blessings.   We toiled
not in the acquisition or establishment of them: they are a
legacy bequeathed us by a *once* hardy, brave, and patriotic,
but *now* lamented and departed race of ancestors.   Theirs was
the task (and nobly they performed it) to possess themselves,
and, through themselves, us, of this goodly land, and to uprear

upon its hills and valleys a political edifice of liberty and equal rights: 'tis ours only to transmit these — the former unprofaned by the foot of an invader, the latter undecayed by the lapse of time and untorn by usurpation — to the latest generation that fate shall permit the world to know. This task, gratitude to our fathers, justice to ourselves, duty to posterity, — all imperatively require us faithfully to perform.

" How, then, shall we perform it? At what point shall we expect the approach of danger? Shall we expect some transatlantic military giant to step the ocean and crush us at a blow? Never! All the armies of Europe, Asia, and Africa combined, with all the treasure of the earth (our own excepted) in their military chest, with a Bonaparte for a commander, could not, by force, take a drink from the Ohio, or make a track on the Blue Ridge, in a trial of a thousand years!

" At what point, then, is the approach of danger to be expected? I answer, if it ever reach us, it must spring up amongst us. It cannot come from abroad. If destruction be our lot, we must ourselves be its author and finisher. As a nation of freemen, we must live through all time, or die by suicide.

" I hope I am not over-wary; but, if I am not, there is even now something of ill-omen amongst us. I mean the increasing disregard for law which pervades the country, the growing disposition to substitute the wild and furious passions in lieu of the sober judgment of courts, and the worse than savage mobs for the executive ministers of justice. This disposition is awfully fearful in any community, and that it now exists in ours, though grating to our feelings to admit it, it would be a violation of truth and an insult to our intelligence to deny. Accounts of outrages committed by mobs form the every-day news of the times. They have pervaded the country from New England to Louisiana; they are neither peculiar to the eternal snows of the former, nor the burning sun of the latter. They are not the creature of climate; neither are they confined to the slaveholding or non-slaveholding States. Alike they spring up among the pleasure-hunting masters of Southern slaves and the order-loving citizens of the land of steady habits. Whatever, then, their cause may be, it is common to the whole country."

The orator then adverts to the doings of recent mobs in various parts of the country, and insists, that, if the spirit that produced them continues to increase, the laws and the government itself must fall before it: bad citizens will be encouraged, and good ones, having no protection against the lawless, will be glad to receive an individual master who will be able to give them the peace and order they desire. That will be the time when the usurper will put down his heel on the neck of the people, and batter down the " fair fabric " of free institutions. " Many great and good men," he says, " sufficiently qualified for any task they should undertake, may ever be found, whose ambition would aspire to nothing beyond a seat in Congress, a gubernatorial or a presidential chair; *but such belong not to the family of the lion or the tribe of the eagle.*[1] What! Think you these places would satisfy an Alexander, a Cæsar, or a Napoleon? Never! Towering genius disdains a beaten path. It seeks regions hitherto unexplored. It sees no distinction in adding story to story upon the monuments of fame erected to the memory of others. It *denies* that it is glory enough to serve under any chief. It *scorns* to tread in the footsteps of any predecessor, however illustrious. It thirsts and burns for distinction; and, if possible, it will have it, whether at the expense of emancipating slaves or enslaving freemen. . . . Another reason which once *was*, but which, to the same extent, *is now no more*, has done much in maintaining our institutions thus far. I mean the powerful influence which the interesting scenes of the Revolution had upon the *passions* of the people as distinguished from their judgment." This influence, the lecturer maintains, was kept alive by the presence of the surviving soldiers of the Revolution, who were in some sort " living histories," and concludes with this striking peroration: —

" But those histories are gone. They *can* be read no more forever. They *were* a fortress of strength; but what invading

[1] The italics are the orator's.

foeman could never do, the silent artillery of time *has done*, — the levelling of its walls. They are gone. They *were* a forest of giant oaks; but the all-resistless hurricane has swept over them, and left only here and there a lonely trunk, despoiled of its verdure, shorn of its foliage, unshading and unshaded, to murmur in a few more gentle breezes, and to combat with its mutilated limbs a few more rude storms, then to sink and be no more. They *were* the pillars of the temple of liberty; and now that they have crumbled away, that temple must fall, unless we, the descendants, supply their places with other pillars hewn from the same solid quarry of sober reason. Passion has helped us, but can do so no more. It will in future be our enemy. Reason — cold, calculating, unimpassioned reason — must furnish all the materials for our future support and defence. Let those materials be moulded into *general intelligence, sound morality*, and, in particular, *a reverence for the Constitution and the laws;* and that we improved to the last, that we revered his name to the last, that during his long sleep we permitted no hostile foot to pass or desecrate his resting-place, shall be that which to learn the last trump shall awaken our WASHINGTON. Upon these let the proud fabric of freedom rest as the rock of its basis, and as truly as has been said of the only greater institution, ' The gates of hell shall not prevail against it.' "

These extracts from a lecture carefully composed by Mr. Lincoln at the mature age of twenty-eight, and after considerable experience in the public service, are worthy of attentive perusal. To those familiar with his sober and pure style at a later age, these sophomoric passages will seem incredible. But they were thought "able and eloquent" by the " Young Men's Lyceum" of Springfield: he was "solicited to furnish a copy for publication," and they were duly printed in " The Sangamon Journal." In the mere matter of rhetoric, they compare favorably with some of his other productions of nearly the same date. This was what he would have called his "growing time; " and it is intensely interesting to witness the processes of such mental growth as his. In time.

gradually, but still rapidly, his style changes completely: the constrained and unnatural attempts at striking and lofty metaphor disappear, and the qualities which produced the Gettysburg address — that model of unadorned eloquence — begin to be felt. He finds the people understand him better when he comes down from his stilts, and talks to them from their own level.

Political discussions at Springfield were apt to run into heated and sometimes unseemly personal controversies. When Douglas and Stuart were candidates for Congress in 1838, they fought like tigers in Herndon's grocery, over a floor that was drenched with slops, and gave up the struggle only when both were exhausted. Then, as a further entertainment to the populace, Mr. Stuart ordered out a " barrel of whiskey and wine."

On the election-day in 1840, it was reported to Mr. Lincoln that one Radford, a contractor on the railroad, had brought up his men, and taken full possession of one of the polling-places. Lincoln started off to the precinct on a slow trot. Radford knew him well, and a little stern advice reversed proceedings without any fighting. Among other remarks, Lincoln said, " Radford, you'll spoil and blow if you live much longer." He wanted to hit Radford, but could get no chance to do so, and contented himself with confiding his intentions to Speed. " I intended just to knock him down, and leave him kicking."

The same year, Col. Baker was making a speech to a promiscuous audience in the court-room, — " a rented room in Hoffman's Row." It will be remembered that Lincoln's office was just above, and he was listening to Baker through a large hole or trap-door in the ceiling. Baker warmed with his theme, and, growing violent and personally offensive, declared at length, " that wherever there was a land-office, there was a Democratic newspaper to defend its corruptions." " This," says John B. Webber, " was a personal attack on my brother, George Webber. I was in the Court House, and in my anger cried, ' Pull him down!' " A scene of great confusion ensued, threatening to end in a general riot, in which Baker was likely to suffer. But just at the critical moment Lincoln's legs were seen coming through the hole; and directly his tall figure was standing between Baker and the audience, gesticulating for silence. "Gentlemen," said he, "let us not disgrace the age and country in which we live. This is a land where freedom of speech is guaranteed. Mr Baker has a right to speak, and ought to be permitted to do so. I am here to protect him, and no man shall take him from this stand if I can prevent it." Webber only recollects that "some one made some soothing, kind remarks," and that he was properly "held until the excitement ceased," and the affair "soon ended in quiet and peace."

In 1838, or 1840, Jesse B. Thomas made an intemperate attack upon the "Long Nine," and especially upon Mr. Lincoln, as the longest and worst of them. Lincoln was not present at the meeting; but being sent for, and informed of what had passed, he ascended the platform, and made a reply which nobody seems to remember, but which everybody describes as a "terrible skinning" of his victim. Ellis says, that, at the close of a furious personal denunciation, he wound up by "mimicking" Thomas, until Thomas actually cried with vexation and anger. Edwards, Speed, Ellis, Davis, and many others, refer to this scene, and, being asked whether Mr. Lincoln could not be vindictive upon occasion, generally respond, "Remember the Thomas skinning."

The most intimate friend Mr. Lincoln ever had, at this or any other time, was probably Joshua F. Speed. In 1836 he settled himself in Springfield, and did a thriving business as a merchant. Ellis was one of his clerks, and so also was William H. Herndon, Mr. Lincoln's future partner. This store was for years Lincoln's familiar haunt. There he came to while away the tedious evenings with Speed and the congenial company that naturally assembled around these choice spirits. He even slept in the store room as often as he slept at home, and here made to Speed the most confidential communications he ever made to mortal man. If he had on

earth "a bosom crony," it was Speed, and that deep and
abiding attachment subsisted unimpaired to the day of Mr.
Lincoln's death.   In truth, there were good reasons why he
should think of Speed with affection and gratitude, for
through life no man rendered him more important services.

One night in December, 1839, Lincoln, Douglas, Baker, and
some other gentlemen of note, were seated at Speed's hospitable fire in the store. " They got to talking politics, got warm,
hot, angry.   Douglas sprang up and said, "Gentlemen, this is
no place to talk politics : we will discuss the questions publicly
with you," and much more in a high tone of banter and defiance.   A few days afterwards the Whigs had a meeting, at
which Mr. Lincoln reported a resolution challenging the Democrats to a joint debate.   The challenge was accepted ; and
Douglas, Calhoun, Lamborn, and Jesse B. Thomas were deputed by the Democrats to meet Logan, Baker, Browning,
and Lincoln on the part of the Whigs.   The intellectual
encounter between these noted champions is still described by
those who witnessed it as " the great debate." It took place
in the Second Presbyterian Church, in the hearing of as many
people as could get into the building, and was adjourned from
night to night.   When Mr. Lincoln's turn came, the audience
was very thin ; but, for all that, his speech was by many persons considered the best one of the series.   To this day, there
are some who believe he had assistance in the preparation of
it.   Even Mr. Herndon accused Speed of having " had a hand
in it," and got a flat denial for his answer.   At all events, the
speech was a popular success, and was written out, and published in " The Sangamon Journal," of March 6, 1840.   The
exordium was a sort of complaint that must have had a very
depressing effect upon both the speaker and his hearers : —

" *Fellow-Citizens,* — It is peculiarly embarrassing to me to
attempt a continuance of the discussion, on this evening, which
has been conducted in this hall on several preceding ones.
It is so, because on each of these evenings there was a much
fuller attendance than now, without any reason for its being

so, except the greater interest the community feel in the speakers who addressed them then, than they do in him who is to do so now. I am, indeed, apprehensive that the few who have attended have done so more to spare me of mortification, than in the hope of being interested in any thing I may be able to say. This circumstance casts a damp upon my spirits which I am sure I shall be unable to overcome during the evening.

"The subject heretofore and now to be discussed is the Sub-Treasury scheme of the present administration, as a means of collecting, safe-keeping, transferring, and disbursing the revenues of the nation, as contrasted with a National Bank for the same purposes. Mr. Douglas has said that we (the Whigs) have not dared to meet them (the Locos) in argument on this question. I protest against this assertion. I say we have again and again, during this discussion, urged facts and arguments against the Sub-Treasury which they have neither dared to deny nor attempted to answer. But lest some may be led to believe that we really wish to avoid the question, I now propose, in my humble way, to urge these arguments again; at the same time begging the audience to mark well the positions I shall take, and the proofs I shall offer to sustain them, and that they will not again allow Mr. Douglas or his friends to escape the force of them by a round and groundless assertion that we dare not meet them in argument.

"Of the Sub-Treasury, then, as contrasted with a National Bank, for the before-enumerated purposes, I lay down the following propositions, to wit: —

"1st. It will injuriously affect the community by its operation on the circulating medium.

"2d. It will be a more expensive fiscal agent.

"3d. It will be a less secure depository for the public money."

Mr. Lincoln's objections to the Sub-Treasury were those commonly urged by its enemies, and have been somewhat conclusively refuted by the operation of that admirable institution from the hour of its adoption to the present. " The extravagant expenditures" of Mr. Van Buren's administration, however, was a standard topic of the Whigs in those days, and, sliding gracefully off from the Sub-Treasury, Mr. Lincoln dilated extensively upon this more attractive subject. This part of his speech was entirely in reply to Mr. Douglas. But, when he came to answer Mr. Lamborn's remarks, he "got in a hard hit" that must have brought down the house.

"Mr. Lamborn insists that the difference between the Van Buren party and the Whigs is, that, although the former sometimes err in practice, they are always correct in principle, whereas the latter are wrong in principle ; and, the better to impress this proposition, he uses a figurative expression in these words : ' The Democrats are vulnerable in the heel, but they are sound in the heart and head.' The first branch of the figure, — that is, that the Democrats are vulnerable in the heel, — I admit is not merely figuratively but literally true. Who that looks but for a moment at their Swartwouts, their Prices, their Harringtons, and their hundreds of others, scampering away with the public money to Texas, to Europe, and to every spot of the earth where a villain may hope to find refuge from justice, can at all doubt that they are most distressingly affected in their heels with a species of ' running itch.' It seems that this malady of their heels operates on the sound-headed and honest-hearted creatures very much like the cork-leg in the comic song did on its owner, which, when he had once got started on it, the more he tried to stop it, the more it would run away. At the hazard of wearing this point threadbare, I will relate an anecdote which seems to be too strikingly in point to be omitted. A witty Irish soldier who was always boasting of his bravery when no danger was near, but who invariably retreated without orders at the first charge of the engagement, being asked by his captain why he did so, replied, ' Captain, I have as brave a heart as Julius Cæsar ever had, but somehow or other, whenever danger approaches, my cowardly legs will run away with it.' So with Mr. Lamborn's party. They take the public money into their hands for the most laudable purpose that wise heads and honest hearts can dictate ; but, before they can possibly get it out again, their rascally vulnerable heels will run away with them."

But, as in the lecture before the Lyceum, Mr. Lincoln reserved his most impressive passage, his boldest imagery, and his most striking metaphor, for a grand and vehement peroration.

"Mr. Lamborn refers to the late elections in the States, and, from their results, confidently predicts every State in the Union will vote for Mr. Van Buren at the next presidential election. Address that argument to cowards and knaves: with the free and the brave it will affect nothing. It may be true: if it must, let it. Many free countries have lost their liberty, and ours may lose hers; but, if she shall, be it my proudest plume, not that I was the last to desert, but that I never deserted her. I know that the great volcano at Washington, aroused and directed by the evil spirit that reigns there, is belching forth the lava of political corruption in a current broad and deep, which is sweeping with frightful velocity over the whole length and breadth· of the land, bidding fair to leave unscathed no green spot or living thing; while on its bosom are riding, like demons on the wave of hell, the imps of that evil spirit, and fiendishly taunting all those who dare to resist its destroying course with the hopelessness of their efforts; and, knowing this, I cannot deny that all may be swept away. Broken by it, I, too, may be; bow to it, I never will. The probability that we may fall in the struggle ought not to deter us from the support of a cause we believe to be just. It shall not deter me. If ever I feel the soul within me elevate and expand to those dimensions, not wholly unworthy of its almighty Architect, it is when I contemplate the cause of my country, deserted by all the world beside, and I standing up boldly, alone, hurling defiance at her victorious oppressors. Here, without contemplating consequences, before Heaven and in face of the world, I swear eternal fealty to the just cause, as I deem it, of the land of my life, my liberty, and my love. And who that thinks with me will not fearlessly adopt that oath that I take? Let none falter who thinks he is right, and we may succeed. But if, after all, we shall fail, be it so : we still shall have the proud consolation of saying to our consciences, and to the departed shade of our country's freedom, that the cause approved of our judgment and adored of our hearts, in disaster, in chains, in torture, in death, we never faltered in defending."

Considering that the times were extremely peaceful, and that the speaker saw no bloodshed except what flowed from the noses of belligerents in the groceries about Springfield, the speech seems to have been unnecessarily defiant.

In 1840 Mr. Lincoln was a candidate for presidential elector on the Harrison ticket, and stumped a large part of the State. He and Douglas followed Judge Treat's court all around the circuit, "and spoke in the afternoons." The Harrison club at Springfield became thoroughly familiar with his voice. But these one-sided affairs were not altogether suited to his temper: through his life he preferred a joint discussion, and the abler the man pitted against him, the better he liked it. He knew he shone in retort, and sought every opportunity to practise it. From 1838 to 1858, he seems to have followed up Douglas as a regular business during times of great political excitement, and only on one or two occasions did he find the " Little Giant " averse to a conflict. Here, in 1840, they came in collision, as they did in 1839, and as they continued to do through twenty or more years, until Lincoln became President of the United States, and Douglas's disappointments were buried with his body. Once during this Harrison campaign they had a fierce discussion before a meeting assembled in the market-house. In the course of his speech, Lincoln imputed to Van Buren the great sin of having voted in the New York State Convention for negro suffrage with a property qualification. Douglas denied the fact; and Lincoln attempted to prove his statement by reading a certain passage from Holland's " Life of Van Buren," containing a letter from Van Buren to one Mr. Fithian. Whereupon " Douglas got mad," snatched up the book, and, tossing it into the crowd, remarked sententiously, although not conclusively, " Damn such a book ! "

" He was very sensitive," says Mr. Gillespie, " where he thought he had failed to come up to the expectations of his friends. I remember a case. He was pitted by the Whigs, in 1840, to debate with Mr. Douglas, the Democratic champion. Lincoln did not come up to the requirements of the occasion. He was conscious of his failure ; and I never saw any man so much distressed. He begged to be permitted to try it again, and was reluctantly indulged ; and in the next effort he transcended our highest expectations. I never heard, and never expect to hear, such a triumphant vindication as he then gave of Whig measures or policy. He never after, to my knowledge, fell below himself."

It must by this time be clear to the reader that Mr. Lincoln was never agitated by any passion more intense than his wonderful thirst for distinction. There is good evidence that it furnished the feverish dreams of his boyhood ; and no man that knew him well can doubt that it governed all his conduct, from the hour when he astonished himself by his oratorical success against Posey and Ewing, in the back settlements of Macon County, to the day when the assassin marked him as the first hero of the restored Union, re-elected to his great office, surrounded by every circumstance that could minister to his pride, or exalt his sensibilities, — a ruler whose power was only less wide than his renown. He never rested in the race he had determined to run; he was ever ready to be honored ; he struggled incessantly for place. There is no instance where an important office seemed to be within his reach, and he did not try to get it. Whatsoever he did in politics, at the bar, in private life, had more or less reference to this great object of his life. It is not meant to be said that he was capable of any shameful act, any personal dishonor, any surrender or concealment of political convictions. In these respects, he was far better than most men. It was not in his nature to run away from the fight, or to desert to the enemy ; but he was quite willing to accept his full share of the fruits of victory.

Born in the humblest circumstances, uneducated, poor,

acquainted with flatboats and groceries, but a stranger to the drawing-room, it was natural that he should seek in a matrimonial alliance those social advantages which he felt were necessary to his political advancement. This was, in fact, his own view of the matter; but it was strengthened and enforced by the counsels of those whom he regarded as friends.

In 1839 Miss Mary, daughter of Hon. Robert S. Todd of Lexington, Ky., came to live with her sister, Mrs. Ninian W. Edwards, at Springfield. Like Miss Owens, Miss Todd had a stepmother, with whom she failed to "agree," and for that reason the Edwardses offered her a home with them. She was young, — just twenty-one, — her family was of the best, and her connections in Illinois among the most refined and distinguished people. Her mother having died when she was a little girl, she had been educated under the care of a French lady, "opposite Mr. Clay's." She was gifted with rare talents, had a keen sense of the ridiculous, a ready insight into the weaknesses of individual character, and a most fiery and ungovernable temper. Her tongue and her pen were equally sharp. High-bred, proud, brilliant, witty, and with a will that bent every one else to her purpose, she took Mr. Lincoln captive the very moment she considered it expedient to do so.

Mr. Lincoln was a rising politician, fresh from the people, and possessed of great power among them: Miss Todd was of aristocratic and distinguished family, able to lead through the awful portals of "good society" whomsoever they chose to countenance. It was thought that a union between them could not fail of numerous benefits to both parties. Mr. Edwards thought so; Mrs. Edwards thought so; and it was not long before Mary Todd herself thought so. She was very ambitious, and even before she left Kentucky announced her belief that she was "destined to be the wife of some future President." For a little while she was courted by Douglas as well as by Lincoln; but she is said to have refused the "Little Giant," "on account of his bad morals." Being asked which of them she intended to have, she an-

MRS. MARY LINCOLN, WIFE OF THE PRESIDENT.

swered, " The one that has the best chance of being President." She decided in favor of Lincoln, and, in the opinion
of some of her husband's friends, aided to no small extent in
the fulfilment of the prophecy which the bestowal of her
hand implied. A friend of Miss Todd was the wife of an
elderly but wealthy gentleman ; and being asked by one of
the Edwards coterie why she had married " such an old,
dried-up husband, such a withered-up old buck," she answered that " He had lots of horses and gold." But Mary
Todd spoke up in great surprise, and said, " Is that true ? *I*
would rather marry a good man, a man of mind, with hope
and bright prospects ahead for position, fame, and power, than
to marry all the horses, gold, and bones in the world."

Mrs. Edwards, Miss Todd's sister, tells us that Mr. Lincoln " was charmed with Mary's wit and fascinated with her
quick sagacity, her will, her nature and culture." " I have
happened in the room," she says, " where they were sitting
often and often, and Mary led the conversation. Lincoln
would listen, and gaze on her as if drawn by some superior
power, — irresistibly so : he listened, but never scarcely said a
word. . . . Lincoln could not hold a lengthy conversation
with a lady, — was not sufficiently educated and intelligent
in the female line to do so."

Mr. Lincoln and Mary were engaged, and their marriage was
only a question of time. But Mr. Lincoln's love-affairs were
destined never to run smoothly, and now one Miss Matilda
Edwards made her " sweet appearance," and brought havoc
in her train. She was the sister of Ninian W. Edwards, and
came to spend a year with her brother. She was very fair,
and soon was the reigning belle. No sooner did Lincoln know
her than he felt his heart change. The other affair, according to the Edwardses, according to Stuart, according to Herndon, according to Lincoln and everybody else, was a " policy
match ;" but *this* was love. For a while he evidently tried
hard to go on as before, but his feelings were too strong to be
concealed. Mr. Edwards endeavored to reconcile matters by
getting his sister to marry Speed ; but the rebellious beauty

refused Speed incontinently (as she did Douglas too), and married Mr. Schuyler Strong. Poor Lincoln never whispered a word of his passion to her: his high sense of honor prevented that, and perhaps she would not have listened to him if it had been otherwise.

At length, after long reflection, in great agony of spirit, Mr. Lincoln concluded that duty required him to make a candid statement of his feelings to the lady who was entitled to his hand. He wrote her a letter, and told her gently but plainly that he did not love her. He asked Speed to deliver it; but Speed advised him to burn it. "Speed," said Mr. Lincoln, "I always knew you were an obstinate man. If you won't deliver it, I'll get some one else to do it." But Speed now had the letter in his hand; and, emboldened by the warm friendship that existed between them, replied, "I shall not deliver it, nor give it to you to be delivered. Words are forgotten, misunderstood, passed by, not noticed in a private conversation; but once put your words in writing, and they stand as a living and eternal monument against you. If you think you have *will* and manhood enough to go and see her, and speak to her what you say in that letter, you may do that." Lincoln went to see her forthwith, and reported to Speed. He said, that, when he made his somewhat startling communication, she rose and said, "'The deceiver shall be deceived: woe is me!' alluding to a young man she had fooled." Mary told him she knew the reason of his change of heart, and released him from his engagement. Some parting endearments took place between them, and then, as the natural result of those endearments, a reconciliation.

We quote again from Mrs. Edwards: —

"Lincoln and Mary were engaged; every thing was ready and prepared for the marriage, even to the supper. Mr. Lincoln failed to meet his engagement. Cause, insanity!

"In his lunacy he declared he hated Mary and loved Miss Edwards. This is true, yet it was not his real feelings. A crazy man hates those he loves when at himself. Often, often, is this the case. The world had it that Mr. Lincoln backed out, and this placed Mary in a peculiar situation ; and to set herself right, and free Mr. Lincoln's mind, she wrote a letter to Mr. Lincoln, stating that she would release him from his engagement. . . . The whole of the year was a crazy spell. Miss Edwards was at our house, say a year. I asked Miss Edwards if Mr. Lincoln ever mentioned the subject of his love to her. Miss Edwards said, ' On my word, he never mentioned such a subject to me : he never even stooped to pay me a compliment.' "

In the language of Mr. Edwards, " Lincoln went as crazy as a loon," and was taken to Kentucky by Speed, who kept him " until he recovered." He " did not attend the Legislature in 1841–2 for this reason."

Mr. Herndon devoutly believes that Mr. Lincoln's insanity grew out of a most extraordinary complication of feelings, — aversion to the marriage proposed, a counter-attachment to Miss Edwards, and a new access of unspeakable tenderness for the memory of Ann Rutledge, — the old love struggling with a new one, and each sending to his heart a sacrificial pang as he thought of his solemn engagement to marry a third person. In this opinion Mr. Speed appears to concur, as shown by his letter below. At all events, Mr. Lincoln's derangement was nearly, if not quite, complete. " We had to remove razors from his room," says Speed, " take away all knives, and other dangerous things. It was terrible." And now Speed determined to do for him what Bowlin Greene had done on a similar occasion at New Salem. Having sold out his store on the 1st of January, 1841, he took Mr. Lincoln with him to his home in Kentucky, and kept him there during most of the summer and fall, or until he seemed sufficiently restored to be given his liberty again at Springfield, when he was brought back to his old quarters. During this period, " he was at times very melancholy," and, by his own admission, " almost contemplated self-destruction." It was about this time that he wrote some gloomy lines under the head of " Suicide," which were published in " The Sangamon Journal." Mr. Herndon remembered something about them ; but, when he went to look for them in the office-file of the " Journal," he found them neatly cut out, — " supposed to have been done," says he, " by Lincoln." Speed's mother was much pained by the " deep depression " of her guest, and gave him a Bible, advising him to read it, to adopt its precepts, and pray for its promises. He acknowledged this attempted service, after he became President, by sending her a photograph of himself, with this inscription: " To my very good friend, Mrs. Lucy G. Speed, from whose pious hands I received an Oxford Bible twenty years ago." But Mrs. Speed's medicine, the best ever offered for a mind diseased, was of no avail in this case. Among other things, he told Speed, referring probably to his inclination to commit suicide, " that he had done nothing to make any human being remember that he had lived, and that to connect his name with the events transpiring in his day and generation, and so impress himself upon them as to link his name with something that would redound to the interest of his fellow-man, was what he desired to live for." Of this conversation he pointedly reminded Speed at the time, or just before the time, he issued the Emancipation Proclamation.

What took place after his return to Springfield cannot be better told than in the words of the friends of both parties. " Mr. Edwards and myself," says Mrs. Edwards, " after the first crash of things, told Mary and Lincoln that they had better not ever marry; that their natures, minds, education, raising, &c., were so different, that they could not live happy as man and wife; had better never think of the subject again. All at once we heard that Mr. Lincoln and Mary had secret meetings at Mr. S. Francis's, editor of ' The Springfield Journal.' Mary said the reason this was so, the cause why it was, was that the world, woman and man, were uncertain and slippery, and that it was best to keep the secret courtship from all eyes and ears. Mrs. Lincoln told Mr. Lincoln, that, though she had released him in the letter spoken of, yet she would hold the question an open one, — that is, that she had not changed her mind, but felt as always. . . . The marriage of Mr. Lincoln and Mary was quick and sudden, —

one or two hours' notice." How poor Mr. Lincoln felt about it, may be gathered from the reminiscences of his friend, J. H. Matheny, who says, "that Lincoln and himself, in 1842, were very friendly; that Lincoln came to him one evening and said, 'Jim, I shall have to marry that girl.'" He was married that evening, but Matheny says, "he looked as if he was going to the slaughter," and that Lincoln "had often told him, directly and individually, that he was driven into the marriage; that it was concocted and planned by the Edwards family; that Miss Todd — afterwards Mrs. Lincoln — was crazy for a week or so, not knowing what to do; and that he loved Miss Edwards, and went to see her, and not Mrs. Lincoln."

The license to marry was issued on the 4th of November, 1842, and on the same day the marriage was celebrated by Charles Dresser, " M.G." With this date carefully borne in mind, the following letters are of surpassing interest. They are relics, not only of a great man, but of a great agony.

The first is from Mr. Speed to Mr. Herndon, and explains the circumstances under which the correspondence took place. Although it is in part a repetition of what the reader already knows, it is of such peculiar value, that we give it in full: —

LOUISVILLE, Nov. 30, 1866.

W. H. HERNDON, ESQ.

Dear Sir, — I enclose you copies of all the letters of any interest from Mr. Lincoln to me.

Some explanation may be needed, that you may rightly understand their import.

In the winter of 1840 and 1841 he was unhappy about his engagement to his wife, — not being entirely satisfied that his *heart* was going with his hand. How much he suffered then on that account, none know so well as myself: he disclosed his whole heart to me.

In the summer of 1841 I became engaged to my wife. He was here on a visit when I courted her; and, strange to say, something of the same feeling which I regarded as so foolish in him took possession of me, and kept me very unhappy from the time of my engagement until I was married.

This will explain the deep interest he manifested in his letters on my account.

If you use the letters (and some of them are perfect gems) do it carefully, so as not to wound the feelings of Mrs. Lincoln.

One thing is plainly discernible: if I had not been married and happy, —far more happy than I ever expected to be,—he would not have married.

I have erased a name which I do not wish published. If I have failed to do it anywhere, strike it out when you come to it. That is the word ——.

I thank you for your last lecture. It is all new to me, but so true to my appreciation of Lincoln's character, that, independent of my knowledge of you, I would almost swear to it.

Lincoln wrote a letter (a long one, which he read to me) to Dr. Drake, of Cincinnati, descriptive of his case. Its date would be in December, 1840, or early in January, 1841. I think that he must have informed Dr. D. of his early love for Miss Rutledge, as there was a part of the letter which he would not read.

It would be worth much to you, if you could procure the original.

Charles D. Drake, of St. Louis, may have his father's papers. The date which I give you will aid in the search.

I remember Dr. Drake's reply, which was, that he would not undertake to prescribe for him without a personal interview. I would advise you to make some effort to get the letter.

Your friend, &c.,

J. F. SPEED.

The first of the papers from Mr. Lincoln's pen is a letter of advice and consolation to his friend, for whom he apprehends the terrible things through which, by the help of that friend, he has himself just passed.

MY DEAR SPEED,—Feeling, as you know I do, the deepest solicitude for the success of the enterprise you are engaged in, I adopt this as the last method I can invent to aid you, in case (which God forbid) you shall need any aid. I do not place what I am going to say on paper, because I can say it better in that way than I could by word of mouth; but, were I to say it orally before we part, most likely you would forget it at the very time when it might do you some good. As I think it reasonable that you will feel very badly sometime between this and the final consummation of your purpose, it is intended that you shall read this just at such a time. Why I say it is reasonable that you will feel very badly yet, is because of three *special causes* added to *the general one* which I shall mention.

The general cause is, that you are naturally of a nervous temperament, and this I say from what I have seen of you personally, and what you have told me concerning your mother at various times, and concerning your brother William at the time his wife died. The first special cause is your *exposure to bad weather* on your journey, which my experience clearly proves to be very severe on defective nerves. The second is the *absence of all business and conversation* of friends, which might divert your mind, give it occasional rest from the intensity of thought which will sometimes wear the sweetest idea threadbare, and turn it to the bitterness of death.

The third is *the rapid and near approach of that crisis on which all your thoughts and feelings concentrate.*

If from all these causes you shall escape, and go through triumphantly, without another " twinge of the soul," I shall be most happily but most egregiously deceived. If, on the contrary, you shall, as I expect you will at some time, be agonized and distressed, let me, who have some reason to speak with judgment on such a subject, beseech you to ascribe it to the causes I have mentioned, and not to some false and ruinous suggestion of the Devil.

" But," you will say, " do not your causes apply to every one engaged in a like undertaking ? " By no means. *The particular causes*, to a greater or less extent, perhaps, do apply in all cases; but the *general one*, — nervous debility, which is the key and conductor of all the particular ones, and without which they would be utterly harmless, though it *does* pertain to you, — *does not* pertain to one in a thousand. It is out of this that the painful difference between you and the mass of the world springs.

I know what the painful point with you is at all times when you are unhappy : it is an apprehension that you do not love her as you should. What nonsense ! How came you to court her ? Was it because you thought she deserved it, and that you had given her reason to expect it ? If it was for that, why did not the same reason make you court Ann Todd, and at least twenty others of whom you can think, and to whom it would apply with greater force than to *her ?* Did you court her for her wealth ? Why, you know she had none. But you say you reasoned yourself into it. What do you mean by that ? Was it not that you found yourself unable to reason yourself out of it ? Did you not think, and partly form the purpose, of courting her the first time you ever saw her or heard of her ? What had reason to do with it at that early stage ? There was nothing at that time for reason to work upon. Whether she was moral, amiable, sensible, or even of good character, you did not, nor could then know, except, perhaps, you might infer the last from the company you found her in.

All you then did or could know of her was her personal *appearance and deportment ;* and these, if they impress at all, impress the heart, and not the head.

Say candidly, were not those heavenly *black eyes* the whole basis of all your early *reasoning* on the subject ? After you and I had once been at the residence, did you not go and take me all the way to Lexington and back, for no other purpose but to get to see her again, on our return on that evening to take a trip for that express object?

What earthly consideration would you take to find her scouting and despising you, and giving herself up to another? But of this you have no apprehension; and therefore you cannot bring it home to your feelings

I shall be so anxious about you, that I shall want you to write by every mail. Your friend,

LINCOLN.

SPRINGFIELD, ILL., Feb. 3, 1842.

DEAR SPEED, — Your letter of the 25th January came to hand to-day. You well know that I do not feel my own sorrows much more keenly than I do yours, when I know of them; and yet I assure you I was not much hurt by what you wrote me of your excessively bad feeling at the time you wrote. Not that I am less capable of sympathizing with you now than ever, not that I am less your friend than ever, but because I hope and believe that your present anxiety and distress about *her* health and *her* life must and will forever banish those horrid doubts which I know you sometimes felt as to the truth of your affection for her. If they can once and forever be removed (and I almost feel a presentiment that the Almighty has sent your present affliction expressly for that object), surely, nothing can come in their stead to fill their immeasurable measure of misery. The death-scenes of those we love are surely painful enough; but these we are prepared for and expect to see: they happen to all, and all know they must happen. Painful as they are, they are not an unlooked-for sorrow. Should she, as you fear, be destined to an early grave, it is indeed a great consolation to know that she is so well prepared to meet it. Her religion, which you once disliked so much, I will venture you now prize most highly.

But I hope your melancholy bodings as to her early death are not well founded. I even hope that ere this reaches you, she will have returned with improved and still-improving health, and that you will have met her, and forgotten the sorrows of the past in the enjoyment of the present. I would say more if I could, but it seems that I have said enough. It really appears to me that you yourself ought to rejoice, and not sorrow, at this indubitable evidence of your undying affection for her.

Why, Speed, if you did not love her, although you might not wish her death, you would most certainly be resigned to it. Perhaps this point is no longer a question with you, and my pertinacious dwelling upon it is a rude intrusion upon your feelings. If so, you must pardon me. You know the hell I have suffered on that point, and how tender I am upon it. You know I do not mean wrong. I have been quite clear of hypo since you left, even better than I was along in the fall. I have seen —— but once. She seemed very cheerful, and so I said nothing to her about what we spoke of.

Old Uncle Billy Herndon is dead, and it is said this evening that Uncle Ben Ferguson will not live. This, I believe, is all the news, and enough at that, unless it were better.

Write me immediately on the receipt of this.

Your friend as ever,

LINCOLN.

SPRINGFIELD, ILL., Feb. 13, 1842.

DEAR SPEED, — Yours of the 1st inst. came to hand three or four days ago. When this shall reach you, you will have been Fanny's husband several days. You know my desire to befriend you is everlasting; that I will never cease while I know how to do any thing.

But you will always hereafter be on ground that I have never occupied, and consequently, if advice were needed, I might advise wrong. I do fondly hope, however, that you will never again need any comfort from abroad. But, should I be mistaken in this, should excessive pleasure still be accompanied with a painful counterpart at times, still let me urge you, as I have ever done, to remember, in the depth and even agony of despondency, that very shortly you are to feel well again. I am now fully convinced that you love her as ardently as you are capable of loving. Your ever being happy in her presence, and your intense anxiety about her health, if there were nothing else, would place this beyond all dispute in my mind. I incline to think it probable that your nerves will fail you occasionally for a while; but once you get them firmly graded now, that trouble is over forever.

I think if I were you, in case my mind were not exactly right, I would avoid being *idle*. I would immediately engage in some business, or go to making preparations for it, which would be the same thing.

If you went through the ceremony calmly, or even with sufficient composure not to excite alarm in any present, you are safe beyond question, and in two or three months, to say the most, will be the happiest of men.

I would desire you to give my particular respects to Fanny; but perhaps you will not wish her to know you have received this, lest she should desire to see it. Make her write me an answer to my last letter to her; at any rate, I would set great value upon a note or letter from her.

Write me whenever you have leisure.

Yours forever,

A. LINCOLN.

P. S. — I have been quite a man since you left.

SPRINGFIELD, Feb. 25, 1842.

DEAR SPEED, — Yours of the 16th inst., announcing that Miss Fanny and you are "no more twain, but one flesh," reached me this morning. I have no way of telling how much happiness I wish you both, though I believe you both can conceive it. I feel somewhat jealous of both of you now: you will be so exclusively concerned for one another, that I shall be forgotten entirely. My acquaintance with Miss Fanny (I call her this, lest you should think I am speaking of your mother) was too short for me to reasonably hope to long be remembered by her; and still I am sure I shall not forget her soon. Try if you cannot remind her of that debt she owes me, — and be sure you do not interfere to prevent her paying it.

I regret to learn that you have resolved to not return to Illinois. I shall be very lonesome without you. How miserable things seem to be arranged in this world! If we have no friends, we have no pleasure; and, if we have them, we are sure to lose them, and be doubly pained by the loss. I did hope she and you would make your home here; but I own I have no right to insist. You owe obligations to her ten thousand times more sacred than you can owe to others, and in that light let them be respected and observed. It is natural that she should desire to remain with her relatives and friends. As to friends, however, *she* could not need them anywhere: she would have them in abundance here.

Give my kind remembrance to Mr. Williamson and his family, particularly Miss Elizabeth; also to your mother, brother, and sisters. Ask little Eliza Davis if she will ride to town with me if I come there again.

And, finally, give Fanny a double reciprocation of all the love she sent me. Write me often, and believe me

Yours forever,
LINCOLN.

P. S. — Poor Easthouse is gone at last. He died a while before day this morning. They say he was very loath to die.   .   .   .

L.

SPRINGFIELD, Feb. 25, 1842.

DEAR SPEED, — I received yours of the 12th, written the day you went down to William's place, some days since, but delayed answering it till I should receive the promised one of the 16th, which came last night. I opened the letter with intense anxiety and trepidation; so much, that, although it turned out better than I expected, I have hardly yet, at the distance of ten hours, become calm.

I tell you, Speed, our forebodings (for which you and I are peculiar) are all the worst sort of nonsense. I fancied, from the time I received your letter of Saturday, that the one of *Wednesday* was never to come, and yet it *did* come, and, what is more, it is perfectly clear, both from its *tone* and *handwriting*, that you were much *happier*, or, if you think the term preferable, *less miserable*, when you wrote *it*, than when you wrote the last one before. You had so obviously improved at the very time I so much fancied you would have grown worse. You say that something indescribably horrible and alarming still haunts you. You will not say *that* three months from now, I will venture. When your nerves once get steady now, the whole trouble will be over forever. Nor should you become impatient at their being even very slow in becoming steady. Again you say, you much fear that that Elysium of which you have dreamed so much is never to be realized. Well, if it shall not, I dare swear it will not be the fault of her who is now your wife. I now have no doubt, that it is the peculiar misfortune of both you and me to dream dreams of Elysium far exceeding all that any thing earthly can realize. Far short of your dreams as you may be, no woman could do more to realize them than that same black-eyed Fanny. If you could but contemplate her through my imagination, it would appear ridiculous to you that any one should for a moment think of being unhappy with her. My old father used to have a saying, that, "If you make a bad bargain, *hug* it all the tighter;" and it occurs to me, that, if the bargain you have just closed can possibly be called a bad one, it is certainly the most pleasant one for applying that maxim to which my fancy can by any effort picture.

I write another letter, enclosing this, which you can show her, if she desires it. I do this because she would think strangely, perhaps, should you tell her that you received no letters from me, or, telling her you do, refuse to let her see them. I close this, entertaining the confident hope that every successive letter I shall have from you (which I here pray may not be few, nor far between) may show you possessing a more steady hand and cheerful heart than the last preceding it.

As ever, your friend,
LINCOLN.

SPRINGFIELD, March 27, 1842.

DEAR SPEED, — Yours of the 10th inst. was received three or four days since. You know I am sincere when I tell you the pleasure its contents gave me was and is inexpressible. As to your farm matter, I have no sympathy with you. *I* have no farm, nor ever expect to have, and consequently have not studied the subject enough to be much interested with it. I can only say that I am glad *you* are satisfied and pleased with it.

But on that other subject, to me of the most intense interest whether in joy or sorrow, I never had the power to withhold my sympathy from you. It cannot be told how it now thrills me with joy to hear you say you are *"far happier than you ever expected to be."* That much I know is enough. I know you too well to suppose your expectations were not, at least, sometimes extravagant, and, if the reality exceeds them all, I say, Enough, dear Lord. I am not going beyond the truth when I tell you, that the short space it took me to read your last letter gave me more pleasure than the total sum of all I have enjoyed since that fatal 1st of January, 1841. Since then it seems to me I should have been entirely happy, but for the never-absent idea that there is *one* still unhappy whom I have contributed to make so. That still kills my soul. I cannot but reproach myself for even wishing to be happy while she is otherwise. She accompanied a large party on the railroad cars to Jacksonville last Monday, and on her return spoke, so that I heard of it, of having enjoyed the trip exceedingly. God be praised for that!

You know with what sleepless vigilance I have watched you ever since the commencement of your affair; and, although I am almost confident it is useless, I cannot forbear once more to say, that I think it is even yet possible for your spirits to flag down and leave you miserable. If they should, don't fail to remember that they cannot long remain so. One thing I can tell you which I know you will be glad to hear, and that is that I have seen —— and scrutinized her feelings as well as I could, and am fully convinced she is far happier now than she has been for the last fifteen months past.

You will see by the last "Sangamon Journal" that I have made a temperance speech on the 22d of February, which I claim that Fanny and you shall read as an act of charity to me; for I cannot learn that anybody else has read it, or is likely to. Fortunately, it is not very long, and I shall deem it a sufficient compliance with my request if one of you listens while the other reads it.

As to your Lockridge matter, it is only necessary to say that there has been no court since you left, and that the next commences to-morrow morning, during which I suppose we cannot fail to get a judgment.

I wish you would learn of Everett what he would take, over and above a discharge, for all trouble we have been at, to take his business out of our hands and give it to somebody else. It is impossible to collect money on that or any other claim here now, and, although you know I am not a very petulant man, I declare I am almost out of patience with Mr. Everett's endless importunity. It seems like he not only writes all the letters he can himself, but gets everybody else in Louisville and vicinity to be constantly writing to us about his claim. I have always said that Mr. Everett is a very clever fellow, and I am very sorry he cannot be obliged; but it does seem to me he ought to know we are interested to collect his claim, and therefore would do it if we could.

I am neither joking nor in a pet when I say we would thank him to transfer his business to some other, without any compensation for what we have done, provided he will see the court cost paid, for which we are security.

The sweet violet you enclosed came safely to hand, but it was so dry, and mashed so flat, that it crumbled to dust at the first attempt to handle it. The juice that mashed out of it stained a place in the letter, which I mean to preserve and cherish for the sake of her who procured it to be sent. My renewed good wishes to her in particular, and generally to all such of your relations who know me.

As ever,
LINCOLN.

SPRINGFIELD, ILL., July 4, 1842.

DEAR SPEED, — Yours of the 16th June was received only a day or two since. It was not mailed at Louisville till the 25th. You speak of the great time that has elapsed since I wrote you. Let me explain that. Your letter reached here a day or two after I had started on the circuit. I was gone five or six weeks, so that I got the letters only a few weeks before Butler started to your country. I thought it scarcely worth while to write you the news which he could and would tell you more in detail. On his return, he told me you would write me soon, and so I waited for your letter. As to my having been displeased with your advice, surely you know better than that. I know you do, and therefore will not labor to convince you. True, that subject is painful to me; but it is not your silence, or the silence of all the world, that can make me forget it. I acknowledge the correctness of your advice too; but, before I resolve to do the one thing or the other, I must gain my confidence in my own ability to keep my resolves when they are made. In that ability you know I once prided myself, as the only or chief gem of my character: that gem I lost, how and where you know too well. I have not yet regained it; and, until I do, I cannot trust myself in any matter of much importance. I believe now, that, had you understood my case at the time as well as I understood yours afterwards, by the aid you would have given me I should have sailed through clear; but that does not now afford me sufficient confidence to begin that or the like of that again.

You make a kind acknowledgment of your obligations to me for your present happiness. I am much pleased with that acknowledgment. But a thousand times more am I pleased, to know that you enjoy a degree of happiness worthy of an acknowledgment. The truth is, I am not sure that there was any went with me in the part I took in your difficulty: I was drawn to it as by fate. If I would, I could not have done less than I did. I always was superstitious: I believe God made me one of the instruments of bringing your Fanny and you together, which union I have no doubt he had fore-ordained. Whatever he designs, he will do for me yet. "Stand still, and see the salvation of the Lord" is my text just now. If, as you say, you have told Fanny *all*, I should have no objection to her seeing this letter, but for its reference to our friend here: let her seeing it depend upon whether she has ever known any thing of my affairs; and, if she has not, do not let her.

I do not think I can come to Kentucky this season. I am so poor, and make so little headway in the world, that I drop back in a month of idleness as much as I gain in a year's sowing. I should like to visit you again. I should like to see that "sis" of yours that was absent when I was there, though I suppose she would run away again, if she were to hear I was coming.

My respects and esteem to all your friends there, and, by your permission, my love to your Fanny.　　　　Ever yours,　　LINCOLN.

SPRINGFIELD, Oct. 5, 1842.

DEAR SPEED, — You have heard of my duel with Shields, and I have now to inform you that the duelling business still rages in this city. Day before yesterday Shields challenged Butler, who accepted, and proposed fighting next morning at sunrising in Bob Allen's meadow, one hundred yards' distance, with rifles. To this Whitesides, Shields's second, said "no," because of the law. Thus ended duel No. 2. Yesterday Whiteside chose to consider himself insulted by Dr. Merryman, so sent him a kind of *quasi*-challenge, inviting him to meet him at the Planter's House in St. Louis, on the next Friday, to settle their difficulty. Merryman made me his friend, and sent W. a note, inquiring to know if he meant his note as a challenge, and, if so, that he would, according to the law in such case made and provided, prescribe the terms of the meeting. W. returned for answer, that, if M. would meet him at the Planter's House as desired, he would challenge him. M. replied in a note, that he denied W.'s right to dictate time and place, but that he (M.) would waive the question of time, and meet him at Louisiana, Mo. Upon my presenting this note to W., and stating verbally its contents, he declined receiving it, saying he had business in St. Louis, and it was as near as Louisiana. Merryman then directed me to notify Whiteside that he should publish the correspondence between them, with such comments as he thought fit. This I did. Thus it stood at bedtime last night. This morning Whiteside, by his friend Shields, is praying for a new trial, on the ground that he was mistaken in Merryman's proposition to meet him at Louisiana, Mo., thinking it was the State of Louisiana. This Merryman hoots at, and is preparing his publication; while the town is in a ferment, and a street-fight somewhat anticipated.

But I began this letter, not for what I have been writing, but to say something on that subject which you know to be of such infinite solicitude to me. The immense sufferings you endured from the first days of September till the middle of February you never tried to conceal from me, and I well understood. You have now been the husband of a lovely woman nearly eight months. That you are happier now than the day you married her, I well know; for without you could not be living. But I have your word for it, too, and the returning elasticity of spirits which is manifested in your letters. But I want to ask a close question, "Are you now in *feeling*, as well as *judgment*, glad you are married as you are?" From anybody but me this would be an impudent question, not to be tolerated; but I know you will pardon it in me. Please answer it quickly, as I am impatient to know.

I have sent my love to your Fanny so often, I fear she is getting tired of it. However, I venture to tender it again,

Yours forever,

LINCOLN.

In the last of these letters, Mr. Lincoln refers to his " duel with Shields." That was another of the disagreeable consequences which flowed from his fatal entanglement with Mary. Not content with managing a timid, although half-frantic and refractory, lover, her restless spirit led her into new fields of adventure. Her pen was too keen to be idle in the political controversies of the time. As a satirical writer, she had no rival of either sex at Springfield, and few, we venture to say, anywhere else. But that is a dangerous talent: the temptations to use it unfairly are numerous and strong; it inflicts so much pain, and almost necessarily so much injustice, upon those against whom it is directed, that its possessor rarely, if ever, escapes from a controversy without suffering from the desperation it provokes. Mary Todd was not disposed to let her genius rust for want of use ; and, finding no other victim handy, she turned her attention to James Shields, " Auditor." She had a friend, one Miss Jayne, afterwards Mrs. Trumbull, who helped to keep her literary secrets, and assisted as much as she could in worrying the choleric Irishman. Mr. Francis, the editor, knew very well that Shields was "a fighting-man ; " but the " pieces " sent him by the wicked ladies were so uncommonly rich in point and humor, that he yielded to a natural inclination, and printed them, one and all. Below we give a few specimens : —

LETTER FROM THE LOST TOWNSHIPS.

LOST TOWNSHIPS, Aug. 27, 1842.

DEAR MR. PRINTER, — I see you printed that long letter I sent you a spell ago: I'm quite encouraged by it, and can't keep from writing again. I think the printing of my letters will be a good thing all round, — it will give me the benefit of being known by the world, and give the world the advantage of knowing what's going on in the Lost Townships, and give your paper respectability besides. So here comes another. Yesterday afternoon I hurried through cleaning up the dinner-dishes, and stepped over to Neighbor S——, to see if his wife Peggy was as well as mought be expected, and hear what they called the baby. Well, when I got there, and just turned round the corner of his log-cabin, there he was setting on the doorstep reading a newspaper.

"How are you, Jeff?" says I.   He sorter started when he heard me, for he hadn't seen me before.

"Why," says he, "I'm mad as the devil, Aunt 'Becca!"

"What about?" says I: "ain't its hair the right color?   None of that non-sense, Jeff: there ain't an honester woman in the Lost Townships than"—

"Than who?" says he: "what the mischief are you about?"

I began to see I was running the wrong trail, and so says I, "Oh! nothing: I guess I was mistaken a little, that's all.   But what is it you're mad about?"

"Why," says he, "I've been tugging ever since harvest getting out wheat and hauling it to the river, to raise State-Bank paper enough to pay my tax this year, and a little school-debt I owe; and now, just as I've got it, here I open this infernal 'Extra Register,' expecting to find it full of 'Glorious Democratic Victories' and 'High-Comb'd Cocks,' when, lo and behold! I find a set of fellows calling themselves *officers of State* have forbidden the tax-col-lectors and school-commissioners to receive State paper at all; and so here it is, dead on my hands.   I don't now believe all the plunder I've got will fetch ready cash enough to pay my taxes and that school-debt."

I was a good deal thunderstruck myself; for that was the first I had heard of the proclamation, and my old man was pretty much in the same fix with Jeff.   We both stood a moment staring at one another, without knowing what to say.   At last says I, "Mr. S——, let me look at that paper."   He handed it to me, when I read the proclamation over.

"There, now," says he, "did you ever see such a piece of impudence and imposition as that?"   I saw Jeff was in a good tune for saying some ill-na-tured things, and so I tho't I would just argue a little on the contrary side, and make him rant a spell if I could.

"Why," says I, looking as dignified and thoughtful as I could, "it seems pretty tough, to be sure, to have to raise silver where there's none to be raised; but then, you see, '*there will be danger of loss*' if it ain't done."

"Loss, damnation!" says he.   "I defy Daniel Webster, I defy King Solo-mon, I defy the world,—I defy—I defy—yes, I defy even you, Aunt 'Becca, to show how the people can lose any thing by paying their taxes in State paper."

"Well," says I, "you see what the *officers of State* say about it, and they are a desarnin' set of men.   But," says I, "I guess you're mistaken about what the proclamation says.   It don't say *the people* will lose any thing by the paper money being taken for taxes.   It only says '*there will be danger of loss;*' and though it is tolerable plain that the people can't lose by paying their taxes in something they can get easier than silver, instead of having to pay silver; and though it is just as plain that the State can't lose by taking State-Bank paper, however low it may be, while she owes the bank more than the whole revenue, and can pay that paper over on her debt, dollar for dollar,—still *there is danger of loss* to the '*officers of State;*' and you know, Jeff, we can't get along without *officers of State*."

"Damn officers of State!" says he: "that's what you Whigs are always hurrahing for."

"Now, don't swear so, Jeff," says I: "you know I belong to the meetin', and swearin' hurts my feelins'."

"Beg pardon, Aunt 'Becca," says he; "but I do say it's enough to make Dr. Goddard swear, to have tax to pay in silver, for nothing only that Ford may get his two thousand a year, and Shields his twenty-four hundred a year, and Carpenter his sixteen hundred a year, and all without 'danger of loss' by taking it in State paper. Yes, yes: it's plain enough now what these *officers of State* mean by 'danger of loss.' Wash, I s'pose, actually lost fifteen hundred dollars out of the three thousand that two of these 'officers of State' let him steal from the treasury, by being compelled to take it in State paper. Wonder if we don't have a proclamation before long commanding us to make up this loss to Wash in silver."

And so he went on till his breath run out, and he had to stop. I couldn't think of any thing to say just then; and so I begun to look over the paper again. "Ay! here's another proclamation, or something like it."

"Another!" says Jeff; "and whose egg is it, pray?"

I looked to the bottom of it, and read aloud, "Your obedient servant, Jas. Shields, Auditor."

"Aha!" says Jeff, "one of them same three fellows again. Well, read it, and let's hear what of it."

I read on till I came to where it says, "*The object of this measure is to suspend the collection of the revenue for the current year.*"

"Now stop, now stop!" says he: "that's a lie a'ready, and I don't want to hear of it."

"Oh! maybe not," says I.

"I say *it — is — a — lie.* Suspend the collection, indeed! Will the collectors, that have taken their oaths to make the collection, DARE to suspend it? Is there any thing in the law requiring them to perjure themselves at the bidding of James Shields? Will the greedy gullet of the penitentiary be satisfied with swallowing *him* instead of all *them*, if they should venture to obey him? And would he not discover some 'danger of loss,' and be off, about the time it came to taking their places?

"And suppose the people attempt to suspend, by refusing to pay, what then? The collectors would just jerk up their horses and cows, and the like, and sell them to the highest bidder for silver in hand, without valuation or redemption. Why, Shields didn't believe that story himself: it was never meant for the truth. If it was true, why was it not writ till five days after the proclamation? Why didn't Carlin and Carpenter sign it as well as Shields? Answer me that, Aunt 'Becca. I say it's a lie, and not a well-told one at that. It grins out like a copper dollar. Shields is a fool as well as a liar. With him truth is out of the question; and, as for getting a good bright passable lie out of him, you might as well try to strike fire from a cake of tallow. I stick to it, it's all an infernal Whig lie!"

" A *Whig* lie! Highty tighty!"

" Yes, a *Whig* lie; and it's just like every thing the cursed British Whigs do. First they'll do some divilment, and then they'll tell a lie to hide it. And they don't care how plain a lie it is: they think they can cram any sort of a one down the throats of the ignorant Locofocos, as they call the Democrats."

" Why, Jeff, you're crazy: you don't mean to say Shields is a Whig!"

" *Yes, I do.*"

" Why, look here! the proclamation is in your own Democratic paper, as you call it."

" I know it; and what of that? They only printed it to let us Democrats see the deviltry the Whigs are at."

" Well, but Shields is the auditor of this Loco — I mean this Democratic State."

" So he is, and Tyler appointed him to office."

" Tyler appointed him?"

" Yes (if you must chaw it over), Tyler appointed him; or, if it wasn't him, it was old Granny Harrison, and that's all one. I tell you, Aunt 'Becca, there's no mistake about his being a Whig. Why, his very looks shows it, — every thing about him shows it: if I was deaf and blind, I could tell him by the smell. I seed him when I was down in Springfield last winter. They had a sort of a gatherin' there one night among the grandees, they called a fair. All the gals about town was there; and all the handsome widows and married women, finickin' about, trying to look like gals, tied as tight in the middle, and puffed out at both ends, like bundles of fodder that hadn't been stacked yet, but wanted stackin' pretty bad. And then they had tables all round the house kivered over with [   ] caps, and pincushions, and ten thousand such little knick-knacks, tryin' to sell 'em to the fellows that were bowin' and scrapin' and kungeerin' about 'em. They wouldn't let no Democrats in, for fear they'd disgust the ladies, or scare the little gals, or dirty the floor. I looked in at the window, and there was this same fellow Shields floatin' about on the air, without heft or earthly substance, just like a lock of cat-fur where cats had been fightin'.

" He was paying his money to this one, and that one, and t'other one, and sufferin' great loss because it wasn't silver instead of State paper; and the sweet distress he seemed to be in, — his very features, in the ecstatic agony of his soul, spoke audibly and distinctly, ' Dear girls, *it is distressing*, but I cannot marry you all. Too well I know how much you suffer; but do, *do* remember, it is not my fault that I am *so* handsome and *so* interesting.'

" As this last was expressed by a most exquisite contortion of his face, he seized hold of one of their hands, and squeezed, and held on to it about a quarter of an hour. ' O my good fellow!' says I to myself, ' if that was one of our Democratic gals in the Lost Townships, the way you'd get a brass pin let into you, would be about up to the head.' He a Democrat! Fiddlesticks! I tell you, Aunt 'Becca, he's a Whig, and no mistake: nobody but a Whig could make such a conceity dunce of himself."

"Well," says I, "maybe he is; but, if he is, I'm mistaken the worst sort. Maybe so, maybe so; but, if I am, I'll suffer by it; I'll be a Democrat if it turns out that Shields is a Whig; considerin' you shall be a Whig if he turns out a Democrat."

"A bargain, by jingoes!" says he; "but how will we find out?"

"Why," says I, "we'll just write, and ax the printer."

"Agreed again!" says he; "and, by thunder! if it does turn out that Shields is a Democrat, I never will" —

"Jefferson, — Jefferson" —

"What do you want, Peggy?"

"Do get through your everlasting clatter sometime, and bring me a gourd of water: the child's been crying for a drink this live-long hour."

"Let it die, then: it may as well die for water as to be taxed to death to fatten *officers of State*."

Jeff run off to get the water, though, just like he hadn't been sayin' any thing spiteful; for he's a raal good-hearted fellow, after all, once you get at the foundation of him.

I walked into the house, and "Why, Peggy," says I, "I declare, we like to forgot you altogether."

"Oh, yes!" says she, "when a body can't help themselves, everybody soon forgets 'em; but, thank God! by day after to-morrow I shall be well enough to milk the cows, and pen the calves, and wring the contrary ones' tails for 'em, and no thanks to nobody."

"Good-evening, Peggy," says I; and so I sloped, for I seed she was mad at me for making Jeff neglect her so long.

And now, Mr. Printer, will you be sure to let us know in your next paper whether this Shields is a Whig or a Democrat? I don't care about it for myself, for I know well enough how it is already; but I want to convince Jeff. It may do some good to let him, and others like him, know *who* and *what* those *officers of State* are. It may help to send the present hypocritical set to where they belong, and to fill the places they now disgrace with men who will do more work for less pay, and take a fewer airs while they are doing it. It ain't sensible to think that the same men who get us into trouble will change their course; and yet it's pretty plain, if some change for the better is not made, it's not long that either Peggy or I, or any of us, will have a cow left to milk, or a calf's tail to wring.

Yours, truly,
REBECCA ——.

LOST TOWNSHIPS, Sept. 8, 1842.

DEAR MR. PRINTER, — I was a-standin' at the spring yesterday a-washin' out butter, when I seed Jim Snooks a-ridin' up towards the house for very life

17

like, when, jist as I was a wonderin' what on airth was the matter with him, he stops suddenly, and ses he, " Aunt 'Becca, here's somethin' for you; " and with that he hands out your letter.   Well, you see I steps out towards him, not thinkin' that I had both hands full of butter; and seein' I couldn't take the letter, you know, without greasin' it, I ses, " Jim, jist you open it, and read it for me."   Well, Jim opens it, and reads it; and would you believe it, Mr. Editor? I was so completely dumfounded, and turned into stone, that there I stood in the sun, a-workin' the butter, and it a-runnin' on the ground, while he read the letter, that I never thunk what I was about till the hull on't run melted on the ground, and was lost.   Now, sir, it's not for the butter, nor the price of the butter, but, the Lord have massy on us, I wouldn't have sich another fright for a whole firkin of it.   Why, when I found out that it was the man what Jeff seed down to the fair that had demanded the author of my letters, threatnin' to take personal satisfaction of the writer, I was so skart that I tho't I should quill-wheel right where I was.

You say that Mr. S. is offended at being compared to cat's fur, and is as mad as a March *hare* (that ain't *fur*), because I told about the squeezin'.   Now, I want you to tell Mr. S, that, rather than fight, I'll make any apology; and, if he wants *personal* satisfaction, let him only come here, and he may squeeze my hand as hard as I squeeze the butter, and, if that ain't personal satisfaction, I can only say that he is the fust man that was not satisfied with squeezin' my hand.   If this should not answer, there is one thing more that I would do rather than get a lickin'.   I have all along expected to die a widow; but, as Mr. S. is rather good-looking than otherwise, I must say I don't care if we compromise the matter by — really, Mr. Printer, I can't help blushin' — but I — it must come out — I — but widewed modesty — well, if I must, I must — wouldn't he — maybe sorter, let the old grudge drap if I was to consent to be — be — h-i-s w-i-f-e?   I know he's a fightin' man, and would rather fight than eat; but isn't marryin' better than fightin', though it does sometimes run into it?   And I don't think, upon the whole, that I'd be sich a bad match neither: I'm not over sixty, and am just four feet three in my bare feet, and not much more round the girth; and for color, I wouldn't turn my back to nary gal in the Lost Townships.   But, after all, maybe I'm countin' my chickins before they're hatched, and dreamin' of matrimonial bliss when the only alternative reserved for me may be a lickin'.   Jeff tells me the way these fire-eaters do is to give the challenged party choice of weapons, &c., which bein' the case, I'll tell you in confidence that I never fights with any thing but broomsticks, or hot water, or a shovelful of coals, or some such thing; the former of which being somewhat like a shillalah, may not be very objectionable to him.   I will give him choice, however, in one thing, and that is, whether, when we fight, I shall wear breeches or he petti-coats; for I presume that change is sufficient to place us on an equality.

Yours, &c.

REBECCA ————.

P. S. — Jist say to your friend, if he concludes to marry rather than fight, I shall only inforce one condition: that is, if he should ever happen to gallant any young gals home of nights from our house, he must not squeeze their hands.

It is by no means a subject of wonder that these publications threw Mr. James Shields into a state of wrath. A thin-skinned, sensitive, high-minded, and high-tempered man, tender of his honor, and an Irishman besides, it would have been strange indeed, if he had not felt like snuffing blood. But his rage only afforded new delights to his tormentors; and when it reached its height, "Aunt 'Becca" transformed herself to "Cathleen," and broke out in rhymes like the following, which Miss Jayne's brother "Bill" kindly consented to "drop" for the amiable ladies.

[For The Journal.]

Ye Jew's-harps awake! The A——s won:
Rebecca the widow has gained Erin's son;
The pride of the North from Emerald Isle
Has been wooed and won by a woman's smile.
The combat's relinquished, old loves all forgot:
To the widow he's bound. Oh, bright be his lot!
In the smiles of the conquest so lately achieved,
Joyful be his bride, "widowed modesty" relieved.
The footsteps of time tread lightly on flowers,
May the cares of this world ne'er darken his hours!
But the pleasures of life are fickle and coy
As the smiles of a maiden sent off to destroy.
Happy groom! in sadness, far distant from thee,
The *Fair* girls dream only of past times of glee
Enjoyed in thy presence; whilst the soft blarnied store
Will be fondly remembered as relics of yore,
And hands that in rapture you oft would have prest
In prayer will be clasped that your lot may be blest.

CATHLEEN.

It was too bad. Mr. Shields could stand it no longer. He sent Gen. Whiteside to Mr. Francis, to demand the name of the person who wrote the letters from the "Lost Townships;" and Mr. Francis told him it was *A. Lincoln.* This information led to a challenge, a sudden scampering off of parties and friends to Missouri, a meeting, an explanation, and a peaceful return.

Abraham Lincoln in the field of honor, sword in hand, manœuvred by a second learned in the *duello*, would be an attractive spectacle under any circumstances. But with a celebrated man for an antagonist, and a lady's humor the occasion, the scene is one of transcendent interest; and the documents which describe it are well entitled to a place in his history. The letter of Mr. Shields's second, being first in date, is first in order.

SPRINGFIELD, Oct. 3, 1842.

To THE EDITOR OF "THE SANGAMON JOURNAL."

Sir, — To prevent misrepresentation of the recent affair between Messrs. Shields and Lincoln, I think it proper to give a brief narrative of the facts of the case, as they came within my knowledge; for the truth of which I hold myself responsible, and request you to give the same publication. An offensive article in relation to Mr. Shields appeared in "The Sangamon Journal" of the 2d September last; and, on demanding the author, Mr. Lincoln was given up by the editor. Mr. Shields, previous to this demand, made arrangements to go to Quincy on public business; and before his return Mr. Lincoln had left for Tremont, to attend the court, with the intention, as we learned, of remaining on the circuit several weeks. Mr. Shields, on his return, requested me to accompany him to Tremont; and, on arriving there, we found that Dr. Merryman and Mr. Butler had passed us in the night, and got there before us. We arrived in Tremont on the 17th ult.; and Mr. Shields addressed a note to Mr. Lincoln immediately, informing him that he was given up as the author of some articles that appeared in "The Sangamon Journal" (one more over the signature having made its appearance at this time), and requesting him to *retract* the offensive allusions contained in said articles in relation to his private character. Mr. Shields handed this note to me to deliver to Mr. Lincoln, and directed me, at the same time, not to enter into any verbal communication, or be the bearer of any verbal explanation, as such were always liable to misapprehension. This note was delivered by me to Mr. Lincoln, stating, at the same time, that I would call at his convenience for an answer. Mr. Lincoln, in the evening of the same day, handed me a letter addressed to Mr. Shields. In this he gave or offered no explanation, but stated therein that he could not submit to answer further, on the ground that Shields's note contained an assumption of facts and also a menace. Mr. Shields then addressed him another note, in which he disavowed all intention to menace, and requested to know whether he (Mr. Lincoln) was the author of either of the articles which appeared in "The Journal," headed "Lost Townships," and signed "Rebecca;" and, if so, he repeated his request of a retraction of the offensive matter in relation to his private character; if not, his denial would be held sufficient. This letter was returned to Mr. Shields unanswered, with a verbal statement "that there could be no further negotiation between them until the first note was withdrawn." Mr. Shields thereupon sent a note designating me as his friend, to which Mr. Lincoln replied by designating Dr. Merryman. These three last notes passed on Monday morning, the 19th. Dr. Merryman handed me Mr. Lincoln's last note when by ourselves. I remarked to Dr. Merryman that the matter was now submitted to us, and that I would propose that he and myself should pledge our words of honor to each other to try to agree upon terms of amicable arrangement, and compel our principals to accept of them. To this he readily assented, and we shook hands upon the pledge. It was then mutually agreed that we should adjourn to Springfield, and there procrastinate the matter, for the purpose of effecting the secret arrangement between him and myself. All this I kept concealed from Mr. Shields. Our horse had got a little lame in going to Tremont, and Dr. Merryman invited me to take a seat in his buggy. I accepted the invitation the more readily, as I thought, that leaving Mr. Shields in Tremont until his horse would be in better condition to travel would facilitate the private agreement between Dr. Merryman and myself. I travelled to Springfield part of the way with him, and part with Mr. Lincoln; but nothing passed between us on the journey in relation to the matter in hand. We arrived in Springfield on Monday night. About noon on Tuesday, to my astonishment, a proposition was made to meet in Missouri, within three miles of Alton, on the next Thursday! The weapons, cavalry broadswords of the largest size; the parties to stand on each side of a barrier, and to be confined to a limited space. As I had not been consulted at all on the subject, and considering the private understanding between Dr. Merryman and myself, and it being known that Mr. Shields was left at Tremont, such a proposition took me by surprise. However, being determined not to violate the laws of the State, I declined agreeing upon the terms until we should meet in Missouri. Immediately after, I called upon Dr. Merryman, and withdrew the pledge of honor between him and myself in relation to a secret arrangement. I started after this to meet Mr. Shields, and met him about twenty miles from Springfield. It was late on Tuesday night when we both reached the city, and learned that Dr. Merryman had left for Missouri, Mr. Lincoln having left before the proposition was made, as Dr. Merryman had himself informed me. The time and place made it necessary to start at once. We left Springfield at eleven o'clock on Tuesday night, travelled all night, and arrived in Hillsborough on Wednesday morning, where we took in Gen. Ewing. From there we went to Alton, where we arrived on Thursday; and, as the proposition required three friends on each side, I was joined by Gen. Ewing and Dr. Hope, as the friends of Mr. Shields.

We then crossed to Missouri, where a proposition was made by Gen. Hardin and Dr. English (who had arrived there in the mean time as mutual friends) to refer the matter to, I think, four friends for a settlement. This I believed Mr. Shields would refuse, and declined seeing him; but Dr. Hope, who conferred with him upon the subject, returned, and stated that Mr. Shields declined settling the matter through any other than the friends he had selected to stand by him on that occasion. The friends of both the parties finally agreed to withdraw the papers (temporarily) to give the friends of Mr. Lincoln an opportunity to explain. Whereupon the friends of Mr. Lincoln, to wit, Messrs. Merryman, Bledsoe, and Butler, made a full and satisfactory explanation in relation to the article which appeared in "The Sangamon Journal" of the 2d, the only one written by him. This was all done without the knowledge or consent of Mr. Shields; and he refused to accede to it until Dr. Hope, Gen. Ewing, and myself declared the apology sufficient, and that we could not sustain him in going further. I think it necessary to state further, that no explanation or apology had been previously offered on the part of Mr. Lincoln to Mr. Shields, and that none was ever communicated by me to him, nor was any ever offered to me, unless a paper read to me by Dr. Merryman after he had handed me the broadsword proposition on Tuesday. I heard so little of the reading of the paper, that I do not know fully what it purported to be; and I was the less inclined to inquire, as Mr. Lincoln was then gone to Missouri, and Mr. Shields not yet arrived from Tremont. In fact, I could not entertain any offer of the kind, unless upon my own responsibility; and that I was not disposed to do after what had already transpired.

I make this statement, as I am about to be absent for some time, and I think it due to all concerned to give a true version of the matter before I leave.

Your obedient servant,
JOHN D. WHITESIDE.

To which Mr. Merryman replied : —

SPRINGFIELD, Oct. 8, 1842.
EDITORS OF "THE JOURNAL."

Gents, — By your paper of Friday, I discover that Gen. Whiteside has published his version of the late affair between Messrs. Shields and Lincoln. I now bespeak a hearing of my version of the same affair, which shall be true and full as to all material facts.

On Friday evening, the 16th of September, I learned that Mr. Shields and Gen. Whiteside had started in pursuit of Mr. Lincoln, who was at Tremont, attending court. I knew that Mr. Lincoln was wholly unpractised both as to the diplomacy and weapons commonly employed in similar affairs; and I felt it my duty, as a friend, to be with him, and, so far as in my power, to prevent any advantage being taken of him as to either his honor or his life. Accordingly, Mr. Butler and myself started, passed Shields and Whiteside in the night, and arrived at Tremont ahead of them on Saturday morning. I told Mr. Lincoln what was brewing, and asked him what course he proposed to himself. He stated that he was wholly opposed to duelling, and would do any thing to avoid it that might not degrade him in the estimation of himself and friends; but, if such *degradation* or a *fight* were the only alternative, he would fight.

In the afternoon Shields and Whiteside arrived, and very soon the former sent to Mr. Lincoln by the latter the following note or letter : —

TREMONT, Sept. 17, 1842.

A. LINCOLN, ESQ. — I regret that my absence on public business compelled me to postpone a matter of private consideration a little longer than I could have desired. It will only be necessary, however, to account for it by informing you that I have been to Quincy on business that would not admit of delay. I will now state briefly the reasons of my troubling you with this communication, the disagreeable nature of which I regret, as I had hoped to avoid any difficulty with any one in Springfield while residing there, by endeavoring to conduct myself in such a way amongst both my political friends and opponents, as to escape the necessity of any. Whilst thus abstaining from giving provocation, I have become the object of slander, vituperation, and personal abuse, which, were I capable of submitting to, I would prove myself worthy of the whole of it.

In two or three of the last numbers of " The Sangamon Journal," articles of the most personal nature, and calculated to degrade me, have made their appearance. On inquiring, I was informed by the editor of that paper, through the medium of my friend, Gen. Whiteside, that you are the author of those articles. This information satisfies me that I have become, by some means or other, the object of your secret hostility. I will not take the trouble of inquiring into the reason of all this; but I will take the liberty of requiring a full, positive, and absolute retraction of all offensive allusions used by you in these communications, in relation to my private character and standing as a man, as an apology for the insults conveyed in them.

This may prevent consequences which no one will regret more than myself.

Your ob't serv't,

JAS. SHIELDS.

[Copy.]

About sunset Gen. Whiteside called again, and received from Mr. Lincoln the following answer to Mr. Shields's note : —

TREMONT, Sept. 17, 1842

JAS. SHIELDS, ESQ. — Your note of to-day was handed me by Gen. Whiteside. In that note, you say you have been informed, through the medium of the editor of " The Journal," that I am the author of certain articles in that paper which you deem personally abusive of you; and, without stopping to inquire whether I really am the author, or to point out what is offensive in them, you demand an unqualified retraction of all that is offensive, and then proceed to hint at consequences.

Now, sir, there is in this so much assumption of facts, and so much of menace as to consequences, that I cannot submit to answer that note any further than I have, and to add, that the consequence to which I suppose you allude would be matter of as great regret to me as it possibly could to you.   Respectfully,

A. LINCOLN.

In about an hour Gen. Whiteside called again with another note from Mr. Shields; but after conferring with Mr. Butler for a long time, say two or three hours, returned without presenting the note to Mr. Lincoln. This was in consequence of an assurance from Mr. Butler that Mr. Lincoln could not receive any communication from Mr. Shields, unless it were a withdrawal of his first note, or a challenge. Mr. Butler further stated to Gen. Whiteside, that, on the withdrawal of the first note, and a proper and gentlemanly request for an explanation, he had no doubt one would be given. Gen. Whiteside admitted that that was the course Mr. Shields ought to pursue, but deplored that his furious and intractable temper prevented his having any influence with him to that end. Gen. W. then requested us to wait with him until Monday morning, that he might endeavor to bring Mr. Shields to reason.

On Monday morning he called and presented Mr. Lincoln the same note as, Mr. Butler says, he had brought on Saturday evening. It was as follows: —

TREMONT, Sept. 17, 1842.

A. LINCOLN, ESQ. — In your reply to my note of this date, you intimate that I assume facts and menace consequences, and that you cannot submit to answer it further. As now, sir, you desire it, I will be a little more particular. The editor of " The Sangamon Journal " gave me to understand that you are the author of an article which appeared, I think, in that paper of the 2d September inst., headed " The Lost Townships," and signed Rebecca or 'Becca. I would therefore take the liberty of asking whether you are the author of said article, or any other over the same signature which has appeared in any of the late numbers of that paper. If so, I repeat my request of an absolute retraction of all offensive allusion contained therein in relation to my private character and standing. If you are not the author of any of the articles, your denial will be sufficient. I will say further, it is not my intention to menace, but to do myself justice.

Your ob't serv't,

[Copy.] JAS. SHIELDS.

This Mr. Lincoln perused, and returned to Gen. Whiteside, telling him verbally, that he did not think it consistent with his honor to negotiate for peace with Mr. Shields, unless Mr. Shields would withdraw his former offensive letter.

In a very short time Gen. Whiteside called with a note from Mr. Shields, designating Gen. Whiteside as his friend, to which Mr. Lincoln instantly replied, designating me as his. On meeting Gen. Whiteside, he proposed that we should pledge our honor to each other that we would endeavor to settle the matter amicably; to which I agreed, and stated to him the only conditions on which it could be so settled; viz., the withdrawal of Mr. Shields's first note; which he appeared to think reasonable, and regretted that the note had been written, — saying, however, that he had endeavored to prevail on Mr. Shields to write a milder one, but had not succeeded. He added, too, that I must promise not to mention it, as he would not dare to let Mr. Shields know that he was negotiating peace; for, said he, " He would chal lenge me next, and as soon cut my throat as not." Not willing that he should suppose my principal less dangerous than his own, I promised not to mention our pacific intentions to Mr. Lincoln or any other person ; and we started for Springfield forthwith.

We all, except Mr. Shields, arrived in Springfield late at night on Monday. We discovered that the affair had, somehow, got great publicity in Springfield, and that an arrest was probable. To prevent this, it was agreed by Mr. Lincoln and myself that he should leave early on Tuesday morning. Accordingly, he prepared the following instructions for my guide, on a suggestion from Mr. Butler that he had reason to believe that an attempt would be made by the opposite party to have the matter accommodated : —

In case Whiteside shall signify a wish to adjust this affair without further difficulty, let him know, that, if the present papers be withdrawn, and a note from Mr. Shields asking to know if I am the author of the articles of which he complains, and asking that I shall make him gentlemanly satisfaction if I am the author, and this without menace or dictation as to what that satisfaction shall be, a pledge is made that the following answer shall be given: —

"I did write the 'Lost Township' letter which appeared in the 'Journal' of the 2d inst., but had no participation in any form in any other article alluding to you. I wrote that wholly for political effect. I had no intention of injuring your personal or private character, or standing as a man or a gentleman; and I did not then think, and do not now think, that that article could produce, or has produced, that effect against you; and, had I anticipated such an effect, would have forborne to write it. And I will add, that your conduct towards me, so far as I knew, had always been gentlemanly, and that I had no personal pique against you, and no cause for any."

If this should be done, I leave it with you to manage what shall and what shall not be published.

If nothing like this is done, the preliminaries of the fight are to be: —

1st, WEAPONS. — Cavalry broadswords of the largest size, precisely equal in all respects, and such as now used by the cavalry company at Jacksonville.

2d, POSITION. — A plank ten feet long, and from nine to twelve inches broad, to be firmly fixed on edge on the ground as the line between us, which neither is to pass his foot over upon forfeit of his life. Next, a line drawn on the ground on either side of said plank and parallel with it, each at the distance of the whole length of the sword and three feet additional from the plank; and the passing of his own such line by either party during the fight shall be deemed a surrender of the contest.

3d, TIME. — On Thursday evening at 5 o'clock, if you can get it so; but in no case to be at a greater distance of time than Friday evening at 5 o'clock.

4th, PLACE. — Within three miles of Alton, on the opposite side of the river, the particular spot to be agreed on by you.

Any preliminary details coming within the above rules, you are at liberty to make at your discretion; but you are in no case to swerve from these rules, or to pass beyond their limits.

In the course of the forenoon I met Gen. Whiteside, and he again intimated a wish to adjust the matter amicably. I then read to him Mr. Lincoln's instructions to an adjustment, and the terms of the hostile meeting, if there must be one, both at the same time.

He replied that it was useless to talk of an adjustment, if it could only be effected by the *withdrawal* of Mr. Shields's paper, for such withdrawal Mr. Shields would never consent to; adding, that he would as soon think of asking Mr. Shields to "butt his brains out against a brick wall as to withdraw that paper." He proceeded: "I see but one course, — that is a desperate remedy: 'tis to tell them, if they will not make the matter up, they must fight us." I replied, that, if he chose to fight Mr. Shields to compel him to do right, he might do so; but as for Mr. Lincoln, he was on the defensive, and, I believed, in the right, and I should do nothing to compel him to do wrong. Such withdrawal having been made indispensable by Mr. Lincoln, I cut the matter short as to an adjustment, and proposed to Gen. Whiteside to accept the terms of the fight, which he refused to do until Mr. Shields's arrival in town, but agreed, verbally, that Mr. Lincoln's friends should procure the broadswords, and take them to the ground. In the afternoon he came to me, saying that some persons were swearing out affidavits to have us arrested, and that he intended to meet Mr. Shields immediately, and proceed to the place designated; lamenting, however, that I would not delay the time, that he might procure the interference of Gov. Ford and Gen. Ewing to mollify Mr. Shields. I told him that an accommodation, except upon the terms I mentioned, was out of the question; that to delay the meeting was to facilitate our arrest; and, as I was determined not to be arrested, I should leave town in fifteen minutes. I then pressed his acceptance of the preliminaries, which he disclaimed upon the ground that it would interfere with his oath of office as Fund Commissioner. I then, with two other friends, went to Jacksonville, where we joined Mr. Lincoln about 11 o'clock on Tuesday night. Wednesday morning we procured the broadswords, and proceeded to Alton, where we arrived about 11, A.M., on Thursday. The other party were in town before us. We crossed the river, and they soon followed. Shortly after, Gen. Hardin and Dr. English presented to Gen. Whiteside and myself the following note: —

ALTON, Sept. 22, 1842.

MESSRS. WHITESIDE AND MERRYMAN. — As the mutual personal friends of Messrs. Shields and Lincoln, but without authority from either, we earnestly desire to see a reconciliation of the misunderstanding which exists between them. Such difficulties should always be arranged amicably, if it is possible to do so with honor to both parties.

Believing ourselves, that such an arrangement can possibly be effected, we respectfully, but earnestly, submit the following proposition for your consideration: —

Let the whole difficulty be submitted to four or more gentlemen, to be selected by yourselves, who shall consider the affair, and report thereupon for your consideration.

JOHN J. HARDIN.
R. W. ENGLISH.

To this proposition Gen. Whiteside agreed: I declined doing so without consulting Mr. Lincoln. Mr. Lincoln remarked, that, as they had accepted the proposition, he would do so, but directed that his friends should make no terms except those first proposed. Whether the adjustment was finally made upon these very terms, and no other, let the following documents attest : —

MISSOURI, Sept. 22, 1842.

GENTLEMEN, — All papers in relation to the matter in controversy between Mr. Shields and Mr. Lincoln having been withdrawn by the friends of the parties concerned, the friends of Mr. Shields ask the friends of Mr. Lincoln to explain all offensive matter in the articles which appeared in "The Sangamon Journal" of the 2d, 9th, and 16th of September, under the signature of "Rebecca," and headed "Lost Townships."

It is due to Gen. Hardin and Mr. English to state that their interference was of the most courteous and gentlemanly character.

JOHN D. WHITESIDE.
WM. LEE D. EWING.
T. M. HOPE.

MISSOURI, Sept. 22, 1842.

GENTLEMEN, — All papers in relation to the matter in controversy between Mr. Lincoln and Mr. Shields having been withdrawn by the friends of the parties concerned, we, the undersigned, friends of Mr. Lincoln, in accordance with your request that explanation of Mr. Lincoln's publication in relation to Mr. Shields in "The Sangamon Journal" of the 2d, 9th, and 16th of September be made, take pleasure in saying, that, although Mr. Lincoln was the writer of the article signed "Rebecca" in the "Journal" of the 2d, and that only, yet he had no intention of injuring the personal or private character or standing of Mr. Shields as a gentleman or a man, and that Mr. Lincoln did not think, nor does he now think, that said article could produce such an effect; and, had Mr. Lincoln anticipated such an effect, he would have forborne to write it. We will further state, that said article was written solely for political effect, and not to gratify any personal pique against Mr. Shields, for he had none, and knew of no cause for any It is due to Gen. Hardin and Mr. English to say that their interference was of the most courteous and gentlemanly character.

E. H. MERRYMAN.
A. T. BLEDSOE.
WM. BUTLER.

Let it be observed now, that Mr. Shields's friends, after agreeing to the arbitrament of four disinterested gentlemen, declined the contract, saying that Mr. Shields wished his own friends to act for him. They then proposed that we should explain without any withdrawal of papers. This was promptly and firmly refused, and Gen. Whiteside himself pronounced the papers withdrawn. They then produced a note requesting us to "disavow" all offensive intentions in the publications, &c., &c. This we declined answering, and only responded to the above request for an explanation.

These are the material facts in relation to the matter, and I think present the case in a very different light from the garbled and curtailed statement of Gen. Whiteside. Why he made that statement I know not, unless he wished to detract from the honor of Mr. Lincoln. This was ungenerous, more particularly as he on the ground requested us not to make in our explanation any quotations from the " Rebecca papers ; " also not to make *public the terms of reconciliation*, and to unite with them in defending the honorable character of the adjustment.

Gen. W., in his publication, says, " The friends of both parties agreed to withdraw the papers (temporarily) to give the friends of Mr. Lincoln an opportunity to explain." This I deny. I say the papers were withdrawn to enable Mr. Shields's friends to *ask* an explanation ; and I appeal to the documents for proof of my position.

By looking over these documents, it will be seen that Mr. Shields had not before asked for an *explanation*, but had all the time been dictatorily insisting on a *retraction*.

Gen. Whiteside, in his communication, brings to light much of Mr. Shields's manifestations of bravery behind the scenes. I can do nothing of the kind for Mr. Lincoln. He took his stand when I first met him at Tremont, and maintained it *calmly* to the last, without difficulty or difference between himself and his friends.

I cannot close this article, lengthy as it is, without testifying to the honorable and gentlemanly conduct of Gen. Ewing and Dr. Hope, nor indeed can I say that I saw any thing objectionable in the course of Gen. Whiteside up to the time of his communication. This is so replete with prevarication and misrepresentation, that I cannot accord to the General that candor which I once supposed him to possess. He complains that I did not procrastinate time according to agreement. He forgets that by his own act he cut me off from that chance in inducing me, by promise, not to communicate our secret contract to Mr. Lincoln. Moreover, I could see no consistency in wishing for an extension of time at that stage of the affair, when in the outset they were in so precipitate a hurry, that they could not wait three days for Mr. Lincoln to return from Tremont, but must hasten there, apparently with the intention of bringing the matter to a speedy issue. He complains, too, that, after inviting him to take a seat in my buggy, I never broached the subject to him on our route here. But was I, the defendant in the case, with a challenge hanging over me, to make advances, and beg a reconciliation ? Absurd ! Moreover, the valorous general forgets that he beguiled the tedium of the journey by recounting to me his exploits in many a well-fought battle, — dangers by " flood and field " in which I don't believe he ever participated, — doubtless with a view to produce a salutary effect on my nerves, and impress me with a proper notion of his fire-eating propensities.

One more main point of his argument, and I have done. The General seems to be troubled with a convenient shortness of memory on some occasions. He does not remember that any explanations were offered at any time, unless it were a paper read when the " broadsword proposition " was tendered, when his mind was so confused by the anticipated clatter of broadswords, or *something else*, that he did " not know fully what it purported to be." The truth is, that by unwisely refraining from mentioning it to his principal, he placed himself in a dilemma which he is now endeavoring to shuffle out of. By his inefficiency, and want of knowledge of those laws which govern gentlemen in matters of this kind, he has done great injustice to his principal, a gentleman who I believe is ready at all times to vindicate his honor manfully, but who has been unfortunate in the selection of his friend; and this fault he is now trying to wipe out by doing an act of still greater injustice to Mr. Lincoln.

E. H. MERRYMAN.

And so Mr. Lincoln acknowledged himself to have been the author of one of the " Lost Township Letters." Whether he was or not, was known only perhaps to Miss Todd and himself. At the time of their date, he was having secret meetings with her at Mr. Francis's house, and endeavoring to nerve himself to the duty of marrying her, with what success the letters to Speed are abundant evidence. It is probable that Mary composed them fresh from these stolen conferences; that some of Mr. Lincoln's original conceptions and peculiarities of style unwittingly crept into them, and that here and there he altered and amended the manuscript before it went to the printer. Such a connection with a lady's productions made it obligatory upon him to defend them. But why avow one, and disavow the rest? It is more than likely that he was determined to take just enough responsibility to fight upon, provided Shields should prove incorrigible, and not enough to prevent a peaceful issue, if the injured gentleman should be inclined to accept an apology.

After his marriage, Mr. Lincoln took up his residence at the " Globe Tavern," where he had a room and boarding for man and wife for the moderate sum of four dollars per week. But, notwithstanding cheap living, he was still as poor as ever, and gave " poverty " as one of his reasons for not paying a friendly visit which seemed to be expected of him.

At the bar and in political affairs he continued to work with as much energy as before, although his political prospects seem just now to have suffered an unexpected eclipse. In 1843, Lincoln, Hardin, and Baker were candidates for the Whig congressional nomination; but between Hardin and

Baker there was "bitter hostility," and between Baker and Lincoln "suspicion and dislike." The contest was long and fierce; but, before it was over, Lincoln reluctantly withdrew in favor of Baker. He had had a hard time of it, and had been compelled to meet accusations of a very strange character. Among other things, he was charged with being an aristocrat; with having deserted his old friends, the people, by marrying a proud woman on account of her blood and family. This hurt him keenly, and he took great pains to disprove it; but this was not all. He was called an infidel by some, a Presbyterian here, an Episcopalian there; so that by turns he incurred the hostility of all the most powerful religious societies in the district.

On the 24th of March, he wrote to Mr. Speed as follows: —

SPRINGFIELD, March 24, 1843.

DEAR SPEED, — . . . We had a meeting of the Whigs of the county here on last Monday to appoint delegates to a district convention; and Baker beat me, and got the delegation instructed to go for him. The meeting, in spite of my attempt to decline it, appointed me one of the delegates; so that, in getting Baker the nomination, I shall be fixed a good deal like a fellow who is made a groomsman to a man that has cut him out, and is marrying his own dear "gal." About the prospects of your having a namesake at our town, can't say exactly yet.

A. LINCOLN.

He was now a Baker delegate, pledged to get him the nomination if he could; and yet he was far from giving up the contest in his own behalf. Only two days after the letter to Speed, he wrote to Mr. Morris: —

SPRINGFIELD, ILL., March 26, 1843.

FRIEND MORRIS, — Your letter of the 23d was received on yesterday morning, and for which (instead of an excuse, which you thought proper to ask) I tender you my sincere thanks. It is truly gratifying to me to learn, that, while the people of Sangamon have cast me off, my old friends of Menard, who have known me longest and best, stick to me. It would astonish, if not amuse, the older citizens (a stranger, friendless, uneducated, penniless boy, working on a flat-boat at ten dollars per month) to learn that I have been put down here as the candidate of pride, wealth, and aristocratic family distinction. Yet so, chiefly, it was. There was, too, the strangest combination of church-influence against me. Baker is a Campbellite; and therefore, as I suppose, with few exceptions, got all that church.

My wife has some relations in the Presbyterian churches, and some with the Episcopal churches; and therefore, wherever it would tell, I was set down as either the one or the other, while it was everywhere contended that no Christian ought to go for me, because I belonged to no church, was suspected of being a deist, and had talked about fighting a duel. With all these things, Baker, of course, had nothing to do. Nor do I complain of them. As to his own church going for him, I think that was right enough; and as to the influences I have spoken of in the other, though they were very strong, it would be grossly untrue and unjust to charge that they acted upon them in a body, or were very near so. I only mean that those influences levied a tax of a considerable per cent upon my strength throughout the religious controversy. But enough of this.

You say, that, in choosing a candidate for Congress, you have an equal right with Sangamon; and in this you are undoubtedly earnest. In agreeing to withdraw if the Whigs of Sangamon should go against me, I did not mean that they alone were worth consulting, but that if she, with her heavy delegation, should be against me, it would be impossible for me to succeed; and therefore I had as well decline. And in relation to Menard having rights, permit me fully to recognize them, and to express the opinion, that, if she and Mason act circumspectly, they will in the convention be able so far to enforce their rights as to decide absolutely which *one* of the candidates shall be successful. Let me show the reason of this. Hardin, or some other Morgan candidate, will get Putnam, Marshall, Woodford, Tazewell, and Logan, — make sixteen. Then you and Mason, having three, can give the victory to either side.

You say you shall instruct your delegates for me, unless I object. I certainly shall not object. That would be too pleasant a compliment for me to tread in the dust. And besides, if any thing should happen (which, however, is not probable) by which Baker should be thrown out of the fight, I would be at liberty to accept the nomination if I could get it. I do, however, feel myself bound not to hinder him in any way from getting the nomination. I should despise myself were I to attempt it. I think, then, it would be proper for your meeting to appoint three delegates, and to instruct them to go for some one as a *first* choice, some one else as a *second*, and perhaps some one as a *third;* and, if in those instructions I were named as the first choice, it would gratify me very much.

If you wish to hold the balance of power, it is important for you to attend to and secure the vote of Mason also. You should be sure to have men appointed delegates that you know you can safely confide in. If yourself and James Short were appointed for your county, all would be safe; but whether Jim's woman affair a year ago might not be in the way of his appointment is a question. I don't know whether you know it, but I know him to be as honorable a man as there is in the world. You have my permission, and even request, to show this letter to Short; but to no one else, unless it be a very particular friend, who you know will not speak of it.

Yours as ever,
A. LINCOLN.

P. S. — Will you write me again?

To MARTIN M. MORRIS, Petersburg, Ill.

And finally to Speed on the same subject: —

SPRINGFIELD, May 18, 1843.

DEAR SPEED, — Yours of the 9th inst. is duly received, which I do not meet as a "bore," but as a most welcome visitor. I will answer the business part of it first.

.   .   .   .

In relation to our Congress matter here, you were right in supposing I would support the nominee. Neither Baker nor I, however, is the man, but *Hardin*, so far as I can judge from present appearances. We shall have no split or trouble about the matter, — all will be harmony. In relation to the "coming events" about which Butler wrote you, I had not heard one word before I got your letter; but I have so much confidence in the judgment of a Butler on such a subject, that I incline to think there may be some reality in it. What day does Butler appoint? By the way, how do "events" of the same sort come on in your family? Are you possessing houses and lands, and oxen and asses, and men-servants and maid-servants, and begetting sons and daughters? We are not keeping house, but boarding at the Globe Tavern, which is very well kept now by a widow lady of the name of Beck. Our room (the same Dr. Wallace occupied there) and boarding only costs us four dollars a week. Ann Todd was married something more than a year since to a fellow by the name of Campbell, and who, Mary says, is pretty much of a "dunce," though he has a little money and property. They live in Boonville, Mo., and have not been heard from lately enough for me to say any thing about her health. I reckon it will scarcely be in our power to visit Kentucky this year. Besides poverty and the necessity of attending to business, those "coming events," I suspect, would be somewhat in the way. I most heartily wish you and your Fanny would not fail to come. Just let us know the time, and we will have a room provided for you at our house, and all be merry together for a while. Be sure to give my respects to your mother and family: assure her, that, if I ever come near her, I will not fail to call and see her. Mary joins in sending love to your Fanny and you.

Yours as ever,
A. LINCOLN.

JOSHUA F. SPEED.

After the "race," still smarting from the mortification of defeat, and the disappointment of a cherished hope, he took his old friend Jim Matheny away off to a solitary place in the woods, "and then and there," "with great emphasis," protested that he had not grown proud, and was not an aristocrat. "Jim," said he, in conclusion, "I am now, and always shall be, the same Abe Lincoln that I always was."

18

CHAPTER XII.

IN 1844 Mr. Lincoln was again a candidate for elector on the Whig ticket. Mr. Clay, as he has said himself, was his "*beau-ideal* of a statesman," and he labored earnestly and as effectually as any one else for his election. For the most part, he still had his old antagonists to meet in the Springfield region, chief among whom this year was John Calhoun. With him and others he had joint debates, running through several nights, which excited much popular feeling. One of his old friends and neighbors, who attended all these discussions, speaks in very enthusiastic terms of Mr. Calhoun, and, after enumerating his many noble gifts of head and heart, concludes that " Calhoun came nearer of whipping Lincoln in debate than Douglas did."

Mr. Lincoln made many speeches in Illinois, and finally, towards the close of the campaign, he went over into Indiana, and there continued " on the stump " until the end. Among other places he spoke at Rockport on the Ohio, — where he had first embarked for New Orleans with Gentry, — at Gentryville, and at a place in the country about two miles from the cabin where his father had lived. While he was in the midst of his speech at Gentryville, his old friend, Nat Grigsby, entered the room. Lincoln recognized him on the instant, and, stopping short in his remarks, cried out, " There's Nat ! " Without the slightest regard for the proprieties of the occasion, he suspended his address totally, and, striding from the platform, began scrambling through the audience and over the benches, toward the modest Nat, who stood near the door. When he

274

reached him, Lincoln shook his hand " cordially ; " and, after felicitating himself sufficiently upon the happy meeting, he returned to the platform, and finished his speech. When that was over, Lincoln could not make up his mind to part with Nat, but insisted that they must sleep together. Accordingly, they wended their way to Col. Jones's, where that fine old Jackson Democrat received his distinguished " clerk " with all the honors he could show him. Nat says, that in the night a cat " began mewing, scratching, and making a fuss generally." Lincoln got up, took the cat in his hands, and stroking its back " gently and kindly," made it sparkle for Nat's amusement. He then " gently " put it out of the door, and, returning to bed, " commenced telling stories and talking over old times."

It is hardly necessary to say, that the result of the canvass was a severe disappointment to Mr. Lincoln. No defeat but his own could have given him more pain ; and thereafter he seems to have attended quietly to his own private business until the Congressional canvass of 1846.

It was thought for many years by some persons well informed, that between Lincoln, Logan, Baker, and Hardin, — four very conspicuous Whig leaders, — there was a secret personal understanding that they four should " rotate " in Congress until each had had a term. Baker succeeded Hardin in 1844; Lincoln was elected in 1846, and Logan was nominated, but defeated, in 1848. Lincoln publicly declined to contest the nomination with Baker in 1844; Hardin did the same for Lincoln in 1846 (although both seem to have acted reluctantly), and Lincoln refused to run against Logan in 1848. Col. Matheny and others insist, with great show of reason, that the agreement actually existed ; and, if such was the case, it was practically carried out, although Lincoln was a candidate against Baker, and Hardin against Lincoln, as long as either of them thought there was the smallest prospect of success. They might have done this, however, merely to keep other and less tractable candidates out of the field. That Lincoln would cheerfully have made such a bargain to insure himself a seat in Congress, there can be no doubt; but the supposition that he did do it can scarcely be reconciled with the feeling displayed by him in the conflict with Baker, or the persistency of Hardin, to a very late hour, in the contest of 1846.

At all events, Mr. Lincoln and Gen. Hardin were the two, and the only two, candidates for the Whig nomination in 1846. The contest was much like the one with Baker, and Lincoln was assailed in much the same fashion. He was called a deist and an infidel, both before and after his nomination, and encountered in a less degree the same opposition from the members of certain religious bodies that had met him before. But with Hardin he maintained personal relations the most friendly. The latter proposed to alter the mode of making the nomination; and, in the letter conveying this desire to Mr. Lincoln, he also offered to stipulate that each candidate should remain within the limits of his own county. To this Mr. Lincoln replied, " As to your proposed stipulation that all the candidates shall remain in their own counties, and restrain their friends to the same, it seems to me, that, on reflection, you will see the fact of your having been in Congress has, in various ways, so spread your name in the district as to give you a decided advantage in such a stipulation. I appreciate your desire to keep down excitement, and I promise you to ' keep cool' under the circumstances."

On the 26th of February, 1846, " The Journal " contained Gen. Hardin's card declining to be " longer considered a candidate," and in its editorial comments occurred the following: " We have had, and now have, no doubt that he (Hardin) has been, and now is, a great favorite with the Whigs of the district. He states, in substance, that there was never any understanding on his part that his name was not to be presented in the canvasses of 1844 and 1846. This, we believe, is strictly true. Still, the doings of the Pekin Convention did seem to point that way; and the general's voluntary declination as to the canvass of 1844 was by many construed into an acquiescence on his part. These things had led many of his most devoted friends to not expect him to be a candi-

date at this time. Add to this the relation that Mr. Lincoln
bears, and has borne, to the party, and it is not strange that
many of those who are as strongly devoted to Gen. Hardin
as they are to Mr. Lincoln should prefer the latter at this
time. We do not entertain a doubt, that, if we could reverse
the positions of the two men, that a very large portion of
those who now have supported Mr. Lincoln most warmly
would have supported Gen. Hardin quite as warmly." This
article was admirably calculated to soothe Gen. Hardin, and
to win over his friends. It was wise and timely. The editor
was Mr. Lincoln's intimate friend. It is marked by Mr. Lincoln's style, and has at least one expression which was peculiar to him.

In its issue of May 7, " The Journal" announced the nomination as having been made at Petersburg, on the Friday
previous, and said further, " This nomination was, of course,
anticipated, there being no other candidate in the field. Mr.
Lincoln, we all know, is a good Whig, a good man, an able
speaker, and richly deserves, as he enjoys, the confidence of
the Whigs of this district and of the State."

Peter Cartwright, the celebrated pioneer Methodist preacher, noted for his piety and combativeness, was Mr. Lincoln's
competitor before the people. We know already the nature
of the principal charges against Mr. Lincoln's personal character; and these, with the usual criticism upon Whig policy,
formed the staple topics of the campaign on the Democratic
side. But Peter himself did not escape with that impunity
which might have been expected in the case of a minister of
the gospel. Rough tongues circulated exaggerated stories of
his wicked pugnacity and his worldly-mindedness, whilst the
pretended servant of the Prince of peace. Many Democrats
looked with intense disgust upon his present candidacy, and
believed, that, by mingling in politics, he was degrading his
office and polluting the Church. One of these Democrats told
Mr. Lincoln what he thought, and said, that, although it was
a hard thing to vote against his party, he would do it if it
should be necessary to defeat Cartwright. Mr. Lincoln told

him, that on the day of the election he would give him a
candid opinion as to whether the vote was needed or not
Accordingly, on that day, he called upon the gentleman,
and said, "I have got the preacher, . . . and don't want
your vote."

Clay's majority in this district in 1844 had been but nine
hundred and fourteen; whereas it now gave Mr. Lincoln a
majority of fifteen hundred and eleven, in a year which had
no Presidential excitements to bring out electors. In 1848
Gen. Taylor's majority was smaller by ten, and the same year
the Whig candidate for Congress was defeated by a hundred
and six.

In the following letter to Mr. Speed, he intimates that the
first sensations of pleasure attending his new distinction were
not of long duration; at least, that there were moments in
which, if he did not forget his greatness, it afforded him
little joy.

SPRINGFIELD, Oct. 22, 1846.

DEAR SPEED, —

   .   .   .   .   .   .

You no doubt assign the suspension of our correspondence to the true
philosophic cause; though it must.be confessed by both of us, that this is
rather a cold reason for allowing a friendship such as ours to die out by
degrees. I propose now, that, upon receipt of this, you shall be considered
in my debt, and under obligations to pay soon, and that neither shall remain
long in arrears hereafter. Are you agreed?

Being elected to Congress, though I am very grateful to our friends for
having done it, has not pleased me as much as I expected.

We have another boy, born the 10th of March. He is very much such a
child as Bob was at his age, rather of a longer order. Bob is "short and
low," and expect always will be. He talks very plainly, — almost as plainly
as anybody. He is quite smart enough. I sometimes fear he is one of the
little rare-ripe sort, that are smarter at about five than ever after. He has
a great deal of that sort of mischief that is the offspring of much animal
spirits. Since I began this letter, a messenger came to tell me Bob was
lost; but by the time I reached the house his mother had found him, and had
him whipped; and by now, very likely, he is run away again. Mary has
read your letter, and wishes to be remembered to Mrs. S. and you, in which
I most sincerely join her.

As ever yours,

A. LINCOLN.

At the meeting of the Thirtieth Congress Mr. Lincoln took his seat, and went about the business of his office with a strong determination to do something memorable. He was the only Whig member from Illinois, and would be carefully watched. His colleagues were several of them old acquaintances of the Vandalia times. They were John McClernand, O. B. Ficklin, William A. Richardson, Thomas J. Turner, Robert Smith, and John Wentworth (Long John). And at this session that alert, tireless, ambitious little man, Stephen A. Douglas, took his seat in the Senate.

The roll of this House shone with an array of great and brilliant names. Robert C. Winthrop was the Speaker. On the Whig side were John Quincy Adams, Horace Mann, Hunt of New York, Collamer of Vermont, Ingersoll of Pennsylvania, Botts and Goggin of Virginia, Morehead of Kentucky, Caleb B. Smith of Indiana, Stephens and Toombs of Georgia, Gentry of Tennessee, and Vinton and Schenck of Ohio. On the Democratic side were Wilmot of Pennsylvania, McLane of Maryland, McDowell of Virginia, Rhett of South Carolina, Cobb of Georgia, Boyd of Kentucky, Brown and Thompson of Mississippi, and Andrew Johnson and George W. Jones of Tennessee. In the Senate were Webster, Calhoun, Benton, Berrien, Clayton, Bell, Hunter, and William R. King.

The House organized on the 6th; and the day previous to that Mr. Lincoln wrote to his friend and partner, William H. Herndon : —

WASHINGTON, Dec. 5, 1847.

DEAR WILLIAM, — You may remember that about a year ago a man by the name of Wilson (James Wilson, I think) paid us twenty dollars as an advance fee to attend to a case in the Supreme Court for him, against a Mr. Campbell, the record of which case was in the hands of Mr. Dixon of St. Louis, who never furnished it to us. When I was at Bloomington last fall, I met a friend of Wilson, who mentioned the subject to me, and induced me to write to Wilson, telling him that I would leave the ten dollars with you which had been left with me to pay for making abstracts in the case, so that the case may go on this winter; but I came away, and forgot to do it. What I want now is to send you the money to be used accordingly, if any one comes on to start the case, or to be retained by you if no one does.

There is nothing of consequence new here. Congress is to organize to-morrow. Last night we held a Whig caucus for the House, and nominated Winthrop of Massachusetts for Speaker, Sargent of Pennsylvania for Sergeant-at-arms, Homer of New Jersey Doorkeeper, and McCormick of District of Columbia Postmaster. The Whig majority in the House is so small, that, together with some little dissatisfaction, leaves it doubtful whether we will elect them all.

This paper is too thick to fold, which is the reason I send only a half-sheet.

Yours as ever,

A. LINCOLN.

Again on the 13th, to the same gentleman: —

WASHINGTON, Dec. 13, 1847.

DEAR WILLIAM, — Your letter advising me of the receipt of our fee in the bank-case is just received, and I don't expect to hear another as good a piece of news from Springfield while I am away. I am under no obligations to the bank; and I therefore wish you to buy bank certificates, and pay my debt there, so as to pay it with the least money possible. I would as soon you should buy them of Mr. Ridgely, or any other person at the bank, as of any one else, provided you can get them as cheaply. I suppose, after the bank-debt shall be paid, there will be some money left, out of which I would like to have you pay Lavely and Stout twenty dollars, and Priest and somebody (oil-makers) ten dollars, for materials got for house-painting. If there shall still be any left, keep it till you see or hear from me.

I shall begin sending documents so soon as I can get them. I wrote you yesterday about a " Congressional Globe." As you are all so anxious for me to distinguish myself, I have concluded to do so before long.

Yours truly,

A. LINCOLN.

Mr. Lincoln was a member of the Committee on Post-offices and Post-roads, and in that capacity had occasion to study the claim of a mail-contractor who had appealed to Congress against a decision of the Department. Mr. Lincoln made a speech on the case, in which, being his first, he evidently felt some pride, and reported progress to his friends at home: —

WASHINGTON, Jan. 8, 1848.

DEAR WILLIAM, — Your letter of Dec. 27 was received a day or two ago. I am much obliged to you for the trouble you have taken, and promise to take, in my little business there. As to speech-making, by way of getting the hang of the House, I made a little speech two or three days ago, on a post-office question of no general interest. I find speaking *here* and *elsewhere* about the same thing. I was about as badly scared, and no worse, as I am when I speak in court. I expect to make one within a week or two, in which I hope to succeed well enough to wish you to see it.

It is very pleasant to me to learn from you that there are some who desire that I should be re-elected. I most heartily thank them for the kind partiality; and I can say, as Mr. Clay said of the annexation of Texas, that "*personally* I would not object" to a re-election, although I thought at the time, and still think, it would be quite as well for me to return to the law at the end of a single term. I made the declaration, that I would not be a candidate again, more from a wish to deal fairly with others, to keep peace among our friends, and to keep the district from going to the enemy, than for any cause personal to myself; so that, if it should so happen *that nobody else wishes to be elected*, I could not refuse the people the right of sending me again. But to enter myself as a competitor of others, or to authorize any one so to enter me, is what my word and honor forbid.

I get some letters intimating a probability of so much difficulty amongst our friends as to lose us the district; but I remember such letters were written to Baker when my own case was under consideration, and I trust there is no more ground for such apprehension now than there was then.

Remember I am always glad to receive a letter from you.

Most truly your friend,
A. LINCOLN.

Thoroughly hostile to Polk, and hotly opposed to the war, Mr. Lincoln took an active, although not a leading part in the discussions relating to the commencement and conduct of the latter. He was politician enough, however, to go with the majority of his party in voting supplies to the troops, and thanks to the generals, whilst censuring the President by solemnly declaring that the "war was unnecessarily and unconstitutionally begun by the President of the United States." But his position, and the position of the Whigs, will be made sufficiently apparent by the productions of his own pen.

On the 22d of December, 1847, Mr. Lincoln introduced a preamble and resolutions, which attained great celebrity in Illinois under the title of "Spot Resolutions," and in all probability lost the party a great many votes in the Springfield district. They were as follows: —

WHEREAS, The President of the United States, in his Message of May 11, 1846, has declared that "the Mexican Government not only refused to receive him [the envoy of the United States], or listen to his propositions, but, after a long-continued series of menaces, has at last invaded *our territory*, and shed the blood of our fellow-citizens on *our own soil;*"

And again, in his Message of Dec. 8, 1846, that "we had ample cause of war against Mexico long before the breaking out of hostilities; but even then we forbore to take redress into our own hands until Mexico herself became the aggressor, by invading *our soil* in hostile array, and shedding the blood of our citizens;"

And yet again, in his Message of Dec. 7, 1847, that "the Mexican Government refused even to hear the terms of adjustment which he [our minister of peace] was authorized to propose, and finally, under wholly unjustifiable pretexts, involved the two countries in war, by invading the territory of the State of Texas, striking the first blow, and shedding the blood of our citizens on *our own soil;*" and,

WHEREAS, This House is desirous to obtain a full knowledge of all the facts which go to establish whether the particular spot on which the blood of our citizens was so shed was or was not at that time "*our own soil;*" therefore,

Resolved by the House of Representatives, That the President of the United States be respectfully requested to inform this House, —

1st. Whether the spot on which the blood of our citizens was shed, as in his Messages declared, was or was not within the territory of Spain, at least after the treaty of 1819, until the Mexican revolution.

2d. Whether that spot is or is not within the territory which was wrested from Spain by the revolutionary government of Mexico.

3d. Whether that spot is or is not within a settlement of people, which settlement has existed ever since long before the Texas revolution, and until its inhabitants fled before the approach of the United States army.

4th. Whether that settlement is or is not isolated from any and all other settlements by the Gulf and the Rio Grande on the south and west, and by wide, uninhabited regions on the north and east.

5th. Whether the people of that settlement, or a majority of them, or any of them, have ever submitted themselves to the government or laws of Texas or of the United States, by consent or by compulsion, either by accepting office, or voting at elections, or paying tax, or serving on juries, or having process served upon them, or in any other way.

6th. Whether the people of that settlement did or did not flee from the approach of the United States army, leaving unprotected their homes and their growing crops, *before* the blood was shed, as in the Messages stated; and whether the first blood, so shed, was or was not shed within the enclosure of one of the people who had thus fled from it.

7th. Whether our *citizens*, whose blood was shed, as in his Messages declared, were or were not at that time armed officers and soldiers, sent into that settlement by the military order of the President, through the Secretary of War.

8th. Whether the military force of the United States was or was not so sent into that settlement after Gen. Taylor had more than once intimated to the War Department, that, in his opinion, no such movement was necessary to the defence or protection of Texas.

Mr. Lincoln improved the first favorable opportunity (Jan. 12, 1848), to address the House in the spirit of the " Spot Resolutions."

In Committee of the Whole House, Jan. 12, 1848.

Mr. Lincoln addressed the Committee as follows : —

MR. CHAIRMAN, — Some, if not at all, of the gentlemen on the other side of the House, who have addressed the Committee within the last two days, have spoken rather complainingly, if I have rightly understood them, of the vote given a week or ten days ago, declaring that the war with Mexico was unnecessarily and unconstitutionally commenced by the President. I admit that such a vote should not be given in mere party wantonness, and that the one given is justly censurable, if it have no other or better foundation. I am one of those who joined in that vote, and did so under my best impression of the *truth* of the case. How I got this impression, and how it may possibly be removed, I will now try to show. When the war began, it was my opinion that all those who, because of knowing too *little*, or because of knowing too *much*, could not conscientiously approve the conduct of the President (in the beginning of it), should, nevertheless, as good citizens and patriots, remain silent on that point, at least till the war should be ended. Some leading Democrats, including ex-President Van Buren, have taken this same view, as I understand them ; and I adhered to it, and acted upon it, until since I took my seat here ; and I think I should still adhere to it, were it not that the President and his friends will not allow it to be so. Besides the continual effort of the President to argue every silent vote given for supplies into an indorsement of the justice and wisdom of his conduct ; besides that singularly candid paragraph in his late Message, in which he tells us that Congress, with great unanimity (only two in the Senate and fourteen in the House dissenting), had declared that " by the act of the Republic of Mexico a state of war exists between that government and the United States ; " when the same journals that informed him of this also informed him, that, when that declaration stood disconnected from the question of supplies, sixty-seven in the House, and not fourteen merely, voted against it ; besides this open attempt to prove by telling the *truth* what he could not prove by telling the *whole truth*, demanding of all who will not submit to be misrepresented, in justice to themselves, to speak out; besides all this, one of my colleagues [Mr. Richardson], at a very early day in the session, brought in a set of resolutions expressly indorsing the original justice of the war on the part of the President. Upon these resolutions, when they shall be put on their passage, I shall be *compelled* to vote; so that I cannot be silent if I would. Seeing this, I went about preparing myself to give the vote understandingly when it should come. I carefully examined the President's Messages, to ascertain what he himself had said and proved upon the point. The result of this examination was to make the impression, that, taking for true all the President states as facts, he falls far short of proving his justification; and that the President would have gone further with his proof, if it had not been for the small matter that the *truth* would not permit him. Under the impression thus made, I gave the vote before mentioned. I propose now to give concisely the process of the examination I made, and how I reached the conclusion I did.

The President, in his first Message of May, 1846, declares that the soil was *ours* on which hostilities were commenced by Mexico; and he repeats that declaration, almost in the same language, in each successive annual Message, — thus showing that he esteems that point a highly essential one. In the importance of that point I entirely agree with the President. To my judgment, it is the *very point* upon which he should be justified or condemned. In his Message of December, 1846, it seems to have occurred to him, as is certainly true, that title, ownership to soil, or any thing else, is not a simple fact, but is a conclusion following one or more simple facts; and that it was incumbent upon him to present the facts from which he concluded the soil was ours on which the first blood of the war was shed.

Accordingly, a little below the middle of page twelve, in the Message last referred to, he enters upon that task; forming an issue and introducing testimony, extending the whole to a little below the middle of page fourteen. Now, I propose to try to show that the whole of this, issue and evidence, is, from beginning to end, the sheerest deception. The issue, as he presents it, is in these words: "But there are those who, conceding all this to be true, assume the ground that the true western boundary of Texas is the Nueces, instead of the Rio Grande; and that, therefore, in marching our army to the east bank of the latter river, we passed the Texan line, and invaded the Territory of Mexico." Now, this issue is made up of two affirmatives, and no negative. The main deception of it is, that it assumes as true, that *one* river or the *other* is necessarily the boundary, and cheats the superficial thinker entirely out of the idea that *possibly* the boundary is somewhere *between* the two, and not actually at either. A further deception is, that it will let in *evidence* which a true issue would exclude. A true issue made by the President would be about as follows: " I say the soil *was ours* on which the first blood was shed; there are those who say it was not."

I now proceed to examine the President's evidence, as applicable to such an issue. When that evidence is analyzed, it is all included in the following propositions : —

1. That the Rio Grande was the western boundary of Louisiana, as we purchased it of France in 1803.

2. That the Republic of Texas always *claimed* the Rio Grande as her western boundary.

3. That, by various acts, she had claimed it *on paper.*

4. That Santa Anna, in his treaty with Texas, recognized the Rio Grande as her boundary.

5. That Texas *before*, and the United States *after* annexation, had *exercised* jurisdiction *beyond* the Nueces, *between* the two rivers.

6. That our Congress *understood* the boundary of Texas to extend beyond the Nueces.

Now for each of these in its turn : —

His first item is, that the Rio Grande was the western boundary of Louisiana, as we purchased it of France in 1803 ; and, seeming to expect this to be disputed, he argues over the amount of nearly a page to prove it true ; at the end of which, he lets us know, that, by the treaty of 1819, we sold to Spain the whole country, from the Rio Grande eastward to the Sabine. Now, admitting for the present, that the Rio Grande was the boundary of Louisiana, what, under Heaven, had that to do with the *present* boundary between us and Mexico ? How, Mr. Chairman, the line that once divided your land from mine can *still* be the boundary between us *after* I have sold my land to you, is, to me, beyond all comprehension. And how any man, with an honest purpose only of proving the truth, could ever have *thought* of introducing such a fact to prove such an issue, is equally incomprehensible. The outrage upon common *right*, of seizing as our own what we have once sold, merely because it *was* ours *before* we sold it, is only equalled by the outrage on common *sense* of any attempt to justify it.

The President's next piece of evidence is, that " The Republic of Texas always *claimed* this river (Rio Grande) as her western boundary." That is not true, in fact. Texas *has* claimed it, but she has not *always* claimed it. There is, at least, one distinguished exception. Her State Constitution — the public's most solemn and well-considered act, that which may, without impropriety, be called her last will and testament, revoking all others — makes no such claim. But suppose she had always claimed it. Has not Mexico always claimed the contrary ? So that there is but *claim* against *claim*, leaving nothing proved until we get back of the claims, and find which has the better *foundation.*

Though not in the order in which the President presents his evidence, I now consider that class of his statements which are, in substance, nothing more than that Texas has, by various acts of her Convention and Congress, claimed the Rio Grande as her boundary — *on paper.* I mean here what

he says about the fixing of the Rio Grande as her boundary in her old constitution (not her State Constitution), about forming congressional districts,
counties, &c.   Now, all this is but naked *claim ;* and what I have already said
about claims is strictly applicable to this.   If I should claim your land by
word of mouth, that certainly would not make it mine ; and if I were to
claim it by a deed which I had made myself, and with which you had
nothing to do, the claim would be quite the same in substance, or rather in
utter nothingness.

I next consider the President's statement that Santa Anna, in his *treaty*
with Texas, recognized the Rio Grande as the western boundary of Texas.
Besides the position so often taken that Santa Anna, while a prisoner of
war, a captive, *could* not bind Mexico by a treaty, which I deem conclusive, — besides this, I wish to say something in relation to this treaty, so
called by the President, with Santa Anna.   If any man would like to be
amused by a sight at that *little* thing, which the President calls by that *big*
name, he can have it by turning to "Niles's Register," vol. l. p. 336.
And if any one should suppose that "Niles's Register" is a curious reposi-
tory of so mighty a document as a solemn treaty between nations, I can
only say that I learned, to a tolerable degree of certainty, by inquiry at the
State Department, that the President himself never saw it anywhere else.
By the way, I believe I should not err if I were to declare, that, during the
first ten years of the existence of that document, it was never by anybody
called a treaty; that it was never so called till the President, in his extremity, attempted, by so calling it, to wring something from it in justification
of himself in connection with the Mexican war.   It has none of the dis-
tinguishing features of a treaty.   It does not call itself a treaty.   Santa
Anna does not therein assume to bind Mexico : he assumes only to act as
president, commander-in-chief of the Mexican army and navy ; stipulates
that the then present hostilities should cease, and that he would not *himself*
take up arms, nor *influence* the Mexican people to take up arms, against
Texas during the existence of the war of independence.   He did not recognize the independence of Texas ; he did not assume to put an end to the
war, but clearly indicated his expectation of its continuance ; he did not
say one word about boundary, and most probably never thought of it.   It *is*
stipulated therein that the Mexican forces should evacuate the Territory of
Texas, *passing to the other side of the Rio Grande;* and in another article it
is stipulated, that, to prevent collisions between the armies, the Texan army
should not approach nearer than within five leagues, — of *what* is not said ;
but clearly, from the object stated, it is of the Rio Grande.   Now, if this
is a treaty recognizing the Rio Grande as the boundary of Texas, it contains the singular feature of stipulating that Texas shall not go within five
leagues of *her own* boundary.

Next comes the evidence of Texas before annexation, and the United
States afterwards, exercising jurisdiction beyond the Nueces, and *between*

the two rivers. This actual *exercise* of jurisdiction is the very class or quality of evidence we want. It is excellent so far as it goes; but does it go far enough? He tells us it went *beyond* the Nueces; but he does not tell us it went *to* the Rio Grande. He tells us jurisdiction was exercised *between* the two rivers; but he does not tell us it was exercised over *all* the territory between them. Some simple-minded people think it possible to cross one river and go beyond it, without going all the way to the next; that jurisdiction may be exercised *between* two rivers without covering *all* the country between them. I know a man, not very unlike myself, who exercises jurisdiction over a piece of land between the Wabash and the Mississippi; and yet so far is this from being *all* there is between those rivers, that it is just a hundred and fifty-two feet long by fifty wide, and no part of it much within a hundred miles of either. He has a neighbor between him and the Mississippi, — that is, just across the street, in that direction, — whom, I am sure, he could neither *persuade* nor *force* to give up his habitation; but which, nevertheless, he could certainly annex, if it were to be done by merely standing on his own side of the street and claiming it, or even sitting down and writing a deed for it.

But next, the President tells us, the Congress of the United States *understood* the State of Texas they admitted into the Union to extend *beyond* the Nueces. Well, I suppose they did. — I certainly so understand it, — but how *far* beyond? That Congress did *not* understand it to extend clear to the Rio Grande, is quite certain by the fact of their joint resolutions for admission, expressly leaving all questions of boundary to future adjustment. And it may be added, that Texas herself is proved to have had the same understanding of it that our Congress had, by the fact of the exact conformity of her new Constitution to those resolutions.

I am now through the whole of the President's evidence; and it is a singular fact, that, if any one should declare the President sent the army into the midst of a settlement of Mexican people, who had never submitted, by consent or by force, to the authority of Texas or of the United States, and that *there*, and *thereby*, the first blood of the war was shed, there is not one word in all the President has said which would either admit or deny the declaration. In this strange omission chiefly consists the deception of the President's evidence, — an omission which, it does seem to me, could scarcely have occurred but by design. My way of living leads me to be about the courts of justice; and there I have sometimes seen a good lawyer, struggling for his client's neck in a desperate case, employing every artifice to work round, befog, and cover up with many words, some position pressed upon him by the prosecution, which he *dared* not admit, and yet *could* not deny. Party bias may help to make it appear so; but, with all the allowance I can make for such bias, it still does appear to me that just such, and from just such necessity, are the President's struggles in this case.

Some time after my colleague (Mr. Richardson) introduced the resolutions

I have mentioned, I introduced a preamble, resolution, and interrogatories, intended to draw the President out, if possible, on this hitherto untrodden ground. To show their relevancy, I propose to state my understanding of the true rule for ascertaining the boundary between Texas and Mexico. It is, that, *wherever* Texas was *exercising* jurisdiction was hers; and wherever Mexico was exercising jurisdiction was hers; and that whatever separated the actual exercise of jurisdiction of the one from that of the other was the true boundary between them. If, as is probably true, Texas was exercising jurisdiction along the western bank of the Nueces, and Mexico was exercising it along the eastern bank of the Rio Grande, then *neither* river was the boundary, but the uninhabited country between the two was. The extent of our territory in that region depended, not on any *treaty-fixed* boundary (for no treaty had attempted it), but on revolution. Any people anywhere, being inclined and having the power, have the *right* to rise up and shake off the existing government, and form a new one that suits them better. This is a most valuable, a most sacred right, — a right which, we hope and believe, is to liberate the world. Nor is this right confined to cases in which the whole people of an existing government may choose to exercise it. Any portion of such people that *can* may revolutionize, and make their *own* of so much of the territory as they inhabit. More than this, a *majority* of any portion of such people may revolutionize, putting down a *minority*, intermingled with or near about them, who may oppose their movements. Such minority was precisely the case of the Tories of our own Revolution. It is a quality of revolutions not to go by old lines or old laws, but to break up both, and make new ones. As to the country now in question, we bought it of France in 1803, and sold it to Spain in 1819, according to the President's statement. After this, all Mexico, including Texas, revolutionized against Spain; and, still later, Texas revolutionized against Mexico. In my view, just so far as she carried her revolution, by obtaining the *actual*, willing or unwilling, submission of the people, *so far* the country was hers, and no farther.

Now, sir, for the purpose of obtaining the very best evidence as to whether Texas had actually carried her revolution to the place where the hostilities of the present war commenced, let the President answer the interrogatories I proposed, as before mentioned, or some other similar ones. Let him answer fully, fairly, and candidly. Let him answer with *facts*, and not with arguments. Let him remember he sits where Washington sat; and, so remembering, let him answer as Washington would answer. As a nation *should* not, and the Almighty *will* not, be evaded, so let him attempt no evasion, no equivocation. And if, so answering, he can show that the soil was ours where the first blood of the war was shed; that it was not within an inhabited country, or, if within such, that the inhabitants had submitted themselves to the civil authority of Texas, or of the United States, and that the same is true of the site of Fort Brown, then I am with him for his justification. In that case, I shall be most happy to reverse the vote I gave the other day. I have a selfish motive for desiring that the President may do this : I expect to give some votes, in connection with the war, which, without his so doing, will be of doubtful propriety, in my own judgment, but which will be free from the doubt if he does so. But if he *cannot* or *will not* do this, — if, on any pretence, or no pretence, he shall refuse or omit it, — then I shall be fully convinced of what I more than suspect already, — that he is deeply conscious of being in the wrong ; that he feels the blood of this war, like the blood of Abel, is crying to Heaven against him ; that he ordered Gen. Taylor into the midst of a peaceful Mexican settlement, purposely to bring on a war ; that, originally having some strong motive — what I will not stop now to give my opinion concerning — to involve the two countries in a war, and trusting to escape scrutiny by fixing the public gaze upon the exceeding brightness of military glory, — that attractive rainbow that rises in showers of blood, that serpent's eye that charms to destroy, — he plunged into it, and has swept *on* and *on*, till, disappointed in his calculation of the ease with which Mexico might be subdued, he now finds himself he knows not where. How like the half-insane mumbling of a fever-dream is the whole war part of the late Message ! At one time telling us that Mexico has nothing whatever that we can get but territory ; at another, showing us how we can support the war by levying contributions on Mexico. At one time urging the national honor, the security of the future, the prevention of foreign interference, and even the good of Mexico herself, as among the objects of the war ; at another, telling us that, " to reject indemnity by refusing to accept a cession of territory, would be to abandon all our just demands, and to wage the war, bearing all its expenses, *without a purpose or definite object.*" So, then, the national honor, security of the future, and every thing but territorial indemnity, may be considered the *no purposes* and *indefinite* objects of the war ! But having it now settled that territorial indemnity is the only object, we are urged to seize, by legislation here, all that he was content to take a few months ago, and the whole province of Lower California to boot, and to still carry on the war, — to take *all* we are fighting for, and *still* fight on. Again, the President is resolved, under all circumstances, to have full territorial indemnity for the expenses of the war ; but he forgets to tell us how we are to get the *excess* after those expenses shall have surpassed the value of the *whole* of the Mexican territory. So, again, he insists that the separate national existence of Mexico shall be maintained ; but he does not tell us *how* this can be done after we shall have taken *all* her territory. Lest the questions I here suggest be considered speculative merely, let me be indulged a moment in trying to show they are not.

The war has gone on some twenty months ; for the expenses of which, together with an inconsiderable old score, the President now claims about one-half of the Mexican territory, and that by far the better half, so far as

19

concerns our ability to make any thing out of it. It is comparatively uninhabited; so that we could establish land-offices in it, and raise some money
in that way. But the other half is already inhabited, as I understand it,
tolerably densely for the nature of the country; and all its lands, or all that
are valuable, already appropriated as private property. How, then, are we
to make any thing out of these lands with this encumbrance on them, or
how remove the encumbrance? I suppose no one will say we should kill
the people, or drive them out, or make slaves of them, or even confiscate
their property? How, then, can we make much out of this part of the territory? If the prosecution of the war has, in expenses, already equalled
the *better* half of the country, how long its future prosecution will be in
equalling the less valuable half is not a *speculative* but a *practical* question,
pressing closely upon us; and yet it is a question which the President seems
never to have thought of.

As to the mode of terminating the war and securing peace, the President
is equally wandering and indefinite. First, it is to be done by a more vigorous prosecution of the war in the vital parts of the enemy's country; and,
after apparently talking himself tired on this point, the President drops
down into a half-despairing tone, and tells us, that " with a people distracted
and divided by contending factions, and a government subject to constant
changes, by successive revolutions, *the continued success of our arms may fail
to obtain a satisfactory peace.*" Then he suggests the propriety of wheedling
the Mexican people to desert the counsels of their own leaders, and, trusting
in our protection, to set up a government from which we can secure a satisfactory peace, telling us that, " *this may become the only mode of obtaining such
a peace.*" But soon he falls into doubt of this, too, and then drops back on
to the already half-abandoned ground of "more vigorous prosecution." All
this shows that the President is in no wise satisfied with his own positions.
First, he takes up one, and, in attempting to argue us into it, he argues
himself *out* of it; then seizes another, and goes through the same process;
and then, confused at being able to think of nothing new, he snatches up
the old one again, which he has some time before cast off. His mind, tasked
beyond its power, is running hither and thither, like some tortured creature
on a burning surface, finding no position on which it can settle down and be
at ease.

Again, it is a singular omission in this Message, that it nowhere intimates
when the President expects the war to terminate. At its beginning, Gen.
Scott was, by this same President, driven into disfavor, if not disgrace, for
intimating that peace could not be conquered in less than three or four
months. But now at the end of about twenty months, during which time
our arms have given us the most splendid successes, — every department,
and every part, land and water, officers and privates, regulars and volunteers, doing all that men could do, and hundreds of things which it had ever
before been thought that men could *not* do, — after all this, this same Presi-

dent gives us a long Message without showing us that, *as to the end*, he has himself even an imaginary conception. As I have before said, he knows not where he is. He is a bewildered, confounded, and miserably perplexed man. God grant he may be able to show that there is not something about his conscience more painful than all his mental perplexity.

This speech he hastened to send home as soon as it was printed; for, while throughout he trod on unquestionable Whig ground, he had excellent reasons to fear the result. The following is the first letter to Mr. Herndon after the delivery of the speech, and notifying him of the fact: —

WASHINGTON, Jan. 19, 1848.

DEAR WILLIAM, — Enclosed you find a letter of Louis W. Candler. What is wanted is, that you shall ascertain whether the claim upon the note described has received any dividend in the Probate Court of Christian County, where the estate of Mr. Overton Williams has been administered on. If nothing is paid on it, withdraw the note and send it to me, so that Candler can see the indorser of it. At all events, write me all about it, till I can somehow get it off hands. I have already been bored more than enough about it; not the least of which annoyance is his cursed, unreadable, and ungodly handwriting.

I have made a speech, a copy of which I will send you by next mail.

Yours as ever,

A. LINCOLN.

About the last of January, or the first of February, he began to hear the first murmurs of alarm and dissatisfaction from his district. He was now on the defensive, and compelled to write long and tedious letters to pacify some of the Whigs. Of this character are two extremely interesting epistles to Mr. Herndon: —

WASHINGTON, Feb. 1, 1848.

DEAR WILLIAM, — Your letter of the 19th ult. was received last night, and for which I am much obliged. The only thing in it that I wish to talk to you about at once is, that, because of my vote for Ashmun's amendment, you fear that you and I disagree about the war. I regret this, not because of any fear we shall remain disagreed after you have read this letter, but because if *you* misunderstand, I fear other good friends may also. That vote affirms, that the war was unnecessarily and unconstitutionally commenced by the President; and I will stake my life, that, if you had been in my place, you would have voted just as I did. Would you have voted what you felt and knew to be a lie? I know you would not. Would you have gone out of the House, — skulked the vote? I expect not. If you had skulked one vote, you would have had to skulk many more before the end of the session. Richardson's resolutions, introduced before I made any move, or gave any vote upon the subject, make the direct question of the justice of the war; so that no man can be silent if he would. You are compelled to speak; and your only alternative is to tell the *truth* or tell a *lie*. I cannot doubt which you would do.

This vote has nothing to do in determining my votes on the questions of supplies. I have always intended, and still intend, to vote supplies; perhaps not in the precise form recommended by the President, but in a better form for all purposes, except Locofoco party purposes. It is in this particular you seem mistaken. The Locos are untiring in their efforts to make the impression that all who vote supplies, or take part in the war, do, of necessity, approve the President's conduct in the beginning of it; but the Whigs have, from the beginning, made and kept the distinction between the two. In the very first act nearly all the Whigs voted *against* the preamble declaring that war existed by the act of Mexico; and yet nearly all of them voted *for* the supplies. As to the Whig men who have participated in the war, so far as they have spoken to my hearing, they do not hesitate to denounce as unjust the President's conduct in the beginning of the war. They do not suppose that such denunciation is directed by undying hatred to them, as "The Register" would have it believed. There are two such Whigs on this floor (Col. Haskell and Major James). The former fought as a colonel by the side of Col. Baker, at Cerro Gordo, and stands side by side with me in the vote that you seem dissatisfied with. The latter, the history of whose capture with Cassius Clay you well know, had not arrived here when that vote was given; but, as I understand, he stands ready to give just such a vote whenever an occasion shall present. Baker, too, who is now here, says the truth is undoubtedly that way; and, whenever he shall speak out, he will say so. Col. Donaphin, too, the favorite Whig of Missouri, and who overrun all Northern Mexico, on his return home, in a public speech at St. Louis, condemned the administration in relation to the war, if I remember. G. T. M. Davis, who has been through almost the whole war, declares in favor of Mr. Clay; from which I infer that he adopts the sentiments of Mr. Clay, generally at least. On the other hand, I have heard of but one Whig who has been to the war attempting to justify the President's conduct. That one was Capt. Bishop; editor of "The Charleston Courier," and a very clever fellow. I do not mean this letter for the public, but for you. Before it reaches you, you will have seen and read my pamphlet speech, and, perhaps, scared anew by it. After you get over your scare, read it over again, sentence by sentence, and tell me honestly what you think of it. I condensed all I could for fear of being cut off by the hour rule; and, when I got through, I had spoken but forty-five minutes.   Yours forever,

A. LINCOLN.

WASHINGTON, Feb. 15, 1848.

DEAR WILLIAM, — Your letter of the 29th January was received last night. Being exclusively a constitutional argument, I wish to submit some reflections upon it in the same spirit of kindness that I know actuates you. Let me first state what I understand to be your position. It is, that, if it shall become necessary *to repel invasion*, the President may, without violation of the Constitution, cross the line, and *invade* the territory of another country; and that whether such *necessity* exists in any given case, the President is the *sole* judge.

Before going farther, consider well whether this is, or is not, your position. If it is, it is a position that neither the President himself, nor any friend of his, so far as I know, has ever taken. Their only positions are, first, that the soil was ours where the hostilities commenced; and second, that, whether it was rightfully *ours* or not, *Congress had annexed it*, and the President, for that reason, was bound to defend it, both of which are as clearly proved to be false in fact as you can prove that your house is mine. That soil was not ours; and Congress did not annex, or attempt to annex it. But to return to your position. Allow the President to invade a neighboring nation whenever *he* shall deem it necessary to repel an invasion, and you allow him to do so *whenever he may choose to say* he deems it necessary for such purpose, and you allow him to make war at pleasure. Study to see if you can fix *any limit* to his power in this respect, after having given him so much as you propose. If to-day he should choose to say he thinks it necessary to invade Canada, to prevent the British from invading us, how could you stop him? You may say to him, "I see no probability of the British invading us;" but he will say to you, "Be silent: I see it, if you don't."

The provision of the Constitution giving the war-making power to Congress was dictated, as I understand it, by the following reasons: kings had always been involving and impoverishing their people in wars, pretending generally, if not always, that the good of the people was the object. This our convention understood to be the most oppressive of all kingly oppressions; and they resolved to so frame the Constitution that *no one man* should hold the power of bringing this oppression upon us. But your view destroys the whole matter, and places our President where kings have always stood.

Write soon again.

Yours truly,

A. LINCOLN.

But the Whig National Convention to nominate a candidate for the Presidency was to meet at Philadelphia on the 1st of June, and Mr. Lincoln was to be a member. He was not a Clay man: he wanted a candidate that could be elected; and he was for "Old Rough," as the only available material at hand. But let him explain himself : —

WASHINGTON, April 30, 1848.

DEAR WILLIAMS, — I have not seen in the papers any evidence of a movement to send a delegate from your circuit to the June Convention. I wish to say that I think it all important that a delegate should be sent. Mr. Clay's chance for an election is just no chance at all. He might get New York ; and that would have elected in 1844, but it will not now, because he must now, at the least, lose Tennessee, which he had then, and in addition the fifteen *new* votes of Florida, Texas, Iowa, and Wisconsin. I know our good friend Browning is a great admirer of Mr. Clay, and I therefore fear he is favoring his nomination. If he is, ask him to discard feeling, and try if he can possibly, as a matter of judgment, count the votes necessary to elect him.

In my judgment we can elect nobody but Gen. Taylor ; and we cannot elect him without a nomination. Therefore don't fail to send a delegate.

Your friend as ever,

A. LINCOLN.

To ARCHIBALD WILLIAMS, ESQ.

WASHINGTON, June 12, 1848.

DEAR WILLIAMS, — On my return from Philadelphia, where I had been attending the nomination of " Old Rough," I found your letter in a mass of others which had accumulated in my absence. By many, and often, it had been said they would not abide the nomination of Taylor; but, since the deed has been done, they are fast falling in, and in my opinion we shall have a most overwhelming, glorious triumph. One unmistakable sign is, that all the odds and ends are with us, — Barnburners, Native Americans, Tyler men, disappointed, office-seeking Locofocos, and the Lord knows what. This is important, if in nothing else, in showing which way the wind blows. Some of the sanguine men here set down all the States as certain for Taylor but Illinois, and it is doubtful. Cannot something be done even in Illinois ? Taylor's nomination takes the Locos on the blind side. It turns the war thunder against them. The war is now to them the gallows of Haman, which they built for us, and on which they are doomed to be hanged themselves.

Excuse this short letter. I have so many to write that I cannot devote much time to any one.

Yours as ever,

A. LINCOLN.

But his young partner in the law gave him a great deal of annoyance. Mr. Herndon seems to have been troubled by patriotic scruples. He could not understand how the war had

been begun unconstitutionally and unnecessarily by President
Polk, nor how the Whigs could vote supplies to carry on the
war without indorsing the war itself.   Besides all this, he
sent news of startling defections; and the weary Representative took up his pen again and again to explain, defend, and
advise : —

WASHINGTON, June 22, 1848.

DEAR WILLIAM, — Last night I was attending a sort of caucus of the
Whig members, held in relation to the coming Presidential election.   The
whole field of the nation was scanned; and all is high hope and confidence.
Illinois is expected to better her condition in this race.   Under these circumstances, judge how heart-rending it was to come to my room and find and
read your discouraging letter of the 15th.   We have made no gains, but have
lost " H. R. Robinson. Turner, Campbell, and four or five more."   Tell Arney
to reconsider, if he would be saved.   Baker and I used to do something, but
I think you attach more importance to our absence than is just.   There is
another cause : in 1840, for instance, we had two Senators and five Representatives in Sangamon; now, we have part of one Senator and two Representatives.   With quite one-third more people than we had then, we have
only half the sort of offices which are sought by men of the speaking sort of
talent.   This, I think, is the chief cause.   Now, as to the young men.   You
must not wait to be brought forward by the older men.   For instance, do
you suppose that I should ever have got into notice if I had waited to be
hunted up and pushed forward by older men.   You young men get together
and form a Rough and Ready Club, and have regular meetings and speeches.
Take in everybody that you can get.   Harrison, Grimsley, Z. A. Enos, Lee
Kimball, and C. W. Matheny will do to begin the thing; but, as you go
along, gather up all the shrewd, wild boys about town, whether just of age or
a little under age, — Chris. Logan, Reddick Ridgely, Lewis Zwizler, and
hundreds such.   Let every one play the part he can play best, — some speak,
some sing, and all hollow.   Your meetings will be of evenings; the older
men, and the women, will go to hear you; so that it will not only contribute
to the election of " Old Zack," but will be an interesting pastime, and im-
proving to the intellectual faculties of all engaged.   Don't fail to do this.

You ask me to send you all the speeches made about "Old Zack," the
war, &c., &c.   Now, this makes me a little impatient.   I have regularly sent
you "The Congressional Globe" and "Appendix," and you cannot have examined them, or you would have discovered that they contain every speech made
by every man in both Houses of Congress, on every subject, during the session.
Can I send any more?   Can I send speeches that nobody has made?   Thinking it would be most natural that the newspapers would feel interested to give
at least some of the speeches to their readers, I, at the beginning of the session,
made arrangements to have one copy of "The Globe" and "Appendix"

regularly sent to each Whig paper of the district. And yet, with the exception of my own little speech, which was published in two only of the then five, now four, Whig papers, I do not remember having seen a single speech, or even extract from one, in any single one of those papers. With equal and full means on both sides, I will venture that "The State Register" has thrown before its readers more of Locofoco speeches in a month than all the Whig papers of the district have done of Whig speeches during the session.

If you wish a full understanding of the war, I repeat what I believe I said to you in a letter once before, that the whole, or nearly so, is to be found in the speech of Dixon of Connecticut. This I sent you in pamphlet, as well, as in "The Globe." Examine and study every sentence of that speech thoroughly, and you will understand the whole subject.

You ask how Congress came to declare that war had existed by the act of Mexico. Is it possible you don't understand that yet? You have at least twenty speeches in your possession that fully explain it. I will, however, try it once more. The news reached Washington of the commencement of hostilities on the Rio Grande, and of the great peril of Gen. Taylor's army. Everybody, Whigs and Democrats, was for sending them aid, in men and money. It was necessary to pass a bill for this. The Locos had a majority in both Houses, and they brought in a bill with a preamble, saying, *Whereas,* War exists by the act of Mexico, therefore we send Gen. Taylor money. The Whigs moved to strike out the preamble, so that they could vote to send the men and money, without saying any thing about how the war commenced; but, being in the minority, they were voted down, and the preamble was retained. Then, on the passage of the bill, the question came upon them, "Shall we vote *for* preamble and bill both together, or against both together?" They did not want to vote *against* sending help to Gen. Taylor, and therefore they voted *for* both together. Is there any difficulty in understanding this? Even my little speech shows how this was; and, if you w'll go to the library, you may get "The Journal" of 1845–46, in which you can find the whole for yourself.

We have nothing published yet with special reference to the Taylor race; but we soon will have, and then I will send them to everybody. I made an internal-improvement speech day before yesterday, which I shall send home as soon as I can get it written out and printed, — and which I suppose nobody will read.

Your friend as ever,

A. LINCOLN.

————

WASHINGTON, July 10, 1848.

DEAR WILLIAM, — Your letter covering the newspaper slips was received last night. The subject of that letter is exceedingly painful to me; and I cannot but think there is some mistake in your impression of the motives of the old men. I suppose I am now one of the old men; and I declare, on my veracity, which I think is good with you, that nothing could afford me more satisfaction than to learn that you and others of my young friends at home were doing battle in the contest, and endearing themselves to the people, and taking a stand far above any I have ever been able to reach in their admiration. I cannot conceive that other old men feel differently. Of course, I cannot demonstrate what I say; but I was young once, and I am sure I was never ungenerously thrust back. I hardly know what to say. The way for a young man to rise is to improve himself every way he can, never suspecting that anybody wishes to hinder him. Allow me to assure you that suspicion and jealousy never did help any man in any situation. There may sometimes be ungenerous attempts to keep a young man down; and they will succeed, too, if he allows his mind to be diverted from its true channel, to brood over the attempted injury. Cast about, and see if this feeling has not injured every person you have ever known to fall into it.

Now, in what I have said, I am sure you will suspect nothing but sincere friendship. I would save you from a fatal error. You have been a laborious, studious young man. You are far better informed on almost all subjects than I have ever been. You cannot fail in any laudable object, unless you allow your mind to be improperly directed. I have some the advantage of you in the world's experience, merely by being older; and it is this that induces me to advise.

You still seem to be a little mistaken about "The Congressional Globe" and "Appendix." They contain *all* of the speeches that are published in any way. My speech and Dayton's speech, which you say you got in pamphlet form, are both, word for word, in the "Appendix." I repeat again, all are there.

Your friend, as ever,

A. LINCOLN.

The "internal-improvement" speech to which Mr. Lincoln alludes in one of these letters was delivered on the 20th of June, and contained nothing remarkable or especially characteristic. It was in the main merely the usual Whig argument in favor of the constitutionality of Mr. Clay's "American System."

But, after the nominations at Baltimore and Philadelphia, everybody in either House of Congress who could compose any thing at all "on his legs," or in the closet, felt it incumbent upon him to contribute at least one electioneering speech to the political literature of the day. At last, on the 27th of July, Mr. Lincoln found an opportunity to make his. Few like it have ever been heard in either of those venerable chambers. It is a common remark of those who know nothing of the subject, that Mr. Lincoln was devoid of imagination; but the reader of this speech will entertain a different opinion. It opens to us a mind fertile in images sufficiently rare and striking, but of somewhat questionable taste. It must have been heard in amazement by those gentlemen of the House who had never known a Hanks, or seen a New Salem.

SPEECH ON THE PRESIDENCY AND GENERAL POLITICS.

DELIVERED IN THE HOUSE, JULY 27, 1848.

Mr. Speaker, — Our Democratic friends seem to be in great distress because they think our candidate for the Presidency don't suit *us*. Most of them cannot find out that Gen. Taylor has any principles at all; some, however, have discovered that he has *one*, but that that one is entirely wrong. This one principle is his position on the veto power. The gentleman from Tennessee (Mr. Stanton), who has just taken his seat, indeed, has said there is very little, if any, difference on this question between Gen. Taylor and all the Presidents; and he seems to think it sufficient detraction from Gen. Taylor's position on it, that it has nothing new in it. But all others whom I have heard speak assail it furiously. A new member from Kentucky (Mr. Clarke) of very considerable ability, was in particular concern about it. He thought it altogether novel and unprecedented for a President, or a Presidential candidate, to think of approving bills whose constitutionality may not be entirely clear to his own mind. He thinks the ark of our safety is gone, unless Presidents shall always veto such bills as, in their judgment, may be of *doubtful* constitutionality. However clear Congress may be of their authority to pass any particular act, the gentleman from Kentucky thinks the President must veto it if *he* has *doubts* about it. Now, I have neither time nor inclination to argue with the gentleman on the veto power as an original question; but I wish to show that Gen. Taylor, and not he, agrees with the earliest statesmen on this question. When the bill chartering the first Bank of the United States passed Congress, its constitutionality was questioned; Mr. Madison, then in the House of Representatives, as well as others, had opposed it on that ground. Gen. Washington, as President, was called on to approve or reject it. He sought and obtained, on the constitutional question, the separate written opinions of Jefferson, Hamilton, and Edmund Randolph; they then being respectively Secretary of State, Secretary of the Treasury, and Attorney-General. Hamilton's opinion was for the power; while Randolph's and Jefferson's were both against it. Mr. Jefferson, in his letter dated Feb. 15, 1791, after giving his opinion decidedly against the constitutionality of that bill, closed with the paragraph which I now read : —

"It must be admitted, however, that, unless the President's mind, on a view of every thing which is urged for and against this bill, is tolerably clear that it is unauthorized by the Constitution; if the pro and the con hang so even as to balance his judgment, a just respect for the wisdom of the Legislature would naturally decide the balance in favor of their opinion; it is chiefly for cases where they are clearly misled by error, ambition, or interest, that the Constitution has placed a check in the negative of the President."

Gen. Taylor's opinion, as expressed in his Allison letter, is as I now read : —

"The power given by the veto is a high conservative power, but, in my opinion, should never be exercised, except in cases of clear violation of the Constitution, or manifest haste and want of consideration by Congress.

It is here seen, that, in Mr. Jefferson's opinion, if, on the constitutionality of any given bill, the President *doubts*, he is not to veto it, as the gentleman from Kentucky would have him to do, but is to defer to Congress, and approve it. And if we compare the opinions of Jefferson and Taylor, as expressed in these paragraphs, we shall find them more exactly alike than we can often find any two expressions having any literal difference. None but interested fault-finders can discover any substantial variation.

But gentlemen on the other side are unanimously agreed that Gen. Taylor has no other principle. They are in utter darkness as to his opinions on any of the questions of policy which occupy the public attention. But is there any doubt as to what he will *do* on the prominent question, if elected? Not the least. It is not possible to know what he will or would do in every imaginable case, because many questions have passed away, and others doubtless will arise, which none of us have yet thought of; but on the prominent questions of currency, tariff, internal improvements, and Wilmot Proviso, Gen. Taylor's course is at least as well defined as is Gen. Cass's. Why, in their eagerness to get at Gen. Taylor, several Democratic members here have desired to know whether, in case of his election, a bankrupt-law is to be established. Can they tell us Gen. Cass's opinion on this question? (Some member answered, "He is against it.") Ay, how do you know he is? There is nothing about it in the platform, nor elsewhere, that I have seen. If the gentleman knows any thing which I do not, he can show it. But to return : Gen. Taylor, in his Allison letter, says, —

"Upon the subject of the tariff, the currency, the improvement of our great highways, rivers, lakes, and harbors, the will of the people, as expressed through their Representatives in Congress, ought to be respected and carried out by the Executive."

Now, this is the whole matter: in substance, it is this: The people say to Gen. Taylor, "If you are elected, shall we have a national bank?" He answers, " *Your* will, gentlemen, not *mine.*" — " What about the tariff ? " — " Say yourselves." — " Shall our rivers and harbors be improved ? " — " Just as you please." — " If you desire a bank, an alteration of the tariff, internal improvements, any or all, I will not hinder you : if you do not desire them, I will not attempt to force them on you. Send up your members of Congress from the various districts, with opinions according to your own, and if they are for these measures, or any of them, I shall have nothing to oppose : if they are not for them, I shall not, by any appliances whatever, attempt to dragoon them into their adoption." Now, can there be any difficulty in understanding this ? To you, Democrats, it may not seem like principle ; but surely you cannot fail to perceive the position plain enough. The distinction between it and the position of your candidate is broad and obvious, and I admit you have a clear right to show it is wrong, if you can ; but you have no right to pretend you cannot see it at all. We see it, and to us it appears like principle, and the best sort of principle at that, — the principle of allowing the people to do as they please with their own business. My friend from Indiana (Mr. C. B. Smith) has aptly asked, " Are you willing to trust the people ? " Some of you answered substantially, " We are willing to trust the people ; but the President is as much the representative of the people as Congress." In a certain sense, and to a certain extent, he is the representative of the people. He is elected by them as well as Congress is. But can he, in the nature of things, know the wants of the people as well as three hundred other men coming from all the various localities of the nation ? If so, where is the propriety of having a Congress ? That the Constitution gives the President a negative on legislation, all know ; but that this negative should be so combined with platforms and other appliances as to enable him, and, in fact, almost compel him, to take the whole of legislation into his own hands, is what we object to, is what Gen. Taylor objects to, and is what constitutes the broad distinction between you and us. To thus transfer legislation is clearly to take it from those who understand with minuteness the interests of the people, and give it to one who does not and cannot so well understand it. I understand your idea, — that if a Presidential candidate avow his opinion upon a given question, or rather upon all questions, and the people, with full knowledge of this, elect him, they thereby distinctly approve all those opinions. This, though plausible, is a most pernicious deception. By means of it, measures are adopted or rejected contrary to the wishes of the whole of one party, and often nearly half of the other. The process is this : Three, four, or half a dozen questions are prominent at a given time ; the party selects its candidate, and he takes his position on each of these questions. On all but one his positions have already been indorsed at former elections, and his party fully committed to them ; but that one is new, and a large portion of them are against it. But what are they to do ? The whole are strung together, and they must take all or reject all. They cannot take what they like, and leave the rest. What they are already committed to being the majority, they shut their eyes and gulp the whole. Next election, still another is introduced in the same way. If we run our eyes along the line of the past, we shall see that almost, if not quite, all the articles of the present Democratic creed have been at first forced upon the party in this very way. And just now, and just so, opposition to internal improvements is to be established if Gen. Cass shall be elected. Almost half the Democrats here are for improvements, but they will vote for Cass; and, if he succeeds, their votes will have aided in closing the doors against improvements. Now, this is a process which we think is wrong. We prefer a candidate, who, like Gen. Taylor, will allow the people to have their own way, regardless of his private opinion; and I should think the internal-improvement Democrats, at least, ought to prefer such a candidate. He would force nothing on them which they don't want; and he would allow them to have improvements which their own candidate, if elected, will not.

Mr. Speaker, I have said Gen. Taylor's position is as well defined as is that of Gen. Cass. In saying this, I admit I do not certainly know what he would do on the Wilmot Proviso. I am a Northern man, or, rather, a Western Free State man, with a constituency I believe to be, and with personal feelings I know to be, against the extension of slavery. As such, and with what information I have, I hope and *believe* Gen. Taylor, if elected, would not veto the proviso; but I do not *know* it. Yet, if I knew he would, I still would vote for him. I should do so, because, in my judgment, his election alone can defeat Gen. Cass; and because, *should* slavery thereby go into the territory we now have, just so much will certainly happen by the election of Cass, and, in addition, a course of policy leading to new wars, new acquisitions of territory, and still farther extensions of slavery. One of the two is to be President; which is preferable?

But there is as much doubt of Cass on improvements as there is of Taylor on the proviso. I have no doubt myself of Gen. Cass on this question, but I know the Democrats differ among themselves as to his position. My internal-improvement colleague (Mr. Wentworth) stated on this floor the other day, that he was satisfied Cass was for improvements, because he had voted for all the bills that he (Mr. W.) had. So far, so good. But Mr. Polk vetoed some of these very bills; the Baltimore Convention passed a set of resolutions, among other things, approving these vetoes; and Cass declares, in his letter accepting the nomination, that he has carefully read these resolutions, and that he adheres to them as firmly as he approves them cordially. In other words, Gen. Cass voted for the bills, and thinks the President did right to veto them; and his friends here are amiable enough to consider him as being on one side or the other, just as one or the other may correspond with their own respective inclinations. My colleague admits that the platform declares against the constitutionality of a general system of improvement, and that Gen. Cass indorses the platform; but he still thinks Gen.

Cass is in favor of some sort of improvements. Well, what are they? As he is against *general* objects, those he is *for* must be *particular* and *local*. Now, this is taking the subject precisely by the wrong end. *Particularity* — expending the money of the *whole* people for an object which will benefit only a *portion* of them — is the greatest real objection to improvements, and has been so held by Gen. Jackson, Mr. Polk, and all others, I believe, till now. But now, behold, the objects most general, nearest free from this objection, are to be rejected, while those most liable to it are to be embraced. To return: I cannot help believing that Gen. Cass, when he wrote his letter of acceptance, well understood he was to be claimed by the advocates of both sides of this question, and that he then closed the door against all further expressions of opinion, purposely to retain the benefits of that double position. His subsequent equivocation at Cleveland, to my mind, proves such to have been the case.

One word more, and I shall have done with this branch of the subject. You Democrats and your candidate, in the main, are in favor of laying down in advance a platform, — a set of party positions, as a unit; and then of enforcing the people, by every sort of appliance, to ratify them, however unpalatable some of them may be. We and our candidate are in favor of making Presidential elections and the legislation of the country distinct matters; so that the people can elect whom they please, and afterward legislate just *as* they please, without any hinderance, save only so much as may guard against infractions of the Constitution, undue haste, and want of consideration. The difference between us is clear as noonday. That we are right, we cannot doubt. We hold the true republican position. In leaving the people's business in their hands, we cannot be wrong. We are willing, and even anxious, to go to the people on this issue.

But I suppose I cannot reasonably hope to convince you that we have any principles. The most I can expect is, to assure you that we think we have, and are quite contented with them. The other day, one of the gentlemen from Georgia (Mr. Iverson), an eloquent man, and a man of learning, so far as I can judge, not being learned myself, came down upon us astonishingly. He spoke in what "The Baltimore American" calls the "scathing and withering style." At the end of his second severe flash I was struck blind, and found myself feeling with my fingers for an assurance of my continued physical existence. A little of the bone was left, and I gradually revived. He eulogized Mr. Clay in high and beautiful terms, and then declared that we had deserted all our principles, and had turned Henry Clay out, like an old horse, to root. This is terribly severe. It cannot be answered by argument; at least, I cannot so answer it. I merely wish to ask the gentleman if the Whigs are the only party he can think of, who sometimes turn old horses out to root? Is not a certain Martin Van Buren an old horse which your own party have turned out to root? and is he not rooting a little to your discomfort about now? But, in not nominating Mr. Clay, we deserted our principles, you say. Ah! in what? Tell us, ye men of principles, what principle we violated? We say you did violate principle in discarding Van Buren, and we can tell you how. You violated the primary, the cardinal, the one great living principle of all Democratic representative government, — the principle that the representative is bound to carry out the known will of his constituents. A large majority of the Baltimore Convention of 1844 were, by their constituents, instructed to procure Van Buren's nomination if they could. In violation, in utter, glaring contempt of this, you rejected him, — rejected him, as the gentleman from New York (Mr. Birdsall), the other day expressly admitted, for *availability*, — that same " general availability " which you charge upon us, and daily chew over here, as something exceedingly odious and unprincipled. But the gentleman from Georgia (Mr. Iverson) gave us a second speech yesterday, all well considered and put down in writing, in which Van Buren was scathed and withered a " few " for his present position and movements. I cannot remember the gentleman's precise language, but I do remember he put Van Buren down, down, till he got him where he was finally to " stink " and " rot."

Mr. Speaker, it is no business or inclination of mine to defend Martin Van Buren. In the war of extermination now waging between him and his old admirers, I say, Devil take the hindmost — and the foremost. But there is no mistaking the origin of the breach; and, if the curse of " stinking " and " rotting " is to fall on the first and greatest violators of principle in the matter, I disinterestedly suggest, that the gentleman from Georgia and his present co-workers are bound to take it upon themselves.

.   .   .   .

While I have Gen. Cass in hand, I wish to say a word about his political principles. As a specimen, I take the record of his progress on the Wilmot Proviso. In " The Washington Union " of March 2, 1847, there is a report of the speech of Gen. Cass, made the day before in the Senate, on the Wilmot Proviso, during the delivery of which, Mr. Miller of New Jersey is reported to have interrupted him as follows, to wit: —

" Mr. Miller expressed his great surprise at the change in the sentiments of the Senator from Michigan, who had been regarded as the great champion of freedom in the North-west, of which he was a distinguished ornament. Last year the Senator from Michigan was understood to be decidedly in favor of the Wilmot Proviso; and, as no reason had been stated for the change, he (Mr. Miller) could not refrain from the expression of his extreme surprise."

To this, Gen. Cass is reported to have replied as follows, to wit: —

" Mr. Cass said, that the course of the Senator from New Jersey was most extraordinary. Last year he (Mr. Cass) should have voted for the proposition had it come up. But circumstances had altogether changed. The honorable Senator then read several passages from the remarks as given above which he had committed to writing, in order to refute such a charge as that of the Senator from New Jersey."

In the "remarks above committed to writing," is one numbered 4, as follows, to wit : —

"4th. Legislation would now be wholly imperative, because no territory hereafter to be acquired can be governed without an act of Congress providing for its government. And such an act, on its passage, would open the whole subject, and leave the Congress called on to pass it free to exercise its own discretion, entirely uncontrolled by any declaration found in the statute-book."

In "Niles's Register," vol. lxxiii., p. 293, there is a letter of Gen. Cass to A. O. P. Nicholson of Nashville, Tenn., dated Dec. 24, 1847, from which the following are correct extracts : —

"The Wilmot Proviso has been before the country some time. It has been repeatedly discussed in Congress, and by the public press. I am strongly impressed with the opinion that a great change has been going on in the public mind upon this subject, — in my own as well as others ; and that doubts are resolving themselves into convictions, that the principle it involves should be kept out of the national Legislature, and left to the people of the Confederacy in their respective local governments.

"Briefly, then, I am opposed to the exercise of any jurisdiction by Congress over this matter ; and I am in favor of leaving the people of any territory which may be hereafter acquired, the right to regulate it themselves, under the general principles of the Constitution. Because,

"1. I do not see in the Constitution any grant of the requisite power to Congress ; and I am not disposed to extend a doubtful precedent beyond its necessity, — the establishment of territorial governments when needed, — leaving to the inhabitants all the rights compatible with the relations they bear to the Confederation."

These extracts show, that, in 1846, Gen. Cass was for the Proviso *at once* : that, in March, 1847, he was still for it, *but not just then ;* and that in December, 1847, he was *against* it altogether. This is a true index to the whole man. When the question was raised in 1846, he was in a blustering hurry to take ground for it. He sought to be in advance, and to avoid the uninteresting position of a mere follower ; but soon he began to see glimpses of the great Democratic ox-gad waving in his face, and to hear indistinctly a voice saying, "Back!" "Back, sir!" "Back a little!" He shakes his head, and bats his eyes, and blunders back to his position of March, 1847 ; but still the gad waves, and the voice grows more distinct, and sharper still, — "Back, sir!" "Back, I say!" "Further back!" and back he goes to the position of December, 1847 ; at which the gad is still, and the voice soothingly says, "So!" "Stand still at that."

Have no fears, gentlemen, of your candidate : he exactly suits you, and we congratulate you upon it. However much you may be distressed about *our* candidate, you have all cause to be contented and happy with your own. If elected, he may not maintain all, or even any, of his positions previously taken; but he will be sure to do whatever the party exigency, for the time being, may require; and that is precisely what you want. He and Van Buren are the same " manner of men; " and, like Van Buren, he will never desert *you* till you first desert *him*.

[After referring at some length to extra " charges" of Gen. Cass upon the Treasury, Mr. Lincoln continued : —]

But I have introduced Gen. Cass's accounts here chiefly to show the wonderful physical capacities of the man. They show that he not only did the labor of several men at the same *time*, but that he often did it, at several *places* many hundred miles apart, *at the same time*. And at eating, too, his capacities are shown to be quite as wonderful. From October, 1821, to May, 1822, he ate ten rations a day in Michigan, ten rations a day here in Washington, and nearly five dollars' worth a day besides, partly on the road between the two places. And then there is an important discovery in his example, — the art of being paid for what one eats, instead of having to pay for it. Hereafter, if any nice young man shall owe a bill which he cannot pay in any other way, he can just board it out. Mr. Speaker, we have all heard of the animal standing in doubt between two stacks of hay, and starving to death : the like of that would never happen to Gen. Cass. Place the stacks a thousand miles apart, he would stand stock-still, midway between them, and eat them both at once; and the green grass along the line would be apt to suffer some, too, at the same time. By all means make him President, gentlemen. He will feed you bounteously — if — if — there is any left after he shall have helped himself.

But as Gen. Taylor is, par excellence, the hero of the Mexican War, and as you Democrats say we Whigs have always opposed the war, you think it must be very awkward and embarrassing for us to go for Gen. Taylor. The declaration that we have always opposed the war is true or false accordingly as one may understand the term " opposing the war." If to say " the war was unnecessarily and unconstitutionally commenced by the President," be opposing the war, then the Whigs have very generally opposed it. Whenever they have spoken at all, they have said this; and they have said it on what has appeared good reason to them : the marching an army into the midst of a peaceful Mexican settlement, frightening the inhabitants away, leaving their growing crops and other property to destruction, to *you* may appear a perfectly amiable, peaceful, unprovoking procedure; but it does not appear so to *us*. So to call such an act, to us appears no other than a naked, impudent absurdity, and we speak of it accordingly. But if when the war had begun, and had become the cause of the country, the giving of our money and our blood, in common with yours, was support of the war, then it is not true that we have always opposed the war. With few individual exceptions, you have constantly had our votes here for all the necessary supplies. And, more than this, you have had the services, the blood, and the lives of our political brethren in every trial, and on every field. The beardless boy and the mature

20

man, the humble and the distinguished, — you have had them. Through
suffering and death, by disease and in battle, they have endured and fought
and fallen with you. Clay and Webster each gave a son, never to be returned. From the State of my own residence, besides other worthy but less
known Whig names, we sent Marshall, Morrison, Baker, and Hardin: they
all fought, and one fell, and in the fall of that one we lost our best Whig
man. Nor were the Whigs few in number, or laggard in the day of danger.
In that fearful, bloody, breathless struggle at Buena Vista, where each man's
hard task was to beat back five foes or die himself, of the five high officers
who perished, four were Whigs.

In speaking of this, I mean no odious comparison between the lion-hearted
Whigs and Democrats who fought there. On other occasions, and among
the lower officers and privates on *that* occasion, I doubt not the proportion
was different. I wish to do justice to all. I think of all those brave men as
Americans, in whose proud fame, as an American, I, too, have a share. Many
of them, Whigs and Democrats, are my constituents and personal friends;
and I thank them, — more than thank them, — one and all, for the high,
imperishable honor they have conferred on our common State.

But the distinction between the cause of the *President* in beginning the
war, and the cause of the *country* after it was begun, is a distinction which
you cannot perceive. To *you*, the President and the country seem to be all
one. You are interested to see no distinction between them; and I venture
to suggest that *possibly* your interest blinds you a little. We see the distinction, as we think, clearly enough; and our friends, who have fought in the
war, have no difficulty in seeing it also. What those who have fallen would
say, were they alive and here, of course we can never know; but with those
who have returned there is no difficulty. Col. Haskell and Major Gaines,
members here, both fought in the war; and one of them underwent extraordinary perils and hardships; still they, like all other Whigs here, vote on the
record that the war was unnecessarily and unconstitutionally commenced by
the President. And even Gen. Taylor himself, the noblest Roman of them
all, has declared that, as a citizen, and particularly as a soldier, it is sufficient
for him to know that his country is at war with a foreign nation, to do all in
his power to bring it to a speedy and honorable termination, by the most
vigorous and energetic operations, without inquiring about its justice, or any
thing else connected with it.

Mr. Speaker, let our Democratic friends be comforted with the assurance
that we are content with our position, content with our company, and content with our candidate; and that although they, in their generous sympathy, think we ought to be miserable, we really are not, and that they may
dismiss the great anxiety they have on *our* account.[1]

---

[1] The following passage has generally been omitted from this speech, as published in
the "Lives of Lincoln." The reason for the omission is quite obvious.

"But the gentleman from Georgia further says, we have deserted all our principles, and

Congress adjourned on the 14th of August; but Mr. Lincoln went up to New England, and made various campaign

taken shelter under Gen. Taylor's military coat-tail; and he seems to think this is exceedingly degrading. Well, as his faith is, so be it unto him. But can he remember no other military coat-tail, under which a certain other party have been sheltering for near a quarter of a century? Has he no acquaintance with the ample military coat-tail of Gen. Jackson? Does he not know that his own party have run the last five Presidential races under that coat-tail? and that they are now running the sixth under the same cover? Yes, sir, that coat-tail was used, not only for Gen. Jackson himself, but has been clung to with the grip of death by every Democratic candidate since. You have never ventured, and dare not now venture, from under it. Your campaign papers have constantly been · Old Hickories,' with rude likenesses of the old general upon them; hickory poles and hickory brooms your never-ending emblems. Mr. Polk himself was ' Young Hickory,' ' Little Hickory,' or something so; and even now your campaign paper here is proclaiming that Cass and Butler are of the 'Hickory stripe.' No, sir, you dare not give it up. Like a horde of hungry ticks, you have stuck to the tail of the Hermitage lion to the end of his life; and you are still sticking to it, and drawing a loathsome sustenance from it, after he is dead. A fellow once advertised that he had made a discovery by which he could make a new man out of an old one, and have enough of the stuff left to make a little yellow dog. Just such a discovery has Gen. Jackson's popularity been to you. You not only twice made President of him out of it, but you have enough of the stuff left to make Presidents of several comparatively small men since; and it is your chief reliance now to make still another.

"Mr. Speaker, old horses and military coat-tails, or tails of any sort, are not figures of speech such as I would be the first to introduce into discussions here; but, as the gentleman from Georgia has thought fit to introduce them, he and you are welcome to all you have made, or can make, by them. If you have any more old horses, trot them out; any more tails, just cock them, and come at us.

"I repeat, I would not introduce this mode of discussion here; but I wish gentlemen on the other side to understand, that the use of degrading figures is a game at which they may find themselves unable to take all the winnings. [" We give it up."] Ay, you give it up, and well you may; but for a very different reason from that which you would have us understand. The point — the power to hurt — of all figures, consists in the *truthfulness* of their application; and, understanding this, you may well give it up. They are weapons which hit you, but miss us.

"But, in my hurry, I was very near closing on this subject of military tails before I was done with it. There is one entire article of the sort I have not discussed yet; I mean the military tail you Democrats are now engaged in dovetailing on to the great Michigander. Yes, sir, all his biographers (and they are legion) have him in hand, tying him to a military tail, like so many mischievous boys tying a dog to a bladder of beans. True, the material is very limited, but they are at it might and main. He *in*vaded Canada without resistance, and he *out*vaded it without pursuit. As he did both under orders, I suppose there was, to him, neither credit nor discredit; but they are made to constitute a large part of the tail. He was not at Hull's surrender, but he was close by; he was volunteer aid to Gen. Harrison on the day of the battle of the Thames; and, as you said in 1840 Harrison was picking whortleberries two miles off while the battle was fought, I suppose it is a just conclusion, with you, to say Cass was aiding Harrison to pick whortleberries. This is about all, except the mooted question of the broken sword. Some authors say he broke it; some say he threw it away; and some others, who ought to know, say nothing about it. Perhaps it would be a fair historical compromise to say, if he did not break it, he did not do any thing else with it.

"By the way, Mr. Speaker, did you know I am a military hero? Yes, sir: in the days of the Black-Hawk War, I fought, bled, and came away. Speaking of Gen. Cass's career reminds me of my own. I was not at Stillman's defeat, but I was about as near it as Cass was to Hull's surrender; and, like him, I saw the place very soon afterwards. It is quite certain I did not break my sword, for I had none to break; but I bent my musket pretty

speeches before he returned home. They were not preserved, and were probably of little importance.

Soon after his return to Washington, to take his seat at the
second session of the Thirtieth Congress, he received a letter
from his father, which astonished and perhaps amused him.
His reply intimates grave doubts concerning the veracity of
his correspondent.

WASHINGTON, Dec. 24, 1848.

MY DEAR FATHER, — Your letter of the 7th was received night before
last. I very cheerfully send you the twenty dollars, which sum you say is
necessary to save your land from sale. It is singular that you should have
forgotten a judgment against you; and it is more singular that the plaintiff should have let you forget it so long; particularly as I suppose you
always had property enough to satisfy a judgment of that amount. Before
you pay it, it would be well to be sure you have not paid, or at least that you
cannot prove you have paid it.

Give my love to mother and all the connections.

Affectionately your son,

A. LINCOLN.

The second session was a quiet one. Mr. Lincoln did
nothing to attract public attention in any marked degree. He
attended diligently and unobtrusively to the ordinary duties
of his office, and voted generally with the Whig majority.
One Mr. Gott, however, of New York, offered a resolution
looking to the abolition of the slave-trade in the District
of Columbia, and Mr. Lincoln was one of only three or four
Northern Whigs who voted to lay the resolution on the table.
At another time, however, Mr. Lincoln proposed a substitute
for the Gott resolution, providing for gradual and compensated emancipation, with the consent of the people of the
District, to be ascertained at a general election. This meas-

badly on one occasion. If Cass broke his sword, the idea is, he broke it in desperation: I
bent the musket by accident. If Gen. Cass went in advance of me picking whortleberries,
I guess I surpassed him in charges upon the wild onions. If he saw any live fighting Indians, it was more than I did, but I had a good many bloody struggles with the mosquitoes;
and, although I never fainted from loss of blood, I can truly say I was often very hungry.

"Mr. Speaker, if ever I should conclude to doff whatever our Democratic friends may
suppose there is of black-cockade Federalism about me, and, thereupon, they shall take me
up as their candidate for the Presidency, I protest that they shall not make fun of me, as
they have of Gen. Cass, by attempting to write me into a military hero."

ure he evidently abandoned, and it died a natural death among the rubbish of "unfinished business." His record on the Wilmot Proviso has been thoroughly exposed, both by himself and Mr. Douglas, and in the Presidential campaign by his friends and foes. He said himself, that he had voted for it " about forty-two times." It is not likely that he had counted the votes when he made this statement, but spoke according to the best of his " knowledge and belief."

The following letters are printed, not because they illustrate the author's character more than a thousand others would, but because they exhibit one of the many perplexities of Congressional life.

SPRINGFIELD, April 25, 1849.

DEAR THOMPSON, — A tirade is still kept up against me here for recommending T. R. King. This morning it is openly avowed that my supposed influence at Washington shall be broken down generally, and King's prospects defeated in particular. Now, what I have done in this matter, I have done at the request of you and some other friends in Tazewell; and I therefore ask you to either admit it is wrong, or come forward and sustain me. If the truth will permit, I propose that you sustain me in the following manner: copy the enclosed scrap in your own handwriting, and get everybody (not three or four, but three or four hundred) to sign it, and then send it to me. Also, have six, eight, or ten of our best known Whig friends there to write me individual letters, stating the truth in this matter as they understand it. Don't neglect or delay in the matter. I understand information of an indictment having been found against him about three years ago for gaming, or keeping a gaming-house, has been sent to the Department. I shall try to take care of it at the Department till your action can be had and forwarded on.

Yours as ever,

A. LINCOLN.

WASHINGTON, June 5, 1849.

DEAR WILLIAM, — Your two letters were received last night. I have a great many letters to write, and so cannot write very long ones. There must be some mistake about Walter Davis saying I promised him the Post-office. I did not so promise him. I did tell him, that, if the distribution of the offices should fall into my hands, he should have something; and, if I shall be convinced he has said any more than this, I shall be disappointed.

I said this much to him, because, as I understand, he is of *good charac-*

ter, is one of the *young* men, is of the *mechanics*, and always *faithful*, and never troublesome, a Whig and is *poor*, with the support of a widow-mother thrown almost exclusively on him by the death of his brother. If these are wrong reasons, then I have been wrong; but I have certainly not been selfish in it, because, in my greatest need of friends, he was against me and for Baker.

Yours as ever,

A. LINCOLN.

P. S. — Let the above be confidential.

CHAPTER XIII.

LIKE most other public men in America, Mr. Lincoln made his bread by the practice of his profession, and the better part of his fame by the achievements of the politician. He was a lawyer of some note, and, compared with the crowds who annually take upon themselves the responsible office of advocate and attorney, he might very justly have been called a good one; for he regarded his office as a trust, and selected and tried his cases, not with a view to personal gain, but to the administration of justice between suitors. And here, midway in his political career, it is well enough to pause, and take a leisurely survey of him in his other character of country lawyer, from the time he entered the bar at Springfield until he was translated from it to the Presidential chair. It is unnecessary to remind the reader (for by this time it must be obvious enough) that the aim of the writer is merely to present facts and contemporaneous opinions, with as little comment as possible.

In the courts and at the bar-meetings immediately succeeding his death, his professional brethren poured out in volumes their testimony to his worth and abilities as a lawyer. But, in estimating the value of this testimony, it is fair to consider the state of the public mind at the time it was given, — the recent triumph of the Federal arms under his direction; the late overwhelming indorsement of his administration; the unparalleled devotion of the people to his person as exhibited at the polls; the fresh and bitter memories of the hideous tragedy that took him off; the furious and deadly passions it inspired in the one party, and the awe, indignation, and terror it inspired in the other. It was no time for nice and critical examinations, either of his mental or his moral character; and it might have been attended with personal danger to attempt them. For days and nights together it was considered treason to be seen in public with a smile on the face. Men who spoke evil of the fallen chief, or even ventured a doubt concerning the ineffable purity and saintliness of his life, were pursued by mobs, were beaten to death with paving-stones, or strung up by the neck to lamp-posts. If there was any rivalry, it was as to who should be foremost and fiercest among his avengers, who should canonize him in the most solemn words, who should compare him to the most sacred character in all history, sacred and profane. He was prophet, priest, and king; he was Washington; he was Moses; and there were not wanting even those who likened him to the God and Redeemer of all the earth. These latter thought they discovered in his lowly origin, his kindly nature, his benevolent precepts, and the homely anecdotes in which he taught the people, strong points of resemblance between him and the divine Son of Mary. Even at this day, men are not wanting in prominent positions in life, who knew Mr. Lincoln well, and who do not hesitate to make such a comparison.

For many years, Judge David Davis was the near friend and the intimate associate of Mr. Lincoln. He presided in the court where Lincoln was oftenest heard: year in and year out they travelled together from town to town, from county to county, riding frequently in the same conveyance, and lodging in the same room. Although a judge on the bench, Mr. Davis watched the political course of his friend with affectionate solicitude, and more than once interposed most effectually to advance his fortunes. When Mr. Lincoln ascended to the Presidency, it was well understood that no man enjoyed more confidential relations with him than Judge Davis. At the first opportunity, he commissioned Judge Davis an Associate Justice of that august tribunal, the Supreme

HON. DAVID DAVIS, JUDGE OF THE SUPREME COURT OF THE U. S.

Court of the United States; and, upon his death, Judge Davis administered upon his estate at the request of his family. Add to this the fact, that, among American jurists, Judge Davis's fame is, if not peerless, at least not excelled by that of any man whose reputation rests upon his labors as they appear in the books of Reports, and we may very fairly consider him a competent judge of the professional character of Mr. Lincoln.

At Indianapolis, Judge Davis spoke of him as follows: —

"I enjoyed for over twenty years the personal friendship of Mr. Lincoln. We were admitted to the bar about the same time, and travelled for many years what is known in Illinois as the Eighth Judicial Circuit. In 1848, when I first went on the bench, the circuit embraced fourteen counties, and Mr. Lincoln went with the court to every county. Railroads were not then in use, and our mode of travel was either on horseback or in buggies.

"This simple life he loved, preferring it to the practice of the law in a city, where, although the remuneration would be greater, the opportunity would be less for mixing with the great body of the people, who loved him, and whom he loved. Mr. Lincoln was transferred from the bar of that circuit to the office of President of the United States, having been without official position since he left Congress in 1849. In all the elements that constitute the great lawyer, he had few equals. He was great both at *nisi prius* and before an appellate tribunal. He seized the strong points of a cause, and presented them with clearness and great compactness. His mind was logical and direct, and he did not indulge in extraneous discussion. Generalities and platitudes had no charms for him. An unfailing vein of humor never deserted him; and he was always able to chain the attention of court and jury, when the cause was the most uninteresting, by the appropriateness of his anecdotes.

"His power of comparison was large, and he rarely failed in a legal discussion to use that mode of reasoning. The framework of his mental and moral being was honesty, and a wrong cause was poorly defended by him. The ability which some eminent lawyers possess, of explaining away the bad points of a cause by ingenious sophistry, was denied him. In order to bring into full activity his great powers, it was necessary that he should be convinced of the right and justice of the matter which he advocated. When so convinced, whether the cause was great or small, he was usually successful. He read law-books but little, except when the cause in hand made it necessary; yet he was usually self-reliant, depending on his own resources, and rarely consulting his brother lawyers, either on the management of his case or on the legal questions involved.

"Mr. Lincoln was the fairest and most accommodating of practitioners, granting all favors which he could do consistently with his duty to his client, and rarely availing himself of an unwary oversight of his adversary.

"He hated wrong and oppression everywhere; and many a man whose fraudulent conduct was undergoing review in a court of justice has writhed under his terrific indignation and rebukes. He was the most simple anc unostentatious of men in his habits, having few wants, and those easily supplied. To his honor be it said, that he never took from a client, even when the cause was gained, more than he thought the service was worth and the client could reasonably afford to pay. The people where he practised law were not rich, and his charges were always small.

"When he was elected President, I question whether there was a lawyer in the circuit, who had been at the bar as long a time, whose means were not larger. It did not seem to be one of the purposes of his life to accumulate a fortune. In fact, outside of his profession, he had no knowledge of the way to make money, and he never even attempted it.

"Mr. Lincoln was loved by his brethren of the bar; and no body of men will grieve more at his death, or pay more sincere tributes to his memory. His presence on the circuit was watched for with interest, and never failed to produce joy and hilarity. When casually absent, the spirits of both bar and people were depressed. He was not fond of controversy, and would compromise a lawsuit whenever practicable."

More or other evidence than this may, perhaps, be superfluous. Such an eulogium, from such a source, is more than sufficient to determine the place Mr. Lincoln is entitled to occupy in the history, or, more properly speaking, the traditions, of the Western bar. If Sir Matthew Hale had spoken thus of any lawyer of his day, he would have insured to the subject of his praise a place in the estimation of men only less conspicuous and honorable than that of the great judge himself. At the risk, however, of unnecessary accumulation, we venture to record an extract from Judge Drummond's address at Chicago : —

"With a probity of character known to all, with an intuitive insight into the human heart, with a clearness of statement which was in itself an argument, with uncommon power and felicity of illustration, — often, it is true, of a plain and homely kind, — and with that sincerity and earnestness of manner which carried conviction, he was, perhaps, one of the most successful jury lawyers we ever had in the State. He always tried a case fairly and honestly. He never intentionally misrepresented the evidence of a witness, nor the argument of an opponent. He met both squarely, and, if he could not explain the one or answer the other, substantially admitted it. He never misstated the law, according to his own intelligent view of it. Such was the transparent candor and integrity of his nature, that he could not well, or strongly, argue a side or a cause that he thought wrong. Of course, he felt it his duty to say what could be said, and to leave the decision to others ; but there could be seen in such cases the inward struggles of his own mind. In trying a case, he might occasionally dwell too long upon, or give too much importance to, an inconsiderable point ; but this was the exception, and generally he went straight to the citadel of the cause or question, and struck home there, knowing, if that were won, the outworks would necessarily fall. He could hardly be called very learned in his profession, and yet he rarely tried a cause without fully understanding the law applicable to it ; and I have no hesitation in saying he was one of the ablest lawyers I have ever known. If he was forcible before a jury, he was equally so with the court. He detected, with unerring sagacity, the weak points of an opponent's argument, and pressed his own views with overwhelming strength. His efforts were quite unequal ; and it might happen that he would not, on some occasions, strike one as at all remarkable. But let him be thoroughly roused, — let him feel that he was right, and that some principle was involved in his cause, — and he would come out with an earnestness of conviction, a power of argument, and a wealth of illustration, that I have never seen surpassed."

Mr. Lincoln's partnership with John T. Stuart began on the 27th of April, 1837, and continued until the 14th of April, 1841, when it was dissolved, in consequence of Stuart's election to Congress. In that same year (1841), Mr. Lincoln united in practice with Stephen T. Logan, late presiding judge of the district, and they remained together until 1845.

Soon afterwards he formed a copartnership with William H. Herndon, his friend, familiar, and, we may almost say, biographer, — a connection which terminated only when the senior partner took an affectionate leave of the old circuit, the old office, home, friends, and all familiar things, to return no more until he came a blackened corpse. "He once told me of you," says Mr. Whitney in one of his letters to Mr. Herndon, "that he had taken you in as partner, supposing that you had a system, and would keep things in order, but that he found that you had no more system than he had, but that you were a fine lawyer; so that he was doubly disappointed." [1]

As already stated by Judge Davis, Mr. Lincoln was not "a great reader of law-books;" but what he knew he knew well, and within those limits was self-reliant and even intrepid. He was what is sometimes called "a case-lawyer," — a man who reasoned almost entirely to the court and jury from analogous causes previously decided and reported in the books, and not from the elementary principles of the law, or the great underlying reasons for its existence. In consultation he was cautious, conscientious, and painstaking, and was seldom prepared to advise, except after careful and tedious examination of the authorities. He did not consider himself bound to take every case that was brought to him, nor to press all the

---

[1] The following letter exhibits the character of his early practice, and gives us a glimpse into his social and political life: —

SPRINGFIELD, Dec. 23, 1839.

DEAR ——, — Dr. Henry will write you all the political news. I write this about some little matters of business. You recollect you told me you had drawn the Chicago Masack money, and sent it to the claimants. A d——d hawk-billed Yankee is here besetting me at every turn I take, saying that Robert Kenzie never received the eighty dollars to which he was entitled.

Can you tell any thing about the matter? Again, old Mr. Wright, who lives up South Fork somewhere, is teasing me continually about some *deeds*, which he says he left with you, but which I can find nothing of. Can you tell where they are? The Legislature is in session, and has suffered the bank to forfeit its charter without *benefit of clergy*. There seems but little disposition to resuscitate it.

Whenever a letter comes from you to Mrs. ——, I carry it to her, and then I see Betty: she is a tolerable nice *fellow* now. Maybe I will write again when I get more time.

Your friend as ever,

A. LINCOLN.

P. S. — The Democratic giant is here, but he is not now worth talking about.

A. L.

points in favor of a client who in the main was right and entitled to recover. He is known to have been many times on the verge of quarrelling with old and valued friends, because he could not see the justice of their claims, and, therefore, could not be induced to act as their counsel. Henry McHenry, one of his New-Salem associates, brought him a case involving the title to a piece of land. McHenry had placed a family in a cabin which Mr. Lincoln believed to be situated on the other side of the adversary's line. He told McHenry that he must move the family out. " McHenry said he should not do it. ' Well,' said Mr. Lincoln, ' if you do not, I shall not attend to the suit.' McHenry said he did not care a d—n whether he did or not; that he (Lincoln) was not all the lawyer there was in town. Lincoln studied a while, and asked about the location of the cabin, . . . and then said, ' McHenry, you are right: I will attend to the suit,' and did attend to it, and gained it; and that was all the harsh word that passed."

" A citizen of Springfield," says Mr. Herndon, " who visited our office on business about a year before Mr. Lincoln's nomination, relates the following : —

" ' Mr. Lincoln was seated at his table, listening very attentively to a man who was talking earnestly in a low tone. After the would-be client had stated the facts of his case, Mr. Lincoln replied, " Yes, there is no reasonable doubt but that I can gain your case for you. I can set a whole neighborhood at loggerheads; I can distress a widowed mother and her six fatherless children, and thereby get for you six hundred dollars, which rightfully belongs, it appears to me, as much to the woman and her children as it does to you. You must remember that some things that are legally right are not morally right. I shall not take your case, but will give you a little advice, for which I will charge you nothing. You seem to be a sprightly, energetic man. I would advise you to try your hand at making six hundred dollars in some other way." ' "

In the summer of 1841, Mr. Lincoln was engaged in a curious case. The circumstances impressed him very deeply with

the insufficiency and danger of " circumstantial evidence ; '
so much so, that he not only wrote the following account of
it to Speed, but another more extended one, which was printed
in a newspaper published at Quincy, Ill.   His mind was full
of it : he could think of nothing else.   It is apparent that in
his letter to Speed he made no pause to choose his words :
there is nothing constrained, and nothing studied or deliberate
about it ; but its simplicity, perspicuity, and artless grace
make it a model of English composition.   What Goldsmith
once said of Locke may better be said of this letter : " He
never says more nor less than he ought, and never makes use
of a word that he could have changed for a better."

SPRINGFIELD, June 19, 1841.

DEAR SPEED, — We have had the highest state of excitement here for
a week past that our community has ever witnessed ; and although the
public feeling is somewhat allayed, the curious affair which aroused it is
very far from being over yet, cleared of mystery.   It would take a quire of
paper to give you any thing like a full account of it, and I therefore only
propose a brief outline.   The chief personages in the drama are Archibald
Fisher, supposed to be murdered, and Archibald Trailor, Henry Trailor, and
William Trailor, supposed to have murdered him.   The three Trailors are
brothers : the first, Arch., as you know, lives in town ; the second, Henry, in
Clary's Grove ; and the third, William, in Warren County ; and Fisher, the
supposed *murdered*, being without a family, had made his home with William.
On Saturday evening. being the 29th of May, Fisher and William came to
Henry's in a one-horse dearborn, and there staid over Sunday ; and on
Monday all three came to Springfield (Henry on horseback), and joined
Archibald at Myers's, the Dutch carpenter.   That evening at supper Fisher
was missing, and so next morning some ineffectual search was made for him ;
and on Tuesday, at 1 o'clock, P.M., William and Henry started home without him.   In a day or two Henry and one or two of his Clary-Grove neighbors came back for him again, and advertised his disappearance in the
papers.   The knowledge of the matter thus far had not been general, and
here it dropped entirely, till about the 10th inst., when Keys received a letter
from the postmaster in Warren County, that William had arrived at home,
and was telling a very mysterious and improbable story about the disappearance of Fisher, which induced the community there to suppose he had been
disposed of unfairly.   Keys made this letter public, which immediately set
the whole town and adjoining county agog.   And so it has continued until
yesterday.   The mass of the people commenced a systematic search for the

dead body, while Wickersham was despatched to arrest Henry Trailor at the Grove, and Jim Maxcy to Warren to arrest William. On Monday last, Henry was brought in, and showed an evident inclination to insinuate that he knew Fisher to be dead, and that Arch. and William had killed him. He said he guessed the body could be found in Spring Creek, between the Beardstown Road and Hickox's mill. Away the people swept like a herd of buffalo, and cut down Hickox's mill-dam *nolens volens*, to draw the water out of the pond, and then went up and down, and down and up the creek, fishing and raking, and raking and ducking, and diving for two days, and, after all, no dead body found. In the mean time a sort of a scuffling-ground had been found in the brush in the angle, or point, where the road leading into the woods past the brewery, and the one leading in past the brick grove meet. From the scuffle-ground was the sign of something about the size of a man having been dragged to the edge of the thicket, where joined the track of some small wheeled carriage drawn by one horse, as shown by the road-tracks. The carriage-track led off toward Spring Creek. Near this drag-trail Dr. Merryman found two hairs, which, after a long scientific examination, he pronounced to be triangular human hair, which term, he says, includes within it the whiskers, the hair growing under the arms, and on other parts of the body; and he judged that these two were of the whiskers, because the ends were cut, showing that they had flourished in the neighborhood of the razor's operations. On Thursday last Jim Maxcy brought in William Trailor from Warren. On the same day Arch. was arrested, and put in jail. Yesterday (Friday) William was put upon his examining trial before May and Lavely. Archibald and Henry were both present. Lamborn prosecuted, and Logan, Baker, and your humble servant defended. A great many witnesses were introduced and examined, but I shall only mention those whose testimony seemed most important. The first of these was Capt. Ransdell. He swore, that, when William and Henry left Springfield for home on Tuesday before mentioned, they did not take the direct route, — which, you know, leads by the butcher-shop, — but that they followed the street north until they got opposite, or nearly opposite, May's new house, after which he could not see them from where he stood; and it was afterwards proved, that, in about an hour after they started, they came into the street by the butcher's shop from towards the brick-yard. Dr. Merryman and others swore to what is stated about the scuffle-ground, drag-trail, whiskers, and carriage-tracks. Henry was then introduced by the prosecution. He swore, that, when they started for home, they went out north, as Ransdell stated, and turned down west by the brick-yard into the woods, and there met Archibald; that they proceeded a small distance farther, when he was placed as a sentinel to watch for and announce the approach of any one that might happen that way; that William and Arch. took the dearborn out of the road a small distance to the edge of the thicket, where they stopped, and he saw them lift the body of a man into it; that they then moved off with the carriage in the direction of Hickox's mill, and he loitered about for something like an hour, when William returned with the carriage, but without Arch., and said they had put *him* in a safe place; that they went somehow, he did not know exactly how, into the road close to the brewery, and proceeded on to Clary's Grove. He also stated that some time during the day William told him that he and Arch. had killed Fisher the evening before; that the way they did it was by him (William) knocking him down with a club, and Arch. then choking him to death. An old man from Warren, called Dr. Gilmore, was then introduced on the part of the defence. He swore that he had known Fisher for several years; that Fisher had resided at his house a long time at each of two different spells, — once while he built a barn for him, and once while he was doctored for some chronic disease; that two or three years ago Fisher had a serious hurt in his head by the bursting of a gun, since which he had been subject to continued bad health and occasional aberration of mind. He also stated that on last Tuesday, being the same day that Maxcy arrested William Trailor, he (the doctor) was from home in the early part of the day, and on his return, about 11 o'clock, found Fisher at his house in bed, and apparently very unwell; that he asked him how he had come from Springfield; that Fisher said he had come by Peoria, and also told of several other places he had been at, more in the direction of Peoria, which showed that he at the time of speaking did not know where he had been wandering about in a state of derangement. He further stated, that in about two hours he received a note from one of Trailor's friends, advising him of his arrest, and requesting him to go on to Springfield as a witness, to testify as to the state of Fisher's health in former times; that he immediately set off, calling up two of his neighbors as company, and, riding all evening and all night, overtook Maxcy and William at Lewiston in Fulton County. That Maxcy refusing to discharge Trailor upon his statement, his two neighbors returned, and he came on to Springfield. Some question being made as to whether the doctor's story was not a fabrication, several acquaintances of his (among whom was the same postmaster who wrote to Keys, as before mentioned) were introduced as sort of compurgators, who swore that they knew the doctor to be of good character for truth and veracity, and generally of good character in every way. Here the testimony ended, and the Trailors were discharged, Arch. and William expressing, both in word and manner, their entire confidence that Fisher would be found alive at the doctor's by Galloway, Mallory, and Myers, who a day before had been despatched for that purpose; while Henry still protested that no power on earth could ever show Fisher alive. Thus stands this curious affair. When the doctor's story was first made public, it was amusing to scan and contemplate the countenances, and hear the remarks, of those who had been actively engaged in the search for the dead body: some looked quizzical, some melancholy, and some furiously angry. Porter, who had been very active, swore he always knew the man was not dead, and that he had not stirred an inch to hunt for him: Langford, who had taken the lead in cutting down Hickox's mill-dam, and wanted to hang Hickox for objecting, looked most awfully woebegone; he seemed the "*wictim of hunrequited affection,*" as represented in the comic almanacs we used to laugh over. And Hart, the little drayman that hauled Molly home once, said it was too *damned* bad to have so much trouble, and no hanging, after all.

I commenced this letter on yesterday, since which I received yours of the 13th. I stick to my promise to come to Louisville. Nothing new here, except what I have written. I have not seen —— since my last trip; and I am going out there as soon as I mail this letter.

Yours forever,

LINCOLN.

On the 3d of December, 1839, Mr. Lincoln was admitted to practice in the Circuit Court of the United States; and on the same day the names of Stephen A. Douglas, S. H. Treat, Schuyler Strong, and two other gentlemen, were placed on the same roll. The "Little Giant" is always in sight!

The first speech he delivered in the Supreme Court of the State was one the like of which will never be heard again, and must have led the judges to doubt the sanity of the new attorney. We give it in the form in which it seems to be authenticated by Judge Treat: —

"A case being called for hearing in the Court, Mr. Lincoln stated that he appeared for the appellant, and was ready to proceed with the argument. He then said, 'This is the first case I have ever had in this court, and I have therefore examined it with great care. As the Court will perceive, by looking at the abstract of the record, the only question in the case is one of authority. I have not been able to find any authority sustaining *my* side of the case, but I *have found* several cases directly in point on the *other* side. I will now give *these* cases, and then submit the case.'"

The testimony of all the lawyers, his contemporaries and rivals, is in the same direction. "But Mr. Lincoln's love of justice and fair play," says Mr. Gillespie, "was his predominating trait. I have often listened to him when I thought he would certainly state his case out of Court. It was not in his nature to assume, or to attempt to bolster up, a false position. He would abandon his case first. He did so in the

21

case of Buckmaster for the use of Denham *vs.* Beenes and
Arthur, in our Supreme Court, in which I happened to be
opposed to him. Another gentleman, less fastidious, took
Mr. Lincoln's place, and gained the case."

In the Patterson trial — a case of murder which attained
some celebrity — in Champaign County, Ficklin and Lamon
prosecuted, and Lincoln and Swett defended. After hearing
the testimony, Mr. Lincoln felt himself morally paralyzed,
and said, "Swett, the man is guilty: you defend him; I
can't." They got a fee of five hundred or a thousand dollars;
of which Mr. Lincoln declined to take a cent, on the ground
that it justly belonged to Swett, whose ardor, courage, and
eloquence had saved the guilty man from justice.

It was probably his deep sense of natural justice, his irresistible propensity to get at the equities of the matter in
hand, that made him so utterly impatient of all arbitrary or
technical rules. Of these he knew very little, — less than an
average student of six months: "Hence," says Judge Davis,
"a child could make use of the simple and technical rules,
the means and mode of getting at justice, better than Lincoln
could." "In this respect," says Mr. Herndon, "I really
think he was very deficient."

Sangamon County was originally in the First Judicial Circuit; but under the Constitution of 1848, and sundry changes
in the Judiciary Acts, it became the Eighth Circuit. It was in
1848 that Judge Davis came on the bench for the first time.
The circuit was a very large one, containing fourteen counties, and comprising the central portion of the State. Lincoln travelled all over it — first with Judge Treat and then
with Judge Davis — twice every year, and was thus absent
from Springfield and home nearly, if not quite, six months
out of every twelve. "In my opinion," says Judge Davis,
"Lincoln was as happy as *he* could be, on this circuit, and
happy in no other place. This was his place of enjoyment. As
a general rule, of a Saturday evening, when all the lawyers
would go home [the judge means those who were close
enough to get there and back by the time their cases were

called] and see their families and friends, Lincoln would refuse to go." "It was on this circuit," we are told by an authority equally high, " that he shone as a *nisi prius* law-yer; it was on this circuit Lincoln thought, spoke, and acted; it was on this circuit that the people met, greeted, and cheered on the man; it was on this circuit that he cracked his jokes, told his stories, made his money, and was happy as nowhere in the world beside." When, in 1857, Sangamon County was cut off from the Eighth Circuit by the act creating the Eighteenth, " Mr. Lincoln would still continue with Judge Davis, first finishing his business in Sangamon."

On his return from one of these long journeys, he found that Mrs. Lincoln had taken advantage of his absence, and, with the connivance and assistance of his neighbor, Gourly, had placed a second story and a new roof on his house. Approaching it for the first time after this rather startling alteration, and pretending not to recognize it, he called to a man on the street, " Stranger, can you tell me where Lincoln lives? He used to live here."

When Mr. Lincoln first began to " ride the circuit," he was too poor to own horseflesh or vehicle, and was compelled to borrow from his friends. But in due time he became the pro-prietor of a horse, which he fed and groomed himself, and to which he was very much attached. On this animal he would set out from home, to be gone for weeks together, with no baggage but a pair of saddle-bags, containing a change of linen, and an old cotton umbrella, to shelter him from sun or rain. When he got a little more of this world's goods, he set up a one-horse buggy, — a very sorry and shabby-looking affair, which he generally used when the weather promised to be bad. But the lawyers were always glad to see him, and the landlords hailed his coming with pleasure. Yet he was one of those peculiar, gentle, uncomplaining men, whom those servants of the public who keep " hotels " would gene-rally put off with the most indifferent accommodations. It was a very significant remark of a lawyer thoroughly acquainted with his habits and disposition, that "Lincoln was never seated next the landlord at a crowded table, and never got a chicken liver or the best cut from the roast." If rooms were scarce, and one, two, three, or four gentlemen were required to lodge together, in order to accommodate some surly man who "stood upon his rights," Lincoln was sure to be one of the unfortunates. Yet he loved the life, and never went home without reluctance.

From Mr. S. C. Parks of Lincoln, himself a most reputable lawyer, we have two or three anecdotes, which we give in his own language : —

"I have often said, that, for a man who was for the quarter of a century *both* a *lawyer* and a *politician*, he was the most honest man I ever knew. He was not only morally honest, but intellectually so. He could not reason falsely : if he attempted it, he failed. In politics he never would try to mislead. At the bar, when he thought he was wrong, he was the weakest lawyer I ever saw. You know this better than I do. But I will give you an example or two which occurred in this county, and which you may not remember.

"A man was indicted for larceny : Lincoln, Young, and myself defended him. Lincoln was satisfied by the evidence that he was guilty, and ought to be convicted. He called Young and myself aside, and said, 'If you can say any thing for the man, do it. I can't : if I attempt, the jury will see that I think he is guilty, and convict him, of course.' The case was submitted by us to the jury without a word. The jury failed to agree ; and before the next term the man died. Lincoln's honesty undoubtedly saved him from the penitentiary.

"In a closely-contested civil suit, Lincoln had proved an account for his client, who was, though he did not know it at the time, a very slippery fellow. The opposing attorney then proved a receipt clearly covering the entire cause of action. By the time he was through, Lincoln was missing. The court sent for him to the hotel. 'Tell the judge,' said he, 'that I can't come: *my hands are dirty ; and I came over to clean them !*'

" In the case of Harris and Jones *vs.* Buckles, Harris wanted Lincoln to assist you and myself. His answer was characteristic : ' Tell Harris it's no use to *waste money on me* in that case : he'll get beat.' "

Mr. Lincoln was prone to adventures in which *pigs* were the other party. The reader has already enjoyed one from the pen of Miss Owen ; and here is another, from an incorrigible humorist, a lawyer, named J. H. Wickizer : —

" In 1855 Mr. Lincoln and myself were travelling by buggy from Woodford County Court to Bloomington, Ill. ; and, in passing through a little grove, we suddenly heard the terrific squealing of a little pig near by us. Quick as thought Mr. Lincoln leaped out of the buggy, seized a club, pounced upon the old sow, and beat her lustily : she was in the act of eating one of her young ones. Thus he saved the pig, and then remarked, ' By jing ! the unnatural old brute shall not devour her own progeny !' This, I think, was his first proclamation of freedom."

But Mr. Wickizer gives us another story, which most happily illustrates the readiness of Mr. Lincoln's wit : —

" In 1858, in the court at Bloomington, Mr. Lincoln was engaged in a case of no great importance ; but the attorney on the other side, Mr. S——, a young lawyer of fine abilities (now a judge of the Supreme Court of the State), was always very sensitive about being beaten, and in this case manifested unusual zeal and interest. The case lasted until late at night, when it was finally submitted to the jury. Mr. S—— spent a sleepless night in anxiety, and early next morning learned, to his great chagrin, that he had lost the case. Mr. Lincoln met him at the Court House, and asked him what had become of his case. With lugubrious countenance and melancholy tone, Mr. S—— said, ' It's gone to hell.' — ' Oh, well !' replied Lincoln, ' then you'll see it again !' "

Although the humble condition and disreputable character of some of his relations and connections were the subject of constant annoyance and most painful reflections, he never tried to shake them off, and never abandoned them when they needed his assistance. A son of his foster-brother, John Johnston, was arrested in —— County for stealing a watch. Mr. Lincoln went to the same town to address a mass meeting while the poor boy was in jail. He waited until the dusk of the evening, and then, in company with Mr. H. C. Whitney, visited the prison. " Lincoln knew he was guilty," says Mr. Whitney, " and was very deeply affected, — more than I ever saw him. At the next term of the court, upon the State's Attorney's consent, Lincoln and I went to the prosecution witnesses, and got them to come into open court, and state that they did not care to presecute." The boy was released; and that evening, as the lawyers were leaving the town in their buggies, Mr. Lincoln was observed to get down from his, and walk back a short distance to a poor, distressed-looking young man who stood by the roadside. It was young Johnston. Mr. Lincoln engaged for a few moments apparently in earnest and nervous conversation with him, then giving him some money, and returning to his buggy, drove on.

A thousand tales could be told of Mr. Lincoln's amusing tricks and eccentricities on these quiet rides from county to county, in company with judges and lawyers, and of his quaint sayings and curious doings at the courts in these Western villages. But, much against our will, we are compelled to make selections, and present a few only, which rest upon the most undoubted authority.

It is well known that he used to carry with him, on what Mr. Stuart calls " the tramp around the circuit, " ordinary school-books, — from Euclid down to an English grammar, — and study them as he rode along, or at intervals of leisure in the towns where he stopped. He supplemented these with a copy of Shakspeare, got much of it by rote, and recited long passages from it to any chance companion by the way.

He was intensely fond of cutting wood with an axe; and he was often seen to jump from his buggy, seize an axe out of the hands of a roadside chopper, take his place on the log in the most approved fashion, and, with his tremendous long strokes, cut it in two before the man could recover from his surprise.

It was this free life that charmed him, and reconciled him to existence. Here he forgot the past, with all its cruelties and mortifications: here were no domestic afflictions to vex his weary spirit and to try his magnanimous heart.

" After he had returned from Congress," says Judge Davis, " and had lost his practice, Goodrich of Chicago proposed to him to open a law-office in Chicago, and go into partnership with him. Goodrich had an extensive practice there. Lincoln refused to accept, and gave as a reason, that he tended to consumption ; that, if he went to Chicago, he would have to sit down and study hard, and it would kill him ; that he would rather go around the circuit — the Eighth Judicial Circuit — than to sit down and die in Chicago."

In the summer of 1857, at a camp-meeting in Mason County, one Metzgar was most brutally murdered. The affray took place about half a mile from the place of worship, near some wagons loaded with liquors and provisions. Two men, James H. Norris and William D. Armstrong, were indicted for the crime. Norris was tried in Mason County, convicted of manslaughter, and sentenced to the penitentiary for the term of eight years. But Armstrong, the popular feeling being very high against him in Mason, " took a change of venue to Cass County," and was there tried (at Beardstown) in the spring of 1858. Hitherto Armstrong had had the services of two able counsellors, but now their efforts were supplemented by those of a most determined and zealous volunteer.

Armstrong was the son of Jack and Hannah Armstrong of New Salem, the child whom Mr. Lincoln had rocked in the cradle while Mrs. Armstrong attended to other household duties. His life was now in imminent peril: he seemed clearly guilty ; and, if he was to be saved, it must be by the interposition of some power which could deface that fatal record in the Norris trial, refute the senses of witnesses, and make a jury forget themselves and their oaths. Old Hannah had one friend whom she devoutly believed could accomplish this. She wrote to Mr. Lincoln, and he replied that he would defend the boy. (She says she has lost his letter.) Afterwards she visited him at Springfield, and prepared him for the event as well as she could, with an understanding weakened by a long strain of severe and almost hopeless reflection.

When the trial came on, Mr. Lincoln appeared for the defence. His colleague, Mr. Walker, had possessed him of the record in the Norris case; and, upon close and anxious examination, he was satisfied that the witnesses could, by a well-sustained and judicious cross-examination, be made to contradict each other in some important particulars. Mr. Walker "handled" the victims of this friendly design, while Mr. Lincoln sat by and suggested questions. Nevertheless, to the unskilled mind, the testimony seemed to be absolutely conclusive against the prisoner, and every word of it fell like a new sentence of death. Norris had beaten the murdered man with a club from behind, while Armstrong had pounded him in the face with a slung-shot deliberately prepared for the occasion; and, according to the medical men, either would have been fatal without the other. But the witness whose testimony bore hardest upon Armstrong swore that the crime was committed about eleven o'clock at night, and that he saw the blows struck by the light of a moon nearly full, and standing in the heavens about where the sun would stand at ten o'clock in the morning. It is easy to pervert and even to destroy evidence like this; and here Mr. Lincoln saw an opportunity which nobody had dreamed of on the Norris trial. He handed to an officer of the court an almanac, and told him to give it back to him when he should call for it in presence of the jury. It was an almanac of the year previous to the murder.

"Mr. Lincoln," says Mr. Walker, "made the closing argument for the defence. At first he spoke slowly, and carefully reviewed the whole testimony, — picked it all to pieces, and showed that the man had not received his wounds at the place or time named by the witnesses, *but afterwards, and at*

the hands of some one else."   " The evidence bore heavily upon
his client," says Mr. Shaw, one of the counsel for the prosecution.   " There were many witnesses, and each one seemed to
add one more cord that seemed to bind him down, until Mr.
Lincoln was something in the situation of Gulliver after his
first sleep in Lilliput.   But, when he came to talk to the jury
(that was always his forte), he resembled Gulliver again.   He
skilfully untied here and there a knot, and loosened here and
there a peg, until, fairly getting warmed up, he raised himself in his full power, and shook the arguments of his opponents from him as if they were cobwebs."   In due time he
called for the almanac, and easily proved by it, that, at the time
the main witness declared the moon was shining in great splen-
dor, there was, in fact, no moon at all, but black darkness
over the whole scene.   In the " roar of laughter " and undisguised astonishment succeeding this apparent demonstration,
court, jury, and counsel forgot to examine that seemingly conclusive almanac, and let it pass without a question concerning
its genuineness.[1]

In conclusion, Mr. Lincoln drew a touching picture of Jack
Armstrong (whose gentle spirit alas! had gone to that place
of coronation for the meek), and Hannah, — this sweet-faced

[1] Mr. E. J. Loomis, assistant in charge of the " Nautical Almanac" office, Washington,
D.C., under date of Aug. 1, 1871, says, —

" Referring to the ' Nautical Almanac' for 1857, I find, that, between the hours of ten
and eleven o'clock on the night of the 29th of August, 1857, the moon was within one hour
of setting.

" The computed time of its setting on that night is 11 h. 57 m., — three minutes before
midnight.

" The moon was only two days past its first quarter, and could hardly be mistaken for
' nearly full.' "

" In the case of the People *vs.* Armstrong, I was assisting prosecuting counsel.   The
prevailing belief at that time, and I may also say at the present, in Cass County, was
as follows : —

" Mr. Lincoln, previous to the trial, handed an almanac of the year previous to the murder to an officer of the court, stating that he might call for one during the trial, and, if he
did, to send him that one.   An important witness for the People had fixed the time of the
murder to be in the night, near a camp-meeting; ' that the moon was about in the same
place that the sun would be at ten o'clock in the morning, and was nearly full,' therefore he
could see plainly, &c.   At the proper time, Mr. Lincoln called to the officer for an almanac; and the one prepared for the occasion was shown by Mr. Lincoln, he reading from it
at the time referred to by the witness ' *The moon had already set;* ' that in the roar of laughter the jury and opposing counsel forgot to look at the date.   Mr. Carter, a lawyer of this

old lady with the silver locks, — welcoming to their humble cabin a strange and penniless boy, to whom Jack, with that Christian benevolence which distinguished him through life, became as a father, and the guileless Hannah even more than a mother. The boy, he said, stood before them pleading for the life of his benefactors' son, — the staff of the widow's declining years.

"The last fifteen minutes of his speech," his colleague declares, "was as eloquent as I ever heard; and such the power and earnestness with which he spoke to that jury, that all sat as if entranced, and, when he was through, found relief in a gush of tears." "He took the jury by storm," says one of the prosecutors. "There were tears in Mr. Lincoln's eyes while he spoke, but they were genuine. His sympathies were fully enlisted in favor of the young man, and his terrible sincerity could not help but arouse the same passion in the jury. I have said a hundred times that it was Lincoln's *speech* that saved that criminal from the gallows." In the language of Hannah, who sat by enchanted, "he told the stories about our first acquaintance, — what I did for him, and how I did it;" and she thinks it "was *truly* eloquent."

"As to the trial," continues Hannah, "Lincoln said to me, 'Hannah, your son will be cleared before sundown.' He and the other lawyers addressed the jury, and closed the case. *I went down at Thompson's pasture*: Stator came to me, and told me soon that my son was cleared and a free man. I went

city (Beardstown), who was present at, but not engaged in, the Armstrong case, says he is satisfied that the almanac was of the year previous, and thinks he examined it at the time. This was the general impression in the court-room. I have called on the sheriff who offici-ated at that time (James A. Dick), who says that he saw a 'Goudy's Almanac' lying upon Mr. Lincoln's table during the trial, and that Mr. Lincoln took it out of his own pocket. Mr. Dick does not know the date of it. I have seen several of the petit jurymen who sat upon the case, who only recollect that the almanac *floored* the witness. But one of the jurymen, the foreman, Mr. Milton Logan, says that it was the one for the year of the mur-der, and no trick about it; that he is willing to make an affidavit that he examined it as to date, and that it was an almanac of the year of the murder. My own opinion is, that when an almanac was called for by Mr. Lincoln, *two* were brought, one of the year of the mur-der, and one of the year previous; that Mr. Lincoln was entirely innocent of any deception in the matter. I the more think this, from the fact that Armstrong was not cleared by any want of testimony against him, but by the irresistible appeal of Mr. Lincoln in his favor."—HENRY SHAW.

up to the Court House: the jury shook hands with me, so did the Court, so did Lincoln. We were all affected, and tears streamed down Lincoln's eyes. He then remarked to me, 'Hannah, what did I tell you? I pray to God that William may be a good boy hereafter; that this lesson may prove in the end a good lesson to him and to all.' . . . After the trial was over, Lincoln came down to where I was in Beardstown. I asked him what he charged me; told him I was poor. He said, 'Why, Hannah, I sha'n't charge you a cent, — never. Any thing I can do for you I will do for you willing and freely without charges.' He wrote to me about some land which some men were trying to get from me, and said, 'Hannah, they can't get your land. Let them try it in the Circuit Court, and then you appeal it; bring it to Supreme Court, and I and Herndon will attend to it for nothing.'"

This boy William enlisted in the Union army. But in 1863 Hannah concluded she "wanted" him. She does not say that William was laboring under any disability, or that he had any legal right to his discharge. She merely "wanted" him, and wrote Mr. Lincoln to that effect. He replied promptly by telegraph: —

SEPTEMBER, 1863.

MRS. HANNAH ARMSTRONG, — I have just ordered the discharge of your boy William, as you say, now at Louisville, Ky.

A. LINCOLN.

For many years Mr. Lincoln was the attorney of the Illinois Central Railway Company; and, having rendered in some recent causes most important and laborious services, he presented a bill in 1857 for five thousand dollars. He pressed for his money, and was referred to some under-official who was charged with that class of business. Mr. Lincoln would probably have modified his bill, which seemed exorbitant as charges went among country lawyers, but the company treated him with such rude insolence, that he contented himself with a formal demand, and then immediately instituted suit on the claim. The case was tried at Bloomington before Judge Davis; and, upon affidavits of N. B. Judd, O. H.

Browning, S. T. Logan, and Archy Williams, respecting the value of the services, was decided in favor of the plaintiff, and judgment given for five thousand dollars. This was much more money than Mr. Lincoln had ever had at one time.

In the summer of 1859 Mr. Lincoln went to Cincinnati to argue the celebrated McCormick reaping-machine case. Mr. Edwin M. Stanton, whom he never saw before, was one of his colleagues, and the leading counsel in the case; and although the other gentlemen engaged received him with proper respect, Mr. Stanton treated him with such marked and habitual discourtesy, that he was compelled to withdraw from the case. When he reached home he said that he had " never been so brutally treated as by that man Stanton ; " and the facts justified the statement.

STEPHEN T. LOGAN.

CHAPTER XIV.

WE have seen already, from one of his letters to Mr. Herndon, that Mr. Lincoln was personally quite willing to be a candidate for Congress the second time. But his "honor" forbade: he had given pledges, and made private arrangements with other gentlemen, to prevent "the district from going to the enemy." Judge Logan was nominated in his place; and, although personally one of the most popular men in Illinois, he was sadly beaten, in consequence of the record which the Whig party had made "against the war." It was well as it was; for, if Mr. Lincoln had been the candidate, he would have been still more disastrously defeated, since it was mainly the votes he had given in Congress which Judge Logan found it so difficult to explain and impossible to defend.

Mr. Lincoln was an applicant, and a very urgent one, for the office of Commissioner of the General Land-Office in the new Whig administration. He moved his friends to urge him in the newspapers, and wrote to some of his late associates in Congress (among them Mr. Schenck of Ohio), soliciting their support. But it was all of no avail; Mr. Justin Butterfield (also an Illinoisian) beat him "in the race to Washington," and got the appointment. It is said by one of Mr. Lincoln's numerous biographers, that he often laughed over his failure to secure this great office, pretending to think it beneath his merits; but we can find no evidence of the fact alleged, and have no reason to believe it.

Mr. Fillmore subsequently offered him the governorship of

Oregon. The news reached him whilst away at court at Tremont or Bloomington. Mr. Stuart and others "coaxed him to take it;" the former insisting that Oregon would soon become a State, and he one of its senators. Mr. Lincoln saw it all, and said he would accept "if his wife would consent." But his wife "refused to do so;" and time has shown that she was right, as she usually was when it came to a question of practical politics.

From the time of his retirement from Congress to 1854, when the repeal of the Missouri Compromise and the Kansas-Nebraska Bill broke the hollow truce of 1856, which Mr. Clay and his compeers fondly regarded as a peace, Mr. Lincoln's life was one of comparative political inactivity. He did not believe that the sectional agitations could be permanently stilled by the devices which then seemed effectual to the foremost statesmen of either party and of both sections. But he was not disposed to be forward in the renewal of them. He probably hoped against conviction that time would allay the animosities which endangered at once the Union and the principles of free government, which had thus far preserved a precarious existence among the North American States.

Coming home to Springfield from the Tremont court in 1850 in company with Mr. Stuart, he said, "The time will come when we must all be Democrats or Abolitionists. When that time comes, my mind is made up. The 'slavery question' can't be compromised." — "So is my mind made up," replied his equally firm companion; and at that moment neither doubted on which side he would find the other when the great struggle took place.

The Whig party everywhere, in Congress and in their conventions, local and national, accepted the compromise of 1850 under the leadership of Mr. Clay and Mr. Webster. Mr. Lincoln did the same; for, from the hour that party lines were distinctly and closely drawn in his State, he was an unswerving party man. But although he said nothing against those measures, and much in favor of them, it is clear that he accepted the result with reluctance. He spoke out his disapproval of the Fugitive Slave Law as it was passed, believing and declaring wherever he went, that a negro man apprehended as a slave should have the privilege of a trial by jury, instead of the summary processes provided by the law.

"Mr. Lincoln and I were going to Petersburg in 1850, I think," says Mr. Herndon. "The political world was dead: the compromises of 1850 seemed to settle the negro's fate. Things were stagnant; and all hope for progress in the line of freedom seemed to be crushed out. Lincoln was speculating with me about the deadness of things, and the despair which arose out of it, and deeply regretting that his human strength and power were limited by his nature to rouse and stir up the world. He said gloomily, despairingly, sadly, 'How hard, oh! how hard it is to die and leave one's country no better than if one had never lived for it! The world is dead to hope, deaf to its own death-struggle, made known by a universal cry, What is to be done? Is any thing to be done? Who can do any thing? and how is it to be done? Did you ever think of these things?'"

In 1850 Mr. Lincoln again declined to be a candidate for Congress; and a newspaper called "The Tazewell Mirror" persisting in naming him for the place, he published a letter, refusing most emphatically to be considered a candidate. The concluding sentence alleged that there were many men among the Whigs of the district who would be as likely as he to bring "the district right side up."

Until the death of his excellent step-mother, Sarah Bush Lincoln, Mr. Lincoln never considered himself free for a moment from the obligation to look after and care for her family. She had made herself his mother; and he regarded her and her children as near relatives, — much nearer than any of the Hankses.

The limit of Thomas Lincoln's life was rapidly approaching. Mrs. Chapman, his step-daughter, wrote Mr. Lincoln to that effect; and so did John Johnston. He began to fear that the straitened circumstances of the household might make them think twice before they sent for a doctor, or procured other comforts for the poor old man, which he needed, per-haps, more than drugs. He was too busy to visit the dying man, but sent him a kind message, and directed the family to get whatever was wanted upon his credit.

SPRINGFIELD, Jan. 12, 1851.

DEAR BROTHER, — On the day before yesterday I received a letter from Harriet, written at Greenup. She says she has just returned from your house, and that father is very low, and will hardly recover. She also says that you have written me two letters, and that, although you do not expect me to come now, you wonder that I do not write. I received both your let-ters; and, although I have not answered them, it is not because I have for-gotten them, or not been interested about them, but because it appeared to me I could write nothing which could do any good. You already know I desire that neither father nor mother shall be in want of any comfort, either in health or sickness, while they live; and I feel sure you have not failed to use my name, if necessary, to procure a doctor or any thing else for father in his present sickness. My business is such that I could hardly leave home now, if it were not, as it is, that my own wife is sick a-bed. (It is a case of baby sickness, and, I suppose, is not dangerous.) I sincerely hope father may yet recover his health; but, at all events, tell him to remember to call upon and confide in our great and good and merciful Maker, who will not turn away from him in any extremity. He notes the fall of a sparrow, and numbers the hairs of our heads; and he will not forget the dying man who puts his trust in him. Say to him, that, if we could meet now, it is doubtful whether it would not be more painful than pleasant; but that, if it be his lot to go now, he will soon have a joyous meeting with loved ones gone before, and where the rest of us, through the help of God, hope ere long to join them.

Write me again when you receive this.

Affectionately,

A. LINCOLN.

Before and after the death of Thomas Lincoln, John Johns-ton and Mr. Lincoln had a somewhat spirited correspondence regarding John's present necessities and future plans. John was idle, thriftless, penniless, and as much disposed to rove as poor old Tom had been in his earliest and worst days. This lack of character and enterprise on John's part added seriously to Mr. Lincoln's anxieties concerning his step-mother, and greatly embarrassed his attempts to provide for her. At length he wrote John the following energetic exhortation, coupled with a most magnanimous pecuniary offer. It is the letter promised in a previous chapter, and makes John an intimate acquaintance of the reader : —

DEAR JOHNSTON, — Your request for eighty dollars, I do not think it best to comply with now. At the various times when I have helped you a little, you have said to me, " We can get along very well now ; " but in a very short time I find you in the same difficulty again. Now, this can only happen by some defect in your conduct. What that defect is, I think I know. You are not *lazy*, and still you are an *idler*. I doubt whether, since I saw you, you have done a good whole day's work in any one day. You do not very much dislike to work, and still you do not work much, merely because it does not seem to you that you could get much for it. This habit of uselessly wasting time is the whole difficulty ; and it is vastly important to you, and still more so to your children, that you should break the habit. It is more important to them, because they have longer to live, and can keep out of an idle habit before they are in it easier than they can get out after they are in.

You are now in need of some money ; and what I propose is, that you shall go to work, " tooth and nail," for somebody who will give you money for it. Let father and your boys take charge of things at home, prepare for a crop, and make the crop, and you go to work for the best money-wages, or in discharge of any debt you owe, that you can get ; and, to secure you a fair reward for your labor, I now promise you, that, for every dollar you will, between this and the first of next May, get for your own labor, either in money or as your own indebtedness, I will then give you one other dollar. By this, if you hire yourself at ten dollars a month, from me you will get ten more, making twenty dollars a month for your work. In this I do not mean you shall go off to St. Louis, or the lead-mines, or the gold-mines in California ; but I mean for you to go at it for the best wages you can get close to home, in Cole's County. Now, if you will do this, you will be soon out of debt, and, what is better, you will have a habit that will keep you from getting in debt again. But, if I should now clear you out of debt, next year you would be just as deep in as ever. You say you would almost give your place in heaven for $70 or $80. Then you value your place in heaven very cheap ; for I am sure you can, with the offer I make, get the seventy or eighty dollars for four or five months' work. You say, if I will furnish you the money, you will deed me the land, and, if you don't pay the money back, you will deliver possession. Nonsense ! If you can't now live with the land, how will you then live without it ? You have always been kind to me, and I do not mean to be unkind to you. On the contrary, if you will but follow my advice, you will find it worth more than eighty times eighty dollars to you.

Affectionately your brother,

A. LINCOLN

Again he wrote : —

SHELBYVILLE, Nov. 4, 1851.

DEAR BROTHER, — When I came into Charleston day before yesterday, I learned that you are anxious to sell the land where you live, and move to Missouri. I have been thinking of this ever since, and cannot but think such a notion is utterly foolish. What can you do in Missouri better than here ? Is the land any richer ? Can you there, any more than here, raise corn and wheat and oats without work ? Will anybody there, any more than here, do your work for you ? If you intend to go to work, there is no better place than right where you are : if you do not intend to go to work, you cannot get along anywhere. Squirming and crawling about from place to place can do no good. You have raised no crop this year ; and what you really want is to sell the land, get the money, and spend it. Part with the land you have, and, my life upon it, you will never after own a spot big enough to bury you in. Half you will get for the land you will spend in moving to Missouri, and the other half you will eat and drink and wear out, and no foot of land will be bought. Now, I feel it is my duty to have no hand in such a piece of foolery. I feel that it is so even on your own account, and particularly on *mother's* account. The eastern forty acres I intend to keep for mother while she lives : if you *will not cultivate it*, it will rent for enough to support her ; at least, it will rent for something. Her dower in the other two forties she can let you have, and no thanks to me. Now, do not misunderstand this letter : I do not write it in any unkindness. I write it in order, if possible, to get you to *face* the truth, which truth is, you are destitute because you have idled away all your time. Your thousand pretences for not getting along better are all nonsense : they deceive nobody but yourself. *Go to work* is the only cure for your case.

A word to mother. Chapman tells me he wants you to go and live with him. If I were you, I would try it a while. If you get tired of it (as I think you will not), you can return to your own home. Chapman feels very kindly to you ; and I have no doubt he will make your situation very pleasant.

Sincerely your son,

A. LINCOLN.

And again : —

SHELBYVILLE, Nov. 9, 1851.

DEAR BROTHER, — When I wrote you before, I had not received your letter. I still think as I did ; but if the land can be sold so that I get three hundred dollars to put to interest for mother, I will not object, if she does not. But, before I will make a deed, the money must be had, or secured beyond all doubt, at ten per cent.

As to Abram, I do not want him, *on my own account ;* but I understand he wants to live with me, so that he can go to school, and get a fair start in the world, which I very much wish him to have. When I reach home, if I can make it convenient to take, I will take him, provided there is no mistake between us as to the object and terms of my taking him.

In haste as ever,

A. LINCOLN.

On the 1st of July, 1852, Mr. Lincoln was chosen by a public meeting of his fellow-citizens at Springfield to deliver in their hearing a eulogy upon the life and character of Henry Clay; and on the 16th of the same month he complied with their request. Such addresses are usually called orations; but this one scarcely deserved the name. He made no effort to be eloquent, and in no part of it was he more than ordinarily animated. It is true that he bestowed great praise upon Mr. Clay; but it was bestowed in cold phrases and a tame style, wholly unlike the bulk of his previous compositions. In truth, Mr. Lincoln was never so devoted a follower of Mr. Clay as some of his biographers have represented him. He was for another man in 1836, most probably for another in 1840, and very ardently for another in 1848. Dr. Holland credits him with a visit to Mr. Clay at Ashland, and an interview which effectually cooled his ardor in behalf of the brilliant statesman. But, in fact, Mr. Lincoln never troubled himself to make such a pilgrimage to see or hear any man, — much less Mr. Clay. None of his friends — Judge Davis, Mr. Herndon, Mr. Speed, or any one else, so far as we are able to ascertain — ever heard of the visit. If it had been made at any time after 1838, it could scarcely have been concealed from Mr. Speed; and we are compelled to place it along with the multitude of groundless stories which have found currency with Mr. Lincoln's biographers.

If the address upon Clay is of any historical value at all, it is because it discloses Mr. Lincoln's unreserved agreement with Mr. Clay in his opinions concerning slavery and the proper method of extinguishing it. They both favored gradual emancipation by the voluntary action of the people of the Slave States, and the transportation of the whole negro population to Africa as rapidly as they should be freed from service to their masters : it was a favorite scheme with Mr. Lincoln then, as it was long after he became President of the United States. " Compensated " and " voluntary emancipation," on the one hand, and " colonization " of the freedmen on the other, were essential parts of every " plan " which sprung out of his own individual mind. On this occasion, after quoting Mr. Clay, he said, " This suggestion of the possible ultimate redemption of the African race and African continent was made twenty-five years ago. Every succeeding year has added strength to the hope of its realization. May it indeed be realized! Pharaoh's country was cursed with plagues, and his hosts were drowned in the Red Sea, for striving to retain a captive people who had already served them more than four hundred years. May like disasters never befall us ! If, as the friends of colonization hope, the present and coming generations of our countrymen shall by any means succeed in freeing our land from the dangerous presence of slavery, and at the same time restoring a captive people to their long-lost fatherland, with bright prospects for the future, and this, too, so gradually that neither races nor individuals shall have suffered by the change, it will indeed be a glorious consummation. And if to such a consummation the efforts of Mr. Clay shall have contributed, it will be what he most ardently wished ; and none of his labors will have been more valuable to his country and his kind."

During the campaign of 1852, Judge Douglas took the stump for Pierce " in twenty-eight States out of the thirty-one." His first speech was at Richmond, Va. It was published extensively throughout the Union, and especially in Illinois. Mr. Lincoln felt an ardent desire to answer it, and, according to his own account, got the " permission " of the " Scott Club " of Springfield to make the speech under its auspices. It was a very poor effort. If it was distinguished by one quality above another, it was by its attempts at humor ; and all those attempts were strained and affected, as well as very coarse. He displayed a jealous and petulant temper from the first sentence to the last, wholly beneath the dignity of the occasion and the importance of the topic. Considered as a whole, it may be said that none of his public performances was more unworthy of its really noble author than this one. The reader has doubtless observed in the course of this narrative, as he will in the future, that Mr. Douglas's great success in obtaining place and distinction was a standing offence to Mr. Lincoln's self-love and individual ambition. He was intensely jealous of him, and longed to pull him down, or outstrip him in the race for popular favor, which they united in considering " the chief end of man." Some of the first sentences of this speech before the " Scott Club " betray this feeling in a most unmistakable and painful manner. " This speech [that of Mr. Douglas at Richmond] has been published with high commendations in at least one of the Democratic papers in this State, and I suppose it has been and will be in most of the others. When I first saw it and read it, I was reminded of old times, *when Judge Douglas was not so much greater man than all the rest of us, as he is now*, — of the Harrison campaign twelve years ago, when I used to hear and *try* to answer many of his speeches ; and believing that the Richmond speech, though marked with the same species of ' shirks and quirks ' as the old ones, was not marked with any greater ability, I was seized with a strange inclination to attempt an answer to it ; and this inclination it was that prompted me to seek the privilege of addressing you on this occasion."

In the progress of his remarks, Mr. Lincoln emphatically indorsed Mr. Douglas's great speech at Chicago in 1850, in defence of the compromise measures, which Mr. Lincoln pronounced the work of no party, but which, " for praise or blame," belonged to Whigs and Democrats alike. The rest of the address was devoted to a humorous critique upon Mr. Douglas's language in the Richmond speech, to ridicule of the campaign biographies of Pierce, to a description of Gens. Shields and Pierce wallowing in the ditch in the midst of a battle, and to a most remarkable account of a militia muster which might have been seen at Springfield a few years previous. Mr. Douglas had expressed great confidence in the sober judgment of the people, and at the same time had, rather inconsistently as well as indecently, declared that Providence had saved us from one military administration by the timely removal of Gen. Taylor. To this Mr. Lincoln alluded in his closing paragraph, which is given as a fair sample of the whole: —

"Let us stand by our candidate as faithfully as he has always stood by our country, and I much doubt if we do not perceive a slight abatement in Judge Douglas's confidence in Providence, as well as in the people. I suspect that confidence is not more firmly fixed with the judge than it was with the old woman whose horse ran away with her in a buggy. She said she 'trusted in Providence till the britchin' broke, and then she didn't know what on airth *to* do.' The chance is, the judge will see the 'britchin' broke;' and then he can at his leisure bewail the fate of Locofocoism as the victim of misplaced confidence."

On the 4th of January, 1854, Mr. Douglas, Chairman of the Committee on Territories, of the Senate of the United States, reported a bill to establish a territorial government in Nebraska. This bill contained nothing in relation to the Missouri Compromise, which still remained upon the statute-book, although the principle on which it was based had been violated in the Compromise legislation of 1850. A Whig Senator from Kentucky gave notice, that, when the Committee's bill came before the Senate, he would move an amendment repealing the Missouri Compromise. With this admonition in mind, the Committee instructed Mr. Douglas to report a substitute, which he did on the 23d of the same month. The substitute made two Territories out of Nebraska, and called one of them Kansas. It annulled the Missouri Compromise, forbade its application to Kansas, Nebraska, or any other territory, and, as amended and finally passed, fixed the following rules: . . . "It being the true intent and meaning of this act not to legislate slavery into any Territory or State, nor to exclude it therefrom, but to leave the

people thereof perfectly free to form and regulate their
domestic institutions in their own way, subject only to the
Constitution of the United States." Mr. Douglas had long
since denounced his imprecations upon "the ruthless hand"
that should disturb that ancient compact of peace between
the sections; and now he put forth his own ingenious hand
to do the deed, and to take the curse, in both of which he
was eminently successful. Not that the Missouri Act may
not have been repugnant to the Constitution, for no court
had ever passed upon it; but it was enacted for a holy purpose, was venerable in age, was consecrated in the hearts of
the people by the unsurpassed eloquence of the patriots
of a previous generation, and having the authority of law,
of reason, and of covenant, it had till then preserved the
Union, as its authors designed it should; and, being in truth
a sacred thing, it was not a proper subject for the "ruthless"
interference of mere politicians, like those who now devoted
it to destruction. If, upon a regularly heard and decided
issue, the Supreme Court should declare it unconstitutional,
the recision of the compact could be attributed to no party,—
neither to slavery nor to antislavery,—and the peace of the
country might still subsist. But its repeal by the party that
did it—a coalition of Southern Whigs and Democrats with
Northern Democrats—was evidence of a design to carry
slavery into the region north of 36° 30'; or the legislation was
without a purpose at all. It was the first aggression of the
South; but be it remembered in common justice, that she
was tempted to it by the treacherous proffers of a restless but
powerful Northern leader, who asked no recompense but her
electoral votes. In due time he opened her eyes to the
nature of the fraud; and, if he carried through the Kansas-
Nebraska Act to catch the votes of the South in 1856, it cost
him no inconvenience to give it a false and startling construction to catch the votes of the North in 1860. In the
repeal of the Compromise, the Northern Democrats submitted
with reluctance to the dictation of Douglas and the South. It
was the great error of the party,—the one disastrous error of

all its history.   The party succeeded in 1856 only by the nomination of Mr. Buchanan, who was out of the country when the
Kansas-Nebraska Act was passed, and who was known to have
opposed it.   But the questions which grew out of it, the false
and disingenuous construction of the act by its author, the
slavery agitations in Kansas and throughout the country,
disrupted the party at Charleston, and made possible Mr.
Lincoln's election by a minority of the votes cast.   And to the
Whig party, whose Senators and Representatives from the
South voted for the Douglas Bill in a body, the renewal
of the slavery agitation, invited and insured by their action,
was the signal of actual dissolution.

Up to this date, Mr. Lincoln's views of slavery, and how
they were formed, are as well known to the reader as they
can be made known from the materials left behind for a history
of them.   It is clear that his *feelings* on the subject were
inspired by individual cases of apparent hardship which had
come under his observation.   John Hanks, on the last trip to
New Orleans, was struck by Lincoln's peculiarly active sympathy for the servile race, and insists, that, upon sight of their
wrongs, "the iron entered his heart."   In a letter to Mr.
Speed, which will shortly be presented, Mr. Lincoln confesses
to a similar experience in 1841, and speaks with great bitterness of the pain which the actual presence of chained and
manacled slaves had given him.   Indeed, Mr. Lincoln was
not an ardent sympathizer with sufferings of any sort, which
he did not witness with the eye of flesh.   His compassion
might be stirred deeply by an object present, but never by
an object absent and unseen.   In the former case he would
most likely extend relief, with little inquiry into the merits
of the case, because, as he expressed it himself, it "took a
pain out of his own heart;" and he devoutly believed that
every such act of charity or mercy sprung from motives
purely selfish.   None of his public acts, either before or after
he became President, exhibits any special tenderness for the
African race, or any extraordinary commiseration of their
lot.   On the contrary, he invariably, in words and deeds,

postponed the interests of the blacks to the interests of the whites, and expressly subordinated the one to the other. When he was compelled, by what he deemed an overruling necessity, founded on both military and political considerations, to declare the freedom of the public enemy's slaves, he did so with avowed reluctance, and took pains to have it understood that his resolution was in no wise affected by sentiment. He never at any time favored the admission of negroes into the body of electors, in his own State or in the States of the South. He claimed that those who were incidentally liberated by the Federal arms were poor-spirited, lazy, and slothful; that they could be made soldiers only by force, and willing laborers not at all; that they seemed to have no interest in the cause of their own race, but were as docile in the service of the Rebellion as the mules that ploughed the fields or drew the baggage-trains; and, as a people, were useful only to those who were at the same time their masters and the foes of those who sought their good. With such views honestly formed, it is no wonder that he longed to see them transported to Hayti, Central America, Africa, or anywhere, so that they might in no event, and in no way, participate in the government of his country. Accordingly, he was, from the beginning, as earnest a colonizationist as Mr. Clay, and, even during his Presidency, zealously and persistently devised schemes for the deportation of the negroes, which the latter deemed cruel and atrocious in the extreme. He believed, with his rival, that this was purely a " white man's government; " but he would have been perfectly willing to share its blessings with the black man, had he not been very certain that the blessings would disappear when divided with such a partner. He was no Abolitionist in the popular sense; did not want to break over the safeguards of the Constitution to interfere with slavery where it had a lawful existence; but, wherever his power rightfully extended, he was anxious that the negro should be protected, just as women and children and unnaturalized men are pro-

tected, in life, limb, property, reputation, and every thing that
nature or law makes sacred.   But this was all: he had no
notion of extending to the negro the *privilege* of *governing*
him and other white men, by making him an elector.   That
was a political trust, an office to be exercised only by the
superior race.

It was therefore as a white man, and in the interests of
white men, that he threw himself into the struggle to keep
the blacks out of the Territories.   He did not want them
there either as slaves or freemen; but he wanted them less
as slaves than as freemen.   He perceived clearly enough the
motives of the South in repealing the Missouri Compromise.
It did, in fact, arouse him "like a fire-bell in the night."   He
felt that a great conflict impended; and, although he had
as yet no idea that it was an "irrepressible conflict between
opposing and enduring forces," which must end in making
all free or all slave, he thought it was serious enough to
demand his entire mind and heart; and he freely gave them
both.

Mr. Gillespie gives the substance of a conversation with
him, which, judging from the context, must have taken place
about this time.   Prefacing with the remark that the slavery
question was the only one "on which he (Mr. Lincoln)
would become excited," he says, —

"I recollect meeting with him once at Shelbyville, when
he remarked that something must be done, or slavery would
overrun the whole country.   He said there were about
six hundred thousand non-slaveholding whites in Kentucky
to about thirty-three thousand slaveholders; that, in the
convention then recently held, it was expected that the delegates would represent these classes about in proportion to
their respective numbers; but, when the convention assembled, there was not a single representative of the non-
slaveholding class: every one was in the interest of the
slaveholders; 'and,' said he, 'the thing is spreading like
wildfire over the country.   In a few years we will be ready
to accept the institution in Illinois, and the whole country

will adopt it.' I asked him to what he attributed the change that was going on in public opinion. He said he had put that question to a Kentuckian shortly before, who answered by saying, ' You might have any amount of land, money in your pocket, or bank-stock, and, while travelling around, nobody would be any wiser; but, if you had a darkey trudging at your heels, everybody would see him, and know that you owned a slave.' ' It is the most glittering, ostentatious, and displaying property in the world; and now,' says he, ' if a young man goes courting, the only inquiry is, how many negroes he or she owns. The love for slave property was swallowing up every other mercenary possession. Its ownership betokened, not only the possession of wealth, but indicated the gentleman of leisure, who was above and scorned labor.' These things Mr. Lincoln regarded as highly seductive to the thoughtless and giddy-headed young men who looked upon work as vulgar and ungentlemanly. Mr. Lincoln was really excited, and said, with great earnestness, that this spirit ought to be met, and, if possible, checked; that slavery was a great and crying injustice, an enormous national crime, and that we could not expect to escape punishment for it. I asked him how he would proceed in his efforts to check the spread of slavery. *He confessed he did not see his way clearly. I think he made up his mind from that time that he would oppose slavery actively.* I know that Mr. Lincoln always contended that no man had any right other than mere brute force gave him to a slave. He used to say that it was singular that the courts would hold that a man never lost his right to his property that had been stolen from him, but that he instantly lost his right to himself if he was stolen. Mr. Lincoln always contended that the cheapest way of getting rid of slavery was for the nation to buy the slaves, and set them free."

If the passage of the Kansas-Nebraska Bill awakened Lincoln from his dream of security regarding the slavery question, which he hoped had been put to rest by the compromises of 1820 and 1850, it did the same with all like-minded people in the North.   From that moment the Abolitionists, on the one hand, discerned a hope, not only of restricting slavery, but of ultimate emancipation; and the Southern Disunionists, on the other, who had lately met with numerous and signal defeats in their own section, perceived the means of inflaming the popular heart to the point of disunion.   A series of agitations immediately began, — incessant, acrimonious, and in Kansas murderous and bloody, — which destroyed the Whig party at once, and continued until they severed the Democratic party at Charleston.   All other issues were as chaff to this, — slavery or no slavery in the Territories, — while the discussion ranged far back of this practical question, and involved the much broader one, whether slavery possessed inherent rights under the Constitution.   The Whigs South having voted for the repeal of the compromise, and the Whigs North against it, that party was practically no more.   Some of its members went into the Know-Nothing lodges; some enlisted under the Abolition flag, and others drifted about and together until they formed themselves into a new organization, which they called Republican.   It was a disbanded army; and, released from the authority of discipline and party tradition, a great part of the members engaged for a while in political operations of a very disreputable character.   But the better class, having kept themselves unspotted from the pollution of Know-Nothingism, gradually but speedily formed the Republican party, which in due time drew into its mighty ranks nearly all the elements of opposition to the Democracy.   Such a Whig was Mr. Lincoln, who lost no time in taking his ground.   In Illinois the new party was not (in 1854) either Abolitionist, Republican, Know-Nothing, Whig, or Democratic, for it was composed of odds and ends of all; but simply the Anti-Nebraska party, of which Mr. Lincoln soon became the acknowledged leader.

Returning from Washington, Mr. Douglas attempted to speak at Chicago; but he was not heard, and, being hissed and hooted by the populace of the city, betook himself to more complaisant audiences in the country.   Early in October, the State Fair being in progress there, he spoke at Springfield. His speech was ingenious, and, on the whole, able : but he was on the defensive ; and the consciousness of the fact, both on his own part and that of the audience, made him seem weaker than he really was. By common consent the Anti-Nebraska men put up Mr. Lincoln to reply ; and he did reply with such power as he had never exhibited before. He was not the Lincoln who had spoken that tame address over Clay in 1852, or he who had deformed his speech before the " Scott Club " with petty jealousies and gross vulgarisms, but a new and greater Lincoln, the like of whom no one in that vast multitude had ever heard before. He felt that he was addressing the people on a living and vital question, not merely for the sake of speaking, but to produce conviction, and achieve a great practical result. How he succeeded in his object may be gathered from the following extracts from a leading editorial in " The Springfield Journal," written by Mr. Herndon : —

" This Anti-Nebraska speech of Mr. Lincoln was the profoundest, in our opinion, that he has made in his whole life. He felt upon his soul the truths burn which he uttered, and all present felt that he was true to his own soul. His feelings once or twice swelled within, and came near stifling utterance. . . . He quivered with emotion. The whole house was as still as death.

" He attacked the Nebraska Bill with unusual warmth and energy ; and all felt that a man of strength was its enemy, and that he intended to blast it if he could by strong and manly efforts. He was most successful, and the house approved the glorious triumph of truth by loud and continued huzzas. Women waved their white handkerchiefs in token of woman's silent but heartfelt assent. Douglas felt the sting : the animal within was roused, because he frequently interrupted Mr. Lincoln. His friends felt that he was crushed by Lincoln's powerful argument, manly logic, and illustrations from nature around us. The Nebraska Bill was shivered, and, like a tree of the forest, was torn and rent asunder by hot bolts of truth.

. . . Mr. Lincoln exhibited Douglas in all the attitudes he could be placed in a friendly debate. He exhibited the bill in all its aspects to show its humbuggery and falsehood; and, when thus torn to rags, cut into slips, held up to the gaze of the vast crowd, a kind of scorn and mockery was visible upon the face of the crowd and upon the lips of the most eloquent speaker. . . . At the conclusion of this speech, every man, woman, and child felt that it was unanswerable. . . . He took the heart captive, and broke like a sun over the understanding."

Mr. Douglas rose to reply. He was excited, angry, imperious in his tone and manner, and his voice loud and shrill. Shaking his forefinger at the Democratic malecontents with furious energy, and declaiming rather than debating, he occupied to little purpose the brief interval remaining until the adjournment for supper. Then, promising to resume his address in the evening, he went his way; and that audience " saw him no more." Evening came, but not the orator. Many fine speeches were made during the continuance of that fair upon the one absorbing topic, — speeches by the ablest men in Illinois, — Judge Trumbull, Judge Breese, Col. Taylor (Democratic recusants), and Stephen A. Douglas and John Calhoun (then Surveyor-General of Nebraska). But it is no shame to any one of these, that their really impressive speeches were but slightly appreciated, nor long remembered, beside Mr. Lincoln's splendid and enduring performance, — enduring in the memory of his auditors, although preserved upon no written or printed page.

Among those whom the State Fair brought to Springfield for political purposes, were some who were neither Whigs, Democrats, Know-Nothings, nor yet mere Anti-Nebraska men: there were the restless leaders of the then insignificant Abolition faction. Chief among them was Owen Lovejoy; and second to him, if second to any, was William H. Herndon. But the position of this latter gentleman was one of singular embarrassment. According to himself, he was an Abolitionist " sometime before he was born," and hitherto he had made his

" calling and election sure " by every word and act of a life
devoted to political philanthropy and disinterested political
labors. While the two great national parties divided the
suffrages of the people, North and South, every thing in his
eyes was " dead." He detested the bargains by which those
parties were in the habit of composing sectional troubles,
and sacrificing the " principle of freedom." When the Whig
party " paid its breath to time," he looked upon its last ago-
nies as but another instance of divine retribution. He had
no patience with time-servers, and regarded with indignant
contempt the " policy " which would postpone the natural
rights of an enslaved race to the success of parties and politicians. He stood by at the sacrifice of the Whig party in
Illinois with the spirit of Paul when he " held the clothes of
them that stoned Stephen." He believed it was for the best,
and hoped to see a new party rise in its place, great in the
fervor of its faith, and animated by the spirit of Wilberforce,
Garrison, and the Lovejoys. He was a fierce zealot, and
gloried proudly in his title of " fanatic ; " for it was his conviction that fanatics were at all times the salt of the earth,
with power to save it from the blight that follows the wickedness of men. He believed in a God, but it was the God of
nature, — the God of Socrates and Plato, as well as the God
of Jacob. He believed in a Bible, but it was the open scroll
of the universe ; and in a religion clear and well defined, but
it was a religion that scorned what he deemed the narrow
slavery of verbal inspiration. Hot-blooded, impulsive, brave
morally and physically, careless of consequences when moved
by a sense of individual duty, he was the very man to receive
into his inmost heart the precepts of Mr. Seward's " higher
law." If he had pledged faith to slavery, no peril of life
or body could have induced him to violate it. But he held
himself no party to the compromises of the Constitution, nor
to any law which recognized the justice of human bondage ;
and he was therefore free to act as his God and nature
prompted.

Now, Mr. Herndon had determined to make an Abolitionist

out of Mr. Lincoln when the proper time should arrive ; and that time would be only when Mr. Lincoln could change front and " come out " without detriment to his personal aspirations. For, although Mr. Herndon was a zealot in the cause, he loved his partner too dearly to wish him to espouse it while it was unpopular and politically dangerous to belong to it. " I cared nothing for the ruin of myself," said he ; " but I did not wish to see Mr. Lincoln sacrificed." He looked forward to a better day, and, in the mean time, was quite willing that Mr. Lincoln should be no more than a nominal Whig, or a strong Anti-Nebraska man ; being quite sure, that, when the auspicious moment arrived, he would be able to present him to his brethren as a convert over whom there would surely be great joy. Still, there was a bare chance that he might lose him. Mr. Lincoln was beset by warm friends and by old coadjutors, and besought to pause in his antislavery course while there was yet time. Among these there was none more earnest or persuasive than John T. Stuart, who was but the type of a class. Tempted on the one side to be a Know-Nothing, and on the other side to be an Abolitionist, Mr. Lincoln said, as if in some doubt of his real position, " I *think* I am still a Whig." But Mr. Herndon was more than a match for the full array against him. An earnest man, instant in season and out of season, he spoke with the eloquence of apparent truth and of real personal love. Moreover, Mr. Lincoln's preconceptions inclined him to the way in which Mr. Herndon desired him to walk ; and it is not surprising that in time he was, not only almost, but altogether, persuaded by a friend and partner, whose opportunities to reach and convince his wavering mind were daily and countless. " From 1854 to 1860," says Mr. Herndon, " I kept putting in Lincoln's hands the speeches and sermons of Theodore Parker, the speeches of Phillips and Beecher. I took ' The Antislavery Standard ' for years before 1856, ' The Chicago Tribune,' and ' The New York Tribune ; ' kept them in my office, kept them purposely on my table, and would read to Lincoln good, sharp, and solid things well put. Lincoln was a

JOHN T. STUART.

natural antislavery man, as I think, and yet he needed watching, — needed hope, faith, energy; and I think I warmed him. Lincoln and I were just the opposite one of another. He was cautious and practical; I was spontaneous, ideal, and speculative. He arrived at truths by reflection; I, by intuition; he, by reason; I, by my soul. He calculated; I went to toil asking no questions, never doubting. Lincoln had great faith in my intuitions, and I had great faith in his reason."

Of course such a man as we have described Mr. Herndon to be could have nothing but loathing and disgust for the secret oaths, the midnight lurking, and the proscriptive spirit of Know-Nothingism. "A number of gentlemen from Chicago," says he, "among them the editor of ' The Star of the West,' an Abolitionist paper published in Chicago, waited on me in my office, and asked my advice as to the policy of going into Know-Nothing Lodges, and ruling them for freedom. I opposed it as being wrong in principle, as well as a fraud on the lodges, and wished to fight it out in open daylight. Lincoln was opposed to Know-Nothingism, but did not say much in 1854 or 1855 (did afterwards). I told Lincoln what was said, and argued the question with him often, insisting that, as we were advocating *freedom for the slave in tendency* under the Kansas-Nebraska Bill, it was radically wrong to enslave the religious ideas and faith of men. The gentlemen who waited on me as before stated asked me if I thought that Mr. Lincoln could be trusted for freedom. I said to them, ' Can you trust yourselves? If you can, you can trust Lincoln forever.' "

With this explanation of the political views of Mr. Herndon, and his personal relations to Mr. Lincoln, the reader will more easily understand what follows.

"This State Fair," continues Mr. Herndon, " called thousands to the city. We Abolitionists all assembled here, taking advantage of the fair to organize and disseminate our ideas. As soon as Lincoln had finished his speech, Lovejoy, who had been in the hall, rushed up to the stand, and notified the crowd that there would be a meeting there in the evening:

subject, *Freedom.* I had been with the Abolitionists that day, and knew their intentions: namely, to force Lincoln with our organization, and to take broader and deeper and more radical views and ideas than in his speech, which was simply *Historic Kansas.* . . . He (Lincoln) had not then announced himself for freedom, only discussed the inexpediency of repealing the Missouri Compromise Line. The Abolitionists that day determined to make Lincoln take a stand. I determined he should *not at that time,* because the time had not yet come when Lincoln should show his hand. When Lovejoy announced the Abolition gathering in the evening, I rushed to Lincoln, and said, 'Lincoln, go home; take Bob and the buggy, and leave the county: go quickly, go right off, and never mind the order of your going.' Lincoln took a hint, got his horse and buggy, and did leave quickly, not noting the order of his going. He staid away till all conventions and fairs were over."

But the speech against the repeal of the Compromise signally impressed all parties opposed to Mr. Douglas's late legislation, — Whigs, Abolitionists, and Democratic Freesoilers, — who agreed with perfect unanimity, that Mr. Lincoln should be pitted against Mr. Douglas wherever circumstances admitted of their meeting. As one of the evidences of this sentiment, Mr. William Butler drew up a paper addressed to Mr. Lincoln, requesting and "urging him to follow Douglas up until the election." It was signed by Mr. Butler, William Jayne, P. P. Eads, John Cassady, B. F. Irwin, and many others. Accordingly, Lincoln "followed" Douglas to Peoria, where the latter had an appointment, and again replied to him, in much the same spirit, and with the same arguments, as before. The speech was really a great one, almost perfectly adapted to produce conviction upon a doubting mind. It ought to be carefully read by every one who desires to know Mr. Lincoln's power as a debater, after his intellect was matured and ripened by years of hard experience. On the general subject of slavery and negroes in the Union, he spoke as follows: —

" Before proceeding, let me say, I think I have no prejudice against the Southern people: they are just what we would be in their situation. If slavery did not now exist among them, they would not introduce it: if it did now exist amongst us, we should not instantly give it up. This I believe of the masses North and South. Doubtless there are individuals on both sides who would not hold slaves under any circumstances, and others would gladly introduce slavery anew if it were out of existence. We know that some Southern men do free their slaves, go North, and become tip-top Abolitionists; while some Northern men go South, and become cruel slave-masters.

" When Southern people tell us they are no more responsible for the origin of slavery than we, I acknowledge the fact. When it is said that the institution exists, and that it is very difficult to get rid of it in any satisfactory way, I can understand and appreciate the saying. *I surely will not blame them for not doing what I should not know how to do myself. If all earthly power were given me, I should not know what to do as to the existing institution.* My first impulse would be to free all the existing slaves, and send them to Liberia, — to their own native land; but a moment's reflection would convince me that whatever of high hope (as I think there is) there may be in this, in the long run, its sudden execution is impossible. If they were all landed there in a day, they would all perish in the next ten days; and there are not surplus shipping and surplus money enough in the world to carry them there in many times ten days. What then? Free them all, and keep them among us as underlings? Is it quite certain that this betters their condition? *I think I would not hold* one in slavery at any rate, yet the point is not clear enough to me to denounce people upon. What next? Free them, and make them politically and socially our equals? My own feelings will not admit of this; and, if mine would, we all know that those of the great mass of white people would not. Whether this feeling accords with justice and sound judgment is not the sole question, if, indeed, it is any part of it. A universal feeling, whether well or ill founded, cannot be safely disregarded. *We cannot, then, make them equals.* It does seem to me that systems of gradual emancipation might be adopted; but for their tardiness in this I will not undertake to judge our brethren of the South. When they remind us of their constitutional rights, I acknowledge them, not grudgingly, but fully and fairly; *and I would give them any legislation for the reclaiming of their fugitives which should not in its stringency be more likely to carry a free man into slavery than our ordinary criminal laws are to hang an innocent one.*

" But all this, to my judgment, furnishes no more excuse for permitting slavery to go into our own free territory than it would for reviving the African slave-trade by law. The law which forbids the bringing of slaves *from* Africa, and that which has so long forbidden the taking them *to* Nebraska, can hardly be distinguished on any moral principle; and the repeal of the former could find quite as plausible excuses as that of the latter.

.   .   .   .

" But Nebraska is urged as a great Union-saving measure. Well, I, too, go for saving the Union. Much as I hate slavery, I would consent to the extension of it, rather than see the Union dissolved, just as I would consent to any great evil to avoid a greater one. But, when I go to Union-saving, I must believe, at least, that the means I employ have adaptation to the end. To my mind, Nebraska has no such adaptation. ' It hath no relish of salvation in it.' It is an aggravation, rather, of the only one thing which ever endangers the Union. When it came upon us, all was peace and quiet. The nation was looking to the forming of new bonds of Union, and a long course of peace and prosperity seemed to lie before us. In the whole range of possibility, there scarcely appears to me to have been any thing out of which the slavery agitation could have been revived, except the project of repealing the Missouri Compromise. Every inch of territory we owned already had a definite settlement of the slavery question, and by which all parties were pledged to abide. Indeed, there was no uninhabited country on the continent which we could acquire, if we except some extreme Northern regions, which are wholly out of the question. In this state of the case, the Genius of Discord himself could scarcely have invented a way of getting us by the ears, but by turning back and destroying the peace measures of the past.

.   .   .   .

"The structure, too, of the Nebraska Bill is very peculiar. The people are to decide the question of slavery for themselves; but *when* they are to decide, or *how* they are to decide, or whether, when the question is once decided, it is to remain so, or is to be subject to an indefinite succession of new trials, the law does not say. Is it to be decided by the first dozen settlers who arrive there, or is it to await the arrival of a hundred? Is it to be decided by a vote of the people, or a vote of the Legislature, or, indeed, on a vote of any sort? To these questions the law gives no answer. There is a mystery about this; for, when a member proposed to give the Legislature express authority to exclude slavery, it was hooted down by the friends of the bill. This fact is worth remembering. Some Yankees in the East are sending emigrants to Nebraska to exclude slavery from it; and, so far as I can judge, they expect the question to be decided by voting in some way or other. But the Missourians are awake too. They are within a stone's-throw of the contested ground. They hold meetings and pass resolutions, in which not the slightest allusion to voting is made. They resolve that slavery already exists in the Territory; that more shall go there; and that they, remaining in Missouri, will protect it, and that Abolitionists shall be hung or driven away. Through all this, bowie-knives and six-shooters are seen plainly enough, but never a glimpse of the ballot-box. And really, what is the result of this? Each party within having numerous and determined backers without, is it not probable that the contest will come to blows and bloodshed? Could there be a more apt invention to bring about a collision and violence on

the slavery question than this Nebraska project is? I do not
charge or believe that such was intended by Congress; but
if they had literally formed a ring, and placed champions
within it to fight out the controversy, the fight could be no
more likely to come off than it is. And, if this fight should
begin, is it likely to take a very peaceful, Union-saving turn?
Will not the first drop of blood so shed be the real knell
of the Union?"

No one in Mr. Lincoln's audience appreciated the force of
this speech more justly than did Mr. Douglas himself. He
invited the dangerous orator to a conference, and frankly proposed a truce. What took place between them was explicitly
set forth by Mr. Lincoln to a little knot of his friends, in the
office of Lincoln & Herndon, about two days after the election. We quote the statement of B. F. Irwin, explicitly
indorsed by P. L. Harrison and Isaac Cogdale, all of whom
are already indifferently well known to the reader. "W. H.
Herndon, myself, P. L. Harrison, and Isaac Cogdale were
present. What Lincoln said was about this: that the day
after the Peoria debate in 1854, Douglas came to him (Lincoln), and flattered him that he (Lincoln) understood the
Territorial question from the organization of the government
better than all the opposition in the Senate of the United
States; and he did not see that he could make any thing by
debating it with him; and then reminded him (Lincoln) of
the trouble they had given him, and remarked that Lincoln
had given him more trouble than all the opposition in the
Senate combined; and followed up with the proposition, that
he would go home, and speak no more during the campaign,
if Lincoln would do the same: to which proposition Lincoln
acceded." This, according to Mr. Irwin's view of the thing,
was running Douglas "into his hole," and making "him
holler, Enough."

Handbills and other advertisements announced that Judge
Douglas would address the people of Lacon the day following
the Peoria encounter; and the Lacon Anti-Nebraska people
sent a committee to Peoria to secure Mr. Lincoln for a speech

in reply. He readily agreed to go, and on the way said not a word of the late agreement to the gentleman who had him in charge. Judge Douglas observed the same discreet silence among his friends. Whether they had both agreed to go to Lacon before this agreement was made, or had mutually contrived this clever mode of deception, cannot now be determined. But, when they arrived at Lacon, Mr. Douglas said he was too hoarse to speak, although, " a large portion of the people of the county assembled to hear him." Mr. Lincoln, with unheard-of magnanimity, " informed his friends that he would not like to take advantage of the judge's indisposition, and would not address the people." His friends could not see the affair in the same light, and " pressed him for a speech ; " but he persistently and unaccountably " refused."

Of course, Mr. Lincoln and Mr. Douglas met no more during the campaign. Mr. Douglas did speak at least once more (at Princeton), but Mr. Lincoln scrupulously observed the terms of the agreement. He came home, wrote out his Peoria speech, and published it in seven consecutive issues of " The Illinois Daily Journal ; " but he never spoke nor thought of speaking again. When his friends insisted upon having a reason for this most unexpected conduct, he gave the answer already quoted from Mr. Irwin.

The election took place on the 7th of November. During his absence, Mr. Lincoln had been announced as a candidate for the House of Representatives of the Illinois Legislature. William Jayne took the responsibility of making him a candidate. Mrs. Lincoln, however, " saw Francis, the editor, and had Lincoln's name taken out." When Mr. Lincoln returned, Jayne (Mrs. Lincoln's old friend " Bill ") went to see him. " I went to see him," says Jayne, " in order to get his consent to run. This was at his house. He was then the saddest man I ever saw, — the gloomiest. He walked up and down the floor, almost crying ; and to all my persuasions to let his name stand in the paper, he said, ' No, I can't. You don't know all. I say you don't begin to know one-half, and that's enough.' I did, however, go and have his name re-instated ;

and there it stood.   He and Logan were elected by about six hundred majority." Mr. Jayne had caused originally both Judge Logan and Mr. Lincoln to be announced, and they were both elected.   But, after all, Mrs. Lincoln was right, and Jayne and Lincoln were both wrong.   Mr. Lincoln was a well-known candidate for the United States Senate, in the place of Mr. Shields, the incumbent, who had voted for the Kansas-Nebraska Bill; and, when the Legislature met and showed a majority of Anti-Nebraska men, he thought it a necessary preliminary of his candidacy that he should resign his seat in the House.   He did so, and Mr. Jayne makes the following acknowledgment: "Mr. Lincoln resigned his seat, finding out that the Republicans, the Anti-Nebraska men, had carried the Legislature.   A. M. Broadwell ran as a Whig Anti-Nebraska man, and was badly beaten.   "The people of Sangamon County was down on Lincoln, — hated him." None can doubt that even the shame of taking a woman's advice might have been preferable to this!

But Mr. Lincoln "had set his heart on going to the United States Senate."   Counting in the Free-soil Democrats, who had revolted against Mr. Douglas's leadership, and been largely supported by the Whigs in the late elections, there was now on joint ballot a clear Anti-Nebraska majority of two.   A Senator was to be chosen to succeed Mr. Shields; and Mr. Lincoln had a right to expect the place.   He had fairly earned the distinction, and nobody in the old Whig party was disposed to withhold it.   But a few Abolitionists doubted his fidelity to their extreme views; and five Anti-Nebraska Senators and Representatives, who had been elected as Democrats, preferred to vote for a Senator with antecedents like their own.   The latter selected Judge Trumbull as their candidate, and clung to him manfully through the whole struggle.   They were five only in number; but in the situation of affairs then existing they were the sovereign five. They were men of conceded integrity, of good abilities in debate, and extraordinary political sagacity.   Their names ought to be known to posterity, for their unfriendliness at this juncture saved Mr. Lincoln to the Republicans of Illinois, to be brought forward at the critical moment as a fresh and original candidate for the Presidency. They were Judd of Cook County, Palmer of Macoupin, Cook of La Salle, Baker and Allen of Madison. They called themselves Democrats, and, with the modesty peculiar to bolters, claimed to be the only " Simon-pure." " They could not act with the Democrats from principle, and would not act with the Whigs from policy; " but, holding off from the caucuses of both parties, they demanded that all Anti-Nebraska should come to them, or sacrifice the most important fruits of their late victory at the polls. But these were not the only enemies Mr. Lincoln could count in the body of his party. The Abolitionists suspected him, and were slow to come to his support. Judge Davis went to Springfield, and thinks he " got some " of this class " to go for " him ; but it is probable they were " got " in another way. Mr. Lovejoy was a member, and required, as the condition of his support and that of his followers, that Mr. Lincoln should pledge himself to favor the exclusion of slavery from *all* the Territories of the United States. This was a long step in advance of any that Mr. Lincoln had previously taken. He was, as a matter of course, opposed to the introduction of slavery into the Territories north of the line of 36° 30′ ; but he had, up to this time, regarded all south of that as being honestly open to slavery. The villany of obliterating that line, and the necessity of its immediate restoration, — in short, the perfect sanctity of the Missouri settlement, — had formed the burden of all his speeches in the preceding canvass. But these opinions by no means suited the Abolitionists, and they required him to change them forthwith. He thought it would be wise to do so, considering the peculiar circumstances of his case ; but, before committing himself finally, he sought an understanding with Judge Logan. He told the judge what he was disposed to do, and said he would act upon the inclination, if the judge would not regard it as " treading upon his toes." The judge said he was opposed to the doctrine proposed ; but, for the sake of the cause in hand, he would cheerfully risk his "toes." And so the Abolitionists were accommodated: Mr. Lincoln quietly made the pledge, and they voted for him.

On the eighth day of February, 1855, the two Houses met in convention to choose a Senator. On the first ballot, Mr. Shields had forty-one votes, and three Democratic votes were scattered. Mr. Lincoln had forty-five, Mr. Trumbull five, and Mr. Koerner two. On the seventh ballot, the Democrats left Shields, and, with two exceptions, voted for Gov. Matteson. In addition to the party strength, Matteson received also the votes of two of the anti-Nebraska Democrats. That stout little knot, it was apparent, was now breaking up. For many reasons the Whigs detested Matteson most heartily, and dreaded nothing so much as his success. But of that there now appeared to be great danger; for, unless the Whigs abandoned Lincoln and went for Trumbull, the five Anti-Nebraska men would unite on Matteson, and elect him. Mr. Gillespie went to Lincoln for advice. "He said unhesitatingly, 'You ought to drop me, and go for Trumbull: that is the only way you can defeat Matteson.' Judge Logan came up about that time, and insisted on running Lincoln still; but the latter said, 'If you do, you will lose both Trumbull and myself; and I think the cause, in this case, is to be preferred to men.' We adopted his suggestion, and turned upon Trumbull, and elected him, although it grieved us to the heart to give up Mr. Lincoln. This, I think, shows that Mr. Lincoln was capable of sinking himself for the cause in which he was engaged." It was with great bitterness of spirit that the Whigs accepted this hard alternative. Many of them accused the little squad of Anti-Nebraska Democrats of " ungenerous and selfish " motives. One of them, "Mr. Waters of McDonough, was especially indignant, and utterly refused to vote for Mr. Trumbull at all. On the last ballot he threw away his ballot on Mr. Williams."

" Mr. Lincoln was very much disappointed," says Mr. Parks, a member of the Legislature, and one of Mr. Lincoln's special friends; "for I think, that, at that time, it was the height of his ambition to get into the United States Senate. He manifested, however, no bitterness towards Mr. Judd, or the other Anti-Nebraska Democrats, by whom politically he was beaten, but evidently thought that their motives were right. He told me several times afterwards, that the election of Trumbull was the best thing that could have happened."

In the great campaign of 1858, Mr. Douglas on various occasions insisted, that, in 1854, Mr. Lincoln and Judge Trumbull, being until then political enemies, had formed a secret agreement to abolitionize, the one the Whig, and the other the Democratic party; and, in order that neither might go unrewarded for a service so timely and patriotic, Mr. Trumbull had agreed on the one hand that Mr. Lincoln should have Shields's seat in the United States Senate (in 1855); and Mr. Lincoln had agreed, on the other, that Judge Trumbull should have Douglas's seat (in 1859). But Mr. Douglas alleged, that, when the first election (in 1854) came on, Judge Trumbull treated his fellow-conspirator with shameful duplicity, and cheated himself into the Senate just four years in advance of his appointed time; that, Mr. Lincoln's friends being greatly incensed thereat, Col. James H. Matheny, Mr. Lincoln's "friend and manager for twenty years," exposed the plot and the treachery; that, in order to silence and conciliate the injured party, Mr. Lincoln was promised the senatorial nomination in 1858, and thus a second time became a candidate in pursuance of a bargain more than half corrupt. But it is enough to say here, that Mr. Lincoln explicitly and emphatically denied the accusation as often as it was made, and bestowed upon the character of Judge Trumbull encomiums as lofty and as warm as he ever bestowed upon any contemporary. With the exception of Col. Matheny, we find none of Mr. Lincoln's peculiar friends complaining of Judge Trumbull; but as many of them as have spoken in the records before us (and they are numerous and prominent) speak of the purity, devotion, and excellence of Judge Trumbull in the most unreserved and unaffected manner. In fact and in

truth, he did literally nothing to advance his own interest:
he solicited no vote, and got none which did not come to him
by reason of the political necessities of the time.   His election consolidated the Anti-Nebraska party in the State, and,
in the language of Mr. Parks, his "first encounter with Mr.
Douglas in the Senate filled the people of Illinois with admiration for his abilities; and the ill feeling caused by his election gradually passed away."

But Mr. Douglas had a graver charge to make against Mr.
Lincoln than that of a simple conspiracy with Trumbull to
dispose of a great office.   He seems to have known nothing of
Mr. Lincoln's secret understanding with Lovejoy and his associates; but he found, that, on the day previous to the election
for Senator, Lovejoy had introduced a series of extreme antislavery resolutions; and with these he attempted to connect
Mr. Lincoln, by showing, that, with two exceptions, every
member who voted for the resolutions on the 7th of February voted also for Mr. Lincoln on the 8th.   The first
of the resolutions favored the restoration of the prohibition of slavery north of 36° 30′, and also a similar prohibition
as to "*all* territory which now belongs to the United States,
or which may hereafter come under their jurisdiction."
The second resolution declared against the admission of
any Slave State, no matter out of what Territory, or in what
manner formed; and the third demanded, first, the unconditional repeal of the Fugitive-Slave Law, or, failing that,
the right of *habeas corpus* and trial by jury for the person
claimed as a slave.   The first resolution was carried by a
strict party vote; while the second and third were defeated.   But Mr. Douglas asserted that Mr. Lincoln was
committed in favor of all three, because the members that
supported them subsequently supported him.   Of all this
Mr. Lincoln took no further notice than to say that Judge
Douglas might find the Republican platform in the resolutions of the State Convention of that party, held at Bloomington in 1856.   In fact, he maintained a singular reticence
about the whole affair, probably dreading to go into it too

deeply, lest his rival should unearth the private pledge to Lovejoy, of which Judge Logan has given us the history. When Judge Douglas produced a set of resolutions which he said had been passed by the Abolitionists at their Convention at Springfield, during the State Fair (the meeting alluded to by Mr. Herndon), and asserted that Mr. Lincoln was one of the committee that reported them, the latter replied with great spirit, and said what he could say with perfect truth, — that he was not near Springfield when that body met, and that his name had been used without his consent.

CHAPTER XV.

MR. LINCOLN predicted a bloody conflict in Kansas as the immediate effect of the repeal of the Missouri restriction. He had not long to wait for the fulfilment of his prophecy: it began, in fact, before he spoke; and if blood had not actually flowed on the plains of Kansas, occurrences were taking place on the Missouri border which could not avoid that result. The South invited the struggle by repealing a time-honored compromise, in such a manner as to convince the North that she no longer felt herself bound by any Congressional restrictions upon the institution of slavery; and that she intended, as far as her power would permit, to push its existence into all the Territories of the Union. The Northern States accepted the challenge promptly. The people of the Free States knew how to colonize and settle new Territories. The march of their westward settlements had for years assumed a steady tread as the population of these States augmented, and the facility for emigrating increased. When, therefore, the South threw down the barriers which had for thirty years consecrated all the Territories north of 36° 30′ to free labor, and announced her intention of competing therein for the establishment of her " peculiar institution," the North responded by using the legitimate means at her command to throw into the exposed regions settlers who would organize the Territories in the interest of free labor. The " irrepressible conflict " was therefore opened in the Territories, with the people of the two sections of the country arrayed against each other as participants in, as well as spec-

366

tators of, the contest. As participants, each section aided its representatives. The struggle opened in Kansas, and in favor of the South. During the passage of the bill organizing the Territory, preparations had been extensively made along the Missouri border, by " Blue Lodges " and " Social Bands," for the purpose of getting control of its Territorial government. The whole eastern border of the Territory was open to these marauders ; and they were not slow to embrace the opportunity of meeting their enemies with so many advantages in their favor. Public meetings were held in many of the frontier counties of Missouri, in which the people were not only advised to go over and take early possession of the Territory, but to hold themselves in readiness to remove all emigrants who should go there under the auspices of the Northern Aid Societies. It was with these " Border Ruffians," and some volunteers from Alabama and South Carolina, with a few vagabond " colonels " and " generals " from the Slave States generally, that the South began the struggle. Of course, the North did not look with complacency upon such a state of things. If the repeal of the Missouri Compromise startled the people of the Free States from their sense of security, the manner of applying " popular sovereignty," as indicated at its first introduction, was sufficient to arouse public sentiment to an unwonted degree. Kansas became at once a subject of universal interest. Societies were formed for throwing into her borders, with the utmost expedition, settlers who could be relied upon to mould her government in the interest of freedom. At the same time there was set in train all the political machinery that could be used to agitate the question, until the cry of " Bleeding Kansas " was heard throughout the land.

It is not necessary in this connection to set down, in order, the raids, assassinations, burnings, robberies, and election frauds which followed. Enough if their origin and character be understood. For this present purpose, a brief summary only will be given of what occurred during the long struggle to make Kansas a Slave State ; for upon the practical issues which arose during the contest followed the discussions between Mr. Lincoln and Mr. Douglas, upon the merits of which the former was carried into the Presidential office.

The first Territorial governor appointed under the provisions of the Kansas-Nebraska Act was Andrew H. Reeder of Pennsylvania. He was appointed by President Pierce. He reached Kansas in the autumn of 1854, and proceeded to establish a Territorial Government. The first election was for a delegate to Congress. By the aid of the people of Missouri, it resulted in favor of the Democrats. The governor then ordered an election for a first Territorial Legislature, to be held on the 31st of March, 1855. To this election the Missourians came in greater force than before; and succeeded in electing proslavery men to both Houses of the Legislature, with a single exception in each house. The governor, a proslavery man, set aside the returns in six districts, as being fraudulent; whereupon new elections were held, which, with one exception, resulted in favor of the Free-State men. These parties, however, were refused their seats in the Legislature; while the persons chosen at the previous election were accepted.

The Legislature thus organized proceeded to enact the most hostile measures against the Free-State men. Many of these acts were promptly vetoed by the governor. The Legislature then petitioned the President for his removal. Their wishes were complied with; and Wilson G. Shannon of Ohio was appointed in his stead. In the mean time, the Free-State men entirely repudiated the Legislature, and refused to be bound by its enactments.

Such was the situation in Kansas when Mr. Lincoln addressed to Mr. Speed the following letter: —

SPRINGFIELD, Aug. 24, 1855.

DEAR SPEED, — You know what a poor correspondent I am. Ever since I received your very agreeable letter of the 22d of May, I have been intending to write you an answer to it. You suggest that in political action now you and I would differ. I suppose we would; not quite as much, however, as you may think. You know I dislike slavery; and you fully admit the abstract wrong of it. So far there is no cause of difference. But you say, that, sooner than yield your legal right to the slave, — especially at the bidding of those who are not themselves interested, — you would see the Union dissolved. I am not aware that *any one* is bidding you yield that right: very certainly *I* am not. I leave that matter entirely to yourself. I also acknowledge *your* rights and *my* obligations under the Constitution in regard to your slaves. I confess I hate to see the poor creatures hunted down, and caught and carried back to their stripes and unrequited toils; but I bite my lip, and keep quiet. In 1841 you and I had together a tedious low-water trip on a steamboat from Louisville to St. Louis. You may remember, as I well do, that, from Louisville to the mouth of the Ohio, there were on board ten or a dozen slaves shackled together with irons. That sight was a continued torment to me; and I see something like it every time I touch the Ohio, or any other slave border. It is not fair for you to assume that I have no interest in a thing which has, and continually exercises, the power of making me miserable. You ought rather to appreciate how much the great body of the Northern people do crucify their feelings, in order to maintain their loyalty to the Constitution and the Union. I do oppose the extension of slavery because my judgment and feeling so prompt me; and I am under no obligations to the contrary. If for this you and I must differ, differ we must. You say, if you were President, you would send an army, and hang the leaders of the Missouri outrages upon the Kansas elections; still, if Kansas fairly votes herself a Slave State, she must be admitted, or the Union must be dissolved. But how if she votes herself a Slave State *unfairly*, — that is, by the very means for which you say you would hang men? Must she still be admitted, or the Union dissolved? That will be the phase of the question when it first becomes a practical one. In your assumption that there may be a fair decision of the slavery question in Kansas, I plainly see you and I would differ about the Nebraska law. I look upon that enactment, not as a *law*, but a *violence* from the beginning. It was conceived in violence, is maintained in violence, and is being executed in violence. I say it was *conceived* in violence, because the destruction of the Missouri Compromise, under the circumstances, was nothing less than violence. It was passed in violence, because it could not have passed at all but for the votes of many members in violence of the known will of their constituents. It is *maintained* in violence, because the elections since clearly demand its repeal; and the demand is openly disregarded.

You say men ought to be hung for the way they are executing that law; and *I* say the way it is being executed is quite as good as any of its antecedents. It is being executed in the precise way which was intended from the first; else why does no Nebraska man express astonishment or condemnation? Poor Reeder is the only public man who has been silly enough to believe that any thing like fairness was ever intended; and he has been bravely undeceived.

That Kansas will form a slave constitution, and with it will ask to be admitted into the Union, I take to be already a settled question, and so
24

settled by the very means you so pointedly condemn. By every principle of law ever held by any court, North or South, every negro taken to Kansas is free; yet, in utter disregard of this, — in the spirit of violence merely, — that beautiful Legislature gravely passes a law to hang any man who shall venture to inform a negro of his legal rights. This is the substance and real object of the law. If, like Haman, they should hang upon the gallows of their own building, I shall not be among the mourners for their fate. In my humble sphere, I shall advocate the restoration of the Missouri Compromise so long as Kansas remains a Territory; and when, by all these foul means, it seeks to come into the Union as a Slave State, I shall oppose it. I am very loath, in any case, to withhold my assent to the enjoyment of property *acquired* or *located* in good faith; but I do not admit that *good faith* in taking a negro to Kansas to be held in slavery is a probability with any man. Any man who has sense enough to be the controller of his own property has too much sense to misunderstand the outrageous character of the whole Nebraska business. But I digress. In my opposition to the admission of Kansas, I shall have some company; but we may be beaten. If we are, I shall not, on that account, attempt to dissolve the Union. I think it probable, however, we shall be beaten. Standing as a unit among yourselves, you can, directly and indirectly, bribe enough of our men to carry the day, as you could on the open proposition to establish a monarchy. Get hold of some man in the North whose position and ability is such that he can make the support of your measure, whatever it may be, a *Democratic party necessity*, and the thing is done. *Apropos* of this, let me tell you an anecdote. Douglas introduced the Nebraska Bill in January. In February afterwards, there was a called session of the Illinois Legislature. Of the one hundred members composing the two branches of that body, about seventy were Democrats. These latter held a caucus, in which the Nebraska Bill was talked of, if not formally discussed. It was thereby discovered that just three, and no more, were in favor of the measure. In a day or two Douglas's orders came on to have resolutions passed approving the bill; and they were passed by large majorities!!! The truth of this is vouched for by a bolting Democratic member. The masses, too, Democratic as well as Whig, were even nearer unanimous against it; but, as soon as the party necessity of supporting it became apparent, the way the Democracy began to see the *wisdom* and *justice* of it was perfectly astonishing.

You say, that, if Kansas fairly votes herself a Free State, as a Christian you will rather rejoice at it. All decent slaveholders *talk* that way; and I do not doubt their candor. But they never *vote* that way. Although in a private letter, or conversation, you will express your preference that Kansas shall be free, you would vote for no man for Congress who would say the same thing publicly. No such man could be elected from any district in a Slave State. You think Stringfellow & Co. ought to be hung; and yet, at the next Presidential election, you will vote for the exact type and representative of Stringfellow. The slave-breeders and slave-traders are a small, odious, and detested class among you; and yet in politics they dictate the course of all of you, and are as completely your masters as you are the master of your own negroes. You inquire where I now stand. That is a disputed point. I think I am a Whig; but others say there are no Whigs, and that I am an Abolitionist. When I was at Washington, I voted for the Wilmot Proviso as good as forty times; and I never heard of any one attempting to unwhig me for that. I now do no more than oppose the extension of slavery. I am not a Know-Nothing: that is certain. How could I be? How can any one who abhors the oppression of negroes be in favor of degrading classes of white people? Our progress in degeneracy appears to me to be pretty rapid. As a nation, we began by declaring that "*all men are created equal.*" We now practically read it "all men are created equal, except negroes." When the Know-Nothings get control, it will read "all men are created equal, except negroes and foreigners and Catholics." When it comes to this, I should prefer emigrating to some country where they make no pretence of loving liberty, — to Russia, for instance, where despotism can be taken pure, and without the base alloy of hypocrisy.

Mary will probably pass a day or two in Louisville in October. My kindest regards to Mrs. Speed. On the leading subject of this letter, I have more of her sympathy than I have of yours; and yet let me say I am

Your friend forever,

A. LINCOLN.

Gov. Shannon arrived in the Territory Sept. 1, 1855. On his way thither, he declared himself in favor of making Kansas a Slave State. He found affairs in a turbulent condition, which his policy by no means tended to mitigate or assuage. The Free-State party held a mass-meeting at Big Springs in the early part of September, at which they distinctly and earnestly repudiated the legislative government, which claimed to have been elected in March, as well as all laws passed by it; and they decided not to participate in an election for a delegate to Congress, which the Legislature had appointed to be held on the 1st of October following. They also held a Delegate Convention at Topeka, on the 19th of September, and appointed an Executive Committee for the Territory; and also an election for a Delegate to Congress, to be held on the second Tuesday in October. These two rival elections for a congressional delegate took place on different days; at the former of which, Whitfield, representing the proslavery party, was elected; while at the other, Gov. Reeder, representing the Free-State party, was chosen. On the 23d of October, the Free-State party held a constitutional Convention at Topeka, and formed a State constitution in their interest, under the provisions of which they subsequently acted, and also asked for admission into the Union.

While we are upon this phase of the Kansas question, it may not be amiss to postpone the relation of some intermediate events, in order to give the reader the benefit of an expression of Mr. Lincoln's views, which thus far has found place in no printed record.

Sometime in 1856 an association of Abolitionists was formed in Illinois to go to Kansas and aid the Free-State men in opposing the Government. The object of those engaged in this work was, in their opinion, a very laudable one, — no other than the defence of freedom, which they thought foully menaced in that far-off region. Among these gentlemen, and one of the most courageous and disinterested, was William H. Herndon. He says, —

"Mr. Lincoln was informed of our intents by some means. Probably the idea of resistance was more known than I now remember. He took the first opportunity he could to dissuade us from our partially-formed purpose. We spoke of liberty, justice, and God's higher law, and invoked the spirit of these as our holiest inspiration. In 1856 he addressed us on this very subject, substantially in these words : —

"'Friends, I agree with you in Providence; but I believe in the providence of the most men, the largest purse, and the longest cannon. You are in the minority, — in a sad minority; and you can't hope to succeed, reasoning from all human experience. You would rebel against the Government, and redden your hands in the blood of your countrymen. If you are in the minority, as you are, *you can't succeed*. I say again and again, against the Government, with a great majority of its best citizens backing it, and when they have the most men, the longest purse, and the biggest cannon, you can't succeed.

If you have the majority, as some of you say you have, you can succeed with the ballot, throwing away the bullet. You can peaceably, then, redeem the Government, and preserve the liberties of mankind, through your votes and voice and moral influence. Let there be peace. In a democracy, where the majority rule by the ballot through the forms of law, these physical rebellions and bloody resistances are radically wrong, unconstitutional, and are treason. Better bear the ills you have than fly to those you know not of. Our own Declaration of Independence says, that governments long established, for trivial causes should not be resisted. Revolutionize through the ballot-box, and restore the Government once more to the affections and hearts of men, by making it express, as it was intended to do, the highest spirit of justice and liberty. Your attempt, if there be such, to resist the laws of Kansas by force, is criminal and wicked; and all your feeble attempts will be follies, and end in bringing sorrow on your heads, and ruin the cause you would freely die to preserve!'

"This little speech," continues Mr. Herndon, "is not in print. It is a part of a much longer one, likewise not in print. This speech squelched the ideas of physical resistance, and directed our energies through other more effective channels, which his wisdom and coolness pointed out to us. This little speech, so timely and well made, saved many of us from great follies, if not our necks from the halter. The man who uttered it is no more; but this little speech, I hope, shall not soon be forgotten. Mr. Lincoln himself, after this speech, subscribed money to the people of Kansas *under conditions*, which I will relate in other ways. He was not alone in his gifts: I signed the same paper, I think, for the same amount, most cheerfully; and would do it again, only doubling the sum, adding no conditions, only the good people's wise discretion."

Early in 1856 it became painfully apparent to Mr. Lincoln that he must take a decisive stand upon the questions of the day, and become a Know-Nothing, a Democrat, a Republican, or an Abolitionist. Mere "Anti-Nebraska" would answer no longer: the members of that ephemeral coalition were seeking more permanent organizations. If interrogated concerning his position, he would probably have answered still, "I think I am a Whig." With the Abolition or Liberty party, he had thus far shown not a particle of sympathy. In 1840, 1844, 1848, and 1852, the Abolitionists, Liberty-men, or Free-Soilers, ran candidates of their own for the Presidency, and made no little noise and stir in the politics of the country; but they were as yet too insignificant in number to claim the adhesion of a practical man like Mr. Lincoln. In fact, his partner, one of the most earnest of them all, had not up to this time desired his fellowship. But now Mr. Herndon thought the hour had arrived when his hero should declare himself in unmistakable terms. He found, however, one little difficulty in the way: he was not precisely certain of his hero. Mr. Lincoln might go that way, and he might go the other way: his mind was not altogether made up; and there was no telling on which side the decision would fall. "He was button-holed by three ideas, and by men belonging to each class: first, he was urged to remain a Whig; secondly, he was urged to become a Know-Nothing, Say-Nothing, Do-Nothing; and, thirdly, he was urged to be baptized in Abolitionism: and in my imagination I can see Lincoln strung out three ways. At last two cords were snapped, he flying to Freedom."

And this is the way the cords were snapped: Mr. Herndon drew up a paper to be signed by men of his class in politics, calling a county convention to elect delegates to the State convention at Bloomington. "Mr. Lincoln was then backward," says Mr. Herndon, "dodge-y, — so and so. I was determined to make him take a stand, if he would not do it willingly, which he might have done, as he was naturally inclined Abolitionward. Lincoln was absent when the call was signed, and circulated here. I signed Mr. Lincoln's name without authority; had it published in "The Journal." John T. Stuart was keeping his eye on Lincoln, with the view of keeping him on his side, — the totally-dead conservative side. Mr. Stuart saw the published call, and grew mad; rushed into my office, seemed mad, horrified, and said to me, 'Sir, did Mr. Lincoln sign that Abolition call which is published this morning?' I answered, 'Mr. Lincoln did not sign that call.' — 'Did Lincoln authorize you to sign it?' said Mr. Stuart. 'No: he never authorized me to sign it.' — 'Then do you know that you have ruined Mr. Lincoln?' — 'I did not know that I had ruined Mr. Lincoln; did not intend to do so; thought he was a made man by it; that the time had come when conservatism was a crime and a blunder.' — 'You, then, take the responsibility of your acts; do you?' — 'I do, most emphatically.'

"However, I instantly sat down and wrote to Mr. Lincoln, who was then in Pekin or Tremont, — possibly at court. He received my letter, and instantly replied, either by letter or telegraph, — most likely by letter, — that he adopted *in toto* what I had done, and promised to meet the radicals — Lovejoy, and suchlike men — among us."

At Bloomington Lincoln was the great figure. Beside him all the rest — even the oldest in the faith and the strongest in the work — were small. Yet he was universally regarded as a recent convert, although the most important one that could be made in the State of Illinois. "We met at Bloomington; and it was there," says Mr. Herndon in one of his lectures, "that Mr. Lincoln was baptized, and joined our church. He made a speech to us. I have heard or read all Mr. Lincoln's great speeches; and I give it as my opinion, on my best judgment, that the Bloomington speech was the grand effort of his life. Heretofore, and up to this moment, he had simply argued the slavery question on grounds of policy, — on what are called the statesman's grounds, — never reaching the question of the radical and the eternal right. Now he was newly baptized and freshly born: he had the fervor of a new convert; the smothered flame broke out; enthusiasm unusual to him blazed up; his eyes were aglow with an inspiration; he felt justice; his heart was alive to the right; his sympathies, remarkably deep for him, burst forth, and he stood before the throne of the eternal Right, in presence of his God, and then and there unburdened his penitential and fired soul.   This speech was fresh, new, genuine, odd, original; filled with fervor not unmixed with a divine enthusiasm; his head breathing out through his tender heart its truths, its sense of right, and its feeling of the good and for the good.   This speech was full of fire and energy and force: it was logic; it was pathos; it was enthusiasm; it was justice, equity, truth, right, and the good, set ablaze by the divine fires of a soul maddened by the wrong; it was hard, heavy, knotty, gnarly, edged, and heated.   I attempted for about fifteen minutes, as was usual with me then, to take notes; but at the end of that time I threw pen and paper to the dogs, and lived only in the inspiration of the hour.   If Mr. Lincoln was six feet four inches high usually, *at Bloomington* he was seven feet, and inspired at that.   From that day to the day of his death, he stood firm on the right.   He felt his great cross, had his great idea, nursed it, kept it, taught it to others, and in his fidelity bore witness of it to his death, and finally sealed it with his precious blood."

If any thing in the foregoing description by Mr. Herndon seems extravagant to the reader, something must be pardoned to the spirit of a patient friend and an impatient teacher, who saw in this scene the first fruits of his careful husbandry, and the end of his long vigil.   He appears to have participated even then in the belief which Mr. Lincoln himself avowed, — that the latter was designed by the Dispenser of all things to occupy a great place in the world's history; and he felt that that day's doings had fixed his political character forever. The Bloomington Convention was called " Republican," and the Republican party of Illinois was there formed: but the most noted Abolitionists were in it, the spirit of the Lovejoys was present; and Mr. Herndon had a right to say, that, if Mr. Lincoln was not an Abolitionist, he was tending " Abolitionward " so surely that no doubt could be entertained of his ultimate destination.   But, after all, the resolutions of the convention were very "moderate."   They merely denounced the administration for its course regarding Kansas, stigmatized

WILLIAM H. HERNDON.

the repeal of the Missouri Compromise as an act of bad faith, and opposed " the extension of slavery into Territories heretofore free." It was surely not because Mr. Lincoln was present, and aiding at the passage of such resolutions, that Mr. Herndon and others thereafter regarded him as a " new-born " Abolitionist. It must have been the general warmth of his speech against the South, — his manifest detestation of slaveholders and slaveholding, as exhibited in his words, — which led them to believe that his feelings at least, if not his opinions, were similar to theirs. But the reader will see, nevertheless, as we get along in our history, that the Bloomington resolutions were the actual standard of Mr. Lincoln's views; that he continued to express his determination to maintain the rights of the Slave States under the Constitution, and to make conspicuously plain his abhorrence of negro suffrage and negro equality. He certainly disliked the Southern politicians very much; but even that sentiment, growing daily more fierce and ominous in the masses of the new party, was in his case counterbalanced by his prejudices or his caution, and he never saw the day when he would willingly have clothed the negroes with political privileges.

Notwithstanding the conservative character of the resolutions, the proceedings of the Bloomington Convention were alarming to a portion of the community, and seem to have found little favor with the people of Springfield. About five days after its adjournment, Herndon and Lincoln bethought them of holding a ratification meeting. Mr. Herndon got out huge posters, announcing the event, and employed a band of musicians to parade the streets and " drum up a crowd." As the hour of meeting drew near, he " lit up the Court House with many blazes," rung the bells, and blew a horn. At seven o'clock the meeting should have been called to order, but it turned out to be extremely slim. There was nobody present, with all those brilliant lights, but A. Lincoln, W. H. Herndon, and John Pain. " When Lincoln came into the court-room," says the bill-poster and horn-blower of this great demonstration, " he came with a sadness and a sense of the

ludicrous on his face. He walked to the stand, mounted it
in a kind of mockery, — mirth and sadness all combined, —
and said, 'Gentlemen, this meeting is larger than I *knew* it
would be. I knew that Herndon and myself would come,
but I did not know that any one else would be here; and yet
another has come, — you, John Pain. These are sad times,
and seem out of joint. All seems dead, dead, dead: but the
age is not yet dead; it liveth as sure as our Maker liveth.
Under all this seeming want of life and motion, the world
does move nevertheless. Be hopeful. And now let us adjourn, and appeal to the people.'

"This speech is in substance just as he delivered it, and
substantially in the same sad but determined spirit; and so we
did adjourn, did go out, and did witness the fact that 'the
world was not dead.'"

The Bloomington Convention sent delegates to the general
Republican Convention, which was to be held at Philadelphia
in June. That body was to nominate candidates for the
Presidency and Vice-Presidency, and high hopes were entertained of their success. But much remained to be done before such a revolution in sentiment could be expected. The
American or Know-Nothing party — corrupt, hideous, and
delusive, but still powerful — had adopted the old Whig platform on the several slavery questions, and planted itself de-
cisively against the agitations of the Anti-Nebraska men and
the Republicans. A "National Council" had taken this position for it the year previous, in terms beside which the resolutions of the Whigs and Democrats in 1852 were mild and
inexpressive. Something, therefore, must be done to get this
great organization out of the way, or to put its machinery
under "Republican" control. We have seen a party of gentlemen from Chicago proposing to go into the lodges, and
"rule them for freedom." Mr. Herndon and Mr. Lincoln rejected the plot with lofty indignation; but a section of the
Free-Soil politicians were by no means so fastidious. They
were for the most part bad, insincere, trading men, with
whom the profession of principles of any kind was merely a

convenient disguise, and who could be attached to no party, except from motives of self-interest. As yet, they were not quite certain whether it were possible to raise more hatred in the Northern mind against foreigners and Catholics than against slaveholders; and they prudently determined to be in a situation to try either. Accordingly, they went into the lodges, took the oaths, swore to stand by the platform of the " National Council " of 1855, and were perfectly ready to do that, or to betray the organization to the Republicans, as the prospect seemed good or bad. Believing the latter scheme to be the best, upon deliberation, they carried it out as far as in them lay, and then told the old, grim, honest, antislavery men, with whom they again sought association, that they had joined the Know-Nothings, and sworn irrevocable oaths to proscribe foreigners and Catholics, solely that they might rule the order " for freedom ; " and, the Republicans stand- ing in much need of aid just then, the excuse was con- sidered very good. But it was too shameless a business for Lincoln and Herndon; and they most righteously de- spised it.

In February, 1856, the Republicans held what Mr. Greeley styles their " first National Convention," at Pittsburg ; but they made no nominations there. At the same time, a Know- Nothing American " National Council " was sitting at Phila- delphia (to be followed by a nominating convention) ; and the Republicans at Pittsburg had not adjourned before they got news by telegraph, that the patriots who had entered the lodges on false pretences were achieving a great success : the American party was disintegrating, and a great section of it falling away to the Republicans. A most wonderful political feat had been performed, and the way was now apparently clear for a union of the all-formidable anti-Democratic ele- ments in the Presidential canvass.

On the 17th of June the National Republican Conven- tion met at Philadelphia, and nominated John C. Fremont for President, and William L. Dayton for Vice-President. Mr. Williams, Chairman of the Illinois Delegation, presented to the convention the name of Abraham Lincoln for the latter office ; and it was received with great enthusiasm by some of the Western delegates. He received, however, but 110 votes, against 259 for Mr. Dayton, and 180 scattered ; and Mr. Dayton was immediately thereafter unanimously declared the nominee.

While this convention was sitting, Mr. Lincoln was attending court at Urbana, in Champaign County. When the news reached that place that Mr. Dayton had been nominated, and " Lincoln had received 110 votes," some of the lawyers insisted that the latter must have been " our [their] Lincoln ; " but he said, " No, it could not be: it must have been the *great* Lincoln from Massachusetts." He utterly refused to believe in the reality of this unexpected distinction until he saw the proceedings in full. He was just then in one of his melancholy moods, his spirits depressed, and his heart suffering the miseries of a morbid mind.

With an indorsement of the " self-evident truths " and " inalienable rights " of the Declaration of Independence, the Republican Convention adopted the following as the practical and essential features of its platform : —

" *Resolved*, . . . That we deny the authority of Congress, of a territorial Legislature, of any individual, or association of individuals, to give legal existence to slavery in any Territory of the United States while the present Constitution shall be maintained.

" *Resolved*, That the Constitution confers upon Congress sovereign power over the Territories of the United States for their government; and that, in the exercise of this power, it is both the right and the duty of Congress to prohibit in the Territories those twin relics of barbarism, — polygamy and slavery."

The National Democratic Convention had already placed in nomination Buchanan and Breckenridge. Their platform denounced as sectional the principles and purposes of their opponents ; re-affirmed " the principles contained in the organic laws establishing the Territories of Kansas and Nebraska, as embodying the only sound and safe solution of the slavery question," and declared further, —

" That by the uniform application of Democratic principles to the organization of Territories and the admission of new States, with or without slavery as they may elect, the equal rights of all the States will be preserved intact, the original compacts of the Constitution maintained inviolate, and the perpetuity and expansion of the Union insured to its utmost capacity of embracing, in peace and harmony, every future American State that may be constituted or annexed with a republican form of government."

Mr. Lincoln was again a candidate for the office of Presidential elector, and made a thorough and energetic canvass. Some of his speeches were very striking ; and probably no man in the country discussed the main questions in that campaign — Kansas, and slavery in the Territories — in a manner more original and persuasive. From first to last, he scouted the intimation that the election of Fremont would justify a dissolution of the Union, or that it could possibly become even the occasion of a dissolution. In his eyes, the apprehensions of disunion were a " humbug ; " the threat of it mere bluster, and the fear of it silly timidity.

In the heat of the canvass, Mr. Lincoln wrote the following perfectly characteristic letter, — marked " Confidential : " —

SPRINGFIELD, Sept. 8, 1856.

HARRISON MALTBY, ESQ.

Dear Sir, — I understand you are a Fillmore man. Let me prove to you that every vote withheld from Fremont and given to Fillmore *in this State* actually lessens Fillmore's chance of being President.

Suppose Buchanan gets all the Slave States and Pennsylvania, and *any other* one State besides ; *then he is elected*, no matter who gets all the rest.

But suppose Fillmore gets the two Slave States of Maryland and Kentucky ; then Buchanan *is not elected :* Fillmore goes into the House of Representatives, and may be made President by a compromise.

But suppose, again, Fillmore's friends throw away a few thousand votes on him in Indiana and Illinois : it will inevitably give these States to Buchanan, which will more than compensate him for the loss of Maryland and Kentucky ; will elect him, and leave Fillmore no chance in the H. R., or out of it.

This is as plain as adding up the weights of three small hogs.   As Mr. Fillmore has no possible chance to carry Illinois *for himself*, it is plainly to his interest to let Fremont take it, and thus keep it out of the hands of Buchanan.   Be not deceived.   Buchanan is the hard horse to beat in this race.   Let him have Illinois, and nothing can beat him; *and he will get Illinois* if men persist in throwing away votes upon Mr. Fillmore.   Does some one persuade you that Mr. Fillmore can carry Illinois?   Nonsense!   There are over seventy newspapers in Illinois opposing Buchanan, only three or four of which support Mr. Fillmore, *all* the rest going for Fremont.   Are not these newspapers a fair index of the proportion of the votes?   If not, tell me why.

Again, of these three or four Fillmore newspapers, *two*, at least, are supported in part by the Buchanan men, as I understand.   Do not they know where the shoe pinches?   They know the Fillmore movement helps *them*, and therefore they *help it*.

Do think these things over, and then act according to your judgment.

Yours very truly,
A. LINCOLN.

(Confidential.)

This letter was discovered by the Buchanan men, printed in their newspapers, and pronounced, as its author anticipated, "a mean trick."   It was a dangerous document to them, and was calculated to undermine the very citadel of their strength.

Mr. Lincoln was still in imperfect fellowship — if, indeed, in any fellowship at all — with the extreme Abolitionists. He had met with Lovejoy and his followers at Bloomington, and was apparently co-operating with them for the same party purposes; but the intensity of his opposition to their radical views is intimated very strongly in this letter to Mr. Whitney: —

SPRINGFIELD, July 9, 1856.

DEAR WHITNEY, — I now expect to go to Chicago on the 15th, and I probably shall remain there or thereabout for about two weeks.

It turned me blind when I first heard Swett was beaten and Lovejoy nominated; but, after much anxious reflection, I really believe it is best to let it stand.   This, of course, I wish to be confidential.

Lamon did get your deeds.   I went with him to the office, got them, and put them in his hands myself.

Yours very truly,
A. LINCOLN.

In June, 1857, Judge Douglas made a speech at Springfield, in which he attempted to vindicate the wisdom and fairness of the law under which the people of Kansas were about to choose delegates to a convention to be held at Lecompton to frame a State constitution. He declared with emphasis, that, if the Free-State party refused to vote at this election, they alone would be blamable for the proslavery constitution which might be formed. The Free-State men professed to have a vast majority, — " three-fourths," " four-fifths," " nine-tenths," of the voters of Kansas. If these wilfully staid away from the polls, and allowed the minority to choose the delegates and make the constitution, Mr. Douglas thought they ought to abide the result, and not oppose the constitution adopted. Mr. Douglas's speech indicated clearly that he himself would countenance no opposition to the forthcoming Lecompton Convention, and that he would hold the Republican politicians responsible if the result failed to be satisfactory to them.

Judge Douglas seldom spoke in that region without provoking a reply from his constant and vigilant antagonist. Mr. Lincoln heard this speech with a critical ear, and then, waiting only for a printed report of it, prepared a reply to be delivered a few weeks later. The speeches were neither of them of much consequence, except for the fact that Judge Douglas seemed to have plainly committed himself in advance to the support of the Lecompton Constitution. Mr. Lincoln took that much for granted; and, arguing from sundry indications that the election would be fraudulently conducted, he insisted that Mr. Douglas himself, as the author of the Kansas-Nebraska Bill, and the inventor of " popular sovereignty," had made this " outrage " possible. He did not believe there were any " Free-State Democrats " in Kansas to make it a Free State without the aid of the Republicans, whom he held to be a vast majority of the population. The latter, he contended, were not *all* registered; and, because *all* were not registered, he thought none ought to vote. But Mr. Lincoln advised no bloodshed, no civil war, no roadside assassinations. Even if an incomplete registry might justify a majority of the people in an obstinate refusal to participate in the regulation of their own affairs, it certainly would not justify them in taking up arms to oppose all government in the Territory; and Mr. Lincoln did not say so. We have seen already how, in the "little speech" reported by Mr. Herndon, he deprecated "all physical rebellions" in this country, and applied his views to this case.

Mr. Lincoln also discussed the Dred-Scott Decision at some length; and, while doing so, disclosed his firm belief, that, in some respects, such as "life, liberty, and the pursuit of happiness," the negroes were made by the Declaration of Independence the equals of white men. But it did not follow from this that he was in favor of political or social equality with them. "There is," said he, "a natural disgust in the minds of nearly all the white people to the idea of an indiscriminate amalgamation of the white and black races; and Judge Douglas evidently is basing his chief hope upon the chances of his being able to appropriate the benefit of this disgust to himself. If he can, by much drumming and repeating, fasten the odium of that idea upon his adversaries, he thinks he can struggle through the storm. He therefore clings to his hope, as a drowning man to the last plank. He makes an occasion for lugging it in from the opposition to the Dred-Scott Decision. He finds the Republicans insisting that the Declaration of Independence includes ALL men, — black as well as white; and forthwith he boldly denies that it includes negroes at all, and proceeds to argue gravely, that all who contend it does, do so only because they want to vote, eat, sleep, and marry with negroes. Now, I protest against the counterfeit logic which concludes, that, because I do not want a black woman for a slave, I must necessarily want her for a wife. I need not have her for either. I can just leave her alone. In some respects, she certainly is not my equal; but in her natural right to eat the bread she earns with her own hands, without asking leave of any one else, she is my equal, and the equal of all others."

These speeches were delivered, the one early and the other late, in the month of June : they present strongly, yet guardedly, the important issues which were to engage Mr. Lincoln and Mr. Douglas in the famous campaign of 1858, and leave us no choice but to look into Kansas, and observe what had taken place and what was happening there.

Violence still (June, 1857) prevailed throughout the Territory. The administration of President Pierce committed itself at the first in support of the proslavery party. It acknowledged the Legislature as the only legal government in the Territory, and gave it military assistance to enforce its enactments. Gov. Shannon, having by his course only served to increase the hostility between the parties, was recalled, and John W. Geary of Pennsylvania was appointed his successor. Gov. Geary, while adopting the policy of the administration, so far as recognizing the Legislative party as the only legally organized government, was yet disposed to see, that, so far as the two parties could be got to act together, each should be fairly protected. This policy, however, soon brought him into collision with some of the proslavery leaders in the Territory ; and, not being sustained by Mr. Buchanan's administration, which had in the mean time succeeded the administration of President Pierce, he resigned his office. Hon. Robert J. Walker of Mississippi was appointed his successor, with Hon. F. P. Stanton of Tennessee as secretary. Both were strong Democrats ; and both were earnest advocates of the policy of the administration, as expressed in the recent presidential canvass, and in Mr. Buchanan's inaugural Message, — the absolute freedom of the people of the Territories to form such governments as they saw fit, subject to the provisions of the Constitution. Gov. Walker and his secretary earnestly set themselves to work to carry out this policy. The governor, in various addresses to the people of the Territory, assured all parties that he would protect them in the free expression of their wishes in the election for a new Territorial legislature ; and he besought the Free-State men to give up their separate Territorial organization, under which

25

they had already applied for admission into the Union, and
by virtue of which they claimed still to have an equitable
legal existence.   The governor was so earnest in his policy,
and so fair-minded in his purposes, that he soon drew upon
himself the opposition of the proslavery party of the Territory, now in a small minority, as well as the enmity of that
party in the States.   He assured the people they should have
a fair election for the new Legislature to be chosen in October
(1857), and which would come into power in January following.   The people took him at his word; and he kept it.
Enormous frauds were discovered in two districts, which were
promptly set aside.   The triumph of the Free-State party
was complete: they elected a legislature in their interest by
a handsome majority.   And now began another phase of the
struggle.   The policy of the Governor and the Secretary was
repudiated at Washington: the former resigned, and the latter was removed.   Meanwhile, a convention held under the
auspices of the old Legislature had formed a new constitution, known as the Lecompton Constitution, which the old
Legislature proposed to submit to the people for ratification
on the 21st of December.   The manner of submitting it was
singular, to say the least.   The people were required to vote
either for the constitution *with* slavery, or the constitution
without slavery.   As *without* slavery the constitution was in
some of its provisions as objectionable as if it upheld slavery,
the Free-State men refused to participate in its ratification.
The vote on its submission, therefore, stood 4,206 for the constitution *with* slavery, and 567 *without* slavery; and it was
this constitution, thus submitted and thus adopted, that Mr.
Buchanan submitted to Congress on the 2d of February, 1858,
as the free expression of the wishes of the people of Kansas;
and its support was at once made an administration measure.
Meantime the new Legislature elected by the people of the
Territory in October submitted this same Lecompton Constitution to the people again, and in this manner: votes to be
given for the constitution *with* slavery and *without* slavery, and
also against the constitution entirely.   The latter manner pre-

vailed ; the vote against the constitution in any form being over ten thousand. Thus the proslavery party in the Territory was overthrown. Under the auspices of the new Free-State Legislature, a constitutional convention was held at Wyandotte, in March, 1859. A Free-State constitution was adopted, under which Kansas was subsequently admitted into the Union.

Before leaving this Kansas question, there is one phase of the closing part of the struggle which it is worth while to note, particularly as it has a direct bearing upon the fortunes of Judge Douglas, and indirectly to the success of Mr. Lincoln. Douglas always insisted that his plan of " popular sovereignty " would give to the people of the Territories the utmost freedom in the formation of their local governments. When Mr. Buchanan attempted to uphold the Lecompton Constitution as being the free choice of the people of Kansas, Judge Douglas at once took issue with the administration on this question, and the Democratic party was split in twain. Up to the time of the vote of the people of the Territory on the constitution, Douglas had been an unswerving supporter of the administration policy in Kansas. His speech at Springfield, in the June previous, could not be misunderstood. He held all the proceedings which led to the Lecompton issue to be in strict accordance, not only with the letter, but the spirit, of the Kansas-Nebraska Act, and with the faith of the Democratic party as expounded by himself. But a few weeks later it became manifest that his opinions had undergone a change. Ominous rumors of a breach with the administration began to circulate among his friends. It was alleged at length that Mr. Douglas's delicate sense of justice had been shocked by the unfairness of certain elections in Kansas : it was even intimated that he, too, considered the Lecompton affair an " outrage " upon the sovereign people of Kansas, and that he would speedily join the Republicans — the special objects of his indignation in the June speech — in denouncing and defeating it. The Kansas-Nebraska Bill had borne its appropriate fruits, — the fruits all along predicted by

Mr. Lincoln, — and Mr. Douglas commended them to any-body's eating but his own. His desertion was sudden and astonishing; but there was method in it, and a reason for it. The next year Illinois was to choose a senator to fill the vacancy created by the expiration of his own term; and the choice lay between the author of the Kansas-Nebraska Bill and its most conspicuous opponent in that State. The news-papers were not yet done publishing Mr. Lincoln's speech, in which occurred the following paragraph : —

" Three years and a half ago Judge Douglas brought for-ward his famous Nebraska Bill. The country was at once in a blaze. He scorned all opposition, and carried it through Congress. Since then he has seen himself superseded in a Presidential nomination by one indorsing the general doc-trine of his measure, but at the same time standing clear of the odium of its untimely agitation and its gross breach of national faith; and he has seen the successful rival constitu-tionally elected, not by the strength of friends, but by the division of his adversaries, being in a popular minority of nearly four hundred thousand votes. He has seen his chief aids in his own State, Shields and Richardson, politically speaking, successively tried, convicted, and executed for an offence not their own, but his. And now he sees his own case standing next on the docket for trial."

CHAPTER XVI.

ALTHOUGH primarily responsible for all that had taken place in Kansas, Mr. Douglas appeared to be suddenly animated by a new and burning zeal in behalf of the Free-State party in the Territory. It struck him very forcibly, just when he needed most to be struck by a new idea, that the Lecompton Constitution was not "the act and deed of the people of Kansas."

Accordingly, Mr. Douglas took his stand against Lecompton at the first note of the long conflict in Congress. We shall make no analysis of the debates, nor set out the votes of senators and representatives which marked the intervals of that fierce struggle between sections, parties, and factions which followed. It is enough to say here, that Mr. Douglas was found speaking and voting with the Republicans upon every phase of the question. He had but one or two followers in the Senate, and a mere handful in the House; yet these were faithful to his lead until a final conference committee and the English Bill afforded an opportunity for some of them to escape. For himself he scorned all compromises, voted against the English Bill, and returned to Illinois to ask the votes of the people upon a winter's record wholly and consistently anti-Democratic. The fact is mentioned, not to obscure the fame of the statesman, nor to impugn the honesty of the politician, but because it had an important influence upon the canvass of the ensuing summer.

During the winter Mr. Douglas held frequent consultations with the leaders of the Republican party. Their meetings were secret, and for that reason the more significant. By this means, harmony of action was secured for the present, and something provided for the future. Mr. Douglas covertly announced himself as a convert to the Republicans, declared his uncompromising enmity to " the slave power," and said that, however he might be distrusted then, he would be seen " fighting their battles in 1860 ; " but for the time he thought it wise to conceal his ultimate intentions. He could manage the Democracy more effectually by remaining with them until better opportunities should occur. " He insisted that he would never be driven from the party, but would remain in it until he exposed the administration and the Disunionists ; and, when he went out, he would go of his own accord. He was in the habit of remarking, that it was policy for him to remain in the party, in order to hold certain of the rank-and-file; so that, if he went over from the Democracy to any other party, he would be able to take the crowd along with him ; and, when he got them all over, he would cut down the bridges, and sink the boats." When asked if he knew precisely where his present course was taking him, he answered repeatedly, " I do ; and I have checked all my baggage, and taken a through ticket."

He was a proselyte not to be despised : his weight might be sufficient to turn the scale in the Presidential election. The Republicans were naturally pleased with his protestations of friendship, and more than pleased with his proffers of active service ; but he was not content with this alone. He contrived to convince many of his late opponents that the Kansas-Nebraska Bill itself was actually conceived in the interests of antislavery, and that the device was the most cunning of political tricks, intended to give back to " freedom " all the vast expanse of territory which the Missouri line had dedicated forever to slavery. " Mr. Douglas's plan for destroying the Missouri line," said one Republican, " and thereby opening the way for the march of freedom beyond the limits forever prohibited by that line, and the opening up of Free States in territory which it was conceded belonged to the Slave States, and its march westward, embracing the whole line of the Pacific from the British possessions to Mexico, struck me as the most magnificent scheme ever conceived by the human mind. This character of conversation, so frequently employed by Mr. Douglas with those with whom he talked, made the deepest impression upon their minds, enlisted them in his behalf, and changed, in almost every instance, their opinion of the man." In support of this view, Mr. Douglas could point to Kansas, where the battle under his bill was being fought out. The Free-State men had, perhaps from the very beginning, been in a majority, and could take possession of the Territory or the new State, as the case might be, whenever they could secure a fair vote. The laboring classes of the North were the natural settlers of the western Territories. If these failed in numbers, the enormous and increasing European immigration was at their back ; and, if both together failed, the churches, aid societies, and anti-slavery organizations were at hand to raise, arm, and equip great bodies of emigrants, as they would regular forces for a public purpose. The South had no such facilities : its social, political, and material conditions made a sudden exodus of its voting population to new countries a thing impossible. It might send here a man with a few negroes, and there another. It might insist vehemently upon its supposed rights in the common Territories, and be ready to fight for them ; but it could never cover the surface of those Territories with cosey farmsteads, or crowd them with intelligent and muscular white men ; and yet these last would inevitably give political character to the rising communities. Such clearly were to be the results of " popular sovereignty," as Mr. Douglas had up to that time maintained it under the Nebraska Bill.

It signified the right of the people of a Territory " to form and regulate their domestic institutions in their own way " when, and not before, they came to frame a State constitution. The Missouri line, on the contrary, had been a sort of convention, which, by common consent, gave all north of it to freedom, and all south of it to slavery. But popular sovereignty disregarded all previous compacts, all ordinances, and all laws. With this doctrine in practice, the North were sure to be victors in every serious contest. But when Mr. Douglas changed ground again, and popular sovereignty became squatter sovereignty, he had reason to boast himself the most efficient, although the wiliest and coolest, antislavery agitator on the continent. The new doctrine implied the right of a handful of settlers to determine the slavery question in their first Legislature. It made no difference whether they did this by direct or " unfriendly legislation : " the result was the same.

"Popular sovereignty! popular sovereignty!" said Mr. Lincoln. " Let us for a moment inquire into this vast matter of popular sovereignty. What is popular sovereignty? We recollect, that, in an early period in the history of this struggle, there was another name for the same thing, — *squatter sovereignty*. It was not exactly popular sovereignty, —squatter sovereignty. What do these terms mean? What do those terms mean when used now? And vast credit is taken by our friend, the Judge, in regard to his support of it, when he declares the last years of his life have been, and all the future years of his life shall be, devoted to this matter of popular sovereignty. What is it? Why, it is the sovereignty of the people! What was squatter sovereignty? I suppose, if it had any significance at all, it was the right of the people to govern themselves, to be sovereign in their own affairs while they were squatted down in a country not their own, while they had squatted on a territory that did not belong to them ; in the sense that a State belongs to the people who inhabit it, when it belongs to the nation. Such right to govern themselves was called 'squatter sovereignty.' "

Again, and on another occasion, but still before Mr. Douglas had substituted " squatter " for " popular " sovereignty, — a feat which was not performed until September, 1859, — Mr. Lincoln said, —

" I suppose almost every one knows, that in this controversy, whatever has been said has had reference to negro slavery. We have not been in a controversy about the right of the people to govern themselves in the ordinary matters of domestic concern in the States and Territories. Mr. Buchanan, in one of his late messages (I think when he sent up the Lecompton Constitution), urged that the main point to which the public attention had been directed was not in regard to the great variety of small domestic matters, but it was directed to negro slavery; and he asserts, that, if the people had had a fair chance to vote on that question, there was no reasonable ground of objection in regard to minor questions. Now, while I think that the people had *not* had given them, or offered them, a fair chance upon that slavery question, still, if there had been a fair submission to a vote upon that main question, the President's proposition would have been true to the uttermost. Hence, when hereafter I speak of popular sovereignty, I wish to be understood as applying what I say to the question of slavery only, not to other minor domestic matters of a Territory or a State.

"Does Judge Douglas, when he says that several of the past years of his life have been devoted to the question of popular sovereignty, and that all the remainder of his life shall be devoted to it, — does he mean to say, that he has been devoting his life to securing to the people of the Territories the right to exclude slavery from the Territories? If he means so to say, he means to deceive; because he and every one knows that the decision of the Supreme Court, which he approves, and makes an especial ground of attack upon me for disapproving, forbids the people of a Territory to exclude slavery. This covers the whole ground, from the settlement of a Territory till it reaches the degree of maturity entitling it to form a State constitution. So far as all that ground is concerned, the judge is not sustaining popular sovereignty, but absolutely opposing it. He sustains the decision which declares that the popular will of the Territories has no constitutional power to exclude slavery during their territorial existence. This being so, the period of time from the first settlement of a territory till it reaches the point of forming a State constitution is not the thing that the Judge has fought for, or is fighting for; but, on the contrary, he has fought for, and is fighting for, the thing that annihilates and crushes out that same popular sovereignty."

It is probable, that, in the numerous private conferences held by Mr. Douglas with Republican leaders in the winter of 1857–8, he managed to convince them that it was, after all, not popular sovereignty, but squatter sovereignty, that he meant to advance as his final and inevitable deduction from " the great principles " of the Nebraska Bill. This he knew, and they were sure, would give antislavery an unbroken round of solid victories in all the Territories. The South feared it much more than they did the Republican theory: it was, in the language of their first orator, " a shortcut to all the ends of Sewardism."

But Mr. Douglas's great difficulty was to produce any belief in his sincerity. At home, in Illinois, the Republicans distrusted him almost to a man; and at Washington, among his peers in the Senate and the House, it seemed necessary for him to repeat his plans and promises very often, and to mingle with them bitter and passionate declamations against the South. At last, however, he succeeded, — partially, at least. Senator Wilson believed him devoutly; Mr. Burlingame said his record was " laid up in light; " Mr. Colfax, Mr. Blair, and Mr. Covode were convinced; and gentlemen of the press began industriously to prepare the way for his entrance into the Republican party. Mr. Greeley was thoroughly possessed by the new idea, and went about propagating and enforcing it with all his might. Among all the grave counsellors employed in furthering Mr. Douglas's defection, it is singular that only one man of·note steadily resisted his admission to a place of leadership in the Republican ranks: Judge Trumbull could not be persuaded; he had no faith in the man who proposed to desert, and had some admonitions to deliver, based upon the history of recent events. He was willing enough to take him " on probation," but wholly opposed to

giving him any power. Covode was employed to mollify
Judge Trumbull; but he met with no success, and went away
without so much as delivering the message with which Mr.
Douglas had charged him. The message was a simple proposition of alliance with the home Republicans, to the effect,
that, if they agreed to return him to the Senate in 1858, he
would fight their Presidential battle in 1860. Judge Trumbull did not even hear it, but he was well assured that Mr.
Douglas was "an applicant for admission into the Republican
party." "It was reported to me at that time," said he, "that
such was the fact; and such appeared to be the universal
understanding among the Republicans at Washington. I will
state another fact, — I almost quarrelled with some of my
best Republican friends in regard to this matter. I was willing to receive Judge Douglas into the Republican party on
probation; but I was not, as these Republican friends were,
willing to receive him, and place him at the head of our
ranks."

Toward the latter part of April, 1858, a Democratic State
Convention met in Illinois, and, besides nominating a ticket for
State officers, indorsed Mr. Douglas. This placed him in the
field for re-election as an Anti-Lecompton Democrat; but it
by no means shook the faith of his recently acquired Republican friends: they thought it very natural, under the circumstances, that his ways should be a little devious, and his policy
somewhat dark. He had always said he could do more
for them by seeming to remain within the Democratic party;
and they looked upon this latest proceeding — his practical
nomination by a Democratic convention — as the foundation
for an act of stupendous treason between that time and the
Presidential election. They continued to press the Republicans of Illinois to make no nomination against him, — to vote
for him, to trust him, to follow him, as a sincere and manifestly a powerful antislavery leader. These representations
had the effect of seducing away, for a brief time, Mr. Washburne and a few others among the lesser politicians of the
State; but, when they found the party at large irrevocably

opposed to the scheme, they reluctantly acquiesced in what they could not prevent, — Mr. Lincoln's nomination. But the plot made a profound impression on Mr. Lincoln's mind : it proved the existence of personal qualities in Mr. Douglas, which, to a simpler man, were unimaginable and inexplicable. A gentleman once inquired of Mr. Lincoln what he thought of Douglas's chances at Charleston. " Well," he replied, " were it not for certain matters that I know transpired, which I regarded at one time among the impossibilities, I would say he stood no possible chance. I refer to the fact, that, in the Illinois contest with myself, he had the sympathy and support of Greeley, of Burlingame, and of Wilson of Massachusetts, and other leading Republicans ; that, at the same time, he received the support of Wise, and the influence of Breckinridge, and other Southern men ; that he took direct issue with the administration, and secured, against all its power, one hundred and twenty-five thousand out of one hundred and thirty thousand Democratic votes cast in the State. A man that can bring such influence to bear with his own exertions may play the devil at Charleston."

From about the 7th to the 16th of June, 1858, Mr. Lincoln was busily engaged writing a speech : he wrote it in scraps, — a sentence now, and another again. It was originally scattered over numberless little pieces of paper, and was only reduced to consecutive sheets and connected form as the hour for its delivery drew near. It was to be spoken on or about the 16th, when the Republican State Convention would assemble at Springfield, and, as Mr. Lincoln anticipated, would nominate him for senator in Congress.

About the 13th of June, Mr. Dubois, the State auditor, entered the office of Lincoln & Herndon, and found Mr. Lincoln deeply intent upon the speech. " Hello, Lincoln ! what *are* you writing ? " said the auditor. " Come, tell me." — " I sha'n't tell you," said Lincoln. " *It is none of your business,* Mr. Auditor. Come, sit down, and let's be jolly."

On the 16th, the convention, numbering, with delegates and alternates, about a thousand men, met, and passed unanimously the following resolution : —

" That Hon. Abraham Lincoln is our first and only choice
for United States senator to fill the vacancy about to be created by the expiration of Mr. Douglas's term of office."

That evening Mr. Lincoln came early to his office, along
with Mr. Herndon. Having carefully locked the door, and
put the key in his own pocket, he pulled from his bosom the
manuscript of his speech, and proceeded to read it slowly
and distinctly. When he had finished the first paragraph, he
came to a dead pause, and turned to his astounded auditor
with the inquiry, " How do you like that? What do you
think of it? " — " I think," returned Mr. Herndon, " it is true ;
but is it entirely *politic* to read or speak it as it is written ? "
— " That makes no difference," Mr. Lincoln said. " That
expression is a truth of all human experience, — ' a house
divided against itself cannot stand ; ' and ' he that runs may
read.' The proposition is indisputably true, and has been
true for more than six thousand years ; and — I *will* deliver it
as written. I want to use some universally known figure,
expressed in simple language as universally known, that may
strike home to the minds of men, in order to rouse them to
the peril of the times. I would rather be *defeated with this
expression in* the speech, and it held up and discussed before
the people, than *to be victorious without it*."

It may be questioned whether Mr. Lincoln had a clear
right to indulge in such a venture, as a representative party
man in a close contest. He had other interests than his own
in charge : he was bound to respect the opinions, and, if possible, secure the success, of the party which had made him
its leader. He knew that the strange doctrine, so strikingly
enunciated, would alienate many well-affected voters. Was
it his duty to cast these away, or to keep them ? He was not
asked to sacrifice any principle of the party, or any opinion
of his own previously expressed, but merely to forego the
trial of an experiment, to withhold the announcement of a
startling theory, and to leave the creed of the party as it came
from the hands of its makers, without this individual supple-
ment, of which they had never dreamed. It is evident that

he had not always been insensible to the force of this reasoning. At the Bloomington Convention he had uttered the
same ideas in almost the same words ; and their novelty,
their tendency, their recognition of a state of incipient civil
war in a country for the most part profoundly peaceful, —
these, and the bloody work which might come of their acceptance by a great party, had filled the minds of some of his
hearers with the most painful apprehensions. The theory
was equally shocking to them, whether as partisans or as
patriots. Among them was Hon. T. Lyle Dickey, who
sought Mr. Lincoln, and begged him to suppress them in
future. He vindicated his speech as he has just vindicated
it in the interview with Mr. Herndon ; but, after much persuasion, he promised at length not to repeat it.

It was now Mr. Herndon's turn to be surprised : the pupil
had outstripped the teacher. He was intensely anxious for Mr.
Lincoln's election : he feared the effect of this speech ; and
yet it was so exactly in accordance with his own faith, that
he could not advise him to suppress it. It might be heresy
to many others, but it was orthodoxy to him ; and he was in
the habit of telling the whole truth, without regard to consequences. If it cost a single defeat now, he was sure that its
potency would one day be felt, and the wisdom of its present
utterance acknowledged. He therefore urged Mr. Lincoln to
speak it as he had written it, and to treat with the scorn of
a prophet those who, having ears, would not hear, and, having
eyes, would not see. The advice was not unacceptable, but
Mr. Lincoln thought he owed it to other friends to counsel
with them also.

About a dozen gentlemen were called to meet in the Library Room in the State House. " After seating them at the
round table," says John Armstrong, one of the number, " he
read that clause or section of his speech which reads, ' a
house divided against itself cannot stand,' &c. He read it
slowly and cautiously, so as to let each man fully understand
it. After he had finished the reading, he asked the opinions
of his friends as to the wisdom or policy of it. Every man

among them condemned the speech in substance and spirit, and especially that section quoted above. They unanimously declared that the whole speech was too far in advance of the times; and they all condemned that section or part of his speech already quoted, as unwise and impolitic, if not false. William H. Herndon sat still while they were giving their respective opinions of its unwisdom and impolicy: then he sprang to his feet and said, 'Lincoln, deliver it just as it reads. If it is in advance of the times, let us — you and I, if no one else — lift the people to the level of this speech now, higher hereafter. The speech is true, wise, and politic, and will succeed now or in the future. Nay, it will aid you, if it will not make you President of the United States.'

" Mr. Lincoln sat still a short moment, rose from his chair, walked backwards and forwards in the hall, stopped and said, ' Friends, I have thought about this matter a great deal, have weighed the question well from all corners, and am thoroughly convinced the time has come when it should be uttered; and if it must be that I must go down because of this speech, then let me go down linked to truth, — die in the advocacy of what is right and just. This nation cannot live on injustice, — " a house divided against itself cannot stand," I say again and again.' This was spoken with some degree of emotion, — the effects of his love of truth, and sorrow from the disagreement of his friends with himself."

On the evening of the 17th this celebrated speech — known since as " The House-divided-against-itself Speech " — was delivered to an immense audience in the hall of the House of Representatives. Mr. Lincoln never penned words which had a more prodigious influence upon the public mind, or which more directly and powerfully affected his own career. It was as follows : —

GENTLEMEN OF THE CONVENTION, — If we could first know where we are, and whither we are tending, we could then better judge what to do, and how to do it. We are now far on into the fifth year since a policy was initiated with the avowed object and confident promise of putting an end to slavery agitation. Under the operation of that policy, that agitation had not only not ceased, but has constantly augmented. In my opinion, it will not cease until a crisis shall have been reached and passed. "A house divided against itself cannot stand." I believe this Government cannot endure permanently half slave and half free. I do not expect the Union to be dissolved, — I do not expect the house to fall; but I do expect it will cease to be divided. It will become all one thing, or all the other. Either the opponents of slavery will arrest the farther spread of it, and place it where the public mind shall rest in the belief that it is in course of ultimate extinction, or its advocates will push it forward till it shall become alike lawful in all the States, — old as well as new, North as well as South.

Have we no tendency to the latter condition? Let any one who doubts carefully contemplate that now almost complete legal combination, — piece of machinery, so to speak, — compounded of the Nebraska doctrine and the Dred-Scott Decision. Let him consider, not only what work the machinery is adapted to do, and how well adapted, but also let him study the history of its construction, and trace, if he can, or rather fail, if he can, to trace, the evidences of design and concert of action among its chief master-workers from the beginning.

But so far Congress only had acted; and an indorsement by the people, real or apparent, was indispensable, to save the point already gained and give chance for more. The New Year of 1854 found slavery excluded from more than half the States by State constitutions, and from most of the national territory by congressional prohibition. Four days later commenced the struggle which ended in repealing that congressional prohibition. This opened all the national territory to slavery, and was the first point gained.

This necessity had not been overlooked, but had been provided for, as well as might be, in the notable argument of "*squatter sovereignty*," otherwise called "*sacred right of self-government;*" which latter phrase, though expressive of the only rightful basis of any government, was so perverted in this attempted use of it as to amount to just this: that, if any one man choose to enslave another, no third man shall be allowed to object. That argument was incorporated into the Nebraska Bill itself, in the language which follows: "It being the true intent and meaning of this act not to legislate slavery into any Territory or State, nor exclude it therefrom, but to leave the people thereof perfectly free to form and regulate their domestic institutions in their own way, subject only to the Constitution of the United States."

Then opened the roar of loose declamation in favor of "squatter sovereignty" and "sacred right of self-government."

"But," said opposition members, "let us be more specific, — let us *amend* the bill so as to expressly declare that the people of the Territory *may* exclude slavery." — "Not we," said the friends of the measure; and down they voted the amendment.

While the Nebraska Bill was passing through Congress, a law-case involving the question of a negro's freedom, by reason of his owner having voluntarily taken him first into a Free State, and then a Territory covered by the congressional prohibition, and held him as a slave, — for a long time in each, — was passing through the United-States Circuit Court for the District of Missouri; and both the Nebraska Bill and lawsuit were brought to a decision in the same month of May, 1854. The negro's name was Dred Scott, which name now designates the decision finally made in the case.

Before the then next Presidential election, the law-case came to, and was argued in, the Supreme Court of the United States; but the decision of it was deferred until *after* the election. Still, *before* the election, Senator Trumbull, on the floor of the Senate, requests the leading advocate of the Nebraska Bill to state *his opinion* whether a people of a Territory can constitutionally exclude slavery from their limits; and the latter answers, "That is a question for the Supreme Court."

The election came. Mr. Buchanan was elected, and the *indorsement*, such as it was, secured. That was the *second* point gained. The indorsement, however, fell short of a clear popular majority by nearly four hundred thousand votes; and so, perhaps, was not overwhelmingly reliable and satisfactory. The outgoing President, in his last annual Message, as impressively as possible echoed back upon the people the weight and authority of the indorsement.

The Supreme Court met again; did not announce their decision, but ordered a re-argument. The Presidential inauguration came, and still no decision of the court; but the incoming President, in his inaugural address, fervently exhorted the people to abide by the forthcoming decision, *whatever it might be.* Then, in a few days, came the decision.

This was the third point gained.

The reputed author of the Nebraska Bill finds an early occasion to make a speech at this Capitol indorsing the Dred-Scott Decision, and vehemently denouncing all opposition to it. The new President, too, seizes the early occasion of the Silliman letter to indorse and strongly construe that decision, and to express his astonishment that any different view had ever been entertained. At length a squabble springs up between the President and the author of the Nebraska Bill, on the mere question of fact whether the Lecompton Constitution was, or was not, in any just sense, made by the people of Kansas; and, in that squabble, the latter declares that all he wants is a fair vote for the people, and that he cares not whether slavery be voted down or voted up. I do not understand his declaration, that he cares not whether slavery be voted down or voted up, to be intended by him other than as an apt definition of the policy he would impress upon the public mind, — the principle for which he declares he has suffered much, and is ready to suffer to the end.

And well may he cling to that principle! If he has any parental feel-

26

ing, well may he cling to it! That principle is the only shred left of his original Nebraska doctrine. Under the Dred-Scott Decision, squatter sovereignty squatted out of existence, — tumbled down like temporary scaffolding; like the mould at the foundery, served through one blast, and fell back into loose sand; helped to carry an election, and then was kicked to the winds. His late joint struggle with the Republicans against the Lecompton Constitution involves nothing of the original Nebraska doctrine. That struggle was made on a point — the right of a people to make their own constitution — upon which he and the Republicans have never differed.

The several points of the Dred-Scott Decision, in connection with Senator Douglas's "care-not" policy, constitute the piece of machinery in its present state of advancement. The working-points of that machinery are, —

First, That no negro slave, imported as such from Africa, and no descendant of such, can ever be a citizen of any State, in the sense of that term as used in the Constitution of the United States.

This point is made in order to deprive the negro, in every possible event, of the benefit of this provision of the United States Constitution, which declares that "The citizens of each State shall be entitled to all the privileges and immunities of citizens in the several States."

Secondly, That, "subject to the Constitution of the United States," neither Congress nor a Territorial Legislature can exclude slavery from any United States Territory.

This point is made in order that individual men may fill up the Territories with slaves, without danger of losing them as property, and thus to enhance the chances of permanency to the institution through all the future.

Thirdly, That whether the holding a negro in actual slavery in a Free State makes him free, as against the holder, the United States courts will not decide, but will leave it to be decided by the courts of any Slave State the negro may be forced into by the master.

This point is made, not to be pressed immediately; but if acquiesced in for a while, and apparently indorsed by the people at an election, then to sustain the logical conclusion, that, what Dred Scott's master might lawfully do with Dred Scott in the free State of Illinois, every other master may lawfully do with any other one or one thousand slaves in Illinois, or in any other Free State.

Auxiliary to all this, and working hand in hand with it, the Nebraska doctrine, or what is left of it, is to educate and mould public opinion, at least Northern public opinion, not to care whether slavery is voted down or voted up.

This shows exactly where we now are, and partially, also, whither we are tending.

It will throw additional light on the latter to go back and run the mind over the string of historical facts already stated. Several things will now appear less dark and mysterious than they did when they were transpiring.

The people were to be left "perfectly free," "subject only to the Constitution." What the Constitution had to do with it, outsiders could not then see. Plainly enough now, it was an exactly fitted niche for the Dred-Scott Decision afterward to come in, and declare that perfect freedom of the people to be just no freedom at all.

Why was the amendment expressly declaring the right of the people to exclude slavery voted down? Plainly enough now: the adoption of it would have spoiled the niche for the Dred-Scott Decision.

Why was the court decision held up? Why even a senator's individual opinion withheld till after the Presidential election? Plainly enough now: the speaking out then would have damaged the "*perfectly free*" argument upon which the election was to be carried.

Why the outgoing President's felicitation on the indorsement? Why the delay of a re-argument? Why the incoming President's advance exhortation in favor of the decision? These things look like the cautious patting and petting of a spirited horse preparatory to mounting him, when it is dreaded that he may give the rider a fall. And why the hasty after-indorsements of the decision by the President and others?

We cannot absolutely know that all these exact adaptations are the result of preconcert. But when we see a lot of framed timbers, different portions of which we know have been gotten out at different times and places, and by different workmen, — Stephen, Franklin, Roger, and James, for instance, — and when we see these timbers joined together, and see they exactly make the frame of a house or a mill, all the tenons and mortises, exactly fitting, and all the lengths and proportions of the different pieces exactly adapted to their respective places, and not a piece too many or too few, — not omitting even scaffolding — or, if a single piece be lacking, we can see the place in the frame exactly fitted and prepared to yet bring such piece in, — in such a case, we find it impossible not to believe that Stephen and Franklin and Roger and James all understood one another from the beginning, and all worked upon a common plan or draft drawn up before the first blow was struck.

It should not be overlooked, that, by the Nebraska Bill, the people of a State as well as Territory were to be left "*perfectly free*," "*subject only to the Constitution*." Why mention a State? They were legislating for Territories, and not for or about States. Certainly the people of a State are and ought to be subject to the Constitution of the United States; but why is mention of this lugged into this merely territorial law? Why are the people of a Territory and the people of a State therein lumped together, and their relation to the Constitution therein treated as being precisely the same?

While the opinion of the court by Chief-Justice Taney, in the Dred-Scott case, and the separate opinions of all the concurring judges, expressly declare that the Constitution of the United States neither permits Congress nor a Territorial Legislature to exclude slavery from any United States

Territory, they all omit to declare whether or not the same Constitution permits a State, or the people of a State, to exclude it. *Possibly*, this was a
mere *omission;* but who can be quite sure, if McLean or Curtis had sought
to get into the opinion a declaration of unlimited power in the people of a
State to exclude slavery from their limits, just as Chase and Mace sought to
get such declaration, in behalf of the people of a Territory, into the Nebraska Bill, — I ask, who can be quite sure that it would not have been voted
down in the one case as it had been in the other?

The nearest approach to the point of declaring the power of a State
over slavery is made by Judge Nelson. He approaches it more than
once, using the precise idea, and almost the language too, of the Nebraska Act. On one occasion his exact language is, " Except in cases
where the power is restrained by the Constitution of the United States,
the law of the State is supreme over the subject of slavery within its jurisdiction."

In what cases the power of the State is so restrained by the United
States Constitution is left an open question, precisely as the same question,
as to the restraint on the power of the Territories, was left open in the
Nebraska Act. Put that and that together, and we have another nice little
niche, which we may ere long see filled with another Supreme Court decision, declaring that the Constitution of the United States does not permit a
State to exclude slavery from its limits. And this may especially be
expected if the doctrine of "care not whether slavery be voted down or
voted up" shall gain upon the public mind sufficiently to give promise that
such a decision can be maintained when made.

Such a decision is all that slavery now lacks of being alike lawful in all
the States. Welcome or unwelcome, such decision is probably coming, and
will soon be upon us, unless the power of the present political dynasty shall
be met and overthrown. We shall lie down pleasantly dreaming that the
people of Missouri are on the verge of making their State free; and we shall
awake to the reality, instead, that the Supreme Court has made Illinois a
Slave State.

To meet and overthrow the power of that dynasty is the work now
before all those who would prevent that consummation. That is what we
have to do. But how can we best do it?

There are those who denounce us openly to their own friends, and yet
whisper softly, that Senator Douglas is the *aptest* instrument there is with
which to effect that object. They do not tell us, nor has he told us, that he
wishes any such object to be effected. They wish us to infer all, from the
facts that he now has a little quarrel with the present head of the dynasty;
and that he has regularly voted with us, on a single point, upon which he
and we have never differed.

They remind us that *he* is a very *great man*, and that the largest of us
are very small ones. Let this be granted. But " a *living dog* is better than

a *dead lion.*" Judge Douglas, if not a *dead* lion for this work, is at least a *caged* and *toothless* one. How can he oppose the advances of slavery? He don't care any thing about it. His avowed mission is impressing the " public heart " to care nothing about it.

A leading Douglas Democrat newspaper thinks Douglas's superior talent will be needed to resist the revival of the African slave-trade. Does Douglas believe an effort to revive that trade is approaching? He has not said so. Does he *really* think so? But, if it is, how can he resist it? For years he has labored to prove it a *sacred right* of white men to take negro slaves into the new Territories. Can he possibly show that it is less a sacred right to buy them where they can be bought cheapest? And unquestionably they can be bought cheaper in Africa than in Virginia.

He has done all in his power to reduce the whole question of slavery to one of a mere right of property; and as such, how can he oppose the foreign slave-trade, — how can he refuse that trade in that " property " shall be " perfectly free," — unless he does it as a *protection* to the home production? And, as the home *producers* will probably not ask the protection, he will be wholly without a ground of opposition.

Senator Douglas holds, we know, that a man may rightfully be wiser to-day than he was yesterday; that he may rightfully change when he finds himself wrong. But can we for that reason run ahead, and infer that he will make any particular change, of which he himself has given no intimation? Can we safely base our action upon any such vague inferences?

Now, as ever, I wish not to misrepresent Judge Douglas's position, question his motives, or do aught that can be personally offensive to him. Whenever, *if ever*, he and we can come together on *principle*, so that our great cause may have assistance from his great ability, I hope to have interposed no adventitious obstacle.

But clearly he is not now with us; he does not pretend to be; he does not promise ever to be. Our cause, then, must be intrusted to, and conducted by, its own undoubted friends, — those whose hands are free, whose hearts are in the work, who do care for the result.

Two years ago the Republicans of the nation mustered over thirteen hundred thousand strong. We did this under the single impulse of resistance to a common danger, with every external circumstance against us. Of strange, discordant, and even hostile elements, we gathered from the four winds, and formed and fought the battle through, under the constant hot fire of a disciplined, proud, and pampered enemy. Did we brave all then to falter now? — *now*, when that same enemy is wavering, dissevered, and belligerent?

The result is not doubtful. We shall not fail, — if we stand firm, we shall not fail. *Wise counsels* may *accelerate* or *mistakes delay* it; but, sooner or later, the victory is *sure* to come.

The speech produced a profound impression upon men of all parties: the Democrats rejoiced in it, and reprobated it; the conservative Republicans received it coldly, and saw in it the sign of certain defeat. In the eyes of the latter it was a disheartening mistake at the outset of a momentous campaign, —a fatal error, which no policy or exertion could retrieve. Alone of all those directly affected by it, the Abolitionists, the compatriots of Mr. Herndon, heard in it the voice of a fearless leader, who had the wisdom to comprehend an unwelcome fact, and the courage to proclaim it at the moment when the delusion of fancied security and peace was most generally and fondly entertained. It was the "irrepressible conflict" which Mr. Seward had been preaching, and to which the one party had given almost as little credit as the other. Except a few ultraists here and there, nobody as yet had actually prepared his armor for this imaginary conflict, to which the nation was so persistently summoned, — and, indeed, none but those few seriously believed in the possibility of its existence. The Republican party had heretofore disavowed the doctrine with a unanimity nearly as great as that exhibited by the little council of Mr. Lincoln's immediate friends. It was therefore to be expected, that, when a slow, cautious, moderate man like Mr. Lincoln came forward with it in this startling fashion, it would carry dismay to his followers, and a cheering assurance to his enemies. But Mr. Lincoln was looking farther than this campaign: he was quietly dreaming of the Presidency, and edging himself to a place in advance, where he thought the tide might take him up in 1860. He was sure that sectional animosities, far from subsiding, would grow deeper and stronger with time; and for that reason the next nominee of the exclusively Northern party must be a man of radical views. "I think," says Mr. Herndon, "the speech was intended to take the wind out of Seward's sails;" and Mr. Herndon is not alone in his opinion.

A day or two after Mr. Lincoln spoke, one Dr. Long came into his office, and delivered to him a foretaste of the remarks he was doomed to hear for several months. " Well, Lincoln," said he, " that foolish speech of yours will kill you, — will defeat you in this contest, and probably for all offices for all ·time to come. I am sorry, sorry, — very sorry : I wish it was wiped out of existence. Don't you wish it, now ? " Mr. Lincoln had been writing during the doctor's lament ; but at the end of it he laid down his pen, raised his head, lifted his spectacles, and, with a look half quizzical, half contemptuous, replied, " Well, doctor, if I had to draw a pen across, and erase my whole life from existence, and I had one poor gift or choice left, as to what I should save from the wreck, I should choose that speech, and leave it to the world unerased."

Leonard Swett, than whom there was no more gifted man, nor a better judge of political affairs, in Illinois, is convinced that " the first ten lines of that speech defeated him." " The sentiment of the ' house divided against itself ' seemed wholly inappropriate," says Mr. Swett. " It was a speech made at the commencement of a campaign, and apparently made for the campaign. Viewing it in this light alone, nothing could have been more unfortunate or inappropriate. It was saying first the wrong thing ; yet he saw that it was an abstract truth, and standing by the speech would ultimately find him in the right place. I was inclined at the time to believe these words were hastily and inconsiderately uttered ; but subsequent facts have convinced me they were deliberate and had been matured . . . In the summer of 1859, when he was dining with a party of his intimate friends at Bloomington, the subject of his Springfield speech was discussed. We all insisted that it was a great mistake ; but he justified himself, and finally said, ' Well, gentlemen, you may think that speech was a mistake ; but I never have believed it was, and you will see the day when you will consider it was the wisest thing I ever said.' "

John T. Stuart was a family connection of the Todds and Edwardses, and thus also of Lincoln. Mr. C. C. Brown married Mr. Stuart's daughter, and speaks of Mr. Lincoln as " our relative." This gentleman says, " The Todd-Stuart-Edwards family, with preacher and priest, dogs and servants, got mad at Mr. Lincoln because he made ' The House-divided-against-itself Speech.' He flinched, dodged, said he would explain, and did explain, in the Douglas debates."

But it was difficult to explain : explanations of the kind are generally more hurtful than the original offence. Accordingly, Mr. Herndon reports in his broad, blunt way, that " Mr. Lincoln met with many cold shoulders for some time, — nay, during the whole canvass with Douglas." At the great public meetings which characterized that campaign, " you could hear, from all quarters in the crowd, Republicans saying, ' Damn that fool speech ! it will be the cause of the death of Lincoln and the Republican party. Such folly ! such nonsense ! Damn it ! ' "

Since 1840 Lincoln and Douglas had appeared before the people, almost as regularly as the elections came round, to discuss, the one against the other, the merits of parties, candidates, and principles. Thus far Mr. Lincoln had been in a certain sense the pursuer : he had lain in wait for Mr. Douglas ; he had caught him at unexpected turns and upon sharp points ; he had mercilessly improved the advantage of Mr. Douglas's long record in Congress to pick apart and to criticise, while his own was so much more humble and less extensive. But now at last they were abreast, candidates for the same office, with a fair field and equal opportunities. It was the great crisis in the lives of both. Let us see what they thought of each other ; and, in the extracts which convey the information, we may also get a better idea of the character of each for candor, generosity, and truthfulness.

Dr. Holland quotes from one of Mr. Lincoln's unpublished manuscripts as follows : —

" Twenty-two years ago, Judge Douglas and I first became acquainted : we were both young then, — he a trifle younger than I. Even then we were both ambitious, — I, perhaps, quite as much so as he. With me the race of ambition has been a failure, — a flat failure ; with him it has been one of splendid success. His name fills the nation, and is not unknown even in foreign lands. I affect no contempt for the high eminence he has reached, — so reached that the oppressed of my species might have shared with me in the elevation, I would rather stand on that eminence than wear the richest crown that ever pressed a monarch's brow."

Again, in the pending campaign, Mr. Lincoln said, "There is still another disadvantage under which we labor, and to which I will invite your attention. It arises out of the relative positions of the two persons who stand before the State as candidates for the Senate. Senator Douglas is of world-wide renown. All the anxious politicians of his party, or who had been of his party for years past, have been looking upon him as certainly, at no distant day, to be the President of the United States. They have seen, in his round, jolly, fruitful face, post-offices, land-offices, marshalships, and cabinet appointments, chargéships and foreign missions, bursting and sprouting out in wonderful exuberance, ready to be laid hold of by their greedy hands. And as they have been gazing upon this attractive picture so long, they cannot, in the little distraction that has taken place in the party, bring themselves to give up the charming hope; but, with greedier anxiety, they rush about him, sustain him, and give him marches, triumphal entries, and receptions, beyond what, even in the days of his highest prosperity, they could have brought about in his favor. On the contrary, nobody has ever expected me to be President. In *my* poor, lean, lank face, nobody has ever seen that any cabbages were sprouting out. These are disadvantages, all taken together, that the Republicans labor under. *We* have to fight this battle upon principle, and principle alone."

Now hear Mr. Douglas. In their first joint debate at Ottawa, he said, "In the remarks I have made on this platform, and the position of Mr. Lincoln upon it, I mean nothing personally disrespectful or unkind to that gentleman. I have known him for nearly twenty-five years. There were many points of sympathy between us when we first got acquainted. We were both comparatively boys, and both struggling with poverty in a strange land. I was a school-teacher in the town of Winchester, and he a flourishing gro-cery-keeper in the town of Salem. He was more successful in his occupation than I was in mine, and hence more fortu-nate in this world's goods. Lincoln is one of those peculiar men who perform with admirable skill every thing which they undertake. I made as good a school-teacher as I could; and, when a cabinet-maker, I made a good bedstead and tables, although my old boss said I succeeded better with bureaus and secretaries than with any thing else; but I believe that Lincoln was always more successful in business than I, for his business enabled him to get into the Legislature. I met him there, however, and had a sympathy with him, because of the up-hill struggle we both had in life. He was then just as good at telling an anecdote as now. He could beat any of the boys wrestling, or running a foot-race, in pitching quoits, or tossing a copper; could ruin more liquor than all of the boys of the town together; and the dignity and impartiality with which he presided at a horse-race or fist-fight excited the admiration and won the praise of everybody that was present and participated. I sympathized with him because he was struggling with difficulties; and so was I. Mr. Lincoln served with me in the Legislature in 1836, when we both retired, and he subsided, or became submerged; and he was lost sight of as a public man for some years. In 1846, when Wilmot introduced his celebrated proviso, and the abolition tornado swept over the country, Lincoln again turned up as a mem-ber of Congress from the Sangamon district. I was then in the Senate of the United States, and was glad to welcome my old friend and companion. Whilst in Congress, he dis-tinguished himself by his opposition to the Mexican War, taking the side of the common enemy against his own coun-try; and, when he returned home, he found that the indig-nation of the people followed him everywhere, and he was again submerged, or obliged to retire into private life, for-gotten by his former friends. He came up again in 1854, just in time to make this abolition or Black Republican platform, in company with Giddings, Lovejoy, Chase, and Fred. Douglas, for the Republican party to stand upon. Trumbull, too, was one of our own contemporaries."

Previous pages of this book present fully enough for our present purpose the issues upon which this canvass was made to turn. The principal speeches, the joint debates, with five separate and independent speeches by Mr. Lincoln, and three by Mr. Douglas, have been collected and published under Mr. Lincoln's supervision in a neat and accessible volume. It is, therefore, unnecessary, and would be unjust, to reprint them here. They obtained at the time a more extensive circulation than such productions usually have, and exerted an influence which is very surprising to the calm reader of the present day.

Mr. Douglas endeavored to prove, from Mr. Lincoln's Springfield speech, that he (Mr. Lincoln) was a self-declared Disunionist, in favor of reducing the institutions of all the States "to a dead uniformity," in favor of abolishing slavery everywhere, — an old-time abolitionist, a negropolist, an amalgamationist. This, with much vaunting of himself for his opposition to Lecompton, and a loud proclamation of "popular sovereignty," made the bulk of Mr. Douglas's speeches.

Mr. Lincoln denied these accusations ; he had no "thought of bringing about civil war," nor yet uniformity of institutions : he would not interfere with slavery where it had a lawful existence, and was not in favor of negro equality or miscegenation. He did, however, believe that Congress had the right to exclude slavery from the Territories, and ought to exercise it. As to Mr. Douglas's doctrine of popular sovereignty, there could be no issue concerning it; for everybody agreed that the people of a Territory might, when they formed a State constitution, adopt or exclude slavery as they pleased. But that a Territorial Legislature possessed exclusive power, or any power at all, over the subject, even Mr Douglas could not assert, inasmuch as the Dred-Scott Decision was plain and explicit the other way; and Mr. Douglas boasted that decision as the rule of his political conduct, and sought to impose it upon all parties as a perfect definition of the rights and duties of government, local and general.

At Ottawa, Mr. Douglas put to Mr. Lincoln a series of questions, which, upon their next meeting (at Freeport), Mr. Lincoln answered as follows: —

I have supposed myself, since the organization of the Republican party at Bloomington, in May, 1856, bound as a party man by the platforms of the party, then and since. If, in any interrogatories which I shall answer, I go beyond the scope of what is within these platforms, it will be perceived that no one is responsible but myself.

Having said thus much, I will take up the judge's interrogatories as I find them printed in "The Chicago Times," and answer them *seriatim.* In order that there may be no mistake about it, I have copied the interrogatories in writing, and also my answers to them. The first one of these interrogatories is in these words: —

Question 1. — " I desire to know whether Lincoln to-day stands, as he did in 1854, in favor of the unconditional repeal of the Fugitive-Slave Law."

Answer. — I do not now, nor ever did, stand in favor of the unconditional repeal of the Fugitive-Slave Law.

Q. 2. — " I desire him to answer whether he stands pledged to-day, as he did in 1854, against the admission of any more Slave States into the Union, even if the people want them."

A. — " I do not now, nor ever did, stand pledged against the admission of any more Slave States into the Union.

Q. 3. — " I want to know whether he stands pledged against the admission of a new State into the Union with such a constitution as the people of that State may see fit to make."

A. — I do not stand pledged against the admission of a new State into the Union, with such a constitution as the people of that State may see fit to make.

Q. 4. — " I want to know whether he stands to-day pledged to the abolition of slavery in the District of Columbia."

A. — I do not stand to-day pledged to the abolition of slavery in the District of Columbia.

Q. 5. — " I desire him to answer whether he stands pledged to the prohibition of the slave-trade between the different States."

A. — I do not stand pledged to the prohibition of the slave-trade between the different States.

Q. 6. — " I desire to know whether he stands pledged to prohibit slavery in all the Territories of the United States, north as well as south of the Missouri Compromise line."

A. — I am impliedly, if not expressly, pledged to a belief in the *right* and *duty* of Congress to prohibit slavery in all the United States Territories. [Great applause.]

Q 7. — " I desire him to answer whether he is opposed to the acquisition of any new territory unless slavery is first prohibited therein."

A. — I am not generally opposed to honest acquisition of territory ; and, in any given case, I would or would not oppose such acquisition, accordingly as I might think such acquisition would or would not agitate the slavery question among ourselves.

Now, my friends, it will be perceived, upon an examination of these questions and answers, that so far I have only answered that I was not *pledged* to this, that, or the other. The judge has not framed his interrogatories to ask me any thing more than this, and I have answered in strict accordance with the interrogatories, and have answered truly that I am not *pledged* at all upon any of the points to which I have answered. But I am not disposed to hang upon the exact form of his interrogatory. I am rather disposed to take up at least some of these questions, and state what I really think upon them.

As to the first one, in regard to the Fugitive-Slave Law, I have never hesitated to say, and I do not now hesitate to say, that I think, under the Constitution of the United States, the people of the Southern States are entitled to a congressional slave law. Having said that, I have had nothing to say in regard to the existing Fugitive-Slave Law, further than that I think it should have been framed so as to be free from some of the objections that pertain to it, without lessening its efficiency. And inasmuch as we are not now in an agitation in regard to an alteration or modification of that law, I would not be the man to introduce it as a new subject of agitation upon the general question of slavery.

In regard to the other question, of whether I am pledged to the admission of any more Slave States into the Union, I state to you very frankly, that I would be exceedingly sorry ever to be put in a position of having to pass upon that question. I should be exceedingly glad to know that there would never be another Slave State admitted into the Union ; but I must add, that, if slavery shall be kept out of the Territories during the Territorial existence of any one given Territory, and then the people shall, having a fair chance and a clear field, when they come to adopt the constitution, do such an extraordinary thing as to adopt a slave constitution, uninfluenced by the actual presence of the institution among them, I see no alternative, if we own the country, but to admit them into the Union. [Applause.]

The third interrogatory is answered by the answer to the second, it being, as I conceive, the same as the second.

The fourth one is in regard to the abolition of slavery in the District of Columbia. In relation to that, I have my mind very distinctly made up. I should be exceedingly glad to see slavery abolished in the District of Columbia. I believe that Congress possesses the constitutional power to abolish it. Yet, as a member of Congress, I should not, with my present views, be in favor of *endeavoring* to abolish slavery in the District of Columbia, unless it would be upon these conditions: *First*, that the abolition should be gradual; *Second*, That it should be on a vote of the majority of qualified voters in the District; and *Third*, That compensation should be made to unwilling owners. With these three conditions, I confess I would be exceedingly glad to see Congress abolish slavery in the District of Columbia, and, in the language of Henry Clay, "sweep from our capital that foul blot upon our nation."

In regard to the fifth interrogatory, I must say here, that as to the question of the abolition of the slave-trade between the different States, I can truly answer, as I have, that I am *pledged* to nothing about it. It is a subject to which I have not given that mature consideration that would make me feel authorized to state a position so as to hold myself entirely bound by it. In other words, that question has never been prominently enough before me to induce me to investigate whether we really have the constitutional power to do it. I could investigate it if I had sufficient time to bring myself to a conclusion upon that subject; but I have not done so, and I say so frankly to you here and to Judge Douglas. I must say, however, that, if I should be of opinion that Congress does possess the constitutional power to abolish slave-trading among the different States, I should still not be in favor of the exercise of that power unless upon some conservative principle as I conceive it, akin to what I have said in relation to the abolition of slavery in the District of Columbia.

My answer as to whether I desire that slavery should be prohibited in all Territories of the United States is full and explicit within itself, and cannot be made clearer by any comments of mine. So I suppose, in regard to the question whether I am opposed to the acquisition of any more territory unless slavery is first prohibited therein, my answer is such that I could add nothing by way of illustration, or making myself better understood, than the answer which I have placed in writing.

Now, in all this the Judge has me, and he has me on the record. I suppose he had flattered himself that I was really entertaining one set of opinions for one place, and another set for another place, — that I was afraid to say at one place what I uttered at another. What I am saying here I suppose I say to a vast audience as strongly tending to abolitionism as any audience in the State of Illinois; and I believe I am saying that which, if it would be offensive to any persons, and render them enemies to myself, would be offensive to persons in this audience.

Mr. Douglas had presented his interrogatories on the 21st of August, and Mr. Lincoln did not answer them until the 27th. They had no meetings between those days ; and Mr. Lincoln had ample time to ponder his replies, and consult his friends. But he did more : he improved the opportunity to prepare a series of insidious questions, which he felt sure Mr. Douglas could not possibly answer without utterly ruining his political prospects. Mr. Lincoln struggled for a great prize, unsuspected by the common mind, but the thought of which was ever present to his own. Mr. Douglas was a standing candidate for the Presidency ; but as yet Mr. Lincoln was a very quiet one, nursing hopes which his modesty prevented him from obtruding upon others. He was wise enough to keep the fact of their existence to himself, and in the mean time to dig pitfalls and lay obstructions in the way of his most formidable competitors. His present purpose was not only to defeat Mr. Douglas for the Senate, but to " kill him," — to get him out of the way finally and forever. If he could make him evade the Dred-Scott Decision, and deny the right of a Southern man to take his negroes into a Territory, and keep them there while it was a Territory, he would thereby sever him from the body of the Democratic party, and leave him the leader of merely a little half-hearted antislavery faction. Under such circumstances, Mr. Douglas could never be the candidate of the party at large ; but he might serve a very useful purpose by running on a separate ticket, and dividing the great majority of conservative votes, which would inevitably elect a single nominee.

Mr. Lincoln went to Chicago, and there intimated to some of his friends what he proposed to do. They attempted to dissuade him, because, as they insisted, if Mr. Douglas should answer that the Dred-Scott Decision might be evaded by the people of a Territory, and slavery prohibited in the face of it, the answer would draw to him the sympathies of the anti-slavery voters, and probably, of itself, defeat Mr. Lincoln. But, so long as Mr. Douglas held to the decision in good faith, he had no hope of more aid from that quarter than he had already received.   It was therefore the part of wisdom to let him alone as to that point.   Mr. Lincoln, on the contrary, looked forward to 1860, and was determined that the South should understand the antagonism between Mr. Douglas's latest conception of "squatter sovereignty," on the one hand, and the Dred-Scott Decision, the Nebraska Bill, and all previous platforms of the party, on the other.   Mr. Douglas taught strange doctrines and false ones ; and Mr. Lincoln thought the faithful, far and near, should know it.   If Mr. Douglas was a schismatic, there ought to be a schism, of which the Republicans would reap the benefit; and therefore he insisted upon his questions.   " That is no business of yours," said his friends.   " Attend exclusively to your senatorial race, and let the slaveholder and Douglas fight out that question among themselves and for themselves.   If you put the question to him, he will answer that the Dred-Scott Decision is simply an abstract rule, having no practical application."— " If he answers that way, he's a dead cock in the pit," responded Mr. Lincoln.   " But that," said they, " is none of your business : you are concerned only about the senatorship." — " No," continued Mr. Lincoln, " not alone *exactly :* I am killing larger game.   The great battle of 1860 is worth a thousand of this senatorial race."

He did accordingly propound the interrogatories as follows : —

1. If the people of Kansas shall, by means entirely unobjectionable in all other respects, adopt a State constitution, and ask admission into the Union under it, before they have the requisite number of inhabitants according to the English Bill, — some ninety-three thousand, — will you vote to admit them ?

2. Can the people of a United States Territory, in any lawful way, against the wish of any citizen of the United States, exclude slavery from its limits ?

3. If the Supreme Court of the United States shall decide that States cannot exclude slavery from their limits, are you in favor of acquiescing in, adopting, and following such decision as a rule of political action ?

4. Are you in favor of acquiring additional territory, in disregard of how such acquisition may affect the nation on the slavery question?

The first and fourth questions Mr. Douglas answered substantially in the affirmative. To the third he replied, that no judge would ever be guilty of the " moral treason " of making such a decision. But to the second — the main question, to which all the others were riders and make-weights — he answered as he was expected to answer. " It matters not," said he, " what way the Supreme Court may hereafter decide as to the abstract question whether slavery may or may not go into a Territory under the Constitution : the people have the lawful means to introduce it or exclude it, as they please, for the reason that slavery cannot exist a day or an hour anywhere, unless it is supported by local police regulations. Those police regulations can only be established by the local Legislature ; and, if the people are opposed to slavery, they will elect representatives to that body who will, by unfriendly legislation, effectually prevent the introduction of it into their midst."

The reply was more than enough for Mr. Lincoln's purpose. It cut Mr. Douglas off from his party, and put him in a state of perfect antagonism to it. He firmly denied the power of Congress to restrict slavery ; and he admitted, that, under the Dred-Scott Decision, all Territories were open to its entrance. But he held, that, the moment the slaveholder passed the boundary of a Territory, he was at the mercy of the squatters, a dozen or two of whom might get together in a legislature, and rob him of the property which the Constitution, the Supreme Court, and Mr. Douglas himself said he had an indefeasible right to take there. Mr. Lincoln knew that the Southern people would feel infinitely safer in the hands of Congress than in the hands of the squatters. If they regarded the Republican mode of excluding slavery as a barefaced usurpation, they would consider Mr. Douglas's system of confiscation by " unfriendly legislation " mere plain stealing. The Republicans said to them, " We will regulate

27

the whole subject by general laws, which you participate with
us in passing;" but Mr. Douglas offered them, as sovereign
judges and legislators, the territorial settlers themselves, —
squatters they might be, — whom the aid societies rushed into
the new Territories for the very purpose of keeping slavery
away. The new doctrine was admirably calculated to alarm
and incense the South; and, following so closely Mr. Douglas's conduct in the Lecompton affair, it was very natural
that he should now be universally regarded by his late
followers as a dangerous heretic and a faithless turncoat.
The result justified Mr. Lincoln's anticipations. Mr. Douglas
did not fully develop his new theory, nor personally promul-
gate it as the fixed tenet of his faction, until the next year,
when he embodied it in the famous article contributed by
him to "Harper's Magazine." But it did its work effectually; and, when parties began to marshal for the great struggle of 1860, Mr. Douglas was found to be, not precisely what
he had promised, — a Republican, "fighting their battles," —
but an independent candidate, upon an independent platform,
dividing the opposition.

Mr. Lincoln pointed out on the spot the wide difference
between Mr. Douglas's present views and those he had previously maintained with such dogged and dogmatic persist-
ence. "The new state of the case" had induced "the Judge
to sheer away from his original ground." The new theory
was false in law, and could have no practical application.
The history of the country showed it to be a naked humbug,
a demagogue's imposture. Slavery was established in all
this country, without "local police regulations" to protect
it. Dred Scott himself was held in a Territory, not only
without "local police regulations" to favor his bondage, but
in defiance of a general law which prohibited it. A man
who believed that the Dred-Scott Decision was the true interpretation of the Constitution could not refuse to negro slavery whatever protection it needed in the Territories without incurring the guilt of perjury. To say that slave property
might be constitutionally confiscated, destroyed, or driven

away from a place where it was constitutionally protected, was such an absurdity as Mr. Douglas alone in this evil strait was equal to ; the proposition meaning, as he said on a subsequent occasion, " no less than that a thing may lawfully be driven away from a place where it has a lawful right to be."

" Of that answer at Freeport," as Mr. Herndon has it, .Douglas " instantly died. The red-gleaming Southern tomahawk flashed high and keen. Douglas was removed out of Lincoln's way. The wind was taken out of Seward's sails (by the House-divided Speech), and Lincoln stood out prominent."

The State election took place on the 2d of November, 1858. Mr. Lincoln had more than four thousand majority of the votes cast; but this was not enough to give him a majority in the Legislature. An old and inequitable apportionment law was still in operation; and a majority of the members chosen under it were, as it was intended by the law-makers they should be, Democrats. In the Senate were fourteen Democrats to eleven Republicans; and in the House, forty Democrats to thirty-five Republicans. Mr. Douglas was, of course, re-elected, and Mr. Lincoln bitterly disappointed. Some one asked Mr. Lincoln how he felt when the returns came in. He replied, " that he felt like the boy that stumped his toe, — ' it hurt too bad to laugh, and he was too big to cry ! ' "

In this canvass Mr. Lincoln earned a reputation as a popular debater second to that of no man in America, — certainly not second to that of his famous antagonist. He kept his temper; he was not prone to personalities; he indulged in few anecdotes, and those of a decent character; he was fair, frank, and manly ; and, if the contest had shown nothing else, it would have shown, at least, that " Old Abe " could behave like a well-bred gentleman under very trying circumstances. His marked success in these discussions was probably no surprise to the people of the Springfield District, who knew him as well as, or better than, they did Mr. Douglas. But in the greater part of the State, and throughout the Union the series of brilliant victories successively won by an obscure man over an orator of such wide experience and renown was received with exclamations of astonishment, alike by listeners and readers. It is true that many believed, or pretended to believe, that he was privately tutored and "crammed" by politicians of greater note than himself; and, when the speeches were at last collected and printed together, it was alleged that Mr. Lincoln's had been re-written or extensively revised by Mr. Judd, Judge Logan, Judge Davis, or some one else of great and conceded abilities.

CHAPTER XVII.

IN the winter of 1858–9, Mr. Lincoln, having no political business on hand, appeared before the public in the character of lecturer, having prepared himself with much care. His lecture was, or might have been, styled, "All Creation is a mine, and every man a miner." He began with Adam and Eve, and the invention of the "fig-leaf apron," of which he gave a humorous description, and which he said was a "joint operation." The invention of letters, writing, printing, of the application of steam, of electricity, he classed under the comprehensive head of "inventions and discoveries," along with the discovery of America, the enactment of patent-laws, and the "invention of negroes, or the present mode of using them." Part of the lecture was humorous; a very small part of it actually witty; and the rest of it so commonplace that it was a genuine mortification to his friends. He delivered it at two or three points, and then declined all further invitations. To one of these he replied, in March, as follows: "Your note, inviting me to deliver a lecture in Galesburgh, is received. I regret to say I cannot do so now: I must stick to the courts a while. I read a sort of a lecture to three different audiences during the last month and this; but I did so under circumstances which made it a waste of no time whatever."

From the Douglas discussion many of the leaders of the Republican party believed, and the reader will agree had some foundation for the belief, that Mr. Lincoln was one of the greatest and best men in the party. It was natural, therefore,

421

that many eyes should be turned towards him for the coming Presidential nomination.   He had all the requisites of an available candidate : he had not been sufficiently prominent in national politics to excite the jealousies of powerful rivals; he was true, manly, able ; he was pre-eminently a man of the people ; he had sprung from a low family in the lowest class of society ; he had been a rail-splitter, a flat-boatman, a grocery-keeper, — every thing that could commend him to the " popular heart."   His manners, his dress, his stories, and his popular name and style of " Honest Old Abe," pointed to him as a man beside whose " running qualities " those of Taylor and Harrison were of slight comparison.   That he knew all this, and thought of it a great deal, no one can doubt; and in the late campaign he had most adroitly opened the way for the realization of his hopes.   But he knew very well that a becoming modesty in a " new man " was about as needful as any thing else. Accordingly, when a Mr. Pickett wrote him on the subject in March, 1859, he replied as follows : " Yours of the 2d instant, inviting me to deliver my lecture on ' Inventions ' in Rock Island, is at hand, and I regret to be unable from press of business to comply therewith.   In regard to the other matter you speak of, I beg that you will not give it a further mention.   I do not think I am fit for the Presidency."

But in April the project began to be agitated in his own town.   On the 27th of that month, he was in the office of " The Central Illinois Gazette," when the editor suggested his name.   Mr. Lincoln, " with characteristic modesty, declined." But the editor estimated his " No " at its proper value ; and he " was brought out in the next issue, May 4."   Thence the movement spread rapidly and strongly.   Many Republicans welcomed it, and, appreciating the pre-eminent fitness of the nomination, saw in it the assurance of certain victory.

The West was rapidly filling with Germans and other inhabitants of foreign birth.   Dr. Canisius, a German, foreseeing Mr. Lincoln's strength in the near future, wrote to inquire what he thought about the restrictions upon naturalization recently adopted in Massachusetts, and whether he favored the fusion of all the opposition elements in the next canvass. He replied, that, as to the restrictions, he was wholly and unalterably opposed to them; and as to fusion, he was ready for it upon "Republican grounds," but upon no other. He would not lower "the Republican standard even by a hair's breadth." The letter undoubtedly had a good effect, and brought him valuable support from the foreign population.

To a gentleman who desired his views about the tariff question, he replied cautiously and discreetly as follows:—

CLINTON, Oct. 11, 1859.

DR. EDWARD WALLACE.

My dear Sir,—I am here just now attending court. Yesterday, before I left Springfield, your brother, Dr. William S. Wallace, showed me a letter of yours, in which you kindly mention my name, inquire for my tariff-views, and suggest the propriety of my writing a letter upon the subject. I was an old Henry-Clay Tariff Whig. In old times I made more speeches on that subject than on any other.

I have not since changed my views. I believe yet, if we could have a moderate, carefully adjusted, protective tariff, so far acquiesced in as not to be a perpetual subject of political strife, squabbles, changes, and uncertainties, it would be better for us. Still, it is my opinion, that, just now, the revival of that question will not *advance the cause itself, or the man who revives it.*

I have not thought much on the subject recently; but my general impression is, that the necessity for a protective tariff will ere long force its old opponents to take it up; and then its old friends can join in and establish it on a more firm and durable basis. We, the old Whigs, have been entirely beaten out on the tariff question; and we shall not be able to re-establish the policy until the absence of it shall have demonstrated the necessity for it in the minds of men heretofore opposed to it. With this view, I should prefer to not now write a public letter upon the subject.

I therefore wish this to be considered confidential.

I shall be very glad to receive a letter from you.

Yours truly,
A. LINCOLN.

In September Mr. Lincoln made a few masterly speeches in Ohio, where Mr. Douglas had preceded him on his new hobby of "squatter sovereignty," or "unfriendly legislation."

He spoke at Columbus, Cincinnati, and several other points, each time devoting the greater part of his address to Mr. Douglas and his theories, as if the habit of combating that illustrious chieftain was hard to break.

In December he went to Kansas, speaking at Elwood, Donaphan, Troy, Atchison, and twice at Leavenworth. Wherever he went, he was met by vast assemblages of people. His speeches were principally repetitions of those previously made in Illinois; but they were very fresh and captivating to his new audiences. These journeys, which turned out to be continuous ovations, spread his name and fame far beyond the limits to which they had heretofore been restricted.

During the winter of 1859–60, he saw that his reputation had reached such a height, that he might honorably compete with such renowned men as Seward, Chase, and Bates, for the Presidential nomination. Mr. Jackson Grimshaw of Quincy urged him very strongly on the point. At length Mr. Lincoln consented to a conference with Grimshaw and some of his more prominent friends. It took place in a committee-room in the State House. Mr. Bushnell, Mr. Hatch (the Secretary of State), Mr. Judd (Chairman of the Republican State Central Committee), Mr. Peck, and Mr. Grimshaw were present, — all of them "intimate friends." They were unanimous in opinion as to the expediency and propriety of making him a candidate. But "Mr. Lincoln, with his characteristic modesty, doubted whether he could get the nomination, even if he wished it, and asked until the next morning to answer us. . . . The next day he authorized us to consider him, and work for him, if we pleased, as a candidate for the Presidency."

It was in October, 1859, that Mr. Lincoln received an invitation to speak in New York. It enchanted him: no event of his life had given him more heartfelt pleasure. He went straight to his office, and, Mr. Herndon says, "looked pleased, not to say *tickled*. He said to me, 'Billy, I am invited to deliver a lecture in New York. Shall I go?'—'By all means,' I replied; 'and it is a good opening too.'—'If you were in my fix, what subject would you choose?' said Lincoln. 'Why, a political one: that's your forte,' I answered." Mr. Herndon remembered his partner's previous " failure, — utter failure," as a lecturer, and, on this occasion, dreaded excessively his choice of a subject. " In the absence of a friend's advice, Lincoln would as soon take the Beautiful for a subject as any thing else, when he had absolutely no sense of it." He wrote in response to the invitation, that he would avail himself of it the coming February, provided he might be permitted to make a political speech, in case he found it inconvenient to get up one of another kind. He had purposely set the day far ahead, that he might thoroughly prepare himself; and it may safely be said, that no effort of his life cost him so much labor as this one. Some of the party managers who were afterwards put to work to verify its statements, and get it out as a campaign document, are alleged to have been three weeks in finding the historical records consulted by him.

On the 25th of February, 1860, he arrived in New York. It was Saturday, and he spent the whole day in revising and retouching his speech. The next day he heard Beecher preach, and on Monday wandered about the city to see the sights. When the committee under whose auspices he was to speak waited upon him, they found him dressed in a sleek and shining suit of new black, covered with very apparent creases and wrinkles, acquired by being packed too closely and too long in his little valise. He felt uneasy in his new clothes and a strange place. His confusion was increased when the reporters called to get the printed slips of his speech in advance of its delivery. Mr. Lincoln knew nothing of such a custom among the orators, and had no slips. He was, in fact, not quite sure that the press would desire to publish his speech. When he reached the Cooper Institute, and was ushered into the vast hall, he was surprised to see the most cultivated men of the city awaiting him on the stand, and an immense audience assembled to hear him. Mr. Bryant introduced him as " an eminent citizen of the West, hitherto known to you only by reputation." Mr. Lincoln then began, in low, monotonous tones, which gradually became louder and clearer, the following speech : —

MR. PRESIDENT AND FELLOW-CITIZENS OF NEW YORK, — The facts with which I shall deal this evening are mainly old and familiar ; nor is there any thing new in the general use I shall make of them. If there shall be any novelty, it will be in the mode of presenting the facts, and the inferences and observations following that presentation.

In his speech last autumn, at Columbus, Ohio, as reported in " The New-York Times," Senator Douglas said, —

" Our fathers, when they framed the government under which we live, understood this question just as well, and even better than we do now."

I fully indorse this, and I adopt it as a text for this discourse. I so adopt it, because it furnishes a precise and agreed starting-point for the discussion between Republicans and that wing of Democracy headed by Senator Douglas. It simply leaves the inquiry, " What was the understanding those fathers had of the questions mentioned ? "

What is the frame of government under which we live ?

The answer must be, " The Constitution of the United States." That Constitution consists of the original, framed in 1787 (and under which the present Government first went into operation), and twelve subsequently framed amendments, the first ten of which were framed in 1789.

Who were our fathers that framed the Constitution ? I suppose the "thirty-nine" who signed the original instrument may be fairly called our fathers who framed that part of the present Government. It is almost exactly true to say they framed it ; and it is altogether true to say they fairly represented the opinion and sentiment of the whole nation at that time. Their names, being familiar to nearly all, and accessible to quite all, need not now be repeated.

I take these "thirty-nine," for the present, as being "our fathers, who framed the Government under which we live."

What is the question which, according to the text, those fathers understood just as well, and even better than we do now ?

It is this : Does the proper division of local from Federal authority, or any thing in the Constitution, forbid our Federal Government control as to slavery in our Federal Territories ?

.Upon this, Douglas holds the affirmative, and Republicans the negative. This affirmative and denial form an issue ; and this issue, this question, is precisely what the text declares our fathers understood better than we.

Let us now inquire whether the "thirty-nine," or any of them, ever acted upon this question ; and, if they did, how they acted upon it, — how they expressed that better understanding.

In 1784, — three years before the Constitution, — the United States then owning the North-western Territory, and no other, the Congress of the Confederation had before them the question of prohibiting slavery in that Territory; and four of the "thirty-nine" who afterward framed the Constitution were in that Congress, and voted on that question. Of these, Roger Sherman, Thomas Mifflin, and Hugh Williamson voted for the prohibition; thus showing, that, in their understanding, no line dividing local from Federal authority, nor any thing else, properly forbade the Federal Government to control as to slavery in Federal territory. The other of the four, James McHenry, voted against the prohibition, showing that, for some cause, he thought it improper to vote for it.

In 1787 — still before the Constitution, but while the Convention was in session framing it, and while the North-western Territory still was the only Territory owned by the United States — the same question of prohibiting slavery in the Territory again came before the Congress of the Confederation; and three more of the "thirty-nine" who afterward signed the Constitution were in that Congress, and voted on the question. They were William Blount, William Few, and Abraham Baldwin; and they all voted for the prohibition, thus showing that, in their understanding, no line dividing local from Federal authority, nor any thing else, properly forbids the Federal Government to control as to slavery in Federal territory. This time the prohibition became a law, being part of what is now well known as the Ordinance of '87.

The question of Federal control of slavery in the Territories seems not to have been directly before the convention which framed the original Constitution; and hence it is not recorded that the "thirty-nine," or any of them, while engaged on that instrument, expressed any opinion on that precise question.

In 1789, by the First Congress which sat under the Constitution, an act was passed to enforce the Ordinance of '87, including the prohibition of slavery in the North-western Territory. The bill for this act was reported by one of the "thirty-nine," — Thomas Fitzsimmons, then a member of the House of Representatives from Pennsylvania. It went through all its stages without a word of opposition, and finally passed both branches without yeas and nays, which is equivalent to a unanimous passage. In this Congress there were sixteen of the "thirty-nine" fathers who framed the original Constitution. They were John Langdon, Nicholas Gilman, William S. Johnson, Roger Sherman, Robert Morris, Thomas Fitzsimmons, William Few, Abraham Baldwin, Rufus King, William Patterson, George Clymer, Richard Bassett, George Read, Pierce Butler, Daniel Carrol, James Madison.

This shows that, in their understanding, no line dividing local from Federal authority, nor any thing in the Constitution, properly forbade Congress to prohibit slavery in the Federal territory; else both their fidelity to correct principle, and their oath to support the Constitution, would have constrained them to oppose the prohibition.

Again, George Washington, another of the "thirty-nine," was then President of the United States, and, as such, approved and signed the bill, thus completing its validity as a law, and thus showing, that, in his understanding, no line dividing local from Federal authority, nor any thing in the Constitution, forbade the Federal Government to control as to slavery in Federal territory.

No great while after the adoption of the original Constitution, North Carolina ceded to the Federal Government the country now constituting the State of Tennessee; and a few years later Georgia ceded that which now constitutes the States of Mississippi and Alabama. In both deeds of cession it was made a condition by the ceding States that the Federal Government should not prohibit slavery in the ceded country. Besides this, slavery was then actually in the ceded country. Under these circumstances, Congress, on taking charge of these countries, did not absolutely prohibit slavery within them. But they did interfere with it, take control of it, even there, to a certain extent. In 1798, Congress organized the Territory of Mississippi. In the act of organization they prohibited the bringing of slaves into the Territory, from any place without the United States, by fine, and giving freedom to slaves so brought. This act passed both branches of Congress without yeas and nays. In that Congress were three of the "thirty-nine" who framed the original Constitution: they were John Langdon, George Read, and Abraham Baldwin. They all, probably, voted for it. Certainly they would have placed their opposition to it upon record, if, in their understanding, any line dividing local from Federal authority, or any thing in the Constitution, properly forbade the Federal Government to control as to slavery in Federal territory.

In 1803 the Federal Government purchased the Louisiana country. Our former territorial acquisitions came from certain of our own States; but this Louisiana country was acquired from a foreign nation. In 1804 Congress gave a territorial organization to that part of it which now constitutes the State of Louisiana. New Orleans, lying within that part, was an old and comparatively large city. There were other considerable towns and settlements, and slavery was extensively and thoroughly intermingled with the people. Congress did not, in the Territorial Act, prohibit slavery; but they did interfere with it, take control of it, in a more marked and extensive way than they did in the case of Mississippi. The substance of the provision therein made, in relation to slaves, was, —

First, That no slave should be imported into the Territory from foreign parts.

Second, That no slave should be carried into it who had been imported into the United States since the first day of May, 1798.

Third, That no slave should be carried into it, except by the owner, and for his own use as a settler; the penalty in all the cases being a fine upon the violator of the law, and freedom to the slave.

This act also was passed without yeas and nays. In the Congress which passed it there were two of the "thirty-nine:" they were Abraham Baldwin and Jonathan Dayton. As stated in the case of Mississippi, it is probable they both voted for it. They would not have allowed it to pass without recording their opposition to it, if, in their understanding, it violated either the line proper dividing local from Federal authority or any provision of the Constitution.

In 1819-20 came and passed the Missouri question. Many votes were taken by yeas and nays, in both branches of Congress, upon the various phases of the general question. Two of the "thirty-nine" — Rufus King and Charles Pinckney — were members of that Congress. Mr. King steadily voted for slavery prohibition and against all compromises; while Mr. Pinckney as steadily voted against slavery prohibition and against all compromises. By this Mr. King showed, that, in his understanding, no line dividing local from Federal authority, nor any thing in the Constitution, was violated by Congress prohibiting slavery in Federal territory; while Mr. Pinckney, by his votes, showed, that, in his understanding, there was some sufficient reason for opposing such prohibition in that case.

The cases I have mentioned are the only acts of the "thirty-nine," or of any of them, upon the direct issue, which I have been able to discover.

To enumerate the persons who thus acted as being four in 1784, three in 1787, seventeen in 1789, three in 1798, two in 1804, and two in 1819-20, — there would be thirty-one of them. But this would be counting John Langdon, Roger Sherman, William Few, Rufus King, and George Read each twice, and Abraham Baldwin four times. The true number of those of the "thirty-nine" whom I have shown to have acted upon the question, which, by the text, they understood better than we, is twenty-three, leaving sixteen not shown to have acted upon it in any way.

Here, then, we have twenty-three out of our "thirty-nine" fathers, who framed the government under which we live, who have, upon their official responsibility and their corporal oaths, acted upon the very question which the text affirms they "understood just as well, and even better than we do now;" and twenty-one of them — a clear majority of the "thirty-nine" — so acting upon it as to make them guilty of gross political impropriety and wilful perjury if, in their understanding, any proper division between local and Federal authority, or any thing in the Constitution they had made themselves, and sworn to support, forbade the Federal Government to control as to slavery in the Federal Territories. Thus the twenty-one acted; and, as actions speak louder than words, so actions under such responsibility speak still louder.

Two of the twenty-three voted against congressional prohibition of slavery in the Federal Territories in the instances in which they acted upon the question; but for what reasons they so voted is not known. They may have done so because they thought a proper division of local from Federal authority, or some provision or principle of the Constitution, stood in the way; or they may, without any such question, have voted against the prohibition, on what appeared to them to be sufficient grounds of expediency. No one who has sworn to support the Constitution can conscientiously vote for what he understands to be an unconstitutional measure, however expedient he may think it; but one may and ought to vote against a measure which he deems constitutional if, at the same time, he deems it inexpedient. It, therefore, would be unsafe to set down even the two who voted against the prohibition as having done so because, in their understanding, any proper division of local from Federal authority, or any thing in the Constitution, forbade the Federal Government to control as to slavery in Federal territory.

The remaining sixteen of the "thirty-nine," so far as I have discovered, have left no record of their understanding upon the direct question of Federal control of slavery in the Federal Territories. But there is much reason to believe that their understanding upon that question would not have appeared different from that of their twenty-three compeers, had it been manifested at all.

For the purpose of adhering rigidly to the text, I have purposely omitted whatever understanding may have been manifested by any person, however distinguished, other than the "thirty-nine" fathers who framed the original Constitution; and, for the same reason, I have also omitted whatever understanding may have been manifested by any of the "thirty-nine" even, on any other phase of the general question of slavery. If we should look into their acts and declarations on those other phases, as the foreign slave-trade, and the morality and policy of slavery generally, it would appear to us, that, on the direct question of Federal control of slavery in Federal Territories, the sixteen, if they had acted at all, would probably have acted just as the twenty-three did. Among that sixteen were several of the most noted anti-slavery men of those times, — as Dr. Franklin, Alexander Hamilton, and Gouverneur Morris; while there was not one now known to have been otherwise, unless it may be John Rutledge of South Carolina.

The sum of the whole is, that of our "thirty-nine" fathers who framed the original Constitution, twenty-one — a clear majority of the whole — certainly understood that no proper division of local from Federal authority, nor any part of the Constitution, forbade the Federal Government to control slavery in the Federal Territories; while all the rest probably had the same understanding. Such, unquestionably, was the understanding of our fathers who framed the original Constitution; and the text affirms that they understood the question better than we.

But, so far, I have been considering the understanding of the question manifested by the framers of the original Constitution. In and by the original instrument, a mode was provided for amending it; and, as I have already stated, the present frame of government under which we live consists of that original, and twelve amendatory articles framed and adopted since. Those who now insist that Federal control of slavery in Federal Territories violates the Constitution point us to the provisions which they suppose it thus violates; and, as I understand, they all fix upon provisions in these amendatory articles, and not in the original instrument. The Supreme Court, in the Dred-Scott case, plant themselves upon the fifth amendment, which provides that "no person shall be deprived of property without due process of law ;" while Senator Douglas and his peculiar adherents plant themselves upon the tenth amendment,· providing that "the powers not granted by the Constitution are reserved to the States respectively and to the people."

Now, it so happens that these amendments were framed by the first Congress which sat under the Constitution, — the identical Congress which passed the act already mentioned, enforcing the prohibition of slavery in the North-western Territory. Not only was it the same Congress, but they were the identical, same individual men, who, at the same time within the session, had under consideration, and in progress toward maturity, these constitutional amendments, and this act prohibiting slavery in all the territory the nation then owned. The constitutional amendments were introduced before, and passed after, the act enforcing the Ordinance of '87; so that, during the whole pendency of the act to enforce the Ordinance, the constitutional amendments were also pending.

That Congress, consisting in all of seventy-six members, including sixteen of the framers of the original Constitution, as before stated, were preeminently our fathers who framed that part of the government under which we live, which is now claimed as forbidding the Federal Government to control slavery in the Federal Territories.

Is it not a little presumptuous in any one at this day to affirm that the two things which that Congress deliberately framed, and carried to maturity at the same time, are absolutely inconsistent with each other? And does not such affirmation become impudently absurd when coupled with the other affirmation, from the same mouth, that those who did the two things alleged to be inconsistent understood whether they were really inconsistent better than we, — better than he who affirms that they are inconsistent?

It is surely safe to assume that the "thirty-nine" framers of the original Constitution, and the seventy-six members of the Congress which framed the amendments thereto, taken together, do certainly include those who may be fairly called "our fathers who framed the government under which we live." And so assuming, I defy any man to show that any one of them ever, in his whole life, declared, that, in his understanding, any proper division of local from Federal authority, or any part of the Constitution, forbade the Federal Government to control as to slavery in the Federal Territories. I go a step farther. I defy any one to show that any living man in the whole world ever did, prior to the beginning of the present century (and I might almost say prior to the beginning of the last half of the present century), declare, that, in his understanding, any proper division of local from Federal authority, or any part of the Constitution, forbade the Federal Government to control as to slavery in the Federal Territories. To those who now so declare, I give, not only " our fathers, who framed the government under which we live," but with them all other living men within the century in which it was framed, among whom to search, and they shall not be able to find the evidence of a single man agreeing with them.

Now, and here, let me guard a little against being misunderstood. I do not mean to say we are bound to follow implicitly in whatever our fathers did. To do so would be to discard all the lights of current experience, — to reject all progress, — all improvement. What I do say is, that, if we would supplant the opinions and policy of our fathers in any case, we should do so upon evidence so conclusive, and argument so clear, that even their great authority, faifly considered and weighed, cannot stand; and most surely not in a case whereof we ourselves declare they understood the question better than we.

If any man, at this day, sincerely believes that a proper division of local from Federal authority, or any part of the Constitution, forbids the Federal Government to control as to slavery in the Federal Territories, he is right to say so, and to enforce his position by all truthful evidence and fair argument which he can. But he has no right to mislead others, who have less access to history and less leisure to study it, into the false belief that " our fathers, who framed the government under which we live," were of the same opinion, thus substituting falsehood and deception for truthful evidence and fair argument. If any man at this day sincerely believes "our fathers, who framed the government under which we live," used and applied principles, in other cases, which ought to have led them to understand that a proper division of local from Federal authority, or some part of the Constitution, forbids the Federal Government to control as to slavery in the Federal Territories, he is right to say so. But he should, at the same time, brave the responsibility of declaring, that, in his opinion, he understands their principles better than they did themselves; and especially should he not shirk that responsibility by asserting that they " understood the question just as well, and even better than we do now."

But enough. Let all who believe that " our fathers, who framed the government under which we live, understood this question just as well, and even better than we do now," speak as they spoke, and act as they acted upon it. This is all Republicans ask, all Republicans desire, in relation to slavery. As those fathers marked it, so let it be again marked, as an evil not to be extended, but to be tolerated and protected only because of and so far as its actual presence among us makes that toleration and protection a necessity. Let all the guaranties those fathers gave it be, not grudgingly, but fully and fairly maintained. For this Republicans contend, and with this, so far as I know or believe, they will be content.

And now, if they would listen, — as I suppose they will not, — I would address a few words to the Southern people.

I would say to them, You consider yourselves a reasonable and a just people; and I consider, that, in the general qualities of reason and justice, you are not inferior to any other people. Still, when you speak of us Republicans, you do so only to denounce us as reptiles, or, at the best, as no better than outlaws. You will grant a hearing to pirates or murderers, but nothing like it to "Black Republicans." In all your contentions with one another, each of you deems an unconditional condemnation of "Black Republicanism" as the first thing to be attended to. Indeed, such condemnation of us seems to be an indispensable prerequisite — license, so to speak — among you to be admitted or permitted to speak at all.

Now can you, or not, be prevailed upon to pause and to consider whether this is quite just to us, or even to yourselves?

Bring forward your charges and specifications, and then be patient long enough to hear us deny or justify.

You say we are sectional. We deny it. That makes an issue; and the burden of proof is upon you. You produce your proof; and what is it? Why, that our party has no existence in your section, — gets no votes in your section. The fact is substantially true; but does it prove the issue? If it does, then in case we should, without change of principle, begin to get votes in your section, we should thereby cease to be sectional. You cannot escape this conclusion; and yet are you willing to abide by it? If you are, you will probably soon find that we have ceased to be sectional, for we shall get votes in your section this very year. You will then begin to discover, as the truth plainly is, that your proof does not touch the issue. The fact that we get no votes in your section is a fact of your making, and not of ours. And if there be fault in that fact, that fault is primarily yours, and remains so until you show that we repel you by some wrong principle or practice. If we do repel you by any wrong principle or practice, the fault is ours; but this brings us to where you ought to have started, — to a discussion of the right or wrong of our principle. If our principle, put in practice, would wrong your section for the benefit of ours, or for any other object, then our principle, and we with it, are sectional, and are justly opposed and denounced as such. Meet us, then, on the question of whether our principle, put in practice, would wrong your section; and so meet it as if it were possible that something may be said on our side. Do you accept the challenge? No? Then you really believe that the principle which our fathers, who framed the government under which we live, thought so clearly right as to adopt it, and indorse it again and again upon their official oaths, is, in fact, so clearly wrong as to demand your condemnation without a moment's consideration.

Some of you delight to flaunt in our faces the warning against sectional parties given by Washington in his Farewell Address. Less than eight years before Washington gave that warning, he had, as President of the United States, approved and signed an act of Congress enforcing the prohi-

28

bition of slavery in the North-western Territory, which act embodied the policy of the Government upon that subject up to and at the very moment he penned that warning; and about one year after he penned it he wrote Lafayette that he considered that prohibition a wise measure, expressing, in the same connection, his hope that we should some time have a confederacy of Free States.

Bearing this in mind, and seeing that sectionalism has since arisen upon this same subject, is that warning a weapon in your hands against us, or in our hands against you? Could Washington himself speak, would he cast the blame of that sectionalism upon us, who sustain his policy, or upon you, who repudiate it? We respect that warning of Washington; and we commend it to you, together with his example pointing to the right application of it.

But you say you are conservative, — eminently conservative; while we are revolutionary, destructive, or something of the sort. What is conservatism? Is it not adherence to the old and tried against the new and untried? We stick to, contend for, the identical old policy on the point in controversy which was adopted by our fathers who framed the government under which we live; while you, with one accord, reject and scout and spit upon that old policy, and insist upon substituting something new. True, you disagree among yourselves as to what that substitute shall be. You have considerable variety of new propositions and plans; but you are unanimous in rejecting and denouncing the old policy of the fathers. Some of you are for reviving the foreign slave-trade; some for a Congressional Slave-code for the Territories; some for Congress forbidding the Territories to prohibit slavery within their limits; some for maintaining slavery in the Territories through the judiciary; some for the " gur-reat pur-rinciple " that, " if one man would enslave another, no third man should object," fantastically called " popular sovereignty; " but never a man among you in favor of Federal prohibition of slavery in Federal Territories, according to the practice of our fathers, who framed the government under which we live. Not one of all your various plans can show a precedent or an advocate in the century within which our Government originated. Consider, then, whether your claim of conservatism for yourselves, and your charge of destructiveness against us, are based on the most clear and stable foundations.

Again, you say we have made the slavery question more prominent than it formerly was. We deny it. We admit that it is more prominent, but we deny that we made it so. It was not we, but you, who discarded the old policy of the fathers. We resisted, and still resist, your innovation; and thence comes the greater prominence of the question. Would you have that question reduced to its former proportions? Go back to that old policy. What has been will be again, under the same conditions. If you would have the peace of the old times, re-adopt the precepts and policy of the old times.

You charge that we stir up insurrections among your slaves. We deny it. And what is your proof? Harper's Ferry! John Brown! John Brown was no Republican; and you have failed to implicate a single Republican in his Harper's Ferry enterprise. If any member of our party is guilty in that matter, you know it, or you do not know it. If you do know it, you are inexcusable to not designate the man, and prove the fact. If you do not know it, you are inexcusable to assert it, and especially to persist in the assertion after you have tried and failed to make the proof. You need not be told that persisting in a charge which one does not know to be true is simply malicious slander.

Some of you admit that no Republican designedly aided or encouraged the Harper's-Ferry affair, but still insist that our doctrines and declarations necessarily lead to such results. We do not believe it. We know we hold to no doctrine, and make no declarations, which were not held to and made by our fathers, who framed the government under which we live. You never deal fairly by us in relation to this affair. When it occurred, some important State elections were near at hand; and you were in evident glee with the belief, that, by charging the blame upon us, you could get an advantage of us in those elections. The elections came; and your expectations were not quite fulfilled. Every Republican man knew, that, as to himself at least, your charge was a slander, and he was not much inclined by it to cast his vote in your favor. Republican doctrines and declarations are accompanied with a continual protest against any interference whatever with your slaves, or with you about your slaves. Surely this does not encourage them to revolt. True, we do, in common with our fathers who framed the government under which we live, declare our belief that slavery is wrong; but the slaves do not hear us declare even this. For any thing we say or do, the slaves would scarcely know there is a Republican party. I believe they would not, in fact, generally know it but for your misrepresentations of us in their hearing. In your political contest among yourselves, each faction charges the other with sympathy with Black Republicanism; and then, to give point to the charge, defines Black Republicanism to simply be insurrection, blood, and thunder among the slaves.

Slave insurrections are no more common now than they were before the Republican party was organized. What induced the Southampton Insurrection, twenty-eight years ago, in which, at least, three times as many lives were lost as at Harper's Ferry? You can scarcely stretch your very elastic fancy to the conclusion that Southampton was got up by Black Republicanism. In the present state of things in the United States, I do not think a general, or even a very extensive slave insurrection, is possible. The indispensable concert of action cannot be attained. The slaves have no means of rapid communication; nor can incendiary free men, black or white, supply it. The explosive materials are everywhere in parcels; but there neither are, nor can be supplied, the indispensable connecting trains.

Much is said by Southern people about the affection of slaves for their masters and mistresses; and a part of it, at least, is true. A plot for an uprising could scarcely be devised and communicated to twenty individuals before some one of them, to save the life of a favorite master or mistress, would divulge it. This is the rule; and the slave revolution in Hayti was not an exception to it, but a case occurring under peculiar circumstances. The gunpowder plot of British history, though not connected with the slaves, was more in point. In that case, only about twenty were admitted to the secret; and yet one of them, in his anxiety to save a friend, betrayed the plot to that friend, and, by consequence, averted the calamity. Occasional poisoning from the kitchen, and open or stealthy assassinations in the field, and local revolts extending to a score or so, will continue to occur as the natural results of slavery; but no general insurrection of slaves, as I think, can happen in this country for a long time. Whoever much fears, or much hopes, for such an event will be alike disappointed.

In the language of Mr. Jefferson, uttered many years ago, " It is still in our power to direct the process of emancipation and deportation peaceably, and in such slow degrees, as that the evil will wear off insensibly; and their places be, *pari passu*, filled up by free white laborers. If, on the contrary, it is left to force itself on, human nature must shudder at the prospect held up."

Mr. Jefferson did not mean to say, nor do I, that the power of emancipation is in the Federal Government. He spoke of Virginia; and, as to the power of emancipation, I speak of the slaveholding States only.

The Federal Government, however, as we insist, has the power of restraining the extension of the institution, — the power to insure that a slave insurrection shall never occur on any American soil which is now free from slavery.

John Brown's effort was peculiar. It was not a slave insurrection. It was an attempt by white men to get up a revolt among slaves, in which the slaves refused to participate. In fact, it was so absurd that the slaves, with all their ignorance, saw plainly enough it could not succeed. That affair, in its philosophy, corresponds with the many attempts, related in history, at the assassination of kings and emperors. An enthusiast broods over the oppression of a people till he fancies himself commissioned by Heaven to liberate them. He ventures the attempt, which ends in little else than in his own execution. Orsini's attempt on Louis Napoleon, and John Brown's attempt at Harper's Ferry, were, in their philosophy, precisely the same. The eagerness to cast blame on old England in the one case, and on New England in the other, does not disprove the sameness of the two things.

And how much would it avail you, if you could, by the use of John Brown, Helper's book, and the like, break up the Republican organization? Human action can be modified to some extent; but human nature cannot be changed. There is a judgment and a feeling against slavery in this nation, which cast at least a million and a half of votes. You cannot destroy that judgment and feeling, that sentiment, by breaking up the political organization which rallies around it. You can scarcely scatter and disperse an army which has been formed into order in the face of your heaviest fire; but, if you could, how much would you gain by forcing the sentiment which created it out of the peaceful channel of the ballot-box, into some other channel? What would that other channel probably be? Would the number of John Browns be lessened or enlarged by the operation?

But you will break up the Union rather than submit to a denial of your constitutional rights.

That has a somewhat reckless sound; but it would be palliated, if not fully justified, were we proposing by the mere force of numbers to deprive you of some right plainly written down in the Constitution. But we are proposing no such thing.

When you make these declarations, you have a specific and well-understood allusion to an assumed constitutional right of yours to take slaves into the Federal Territories, and hold them there as property; but no such right is specifically written in the Constitution. That instrument is literally silent about any such right. We, on the contrary, deny that such a right has any existence in the Constitution, even by implication.

Your purpose then, plainly stated, is, that you will destroy the government, unless you be allowed to construe and enforce the Constitution as you please on all points in dispute between you and us. You will rule or ruin in all events.

This, plainly stated, is your language to us. Perhaps you will say the Supreme Court has decided the disputed constitutional question in your favor. Not quite so. But waiving the lawyer's distinction between dictum and decision, the courts have decided the question for you in a sort of way. The courts have substantially said, it is your constitutional right to take slaves into the Federal Territories, and to hold them there as property.

When I say the decision was made in a sort of way, I mean it was made in a divided court by a bare majority of the judges, and they not quite agreeing with one another in the reasons for making it; that it is so made as that its avowed supporters disagree with one another about its meaning, and that it was mainly based upon a mistaken statement of fact, — the statement in the opinion that "the right of property in a slave is distinctly and expressly affirmed in the Constitution."

An inspection of the Constitution will show that the right of property in a slave is not distinctly and expressly affirmed in it. Bear in mind, the judges do not pledge their judicial opinion that such right is impliedly affirmed in the Constitution; but they pledge their veracity that it is distinctly and expressly affirmed there, — "distinctly," that is, not mingled with any thing else; "expressly," that is, in words meaning just that, without the aid of any inference, and susceptible of no other meaning.

If they had only pledged their judicial opinion that such right is affirmed in the instrument by implication, it would be open to others to show that neither the word "slave" nor "slavery" is to be found in the Constitution, nor the word "property" even, in any connection with language alluding to the things slave or slavery, and that, wherever in that instrument the slave is alluded to, he is called a "person;" and wherever his master's legal right in relation to him is alluded to, it is spoken of as "service or labor due," — as a "debt" payable in service or labor. Also it would be open to show, by contemporaneous history, that this mode of alluding to slaves and slavery, instead of speaking of them, was employed on purpose to exclude from the Constitution the idea that there could be property in man.

To show all this is easy and certain.

When this obvious mistake of the judges shall be brought to their notice, is it not reasonable to expect that they will withdraw the mistaken statement, and reconsider the conclusion based upon it?

And then it is to be remembered that "our fathers, who framed the government under which we live," — the men who made the Constitution, — decided this same constitutional question in our favor long ago, — decided it without a division among themselves, when making the decision; without division among themselves about the meaning of it after it was made, and, so far as any evidence is left, without basing it upon any mistaken statement of facts.

Under all these circumstances, do you really feel yourselves justified to break up this Government, unless such a court decision as yours is shall be at once submitted to, as a conclusive and final rule of political action?

But you will not abide the election of a Republican President. In that supposed event, you say, you will destroy the Union; and then, you say, the great crime of having destroyed it will be upon us!

That is cool. A highwayman holds a pistol to my ear, and mutters through his teeth, "Stand and deliver, or I shall kill you; and then you will be a murderer!"

To be sure, what the robber demanded of me — my money — was my own; and I had a clear right to keep it; but it was no more my own than my vote is my own; and threat of death to me to extort my money, and threat of destruction to the Union to extort my vote, can scarcely be distinguished in principle.

A few words now to Republicans. It is exceedingly desirable that all parts of this great Confederacy shall be at peace, and in harmony, one with another. Let us Republicans do our part to have it so. Even though much provoked, let us do nothing through passion and ill-temper. Even though the Southern people will not so much as listen to us, let us calmly consider their demands, and yield to them if, in our deliberate view of our duty, we possibly can. Judging by all they say and do, and by the subject and nature of their controversy with us, let us determine, if we can, what will satisfy them.

Will they be satisfied if the Territories be unconditionally surrendered to them? We know they will not. In all their present complaints against us, the Territories are scarcely mentioned. Invasions and insurrections are the rage now. Will it satisfy them if, in the future, we have nothing to do with invasions and insurrections? We know it will not. We so know because we know we never had any thing to do with invasions and insurrections; and yet this total abstaining does not exempt us from the charge and the denunciation.

The question recurs, what will satisfy them? Simply this: We must not only let them alone, but we must, somehow, convince them that we do let them alone. This we know by experience is no easy task. We have been so trying to convince them from the very beginning of our organization, but with no success. In all our platforms and speeches we have constantly protested our purpose to let them alone; but this has had no tendency to convince them. Alike unavailing to convince them is the fact that they have never detected a man of us in any attempt to disturb them.

These natural, and apparently adequate means all failing, what will convince them? This, and this only: cease to call slavery *wrong*, and join them in calling it *right*. And this must be done thoroughly,—done in *acts* as well as in *words*. Silence will not be tolerated: we must place ourselves avowedly with them. Douglas's new sedition law must be enacted and enforced, suppressing all declarations that slavery is wrong, whether made in politics, in presses, in pulpits, or in private. We must arrest and return their fugitive slaves with greedy pleasure. We must pull down our Free-State Constitutions. The whole atmosphere must be disinfected from all taint of opposition to slavery, before they will cease to believe that all their troubles proceed from us.

I am quite aware they do not state their case precisely in this way. Most of them would probably say to us, "Let us alone, do nothing to us, and say what you please about slavery." But we do let them alone, have never disturbed them; so that, after all, it is what we say which dissatisfies them. They will continue to accuse us of doing until we cease saying.

I am also aware they have not as yet, in terms, demanded the overthrow of our Free-State constitutions. Yet those constitutions declare the wrong of slavery with more solemn emphasis than do all other sayings against it; and when all these other sayings shall have been silenced, the overthrow of these constitutions will be demanded, and nothing be left to resist the demand. It is nothing to the contrary, that they do not demand the whole of this just now. Demanding what they do, and for the reason they do, they can voluntarily stop nowhere short of this consummation. Holding, as they do, that slavery is morally right, and socially elevating, they cannot cease to demand a full national recognition of it, as a legal right and a social blessing.

Nor can we justifiably withhold this on any ground, save our conviction

that slavery is wrong. If slavery is right, all words, acts, laws, and constitutions against it are themselves wrong, and should be silenced and swept
away. If it is right, we cannot justly object to its nationality, its univer-
sality; if it is wrong, they cannot justly insist upon its extension, its
enlargement. All they ask, we could readily grant, if we thought slavery
right; all we ask, they could as readily grant, if they thought it wrong.
Their thinking it right, and our thinking it wrong, is the precise fact upon
which depends the whole controversy. Thinking it right, as they do, they
are not to blame for desiring its full recognition, as being right; but thinking it wrong, as we do, can we yield to them? Can we cast our votes with
their view, and against our own? In view of our moral, social, and political
responsibilities, can we do this?

Wrong as we think slavery is, we can yet afford to let it alone where it
is, because that much is due to the necessity arising from its actual presence
in the nation; but can we, while our votes will prevent it, allow it to spread
into the national Territories, and to overrun us here in these Free States?

If our sense of duty forbids this, then let us stand by our duty fearlessly
and effectively. Let us be diverted by none of those sophistical contrivances
wherewith we are so industriously plied and belabored, — contrivances such
as groping for some middle ground between the right and the wrong, vain as
the search for a man who should be neither a living man nor a dead man, —
such as a policy of "don't care" on a question about which all true men do
care, — such as Union appeals beseeching true Union men to yield to Disunionists, reversing the divine rule, and calling, not the sinners, but the
righteous, to repentance, — such as invocations to Washington, imploring
men to unsay what Washington said, and undo what Washington did.

Neither let us be slandered from our duty by false accusations against us,
nor frightened from it by menaces of destruction to the Government, nor of
dungeons to ourselves. Let us have faith that right makes might; and in
that faith, let us, to the end, dare to do our duty as we understand it.

The next morning "The Tribune" presented a report of
the speech, but, in doing so, said, " the tones, the gestures,
the kindling eye, and the mirth-provoking look defy the
reporter's skill. . . . No man ever before made such an impression on his first appeal to a New York audience." " The
Evening Post" said, " We have made room for Mr. Lincoln's speech, notwithstanding the pressure of other matters; and our readers will see that it was well worthy of the
deep attention with which it was heard." For the publication of such arguments the editor was " tempted to wish "

that his columns " were indefinitely elastic." And these are but fair evidences of the general tone of the press.

Mr. Lincoln was much annoyed, after his return home, by the allegation that he had sold a " political speech," and had been generally governed by mercenary motives in his Eastern trip. Being asked to explain it, he answered as follows : —

SPRINGFIELD, April 6, 1860.

C. F. McNEILL, ESQ.

Dear Sir, — Reaching home yesterday, I found yours of the 23d March, enclosing a slip from " The Middleport Press." It is not true that I ever charged any thing for a political speech in my life; but this much is true. Last October I was requested by letter to deliver some sort of speech in Mr. Beecher's church in Brooklyn, — $200 being offered in the first letter. I wrote that I could do it in February, provided they would take a political speech if I could find time to get up no other. They agreed; and subsequently I informed them the speech would have to be a political one. When I reached New York, I, for the first, learned that the place was changed to " Cooper Institute." I made the speech, and left for New Hampshire, where I have a son at school, neither asking for pay nor having any offered me. Three days after, a check for $200 was sent to me at N.H.; and I took it, *and did not know it was wrong.* My understanding now is, though I knew nothing of it at the time, that they did charge for admittance at the Cooper Institute, and that they took in more than twice $200.

I have made this explanation to you as a friend; but I wish no explanation made to our enemies. What they want is a squabble and a fuss: and that they can have if we explain; and they cannot have it if we don't.

When I returned through New York from New England, I was told by the gentlemen who sent me the check, that a drunken vagabond in the club, having learned something about the $200, made the exhibition out of which " The Herald " manufactured the article quoted by " The Press " of your town.

My judgment is, and therefore my request is, that you give no denial, and no explanations.

Thanking you for your kind interest in the matter, I remain

Yours truly,

A. LINCOLN.

From New York Mr. Lincoln travelled into New England, to visit his son Robert, who was a student at Harvard; but he was overwhelmed with invitations to address Republican meetings. In Connecticut he spoke at Hartford,

Norwich, New Haven, Meriden, and Bridgeport; in Rhode Island, at Woonsocket; in New Hampshire, at Concord and Manchester. Everywhere the people poured out in multitudes, and the press lavished encomiums. Upon his speech at Manchester, "The Mirror," a neutral paper, passed the following criticisms of his style of oratory, — criticisms familiar enough to the people of his own State: " He spoke an hour and a half with great fairness, great apparent candor, and with wonderful interest. He did not abuse the South, the administration, or the Democrats, or indulge in any personalities, with the exception of a few hits at Douglas's notions. He is far from prepossessing in personal appearance, and his voice is disagreeable; and yet he wins your attention and good-will from the start. . . . He indulges in no flowers of rhetoric, no eloquent passages. He is not a wit, a humorist, or a clown; yet so great a vein of pleasantry and good-nature pervades what he says, gilding over a deep current of practical argument, he keeps his hearers in a smiling mood, with their mouths open ready to swallow all he says. His sense of the ludicrous is very keen; and an exhibition of that is the clincher of all his arguments, — not the ludicrous acts of persons, but ludicrous ideas. Hence he is never offensive, and steals away willingly into his train of belief persons who were opposed to him. For the first half-hour his opponents would agree with every word he uttered; and from that point he began to lead them off little by little, until it seemed as if he had got them all into his fold. He displays more shrewdness, more knowledge of the masses of mankind, than any public speaker we have heard since Long Jim Wilson left for California."

On the morning after the Norwich speech, Mr. Lincoln was met, or is said to have been met, in the cars by a preacher, one Gulliver, — a name suggestive of fictions. Gulliver says he told Mr. Lincoln that he thought his speech " the most remarkable one he ever heard." Lincoln doubted his sincerity; but Gulliver persisted. " Indeed, sir," said he, " I learned more of the art of public speaking last evening than

I could from a whole course of lectures on rhetoric." Lincoln found he had in hand a clerical sycophant, and a little politician at that, — a class of beings whom he most heartily despised. Whereupon he began to quiz the fellow, and told him, for a most " remarkable circumstance," that the professors of Yale College were running all around after him, taking notes of his speeches, and lecturing about him to the classes. " Now," continued he, " I should like very much to know what it was in my speech which you thought so remarkable, and which interested my friend the professor so much ? " Gulliver was equal to the occasion, and answered with an opinion which Mr. Bunsby might have delivered, and died, leaving to the world a reputation perfected by that single saying. " The clearness of your statements," said Gulliver, " the unanswerable style of your reasoning, and especially your illustrations, which were romance and pathos, and fun and logic, all welded together." Gulliver closed the interview with the cant peculiar to his kind. " Mr. Lincoln," said he, " may I say one thing to you before we separate ? " — " Certainly ; any thing you please," replied the good-natured old Abe. " You have just spoken," preached Gulliver, " of the tendency of political life in Washington to debase the moral convictions of our representatives there by the admixture of mere political expediency. You have become, by the controversy with Mr. Douglas, one of our leaders in this great struggle with slavery, which is undoubtedly the struggle of the nation and the age. What I would like to say is this, and I say it with a full heart: Be true to your principles ; *and we will be true to you, and God will be true to us all.*" To which modest, pious, and original observation, Mr. Lincoln responded, " I say Amen to that ! Amen to that ! "

CHAPTER XVIII.

IT was not until May 9 and 10 that the Republican State Convention of Illinois met at Decatur. Mr. Lincoln was present, and is said to have been there as a mere "spectator." He had no special interest in the proceedings, and appears to have had no notion that any business relating to him was to be transacted that day. It was a very large and spirited body, comprising an immense number of delegates, among whom were the most brilliant, as well as the shrewdest men in the party. It was evident that something of more than usual importance was expected to transpire. A few moments after the convention organized, "Old Abe" was seen squatting, or sitting on his heels, just within the door of the Wigwam. Gov. Oglesby rose and said amid increasing silence, "I am informed that a distinguished citizen of Illinois, and one whom Illinois will ever delight to honor, is present; and I wish to move that this body invite him to a seat on the stand." Here the governor paused, as if to tease and dally, and work curiosity up to the highest point; but at length he shouted the magic name "*Abraham Lincoln!*" Not a shout, but a roar of applause, long and deep, shook every board and joist of the Wigwam. The motion was seconded and passed. A rush was made for the hero that sat on his heels. He was seized, and jerked to his feet. An effort was made to "jam him through the crowd" to his place of honor on the stage; but the crowd was too dense, and it failed. Then he was "troosted," — lifted up bodily, — and lay for a few seconds sprawling and kicking upon the heads and shoulders of

444

UNCLE JOHN H'NKS.

the great throng. In this manner he was gradually pushed toward the stand, and finally reached it, doubtless to his great relief, "in the arms of some half-dozen gentlemen," who set him down in full view of his clamorous admirers. "The cheering was like the roar of the sea. Hats were thrown up by the Chicago delegation, as if hats were no longer useful." Mr. Lincoln rose, bowed, smiled, blushed, and thanked the assembly as well as he could in the midst of such a tumult. A gentleman who saw it all says, "I then thought him one of the most diffident and worst-plagued men I ever saw."

At another stage of the proceedings, Gov. Oglesby rose again with another provoking and mysterious speech. "There was," he said, "an old Democrat outside who had something he wished to present to this Convention." — "Receive it!" "Receive it!" cried some. "What is it?" "What is it?" screamed some of the lower Egyptians, who had an idea the old Democrat might want to blow them up with an infernal machine. But the party for Oglesby and the old Democrat was the stronger, and carried the vote with a tremendous hurrah. The door of the Wigwam opened; and a fine, robust old fellow, with an open countenance and bronzed cheeks, marched into the midst of the assemblage, bearing on his shoulder "two small triangular heart rails," surmounted by a banner with this inscription : —

TWO RAILS,

FROM A LOT MADE BY ABRAHAM LINCOLN AND JOHN HANKS, IN THE SANGAMON BOTTOM, IN THE YEAR 1830.

The sturdy bearer was old John Hanks himself, enjoying the great field-day of his life. He was met with wild and tumultuous cheers, prolonged through several minutes; and it was observed that the Chicago and Central-Illinois men put up the loudest and longest. The whole scene was for a time simply tempestuous and bewildering. But it ended at last; and now the whole body, those in the secret and those out of it, clamored like men beside themselves for a speech from Mr.

Lincoln, who in the mean time " blushed, but seemed to shake with inward laughter." In response to the repeated appeals he rose and said, —

" Gentlemen, I suppose you want to know something about those things " (pointing to old John and the rails). " Well, the truth is, John Hanks and I did make rails in the Sangamon Bottom. I don't know whether we made those rails or not; fact is, I don't think they are a credit to the makers " (laughing as he spoke). " But I do know this: I made rails then, and I think I could make better ones than these now."

By this time the innocent Egyptians began to open their eyes: they saw plainly enough now the admirable Presidential scheme unfolded to their view. The result of it all was a resolution declaring that " Abraham Lincoln *is the first choice of the Republican party of Illinois for the Presidency, and instructing the delegates to the Chicago Convention to use all honorable means to secure his nomination, and to cast the vote of the State as a unit for him.*"

The crowd at Decatur, delegates and private citizens, who took part in these proceedings, was estimated at five thousand. Neither the numbers nor the enthusiasm was a pleasant sight to the divided and demoralized Democrats. They disliked to hear so much about " honest Old Abe," " the rail-splitter," " the flat-boatman," " the pioneer." These cries had an ominous sound in their ears. Leaving Decatur on the cars, an old man out of Egypt, devoted to the great principles of Democracy, and excessively annoyed by the demonstration in progress, approached Mr. Lincoln and said, " So you're Abe Lincoln ? " — " That's my name, sir," answered Mr. Lincoln. " They say you're a self-made man," said the Democrat. " Well, yes," said Mr. Lincoln, " what there is of me is self-made." — " Well, all I've got to say," observed the old man, after a careful survey of the statesman before him, " is, that it was a d—n bad job."

In the mean time Mr. Lincoln's claims had been attractively presented to the politicians of other States. So early as

1858, Mr. Herndon had been to Boston partly, if not entirely, on this mission; and latterly Judge Davis, Leonard Swett, and others had visited Ohio, Indiana, Pennsylvania, and Maryland in his behalf. Illinois was, of course, overwhelmingly and vociferously for him.

On the 16th of May, the Republican Convention assembled at Chicago. The city was literally crammed with delegates, alternates, " outside workers," and spectators. No nominating convention had ever before attracted such multitudes to the scene of its deliberations.

The first and second days were spent in securing a permanent organization, and the adoption of a platform. The latter set out by reciting the Declaration of Independence as to the equality of all men, not forgetting the usual quotation about the right to " life, liberty, and the pursuit of happiness." The third resolution denounced disunion in any possible event; the fourth declared the right of each State to " order and control its own domestic institutions according to its own judgment exclusively;" the fifth denounced the administration and its treatment of Kansas, as well as its general support of the supposed rights of the South under the Constitution; the sixth favored " economy;" the seventh denied the " new dogma, that the Constitution, of its own force, carries slavery into any or all of the Territories of the United States;" the eighth denied the " authority of Congress, of a Territorial Legislature, or of any individuals, to give legal existence to slavery in any Territory of the United States;" the ninth called the African slave-trade a " burning shame;" the tenth denounced the governors of Kansas and Nebraska for vetoing certain antislavery bills; the eleventh favored the admission of Kansas; the twelfth was a high-tariff manifesto, and a general stump speech to the mechanics; the thirteenth lauded the Homestead policy; the fourteenth opposed any Federal or State legislation " by which the rights of citizenship, hitherto accorded to immigrants from foreign lands, shall be abridged or impaired," with some pretty words, intended as a further bid for the foreign vote; the fifteenth declared for

"river and harbor improvements," and the sixteenth for a
"Pacific Railroad." It was a very comprehensive "platform;"
and, if all classes for whom planks were provided should be
kind enough to stand upon them, there could be no failure in
the election.

On the third day the balloting for a candidate was to
begin. Up to the evening of the second day, Mr. Seward's
prospects were far the best. It was certain that he would
receive the largest vote on the first ballot; and outside of the
body itself the "crowd" for him was more numerous and
boisterous than for any other, except Mr. Lincoln. For Mr.
Lincoln, however, the "pressure" from the multitude, in the
Wigwam, in the streets, and in the hotels, was tremendous.
It is sufficiently accounted for by the fact that the "spot"
was Chicago, and the State Illinois. Besides the vast numbers who came there voluntarily to urge his claims, and to
cheer for him, as the exigency demanded, his adherents had
industriously "drummed up" their forces in the city and
country, and were now able to make infinitely more noise
than all the other parties put together. There was a large
delegation of roughs there for Mr. Seward, headed by Tom
Hyer, the pugilist. These, and others like them, filled the
Wigwam toward the evening of the second day in expectation that the voting would begin. The Lincoln party found
it out, and determined to call a check to that game. They
spent the whole night in mustering and organizing their
"loose fellows" from far and near, and at daylight the next
morning "took charge" of the Wigwam, filling every available space, and much that they had no business to fill. As
a result, the Seward men were unable to get in, and were
forced to content themselves with curbstone enthusiasm.

Mr. Lincoln seemed to be very sure, all along, that the contest would be ultimately between him and Mr. Seward. The
"Bates men" were supposed to be conservative, that is,
not Abolitionists; and the object of the move in favor of Mr.
Bates was to lower the fanatical tone of the party, and save
the votes of certain "Union men" who might otherwise be

against it. But a Seward man had telegraphed to St. Louis, to the friends of Mr. Bates, to say that Lincoln was as bad as Seward, and to urge them to go for Mr. Seward in case their own favorite should fail. The despatch was printed in " The Missouri Democrat," but was not brought to Mr. Lincoln's attention until the meeting of the Convention. He immediately caught up the paper, and " wrote on its broad margin," " Lincoln agrees with Seward in his irrepressible-conflict idea, and in negro equality ; but he is opposed to Seward's Higher Law." With this he immediately despatched a friend to Chicago, who handed it to Judge Davis or Judge Logan.

Simon Cameron of Pennsylvania was nominally a candidate ; but, in the language of Col. McClure, " it meant nothing : " it was a mere sham, got up to enable Cameron to make a bargain with some real candidate, and thus secure for himself and his friends the lion's share of the spoils in the event of a victory at the polls. The genuine sentiment of the Pennsylvania delegation was divided between Judge Bates and Judge McLean. But Cameron was in a fine position to trade, and his friends were anxious for business. On the evening of the second day, these gentlemen were gratified. A deputation of them — Casey, Sanderson, Reeder, and perhaps others — were invited to the Lincoln Head-quarters at the Tremont House, where they were met by Messrs. Davis, Swett, Logan, and Dole, on the part of Mr. Lincoln. An agreement was there made, that, if the Cameron men would go for Lincoln, and he should be nominated and elected, Cameron should have a seat in his Cabinet, *provided* the Pennsylvania delegation could be got to recommend him. The bargain was fulfilled, but not without difficulty. Cameron's strength was more apparent than real. There was, however, " a certain class of the delegates under his immediate influence ; " and these, with the aid of Mr. Wilmot and his friends, who were honestly for Lincoln, managed to carry the delegation by a very small majority, — " about six."

About the same time a similar bargain was made with the friends of Caleb B. Smith of Indiana ; and with these two

29

contracts quietly ratified, the Lincoln men felt strong and confident on the morning of the third day.

While the candidates were being named, and when the ballotings began, every mention of Mr. Lincoln's name was received with thundering shouts by the vast mass of his adherents by whom the building had been packed. In the phrase of the day, the "outside pressure" was all in his favor. On the first ballot, Mr. Seward had $173\frac{1}{2}$ votes; Mr. Lincoln, 102; Mr. Cameron, $50\frac{1}{2}$; Mr. Chase, 49; Mr. Bates, 48; Mr. Dayton, 14; Mr. McLean, 12; Mr. Collamer, 10; and 6 were scattered. Mr. Cameron's name was withdrawn on the second ballot, according to the previous understanding; Mr. Seward had $184\frac{1}{2}$; Mr. Lincoln, 181; Mr. Chase, $42\frac{1}{2}$; Mr. Bates, 35; Mr. Dayton, 10; Mr. McLean, 8; and the rest scattered. It was clear that the nomination lay between Mr. Seward and Mr. Lincoln, and the latter was receiving great accessions of strength. The third ballot came, and Mr. Lincoln ran rapidly up to $231\frac{1}{2}$ votes; 233 being the number required to nominate. Hundreds of persons were keeping the count; and it was well known, without any announcement, that Mr. Lincoln lacked but a vote and a half to make him the nominee. At this juncture, Mr. Cartter of Ohio rose, and changed four votes from Mr. Chase to Mr. Lincoln. He was nominated. The Wigwam shook to its foundation with the roaring cheers. The multitude in the streets answered the multitude within, and in a moment more all the holiday artillery of Chicago helped to swell the grand acclamation. After a time, the business of the convention proceeded amid great excitement. All the votes that had heretofore been cast against Mr. Lincoln were cast for him before this ballot concluded; and, upon motion, the nomination was made unanimous. The convention then adjourned for dinner, and in the afternoon finished its work by the nomination of Hannibal Hamlin of Maine for Vice-President.

All that day and all the day previous Mr. Lincoln was in Springfield, trying to behave as usual, but watching the proceedings of the Convention, as they were reported by telegraph, with nervous anxiety. Mr. Baker, the friend who had taken "The Missouri Democrat" to Chicago with Mr. Lincoln's pregnant indorsement upon it, returned on the night of the 18th. Early in the morning, he and Mr. Lincoln went to the ball-alley to play at "fives;" but the alley was pre-engaged. They went to an "excellent and neat beer saloon" to play a game of billiards; but the table was occupied. In this strait they contented themselves with a glass of beer, and repaired to "The Journal" office for news.

C. P. Brown says that Lincoln played ball a great deal that day, notwithstanding the disappointment when he went with Baker; and Mr. Zane informs us that he was engaged in the same way the greater part of the day previous. It is probable that he took this physical mode of working off or keeping down the unnatural excitement that threatened to possess him.

About nine o'clock in the morning, Mr. Lincoln came to the office of Lincoln & Herndon. Mr. Zane was then conversing with a student, "Well, boys," said Mr. Lincoln, "what do you know?"—"Mr. Rosette," answered Zane, "who came from Chicago this morning, thinks your chances for the nomination are good." Mr. Lincoln wished to know what Mr. Rosette's opinion was founded upon; and, while Zane was explaining, Mr. Baker entered with a telegram, "which said the names of the candidates for nomination had been announced," and that Mr. Lincoln's had been received with more applause than any other. Mr. Lincoln lay down on a sofa to rest. Soon after, Mr. Brown entered; and Mr. Lincoln said to him, "Well, Brown, do you know any thing?" Brown did not know much; and so Mr. Lincoln, secretly nervous and impatient, rose and exclaimed, "Let's go to the telegraph-office." After waiting some time at the office, the result of the first ballot came over the wire. It was apparent to all present that Mr. Lincoln thought it very favorable. He believed that if Mr. Seward failed to get the nomination, or to "come very near it," on the first ballot, he would fail

altogether. Presently the news of the second ballot arrived,
and Mr. Lincoln showed by his manner that he considered
the contest no longer doubtful. "I've got him," said he.
He then went over to the office of "The Journal," where
other friends were awaiting decisive intelligence. The local
editor of that paper, Mr. Zane, and others, remained behind
to receive the expected despatch. In due time it came: the
operator was intensely excited; at first he threw down his
pencil, but, seizing it again, wrote off the news that threw
Springfield into a frenzy of delight. The local editor picked
it up, and rushed to "The Journal" office. Upon entering
the room, he called for three cheers for the next President.
They were given, and then the despatch was read. Mr. Lincoln seemed to be calm, but a close observer could detect
in his countenance the indications of deep emotion. In the
mean time cheers for Lincoln swelled up from the streets, and
began to be heard throughout the town. Some one remarked,
"Mr. Lincoln, I suppose now we will soon have a book containing your life." — "There is not much," he replied, "in
my past life about which to write a book, as it seems to me."
Having received the hearty congratulations of the company in
the office, he descended to the street, where he was immediately surrounded by "Irish and American citizens;" and, so
long as he was willing to receive it, there was great hand-
shaking and felicitating. "Gentlemen," said the great man
with a happy twinkle in his eye, "you had better come up
and shake my hand while you can: honors elevate some
men, you know." But he soon bethought him of a person
who was of more importance to him than all this crowd.
Looking toward his house, he said, "Well, gentlemen, there
is a little short woman at our house who is probably more
interested in this despatch than I am; and, if you will excuse
me, I will take it up and let her see it."
During the day a hundred guns were fired at Springfield;
and in the evening a great mass meeting "ratified" the nomination, and, after doing so, adjourned to the house of the
nominee. Mr. Lincoln appeared, made a "model" speech,

and invited into his house everybody that could get in. To this the immense crowd responded that they would give him a larger house the next year, and in the mean time beset the one he had until after midnight.

On the following day the Committee of the Convention, with Mr. Ashmun, the president, at its head, arrived at Springfield to notify Mr. Lincoln of his nomination. Contrary to what might have been expected, he seemed sad and dejected. The re-action from excessive joy to deep despondency — a process peculiar to his constitution — had already set in. To the formal address of the Committee, he responded with admirable taste and feeling : —

"Mr. Chairman and Gentlemen of the Committee, — I tender to you, and through you to the Republican National Convention, and all the people represented in it, my profoundest thanks for the high honor done me, which you now formally announce. Deeply and even painfully sensible of the great responsibility which is inseparable from this high honor, — a responsibility which I could almost wish had fallen upon some one of the far more eminent men and experienced statesmen whose distinguished names were before the Convention, I shall, by your leave, consider more fully the resolutions of the Convention, denominated the platform, and, without unnecessary and unreasonable delay, respond to you, Mr. Chairman, in writing, not doubting that the platform will be found satisfactory, and the nomination gratefully accepted. And now I will not longer defer the pleasure of taking you, and each of you, by the hand."

The Committee handed him a letter containing the official notice, accompanied by the resolutions of the Convention ; and to this he replied on the 23d as follows : —

Springfield, Ill., May 23, 1860.

Hon. George Ashmun, President of the Republican National Convention.

Sir, — I accept the nomination tendered me by the Convention over which you presided, and of which I am formally apprised in the letter of yourself and others, acting as a Committee of the Convention for that purpose.

The declaration of principles and sentiments which accompanies your letter meets my approval; and it shall be my care not to violate or disregard it in any part.

Imploring the assistance of Divine Providence, and with due regard to the views and feelings of all who were represented in the Convention; to the rights of all the States and Territories, and people of the nation; to the inviolability of the Constitution, and the perpetual union, harmony, and prosperity of all, — I am most happy to co-operate for the practical success of the principles declared by the Convention.

Your obliged friend and fellow-citizen,

ABRAHAM LINCOLN.

In the mean time the National Democratic Convention had met at Charleston, S.C., and split in twain.　The South utterly repudiated Mr. Douglas's new heresy; and Mr. Douglas insisted that the whole party ought to become heretics with him, and, turning their backs on the Dred-Scott Decision and the Cincinnati Platform, give up slavery in the Territories to the tender mercies of "squatter sovereignty" and "unfriendly legislation."　Neither party to the controversy would be satisfied with a simple re-affirmation of the Cincinnati Platform; for under it Mr. Douglas could go to the North and say that it meant "squatter sovereignty," and Mr. Breckinridge could go to the South and say that it meant Congressional protection to slavery.　In fact, it meant neither, and said neither, but declared, in plain English words, that Congress had no power to interfere with slavery in the Territories; and that, when the Territories were about to become States, they had *all* power to settle the question for themselves.　Gen. B. F. Butler of Massachusetts proposed to heal the ominous divisions in the Convention by the re-adoption of that clear and emphatic provision; but his voice was soon drowned in the clamors of the fiercer disputants.　The differences were irreconcilable.　Mr. Douglas's friends had come there determined to nominate him at any cost; and, in order to nominate him, they dared not concede the platform to the South.　A majority of the Committee on Resolutions reported the Cincinnati Platform, with the Southern interpretation of it; and the minority reported the same platform with a recitation concerning the "differences of opinion" "in the Democratic party," and a pledge to abide by the decision of the Supreme

Court " on the questions of constitutional law," — a pledge supposed to be of little value, since those who gave it were that moment in the very act of repudiating the only decision the Court had ever rendered. The minority report was adopted after a protracted and acrimonious debate, by a vote of one hundred and sixty-five to one hundred and thirty-eight. Thereupon the Southern delegates, most of them under instructions from their State conventions, withdrew, and organized themselves into a separate convention. The remaining delegates, called " the rump " by their Democratic adversaries, proceeded to ballot for a candidate for President, and voted fifty-seven times without effecting a nomination. Mr. Douglas, of course, received the highest number of votes; but, the old two-thirds rule being in force, he failed of a nomination. Mr. Guthrie of Kentucky was his principal competitor; but at one time and another Mr. Hunter of Virginia, Gen. Lane of Oregon, and Mr. Johnson of Tennessee, received flattering and creditable votes. After the fifty-seventh ballot, the Convention adjourned to meet at Baltimore on the 18th of June.

The seceders met in another hall, adopted the majority platform, as the adhering delegates had adopted the minority platform, and then adjourned to meet at Richmond on the second Monday in June. Faint hopes of accommodation were still entertained; and, when the seceders met at Richmond, they adjourned again to Baltimore, and the 28th of June.

The Douglas Convention, assuming to be the regular one, had invited the Southern States to fill up the vacant seats which belonged to them; but, when the new delegates appeared, they were met with the apprehension that their votes might not be perfectly secure for Mr. Douglas, and were therefore, in many instances, lawlessly excluded. This was the signal for another secession: the Border States withdrew; Mr. Butler and the Massachusetts delegation withdrew; Mr. Cushing deserted the chair, and took that of the rival Convention. The " regular " Convention, it was said, was now " the rump of a rump."

On the first ballot for a candidate, Mr. Douglas had $173\frac{1}{2}$ votes; Mr. Guthrie, 10; Mr. Breckinridge, 5; and 3 were scattered. On the second ballot, Mr. Douglas had $181\frac{1}{2}$; Mr. Breckinridge, 5; and Mr. Guthrie, $5\frac{1}{2}$. It was plain that under the two-thirds rule no nomination could be made here. Neither Mr. Douglas nor any one else could receive two-thirds of a full convention. It was therefore resolved that Mr. Douglas, "having received two-thirds of all the votes *given* in *this* Convention," should be declared the nominee. Mr. Fitzpatrick of Alabama was nominated for Vice-President, but declined to stand; and Mr. Johnson of Georgia was substituted for him by the Douglas "National Committee."

In the seceders' Convention, twenty-one States were represented more or less fully. It had no trouble in selecting a candidate. John C. Breckinridge of Kentucky and Joseph Lane of Oregon were unanimously nominated for the offices of President and Vice-President.

In the mean time another party — the "Constitutional Union party" — had met in Baltimore on the 19th of May, and nominated John Bell of Tennessee for President, and Edward Everett of Massachusetts for Vice-President. Its platform was, in brief, "The Constitution of the Country, the Union of the States, and the Enforcement of the Laws." This body was composed for the most part of impenitent Know-Nothings and respectable old-line Whigs.

The spring elections had given the democracy good reason to hope for success in the fall. The commercial classes, the shipping classes, and large numbers of the manufacturers, were thoroughly alarmed for the safety of the great trade dependent upon a political connection with the South. It seemed probable that a great re-action against antislavery agitations might take place. But the division at Charleston, the permanent organization of the two factions at Baltimore, and their mutual and rancorous hostility, completely reversed the delusive prospect. A majority of the whole people of the Union looked forward to a Republican victory with dread, and a large part with actual terror; and yet it was now clear that that majority was fatally bent upon wasting its power in the bitter struggles of the factions which composed it. Mr. Lincoln's election was assured; and for them there was nothing left but to put the house in order for the great convulsion which all our political fathers and prophets had predicted as the necessary consequence of such an event.

On the 6th of November, Abraham Lincoln was elected President of the United States. He received 1,857,610 votes; Mr. Douglas had 1,291,574; Mr. Breckinridge, 850,082; Mr. Bell, 646,124. Against Mr. Lincoln there was a majority of 930,170 of all the votes cast. Of the electoral votes, Mr. Lincoln had 180; Mr. Breckinridge, 72; Mr. Bell, 30; and Mr. Douglas, 12. It is more than likely that Mr. Lincoln owed this, his crowning triumph, to the skill and adroitness with which he questioned Mr. Douglas in the canvass of 1858, and drew out of him those fatal opinions about "squatter sovereignty" and "unfriendly legislation" in the Territories. But for Mr. Douglas's committal to those opinions, it is not likely that Mr. Lincoln would ever have been President.

The election over, Mr. Lincoln was sorely beset by office-seekers. Individuals, deputations, "delegations," from all quarters, pressed in upon him in a manner that might have killed a man of less robust constitution. The hotels of Springfield were filled with gentlemen who came with light baggage and heavy schemes. The party had never been in office: a "clean sweep" of the "ins" was expected; and all the "outs" were patriotically anxious to take the vacant places. It was a party that had never fed; and it was voraciously hungry. Mr. Lincoln and Artemus Ward saw a great deal of fun in it; and in all human probability it was the fun alone that enabled Mr. Lincoln to bear it.

Judge Davis says that Mr. Lincoln had determined to appoint "Democrats and Republicans alike to office." Many things confirm this statement. Mr. Lincoln felt deeply the responsibility of his great trust; and he felt still more keenly the supposed impossibility of administering the government for the sole benefit of an organization which had no existence in one-half of the Union. He was therefore willing, not only to appoint Democrats to office, but to appoint them to the very highest offices within his gift. At this time he thought very highly of Mr. Stephens of Georgia, and would gladly have taken him into his Cabinet but for the fear that Georgia might secede, and take Mr. Stephens along with her. He did actually authorize his friend, Mr. Speed, to offer the Treasury Department to Mr. Guthrie of Kentucky; and Mr. Guthrie, for good reasons of his own, declined it. The full significance of this act of courageous magnanimity cannot be understood without reference to the proceedings of the Charleston Convention, where Mr. Guthrie was one of the foremost candidates. He considered the names of various other gentlemen from the Border States, each of them with good proslavery antecedents. He commissioned Thurlow Weed to place a seat in the Cabinet at the disposal of Mr. Gilmore of North Carolina; but Mr. Gilmore, finding that his State was likely to secede, was reluctantly compelled to decline it. He was, in fact, sincerely and profoundly anxious that the South should be honestly represented in his councils by men who had an abiding-place in the hearts of her people. To accomplish that high purpose, he was forced to go beyond the ranks of his own party; and he had the manliness to do it. He felt that his strength lay in conciliation at the outset: that was his ruling conviction during all those months of preparation for the great task before him. It showed itself, not only in the appointments which he sought to make, but in those which he did make. Harboring no jealousies, entertaining no fears concerning his personal interests in the future, he called around him the most powerful of his late rivals, — Seward, Chase, Bates, — and unhesitatingly gave into their hands powers which most presidents would have shrunk from committing to their equals, and much more to their superiors in the conduct of public affairs.

The cases of Cameron and Smith, however, were very distressing. He had authorized no one to make such bargains for him as had been made with the friends of these men. He would gladly have repudiated the contracts, if it could have been done with honor and safety. For Smith he had great regard, and believed that he had rendered important services in the late elections. But his character was now grossly assailed; and it would have saved Mr. Lincoln serious embarrassments if he had been able to put him aside altogether, and select Mr. Lane or some other Indiana statesman in his place. He wavered long, but finally made up his mind to keep the pledge of his friends; and Smith was appointed.

In Cameron's case the contest was fierce and more protracted. At Chicago, Cameron's agents had demanded that he should have the Treasury Department; but that was too much; and the friends of Mr. Lincoln, tried, pushed, and anxious as they were, declined to consider it. They would say that he should be appointed to *a* Cabinet position, but no more; and to secure this, he must get a majority of the Pennsylvania delegation to recommend him. Mr. Cameron was disposed to exact the penalty of his bond, hard as compliance might be on the part of Mr. Lincoln. But Cameron had many and formidable enemies, who alleged that he was a man notorious for his evil deeds, shameless in his rapacity and corruption, and even more shameless in his mean ambition to occupy exalted stations, for which he was utterly and hopelessly incompetent; that he had never dared to offer himself as a candidate before the people of Pennsylvania, but had more than once gotten high offices from the Legislature by the worst means ever used by a politician; and that it would be a disgrace, a shame, a standing offence to the country, if Mr. Lincoln should consent to put him into his Cabinet. On the other hand, Mr. Cameron had no lack of devoted friends to deny these charges, and to say that his was as "white a soul" as ever yearned for political preferment: they came out to Springfield in numbers, — Edgar Cowan, J. K. Moorehead, Alexander Cummins, Mr. Sanderson, Mr. Casey, and many others, besides Gen. Cameron

himself.   On the ground, of course, were the powerful gentlemen who had made the original contract on the part of
Mr. Lincoln, and who, from first to last, strenuously insisted
upon its fulfilment.   It required a hard struggle to overcome
Mr. Lincoln's scruples; and the whole force was necessarily
mustered in order to accomplish it.   "All that I am in the
world," said he, — " the Presidency and all else, — I owe to
that opinion of me which the people express when they call
me ' honest Old Abe.'   Now, what will they think of their
honest Abe, when he appoints Simon Cameron to be his
familiar adviser ? "

In Pennsylvania it was supposed for a while that Cameron's audacity had failed him, and that he would abandon the
attempt.   But about the 1st of January Mr. Swett, one of
the contracting parties, appeared at Harrisburg, and immediately afterwards Cameron and .some of his friends took
flight to Springfield.   This circumstance put the vigilant
opposition on the alert, and aroused them to a clear sense of
the impending calamity.   The sequel is a painful story ; and
it is, perhaps, better to give it in the words of a distinguished
actor, — Col. Alexander K. McClure.   " I do not know," says
he, " that any went there to oppose the appointment but
myself.   When I learned that Cameron had started to Springfield, and that his visit related to the Cabinet, I at once
telegraphed Lincoln that such an appointment would be
most unfortunate.   Until that time, no one outside a small
circle of Cameron's friends dreamed of Lincoln's calling him
to the Cabinet.   Lincoln's character for honesty was considered a complete guaranty against such a suicidal act.   No
efforts had therefore been made to guard against it.

" In reply to my telegram, Mr. Lincoln answered, requesting
me to come to Springfield at once.   I hastily got letters from
Gov. Curtin, Secretary Slifer, Mr. Wilmot, Mr. Dayton, Mr.
Stevens, and started.   I took no affidavits with me, nor were
any specific charges made against him by me, or by any of
the letters I bore ; but they all sustained me in the allegation, that the appointment would disgrace the administration

and the country, because of the notorious incompetency and public and private villany of the candidate. I spent four hours with Mr. Lincoln alone; and the matter was discussed very fully and frankly. Although he had previously decided to appoint Cameron, he closed our interview by a reconsideration of his purpose, and the assurance that within twenty-four hours he would write me definitely on the subject. He wrote me, as he promised, and stated, that, if I would make specific charges against Mr. Cameron, and produce the proof, he would dismiss the subject. I answered, declining to do so for reasons I thought should be obvious to every one. I believe that affidavits were sent to him, but I had no hand in it.

"Subsequently Cameron regarded his appointment as impossible, and he proposed to Stevens to join in pressing *him*. Stevens wrote me of the fact; and I procured strong letters from the State administration in his favor. A few days after Stevens wrote me a most bitter letter, saying that Cameron had deceived him, and was then attempting to enforce his own appointment. The bond was demanded of Lincoln; and that decided the matter." [1]

---

[1] As this was one of the few public acts which Mr. Lincoln performed with a bad conscience, the reader ought to know the consequences of it; and, because it may not be convenient to revert to them in detail at another place, we give them here, still retaining the language of the eye-witness, Col. McClure: —

. "I saw Cameron the night of the day that Lincoln removed him. We met in the room of a mutual friend, and he was very violent against Lincoln *for removing him without consultation or notice.* His denunciation against the President was extremely bitter, for attempting, as he said, his 'personal as well as his political destruction.' He exhibited the letter, which was all in Mr. Lincoln's handwriting, and was literally as follows. I quote from carefully-treasured recollection: —

"'HON. SIMON CAMERON, SECRETARY OF WAR.

Dear Sir. — I have this day nominated Hon. Edwin M. Stanton to be Secretary of War, and you to be Minister Plenipotentiary to Russia.
                                                          Very truly,
                                                                 A. LINCOLN.'

"I am sure there is no material error in my quotation of the letter.

"Cameron's chief complaint was, that he had no knowledge or intimation of the change until Chase delivered the letter. We were then, as ever before and since, and as we ever shall be, not in political sympathy, but our personal relations were ever kind. Had he been entirely collected, he would probably not have said and done what I heard and witnessed; but he wept like a child, and appealed to me to aid in protecting him against the President's attempt at personal degradation, assuring me that under like circumstances he

As a slight relief to the miseries of his high position, and the doleful tales of the office-hunters, who assailed him morning, noon, and night, Mr. Lincoln ran off to Chicago, where he met with the same annoyances, and a splendid reception besides. Here, however, he enjoyed the great satisfaction of a long private conference with his old friend Speed; and it was then that he authorized him to invite Mr. Guthrie to the Cabinet.

And now he began to think very tenderly of his friends and relatives in Coles County, especially of his good stepmother and her daughters. By the first of February, he concluded that he could not leave his home to assume the vast responsibilities that awaited him without paying them a visit. Accordingly, he left Springfield on the first day of that month, and went straight to Charleston, where Col. Chapman and family resided. He was accompanied by Mr. Marshall, the State Senator from that district, and was entertained at his house. The people crowded by hundreds to see him; and he was serenaded by " both the string and brass bands of the town, but declined making a speech." Early the next morning, he repaired " to his cousin, Dennis Hanks ; " and our jolly old friend Dennis had the satisfaction of seeing a grand levee under his own roof. It was all very pleasant to Mr. Lincoln to see such multitudes of familiar faces smiling upon his wonderful successes. But the chief object of his solicitude was not here; Mrs. Lincoln lived in the southern part of the county, and he was all impatience to see her. As soon, therefore, as he had taken a frugal breakfast with Dennis, he and Col. Chapman started off in a " two-horse buggy " toward Farmington, where his step-mother was living with her daughter, Mrs. Moore. They had much difficulty in crossing " the

would defend me. In my presence the proposition was made and determined upon to ask Lincoln to allow a letter of resignation to be antedated, and to write a kind acceptance of the same in reply. The effort was made, in which Mr. Chase joined, although perhaps ignorant of all the circumstances of the case; and it succeeded. The *record* shows that Mr. Cameron voluntarily resigned; while, in point of fact, he was summarily removed without notice.

" In many subsequent conversations with Mr. Lincoln, he did not attempt to conceal the great misfortune of Cameron's appointment and the painful necessity of his removal."

Kickapoo" River, which was running full of ice ; but they finally made the dangerous passage, and arrived at Farmington in safety. The meeting between him and the old lady was of a most affectionate and tender character. She fondled him as her own "Abe," and he her as his own mother. It was soon arranged that she should return with him to Charleston, so that they might enjoy by the way the unrestricted and uninterrupted intercourse which they both desired above all things, but which they were not likely to have where the people could get at him. Then Mr. Lincoln and Col. Chapman drove to the house of John Hall, who lived "on the old Lincoln farm," where Abe split the celebrated rails, and fenced in the little clearing in 1830. Thence they went to the spot where old Tom Lincoln was buried. The grave was unmarked and utterly neglected. Mr. Lincoln said he wanted to "have it enclosed, and a suitable tombstone erected." He told Col. Chapman to go to a "marble-dealer," ascertain the cost of the work proposed, and write him in full. He would then send Dennis Hanks the money, and an inscription for the stone ; and Dennis would do the rest. (Col. Chapman performed his part of the business, but Mr. Lincoln noticed it no further ; and the grave remains in the same condition to this day.)

"We then returned," says Col. Chapman, "to Farmington, where we found a large crowd of citizens — nearly all old acquaintances — waiting to see him. His reception was very enthusiastic, and appeared to gratify him very much. After taking dinner at his step-sister's (Mrs. Moore), we returned to Charleston, his step-mother coming with us.

"Our conversation during the trip was mostly concerning family affairs. Mr. Lincoln spoke to me on the way down to Farmington of his step-mother in the most affectionate manner ; said she had been his best friend in the world, and that no son could love a mother more than he loved her. He also told me of the condition of his father's family at the time he married his step-mother, and of the change she made in the family, and of the encouragement he (Abe) received from her. . . . He spoke of his father, and related some amusing incidents of the old man; of the bull-dogs' biting the old man on his return from New Orleans; of the old man's escape, when a boy, from an Indian who was shot by his uncle Mordecai. He spoke of his uncle Mordecai as being a man of very great natural gifts, and spoke of his step-brother, John D. Johnston, who had died a short time previous, in the most affectionate manner.

"Arriving at Charleston on our return from Farmington, we proceeded to my residence. Again the house was crowded by persons wishing to see him. The crowd finally became so great, that he authorized me to announce that he would hold a public reception at the Town Hall that evening at seven o'clock; but that, until then, he wished to be left with relations and friends. After supper he proceeded to the Town Hall, where large numbers from the town and surrounding country, irrespective of party, called to see him.

"He left this place Wednesday morning at four o'clock to return to Springfield. . . . Mr. Lincoln appeared to enjoy his visit here remarkably well. His reception by his old acquaintances appeared to be very gratifying to him. They all appeared so glad to see him, irrespective of party, and all appeared so anxious that his administration might be a success, and that he might have a pleasant and honorable career as President."

The parting between Mr. Lincoln and his mother was very touching. She embraced him with deep emotion, and said she was sure she would never behold him again, for she felt that his enemies would assassinate him. He replied, "No, no, mamma: they will not do that. Trust in the Lord, and all will be well: we will see each other again." Inexpressibly affected by this new evidence of her tender attachment and deep concern for his safety, he gradually and reluctantly withdrew himself from the arms of the only mother he had ever known, feeling still more oppressed by the heavy cares which time and events were rapidly augmenting.

The fear that Mr. Lincoln would be assassinated was not

peculiar to his step-mother. It was shared by very many of his neighbors at Springfield; and the friendly warnings he received were as numerous as they were silly and gratuitous. Every conceivable precaution was suggested. Some thought the cars might be thrown from the track; some thought he would be surrounded and stabbed in some great crowd; others thought he might be shot from a house-top as he rode up Pennsylvania Avenue on inauguration day; while others still were sure he would be quietly poisoned long before the 4th of March. One gentleman insisted that he ought, in common prudence, to take his cook with him from Springfield, — one from " among his own female friends."

Mingled with the thousands who came to see him were many of his old New-Salem and Petersburg friends and constituents; and among these was Hannah Armstrong, the wife of Jack and the mother of William. Hannah had been to see him once or twice before, and had thought there was something mysterious in his conduct. He never invited her to his house, or introduced her to his wife; and this circumstance led Hannah to suspect that " there was something wrong between him and her." On one occasion she attempted a sort of surreptitious entrance to his house by the kitchen door; but it ended very ludicrously, and poor Hannah was very much discouraged. On this occasion she made no effort to get upon an intimate footing with his family, but went straight to the State House, where he received the common run of strangers. He talked to her as he would have done in the days when he ran for the Legislature, and Jack was an " influential citizen." Hannah was perfectly charmed, and nearly beside herself with pride and pleasure. She, too, was filled with the dread of some fatal termination to all his glory. " Well," says she, " I talked to him some time, and was about to bid him good-by; had told him that it was the last time I should ever see him: something told me that I should never see him; they would kill him. He smiled, and said jokingly, ' Hannah, if they do kill me, I shall never die another death.' I then bade him good-by."

30

CHAPTER XIX.

IT was now but a few weeks until Mr. Lincoln was to become the constitutional ruler of one of the great nations of the earth, and to begin to expend appropriations, to wield armies, to apportion patronage, powers, offices, and honors, such as few sovereigns have ever had at command. The eyes of all mankind were bent upon him to see how he would solve a problem in statesmanship to which the philosophy of Burke and the magnanimity of Wellington might have been unequal. In the midst of a political canvass in his own State but a few years before, impressed with the gravity of the great issues which then loomed but just above the political horizon, he had been the first to announce, amid the objections and protestations of his friends and political associates, the great truth, that " a house divided against itself cannot stand; " that the perpetuity of the Union depended upon its becoming devoted either to the interests of freedom or slavery. And now, by a turn of fortune unparalleled in history, he had been chosen to preside over the interests of the nation; while, as yet unseen to him, the question that perplexed the founders of the government, which ever since had been a disturbing element in the national life, and had at last arrayed section against section, was destined to reach its final settlement through the fierce struggle of civil war. In many respects his situation was exceptionally trying. He was the first President of the United States elected by a strictly sectional vote. The party which elected him, and the parties which had been defeated, were inflamed by the heat of the canvass. The former, with faith in their principles, and a natural eagerness for the prizes now within their reach, were not disposed to compromise their first success by any lowering of their standard or any concession to the beaten ; while many of the latter saw in the success of the triumphant party an attack on their most cherished rights, and refused in consequence to abide by the result of the contest. To meet so grave an exigency, Mr. Lincoln had neither precedents nor experience to guide him, nor could he turn elsewhere for greater wisdom than he possessed. The leaders of the new party were as yet untried in the great responsibilities which had fallen upon him and them. There were men among them who had earned great reputation as leaders of an opposition; but their eloquence had been expended upon a single subject of national concern. They knew how to depict the wrongs of a subject race, and also how to set forth the baleful effects of an institution like slavery on national character. But was it certain that they were equally able to govern with wisdom and prudence the mighty people whose affairs were now given to their keeping ?

Until the day of his overthrow at Chicago, Mr. Seward had been the recognized chief of the party ; had, like Mr. Lincoln, taught the existence of an irrepressible conflict between the North and the South, and had also inculcated the idea of a law higher than the Constitution, which was of more binding force than any human enactment, until many of his followers had come to regard the Constitution with little respect. It was this Constitution which Mr. Lincoln, having sworn to preserve, protect, and defend, was to attempt to administer to the satisfaction of the minority which had elected him, and which was alone expected to support him. To moderate the passions of his own partisans, to conciliate his opponents in the North, and divide and weaken his enemies in the South, was a task which no mere politician was likely to perform, yet one which none but the most expert of politicians and wisest of statesmen was fitted to undertake. It required moral as well as intellectual qualities of the highest order. William of Orange, with a like duty and similar difficulties, was ready at one time and another to give up the effort in despair, although aided by " the divinity that hedges round a king." Few men believed that Mr. Lincoln possessed a single qualification for his great office. His friends had indicated what they considered his chief merit, when they insisted that he was a very common, ordinary man, just like the rest of " the people," — " Old Abe," a rail-splitter and a story-teller. They said he was good and honest and well-meaning ; but they took care not to pretend that he was great. He was thoroughly convinced that there was too much truth in this view of his character. He felt deeply and keenly his lack of experience in the conduct of public affairs. He spoke then and afterwards about the duties of the Presidency with much diffidence, and said, with a story about a justice of the peace in Illinois, that they constituted his " great first case misunderstood." He had never been a ministerial or an executive officer. His most intimate friends feared that he possessed no administrative ability ; and in this opinion he seems to have shared himself, at least in his calmer and more melancholy moments.

Having put his house in order, arranged all his private business, made over his interest in the practice of Lincoln & Herndon to Mr. Herndon, and requested " Billy," as a last favor, to leave his name on the old sign for four years at least, Mr. Lincoln was ready for the final departure from home and all familiar things. And this period of transition from private to public life — a period of waiting and preparing for the vast responsibilities that were to bow down his shoulders during the years to come — affords us a favorable opportunity to turn back and look at him again as his neighbors saw him from 1837 to 1861.

Mr. Lincoln was about six feet four inches high, — the length of his legs being out of all proportion to that of his body. When he sat down on a chair, he seemed no taller than an average man, measuring from the chair to the crown of his head ; but his knees rose high in front, and a marble placed on the cap of one of them would roll down a steep descent to the hip. He weighed about a hundred and eighty pounds; but he was thin through the breast, narrow across the shoulders, and had the general appearance of a consumptive subject. Standing up, he stooped slightly forward; sitting down, he usually crossed his long legs, or threw them over the arms of the chair, as the most convenient mode of disposing of them. His "head was long, and tall from the base of the brain and the eyebrow;" his forehead high and narrow, but inclining backward as it rose. The diameter of his head from ear to ear was six and a half inches, and from front to back eight inches. The size of his hat was seven and an eighth. His ears were large, standing out almost at right-angles from his head; his cheek-bones high and prominent; his eyebrows heavy, and jutting forward over small, sunken blue eyes; his nose long, large, and blunt, the tip of it rather ruddy, and slightly awry toward the right-hand side; his chin, projecting far and sharp, curved upward to meet a thick, material, lower lip, which hung downward; his cheeks were flabby, and the loose skin fell in wrinkles, or folds; there was a large mole on his right cheek, and an uncommonly prominent Adam's apple on his throat; his hair was dark brown in color, stiff, unkempt, and as yet showing little or no sign of advancing age or trouble; his complexion was very dark, his skin yellow, shrivelled, and "leathery." In short, to use the language of Mr. Herndon, "he was a thin, tall, wiry, sinewy, grizzly, raw-boned man," "looking woe-struck." His countenance was haggard and careworn, exhibiting all the marks of deep and protracted suffering. Every feature of the man — the hollow eyes, with the dark rings beneath; the long, sallow, cadaverous face, intersected by those peculiar deep lines; his whole air; his walk; his long, silent reveries, broken at long intervals by sudden and startling exclamations, as if to confound an observer who might suspect the nature of his thoughts — showed he was a man of sorrows, — not sorrows of to-day or yesterday, but long-treasured and deep, — bearing with him a continual sense of weariness and pain.

He was a plain, homely, sad, weary-looking man, to whom one's heart warmed involuntarily, because he seemed at once miserable and kind.

On a winter's morning, this man could be seen wending his way to the market, with a basket on his arm, and a little boy at his side, whose small feet rattled and pattered over the ice-bound pavement, attempting to make up by the number of his short steps for the long strides of his father. The little fellow jerked at the bony hand which held his, and prattled and questioned, begged and grew petulant, in a vain effort to make his father talk to him. But the latter was probably unconscious of the other's existence, and stalked on, absorbed in his own reflections. He wore on such occasions an old gray shawl, rolled into a coil, and wrapped like a rope around his neck. The rest of his clothes were in keeping. "He did not walk cunningly, — Indian-like, — but cautiously and firmly." His tread was even and strong. He was a little pigeon-toed; and this, with another peculiarity, made his walk very singular. He set his whole foot flat on the ground, and in turn lifted it all at once, — not resting momentarily upon the toe as the foot rose, nor upon the heel as it fell. He never wore his shoes out at the heel and the toe more, as most men do, than at the middle of the sole; yet his gait was not altogether awkward, and there was manifest physical power in his step. As he moved along thus silent, abstracted, his thoughts dimly reflected in his sharp face, men turned to look after him as an object of sympathy as well as curiosity: "his melancholy," in the words of Mr. Herndon, "dripped from him as he walked." If, however, he met a friend in the street, and was roused by a loud, hearty "Good-morning, Lincoln!" he would grasp the friend's hand with one or both of his own, and, with his usual expression of "Howdy, howdy," would detain him to hear a story: something reminded him of it; it happened in Indiana, and it must be told, for it was wonderfully pertinent.

After his breakfast-hour, he would appear at his office, and go about the labors of the day with all his might, displaying prodigious industry and capacity for continuous application, although he never was a fast worker. Sometimes it happened that he came without his breakfast; and then he would have in his hands a piece of cheese, or Bologna sausage, and a few crackers, bought by the way. At such times he did not speak to his partner or his friends, if any happened to be present: the tears were, perhaps, struggling into his eyes, while his pride was struggling to keep them back. Mr. Herndon knew the whole story at a glance: there was no speech between them; but neither wished the visitors to the office to witness the scene; and, therefore, Mr. Lincoln retired to the back office, while Mr. Herndon locked the front one, and walked away with the key in his pocket. In an hour or more the latter would return, and perhaps find Mr. Lincoln calm and collected; otherwise he went out again, and waited until he was so. Then the office was opened, and every thing went on as usual.

When Mr. Lincoln had a speech to write, which happened very often, he would put down each thought, as it struck him, on a small strip of paper, and, having accumulated a number of these, generally carried them in his hat or his pockets until he had the whole speech composed in this odd way, when he would sit down at his table, connect the fragments, and then write out the whole speech on consecutive sheets in a plain, legible handwriting.

His house was an ordinary two-story frame-building, with a stable and a yard: it was a bare, cheerless sort of a place. He planted no fruit or shade trees, no shrubbery or flowers. He did on one occasion set out a few rose-bushes in front of his house; but they speedily perished, or became unsightly for want of attention. Mrs. Wallace, Mrs. Lincoln's sister, undertook "to hide the nakedness" of the place by planting some flowers; but they soon withered and died. He cultivated a small garden for a single year, working in it himself; but it did not seem to prosper, and that enterprise also was abandoned. He had a horse and a cow: the one was fed and curried, and the other fed and milked, by his own hand. When at home, he chopped and sawed all the wood that was used in his house. Late one night he returned home, after an absence of a week or so. His neighbor, Webber, was in bed; but, hearing an axe in use at that unusual hour, he rose to see what it meant. The moon was high; and by its light he looked down into Lincoln's yard, and there saw him in his shirt-sleeves " cutting wood to cook his supper with." Webber turned to his watch, and saw that it was one o'clock. Besides this house and lot, and a small sum of money, Mr. Lincoln had no property, except some wild land in Iowa, entered for him under warrants, received for his service in the Black Hawk War.

Mrs. Wallace thinks " Mr. Lincoln was a domestic man by nature." He was not fond of other people's children, but was extremely fond of his own : he was patient, indulgent, and generous with them to a fault. On Sundays he often took those that were large enough, and walked with them into the country, and, giving himself up entirely to them, rambled through the green fields or the cool woods, amusing and instructing them for a whole day at a time. His method of reading is thus quaintly described. " He would read, generally aloud (couldn't read otherwise), — would read with great warmth, all funny or humorous things; read Shakspeare that way. He was a sad man, an abstracted man. He would lean back, his head against the top of a rocking-chair; sit abstracted that way for minutes, — twenty, thirty minutes, — and all at once would burst out into a joke."

Mrs. Col. Chapman, daughter of Dennis Hanks, and therefore a relative of Mr. Lincoln, made him a long visit previous to her marriage. " You ask me," says she, " how Mr. Lincoln acted at home. I can say, and that truly, he was all that a husband, father, and neighbor should be, — kind and affectionate to his wife and child (' Bob ' being the only one they had when I was with them), and very pleasant to all around him. Never did I hear him utter an unkind word. For instance : one day he undertook to correct his child, and his wife was

MR. LINCOLN'S HOME IN SPRINGFIELD, ILL.

determined that he should not, and attempted to take it from him; but in this she failed. She then tried tongue-lashing, but met with the same fate; for Mr. Lincoln corrected his child as a father ought to do, in the face of his wife's anger, and that, too, without even changing his countenance or making any reply to his wife.

"His favorite way of reading, when at home, was lying down on the floor. I fancy I see him now, lying full-length in the hall of his old house reading. When not engaged reading law-books, he would read literary works, and was very fond of reading poetry, and often, when he would be, or appear to be, in deep study, commence and repeat aloud some piece that he had taken a fancy to, such as the one you already have in print, and 'The Burial of Sir John Moore,' and so on. He often told laughable jokes and stories when he thought we were looking gloomy."

Mr. Lincoln was not supremely happy in his domestic relations: the circumstances of his courtship and marriage alone made that impossible. His engagement to Miss Todd was one of the great misfortunes of his life and of hers. He realized the mistake too late; and when he was brought face to face with the lie he was about to enact, and the wrong he was about to do, both to himself and an innocent woman, he recoiled with horror and remorse. For weeks together, he was sick, deranged, and on the verge of suicide, — a heavy care to his friends, and a source of bitter mortification to the unfortunate lady, whose good fame depended, in a great part, upon his constancy. The wedding garments and the marriage feast were prepared, the very hour had come when the solemn ceremony was to be performed; and the groom failed to appear! He was no longer a free agent: he was restrained, carefully guarded, and soon after removed to a distant place, where the exciting causes of his disease would be less constant and active in their operation. He recovered slowly, and at length returned to Springfield. He spoke out his feelings frankly and truly to the one person most interested in them. But he had been, from the beginning, except in the case of

Ann Rutledge, singularly inconstant and unstable in his relations with the few refined and cultivated women who had been the objects of his attention. He loved Miss Rutledge passionately, and the next year importuned Miss Owens to be his wife. Failing in his suit, he wrote an unfeeling letter about her, apparently with no earthly object but to display his levity and make them both ridiculous. He courted Miss Todd, and at the moment of success fell in love with her relative, and, between the two, went crazy, and thought of ending all his woes with a razor or a pocket-knife. It is not impossible that the feelings of such a man might have undergone another and more sudden change. Perhaps they did. At all events, he was conscientious and honorable and just. There was but one way of repairing the injury he had done Miss Todd, and he adopted it. They were married; but they understood each other, and suffered the inevitable consequences, as other people do under similar circumstances. But such troubles seldom fail to find a tongue; and it is not strange, that, in this case, neighbors and friends, and ultimately the whole country, came to know the state of things in that house. Mr. Lincoln scarcely attempted to conceal it, but talked of it with little or no reserve to his wife's relatives, as well as his own friends. Yet the gentleness and patience with which he bore this affliction from day to day, and from year to year, was enough to move the shade of Socrates. It touched his acquaintances deeply, and they gave it the widest publicity. They made no pause to inquire, to investigate, and to apportion the blame between the parties, according to their deserts. Almost ever since Mr. Lincoln's death, a portion of the press has never tired of heaping brutal reproaches upon his wife and widow; whilst a certain class of his friends thought they were honoring his memory by multiplying outrages and indignities upon her, at the very moment when she was broken by want and sorrow, defamed, defenceless, in the hands of thieves, and at the mercy of spies. If ever a woman grievously expiated an offence not her own, this woman did. In the Herndon manuscripts, there is a mass of particulars under this head ; but Mr. Herndon sums them all up in a single sentence, in a letter to one of Mr. Lincoln's biographers : " All that I know ennobles both."

It would be very difficult to recite all the causes of Mr. Lincoln's melancholy disposition. That it was partly owing to physical causes there can be no doubt. Mr. Stuart says, that in some respects he was totally unlike other people, and was, in fact, a " mystery." Blue-pills were the medicinal remedy which he affected most. But whatever the history or the cause, — whether physical reasons, the absence of domestic concord, a series of painful recollections of his mother, of his father and master, of early sorrows, blows, and hardships, of Ann Rutledge and fruitless hopes, or all these combined, Mr. Lincoln was the saddest and gloomiest man of his time. " I do not think that he knew what happiness was for twenty years," says Mr. Herndon. " Terrible " is the word which all his friends use to describe him in the black mood. " It was terrible ! It was terrible ! " says one and another.

His mind was filled with gloomy forebodings and strong apprehensions of impending evil, mingled with extravagant visions of personal grandeur and power. His imagination painted a scene just beyond the veil of the immediate future, gilded with glory yet tarnished with blood. It was his " destiny," — splendid but dreadful, fascinating but terrible. His case bore little resemblance to those of religious enthusiasts like Bunyan, Cowper, and others. His was more like the delusion of the fatalist, conscious of his star. At all events, he never doubted for a moment but that he was formed for " some great or miserable end." He talked about it frequently and sometimes calmly. Mr. Herndon remembers many of these conversations in their office at Springfield, and in their rides around the circuit. Mr. Lincoln said the impression had grown in him " all his life ; " but Mr. Herndon thinks it was about 1840 that it took the character of a " religious conviction." He had then suffered much, and, considering his opportunities, achieved great things. He was already a leader among men, and a most brilliant career had been promised him by the prophetic enthusiasm of many friends. Thus encouraged and stimulated, and feeling himself growing gradually stronger and stronger, in the estimation of " the plain people," whose voice was more potent than all the Warwicks, his ambition painted the rainbow of glory in the sky, while his morbid melancholy supplied the clouds that were to overcast and obliterate it with the wrath and ruin of the tempest. To him it was fate, and there was no escape or defence. The presentiment never deserted him : it was as clear, as perfect, as certain, as any image conveyed by the senses. He had now entertained it so long, that it was as much a part of his nature as the consciousness of identity. All doubts had faded away, and he submitted humbly to a power which he could neither comprehend nor resist. He was to fall, — fall from a lofty place, and in the performance of a great work. The star under which he was born was at once brilliant and malignant: the horoscope was cast, fixed, irreversible ; and he had no more power to alter or defeat it in the minutest particular than he had to reverse the law of gravitation.

After the election, he conceived that he would not "last" through his term of office, but had at length reached the point where the sacrifice would take place. All precautions against assassination he considered worse than useless. " If they want to kill me," said he, " there is nothing to prevent." He complained to Mr. Gillespie of the small body-guard which his counsellors had forced upon him, insisting that they were a needless encumbrance. When Mr. Gillespie urged the ease and impunity with which he might be killed, and the value of his life to the country, he said, " What is the use of putting up the *gap* when the fence is down all around?"

" It was just after my election in 1860," said Mr. Lincoln to his secretary, John Hay, " when the news had been coming in thick and fast all day, and there had been a great ' hurrah boys !' so that I was well tired out, and went home to rest, throwing myself upon a lounge in my chamber.

Opposite to where I lay was a bureau with a swinging glass upon it; and, in looking in that glass, I saw myself reflected nearly at full length; but my face, I noticed, had two separate and distinct images, the tip of the nose of one being about three inches from the tip of the other. I was a little bothered, perhaps startled, and got up and looked in the glass; but the illusion vanished. On lying down again, I saw it a second time, — plainer, if possible, than before; and then I noticed that one of the faces was a little paler — say five shades — than the other. I got up, and the thing melted away; and I went off, and in the excitement of the hour forgot all about it, — nearly, but not quite, for the thing would once in a while come up, and give me a little pang, as though something uncomfortable had happened. When I went home, I told my wife about it: and a few days after I tried the experiment again, when, sure enough, the thing came back again; but I never succeeded in bringing the ghost back after that, though I once tried very industriously to show it to my wife, who was worried about it somewhat. She thought it was ' a sign ' that I was to be elected to a second term of office, and that the paleness of one of the faces was an omen that I should not see life through the last term."

In this morbid and dreamy state of mind, Mr. Lincoln passed the greater part of his life. But his " sadness, despair, gloom," Mr. Herndon says, " were not of the kind that leads a badly-balanced mind into misanthropy and universal hate and scorn. His humor would assert itself from the hell of misanthropy: it would assert its independence every third hour or day or week. His abstractedness, his continuity of thought, his despair, made him, twice in his life, for two weeks at a time, walk that narrow line that divides sanity from insanity. . . . This peculiarity of his nature, his humor, his wit, kept him alive in his mind. . . . It was those good sides of his nature that made, to him, his life bearable. Mr. Lincoln was a weak man and a strong man by turns."

Some of Mr. Lincoln's literary tastes indicated strongly his prevailing gloominess of mind. He read Byron extensively, especially "Childe Harold," "The Dream," and "Don Juan." Burns was one of his earliest favorites, although there is no evidence that he appreciated highly the best efforts of Burns. On the contrary, "Holy Willie's Prayer" was the only one of his poems which Mr. Lincoln took the trouble to memorize. He was fond of Shakspeare, especially "King Lear," and "The Merry Wives of Windsor." But whatever was suggestive of death, the grave, the sorrows of man's days on earth, charmed his disconsolate spirit, and captivated his sympathetic heart. Solemn-sounding rhymes, with no merit but the sad music of their numbers, were more enchanting to him than the loftiest songs of the masters. Of these were, "Why should the Spirit of Mortal be Proud?" and a pretty commonplace little piece, entitled "The Inquiry." One verse of Holmes's "Last Leaf" he thought was "inexpressibly touching." This verse we give the reader: —

> " The mossy marbles rest
>   On the lips that he has pressed
>   In their bloom ;
>   And the names he loved to hear
>   Have been carved for many a year
>   On the tomb."

Mr. Lincoln frequently said that he lived by his humor, and would have died without it. His manner of telling a story was irresistibly comical, the fun of it dancing in his eyes and playing over every feature. His face changed in an instant: the hard lines faded out of it, and the mirth seemed to diffuse itself all over him, like a spontaneous tickle. You could see it coming long before he opened his mouth, and he began to enjoy the "point" before his eager auditors could catch the faintest glimpse of it. Telling and hearing ridiculous stories was one of his ruling passions. He would go a long way out of his road to tell a grave, sedate fellow a broad story, or to propound to him a conundrum that was not particularly remarkable for its delicacy. If he happened to hear of a man who was known to have something fresh in this line, he would hunt him up, and "swap jokes" with him. Nobody remembers the time when his fund of anecdotes was not apparently inexhaustible. It was so in Indiana; it was so in New Salem, in the Black-Hawk War, in the Legislature, in Congress, on the circuit, on the stump, — everywhere. The most trifling incident "reminded" him of a story, and that story reminded him of another, until everybody marvelled "that one small head could carry all he knew." The "good things" he said were repeated at second-hand, all over the counties through which he chanced to travel; and many, of a questionable flavor, were attributed to him, not because they were his in fact, but because they were like his. Judges, lawyers, jurors, and suitors carried home with them select budgets of his stories, to be retailed to itching ears as "Old Abe's last." When the court adjourned from village to village, the taverns and the groceries left behind were filled with the sorry echoes of his "best." He generally located his little narratives with great precision, — in Kentucky, Indiana, Illinois; and if he was not personally "knowing" to the facts himself, he was intimately acquainted with a gentleman who was.

Mr. Lincoln used his stories variously, — to illustrate or convey an argument; to make his opinions clear to another, or conceal them altogether; to cut off a disagreeable conversation, or to end an unprofitable discussion; to cheer his own heart, or simply to amuse his friends. But most frequently he had a practical object in view, and employed them simply "as labor-saving contrivances."

It was Judge Davis's opinion, that Mr. Lincoln's hilarity was mainly simulated, and that "his stories and jokes were intended to whistle off sadness." "The groundwork of his social nature was sad," says Judge Scott; "but for the fact that he studiously cultivated the humorous, it would have been very sad indeed. His mirth to me always seemed to be put on, and did not properly belong there. Like a plant produced in the hot-bed, it had an unnatural and luxuriant growth."

Although Mr. Lincoln's walk among men was remarkably

pure, the same cannot be said of his conversation. He was endowed by nature with a keen sense of humor, and he found great delight in indulging it. But his humor was not of a delicate quality; it was chiefly exercised in hearing and telling stories of the grosser sort. In this tendency he was restrained by no presence and no occasion. It was his opinion that the finest wit and humor, the best jokes and anecdotes, emanated from the lower orders of the country people. It was from this source that he had acquired his peculiar tastes and his store of materials. The associations which began with the early days of Dennis Hanks continued through his life at New Salem and his career at the Illinois Bar, and did not desert him when, later in life, he arrived at the highest dignities.

Mr. Lincoln indulged in no sensual excesses: he ate moderately, and drank temperately when he drank at all. For many years he was an ardent agitator against the use of intoxicating beverages, and made speeches, far and near, in favor of total abstinence. Some of them were printed; and of one he was not a little proud. He abstained himself, not so much upon principle, as because of a total lack of appetite. He had no taste for spirituous liquors; and, when he took them, it was a punishment to him, not an indulgence. But he disliked sumptuary laws, and would not prescribe by statute what other men should eat or drink. When the temperance men ran to the Legislature to invoke the power of the State, his voice — the most eloquent among them — was silent. He did not oppose them, but quietly withdrew from the cause, and left others to manage it. In 1854 he was induced to join the order called Sons of Temperance, but never attended a single meeting after the one at which he was initiated.

Morbid, moody, meditative, thinking much of himself and the things pertaining to himself, regarding other men as instruments furnished to his hand for the accomplishment of views which he knew were important to him, and, therefore, considered important to the public, Mr. Lincoln was a man

apart from the rest of his kind, unsocial, cold, impassive, —
neither a "good hater" nor a fond friend. He unbent in the
society of those who gave him new ideas, who listened to and
admired him, whose attachment might be useful, or whose
conversation amused him. He seemed to make boon-
companions of the coarsest men on the list of his acquaintances, — "low, vulgar, unfortunate creatures;" but,
as Judge Davis has it, "he used such men as tools, —
things to satisfy him, to feed his desires." He felt sorry
for them, enjoyed them, extracted from them whatever service they were capable of rendering, discarded and forgot
them. If one of them, presuming upon the past, followed
him to Washington with a view to personal profit, Mr. Lincoln would probably take him to his private room, lock the
doors, revel in reminiscences of Illinois, new stories and old,
through an entire evening, and then dismiss his enchanted
crony with nothing more substantial than his blessing. It
was said that "he had no heart;" that is, no personal attach-
ments warm and strong enough to govern his actions. It
was seldom that he praised anybody; and, when he did, it was
not a rival or an equal in the struggle for popularity and
power. His encomiums were more likely to be satirical than
sincere, and sometimes were artfully contrived as mere strata-
gems to catch the applause he pretended to bestow, or at least
to share it in equal parts. No one knew better how to
"damn with faint praise," or to divide the glory of another
by being the first and frankest to acknowledge it. Fully
alive to the fact that no qualities of a public man are so
charming to the people as simplicity and candor, he made
simplicity and candor the mask of deep feelings carefully
concealed, and subtle plans studiously veiled from all eyes
but one. He had no reverence for great men, followed no
leader with blind devotion, and yielded no opinion to mere
authority. He felt that he was as great as anybody, and
could do what another did. It was, however, the supreme
desire of his heart to be right, and to do justice in all the
relations of life. Although some of his strongest passions

31

conflicted more or less directly with this desire, he was conscious of them, and strove to regulate them by self-imposed restraints. He was not avaricious, never appropriated a cent wrongfully, and did not think money for its own sake a fit object of any man's ambition. But he knew its value, its power, and liked to keep it when he had it. He gave occasionally to individual mendicants, or relieved a case of great destitution at his very door; but his alms-giving was neither profuse nor systematic. He never made donations to be distributed to the poor who were not of his acquaintance and very near at hand. There were few entertainments at his house. People were seldom asked to dine with him. To many he seemed inhospitable; and there was something about his house, an indescribable air of exclusiveness, which forbade the entering guest. It is not meant to be said that this came from mere economy. It was not at home that he wished to see company. He preferred to meet his friends abroad, — on a street-corner, in an office, at the Court House, or sitting on nail-kegs in a country store.

Mr. Lincoln took no part in the promotion of local enterprises, railroads, schools, churches, asylums. The benefits he proposed for his fellow-men were to be accomplished by political means alone. Politics were his world, — a world filled with hopeful enchantments. Ordinarily he disliked to discuss any other subject. "In his office," says Mr. Herndon, "he sat down, or spilt himself, on his lounge, read aloud, told stories, talked politics, — never science, art, literature, railroad gatherings, colleges, asylums, hospitals, commerce, education, progress, nothing that interested the world generally," except politics. He seldom took an active part in local or minor elections, or wasted his power to advance a friend. He did nothing out of mere gratitude, and forgot the devotion of his warmest partisans as soon as the occasion for their services had passed. What they did for him was quietly appropriated as the reward of superior merit, calling for no return in kind. He was always ready to do battle for a principle, after a discreet fashion, but never permitted himself to be strongly influenced by the claims of individual men. When he was a candidate himself, he thought the whole canvass and all the preliminaries ought to be conducted with reference to his success. He would say to a man, " Your continuance in the field injures *me*," and be quite sure that he had given a perfect reason for his withdrawal. He would have no " obstacles " in his way ; coveted honors, was eager for power, and impatient of any interference that delayed or obstructed his progress. He worked hard enough at general elections, when he could make speeches, have them printed, and " fill the speaking trump of fame " with his achievements ; but in the little affairs about home, where it was all work and no glory, his zeal was much less conspicuous. Intensely secretive and cautious, he shared his secrets with no man, and revealed just enough of his plans to allure support, and not enough to expose their personal application. After Speed left, he had no intimates to whom he opened his whole mind. This is the unanimous testimony of all who knew him. Feeling himself perfectly competent to manage his own affairs, he listened with deceptive patience to the views of others, and then dismissed the advice with the adviser. Judge Davis was supposed to have great influence over him ; but he declares that he had literally none. " Once or twice," says he, " he asked my advice about the almighty dollar, but never about any thing else."

Notwithstanding his overweening ambition, and the breathless eagerness with which he pursued the objects of it, he had not a particle of sympathy with the great mass of his fellow-citizens who were engaged in similar scrambles for place. " If ever," said he, " American society and the United States Government are demoralized and overthrown, it will come from the voracious desire of office, — this wriggle to live without toil, work, and labor, from which I am not free myself."

Mr. Lincoln was not a demagogue or a trimmer. He never deserted a party in disaster, or joined one in triumph. Nearly the whole of his public life was spent in the service of a party which struggled against hopeless odds, which met with many reverses and few victories. It is true, that about the time he began as a politician, the Whigs in his immediate locality, at first united with the moderate Democrats, and afterwards by themselves, were strong enough to help him to the Legislature as often as he chose to go. But, if the fact had been otherwise, it is not likely that he would have changed sides, or even altered his position in any essential particular, to catch the popular favor. Subsequently he suffered many defeats, — for Congress, for Commissioner of the Land Office, and twice for Senator; but on this account he never faltered in devotion to the general principles of the party, or sought to better his fortune by an alliance with the common enemy. It cannot be denied, that, when he was first a candidate for the Legislature, his views of public policy were a little cloudy, and that his addresses to the people were calculated to make fair weather with men of various opinions; nor that, when first a candidate for United States Senator, he was willing to make a secret bargain with the extreme Abolitionists, and, when last a candidate, to make some sacrifice of opinion to further his own aspirations for the Presidency. The pledge to Lovejoy and the "House-divided Speech" were made under the influence of personal considerations, without reference to the views or the success of those who had chosen and trusted him as a leader for a far different purpose. But this was merely steering between sections of his own party, where the differences were slight and easily reconciled, — manœuvring for the strength of one faction to-day and another to-morrow, with intent to unite them and lead them to a victory, the benefits of which would inure to all. He was not one to be last in the fight and first at the feast, nor yet one to be first in the fight and last at the feast. He would do his whole duty in the field, but had not the slightest objection to sitting down at the head of the table, — an act which he would perform with a modest, homely air, that disarmed envy, and silenced the master when he would say, "Friend, go down lower." His "master" was the "plain people." To be popular was to him the greatest good in life. He had known what it was to be without popularity, and he had known what it was to enjoy it. To gain it or to keep it, he considered no labor too great, no artifice misused or misapplied. His ambition was strong; yet it existed in strict subordination to his sense of party fidelity, and could by no chance or possibility lure him into downright social or political treasons. His path may have been a little devious, winding hither and thither, in search of greater convenience of travel, or the security of a larger company; but it always went forward in the same general direction, and never ran off at right-angles toward a hostile camp. The great body of men who acted with him in the beginning acted with him at the last.

On the whole, he was an honest, although a shrewd, and by no means an unselfish politician. He

"Foresaw
Which way the world began to draw,"

and instinctively drew with it. He had convictions, but preferred to choose his time to speak. He was not so much of a Whig that he could not receive the support of the "nominal" Jackson men, until party lines were drawn so tight that he was compelled to be one thing or the other. He was not so much of a Whig that he could not make a small diversion for White in 1836, nor so much of a White man that he could not lead Harrison's friends in the Legislature during the same winter. He was a firm believer in the good policy of high "protective tariffs;" but, when importuned to say so in a public letter, he declined on the ground that it would do him no good. He detested Know-Nothingism with all his heart; but, when Know-Nothingism swept the country, he was so far from being obtrusive with his views, that many believed he belonged to the order. He was an anti-slavery man from the beginning of his service in the Legislature; but he was so cautious and moderate in the expression of his sentiments, that, when the anti-Nebraska party disintegrated, the ultra-Republicans were any thing but sure of his adherence; and even after the Bloomington Convention he continued to pick

his way to the front with wary steps, and did not take his
place among the boldest of the agitators until 1858, when he
uttered the "House-divided Speech," just in time to take
Mr. Seward's place on the Presidential ticket of 1860.

Any analysis of Mr. Lincoln's character would be defective
that did not include his religious opinions. On such matters
he thought deeply; and his opinions were positive. But perhaps no phase of his character has been more persistently
misrepresented and variously misunderstood, than this of his
religious belief. Not that the conclusive testimony of many
of his intimate associates relative to his frequent expressions
on such subjects has ever been wanting; but his great prominence in the world's history, and his identification with some
of the great questions of our time, which, by their moral import, were held to be eminently religious in their character,
have led many good people to trace in his motives and actions
similar convictions to those held by themselves. His extremely
general expressions of religious faith called forth by the grave
exigencies of his public life, or indulged in on occasions of
private condolence, have too often been distorted out of relation to their real significance or meaning to suit the opinions
or tickle the fancies of individuals or parties.

Mr. Lincoln was never a member of any church, nor did
he believe in the divinity of Christ, or the inspiration of the
Scriptures in the sense understood by evangelical Christians.
His theological opinions were substantially those expounded
by Theodore Parker. Overwhelming testimony out of many
mouths, and none stronger than that out of his own, place
these facts beyond controversy.

When a boy, he showed no sign of that piety which
his many biographers ascribe to his manhood. His step-
mother — herself a Christian, and longing for the least sign
of faith in him — could remember no circumstance that supported her hope. On the contrary, she recollected very well
that he never went off into a corner, as has been said,
to ponder the sacred writings, and to wet the page with

his tears of penitence. He was fond of music; but Dennis
Hanks is clear to the point that it was songs of a very
questionable character that cheered his lonely pilgrimage
through the woods of Indiana. When he went to church at
all, he went to mock, and came away to mimic. Indeed, it is
more than probable that the sort of "religion" which prevailed among the associates of his boyhood impressed him
with a very poor opinion of the value of the article. On the
whole, he thought, perhaps, a person had better be without it.

When he came to New Salem, he consorted with free-
thinkers, joined with them in deriding the gospel history
of Jesus, read Volney and Paine, and then wrote a deliberate
and labored essay, wherein he reached conclusions similar to
theirs. The essay was burnt, but he never denied or regretted its composition. On the contrary, he made it the
subject of free and frequent conversations with his friends at
Springfield, and stated, with much particularity and precision,
the origin, arguments, and objects of the work.

It was not until after Mr. Lincoln's death, that his alleged
orthodoxy became the principal topic of his eulogists; but
since then the effort on the part of some political writers
and speakers to impress the public mind erroneously seems
to have been general and systematic. It is important that
the question should be finally determined; and, in order to
do so, the names of some of his nearest friends are given
below, followed by clear and decisive statements, for which
they are separately responsible. Some of them are gentlemen of distinction, and all of them men of high character,
who enjoyed the best opportunities to form correct opinions.

James H. Matheny says in a letter to Mr. Herndon: —

"I knew Mr. Lincoln as early as 1834-7; know he was an infidel. He
and W. D. Herndon used to talk infidelity in the clerk's office in this city,
about the years 1837-40. Lincoln attacked the Bible and the New Testament on two grounds: first, from the inherent or apparent contradic-
tions under its lids; second, from the grounds of reason. Sometimes he
ridiculed the Bible and New Testament, sometimes seemed to scoff it, though
I shall not use that word in its full and literal sense. I never heard that

Lincoln changed his views, though his personal and political friend from 1834 to 1860. Sometimes Lincoln bordered on atheism. He went far that way, and often shocked me. I was then a young man, and believed what my good mother told me. Stuart & Lincoln's office was in what was called Hoffman's Row, on North Fifth Street, near the public square. It was in the same building as the clerk's office, and on the same floor. Lincoln would come into the clerk's office, where I and some young men — Evan Butler, Newton Francis, and others — were writing or staying, and would bring the Bible with him; would read a chapter; argue against it. Lincoln then had a smattering of geology, if I recollect it. Lincoln often, if not wholly, was an atheist; at least, bordered on it. Lincoln was enthusiastic in his infidelity. As he grew older, he grew more discreet, didn't talk much before strangers about his religion; but to friends, close and bosom ones, he was always open and avowed, fair and honest; but to strangers, he held them off from policy. Lincoln used to quote Burns. Burns helped Lincoln to be an infidel, as I think; at least, he found in Burns a like thinker and feeler. Lincoln quoted 'Tam O'Shanter.' 'What! send one to heaven, and ten to hell!' &c.

"From what I know of Mr. Lincoln and his views of Christianity, and from what I know as honest and well-founded rumor; from what I have heard his best friends say and regret for years; from what he never denied when accused, and from what Lincoln has hinted and intimated, to say no more, — he did write a little book on infidelity at or near New Salem, in Menard County, about the year 1834 or 1835. I have stated these things to you often. Judge Logan, John T. Stuart, yourself, know what I know, and some of you more.

"Mr. Herndon, you insist on knowing something which you know I possess, and got as a secret, and that is, about Lincoln's little book on infidelity. Mr. Lincoln *did* tell me that he *did write a little book on infidelity.* This statement I have avoided heretofore; but, as you strongly insist upon it, — probably to defend yourself against charges of misrepresentations, — I give it you as I got it from Lincoln's mouth."

From Hon. John T. Stuart: —

"I knew Mr. Lincoln when he first came here, and for years afterwards. He was an avowed and open infidel, sometimes bordered on atheism. I have often and often heard Lincoln and one W. D. Herndon, who was a freethinker, talk over this subject. Lincoln went further against Christian beliefs and doctrines and principles than any man I ever heard: he shocked me. I don't remember the exact line of his argument: suppose it was against the inherent defects, so called, of the Bible, and on grounds of reason. Lincoln always denied that Jesus was the Christ of God, — denied that Jesus was the Son of God, as understood and maintained by the Christian Church. The Rev. Dr. Smith, who wrote a letter, tried to convert Lincoln from infidelity so late as 1858, and couldn't do it."

William H. Herndon, Esq.: —

"As to Mr. Lincoln's religious views, he was, in short, an infidel, . . . a theist. He did not believe that Jesus was God, nor the Son of God, — was a fatalist, denied the freedom of the will. Mr. Lincoln told me *a thousand times*, that he did not believe the Bible was the revelation of God, as the Christian world contends. The points that Mr. Lincoln tried to demonstrate (in his book) were: First, That the Bible was not God's revelation; and, Second, That Jesus was not the Son of God. *I assert this on my own knowledge, and on my veracity.* Judge Logan, John T. Stuart, James H. Matheny, and others, will tell you the truth. I say they will confirm what I say, with this exception, — they all make it blacker than I remember it. Joshua F. Speed of Louisville, I think, will tell you the same thing."

Hon. David Davis: —

"I do not know any thing about Lincoln's religion, and do not think any-body knew. The idea that Lincoln talked to a stranger about his religion or religious views, or made such speeches, remarks, &c., about it as are pub-lished, is to me absurd. I knew the man so well: he was the most reticent, secretive man I ever saw, or expect to see. He had no faith, in the Christian sense of the term, — had faith in laws, principles, causes, and effects — philo-sophically: you [Herndon] know more about his religion than any man. You ought to know it, of course."

William H. Hannah, Esq.: —

"Since 1856 Mr. Lincoln told me that he was a kind of immortalist; that he never could bring himself to believe in eternal punishment; that man lived but a little while here; and that, if eternal punishment were man's doom, he should spend that little life in vigilant and ceaseless preparation by never-ending prayer."

Mrs. Lincoln: —

"Mr. Lincoln had no hope and no faith in the usual acceptance of those words."

Dr. C. H. Ray: —

"I do not know how I can aid you. You [Herndon] knew Mr. Lincoln far better than I did, though I knew him well; and you have served up his lead-ing characteristics in a way that I should despair of doing, if I should try. I have only one thing to ask: that you do not give Calvinistic theology a chance to claim him as one of its saints and martyrs. He went to the Old-School Church; but, in spite of that outward assent to the horrible dogmas of the sect, *I have reason from himself* to know that his 'vital purity,' if that means belief in the impossible, was of a negative sort."

I. W. Keys, Esq. : —

"In my intercourse with Mr. Lincoln, I learned that he believed in a Creator of all things, who had neither beginning nor end, and possessing all power and wisdom, established a principle, in obedience to which worlds move, and are upheld, and animal and vegetable life come into existence. A reason he gave for his belief was, that, in view of the order and harmony of all nature which we behold, it would have been more miraculous to have come about by chance than to have been created and arranged by some great thinking power. As to the Christian theory, that Christ is God, or equal to the Creator, he said that it had better be taken for granted; for, by the test of reason, we might become infidels on that subject, for evidence of Christ's divinity came to us in a somewhat doubtful shape; but that the system of Christianity was an ingenious one at least, and perhaps was calculated to do good."

Mr. Jesse W. Fell of Illinois, who had the best opportunities of knowing Mr. Lincoln intimately, makes the following statement of his religious opinions, derived from repeated conversations with him on the subject : —

"Though every thing relating to the character and history of this extraordinary personage is of interest, and should be fairly stated to the world, I enter upon the performance of this duty — for so I regard it — with some reluctance, arising from the fact, that, in stating my convictions on the subject, I must necessarily place myself in opposition to quite a number who have written on this topic before me, and whose views largely pre-occupy the public mind. This latter fact, whilst contributing to my embarrassment on this subject, is, perhaps, the strongest reason, however, why the truth in this matter should be fully disclosed; and I therefore yield to your request. If there were any traits of character that stood out in bold relief in the person of Mr. Lincoln, they were those of truth and candor. He was utterly incapable of insincerity, or professing views on this or any other subject he did not entertain. Knowing such to be his true character, that insincerity, much more duplicity, were traits wholly foreign to his nature, many of his old friends were not a little surprised at finding, in some of the biographies of this great man, statements concerning his religious opinions so utterly at variance with his known sentiments. True, he may have changed or modified those sentiments after his removal from among us, though this is hardly reconcilable with the history of the man, and his entire devotion to public matters during his four years' residence at the national capital. It is possible, however, that this may be the proper solution of this conflict of opinions; or, it may be, that, with no intention on the part of any one to mislead the public mind, those who have represented him as believing in the popular theological views of the times may have misapprehended him, as experience shows to be quite common where no special effort has been made to attain critical accuracy on a subject of this nature. This is the more probable from the well-known fact, that Mr. Lincoln seldom communicated to any one his views on this subject. But, be this as it may, I have no hesitation whatever in saying, that, whilst he held many opinions in common with the great mass of Christian believers, *he did not* believe in what are regarded as the orthodox or evangelical views of Christianity.

"On the innate depravity of man, the character and office of the great Head of the Church, the atonement, the infallibility of the written revelation, the performance of miracles, the nature and design of present and future rewards and punishments (as they are popularly called), and many other subjects, he held opinions utterly at variance with what are usually taught in the Church. I should say that his expressed views on these and kindred topics were such as, in the estimation of most believers, would place him entirely outside the Christian pale. Yet, to my mind, such was not the true position, since his principles and practices and the spirit of his whole life were of the very kind we universally agree to call Christian; and I think this conclusion is in no wise affected by the circumstance that he never attached himself to any religious society whatever.

"His religious views were eminently practical, and are summed up, as I think, in these two propositions: 'the Fatherhood of God, and the brotherhood of man.' He fully believed in a superintending and overruling Providence, that guides and controls the operations of the world, but maintained that law and order, and not their violation or suspension, are the appointed means by which this providence is exercised.

"I will not attempt any specification of either his belief or disbelief on various religious topics, as derived from conversations with him at different times during a considerable period; but, as conveying a general view of his religious or theological opinions, will state the following facts. Some eight or ten years prior to his death, in conversing with him upon this subject, the writer took occasion to refer, in terms of approbation, to the sermons and writings generally of Dr. W. E. Channing; and, finding he was considerably interested in the statement I made of the opinions held by that author, I proposed to present him (Lincoln) a copy of Channing's entire works, which I soon after did. Subsequently, the contents of these volumes, together with the writings of Theodore Parker, furnished him, as he informed me, by his friend and law-partner, Mr. Herndon, became naturally the topics of conversation with us; and though far from believing there was an entire harmony of views on his part with either of those authors, yet they were generally much admired and approved by him.

"No religious views with him seemed to find any favor, except of the practical and rationalistic order; and if, from my recollections on this subject, I was called upon to designate an author whose views most nearly represented Mr. Lincoln's on this subject, I would say that author was Theodore Parker.

"As you have asked from me a candid statement of my recollections on this topic, I have thus briefly given them, with the hope that they may be of some service in rightly settling a question about which — as I have good reason to believe — the public mind has been greatly misled.

"Not doubting that they will accord, substantially, with your own recollections, and that of his other intimate and confidential friends, and with the popular verdict after this matter shall have been properly canvassed, I submit them."

John G. Nicolay, his private secretary at the White House : —

"Mr. Lincoln did not, to my knowledge, in any way change his religious views, opinions, or beliefs, from the time he left Springfield to the day of his death. I do not know just what they were, never having heard him explain them in detail; but I am very sure he gave no outward indication of his mind having undergone any change in that regard while here."

The following letter from Mr. Herndon was, about the time of its date, extensively published throughout the United States, and met with no contradiction from any responsible source.

SPRINGFIELD, Feb. 18, 1870.

MR. ABBOTT, — Some time since I promised you that I would send a letter in relation to Mr. Lincoln's religion. I do so now. Before entering on that question, one or two preliminary remarks will help us to understand why he disagreed with the Christian world in its principles, as well as in its theology. In the first place, Mr. Lincoln's mind was a purely logical mind; secondly, Mr. Lincoln was purely a practical man. He had no fancy or imagination, and not much emotion. He was a realist as opposed to an idealist. As a general rule, it is true that a purely logical mind has not much hope, if it ever has *faith in the unseen and unknown.* Mr. Lincoln had not much hope and no faith in things that lie outside of the domain of demonstration: he was so constituted, so organized, that he could believe nothing unless his senses or logic could reach it. I have often read to him a law point, a decision, or something I fancied: he could not understand it until he took the book out of my hand, and read the thing for himself. He was terribly, vexatiously sceptical. He could scarcely understand any thing, unless he had time and place fixed in his mind.

I became acquainted with Mr. Lincoln in 1834, and I think I knew him well to the day of his death. His mind, when a boy in Kentucky, showed a certain gloom, an unsocial nature, a peculiar abstractedness, a bold and daring scepticism. In Indiana, from 1817 to 1830, it manifested the same qualities or attributes as in Kentucky : it only intensified, developed itself, along those lines, in Indiana. He came to Illinois in 1830, and, after some little roving, settled in New Salem, now in Menard County and State of Illinois. This village lies about twenty miles north-west of this city. It was here that Mr. Lincoln became acquainted with a class of men the world never saw the like of before or since. *They were large men, — large in body and large in mind ;* hard to whip, and never to be fooled. They were a bold, daring, and reckless sort of men ; they were men of their own minds, — believed what was demonstrable ; were men of great common sense. With these men Mr. Lincoln was thrown ; with them he lived, and with them he moved, and almost had his being. They were sceptics all, — scoffers some. These scoffers were good men, and their scoffs were protests against theology, — loud protests against the follies of Christianity : they had never heard of theism and the newer and better religious thoughts of this age. Hence, being natural sceptics, and being bold, brave men, they uttered their thoughts freely : they declared that Jesus was an illegitimate child. . . . They were on all occasions, when opportunity offered, debating the various questions of Christianity among themselves : they took their stand on common sense and on their own souls ; and, though their arguments were rude and rough, no man could overthrow their homely logic. They riddled all divines, and not unfrequently made them sceptics, — disbelievers as bad as themselves. They were a jovial, healthful, generous, social, true, and manly set of people.

It was here, and among these people, that Mr. Lincoln was thrown. About the year 1834, he chanced to come across Volney's " Ruins," and some of Paine's theological works. He at once seized hold of them, and assimilated them into his own being. Volney and Paine became a part of Mr. Lincoln from 1834 to the end of his life. In 1835 he wrote out a small work on " Infidelity," and intended to have it published. The book was an attack upon the whole grounds of Christianity, and especially was it an attack upon the idea that Jesus was *the Christ*, the true and only-begotten Son of God, as the Christian world contends. Mr. Lincoln was at that time in New Salem, keeping store for Mr. Samuel Hill, a merchant and postmaster of that place. Lincoln and Hill were very friendly. Hill, I think, was a sceptic at that time. Lincoln, one day after the book was finished, read it to Mr. Hill, his good friend. Hill tried to persuade him not to make it public, not to publish it. Hill at that time saw in Mr. Lincoln a rising man, and wished him success. Lincoln refused to destroy it, said it should be published. Hill swore it should never see light of day. He had an eye, to Lincoln's popularity, — his present and future success ; and believing, that if the book were published, it would kill Lincoln forever, he snatched it from Lincoln's hand, when Lincoln was not expecting it, and ran it into an old-fashioned tin-plate stove, heated as hot as a furnace; and so Lincoln's book went up to the clouds in smoke. It is confessed by all who heard parts of it, that it was at once able and eloquent; and, if I may judge of it from Mr. Lincoln's subsequent ideas and opinions, often expressed to me and to others in my presence, it was able, strong, plain, and fair. His argument was grounded on the internal mistakes of the Old and New Testaments, and on reason, and on the experiences and observations of men. The criticisms from internal defects were sharp, strong, and manly.

Mr. Lincoln moved to this city in 1837, and here became acquainted with various men of his own way of thinking. At that time they called themselves *free-thinkers*, or *free-thinking men*. I remember all these things distinctly; for I was with them, heard them, and was one of them. Mr. Lincoln here found other works, — Hume, Gibbon, and others, — and drank them in: he made no secret of his views, no concealment of his religion. He boldly avowed himself an infidel. When Mr. Lincoln was a candidate for our Legislature, he was accused of being an infidel, and of having said that Jesus Christ was an illegitimate child: he never denied his opinions, nor flinched from his religious views; he was a true man, and yet it may be truthfully said, that in 1837 his religion was low indeed. In his moments of gloom he would doubt, *if he did not sometimes deny, God*. He made me once erase the name of God from a speech which I was about to make in 1854; and he did this in the city of Washington to one of his friends. I cannot now name the man, nor the place he occupied in Washington: it will be known sometime. I have the evidence, and intend to keep it.

Mr. Lincoln ran for Congress, against the Rev. Peter Cartwright, in the year 1847 or 1848. In that contest he was accused of being an infidel, if not an atheist; he never denied the charge; would not; "*would die first:*" in the first place, because he knew it could and would be proved on him; and in the second place he was too true to his own convictions, to his own soul, to deny it. From what I *know* of Mr. Lincoln, and from what I have heard and verily believe, I can say, First, That he *did not* believe in a special creation, his idea being that all creation was an evolution under law; Secondly, That he *did not* believe that the Bible was a special revelation from God, as the Christian world contends; Thirdly, He *did not* believe in miracles, as understood by the Christian world; Fourthly, *He believed in universal inspiration and miracles under law;* Fifthly, He *did not* believe that Jesus was the Christ, the Son of God, as the Christian world contends; Sixthly, *He believed that all things, both matter and mind, were governed by laws*, universal, absolute, and eternal. All his speeches and remarks in Washington conclusively prove this. Law was to Lincoln *every thing*, and special interferences shams and delusions. I know whereof I speak. I used to loan him Theodore Parker's works: I loaned him Emerson sometimes, and other writers; and he would sometimes read, and sometimes would not, as I suppose, — nay, know.

When Mr. Lincoln left this city for Washington, I know he had undergone no change in his religious opinions or views. He held many of the Christian ideas in abhorrence, and among them there was this one; namely, that God would forgive the sinner for a violation of his laws. Lincoln maintained that God could not forgive; that punishment has to follow the sin; that Christianity was wrong in teaching forgiveness; that it tended to make man sin in the hope that God would excuse, and so forth. Lincoln contended that the minister should teach that God has affixed punishment to sin, and that no repentance could bribe him to remit it. In one sense of the word, Mr. Lincoln was a Universalist, and in another sense he was a Unitarian; but he was a theist, as we now understand that word: he was so fully, freely, unequivocally, boldly, and openly, when asked for his views. Mr. Lincoln was supposed, by many people in this city, to be an atheist; and some still believe it. I can put that supposition at rest forever. I hold a letter of Mr. Lincoln in my hand, addressed to his step-brother, John D. Johnston, and dated the twelfth day of January, 1851. He had heard from Johnston that his father, Thomas Lincoln, was sick, and that no hopes of his recovery were entertained. Mr. Lincoln wrote back to Mr. Johnston these words : —

"I sincerely hope that father may yet recover his health; but, at all events, tell him to remember to call upon and confide in One great and good and merciful Maker, who will not turn away from him in any extremity. He notes the fall of a sparrow, and numbers the hairs of our heads; and he will not forget the dying man who puts his trust in him. Say to him, that, if we could meet now, it is doubtful whether it would not be more painful than pleasant; but that, if it be his lot to go now, he will soon have a joyous meeting with many loved ones gone before, and where the rest of us, through the help of God, hope ere long to join them.   " A. LINCOLN."

So it seems that Mr. Lincoln believed in God and immortality as well as heaven, — a place. He believed in no hell and no punishment in the future world. It has been said to me that Mr. Lincoln wrote the above letter to an old man simply to cheer him up in his last moments, and that the writer did not believe what he said. The question is, Was Mr. Lincoln an honest and truthful man ? If he was, he wrote that letter honestly, believing it. It has to me the sound, the ring, of an honest utterance. I admit that Mr. Lincoln, in his moments of melancholy and terrible gloom, was living on the borderland between theism and atheism, — sometimes quite wholly dwelling in atheism. In his happier moments he would swing back to theism, and dwell lovingly there. It is possible that Mr. Lincoln was not always responsible for what he said or thought, so deep, so intense, so terrible, was his melancholy. I send you a lecture of mine which will help you to see what

I mean.   I maintain that Mr. Lincoln was a deeply-religious man at all times and places, in spite of his *transient doubts.*

Soon after Mr. Lincoln was assassinated, Mr. Holland came into my office, and made some inquiries about him, stating to me his purpose of writing his life.   I freely told him what he asked, and much more.   He then asked me what I thought about Mr. Lincoln's religion, meaning his views of Christianity.   I replied, " *The less said, the better.*"   Mr. Holland has recorded my expression to him (see Holland's " Life of Lincoln," p. 241).   I cannot say what Mr. Holland said to me, as that was private.   It appears that he went and saw Mr. Newton Bateman, Superintendent of Public Instruction in this State.   It appears that Mr. Bateman told Mr. Holland many things, if he is correctly represented in Holland's " Life of Lincoln " (pp. 236–241, inclusive).   I doubt whether Mr. Bateman said in full what is recorded there : I doubt a great deal of it.   I know the whole story is untrue, — untrue in substance, untrue in fact and spirit.   As soon as the " Life of Lincoln " was out, on reading that part here referred to, I instantly sought Mr. Bateman, and found him in his office.   I spoke to him politely and kindly, and he spoke to me in the same manner.   I said substantially to him that Mr. Holland, in order to make Mr. Lincoln a technical Christian, made him a hypocrite ; and so his " Life of Lincoln " quite plainly says.   I loved Mr. Lincoln, and was mortified, if not angry, to see him made a hypocrite.   I cannot now detail what Mr. Bateman said, as it was a private conversation, and I am forbidden to make use of it in public.   If some good gentleman can only get the seal of secrecy removed, I can show what was said and done.   On my word, the world may take it for granted that Holland is wrong, that he does not state Mr. Lincoln's views correctly.   Mr. Bateman, if correctly represented in Holland's " Life of Lincoln," is the only man, the sole and only man, who dare say that Mr. Lincoln believed in Jesus as *the Christ of God,* as the Christian world represents.   This is not a pleasant situation for Mr. Bateman.   I have notes and dates of our conversation ; and the world will sometime know who is truthful, and who is otherwise.   I doubt whether Bateman is correctly represented by Holland.   My notes bear date Dec. 3, 12, and 28, 1866. Some of our conversations were in the spring of 1866 and the fall of 1865.

I do not remember ever seeing the words *Jesus* or *Christ* in print, as uttered by Mr. Lincoln.   If he has used these words, they can be found.   He uses the word *God* but seldom.   I never heard him use the name of Christ or Jesus but to confute the idea that he was *the Christ,* the only and truly begotten Son of God, as the Christian world understands it.   The idea that Mr. Lincoln carried the New Testament or Bible in his bosom or boots, to draw on his opponent in debate, is ridiculous.

.   .   .   .

My dear sir, I now have given you my knowledge, speaking from my own experience, of Mr. Lincoln's religious views.   I speak likewise from the evidences, carefully gathered, of his religious opinions.   I likewise speak from the ears and mouths of many in this city; and, after all careful examination, I declare to your numerous readers, that Mr. Lincoln is correctly represented here, so far as I know what truth is, and how it should be investigated.

Very truly,

W. H. HERNDON.

If ever there was a moment when Mr. Lincoln might have been expected to express his faith in the atonement, his trust in the merits of a living Redeemer, it was when he undertook to send a composing and comforting message to a dying man. He knew, moreover, that his father had been "converted" time and again, and that no exhortation would so effectually console his weak spirit in the hour of dismay and dissolution as one which depicted, in the strongest terms, the perfect sufficiency of Jesus to save the perishing soul. But he omitted it wholly: he did not even mention the name of Jesus, or intimate the most distant suspicion of the existence of a Christ. On the contrary, he is singularly careful to employ the word "*One*" to qualify the word "Maker." It is the Maker, and not the Saviour, to whom he directs the attention of a sinner in the agony of death.

While it is very clear that Mr. Lincoln was at all times an infidel in the orthodox meaning of the term, it is also very clear that he was not at all times equally willing that everybody should know it. He never offered to purge or recant; but he was a wily politician, and did not disdain to regulate his religious manifestations with some reference to his political interests. As he grew older, he grew more cautious; and as his New Salem associates, and the aggressive deists with whom he originally united at Springfield, gradually dispersed, or fell away from his side, he appreciated more and more keenly the violence and extent of the religious prejudices which freedom in discussion from his standpoint would be sure to arouse against him. He saw the immense and augmenting power of the churches, and in times past had practically felt it. The imputation of infidelity had seriously injured him in several of his earlier political contests; and, sobered by age and experience, he was resolved

32

that that same imputation should injure him no more. Aspiring to lead religious communities, he foresaw that he must not appear as an enemy within their gates; aspiring to public honors under the auspices of a political party which persistently summoned religious people to assist in the extirpation of that which is denounced as the " nation's sin," he foresaw that he could not ask their suffrages whilst aspersing their faith. He perceived no reason for changing his convictions, but he did perceive many good and cogent reasons for not making them public.

Col. Matheny alleges, that, from 1854 to 1860, Mr. Lincoln "played a sharp game" upon the Christians of Springfield, "treading their toes," and saying, "Come and convert me." Mr. Herndon is inclined to coincide with Matheny; and both give the obvious explanation of such conduct; that is to say, his morbid ambition, coupled with a mortal fear that his popularity would suffer by an open avowal of his deistic convictions. At any rate, Mr. Lincoln permitted himself to be misunderstood and misrepresented by some enthusiastic ministers and exhorters with whom he came in contact. Among these was the Rev. Mr. Smith, then pastor of the First Presbyterian Church of Springfield, and afterwards Consul at Dundee, in Scotland, under Mr. Lincoln's appointment. The abilities of this gentleman to discuss such a topic to the edification of a man like Mr. Lincoln seem to have been rather slender; but the chance of converting so distinguished a person inspired him with a zeal which he might not have felt for the salvation of an obscurer soul. Mr. Lincoln listened to his exhortations in silence, apparently respectful, and occasionally sat out his sermons in church with as much patience as other people. Finding these oral appeals unavailing, Mr. Smith composed a heavy tract out of his own head to suit the particular case. "The preparation of that work," says he, "cost me long and arduous labor;" but it does not appear to have been read. Mr. Lincoln took the "work" to his office, laid it down without writing his name on it, and never took it up again to the knowledge of a man who inhabited that office with him, and who saw it lying on the same spot every day for months. Subsequently Mr. Smith drew from Mr. Lincoln an acknowledgment that his argument was *unanswerable*, — not a very high compliment under the circumstances, but one to which Mr. Smith often referred afterwards with great delight. He never asserted, as some have supposed, that Mr. Lincoln was converted from the error of his ways; that he abandoned his infidel opinions, or that he united himself with any Christian church. On the contrary, when specially interrogated on these points by Mr. Herndon, he refused to answer, on the ground that Mr. Herndon was not a proper person to receive such a communication from him.

Mr. Newton Bateman is reported to have said that a few days before the Presidential election of 1860, Mr. Lincoln came into his office, closed the door against intrusion, and proposed to examine a book which had been furnished him, at his own request, "containing a careful canvass of the city of Springfield, showing the candidate for whom each citizen had declared his intention to vote at the approaching election. He ascertained that only three ministers of the gospel, out of twenty-three, would vote for him, and that, of the prominent church-members, a very large majority were against him." Mr. Bateman does not say so directly, but the inference is plain that Mr. Lincoln had not previously known what were the sentiments of the Christian people who lived with him in Springfield: he had never before taken the trouble to inquire whether they were for him or against him. At all events, when he made the discovery out of the book, he wept, and declared that he "did not understand it at all." He drew from his bosom a pocket New Testament, and, "with a trembling voice and his cheeks wet with tears," quoted it against his political opponents generally, and especially against Douglas. He professed to believe that the opinions adopted by him and his party were derived from the teachings of Christ; averred that Christ was God; and, speaking of the Testament which he carried in his bosom, called it "this rock, on which

I stand." When Mr. Bateman expressed surprise, and told him that his friends generally were ignorant that he entertained such sentiments, he gave this answer quickly: "I know they are : I am obliged to appear different to them." Mr. Bateman is a respectable citizen, whose general reputation for truth and veracity is not to be impeached ; but his story, as reported in Holland's Life, is so inconsistent with Mr. Lincoln's whole character, that it must be rejected as altogether incredible. From the time of the Democratic split in the Baltimore Convention, Mr. Lincoln, as well as every other politician of the smallest sagacity, knew that his success was as certain as any future event could be. At the end of October, most of the States had clearly voted in a way which left no lingering doubts of the final result of November. If there ever was a time in his life when ambition charmed his whole heart, — if it could ever be said of him that "hope elevated and joy brightened his crest," it was on the eve of that election which he saw was to lift him at last to the high place for which he had sighed and struggled so long. It was not then that he would mourn and weep because he was in danger of not getting the votes of the ministers and members of the churches he had known during many years for his steadfast opponents : he did not need them, and had not expected them. Those who understood him best are very sure that he never, under any circumstances, could have fallen into such weakness — not even when his fortunes were at the lowest point of depression — as to play the part of a hypocrite for their support. Neither is it possible that he was at any loss about the reasons which religious men had for refusing him their support ; and, if he said that he could not understand it at all, he must have spoken falsely. But the worst part of the tale is Mr. Lincoln's acknowledgment that his "friends generally were deceived concerning his religious sentiments, and that he was obliged to appear different to them."

According to this version, which has had considerable currency, he carried a Testament in his bosom, carefully hidden from his intimate associates : he believed that Christ was God ; yet his friends understood him to deny the verity of the gospel :

he based his political doctrines on the teachings of the Bible;
yet before all men, except Mr. Bateman, he habitually acted
the part of an unbeliever and reprobate, because he was
" obliged to appear different to them." How obliged ? What
compulsion required him to deny that Christ was God if he
really believed him to be divine ? Or did he put his political
necessities above the obligations of truth, and oppose Christianity against his convictions, that he might win the favor of
its enemies ? It may be that his mere silence was sometimes
misunderstood ; but he never made an express avowal of any
religious opinion which he did not entertain. He did not
" appear different " at one time from what he was at another,
and certainly he never put on infidelity as a mere mask to
conceal his Christian character from the world. There is no
dealing with Mr. Bateman, except by a flat contradiction.
Perhaps his memory was treacherous, or his imagination led
him astray, or, peradventure, he thought a fraud no harm if
it gratified the strong desire of the public for proofs of Mr.
Lincoln's orthodoxy. It is nothing to the purpose that Mr.
Lincoln said once or twice that he thought this or that portion
of the Scripture was the product of divine inspiration ; for
he was one of the class who hold that all truth is inspired, and
that every human being with a mind and a conscience is a
prophet. He would have agreed much more readily with
one who taught that Newton's discoveries, or Bacon's philosophy, or one of his own speeches, were the works of men
divinely inspired above their fellows.[1] But he never told

---

[1] " As we have bodily senses to lay hold on matter, and supply bodily wants, through
which we obtain, naturally, all needed material things; so we have spiritual faculties to
lay hold on God and supply spiritual wants: through them we obtain all needed spiritual
things. As we observe the conditions of the body, we have nature on our side: as we
observe the law of the soul, we have God on our side. He imparts truth to all men who
observe these conditions: we have direct access to him through reason, conscience, and the
religious faculty, just as we have direct access to nature through the eye, the ear, or the hand.
Through these channels, and by means of a law, certain, regular, and universal as gravitation, God inspires men, makes revelation of truth; for is not truth as much a phenomenon
of God as motion of matter ? Therefore, if God be omnipresent and omniactive, this inspiration is no miracle, but a regular mode of God's action on conscious spirit, as gravitation on unconscious matter. It is not a rare condescension of God, but a universal uplift-
ing of man. To obtain a knowledge of duty, a man is not sent away, outside of himself, to
ancient documents: for the only rule of faith and practice, the Word, is very nigh him, even

any one that he accepted Jesus as the Christ, or performed
a single one of the acts which necessarily follow upon
such a conviction. At Springfield and at Washington he
was beset on the one hand by political priests, and on the
other by honest and prayerful Christians. He despised the
former, respected the latter, and had use for both. He said
with characteristic irreverence, that he would not undertake
to "run the churches by military authority;" but he was, nevertheless, alive to the importance of letting the churches "run"
themselves in the interest of his party. Indefinite expressions about "Divine Providence," the "justice of God," "the
favor of the Most High," were easy, and not inconsistent with
his religious notions. In this, accordingly, he indulged freely;
but never in all that time did he let fall from his lips or his pen
an expression which remotely implied the slightest faith in
Jesus as the Son of God and the Saviour of men.

in his heart, and by this Word he is to try all documents whatsoever. Inspiration, like
God's omnipresence, is not limited to the few writers claimed by the Jews, Christians, or
Mohammedans, but is co-extensive with the race. As God fills all space, so all spirit; as he
influences and constrains unconscious and necessitated matter, so he inspires and helps
free, unconscious man.

"This theory does not make God limited, partial, or capricious: it exalts man. While it
honors the excellence of a religious genius of a Moses or a Jesus, it does not pronounce
their character monstrous, as the supernatural, nor fanatical, as the rationalistic theory;
but natural, human, and beautiful, revealing the possibility of mankind. Prayer — whether
voluntative or spontaneous, a word or a feeling, felt in gratitude, or penitence, or joy, or
resignation — is not a soliloquy of the man, not a physiological function, nor an address to
a deceased man, but a sally into the infinite spiritual world, whence we bring back light and
truth. There are windows towards God, as towards the world. There is no intercessor,
angel, mediator, between man and God; for man can speak, and God hear, each for himself. He requires no advocate to plead for men, who need not pray by attorney. Each
man stands close to the omnipresent God; may feel his beautiful presence, and have
familiar access to the All-Father; get truth at first hand from its Author. Wisdom, right-
eousness, and love are the Spirit of God in the soul of man: wherever these are, and just
in proportion to their power, there is inspiration from God. Thus God is not the author of
confusion, but concord. Faith and knowledge and revelation and reason tell the same
tale, and so legitimate and confirm each one another.

"God's action on matter and on man is, perhaps, the same thing to him, though it appear
differently modified to us. But it is plain, from the nature of things, that there can be but
one kind of inspiration, as of truth, faith, or love: it is the direct and intuitive perception
of some truth, either of thought or of sentiment. There can be but one mode of inspiration: it is the action of the Highest within the soul, the divine presence imparting light;
this presence, as truth, justice, holiness, love, infusing itself into the soul, giving it new
life; the breathing-in of the Deity; the in-come of God to the soul, in the form of truth
through the reason, of right through the conscience, of love and faith through the affections and religious element. Is inspiration confined to theological matter alone? Most
certainly not." — PARKER's *Discourse pertaining to Religion.*

The effect of Mr. Lincoln's unbelief did not affect his constitutional love of justice. Though he rejected the New Testament as a book of divine authority, he accepted the practical part of its precepts as binding upon him by virtue of the natural law. The benevolence of his impulses served to keep him, for the most part, within the limits to which a Christian is confined by the fear of God. It is also true beyond doubt that he was greatly influenced by the reflected force of Christianity. If he did not believe it, the masses of the " plain people " did; and no one ever was more anxious to do " whatsoever was of good report among men." To qualify himself as a witness or an officer it was frequently necessary that he should take oaths; and he always appealed to the Christian's God either by laying his hand upon the Gospels, or by some other form of invocation common among believers. Of course the ceremony was superfluous, for it imposed no religious obligation upon him; but his strong innate sense of right was sufficient to make him truthful without that high and awful sanction which faith in divine revelation would have carried with it.

Mr. Lincoln was by no means free from a kind of belief in the supernatural. While he rejected the great facts of Christianity, as wanting the support of authentic evidence, his mind was readily impressed with the most absurd superstitions.[1] He lived constantly in the serious conviction that he was himself the subject of a special decree, made by some unknown and mysterious power, for which he had no name. The birth and death of Christ, his wonderful works, and his resurrection as " the first-fruits of them that slept," Mr. Lincoln

[1] " He had great faith in the strong sense of country people; and he gave them credit for greater intelligence than most men do. If he found an idea prevailing generally amongst them, he believed there was something in it, although it might not harmonize with science. He had great faith in the virtues of the ' mad-stone,' although he could give no reason for it, and confessed that it looked like superstition. But, he said, he found the people in the neighborhood of these stones fully impressed with a belief in their virtues from actual experiment; and that was about as much as we could ever know of the properties of medicines." — *Gillespie.*

" When his son ' Bob ' was supposed to have been bitten by a rabid dog, Mr. Lincoln took him to Terre Haute, Ia., where there was a mad-stone, with the intention of having it applied, and, it is presumed, did so." — *Mrs. Wallace.*

denied, because they seemed naturally improbable, or inconsistent with his "philosophy so called;" but his perverted credulity terrified him when he saw two images of himself in a mirror.

It is very probable that much of Mr. Lincoln's unhappiness, the melancholy that "dripped from him as he walked," was due to his want of religious faith. When the black fit was on him, he suffered as much mental misery as Bunyan or Cowper in the deepest anguish of their conflicts with the evil one. But the unfortunate conviction fastened upon him by his early associations, that there was no truth in the Bible, made all consolation impossible, and penitence useless. To a man of his temperament, predisposed as it was to depression of spirits, there could be no chance of happiness, if doomed to live without hope and without God in the world. He might force himself to be merry with his chosen comrades; he might "banish sadness" in mirthful conversation, or find relief in a jest; gratified ambition might elevate his feelings, and give him ease for a time: but solid comfort and permanent peace could come to him only through "a correspondence fixed with heaven." The fatal misfortune of his life, looking at it only as it affected him in this world, was the influence at New Salem and Springfield which enlisted him on the side of unbelief. He paid the bitter penalty in a life of misery.

"It was a grievous sin in Cæsar;
And grievously hath Cæsar answered it."

CHAPTER XX.

ON the 11th of February, 1861, the arrangements for Mr. Lincoln's departure from Springfield were completed. It was intended to occupy the time remaining between that date and the 4th of March with a grand tour from State to State and city to city. One Mr. Wood, "recommended by Senator Seward," was the chief manager. He provided special trains to be preceded by pilot engines all the way through.

It was a gloomy day : heavy clouds floated overhead, and a cold rain was falling. Long before eight o'clock, a great mass of people had collected at the station of the Great Western Railway to witness the event of the day. At precisely five minutes before eight, Mr. Lincoln, preceded by Mr. Wood, emerged from a private room in the dépôt building, and passed slowly to the car, the people falling back respectfully on either side, and as many as possible shaking his hands. Having finally reached the train, he ascended the rear platform, and, facing about to the throng which had closed around him, drew himself up to his full height, removed his hat, and stood for several seconds in profound silence. His eye roved sadly over that sea of upturned faces ; and he thought he read in them again the sympathy and friendship which he had often tried, and which he never needed more than he did then. There was an unusual quiver in his lip, and a still more unusual tear on his shrivelled cheek. His solemn manner, his long silence, were as full of melancholy eloquence as any words he could have uttered. What did he think of? Of the mighty changes which had lifted him from the lowest to the highest estate on earth? Of the weary road which had brought him to this lofty summit? Of his poor mother lying beneath the tangled underbrush in a distant forest? Of that other grave in the quiet Concord cemetery? Whatever the particular character of his thoughts, it is evident that they were retrospective and painful. To those who were anxiously waiting to catch words upon which the fate of the nation might hang, it seemed long until he had mastered his feelings sufficiently to speak. At length he began in a husky tone of voice, and slowly and impressively delivered his farewell to his neighbors. Imitating his example, every man in the crowd stood with his head uncovered in the fast-falling rain.

"FRIENDS, — No one who has never been placed in a like position can understand my feelings at this hour, nor the oppressive sadness I feel at this parting. For more than a quarter of a century I have lived among you, and during all that time I have received nothing but kindness at your hands. Here I have lived from my youth, until now I am an old man. Here the most sacred ties of earth were assumed. Here all my children were born; and here one of them lies buried. To you, dear friends, I owe all that I have, all that I am. *All the strange, checkered past seems to crowd now upon my mind.* To-day I leave you. I go to assume a task more difficult than that which devolved upon Washington. Unless the great God, who assisted him, shall be with and aid me, I must fail; but if the same omniscient mind and almighty arm that directed and protected him shall guide and support me, I shall not fail, — I shall succeed. Let us all pray that the God of our fathers may not forsake us now. To him I commend you all. Permit me to ask, that, with equal security and faith, you will invoke his wisdom and guidance for me. With these few words I must leave you: for how long I know not. Friends, one and all, I must now bid you an affectionate farewell."

"It was a most impressive scene," said the editor of "The Journal." "We have known Mr. Lincoln for many years; we have heard him speak upon a hundred different occasions; but we never saw him so profoundly affected, nor did he ever utter an address which seemed to us so full of simple and touching eloquence, so exactly adapted to the occasion, so worthy of the man and the hour."

At eight o'clock the train rolled out of Springfield amid the cheers of the populace. Four years later a funeral train, covered with the emblems of splendid mourning, rolled into the same city, bearing a discolored corpse, whose obsequies were being celebrated in every part of the civilized world.

Along with Mr. Lincoln's family in the special car were Gov. Yates, Ex-Gov. Moore, Dr. Wallace (Mr. Lincoln's brother-in-law), Mr. Judd, Mr. Browning, Judge Davis, Col. Ellsworth, Col. Lamon, and private secretaries Nicolay and Hay.

It has been asserted that an attempt was made to throw the train off the track between Springfield and Indianapolis, and also that a hand grenade was found on board at Cincinnati, but no evidence of the fact is given in either case, and none of the Presidential party ever heard of these murderous doings until they read of them in some of the more imaginative reports of their trip.

Full accounts of this journey were spread broadcast over the country at the time, and have been collected and printed in various books. But, except for the speeches of the President elect, those accounts possess no particular interest at this day; and of the speeches we shall present here only such extracts as express his thoughts and feelings about the impending civil war.

In the heat of the late canvass, he had written the following private letter: —

SPRINGFIELD, ILL., Aug. 15, 1860.
JOHN B. FRY, ESQ.

My dear Sir, — Yours of the 9th, enclosing the letter of Hon. John M. Botts, was duly received. The latter is herewith returned, according to your request. It contains one of the many assurances I receive from the South, that in no probable event will there be any very formidable effort to break up the Union. The people of the South have too much of good sense and good temper to attempt the ruin of the government, rather than see it administered as it was administered by the men who made it. At least, so I hope and believe.

I thank you both for your own letter and a sight of that of Mr. Botts.

Yours very truly,
A. LINCOLN.

The opinion expressed in the letter as to the probability of war does not appear to have undergone any material change or modification during the eventful months which had intervened; for he expressed it in much stronger terms at almost every stage of his progress to Washington.

At Toledo he said, —

"I am leaving you on an errand of national importance, attended, as you are aware, with considerable difficulties. Let us believe, as some poet has expressed it, 'Behind the cloud the sun is shining still.'"

At Indianapolis : —

"I am here to thank you for this magnificent welcome, and still more for the very generous support given by your State to that political cause, which, I think, is the true and just cause of the whole country, and the whole world. Solomon says, 'There is a time to keep silence ;' and when men wrangle by the mouth, with no certainty that they mean the same thing while using the same words, it perhaps were as well if they would keep silence.

"The words 'coercion' and 'invasion' are much used in these days, and often with some temper and hot blood. Let us make sure, if we can, that we do not misunderstand the meaning of those who use them. Let us get the exact definitions of these words, not from dictionaries, but from the men themselves, who certainly deprecate the things they would represent by the use of the words.

"What, then, is coercion? What is invasion? Would the marching of an army into South Carolina, without the consent of her people, and with hostile intent toward them, be invasion? I certainly think it would ; and it would be coercion also, if the South Carolinians were forced to submit. But if the United States should merely hold and retake its own forts and other property, and collect the duties on foreign importations, or even withhold the mails from places where they were' habitually violated, would any or all of these things be invasion or coercion? Do our professed lovers of the Union, who spitefully resolve that they will resist coercion and invasion, understand that such things as these, on the part of the United States, would be coercion or invasion of a State? If so, their idea of means to preserve the object of their great affection would seem to be exceedingly thin and airy. If sick, the little pills of the homœopathist would be much too large for them to swallow. In their view, the Union, as a family relation, would seem to be no regular marriage, but rather a sort of 'free-love' arrangement, to be maintained on passional attraction."

At Columbus : —

" Allusion has been made to the interest felt in relation to the policy of the new administration. In this, I have received from some a degree of credit for having kept silence, from others some depreciation. I still think I was right. In the varying and repeatedly-shifting scenes of the present, *without a precedent which could enable me to judge for the past*, it has seemed fitting, that, before speaking upon the difficulties of the country, I should have gained a view of the whole field. To be sure, after all, I would be at liberty to modify and change the course of policy as future events might make a change necessary.

" I have not maintained silence from any want of real anxiety. *It is a good thing that there is no more than anxiety, for there is nothing going wrong. It is a consoling circumstance, that when we look out there is nothing that really hurts anybody. We entertain different views upon political questions ; but nobody is suffering any thing. This is a most consoling circumstance, and from it I judge that all we want is time and patience, and a reliance on that God who has never forsaken this people.*"

At Pittsburg : —

" Notwithstanding the troubles across the river, *there is really no crisis springing from any thing in the Government itself. In plain words, there is really no crisis, except an artificial one.* What is there now to warrant the condition of affairs presented by our friends ' over the river ' ? Take even their own view of the questions involved, and there is nothing to justify the course which they are pursuing. *I repeat it, then, there is no crisis, except such a one as may be gotten up at any time by turbulent men, aided by designing politicians.* My advice, then, under such circumstances, is *to keep cool.* If the great American people will only *keep their temper on both sides of the line, the trouble will come to an end, and the question which now distracts the country will be settled just as surely as all other difficulties of like character which have originated in this Government have been adjusted. Let the people on both sides keep their self-possession, and, just as other clouds have cleared away in due time, so will this ; and this great nation shall continue to prosper as heretofore.*"

At Cleveland : —

" Frequent allusion is made to the excitement at present existing in our national politics, and it is as well that I should also allude to it here. *I think that there is no occasion for any excitement. The crisis, as it is called, is altogether an artificial crisis. . . . As I said before, this crisis is all artificial ! It has no foundation in fact. It was not ' argued up,' as the saying is, and cannot be argued down. Let it alone, and it will go down itself.*"

Before the Legislature of New York: —

"When the time comes, according to the custom of the Government, I shall speak, and speak as well as I am able for the good of the present and of the future of this country, — for the good of the North and of the South, for the good of one and of the other, and of all sections of it. In the mean time, *if we have patience, if we maintain our equanimity, though some may allow themselves to run off in a burst of passion,* I still have confidence that the Almighty Ruler of the Universe, through the instrumentality of this great and intelligent people, can and will bring us through this difficulty, *as he has heretofore brought us through all preceding difficulties of the country. Relying upon this,* and again thanking you, as I forever shall, in my heart, for this generous reception you have given me, I bid you farewell."

In response to the Mayor of New York City, who had said, " To you, therefore, chosen under the forms of the Constitution, as the head of the Confederacy, we look for a restoration of fraternal relations between the States, — *only to be accomplished by peaceful and conciliatory means,* aided by the wisdom of Almighty God," Mr. Lincoln said, —

"In regard to the difficulties that confront us at this time, and of which you have seen fit to speak *so becomingly and so justly,* I can only say that *I agree with the sentiments expressed.*"

At Trenton: —

"I shall endeavor to take the ground I deem most just to the North, the East, the West, the South, and the whole country. I take it, I hope, in good temper, — certainly with no malice towards any section. *I shall do all that may be in my power to promote a peaceful settlement of all our difficulties. The man does not live who is more devoted to peace than I am, — none who would do more to preserve it. But it may be necessary to put the foot down firmly.* And if I do my duty, and do right, you will sustain me : will you not ? Received, as I am, by the members of a legislature, the majority of whom do not agree with me in political sentiments, I trust that I may have their assistance in piloting the Ship of State through this voyage, surrounded by perils as it is ; for, if it should suffer shipwreck now, there will be no pilot ever needed for another voyage."

At Philadelphia: —

"It is true, as your worthy mayor has said, that there is anxiety among the citizens of the United States at this time. I deem it a happy circumstance that this dissatisfied portion of our fellow-citizens do not point us to any thing in which they are being injured, or are about to be injured ; *for which reason I have felt all the while justified in concluding that the crisis, the panic, the anxiety, of the country at this time is artificial.* If there be those who differ with me upon this subject, they have not pointed out the *substantial difficulty that exists.* I do not mean to say that an artificial panic may not do considerable harm : that it has done such I do not deny. The hope that has been expressed by your mayor, that I may be able to restore peace, harmony, and prosperity to the country, is most worthy of him ; and happy indeed will I be if I shall be able to verify and fulfil that hope. I promise you, in all sincerity, that I bring to the work a sincere heart. Whether I will bring a head equal to that heart, will be for future times to determine. It were useless for me to speak of details or plans now : I shall speak officially next Monday week, if ever. If I should not speak then, it were useless for me to do so now."

At Philadelphia again : —

" Now, *in my view of the present aspect of affairs, there need be no bloodshed or war. There is no necessity for it. I am not in favor of such a course: and I may say, in advance, that there will be no blood shed unless it be forced upon the Government ; and then it will be compelled to act in self-defence.*"

At Harrisburg : —

" I recur for a moment but to repeat some words uttered at the hotel in regard to what has been said about the military support which the General Government may expect from the Commonwealth of Pennsylvania in a proper emergency. *To guard against any possible mistake, do I recur to this. It is not with any pleasure that I contemplate the possibility that a necessity may arise in this country for the use of the military arm.* While I am exceedingly gratified to see the manifestation upon your streets of your military force here, and exceedingly gratified at your promise here to use that force upon a proper emergency ; while I make these acknowledgments, I desire to repeat, in order to *preclude any possible misconstruction, that I do most sincerely hope that we shall have no use for them; that it will never become their duty to shed blood, and most especially never to shed fraternal blood.* I promise that, so far as I have wisdom to direct, if so painful a result shall in any wise be brought about, it shall be through no fault of mine."

Whilst Mr. Lincoln, in the midst of his suite and attendants, was being borne in triumph through the streets of Philadelphia, and a countless multitude of people were shouting themselves hoarse, and jostling and crushing each other around his carriage-wheels, Mr. Felton, the President of the Philadelphia, Wilmington, and Baltimore Railway, was engaged with a private detective discussing the details of an alleged conspiracy to murder him at Baltimore. Some months before, Mr. Felton, apprehending danger to the bridges along his line, had taken this man into his pay, and sent him to Baltimore to spy out and report any plot that might be found for their destruction. Taking with him a couple of other men and a woman, the detective went about his business with the zeal which necessarily marks his peculiar profession. He set up as a stock-broker, under an assumed name, opened an office, and became a vehement Secessionist. His agents were instructed to act with the duplicity which such men generally use, to be rabid on the subject of " Southern rights," to suggest all manner of crimes in vindication of them ; and if, by these arts, corresponding sentiments should be elicited from their victims, the " job " might be considered as prospering. Of course they readily found out what everybody else knew, — that Maryland was in a state of great alarm ; that her people were forming military associations, and that Gov. Hicks was doing his utmost to furnish them with arms, on condition that the arms, in case of need, should be turned against the Federal Government. Whether they detected any plan to burn bridges or not, the chief detective does not relate ; but it appears that he soon deserted that inquiry, and got, or pretended to get, upon a scent that promised a heavier reward. Being intensely ambitious to shine in the professional way, and something of a politician besides, it struck him that it would be a particularly fine thing to discover a dreadful plot to assassinate the President elect ; and he discovered it accordingly. It was easy to get that far : to furnish tangible proofs of an imaginary conspiracy was a more difficult matter. But Baltimore was seething with political excitement ; numerous strangers from the far South crowded its hotels and boarding-houses ; great numbers of mechanics and laborers out of employment encumbered its streets ; and everywhere politicians, merchants, mechanics, laborers, and loafers were engaged in heated discussions about the anticipated war, and the probability of Northern troops being marched through Maryland to slaughter and pillage beyond the Potomac. It would seem like an easy thing to beguile a few individuals of this angry and excited multitude into the expression of some criminal desire; and the opportunity was not wholly lost, although the limited success of the detective under such favorable circumstances is absolutely wonderful. He put his "shadows" upon several persons, whom it suited his pleasure to suspect; and the "shadows" pursued their work with the keen zest and the cool treachery of their kind. They reported daily to their chief in writing, as he reported in turn to his employer. These documents are neither edifying nor useful: they prove nothing but the baseness of the vocation which gave them existence. They were furnished to Mr. Herndon in full, under the impression that partisan feeling had extinguished in him the love of truth, and the obligations of candor, as it had in many writers who preceded him on the same subject-matter. They have been carefully and thoroughly read, analyzed, examined, and compared, with an earnest and conscientious desire to discover the truth, if, perchance, any trace of truth might be in them. The process of investigation began with a strong bias in favor of the conclusion at which the detective had arrived. For ten years the author implicitly believed in the reality of the atrocious plot which these spies were supposed to have detected and thwarted; and for ten years he had pleased himself with the reflection that he also had done something to defeat the bloody purpose of the assassins. It was a conviction which could scarcely have been overthrown by evidence less powerful than the detective's weak and contradictory account of his own case. In that account there is literally nothing to sustain the accusation, and much to rebut it. It is perfectly manifest that there was no conspiracy, — no conspiracy of a hundred, of fifty, of twenty, of three; no definite purpose in the heart of even one man to murder Mr. Lincoln at Baltimore.

33

The reports are all in the form of personal narratives, and for the most relate when the spies went to bed, when they rose, where they ate, what saloons and brothels they visited, and what blackguards they met and "drinked" with. One of them "shadowed" a loud-mouthed, drinking fellow, named Luckett, and another, a poor scapegrace and braggart, named Hilliard. These wretches "drinked" and talked a great deal, hung about bars, haunted disreputable houses, were constantly half-drunk, and easily excited to use big and threatening words by the faithless protestations and cunning management of the spies. Thus Hilliard was made to say that he thought a man who should act the part of Brutus in these times would deserve well of his country; and Luckett was induced to declare that he knew a man who would kill Lincoln. At length the great arch-conspirator — the Brutus, the Orsini, of the New World, to whom Luckett and Hilliard, the "national volunteers," and all such, were as mere puppets — condescended to reveal himself in the most obliging and confiding manner. He made no mystery of his cruel and desperate scheme. He did not guard it as a dangerous secret, or choose his confidants with the circumspection which political criminals, and especially assassins, have generally thought proper to observe. Very many persons knew what he was about, and levied on their friends for small sums — five, ten, and twenty dollars — to further the "captain's" plan. Even Luckett was deep enough in the awful plot to raise money for it ; and when he took one of the spies to a public bar-room, and introduced him to the "captain," the latter sat down and talked it all over without the slightest reserve. When was there ever before such a loud-mouthed conspirator, such a trustful and innocent assassin! His name was Ferrandina, his occupation that of a barber, his place of business beneath Barnum's Hotel, where the sign of the bloodthirsty villain still invites the unsuspecting public to come in for a shave.

"Mr. Luckett," so the spy relates, "said that he was not going home this evening; and if I would meet him at Barr's saloon, on South Street, he would introduce me to Ferrandina.

This was unexpected to me; but I determined to take the chances, and agreed to meet Mr. Luckett at the place named at 7, P.M. Mr. Luckett left about 2.30, P.M.; and I went to dinner.

" I was at the office in the afternoon in hopes that Mr. Felton might call, but he did not; and at 6.15, P.M., I went to supper. After supper, I went to Barr's saloon, and found Mr. Luckett and several other gentlemen there. He asked me to drink, and introduced me to Capt. Ferrandina and Capt. Turner. He eulogized me very highly as a neighbor of his, and told Ferrandina that I was the gentleman who had given the twenty-five dollars he (Luckett) had given to Ferrandina.

" The conversation at once got into politics; and Ferrandina, who is a fine-looking, intelligent-appearing person, became very excited. He shows the Italian in, I think, a very marked degree; and, although excited, yet was cooler than what I had believed was the general characteristic of Italians. He has lived South for many years, and is thoroughly imbued with the idea that the South must rule; that they (Southerners) have been outraged in their rights by the election of Lincoln, and freely justified resorting to any means to prevent Lincoln from taking his seat; and, as he spoke, his eyes fairly glared and glistened, and his whole frame quivered, but he was fully conscious of all he was doing. He is a man well calculated for controlling and directing the ardent-minded: he is an enthusiast, and believes, that, to use his own words, ' murder of any kind is justifiable and right to save the rights of the Southern people.' In all his views he was ably seconded by Capt. Turner.

" Capt. Turner is an American; but although very much of a gentleman, and possessing warm Southern feelings, he is not by any means so dangerous a man as Ferrandina, as his ability for exciting others is less powerful; but that he is a bold and proud man there is no doubt, as also that he is entirely under the control of Ferrandina. In fact, it could not be otherwise: for even I myself felt the influence of this man's strange power; and, wrong though I knew him to be, I felt strangely unable to keep my mind balanced against him.

"Ferrandina said, 'Never, never, shall Lincoln be President. His life (Ferrandina's) was of no consequence: he was willing to give it up for Lincoln's; he would sell it for that Abolitionist's; and as Orsini had given his life for Italy, so was he (Ferrandina) ready to die for his country, and the rights of the South; and, said Ferrandina, turning to Capt. Turner, 'We shall all die together: we shall show the North that we fear them not. Every man, captain,' said he, 'will on that day prove himself a hero. The first shot fired, the main traitor (Lincoln) dead, and all Maryland will be with us, and the South shall be free; and the North must then be ours.' — 'Mr. Hutchins,' said Ferrandina, '*if I alone must do it, I shall: Lincoln shall die in this city.*'

"Whilst we were thus talking, we (Mr. Luckett, Turner, Ferrandina, and myself) were alone in one corner of the barroom; and, while talking, two strangers had got pretty near us. Mr. Luckett called Ferrandina's attention to this, and intimated that they were listening; and we went up to the bar, drinked again at my expense, and again retired to another part of the room, at Ferrandina's request, to see if the strangers would again follow us: whether by accident or design, they again got near us; but of course we were not talking of any matter of consequence. Ferrandina said he suspected they were spies, and suggested that he had to attend a secret meeting, and was apprehensive that the two strangers might follow him; and, at Mr. Luckett's request, I remained with him (Luckett) to watch the movements of the strangers. I assured Ferrandina, that, if they would attempt to follow him, that we would whip them.

"Ferrandina and Turner left to attend the meeting; and, anxious as I was to follow them myself, I was obliged to remain with Mr. Luckett to watch the strangers, which we did for about fifteen minutes, when Mr. Luckett said that he should go to a friend's to stay over night, and I left for my hotel, arriving there at about 9, P.M., and soon retired."

It is in a secret communication between hireling spies and paid informers that these ferocious sentiments are attributed to the poor knight of the soap-pot. No disinterested person would believe the story upon such evidence; and it will appear hereafter, that even the detective felt that it was too weak to mention among his strong points at that decisive moment, when he revealed all he knew to the President and his friends. It is probably a mere fiction. If it had had any foundation in fact, we are inclined to believe that the sprightly and eloquent barber would have dangled at a rope's end long since. He would hardly have been left to shave and plot in peace, while the members of the Legislature, the police-marshal, and numerous private gentlemen, were locked up in Federal prisons. When Mr. Lincoln was actually slain, four years later, and the cupidity of the detectives was excited by enormous rewards, Ferrandina was totally unmolested. But even if Ferrandina really said all that is here imputed to him, he did no more than many others around him were doing at the same time. He drank and talked, and made swelling speeches; but he never took, nor seriously thought of taking, the first step toward the frightful tragedy he is said to have contemplated.

The detectives are cautious not to include in the supposed plot to murder any person of eminence, power, or influence. Their game is all of the smaller sort, and, as they conceived, easily taken, — witless vagabonds like Hilliard and Luckett, and a barber, whose calling indicates his character and associations. They had no fault to find with the governor of the ·State: he was rather a lively trimmer, to be sure, and very anxious to turn up at last on the winning side; but it was manifestly impossible that one in such exalted station could meditate murder. Yet, if they had pushed their inquiries with an honest desire to get at the truth, they might have found much stronger evidence against the governor than that which they pretend to have found against the barber. In the governor's case the evidence is documentary, written, authentic, — over his own hand, clear and conclusive as pen and ink could make it.   As early as the previous November, Gov. Hicks had written the following letter; and, notwithstanding its treasonable and murderous import, the writer became conspicuously loyal before spring, and lived to reap splendid rewards and high honors under the auspices of the Federal Government, as the most patriotic and devoted Union man in Maryland.   The person to whom the letter was addressed was equally fortunate ; and, instead of drawing out his comrades in the field to " kill Lincoln and his men," he was sent to Congress by power exerted from Washington at a time when the administration selected the representatives of Maryland, and performed all his duties right loyally and acceptably.   Shall one be taken, and another left ?   Shall Hicks go to the Senate, and Webster to Congress, while the poor barber is held to the silly words which he is alleged to have sputtered out between drinks in a low groggery, under the blandishments and encouragements of an eager spy, itching for his reward ?

STATE OF MARYLAND, EXECUTIVE CHAMBER,
ANNAPOLIS, Nov. 9, 1860.
HON. E. H. WEBSTER.

My dear Sir, —I have pleasure in acknowledging receipt of your favor introducing a very clever gentleman to my acquaintance (though a Demo'). I regret to say that we have, at this time, no arms on hand to distribute, but assure you at the earliest possible moment your company shall have arms: they have complied with all required on their part.   We have some delay, in consequence of contracts with Georgia and Alabama, ahead of us : we expect at an early day an additional supply, and of first received your people shall be furnished.   Will they be good men to send out to kill Lincoln and his men ? if not, suppose the arms would be better sent South.

How does late election sit with you ?   'Tis too bad.   Harford, nothing to reproach herself for.

Your obedient servant,
THOS. H. HICKS.

With the Presidential party was Hon. Norman B. Judd: he was supposed to exercise unbounded influence over the new President; and with him, therefore, the detective opened communications.   At various places along the route, Mr. Judd was given vague hints of the impending danger, accompanied by the usual assurances of the skill and activity of the patriots who were perilling their lives in a rebel city to save that of the Chief Magistrate. When he reached New York, he was met by the woman who had originally gone with the other spies to Baltimore. She had urgent messages from her chief, — messages that disturbed Mr. Judd exceedingly. The detective was anxious to meet Mr. Judd and the President; and a meeting was accordingly arranged to take place at Philadelphia.

Mr. Lincoln reached Philadelphia on the afternoon of the 21st. The detective had arrived in the morning, and improved the interval to impress and enlist Mr. Felton. In the evening he got Mr. Judd and Mr. Felton into his room at the St. Louis Hotel, and told them all he had learned. He dwelt at large on the fierce temper of the Baltimore Secessionists; on the loose talk he had heard about " fire-balls or hand-grenades; " on a " privateer " said to be moored somewhere in the bay; on the organization called National Volunteers; on the fact, that, eaves-dropping at Barnum's Hotel, he had overheard Marshal Kane intimate that he would not supply a police-force on some undefined occasion, but what the occasion was he did not know. He made much of his miserable victim, Hilliard, whom he held up as a perfect type of the class from which danger was to be apprehended; but, concerning " Captain" Ferrandina and his threats, he said, according to his own account, not a single word. He had opened his case, his whole case, and stated it as strongly as he could. Mr. Judd was very much startled, and was sure that it would be extremely imprudent for Mr. Lincoln to pass through Baltimore in open daylight, according to the published programme. But he thought the detective ought to see the President himself; and, as it was wearing toward nine o'clock, there was no time to lose. It was agreed that the part taken by the detective and Mr. Felton should be kept secret from every one but the President. Mr. Sanford, President of the American Telegraph Company, had also been co-operating in the business; and the same stipulation was made with regard to him.

Mr. Judd went to his own room at the Continental, and the detective followed. The crowd in the hotel was very dense, and it took some time to get a message to Mr. Lincoln. But it finally reached him, and he responded in person. Mr. Judd introduced the detective; and the latter told his story over again, with a single variation: this time he mentioned the name of Ferrandina along with Hilliard's, but gave no more prominence to one than to the other.

Mr. Judd and the detective wanted Lincoln to leave for Washington that night. This he flatly refused to do. He had engagements with the people, he said, — to raise a flag over Independence Hall in the morning, and to exhibit himself at Harrisburg in the afternoon; and these engagements he would not break in any event. But he would raise the flag, go to Harrisburg, "get away quietly" in the evening, and permit himself to be carried to Washington in the way they thought best. Even this, however, he conceded with great reluctance. He condescended to cross-examine the detective on some parts of his narrative, but at no time did he seem in the least degree alarmed. He was earnestly requested not to communicate the change of plan to any member of his party, except Mr. Judd, nor permit even a suspicion of it to cross the mind of another. To this he replied, that he would be compelled to tell Mrs. Lincoln; "and he thought it likely that she would insist upon W. H. Lamon going with him; but, aside from that, no one should know."

In the mean time, Mr. Seward had also discovered the conspiracy. He despatched his son to Philadelphia to warn the President elect of the terrible plot into whose meshes he was about to run. Mr. Lincoln turned him over to Judd, and Judd told him they already knew all about it. He went away with just enough information to enable his father to anticipate the exact moment of Mr. Lincoln's surreptitious arrival in Washington.

Early on the morning of the 22d, Mr. Lincoln raised the flag over Independence Hall, and departed for Harrisburg. On the way, Mr. Judd "gave him a full and precise detail of the arrangements that had been made " the previous night. After the conference with the detective, Mr. Sanford, Col. Scott, Mr. Felton, railroad and telegraph officials, had been sent for, and came to Mr. Judd's room. They occupied nearly the whole of the night in perfecting the plan. It was finally understood that about six o'clock the next evening Mr. Lincoln should slip away from the Jones Hotel, at Harrisburg, in company with a single member of his party. A special car and engine would be provided for him on the track outside the dépôt. All other trains on the road would be "side-tracked" until this one had passed. Mr. Sanford would forward skilled "telegraph-climbers," and see that all the wires leading out of Harrisburg were cut at six o'clock, and kept down until it was known that Mr. Lincoln had reached Washington in safety. The detective would meet Mr. Lincoln at the West Philadelphia dépôt with a carriage, and conduct him by a circuitous route to the Philadelphia, Wilmington, and Baltimore dépôt. Berths for four would be pre-engaged in the sleeping-car attached to the regular midnight train for Baltimore. This train Mr. Felton would cause to be detained until the conductor should receive a package, containing important "government despatches," addressed to "E. J. Allen, Willard's Hotel, Washington." This package was made up of old newspapers, carefully wrapped and sealed, and delivered to the detective to be used as soon as Mr. Lincoln was lodged in the car. Mr. Lincoln approved of the plan, and signified his readiness to acquiesce. Then Mr. Judd, forgetting the secrecy which the spy had so impressively enjoined, told Mr. Lincoln that the step he was about to take was one of such transcendent importance, that he thought "it should be communicated to the other gentlemen of the party." Mr. Lincoln said, "You can do as you like about that." Mr. Judd now changed his seat; and Mr. Nicolay, whose suspicions seem to have been aroused by this mysterious conference, sat down beside him, and said, "Judd, there is something *up*. What is it, if it is proper that I should know?"—"George," answered Judd, "there is no necessity for your knowing it. One man can keep a matter better than two."

Arrived at Harrisburg, and the public ceremonies and speech-making over, Mr. Lincoln retired to a private parlor in the Jones House; and Mr. Judd summoned to meet him Judge Davis, Col. Lamon, Col. Sumner, Major Hunter, and Capt. Pope. The three latter were officers of the regular army, and had joined the party after it had left Springfield. Judd began the conference by stating the alleged fact of the Baltimore conspiracy, how it was detected, and how it was proposed to thwart it by a midnight expedition to Washington by way of Philadelphia. It was a great surprise to most of those assembled. Col. Sumner was the first to break silence. " That proceeding," said he, " will be a damned piece of cowardice." Mr. Judd considered this a " pointed hit," but replied that " that view of the case had already been presented to Mr. Lincoln." Then there was a general interchange of opinions, which Sumner interrupted by saying, " I'll get a squad of cavalry, sir, and *cut* our way to Washington, sir!" — " Probably before that day comes," said Mr. Judd, " the inauguration day will have passed. It is important that Mr. Lincoln should be in Washington that day." Thus far Judge Davis had expressed no opinion, but " had put various questions to test the truthfulness of the story." He now turned to Mr. Lincoln, and said, " You personally heard the detective's story. You have heard this discussion. What is your judgment in the matter ? " — " I have listened," answered Mr. Lincoln, " to this discussion with interest. I see no reason, no good reason, to change the programme ; and I am for carrying it out as arranged by Judd." There was no longer any dissent as to the plan itself ; but one question still remained to be disposed of. Who should accompany the President on his perilous ride ? Mr. Judd again took the lead, declaring that he and Mr. Lincoln had previously determined that but one man ought to go, and that Col. Lamon had been selected as the proper person. To this Sumner violently demurred. " *I* have undertaken," he exclaimed, " to see Mr. Lincoln to Washington."

Mr. Lincoln was hastily dining when a close carriage was

brought to the side-door of the hotel. He was called, hurried to his room, changed his coat and hat, and passed rapidly through the hall and out of the door. As he was stepping into the carriage, it became manifest that Sumner was determined to get in also. "Hurry with him," whispered Judd to Lamon, and at the same time, placing his hand on Sumner's shoulder, said aloud, "One moment, colonel!" Sumner turned around; and, in that moment, the carriage drove rapidly away. "A madder man," says Mr. Judd, "you never saw."

Mr. Lincoln and Col. Lamon got on board the car without discovery or mishap. Besides themselves, there was no one in or about the car but Mr. Lewis, general superintendent of the Pennsylvania Central Railroad, and Mr. Franciscus, superintendent of the division over which they were about to pass. As Mr. Lincoln's dress on this occasion has been much discussed, it may be as well to state that he wore a soft, light felt hat, drawn down over his face when it seemed necessary or convenient, and a shawl thrown over his shoulders, and pulled up to assist in disguising his features when passing to and from the carriage. This was all there was of the "Scotch cap and cloak," so widely celebrated in the political literature of the day.

At ten o'clock they reached Philadelphia, and were met by the detective, and one Mr. Kinney, an under-official of the Philadelphia, Wilmington, and Baltimore Railroad. Lewis and Franciscus bade Mr. Lincoln adieu. Mr. Lincoln, Col. Lamon, and the detective seated themselves in a carriage, which stood in waiting, and Mr. Kinney got upon the box with the driver. It was a full hour and a half before the Baltimore train was to start; and Mr. Kinney found it necessary "to consume the time by driving northward in search of some imaginary person."

On the way through Philadelphia, Mr. Lincoln told his companions about the message he had received from Mr. Seward. This new discovery was infinitely more appalling than the other. Mr. Seward had been informed "that about *fifteen thousand men* were organized to prevent his (Lincoln's) passage through Baltimore, and that arrangements were made by these parties *to blow up the railroad track, fire the train,*" &c. In view of these unpleasant circumstances, Mr. Seward recommended a change of route. Here was a plot big enough to swallow up the little one, which we are to regard as the peculiar property of Mr. Felton's detective. Hilliard, Ferrandina, and Luckett disappear among the " fifteen thousand ; " and their maudlin and impotent twaddle about the " abolition tyrant " looks very insignificant beside the bloody massacre, conflagration, and explosion now foreshadowed.

As the moment for the departure of the Baltimore train drew near, the carriage paused in the dark shadows of the dépôt building. It was not considered prudent to approach the entrance. The spy passed in first, and was followed by Mr. Lincoln and Col. Lamon. An agent of the former directed them to the sleeping-car, which they entered by the rear door. Mr. Kinney ran forward, and delivered to the conductor the " important package " prepared for the purpose ; and in three minutes the train was in motion. The tickets for the whole party had been procured beforehand. Their berths were ready, but had only been preserved from invasion by the statement, that they were retained for a sick man and his attendants. The business had been managed very adroitly by the female spy, who had accompanied her employer from Baltimore to Philadelphia to assist him in this the most delicate and important affair of his life. Mr. Lincoln got into his bed immediately ; and the curtains were drawn together. When the conductor came around, the detective handed him the " sick man's " ticket ; and the rest of the party lay down also. None of " our party appeared to be sleepy," says the detective ; " but we all lay quiet, and nothing of importance transpired." " Mr. Lincoln is very homely," said the woman in her " report," " and so very tall, that he could not lay straight in his berth." During the night Mr. Lincoln indulged in a joke or two, in an undertone ; but, with that exception, the " two sections " occupied by them were perfectly silent. The detective said he had men stationed at various places along the road to let him

know "if all was right;" and he rose and went to the platform occasionally to observe their signals, but returned each
time with a favorable report.

At thirty minutes after three, the train reached Baltimore.
One of the spy's assistants came on board, and informed him
"in a whisper that all was right." The woman got out of
the car. Mr. Lincoln lay close in his berth; and in a few
moments the car was being slowly drawn through the quiet
streets of the city toward the Washington dépôt. There again
there was another pause, but no sound more alarming than the
noise of shifting cars and engines. The passengers, tucked
away on their narrow shelves, dozed on as peacefully as if Mr.
Lincoln had never been born, until they were awakened by the
loud strokes of a huge club against a night-watchman's box,
which stood within the dépôt and close to the track. It was
an Irishman, trying to arouse a sleepy ticket-agent, comforta-
bly ensconced within. For twenty minutes the Irishman
pounded the box with ever-increasing vigor, and, at each report
of his blows, shouted at the top of his voice, " Captain! it's
four o'clock! it's four o'clock!" The Irishman seemed to
think that time had ceased to run at four o'clock, and, making
no allowance for the period consumed by his futile exercises,
repeated to the last his original statement that it was four
o'clock. The passengers were intensely amused; and their
jokes and laughter at the Irishman's expense were not lost
upon the occupants of the " two sections" in the rear. " Mr.
Lincoln," says the detective, appeared " to enjoy it very much,
and made several witty remarks, showing that he was as full
of fun as ever."

In due time the train sped out of the suburbs of Baltimore;
and the apprehensions of the President and his friends diminished with each welcome revolution of the wheels. At six
o'clock the dome of the Capitol came in sight; and a moment
later they rolled into the long, unsightly building, which forms
the Washington dépôt. They passed out of the car unob-
served, and pushed along with the living stream of men and
women toward the outer door. One man alone in the great

crowd seemed to watch Mr. Lincoln with special attention. Standing a little on one side, he "looked very sharp at him," and, as he passed, seized hold of his hand, and said in a loud tone of voice, "Abe, you can't play that on me." The detective and Col. Lamon were instantly alarmed. One of them raised his fist to strike the stranger; but Mr. Lincoln caught his arm, and said, "Don't strike him! don't strike him! It is Washburne. Don't you know him?" Mr. Seward had given to Mr. Washburne a hint of the information received through his son; and Mr. Washburne knew its value as well as another. For the present, the detective admonished him to keep quiet; and they passed on together. Taking a hack, they drove towards Willard's Hotel. Mr. Lincoln, Mr. Washburne, and the detectives got out in the street, and approached the ladies' entrance; while Col. Lamon drove on to the main entrance, and sent the proprietor to meet his distinguished guest at the side door. A few minutes later Mr. Seward arrived, and was introduced to the company by Mr. Washburne. He spoke in very strong terms of the great danger which Mr. Lincoln had so narrowly escaped, and most heartily applauded the wisdom of the "secret passage." "I informed Gov. Seward of the nature of the information I had," says the detective, "and that I had no information of any large organization in Baltimore; but the Governor reiterated that he had conclusive evidence of this."

It soon became apparent that Mr. Lincoln wished to be left alone. He said he was "rather tired;" and, upon this intimation, the party separated. The detective went to the telegraph-office, and loaded the wires with despatches, containing the pleasing intelligence that "Plums" had brought "Nuts" through in safety. In the spy's cipher the President elect was reduced to the undignified title of "Nuts."

That same day Mr. Lincoln's family and suite passed through Baltimore on the special train intended for him. They saw no sign of any disposition to burn them alive, or to blow them up with gunpowder, but went their way unmolested and very happy.

Mr. Lincoln soon learned to regret the midnight ride. His

friends reproached him, his enemies taunted him. He was convinced that he had committed a grave mistake in yielding to the solicitations of a professional spy and of friends too easily alarmed. He saw that he had fled from a danger purely imaginary, and felt the shame and mortification natural to a brave man under such circumstances. But he was not disposed to take all the responsibility to himself, and frequently upbraided the writer for having aided and assisted him to demean himself at the very moment in all his life when his behavior should have exhibited the utmost dignity and composure.

The news of his surreptitious entry into Washington occasioned much and varied comment throughout the country; but important events followed it in such rapid succession, that its real significance was soon lost sight of. Enough that Mr. Lincoln was safely at the capital, and in a few days would in all probability assume the power confided to his hands.

If before leaving Springfield he had become weary of the pressure upon him for office, he found no respite on his arrival at the focus of political intrigue and corruption. The intervening days before his inauguration were principally occupied in arranging the construction of his Cabinet. He was pretty well determined on this subject before he reached Washington; but in the minds of the public, beyond the generally accepted fact, that Mr. Seward was to be the Premier of the new administration, all was speculation and conjecture. From the circumstances of the case, he was compelled to give patient ear to the representations which were made him in favor of or against various persons or parties, and to hold his final decisions till the last moment, in order that he might decide with a full view of the requirements of public policy and party fealty.

The close of this volume is not the place to enter into a detailed history of the circumstances which attended the inauguration of Mr. Lincoln's administration, nor of the events which signalized the close of Mr. Buchanan's. The history of the former cannot be understood without tracing its relation to that of the latter, and both demand more impartial consideration than either has yet received.

The 4th of March, 1861, at last arrived; and at noon on that day the administration of James Buchanan was to come to a close, and that of Abraham Lincoln was to take its place. Mr. Lincoln's feelings, as the hour approached which was to invest him with greater responsibilities than had fallen upon any of his predecessors, may readily be imagined by the readers of the foregoing pages. If he saw in his elevation another step towards the fulfilment of that destiny which at times he believed awaited him, the thought served but to tinge with a peculiar, almost poetic sadness, the manner in which he addressed himself to the solemn duties of the hour.

The morning opened pleasantly. At an early hour he gave his inaugural address its final revision. Extensive preparations had been made to render the occasion as impressive as possible. By nine o'clock the procession had begun to form, and at eleven o'clock it commenced to move toward Willard's Hotel. Mr. Buchanan was still at the Capitol, signing bills till the official term of his office expired. At half-past twelve he called for Mr. Lincoln; and, after a delay of a few moments, both descended, and entered the open barouche in waiting for them. Shortly after, the procession took up its line of march for the Capitol.

Apprehensions existed, that possibly some attempt might be made to assassinate Mr. Lincoln; and accordingly his carriage was carefully surrounded by the military and the Committee of Arrangements. By order of Gen. Scott, troops were placed at various points about the city, as well as on the tops of some of the houses along the route of the procession.

The Senate remained in session till twelve o'clock, when Mr. Breckinridge, in a few well-chosen words, bade the senators farewell, and then conducted his successor, Mr. Hamlin, to the chair. At this moment, members and members elect of the House of Representatives, and the Diplomatic Corps, entered the chamber. At thirteen minutes to one, the Judges of the Supreme Court were announced; and on their entrance, headed by the venerable Chief-Justice Taney, all on the floor arose, while they moved slowly to the seats assigned them at the right of the Vice-President, bowing to that officer as they passed. At fifteen minutes past one, the Marshal-in-Chief entered the chamber ushering in the President and President elect. Mr. Lincoln looked pale, and wan, and anxious. In a few moments, the Marshal led the way to the platform at the eastern portico of the Capitol, where preparations had been made for the inauguration ceremony; and he was followed by the Judges of the Supreme Court, Sergeant-at-Arms of the Senate, the Committee of Arrangements, the President and President elect, Vice-President, Secretary of the Senate, Senators, Diplomatic Corps, Heads of Departments, and others in the chamber.

On arriving at the platform, Mr. Lincoln was introduced to the assembly, by the Hon. E. D. Baker, United States Senator from Oregon. Stepping forward, in a manner deliberate and impressive, he read in a clear, penetrating voice, the following

INAUGURAL ADDRESS.

FELLOW-CITIZENS OF THE UNITED STATES:—

In compliance with a custom as old as the Government itself, I appear before you to address you briefly, and to take, in your presence, the oath prescribed by the Constitution of the United States to be taken by the President before he enters on the execution of his office.

I do not consider it necessary, at present, for me to discuss those matters of administration about which there is no special anxiety or excitement. Apprehension seems to exist among the people of the Southern States, that, by the accession of a Republican administration, their property and their peace and personal security are to be endangered. There has never been any reasonable cause for such apprehension. Indeed, the most ample evidence to the contrary has all the while existed, and been open to their inspection. It is found in nearly all the published speeches of him who now addresses you. I do but quote from one of those speeches, when I declare, that "I have no purpose, directly or indirectly, to interfere with the institution of slavery in the States where it exists." I believe I have no lawful right to do so; and I have no inclination to do so. Those who nominated and elected me did so with the full knowledge that I had made this and many similar declarations, and had never recanted them. And, more than this, they placed in the platform, for my acceptance, and as a law to themselves and to me, the clear and emphatic resolution which I now read : —

"*Resolved*, That the maintenance inviolate of the rights of the States, and especially the right of each State to order and control its own domestic institutions according to its own judgment exclusively, is essential to that balance of power on which the perfection and endurance of our political fabric depend; and we denounce the lawless invasion by armed force of the soil of any State or Territory, no matter under what pretext, as among the gravest of crimes."

I now reiterate these sentiments; and, in doing so, I only press upon the public attention the most conclusive evidence of which the case is susceptible, that the property, peace, and security of no section are to be in any wise endangered by the now incoming administration.

I add, too, that all the protection which, consistently with the Constitution and the laws, can be given, will be cheerfully given to all the States, when lawfully demanded, for whatever cause, as cheerfully to one section as to another.

There is much controversy about the delivering up of fugitives from service or labor. The clause I now read is as plainly written in the Constitution as any other of its provisions : —

"No person held to service or labor in one State under the laws thereof, escaping into another, shall, in consequence of any law or regulation therein, be discharged from such service or labor, but shall be delivered up on claim of the party to whom such service or labor may be due."

It is scarcely questioned that this provision was intended by those who made it for the reclaiming of what we call fugitive slaves; and the intention of the lawgiver is the law.

All members of Congress swear their support to the whole Constitution, — to this provision as well as any other. To the proposition, then, that slaves whose cases come within the terms of this clause "shall be delivered up," their oaths are unanimous. Now, if they would make the effort in good temper, could they not, with nearly equal unanimity, frame and pass a law by means of which to keep good that unanimous oath?

There is some difference of opinion whether this clause should be enforced by national or by State authority; but surely that difference is not a very material one. If the slave is to be surrendered, it can be of but little consequence to him or to others by which authority it is done; and should any one in any case be content that this oath shall go unkept on a merely unsubstantial controversy as to how it shall be kept?

Again, in any law upon this subject, ought not all the safeguards of

NORMAN B. JUDD.

liberty known in civilized and humane jurisprudence to be introduced, so that a free man be not, in any case, surrendered as a slave? And might it not be well at the same time to provide by law for the enforcement of that clause in the Constitution which guarantees that "the citizens of each State shall be entitled to all the privileges and immunities of citizens in the several States"?

I take the official oath to-day with no mental reservations, and with no purpose to construe the Constitution or laws by any hypercritical rules; and, while I do not choose now to specify particular acts of Congress as proper to be enforced, I do suggest, that it will be much safer for all, both in official and private stations, to conform to and abide by all those acts which stand unrepealed, than to violate any of them, trusting to find impunity in having them held to be unconstitutional.

It is seventy-two years since the first inauguration of a President under our national Constitution. During that period, fifteen different and very distinguished citizens have in succession administered the executive branch of the government. They have conducted it through many perils, and generally with great success. Yet, with all this scope for precedent, I now enter upon the same task, for the brief constitutional term of four years, under great and peculiar difficulties.

A disruption of the Federal Union, heretofore only menaced, is now formidably attempted. I hold, that, in the contemplation of universal law and of the Constitution, the Union of these States is perpetual. Perpetuity is implied, if not expressed, in the fundamental law of all national governments. It is safe to assert that no government proper ever had a provision in its organic law for its own termination. Continue to execute all the express provisions of our national Constitution, and the Union will endure forever; it being impossible to destroy it, except by some action not provided for in the instrument itself.

Again, if the United States be not a government proper, but an association of States in the nature of a contract merely, can it, as a contract, be peaceably unmade by less than all the parties who made it? One party to a contract may violate it, — break it, so to speak; but does it not require all to lawfully rescind it? Descending from these general principles, we find the proposition that in legal contemplation the Union is perpetual confirmed by the history of the Union itself.

The Union is much older than the Constitution. It was formed, in fact, by the Articles of Association in 1774. It was matured and continued in the Declaration of Independence in 1776. It was further matured, and the faith of all the then thirteen States expressly plighted and engaged that it should be perpetual, by the Articles of Confederation, in 1778; and, finally, in 1787, one of the declared objects for ordaining and establishing the Constitution was to form a more perfect Union. But, if the destruction of the Union by one or by a part only of the States be lawfully possible, the Union is less than before, the Constitution having lost the vital element of perpetuity.

It follows from these views that no State, upon its own mere motion, can lawfully get out of the Union; that resolves and ordinances to that effect are legally void; and that acts of violence within any State or States against the authority of the United States, are insurrectionary or revolutionary according to circumstances.

I therefore consider, that, in view of the Constitution and the laws, the Union is unbroken; and, to the extent of my ability, I shall take care, as the Constitution itself expressly enjoins upon me, that the laws of the Union shall be faithfully executed in all the States. Doing this, which I deem to be only a simple duty on my part, I shall perfectly perform it, so far as is practicable, unless my rightful masters, the American people, shall withhold the requisite power, or in some authoritative manner direct the contrary.

I trust this will not be regarded as a menace, but only as the declared purpose of the Union that it will constitutionally defend and maintain itself.

In doing this, there need be no bloodshed or violence; and there shall be none unless it is forced upon the national authority.

The power confided to me *will be used to hold, occupy, and possess the property and places belonging to the government*, and collect the duties and imposts; but, beyond what may be necessary for these objects, there will be no invasion, no using of force against or among the people anywhere.

Where hostility to the United States shall be so great and so universal as to prevent competent resident citizens from holding the Federal offices, there will be no attempt to force obnoxious strangers among the people for that object. While the strict legal right may exist of the Government to enforce the exercise of these offices, the attempt to do so would be so irritating, and so nearly impracticable withal, that I deem it better to forego for the time the uses of such offices.

The mails, unless repelled, will continue to be furnished in all parts of the Union.

So far as possible, the people everywhere shall have that sense of perfect security which is most favorable to calm thought and reflection.

The course here indicated will be followed, unless current events and experience shall show a modification or change to be proper; and in every case and exigency my best discretion will be exercised according to the circumstances actually existing, and with a view and hope of a peaceful solution of the national troubles, and the restoration of fraternal sympathies and affections.

That there are persons, in one section or another, who seek to destroy the Union at all events, and are glad of any pretext to do it, I will neither affirm nor deny. But, if there be such, I need address no word to them.

To those, however, who really love the Union, may I not speak? Before entering upon so grave a matter as the destruction of our national fabric, with all its benefits, its memories, and its hopes, would it not be well to ascertain why we do it? Will you hazard so desperate a step, while any portion of the ills you fly from have no real existence? Will you, while the certain ills you fly to are greater than all the real ones you fly from? Will you risk the commission of so fearful a mistake? All profess to be content in the Union if all constitutional rights can be maintained. Is it true, then, that any right, plainly written in the Constitution, has been denied? I think not. Happily the human mind is so constituted, that no party can reach to the audacity of doing this.

Think, if you can, of a single instance in which a plainly written provision of the Constitution has ever been denied. If, by the mere force of numbers, a majority should deprive a minority of any clearly written constitutional right, it might, in a moral point of view, justify revolution: it certainly would, if such right were a vital one. But such is not our case.

All the vital rights of minorities and of individuals are so plainly assured to them by affirmations and negations, guaranties and prohibitions, in the Constitution, that controversies never arise concerning them. But no organic law can ever be framed with a provision specifically applicable to every question which may occur in practical administration. No foresight can anticipate, nor any document of reasonable length contain, express provisions for all possible questions. Shall fugitives from labor be surrendered by National or by State authority? The Constitution does not expressly say. Must Congress protect slavery in the Territories? The Constitution does not expressly say. From questions of this class spring all our constitutional controversies, and we divide upon them into majorities and minorities.

If the minority will not acquiesce, the majority must, or the government must cease. There is no alternative for continuing the government but acquiescence on the one side or the other. If a minority, in such a case, will secede rather than acquiesce, they make a precedent which in turn will ruin and divide them; for a minority of their own will secede from them, whenever a majority refuses to be controlled by such a minority. For instance, why not any portion of a new confederacy, a year or two hence, arbitrarily secede again, precisely as portions of the present Union now claim to secede from it? All who cherish disunion sentiments are now being educated to the exact temper of doing this. Is there such perfect identity of interests among the States to compose a new Union as to produce harmony only, and prevent renewed secession? Plainly, the central idea of secession is the essence of anarchy.

A majority held in restraint by constitutional check and limitation, and always changing easily with deliberate changes of popular opinions and sentiments, is the only true sovereign of a free people. Whoever rejects it does, of necessity, fly to anarchy or to despotism. Unanimity is impossible: the rule of a minority, as a permanent arrangement, is wholly inadmissible; so that, rejecting the majority principle, anarchy or despotism in some form is all that is left.

I do not forget the position assumed by some, that constitutional questions are to be decided by the Supreme Court, nor do I deny that such decisions must be binding in any case upon the parties to a suit, as to the object of that suit; while they are also entitled to very high respect and consideration in all parallel cases by all other departments of the government; and, while it is obviously possible that such decision may be erroneous in any given case, still, the evil effect following it, being limited to that particular case, with the chance that it may be overruled and never become a precedent for other cases, can better be borne than could the evils of a different practice.

At the same time, the candid citizen must confess, that, if the policy of the government upon the vital questions affecting the whole people is to be irrevocably fixed by the decisions of the Supreme Court the instant they are made, as in ordinary litigation between parties in personal actions, the people will have ceased to be their own masters, having to that extent practically resigned their government into the hands of that eminent tribunal.

Nor is there in this view any assault upon the court or the judges. It is a duty from which they may not shrink, to decide cases properly brought before them; and it is no fault of theirs if others seek to turn their decisions to political purposes. One section of our country believes slavery is right and ought to be extended, while the other believes it is wrong and ought not to be extended; and this is the only substantial dispute: and the fugitive-slave clause of the Constitution, and the law for the suppression of the foreign slave-trade, are each as well enforced, perhaps, as any law can ever be in a community where the moral sense of the people imperfectly supports the law itself. The great body of the people abide by the dry, legal obligation in both cases, and a few break over in each. This, I think, cannot be perfectly cured; and it would be worse in both cases after the separation of the sections than before. The foreign slave-trade, now imperfectly suppressed, would be ultimately revived, without restriction, in one section; while fugitive slaves, now only partially surrendered, would not be surrendered at all by the other.

Physically speaking, we cannot separate: we cannot remove our respective sections from each other, nor build an impassable wall between them. A husband and wife may be divorced, and go out of the presence and beyond the reach of each other; but the different parts of our country cannot do this. They cannot but remain face to face; and intercourse, either amicable or hostile, must continue between them. Is it possible, then, to make that intercourse more advantageous or more satisfactory after separation than before? Can aliens make treaties easier than friends can make laws? Can treaties be more faithfully enforced between aliens than laws can among friends? Suppose you go to war, you cannot fight always; and when, after much loss on both sides, and no gain on either, you cease fighting, the identical questions as to terms of intercourse are again upon you.

This country, with its institutions, belongs to the people who inhabit it. Whenever they shall grow weary of the existing government, they can exercise their constitutional right of amending, or their revolutionary right to dismember or overthrow it. I cannot be ignorant of the fact, that many worthy and patriotic citizens are desirous of having the national Constitution amended. While I make no recommendation of amendment, I fully recognize the full authority of the people over the whole subject, to be exercised in either of the modes prescribed in the instrument itself; and I should, under existing circumstances, favor rather than oppose a fair opportunity being afforded the people to act upon it.

I will venture to add, that to me the convention mode seems preferable, in that it allows amendments to originate with the people themselves, instead of only permitting them to take or reject propositions originated by others not especially chosen for the purpose, and which might not be precisely such as they would wish either to accept or refuse. I understand that a proposed amendment to the Constitution (which amendment, however, I have not seen) has passed Congress, to the effect that the Federal Government shall never interfere with the domestic institutions of States, including that of persons held to service. To avoid misconstruction of what I have said, I depart from my purpose not to speak of particular amendments so far as to say, that, holding such a provision to now be implied constitutional law, I have no objection to its being made express and irrevocable.

The chief magistrate derives all his authority from the people, and they have conferred none upon him to fix the terms for the separation of the States. The people themselves, also, can do this if they choose; but the Executive, as such, has nothing to do with it. His duty is to administer the present government as it came to his hands, and to transmit it unimpaired by him to his successor. Why should there not be a patient confidence in the ultimate justice of the people? Is there any better or equal hope in the world? In our present differences, is either party without faith of being in the right? If the Almighty Ruler of nations, with his eternal truth and justice, be on your side of the North, or on yours of the South, that truth and that justice will surely prevail by the judgment of this great tribunal, — the American people. By the frame of the government under which we live, this same people have wisely given their public servants but little power for mischief, and have with equal wisdom provided for the return of that little to their own hands at very short intervals. While the people retain their virtue and vigilance, no administration, by any extreme wickedness or folly, can very seriously injure the Government in the short space of four years.

My countrymen, one and all, think calmly and well upon this whole subject. Nothing valuable can be lost by taking time.

If there be an object to hurry any of you, in hot haste, to a step which you would never take deliberately, that object will be frustrated by taking time ; but no good object can be frustrated by it.

Such of you as are now dissatisfied still have the old Constitution unimpaired, and, on the sensitive point, the laws of your own framing under it ; while the new administration will have no immediate power, if it would, to change either.

If it were admitted that you who are dissatisfied hold the right side in the dispute, there is still no single reason for precipitate action. Intelligence, patriotism, Christianity, and a firm reliance on Him who has never yet forsaken this favored land, are still competent to adjust, in the best way, all our present difficulties.

In your hands, my dissatisfied fellow-countrymen, and not in mine, is the momentous issue of civil war. The Government will not assail you.

You can have no conflict without being yourselves the aggressors. You can have no oath registered in heaven to destroy the Government ; while I shall have the most solemn one to " preserve, protect, and defend " it.

I am loah to close. We are not enemies, but friends. We must not be enemies. Though passion may have strained, it must not break our bonds of affection.

The mystic chords of memory, stretching from every battle-field and patriot grave to every living heart and hearthstone all over this broad land, will yet swell the chorus of the Union, when again touched, as surely they will be, by the better angels of our nature.

This address, so characteristic of its author, and so full of the best qualities of Mr. Lincoln's nature, was well received by the large audience which heard it. Having finished, Mr. Lincoln turned to Chief-Justice Taney, who, with much apparent agitation and emotion, administered to him the following oath : —

"I, Abraham Lincoln, do solemnly swear that I will faithfully execute the office of President of the United States, and will, to the best of my ability, preserve, protect, and defend the Constitution of the United States."

The ceremony concluded, Mr. Lincoln, as President of the United States, in charge of the Committee of Arrangements, was accompanied by Mr. Buchanan back to the Senate-

Chamber, and from there to the Executive Mansion. Here Mr. Buchanan took leave of him, invoking upon his administration a peaceful and happy result; and here for the present we leave him. In another volume we shall endeavor to trace his career as the nation's Chief Magistrate during the ensuing four years.

I was born Feb. 12, 1809, in Hardin County, Kentucky. My parents were both born in Virginia, of undistinguished families — second families, perhaps I should say. My mother, who died in my tenth year, was of a family of the name of Hanks, some of whom now reside in Adams, and others in Macon counties, Illinois. My paternal grandfather, Abraham Lincoln, emigrated from Rockingham County, Virginia, to Kentucky, about 1781 or 2, where, a year or two later, he was killed by indians, not in battle, but by stealth, when he was laboring to open a farm in the forest — His ancestors, who were quakers, went to Virginia from Berks County, Pennsylvania — An effort to identify them with the New England family of the same name ended in nothing more definite, than a similarity of Christian names in both families, such as Enoch, Levi, Mordecai, Solomon, Abraham, and the like —

My father, at the death of his father, was but six years of age; and he grew up, litterally without education. He removed from Kentucky to what is now Spencer county, Indiana, in my eighth year — We reached our new home about the time the State came into the union — It was a wild region, with many bears' and other wild animals, still in the woods — There I grew up. There were some schools, so called, but no qualification was ever required of a teacher, beyond "readin, writin, and cipherin" to the Rule of Three — If a straggler supposed to understand latin, happened to sojourn in

the neighborhood, he was looked upon as a
wizzard— There was absolutely nothing to excite
ambition for education. Of course when I came of
age I did not know much— Still somehow, I could
read, write, and cipher to the Rule of Three, but
that was all— I have not been to school since—
The little advance I now have upon this store of education, I have picked up from time to time under
the pressure of necessity—

I was raised to farm work, which I continued
till I was twentytwo— At twentyone I came to
Illinois, and passed the first year in Illinois—
Macon County— Then I got to New Salem (then
in Sangamon, now in Menard County), where I remained a year as a sort of Clerk in a
store— Then came the Black-Hawk war,
and I was elected a Captain of Volunteers—
a success which gave me more pleasure
than any I have had since— I went the
campaign, was elated, ran for the Legislature the
same year (1832) and was beaten— the only time
I ever have been beaten by the people— The next,
and three succeeding biennial elections, I was elected
on to the Legislature— I was not a candidate
afterwards. During this Legislative period I had
studied law, and removed to Springfield to
make practice it— In 1846 I was once elected
to the lower House of Congress— Was not a candidate for re-election— From 1849 to 1854 both

inclusion, practiced law more assiduously than ever
before— Always a whig in politics, and generally
on the whig electoral tickets, making active canvasses— I was losing interest in politics, when
the repeal of the Missouri Compromise aroused
me again. What I have done since then is
pretty well known—

If any personal description of me is thought desirable,
desirable, it may be said, I am, in height, six
feet, four inches, nearly; lean in flesh, weighing, on
an average, one hundred and eighty pounds; dark
complexion, with coarse black hair, and grey eyes—
no other marks or brands recollected—

J. W. Fell, Esq   Yours very truly
                                        A. Lincoln

                    Washington D.C. March 26, 18⁵⁄₂

We the undersigned hereby certify that the
foregoing statement is in the hand
writing of Abraham Lincoln.
                        David Davis
                        Lyman Trumbull
                        Charles Sumner

APPENDIX.

THE circumstances under which the original of the accompanying *fac-simile* was written are explained in the following letter: —

NATIONAL HOTEL, WASHINGTON, D.C., Feb. 19, 1872.

COLONEL WARD H. LAMON.

Dear Sir, — In compliance with your request, I place in your hands a copy of a manuscript in my possession written by Abraham Lincoln, giving a brief account of his early history, and the commencement of that political career which terminated in his election to the Presidency.

It may not be inappropriate to say, that some time preceding the writing of the enclosed, finding, in Pennsylvania and elsewhere, a laudable curiosity in the public mind to know more about the early history of Mr. Lincoln, and looking, too, to the possibilities of his being an available candidate for the Presidency in 1860, I had on several occasions requested of him this information, and that it was not without some hesitation he placed in my hands even this very modest account of himself, which he did in the month of December, 1859.

To this were added, by myself, other facts bearing upon his legislative and political history, and the whole forwarded to a friend residing in my native county (Chester, Pa.), — the Hon. Joseph J. Lewis, former Commissioner of Internal Revenue, —who made them the basis of an ably-written and somewhat elaborate memoir of the late President, which appeared in the Pennsylvania and other papers of the country in January, 1860, and which contributed to prepare the way for the subsequent nomination at Chicago the following June.

Believing this brief and unpretending narrative, written by himself in his own peculiar vein, — and in justice to him I should add, without the remotest expectation of its ever appearing in public, — with the attending circumstances, may be of interest to the numerous admirers of that historic and truly great man, I place it at your disposal.

I am truly yours,

JESSE W. FELL.

INDEX.

Gentryville, character of the early settlers of, 24; social peculiarities and superstitions of, 42–44.

Gillespie, Mr., testimony of, to Lincoln's sensitiveness, 237.

Gilmore, Mr., of North Carolina, offered a seat in the cabinet, 458.

Godbey, Squire, anecdote of, 140.

Graham, Minter, the schoolmaster of New Salem, instructs Lincoln, 95.

Greeley, Horace, in favor of Douglas, 394, 396.

Green, W. G., an intimate friend of Lincoln, 90.

Green, Bowlin, a devoted friend of Lincoln, 146.

Grigsby, Aaron, marries Lincoln's sister, 45.

Grigsby Nat, amusing meeting of, with Lincoln, 274.

Grigsbys, feud between Lincoln and the, 63.

Gulliver, Rev. Mr. a clerical flatterer, 442.

Guthrie, Mr., of Kentucky, offered a seat in cabinet, 458.

Hamlin, Hannibal, nominated for the vice-presidency, 450; takes his seat as president of the senate, 528.

Hanks, Dennis, a constant companion of Lincoln, 22; value of his testimony, 46, 48.

Hanks family, 12.

Hanks, John, describes Lincoln's early habits, 37; splits rails with him, 49; brings rails into Republican Convention, 445.

Hanks, Nancy, becomes the wife of Thomas Lincoln, 10; characteristics of, 11; death of, 28.

Hannah, William H., statement of, in relation to Lincoln's religious belief, 489.

Hardin, John J., bargains for a seat in Congress, 275.

Hazel, Caleb, Lincoln's first schoolmaster, 16.

Herndon, J. R. 127, 135.

Herndon, "Row," 156.

Herndon William H., lectures on Ann Rutledge, 187; law-partner of Lincoln, 316; determines to make him an Abolitionist, 352; indorses the "House-divided-against-itself" speech, 402; letter relating to Lincoln's religious belief, 489, 492.

Henry, Gen., an officer in the Black-Hawk war, 114.

Hicks, Thomas, treasonable letter of, 518.

Hill, Samuel, burns Lincoln's book, 158.

Hilliard, a Baltimore conspirator, 514.

Holland, J. G., biographer of Lincoln, 3, 408.

"House-divided-against-itself" speech, 399.

"Immortality," the poem on, 166.

Inauguration of President Lincoln, 528.

"Irrepressible conflict," opening of the, 366.

Jackson campaign, 122.

Jayne, William, announces Lincoln as a candidate for the State Legislature, 359.

Johnston, John D., character of, 46; letters of his step-brother to, 337.

Johnson, H. V., nominated for the vice-presidency, 456.

Johnston, Mrs. Sarah, marries Thomas Lincoln, 29; her care of his children, 31; love for Abraham, 39; receives a visit from the president elect, 463; fears of his assassination, 464.

Jones, William, of Gentryville, employs Lincoln as a clerk, 56.

Judd, Norman B., accompanies the presidential party to Philadelphia, 518.

Kansas-Nebraska territorial bill, 342.

Kansas, struggle between the Free-state and Slave-state men in, 366; Reeder appointed governor of, 368; letter of Mr. Lincoln relating to, 368; overthrow of the proslavery party in, 386.